3

D0941062

Yale Western Americana Series, 5

EDITORIAL COMMITTEE

William H. Goetzmann
Archibald Hanna, Jr.
Howard R. Lamar
Robin W. Winks

THE FIELD NOTES OF
CAPTAIN WILLIAM CLARK

1803-1805

edited with an Introduction and Notes by

Ernest Staples Osgood

New Haven and London, Yale University Press, 1964

Copyright © 1964 by Yale University.
Designed by John O. C. McCrillis,
set in Linotype Baskerville type,
and printed in the United States of America by
Connecticut Printers, Incorporated,
Hartford, Connecticut,
and the Meriden Gravure Company,
Meriden, Connecticut.
All rights reserved. This book may not be
reproduced, in whole or in part, in any form
(except by reviewers for the public press),
without written permission from the publishers.

Library of Congress catalog card number: 63–7943

To Frederick W. Beinecke, Yale 1909,
whose generosity made this book possible

CONCORDIA UNIVERSITY LIBRARY
PORTLAND, OR 97211

❦ *Preface* ❦

AMONG the noteworthy collections in the Yale University Library is the Frederick W. and Carrie S. Beinecke Collection of Western Americana. Although Mr. Beinecke's career as a collector has been a comparatively short one, he has brought to it so wide a range of interest and so active a search for materials that his collection already ranks as an equal to many of far longer standing. To his love of the great books of the American West he has added a deep concern for the interests and needs of scholars, not only those at Yale, but all who share his enthusiasm for Western history. Consequently, when he was able to acquire these field notes of William Clark, his first thought was that they should be published and thus made available to historians everywhere. Dr. Osgood, who had already devoted several years to their editing, was prevailed upon to complete their preparation for the press. Mr. Beinecke's generosity made it possible to publish not only the text of the documents but also exact facsimiles. Historians now and for years to come will have occasion to be grateful to him.

ARCHIBALD HANNA
Curator, Yale Collection of Western Americana

❦ *Acknowledgments* ❦

THE OPPORTUNITY to acknowledge the assistance that so many people have given me in preparing this journal for publication is a welcome one. For helping me to transcribe the manuscript, my thanks are due three of my former graduate students, Lucile Kane, Curator of Manuscripts at the Minnesota Historical Society, Robert M. Brown, Chief Archivist of the State of Minnesota, and Marvin L. Kay of the University of Brisbane, Brisbane, Australia. I wish to thank also Dean Theodore C. Blegen of the Graduate School at the University of Minnesota for his support and for providing funds to carry out the project. The interest of my former colleagues in the History Department at the University of Minnesota is gratefully acknowledged. The staffs at the Minnesota Historical Society, the Filson Club in Louisville, Kentucky, the Wisconsin Historical Society, and the Missouri Historical Society furnished me with all assistance. At the National Archives in Washington, Robert Bahmer and his associates gave me encouragement and valuable suggestions. Frank B. Queen, formerly of the Medical School at the University of Oregon, supplied important information on some of the problems related to the health of the exploring party. Willard R. Jillson of Frankfort, Kentucky, was helpful in clearing up a particularly obscure passage in the manuscript. To Donald Jackson, editor of the University of Illinois Press, who generously offered me advance sheets on his book, *The Letters of the Lewis and Clark Expedition*, I shall always be indebted, and his suggestions and advice are gratefully acknowledged. Through the generosity of Frederick W. Beinecke, who gave these field notes of Clark to the Western Americana Collection at Yale University, their publication was assured. Archibald Hanna, Curator of the Western Americana Collection in the Sterling Library at Yale University, has given me constant encouragement and help. My wife has been a good companion during our adventure together up the Missouri River with Captain William Clark.

E. S. O.

New Haven, Connecticut
October 1962

✲ *Contents* ✲

SHORT TITLES

Abel   Annie Heloise Abel, ed., *Tabeau's Narrative,* Norman, Oklahoma, 1939

A.S.P.: *Military Affairs*   American State Papers, *Military Affairs*

A.S.P.: *Public Lands*   American State Papers, *Public Lands*

Bakeless   John Bakeless, *Lewis and Clark,* New York, 1947

Biddle   [Nicholas Biddle, ed.,] *History of the Expedition under the Command of Captains Lewis and Clark . . . ,* 2 vols. Philadelphia and New York [1814]

Carter, *Terr. Paprs.*   Clarence E. Carter, ed., *Territorial Papers of the United States, 13*

Coues, *History*   Elliott Coues, ed., *History of the Expedition under the Command of Lewis and Clark . . . ,* 4 vols. New York, 1893

Coues, *New Light*   Elliott Coues, ed., *New Light on the Early History of the Greater Northwest,* 3 vols. New York, 1897

Coues, *Pike*   Elliott Coues, ed., *The Expeditions of Zebulon Montgomery Pike, 1805–1807,* 3 vols. New York, 1895

Chittenden   Hiram M. Chittenden, *The American Fur Trade of the Far West,* 3 vols. New York, 1902

D.A.B.   *Dictionary of American Biography*

Gass   Patrick Gass, *Gass's Journal of the Lewis and Clark Expedition,* Chicago, 1904

Gates, *Five Fur Traders*   Charles M. Gates, *Five Fur Traders of the Northwest,* Minneapolis, 1933

Hodge   F. W. Hodge, ed., *Handbook of American Indians North of Mexico,* 2 vols. Washington, 1907–10

Houck, *Missouri*   Louis Houck, *History of the Missouri,* 3 vols. Chicago, 1908

Jackson   Donald Jackson, ed., *Letters of the Lewis and Clark Expedition with Related Documents,* Urbana, Illinois, 1962

Masson   L. R. Masson, *Les Bourgeois de la Compagnie du Nord-ouest,* 2 vols. Quebec, 1889–90

Nasatir   A. P. Nasatir, *Before Lewis and Clark: Documents Illustrating the History of the Missouri, 1785–1804,* 2 vols. St. Louis, 1952

O.E.D.   *Oxford English Dictionary*

Ohio Journal   "The Journals of Capt. Meriwether Lewis and Sergeant John Ordway," Wisconsin Historical Society, *Collections, 22,* Madison, 1916

Ordway   "The Journal of . . . John Ordway," Wisconsin Historical Society, *Collections, 22,* Madison, 1916

Reynolds   John Reynolds, *Pioneer History of Illinois,* Chicago, 1887

Thompson, *Narrative*   J. B. Tyrrell, ed., *David Thompson's Narrative of His Explorations in Western America,* Toronto, 1916

Thw.   Reuben Gold Thwaites, ed., *Original Journals of the Lewis and Clark Expedition,* 8 vols. New York, 1904–05

Wheeler   Olin D. Wheeler, *The Trail of Lewis and Clark,* 2 vols. New York, 1926

❧ Introduction ❧

THE RETURNING EXPLORER has never been without an audience as he recounted his adventures. Men of all times and in all places, their minds reaching out from the known and familiar to the new and the strange, have listened to him. From the discovery of the New World until the last mile of coastline had been mapped, the last river ascended, the last mountains crossed, each generation watched and listened. The story of the exploration of the North American continent—by Spaniard and Frenchman, Englishman and American—is a great and compelling chapter in our history. From Quebec on the north to New Spain on the south, from the scattered settlements along the eastern seaboard on beyond the farthest western horizon, the story runs. The Indian alone knew the secrets of this great land; the white man had to penetrate every corner of it before he could call it his own.

Hunters, missionaries, fur traders, soldiers, and government officials moved out into this wilderness and returned, most of them, to report in one way or another on what they had seen and what they had learned. Excitement and danger were always with them along the hunting and war trails of the Indian, beside them on the craft that moved up strange and treacherous rivers, and with them as the long pack train struggled upward to the pass from which they could catch their first glimpse of an unknown and unexplored land.

Many of these forerunners left no account of their wanderings. The adventures of the lone hunter who broke open the first trails were remembered only in tales told in the frontier cabins. Sometimes a name is preserved for us only in the names of trails and streams and frontier posts. However, there is a great body of reports, journals, and letters written by men who went out as official explorers, agents, and servants for government, church, or business—stuff out of which much of the history of the American frontier is fashioned.

These records are more than written words on paper. The stained and worn notebook, the ragged and torn bits of paper are in themselves a tangible record. Words are blotted and crowded together, for often the pen faltered and the mind clouded with fatigue. To hold in one's hand such documents, to examine them and discover in them something more than the information that the words convey, brings one closer to the event, and to the men who wrote them. The records are in a very real sense living history. For the fortunate one who may have come upon such an account which, through accident or neglect, had been lost, his is an unforgettable experience.

Such documents are often of far greater import than a mere narrative of travel with the day to day entries of distances traversed, of events and hazards of the journey. They record the moves in the great game of empire that was being played out on the North American continent. Lewis and Clark and their men were counters on the chessboard of international politics; every scrap of information on the initiation, progress, and completion of their memorable expedition is significant.

The arrival of the party at the mouth of the Missouri in December 1803 was an immediate threat to the oldest empire in the western hemisphere. The great, undefined territory of Louisiana was already lost to France and within a few months it would be taken over by the aggressive Americans, who knew no boundaries in their lust for land and profits. Somewhere to the west the new American Louisiana bordered on Spanish territory. The ancient city of Santa Fe was within striking distance, and beyond the mountain barriers lay California. Once the Americans pushed their outposts toward

New Mexico on the southwest and once they succeeded in getting a foothold on the Pacific coast, the Spanish knew that all the regions north of the Rio Grande were in danger, and they could no longer boast that the South Sea was a Spanish ocean.

When the intentions of the Americans became clear to the Spaniards, their official letters to Mexico City and Madrid were filled with alarm. In great agitation Casa Calvo, Governor General of Louisiana, wrote from New Orleans on March 30, 1804, to Cavallos, Commandant General of the Interior Provinces, that something must be done, for "the moment is a critical one." The Americans were taking "hasty and gigantic steps . . . toward the South Sea, entering by way of the Missouri river and other rivers of the west bank of the Mississippi; furthering their discoveries in that district . . . it is of the greatest importance to restrain in that area the progress of the discoverers who are directing toward that district all their views and voyages . . . making themselves masters of our rich possessions which they desire."[1]

It was too late. By the time Cavallos received this letter, July 18, 1804, the "gigantic step" had been taken. Lewis and Clark had already reached the mouth of the Platte River, six hundred miles on their way.

The story of the exploration of the Lewis and Clark party in 1804–06 is known in detail. Reuben Gold Thwaites transcribed and edited the journals of the two captains together with those of two of their men, Floyd and Whitehouse. These were published in 1904–05 under the title *Original Journals of the Lewis and Clark Expedition*. The manuscript from which this official record of the expedition was compiled is in the form of several small-size notebooks, very different in appearance from the manuscript of the journal published in these pages. Long before the publication of the official record, the journal of another member of the party, Sergeant Gass, was published. In 1916 Milo Quaife discovered the journal of Sergeant Ordway and made this important document a part of the corpus. Maps, letters, and fugitive notes relating to the expedition have found their way into historical collections.

In spite of all the known material dealing with this memorable journey, scholars have had suspicions that there was more to be found. They examined the manuscript notebook journals in the collections of the American Philosophical Society in Philadelphia that had been transcribed by Thwaites, and as they noted the clean appearance of most of them, some wondered if the captains had not first made rough notes, under conditions that would have precluded careful writing, and then used these notes at some later time to post their notebook journals. Were there such notes, and if so, what had happened to them?

The discovery in 1953 in an attic in St. Paul of a second journal, in the form of rough notes in William Clark's handwriting, was a partial answer to their questions. This journal, now in the Western Americana Collection at Yale University, is here presented. It was found among the personal papers of John Henry Hammond, Civil War general, one-time inspector in the employ of the Indian Bureau, frontier entrepreneur, and capitalist. After his death in 1890, his daughter continued to live in the family residence until her death in 1952. Upon the request made by one of the heirs to the estate, the general's papers were turned over to the Minnesota Historical Society for examination. When the curator of manuscripts at the society, Miss Lucile Kane, examined them, she found among them a packet wrapped in a copy of the *National Intelligencer* of Washington, D.C., dated 1805. So tightly was the packet folded that it did not seem possible that it had been opened for years. When I

1. A. P. Nasatir, *Before Lewis and Clark: Documents Illustrating the History of the Missouri, 1785–1804* (St. Louis, 1952), 2, 728.

examined its contents, there was no question that here was a rough journal by William Clark. His handwriting was unmistakable.

Further examination revealed that this journal fell naturally into two parts. The first is Clark's day-by-day account from December 13, 1803 to May 14, 1804, recording the events at Camp Dubois, the winter quarters established by the party opposite the mouth of the Missouri River. This part of the journal is of particular importance, for with the exception of a few scattered notes made by the two captains while at Camp Dubois and published by Thwaites, this is the only record we have of the winter of preparation before the expedition began its actual progress up the great river of the West, the Missouri. The second part, beginning on May 14, 1804, is partly in the form of rough field notes in which Clark recorded the sixteen-hundred-mile trip upriver to the Mandan villages, which the party reached in November. From then on, there are only scattered entries in the journal for the winter of 1804–05. The journal ends on April 3, 1805, four days before the party resumed the voyage up the Missouri on the way to the Pacific.

Using these field notes and enlarging upon them, Clark set down day-by-day entries in his notebook journal, which he started the day the party left Camp Dubois. By April 1805 he had filled three of these pocket-size books, the first of a series of notebooks recording the complete journey from Camp Dubois to the Pacific and the return to St. Louis in November 1806. As has been noted, these notebooks have been published in their entirety by Thwaites, as the official record of the expedition. To distinguish between the journals published by Thwaites and the field notes transcribed and printed in these pages, the term "Notebook Journal" will be used hereafter whenever reference is made to the former.

Field notes such as these must have been taken by both Lewis and Clark during the whole journey, and were used in preparing the full text of the Notebook Journal. If they were not destroyed, there is always the chance that more will some day be brought to light, through some such fortunate circumstance as attended the discovery of those printed here.

Those who have followed the trail of Lewis and Clark should have no complaint as to the paucity of written records. As one expert has pointed out, the party was "the writingest crew" in the history of exploration. Besides the two captains, seven of the men kept journals. Four of these seven have been preserved and published. The impressive literary activity of the party was in part the result of strong encouragement from President Jefferson. Ten months before the expedition moved out of its winter quarters at Camp Dubois and up the Missouri, the writing began. In July 1803, Lewis bade goodbye to Jefferson and took the familiar route across the mountains to the forks of the Ohio. There, after frustrating delays, the keelboat was built and made ready, two pirogues were bought, and skeleton crews recruited. On August 31, 1803, the little flotilla headed down the Ohio, and Lewis made his first entry in the first of the many journals. This journal, referred to hereafter as the Ohio Journal, has been edited by Milo Quaife and published by the Wisconsin Historical Society.

At Louisville, Lewis picked up Clark and continued down the Ohio to the Mississippi and up that river to Kaskaskia on the Illinois shore a few miles below St. Louis. Here he left Clark in command and turned over to him his journal. From then on until the party reached the site of the future Camp Dubois on December 12, 1803, the entries in the Ohio Journal were made by Clark. At Camp Dubois on December 13, Clark appears to have picked up the first sheet of paper that came to hand, a map that he had made of the junction of the Ohio and Mississippi, and to have written down on the reverse side his first entry of the Dubois Journal (Document 1). Until now, despite the abundance of documents relating to the expedition, there has been a gap between the Ohio Journal and the journals of the voyage up the Missouri and back. With the discovery of the Dubois Journal, we have at last what amounts to an unbroken record of the expedition from Pittsburgh to Camp Dubois and from there to the Pacific and back to St. Louis, from August 1803 to November 1806.

The Dubois Journal is more than a daily record. On many loose sheets of paper of all shapes and sizes, the subject matter is set down in no logical order. Interspersed with the daily entries are bits of information as to the country to the north and west gathered from visitors who came to the camp and from some of the men, lists of Indian tribes that would be encountered, comments on the men in Clark's command and thoughts about the problem of discipline, lists of supplies and equipment delivered by the contractor or bought from nearby farmers, plans for loading the keelboat and pirogues, and hastily scribbled notations of things to be done or remembered.

One question that must have been constantly on Clark's mind was the distance that the party must travel to reach its objective, the Pacific, and the time it would take to go and to return. All matters concerning the preparations for the journey were in some way or other related to this question. On a January night when through the walls of his cabin came the muffled growl of the ice floes as they collided at the junction of the two greatest rivers of the continent, Clark set himself to the task of answering the question, "How long, and how far?" Like many another explorer before him, his maps misled more than they helped. The chart, so painstakingly and meticulously drawn up (Document 7), attests not only to the over-all accuracy of his estimates but to his awareness of the importance of arriving at some kind of answer.

No one can turn over the scattered sheets on which the Dubois Journal is written without coming closer to a knowledge and understanding of this great Kentuckian, his devotion and courage, his sense of duty and his full commitment to the great adventure that lay ahead. Clark was not a ready writer as was Lewis, who had had a good education. The Kentucky frontier where Clark grew to manhood did not afford opportunities for a formal education. Doggedly he set himself to the task of keeping a journal. Indeed, one passage that will be noted appears to be a copy-book exercise in composition (Document 7). His orthography is a puzzle but also a delight. As has been said of another great explorer, Martin Frobisher, "When . . . he entered on one of his rare and hazardous adventures with the pen, he created spelling absolutely afresh, in the spirit of simple heroism with which he was always ready to sail out into strange seas" (Havelock Ellis, *Dance of Life,* New York, 1923, p. 165).

Whatever conclusions Clark had reached during the winter, as he tried to foresee the trials ahead, were now to be tested. Spring had come and the ice that had barred all passage had long since gone. The boats were loaded, the party fully outfitted, organized, and ready to move. At this time Clark had to decide what should be done with the journal he had kept at Camp Dubois. Instead of putting it in the hands of someone in St. Louis, or sending it to his brother in Louisville—a step that would seem logical, since it was written before the party began its exploration—Clark took it along with him. An examination of the reproduction of Document 65 proves that Clark had the Dubois Journal with him at Fort Mandan in November 1804. On a large, heavy sheet of paper he had made an entry for November 30. Although this entry gives only the day of the month, the Notebook Journal for the same date in 1804, recounts the same incidents. On the verso Clark had written, "Genl Jonathan Clark Near Louisville, Kentucky." In another position on the sheet he had written the address a second time. If the paper is folded along the old folds, this last address comes on the reverse side of the packet. In the left-hand corner of the sheet Clark wrote, "Notes at Wood River in 1803–4." There can be no doubt that the packet was made up and sealed at Fort Mandan; for when the seal was broken, a hole was made in the manuscript, resulting in a break in one of the sentences in the entry for November 30 (see p. 180). We do not know why Clark decided to take the Dubois Journal up the Missouri, but there can be no doubt that he did.

On the same date on which Clark made his last entry in the Dubois Journal, May 14, 1804, he began a second series of notes, which I shall refer to as the River Journal. It records the sixteen-hundred-mile voyage up the Missouri to the winter quarters established at the Mandan villages, continues with scattered entries through the winter of 1804–05, and ends on April 3, 1805, when the party was ready to continue westward.

As one reads through the pages of the River Journal, many questions arise. There is no doubt that it was written by Clark, with a few exceptions that will be noted in the text. However, at the time he began this journal he also began the first of his three notebook journals, covering the same period, from May 14, 1804, to April 7, 1805. The difference between these and the rough notes published here is striking. They are cleanly written in pocket books with few emendations. In contrast, this journal—for the Dubois period and for the journey up the Missouri—is for the most part written on fragments of paper that were at hand: coverings of letters that Clark or Lewis had received, and small sheets which when measured were found to be the same size as the notebooks carried by the party and from which they were obviously torn. Their appearance reflects the urgency, the hazards, and the unending labor, as the little flotilla fought its way upstream against the relentless current of the mighty river. When Clark wrote at the end of a day's struggle, "We Com too and Camped," the relief that the words convey can be sensed by anyone who examines the bits of paper on which they are written. Crowded, crabbed, and blotted, they are indeed rough notes, these "scripts" as Clark once called them. On one occasion his notes blew overboard and he was compelled to refer to the journals of the men in order to complete his entry for that day. I believe that these notes were in many instances made on the keelboat during the day's voyage. At convenient times Clark wrote up the same entries in his Notebook Journal, using these rough notes for reference.

Having used the rough notes to post his journal, why did Clark keep them? He was carrying out Jefferson's wishes as both he and Lewis understood them. For years the President had seized upon every bit of information about the vast areas that reached westward to the Pacific. No travelers' tales, no speculations, passed unheeded. Even before the purchase of Louisiana, Jefferson was busy with the organization of the party of exploration. The camp at Dubois had been established, the preparations were going forward, before the treaty of 1803 was fulfilled by the transfer of the territory from France to the United States. In the very precise instructions that he gave to Lewis, he insisted that a careful and detailed journal should be kept, not only by the two captains but by any of the men under their command who were literate and who could be induced to make their own records. There were to be as many journals kept as possible, so that in case of accidents from the unforeseeable hazards of travel, some record would be preserved. Jefferson urged that the two captains seize upon every opportunity to communicate with him, for he was deeply concerned and involved in the great enterprise. Both Lewis and Clark felt the responsibility placed upon them by the President and strove to carry out his instructions to the very best of their abilities. In preserving these rough notes, Clark was mindful, I believe, of the wishes of his commander-in-chief. The more journals, the less likelihood that any scrap of information would be lost.

By April 1805 the long winter that had tested the fortitude of the men, often to the limit, was over, and all was in readiness for the party to continue on its way west. The keelboat was waiting to return to St. Louis. The time had come to send to Jefferson the report of their progress for which he had so long and anxiously waited.

Six months before, in September 1804, preparations had been made to send Jefferson such a report of the journey up to that time. Indeed, before the party set out from Camp Dubois, Clark had indicated that at some convenient time one of the pirogues would be sent back with dispatches. By September it was time to carry out this plan. Lewis presumably prepared his reports and Clark made a packet of the rough notes, "those scripts" as he called them, that he had taken from May 14 to September 23. For an outside covering he used a large heavy sheet of paper, on one side of which he had made the entries for September 20–23. On the verso he wrote the following address:

> Genl. Jona Clark
> of
> Kentucky   Sept 20th
> To the 22nd of Septr 1804
> To the Care of Genl. Jona. Clark
> Near Louisville Kty
> To be opened by Capt. W. Clark
> or Capt. Meriwether Lewis. [*See Document 56*]

The question immediately comes to mind why Clark decided to send these rough notes to his brother in Louisville rather than to Jefferson. Any answer to this question would be pure speculation. Certainly the two captains must have known that Jefferson would have welcomed any information, particularly such rough notes as Clark had taken. It has been suggested to me that perhaps Lewis was also keeping a journal for this part of the trip and that he intended to send that to the President. The evidence for this will be presented shortly. In any event, neither Lewis' reports nor Clark's "scripts" were sent downriver: it was impossible to release the pirogue to carry back the packets at this time (see Document 54, p. 139). The only hope of getting information to Jefferson before winter prevented all communication was to meet some trading boat on its way to St. Louis with a crew that could be entrusted with the dispatches. No boat came by, and everything was taken up to Fort Mandan.

However, Jefferson had received some news about the party's progress even before it reached the Fort in November 1804. In a letter to Reuben Lewis, Meriwether's brother, dated Washington, November 6, the President wrote,

> We have lately received through a channel meriting entire confidence, advice that on the
> 4th of Aug. he [Lewis] was at the mouth of the river Plate, 600 miles up the Missouri, where
> he had met a great council of the Missouris, Panïs & Ottos . . . Two of his men has deserted
> from him . . . He was then setting out up the river. One of his boats & half of his men would
> return from his winter quarters. In the Spring he would leave about a fourth where he win-
> tered to make corn for his return & proceed with the other fourth.[2]

A few days later a letter from Auguste Chouteau dated St. Louis, November 20, informed Jefferson that the party would presumably winter at the Mandan villages.[3] These letters show that in early August some trader did meet the party and brought the news to St. Louis. At that time the two cap-

---

2. Donald Jackson, *Letters of the Lewis and Clark Expedition with Related Documents* (Urbana, Ill., 1962), p. 216, hereafter cited as Jackson. Dr. Jackson has presented in a single volume practically all of the pertinent documents re-

lated to the expedition. Those of us who have used these materials scattered in many depositories are indebted to him for bringing them together in such convenient form.

3. Ibid., p. 219 n.

tains were still holding to their original intention of sending one of the pirogues back, and apparently did not wish to trust their dispatches to this person, whoever he was. By September, as noted, it was impossible to send back the pirogue, and no other trader appeared.

Lewis and Clark were, of course, unaware that Jefferson had received any information as to their whereabouts. This added to their concern and to their determination to send as complete a report as possible from Fort Mandan, as soon as the river was open in the spring. The question of what the two captains decided to send is of great importance in any discussion of the provenance of the journal published here.

They had with them at the Fort in April 1805 the Notebook Journal in three separate notebooks, and this journal, composed of rough notes and divided into the sections I have referred to as the Dubois Journal and the River Journal. Part of the River Journal had been wrapped up in September and addressed to Louisville. After September 23, 1804, the River Journal takes on another distinction. It is quite different in physical appearance from the section that precedes it. The entries are in Clark's hand but are written neatly, with few emendations and on large sheets of paper. The size of one of these sheets, Document 60, is 40¾ inches long and 13 wide. These are not rough notes, and could not have been written in the field. They must have been copied from notes for that part of the journey. The question of what happened to the originals, and the significance of this variation in the physical character of the documents, will be considered shortly.

The preparation of reports and dispatches to be sent downriver was only part of the hectic activity at Fort Mandan just before the party ventured westward. The pirogues that had come up the river and the keelboat which was to return to St. Louis were badly in need of repair. Additional pirogues had to be built to carry the men and their provisions. Stores had to be sorted and equipment repaired and made ready. The boxes and crates of specimens had to be packed and loaded onto the keelboat. Both the Notebook Journal and the River Journal reflect the urgency of the days and the pressure that all hands felt. There was little time for writing, as both the journals show.

This is all reflected in a letter Lewis wrote to Jefferson from Fort Mandan on April 7, 1805, the day the party resumed its voyage westward. This letter is of the utmost importance in determining whether the journal was sent downriver. In it Lewis noted that he was forwarding an invoice of specimens and instructions as to their disposal. Then he wrote,

> You will also receive herewith inclosed a part of Capᵗ. Clark's private journal, the other part you will find inclosed in a separate tin box. this journal (is in it's original state, and of course incorrect, but it) will serve to give you the daily detales of our progress, and transactions. (Capᵗ. Clark dose not wish this journal exposed in it's present state.

Lewis went on to say that Clark did not object to having one or more copies made by someone Jefferson might select, who would correct the grammatical errors in it. Indeed, he asked that such copies be made and retained until the party's return, adding that such a copy would aid him in compiling his own journal for publication. Neither he nor Clark objected to Jefferson's showing such copies to qualified persons. He continued by reporting his intention to

> dispatch a canoe with three, perhaps four persons, from the extreem navigable point of the Missouri . . . by the return of this canoe, I shal send you my journal, and some one or two of the best of those kept by my men. I have sent a journal kept by one of the Sergeants [Floyd?],

to Capt Stoddard, my agent at S^t. Louis, in order as much as possible to multiply the chances of saving something.[4]

He added that the men had been encouraged to keep journals, and that seven had done so.

The first point to note in this letter is Lewis' reference to what I believe is the present journal, which he calls a "private journal"; it is being sent in two parts, one part "herewith inclosed" and the other part "inclosed in a separate tin box"; it would give Jefferson "the daily details of our progress, and transactions." The question whether Clark's journal was a private one or not will be discussed later. The more important point is what Lewis meant by the "two parts."

The first answer to this question that comes to mind is, of course, the two parts of the journal printed here, namely the Dubois Journal—December 13, 1803, to May 13, 1804—and the River Journal. I do not think that this is the division Lewis had in mind. The Dubois Journal had been prepared for delivery to Jonathan Clark. There seems to be no good reason for sending it to Jefferson, who was interested in the progress of the party up the Missouri. While the party was at Camp Dubois, Lewis was in constant communication with Jefferson, reporting what went on there and in St. Louis. Evidence, weighty though not conclusive, will be presented shortly to show that the Dubois Journal did go to Jonathan as Clark had intended, and the three notebooks containing the official journal were sent to Jefferson at this time. However, these notebooks could not be one of the two parts referred to here, for Lewis specifically mentions that it was Clark's journal in its original state that was in two parts.

This being the case, the journal Lewis referred to in his letter to Jefferson must be Clark's River Journal, a proposition supported by two pieces of evidence. While Lewis was preparing his reports, Clark took enough time off from his many duties to write, with Lewis' help, a short note to the President. Since we have only the rough draft of the letter, and since it contains evidence bearing on this problem that cannot be overlooked, I present it in its entirety. The portions of the draft that are in Lewis' hand are in italics.

Fort Mandan April 1st 1805

Sir

<As Capt. Lewis has not Leasure to Send   write a correct Coppy journal of our Proceedings & c.> *It being the wish of Capt. Lewis* I take the liberty <by the> request of Captain Lewis to send you to send you for your own perusal perusal, the notes which I have taken in the form of a journal in their original state. You will readily perceive in reading over those notes, that many parts are incorrect, principally owing to the variety [of] information received at different times, *I most sincerely wish that leasure had permitted me to offer them in a more correct form. Receive I pray you my unfained acknoledgements for your friendly recollection of me in your letters to my friend and companion Capt. Lewis, and be assured of the sincere regard with which I have the honor to be your most Obt. & Humble Servt.*[5]

The key sentence in this letter is in Clark's hand, "the notes which I have taken in the form of a journal in their original state." This, I believe, can only refer to the River Journal. It should also be noted that the description "in its original state" is the same that Lewis employed in his letter about Clark's journal.

4. Ibid., p. 231–34; Thwaites, 7, 318–21.   5. Jackson, p. 226; Thwaites, 7, 313.

Related to the problem of the two parts of the journal is the question whether the River Journal as it was found in the attic in St. Paul in 1953 was sent to Jefferson in its entirety. The evidence on this point might easily be overlooked by anyone examining the documents, but it is nonetheless important. At the head of each document on which the River Journal is written there is a notation giving the dates of the entries that were put down on that particular document. Since the journal is on loose sheets of paper, this was obviously done to facilitate their arrangement in chronological order. (There are some fragments not so dated that I have had to fit into their proper places; such arrangement has been noted.) These date headings are in neither Clark's nor Lewis' handwriting. From the character of the ink, they appear to have been written at some time after Clark had written the original. Since they are very brief, giving only the month and day of the month, any conclusion as to their authorship must be tentative. From a comparison of the dates at the heads of letters written by Jefferson and by Nicholas Biddle, it is my present belief that they were written by Biddle, whose part in the handling of these documents will be discussed later.

More important than the question of the authorship of the dates at the head of each document is the point that their consecutive dating is an indication of the unity of the River Journal. All of the papers were in the hands of Jefferson or Biddle (or some unknown person) at the time the dates were written. There is however one exception, Document 67, carrying the entry for November 30, 1804. As has been noted, this sheet was used by Clark at Fort Mandan to wrap up the Dubois Journal, which he addressed to his brother. Therefore, the Dubois Journal presumably went to Louisville and the River Journal to Washington. I have no way of knowing when the two came together as I found them in St. Paul. It is reasonable to suppose that they were combined by Clark at some later date.

To continue with the question of the "two parts" of the journal in its "original state" described by Lewis in his letter to Jefferson, I cannot escape the conclusion that one part was composed of the rough notes of the River Journal from May 14 to September 23, 1804, which Clark had previously sealed up to send to his brother. I believe that the seal was torn at the Mandans, and that these notes were sent downstream with the others intended for Jefferson. Document 56, which had been used as a wrapper, carries the "Biddle" date, as do the other documents that had been in the packet. It is my belief that the other part of the journal was the clean copy of the field notes that Clark took for the remainder of the trip, a copy made during the winter. (This copy also carries the Biddle dating.) That the clean copy is dated in sequence with the rough notes is the basis for my conclusion that it is the second of the two parts of Clark's River Journal. What became of the rough notes from which the copy was made is a question open to speculation which will be referred to again.

It is quite possible that Clark intended to copy all of the rough notes. There is a note of embarrassment in Clark's letter to Jefferson—"I most sincerely wish that leasure had permitted me to offer them in a more correct form." Although this sentence was written by Lewis, it is reasonable to assume it expressed Clark's feeling about the matter. Sometime during the winter he began copying his notes, but the pressure of preparations for continuing the journey, and the need to finish the map he intended to send to Jefferson prevented him from completing the task. He simply combined the uncopied rough notes with the finished clean copy and sent the whole thing as we have it to the President—thus the "two parts," one part enclosed with Lewis' reports and the other in a tin box. There is a more obvious explanation for the phrase "two parts," namely that all of Clark's journal may have been too bulky to have been enclosed in the packet Lewis was making up and it was arbitrarily divided.

In this examination of Lewis' letter to Jefferson one more point needs to be commented upon.

Lewis describes Clark's journal as a "private journal." On these words, and on Clark's expressed wish that he did not want his journal shown to everyone, rests the contention that this was his private diary. Nowhere except in Lewis' letter can I find it referred to as such. Clark merely thought it was not in a "correct form." The day-by-day entries in the Notebook Journal and in this journal are similar but not identical. Matters that under any definition of the term would be regarded as private are found in both. It is inconceivable to me that Clark would record the courses and distances of each day's journey, or the identification of geographical features, in a diary devoted to private matters. Furthermore, Lewis wrote that this journal will "give you [Jefferson] daily detales of our progress and transactions." I do not believe it to be a private journal, in any accepted sense of the word, but a second journal kept for the reasons that I have already given. Clark simply did not want it to be handed around generally until a fair copy had been made.

There is some slight evidence to suggest that Lewis kept his own journal of the trip up the Missouri to the Mandans. In his Mandan letter to Jefferson he assured the President that when the party reached the headwaters of the Missouri, he would send back by canoe his journal and one or two of those kept by the men. There was no opportunity to carry out this plan, and it was not until the party returned to St. Louis that the journals of the two captains were delivered to Jefferson. It is impossible to determine whether the words "my journal" in Lewis' letter refer to a journal he had been keeping from the outset of the expedition or to one he intended to keep for the remainder of the trip.

One other piece of evidence on this point comes to mind. Lewis had a hand in helping Clark write his short note of April 1, 1805, to Jefferson. We must rely on the rough draft quoted above, and too much weight cannot be given to the first two lines, which are in Clark's hand—"As Capt. Lewis has not Leasure to Send write a correct Coppy journal of our Proceedings &c." The letter continues, in Clark's hand, that he is sending his journal in its original state at Lewis' request. About all that can be deduced from this is that the two captains regretted that a correct copy was not being sent. The words apply as well to the journal printed here as they do to a hypothetical journal kept by Lewis. The three Notebook Journals were also sent to the President. All of the entries in the first two are Clark's, with only a few exceptions. In the third notebook Lewis made entries for a ten-day period when Clark was on a hunting trip. One other entry was made by Lewis before the party left Fort Mandan; all the others are in Clark's hand. I do not think there is enough available evidence to support a conclusion that Lewis was keeping a journal on the first leg of the journey.

There is no question in my mind that the three Notebook Journals were sent to the President along with Clark's rough notes. In a letter of Jefferson, December 22, 1805, to Benjamin Smith Barton, the evidence on which this conclusion is based is hardly open to question. Barton, an accomplished botanist, member of the American Philosophical Society, and an old friend of Jefferson, had promised to assist Biddle in preparing the history of the expedition. Because of the importance of this letter, I give it in its entirety:

Washington, Dec. 22, 1805

Dear Sir

Under another cover I send you drawings & specimens of the seed, cotton & leaf of the cotton tree of the Western country, received from Genl. Wilkinson at St. Louis. To these I must add that it appears from the journals of Lewis & Clarke that the boughs of this tree are the sole food of the horses up the Missouri during the winter. Their horses having on a particular occasion gone through extraordinary fatigue, bran of the maïs [maize] was ordered for them, which they refused, preferring their ordinary food the boughs of this tree, a few of which are chopped off from the tree with a hatchet every evening & thrown into their pen. Accept affectionate salutations & assurances of great esteem & respect.

Th. Jefferson[6]

There are two references in Clark's rough notes concerning this Indian practice of feeding horses on cottonwood (pp. 144 and 185). Both are very brief, and lack the details given by Jefferson to Barton. However, if one turns to Lewis' entry in the Notebook Journal for February 12, 1805, one finds the source of Jefferson's information. For purposes of comparison I quote the relevant portion of Lewis' entry:

Drewyer [Drouillard] arrived with the horses about the same time, the horses appeared much fatieged I directed some meal brands [bran] given them . . . but to my astonishment found that they would not eat it but preferred the bark of the cottonwood which forms the principall article of food usually given them by their Indian masters in the winter season . . . the Indians in our neighborhood . . . put their horses in their lodges at night. in this situation the only food of the horse consists of a few sticks of the cottonwood . . .[7]

Jefferson must have had this entry before him when he wrote to Barton. The similarity of the two passages is obvious: the fatigued horses, their refusal to eat bran, and "the particular occasion," Drouillard's arrival with the worn-out animals. When he wrote that this incident was drawn from the journals of Lewis and Clark, he could have meant only the Notebook Journals. I can find no other description of this practice among the Indians in any other material related to the expedition that Jefferson could have seen in December 1805. The brief references in Clark's rough notes could not have been the basis for Jefferson's circumstantial account in his letter to Barton.

It would seem reasonable to expect that Lewis would have notified Jefferson that he was sending along the three Notebook Journals. However, there is nothing in the correspondence that refers to them in any way. One is puzzled by the words in Lewis' Mandan letter, where he wrote that Clark's journal in its original state "will serve to give you the daily detales of our progress and transactions." Certainly if Jefferson was to have the Notebook Journals, he would get a clearer idea of the "progress and transactions" of the party than he could from Clark's rough notes.

It was, of course, a wise decision to send both Clark's rough notes and the Notebook Journals downriver. To expose them to the hazards of travel to the Pacific and back was too great a risk. Furthermore, Jefferson's instructions to Lewis as to the keeping of journals, their preservation, and their transmission to the government had been very specific. He wrote that observations were to be taken "with great pains and accuracy" and "several copies of these, as well as other notes, should be made at leisure times & put into the care of the most trustworthy of your attendants to guard, by multiplying them, against the accidental losses to which they will be exposed." The President went on to say that Lewis should avail himself of any trader "to communicate to us at seasonable intervals, a copy of your journal, notes and observations."[8] The two captains tried to carry out Jefferson's instructions as faithfully as possible by taking and keeping rough notes as well as posting their notebooks and urging the men to do the same. Unable to depend on the safe transmission of documents

---

6. Jackson, p. 272. 7. Thwaites, *1*, 258. 8. Jackson, pp. 61–66; Thwaites, 7, 247–52.

to St. Louis before the spring of 1805, they now prepared to send back nearly all the documents they had, which included the rough notes as well as the Notebook Journals and the journal that Sergeant Floyd had kept until his death in August 1804. Lewis sent the latter to Captain Stoddard at St. Louis.[9]

During those crowded days in early April the two captains found time to write to others who were awaiting news of their progress, and these letters give some additional information on the variety of material, documentary and otherwise, that was sent downriver. Lewis got off a long, descriptive letter to his mother, assuring her of his good health and the high spirits of the party as it prepared for its adventure westward.[10] Clark wrote to his old friend, Governor William Henry Harrison, a long letter full of detail about the trip so far. Those who have been inclined to compare unfavorably Clark's literary efforts with Lewis' should note the straightforward and spare prose of this letter.[11] He also wrote a "hasty scrawl" to his brother-in-law, William Croghan, apologizing for its brevity and adding, "I must therefore take the liberty of refuring you to my brother to whome I have inclosed a Map and some sketches relative to the Indians."[12] Since, as we have seen, two packets had been addressed to his brother Jonathan, Clark's words here are worth notice, particularly if they are considered together with a brief letter to Captain Amos Stoddard at St. Louis. Stoddard was the military commander at St. Louis and the official representative of the United States when the transfer of the territory of Louisiana from France to the United States was consummated. He was in close touch with Lewis and Clark during the whole Dubois period. He had been instructed by the Secretary of War, General Dearborn, to cooperate fully with the two commanders of the exploring party and to afford them every assistance possible. There seems no doubt that the Virginian, the Kentuckian, and the Connecticut Yankee became strong friends. Before Lewis left, he designated Stoddard as his agent in St. Louis, and in the event that Stoddard could not carry out this assignment Charles Gratiot was to take over.

We have only the rough draft of this letter—written, incidentally, on the same sheet of paper as the rough draft of Clark's letter to Jefferson. It does not specify to whom the letter was written, nor does it carry a date. From the wording of the letter, and from the fact that Stoddard was the man chosen by Lewis to receive communications from the party and to forward them, there can be no doubt that Stoddard was the intended recipient. Because of the importance of this letter, I present it in full:

DSir

I must request the favour of you to send by some safe conveyance as early as possible a red box containing some specimens & papers of consequence [?] to my brother Genl. Jonathin Clark of Kentucky as Directed on the top of the Box. R. Worvington the Bearer of this is intrusted with duplicates & papers of considerable consequence which I wish lodged in the hands of my brother in Kentucky be so good as to furnish this man with a publick horse if you have one which may be returned to you by the post rider. I do not think it worth while to enter into a detaill of occurences as Capt. Lewis has written you fully on that subject Yrs. &c.[13]

It may well be that Clark was sending his brother the Dubois Journal which, as we have seen, he took up to Fort Mandan and addressed to Jonathan in November 1804. This would certainly belong

9. Jackson, p. 232; Thwaites, 7, 319.
10. Jackson, pp. 222–25; Thwaites, 7, 309–12.
11. Jackson, pp. 227–30; Thwaites, 7, 314–16.
12. Jackson, p. 230; Thwaites, 7, 317.
13. Jackson, pp. 226–27.

under the heading "papers of consequence." Among the other papers entrusted to Corporal Wafving-ton (who was in command of the soldiers sent back to St. Louis) for delivery to Jonathan with all possible speed were "sketches relative to the Indians" that Clark in his letter to Croghan said he was sending to Louisville. The word "duplicates" suggests that Clark was sending the rough notes that he had made of the trip for the period from September 23, 1804, to April 2, 1805, and from which, as we have noted, he made a clean copy.

There is, however, another explanation for the term "duplicates," suggested by the mention of "rough notes" in a letter written by Clark to Nicholas Biddle in 1811. Before presenting this letter, events that occurred after the return of the party and before the letter to Biddle was written need to be briefly indicated. Both captains knew of Jefferson's interest in seeing the history of the expedition published as soon as possible. This project was delayed, first by the official duties that both men assumed immediately following their return, and then by the death of Lewis in 1809. The task of directing the publication devolved on Clark. Under the constant urging of Jefferson, he finally got in touch with Nicholas Biddle of Philadelphia, who agreed to write the story. It was understood that Clark would help in the enterprise and that Biddle would have at his disposal all the records of the expedition.

In the course of his correspondence with Biddle, Clark wrote from St. Louis, January 24, 1811, the following brief note:

> I hope you have received my several letters my new map, and sundry other papers relative to such information as I could collect. Inclosed I sent you some rough notes which I made at the Mandans the 1st year of my tour, perhaps you may Collect from this something which you may wish to Know. *A Copy of these notes were sent to Mr. Jefferson from the Mandans* &c. I send this as I have sent several other papers thro' the Secty. of War. [Italics mine][14]

If Clark's memory was correct after six years, the rough notes made at the Mandans were copied and the copy was sent to the President. I do not think that this refers to the clean copy of the field notes of the River Journal from September 23, 1804, to April 3, 1805, which went to Jefferson. The rough notes Clark mentions in this letter to Biddle were made at the Mandans, not on the journey upstream. After he made a copy of these for Jefferson, he either carried them to the Pacific and back to St. Louis, or he sent them to someone. He did not destroy them, for they were in his possession in 1811. There is the possibility that these were the "duplicates" mentioned in Clark's letter to Stoddard and which the latter was to send to Jonathan.

It is hazardous to speculate about which of the papers sent to Jefferson might have been the copy of notes made at the Mandans, but there is the following possibility. While the party was at Fort Mandan, Clark prepared for the Secretary of War a tabulated statement containing names, languages, numbers, trade, and general information concerning the Indian tribes that lived along the banks of the Missouri, and with which the party had come in contact thus far on the journey. Thwaites has pointed out that two copies were made, one of which was sent to the Secretary of War and was probably burned when the British raided Washington in 1814.[15] Thwaites found the second copy in the Lewis and Clark collection in the American Philosophical Society. This "Statistical View" with "additional Remarks" was presented to Congress by Jefferson with his message of February 9, 1806.

14. Ibid., pp. 565–66.   15. Thwaites, 6, 80.

It is found in the American State Papers, Indian Affairs, *1*, 705–43, and in the Thwaites edition of the Notebook Journals, Vol. 6, under the heading "Ethnology: Eastern Indians."

To return to Clark's letter of 1811 to Biddle, we see that either he had sent these rough notes to Biddle enclosed with his map and "sundry other papers" or he was sending them with the letter quoted. The last sentence may be confusing, for he told Biddle, "I send this as I have sent several other papers thro' the Secty. of War." It is not unlikely that he was corresponding with Biddle through the Secretary of War and here is telling Biddle that he had sent the copy of rough notes made at the Mandans to the Secretary in 1805 as he had sent other papers. If the above interpretation is correct, then the copy made at Fort Mandan for Jefferson got to him through the Secretary of War, and was later destroyed as Thwaites suggests. The rough notes were retained by Clark and may have gone to Jonathan Clark at Louisville, to be reclaimed by William on his return and then sent to Biddle in 1811.

Although there is no evidence in Jonathan's diary, or in his papers for 1805 and thereafter, that he ever received anything from his brother William, it can, I think, be concluded that a military messenger—Corporal Warfington, perhaps—galloped off to Louisville on a "publick horse" with a bulky package in his saddle bags. Still another bit of evidence may have some bearing on the matter. In the appendix to the Notebook Journals published by Thwaites there is a copy of a newspaper account which appeared in the Boston *Centinel* for July 13, 1805. It appears to have been taken from a story printed in the *Kentucky Gazette* under the dateline Lexington, June 18, 1805. The paper reported the arrival of an express with dispatches from the winter quarters of the exploring party. It went on so say,

> letters were received from Captain *Clark* to his correspondents in *Kentucky*. A gentleman from *Jefferson* County [Louisville?], has obligingly favored the Editor of the *Kentucky Gazette* with the following account, which he obtained from one of the men who returned with the express, and from letters from some of the party.[16]

This means only that Kentucky, and presumably Clark's brother Jonathan, knew of the return of the keelboat, that someone had been interviewed, and that "letters . . . from Captain Clark" and "from some of the party" had been received. The account goes on to say that Lewis and Clark had sent to the President "an accurate journal, with a map of the country through which they passed."

Now we are ready to review the documents which Charles Gratiot, who was acting as Lewis' agent in the absence of Stoddard, received when the keelboat with its diverse cargo tied up at the levee in St. Louis on May 20, 1805.

1. Lewis' letter to Jefferson, April 7, 1805, and with it Clark's River Journal, published here. According to Lewis, part of it was enclosed in his letter and part was in a tin box.

2. Clark's Dubois Journal, published here, probably sent to his brother as "papers of consequence."

3. The three Notebook Journals, perhaps in the two tin boxes that Gratiot forwarded to the Secretary of War.

16. Ibid., 7, 324–26.

4. A copy of the rough notes that Clark took at the Mandans in 1804–05, which in 1811 he remembered he had sent to Jefferson, and which was probably embodied in the *Statistical View of the Indian Nations* that accompanied Jefferson's Message to Congress, February 6, 1806.

5. Possibly the originals of the above. These may be the "Indian Sketches" that Clark said (in his letter to Croghan) he was sending to his brother, or the "duplicates" he referred to in his letter to Stoddard.

6. Clark's map, perhaps a copy, which according to his letter to Croghan he sent to Jonathan.

7. Clark's map which Jefferson received. This will be mentioned later.

8. According to the index of letters received by Jefferson, a "personal letter" from Lewis to Jefferson. This letter has not been found.[17]

9. A letter from Lewis to Jefferson, dated Fort Mandan, March 5, 1805, containing information on the Indians' treatment of snake bite.

10. Lewis' letter to Stoddard, mentioned in Clark's letter to Stoddard.

11. Lewis' letter to his mother, from Fort Mandan, dated March 31, 1805.

12. Clark's short note to Jefferson, from Fort Mandan, dated April 1, 1805.

13. Clark's letter to Stoddard, no date.

14. Clark's letter to Croghan, from Fort Mandan, dated April 2, 1805.

15. Clark's letter to Harrison, from Fort Mandan, dated April 2, 1805.

16. Possibly a letter by Clark to his brother, covering the "papers of consequence."

17. Letters by other members of the party, as suggested by the news item in the Boston *Centinel.*

18. Sergeant Floyd's journal, sent to Stoddard, according to Lewis' Mandan letter of April 7, 1805.

19. Lewis' report to the Secretary of War, including public accounts, muster rolls, and information relating to the Indian country, according to Lewis' Mandan letter of April 7, 1805.

20. An invoice of the specimens collected by the party and enclosed with Lewis' letter to the President, with the information that the boxes and trunks containing them would be forwarded by Captain Stoddard. (On this list was another tin box which, much to my relief, contained only insects and mice.)

17. Jackson, p. 236 n. Jackson believes that this letter, dated March 30, 1805, was a personal report to Jefferson supplementing Lewis' Mandan letter of April 7, 1805, which was for publication and was presented to Congress with Jefferson's message of February 19, 1806 (Jackson, pp. 298–300; Thwaites, 7, 328).

It is impossible to say with certainty that every item listed above was on the keelboat, or that each one got to its intended destination—particularly those I have listed as going to Jonathan Clark. The difficulty Gratiot and Chouteau must have had in sorting out the cargo of the keelboat, I can appreciate.

There was delay. In a letter to the Secretary of War, dated Vincennes, May 27, 1805, a week after the keelboat arrived, Harrison wrote that the dispatches to Washington would be delayed by nearly a fortnight. He added that he had received Clark's letter by express.[18] Chouteau reported on June 15 that the boxes and trunks were on their way to New Orleans. From there on, it would be General Claiborne's responsibility to see that they were shipped by sea to Washington.[19]

It was late June before Jefferson received word that the keelboat had arrived in St. Louis. In a letter to William Eustis dated Washington, June 25, 1805, he wrote,

> I have the pleasure to inform you that one of Capt Lewis' barges returned to St. Louis brings us certain informaton from him. He wintered with the Mandans, 1609 miles up the Missouri . . . all well, and peculiarly cherished by all of the Indian nations. He has sent in his barge 45 deputies from 6 of the principal nations in that quarter who will be joined at St. Louis by those of 3 or 4 nations between the Missouri and the Missisipi, and will come on here.[20]

The long-awaited dispatches arrived in Washington three weeks later. Lewis' Mandan letter with the enclosures was endorsed as received on July 13, 1805. On the next day Jefferson informed General Dearborn that he was sending his servant over with "Lewis's large map."[21] He also got off a letter to General Claiborne saying that in Lewis' letter he had noted that "6 or 8 packages filled with very curious subjects from the upper country" were to be forwarded to him.[22] These arrived at Monticello on August 12.[23]

During the autumn months of 1805 Jefferson found time to go over the journals, including, I believe, this journal in its "original state." In December he was writing to Barton about the use of cottonwood as fodder for Indian ponies, information that he could only have obtained from the Notebook Journal.

I have been unable to find in the documents of this period any direct reference to this journal. In his letter to Barton, Jefferson wrote of the "Lewis and Clark Journals." In a letter, January 12, 1806, to William Dunbar, another member of the American Philosophical Society in frequent correspondence with the President, Jefferson wrote,

> We have Capt. Lewis's notes of the Missouri to his wintering place at Fort Mandan, and a map of the whole country watered by the Missouri & Columbia composed by himself last winter on very extensive information from Indians & traders, in which he expresses a good deal of confidence.[24]

One month later, and a week before his message to Congress in which he reported on the expedition, Jefferson wrote to his friend the Comte de Volney of the news from the west.

> Our last news of Captn Lewis was that he had reached the upper part of the Missouri and

---

18. Jackson, pp. 246–47.
19. Ibid., pp. 248–49.
20. Ibid., p. 249.

21. Ibid., p. 252.
22. Idem.
23. Ibid., pp. 253–54.

24. Ibid., p. 290.

had taken horses to cross the highlands to the Columbia river. He passed the last winter among the Mandans 1610 miles above the mouth of the river. So far he had delineated it with as great accuracy as will probably be ever applied to it, as his courses & distances by mensuration were corrected by almost daily observations of Latitude and Longitude. With his map he sent us specimens or information of the following animals not before known to the northern continent of America.[25]

On February 19, 1806, Congress and the public were officially informed that Jefferson had received Lewis' letter. In his message to Congress he reported:

On the 8th of April, 1805, they [the exploring party] proceeded up the river in pursuance of the objects prescribed to them. A letter of the preceding day, April 7th, from Capt. Lewis is herewith communicated. During his stay among the Mandans he had been able to lay down the Missouri according to courses & distances taken on his passage up to it [Fort Mandan] . . . & to add to the actual survey of this portion of the river a general map of the country between the Mississipi and the Pacific from the 34th to the 54th degree of Latitude . . . Copies of this map are now presented to both houses of Congress. With these I communicate also a statistical view . . .[26]

Clark's name is not mentioned in any of these communications. Jefferson, in all three of the passages quoted above, refers to the map of the Missouri as Lewis' map. But the map was the work of Clark, the cartographer of the exploring party. He had been at work on it from the start of the expedition. According to his letter to Croghan, a copy had been sent to Jonathan. Lewis was in command of the exploration, and it was natural for the President to use Lewis' name in the above statements. In his message to Congress Jefferson's only mention of Clark is to refer to him as second in command. As to this journal in its "original state," Jefferson made no mention of it, for he was obviously carrying out Clark's wishes as expressed in Lewis' Mandan letter of April 7, that it not be handed about and that it should be "retained until our return."

I have attempted to trace this journal from Fort Mandan in April 1805 into the hands of the President. Anyone who attempts to follow it from there to an attic in St. Paul in 1953 is doomed to lose himself in an underbrush of speculation, obscurity, and confusion. There is always the hope that additional material may turn up that will yield enough light so that the trail may be revealed.

Although there are some clues in the documents after 1806, which I shall briefly touch upon, there is nothing substantial enough on which to rest any firm conclusions. The absence of any information as to what happened to these documents is understandable if the reader is reminded of the events following the return of the exploring party to St. Louis. Both captains had long had in mind joint publication of a history of the exploration, and their intention had been ardently encouraged by Jefferson.

However, the publication was long delayed. The appointment of both of the captains to government office soon after their return meant that they were soon involved in official business. Lewis became Governor of the Territory of Louisiana, and Clark took over the duties of Principal Agent of Indian Affairs for the Louisiana Territory. There was little spare time to collect the records of the

---

25. Ibid., p. 291; Thwaites, 7, 327.   26. Jackson, pp. 298–300; Thwaites, 7, 328.

expedition that were already scattered, some in Washington, some in Philadelphia, and probably some in Louisville.

In November 1806, shortly after the party's return, Lewis left St. Louis for Washington. In a letter written ten years later to Correa da Serra, Jefferson gives us the only firm evidence as to what notebooks Lewis had with him when he and the President met in 1806 and what was done with them. Jefferson wrote that Lewis had with him,

> Ten or twelve such pocket volumes, Morocco bound, as that you describe, in which, in his own hand writing, he had journalised all occurences, day by day, as he travelled. They were small 8vos and opened at the end for more convenient writing. Every one had been put into a separate tin case, cemented to prevent injury from wet. But on his return the cases, I presume, had been taken from them, as he delivered me the books uncased . . . we were willing to give to Lewis and Clarke whatever pecuniary benefits might be derived from the publication [of the journals] and therefore left the papers in their hands.[27]

From this letter certain conclusions may be drawn that have some bearing on the provenance of the documents published here. As has been noted above, Jefferson had received the three notebook journals of the trip from May 14, 1804, to April 7, 1805. I have stated on the basis of the available evidence that he also had these field notes used by Clark to write the entries in the three notebooks. Jefferson now had in his hands the morocco-bound notebooks recording the rest of the trip. It is my opinion that Jefferson's words, "we . . . therefore left the papers in their [Lewis' and Clark's] hands," refer to all the papers: these field notes with the exception of the Dubois Journal, the three notebook journals, and the morocco-bound journals. As I have pointed out, the clean and unworn appearance of the latter has led many to believe that they could not have been carried on the trip. Yet Lewis delivered them to Jefferson uncased. Certainly there was not enough time between the arrival of the party at St. Louis and the departure of Lewis for Washington for the two captains to copy whatever rough notes they had into these clean journals. The only reasonable conclusion is that the entries in the morocco notebooks were written from field notes while the trip was being made, and when each notebook was full, it was cemented into one of the tin boxes. Apparently the practice Clark instituted at the outset, of copying the field notes into the notebooks, was continued throughout the whole trip. It is quite possible that during the long winter at Fort Clatsop at the mouth of the Columbia, the two captains were busy copying their field notes of the journey thus far and sealing them up in the tin boxes. For the eastward trip, entries in the notebooks must have been made as the party proceeded. What happened to the field notes? Were they destroyed, were they preserved? There is no answer to this question. Scholars may hope that sometime they may come to light as did those of the journey from Camp Dubois to the Mandans.

Not until September 1809 was Lewis free to leave St. Louis for a second visit to Washington, a journey that ended fatally. His suicide or murder in a tavern on the Natchez Trace on October 11, 1809, shocked the whole country. To Clark it was a shrewd blow, for the two men—so different in temperament and training—had formed one of the most famous friendships in our annals. Now the task of telling the story of their common experience, out of which this friendship had grown, rested on Clark alone. Not only had he lost a beloved companion but the man whose literary talents Clark would be the first to admit were superior to his own.

27. Jackson, pp. 611–13; Thwaites, 7, 394–96.

In the room in which Lewis died were found two trunks. An inventory of their contents was made on November 23, 1809, more than a month following his death. From this list I have selected several items that appear to have some bearing on the problem of gathering together the documents of the expedition. To the left of the inventory column under the heading "Forwarded" there is a notation of the disposition of each item.

Forwarded	Inventory
Depts	One small bundle of Letters & Vouchers—of consequence
W.C. [William Clark]	One Book an Estimate of the western Indians
Th. Jefferson	One Memorandum Book
Pret. U.S. [James Madison]	A Transcript of Records &c.
W.C.	Nine Memorandum books
W.C.	Sixteen Note books bound in red morocco with clasps
Th. Jefferson	One bundle of Misceleans. paprs.
W.C.	Six note books unbound
W.C.	One bundle of Maps &c.
W.C.	One do. [bundle] "Ideas on the Western expedition
W.C.	One do. [bundle] Vocabulary
W.C.	One do. [bundle] Maps & Charts
Th. Jefferson	One Bundle of papers marked A[28]

Although there is no specific mention of Clark's map in this list, Jefferson, in a letter to Correa da Serra written five years later, recalled that it had been among Lewis' papers at the time of his death.

Clark arrived in Washington shortly after he received the news of the death of his friend. There he met Isaac A. Coles, Jefferson's former private secretary who was then acting as secretary for the new President, James Madison. In a letter to Jefferson, dated January 5, 1810, Coles reported that Lewis' trunks had arrived and that "they were opened by Genl. Clarke and my self, when every thing of a public nature was given to the Dept. to which it properly belonged, every thing relating to the expedition to Genl. Clarke, & all that remained is contained in the five little bundles now directed to you."[29]

Appended to the above inventory was a note by Coles, dated Washington, January 10, 1810, describing the condition that the papers were in as he and Clark found them.

The bundles of Papers referred to in the above memorandum were so badly assorted, that no idea could be given of them by any terms of general description. Many of the bundles containing at once, Papers of a public nature—Papers intirely private, some important & some otherwise with accts. Receipts, & &. They were all carefully looked over, & put in separate bundles. . . . Everything relating to the expedition [was given] to Genl. Clarke.[30]

28. Jackson, pp. 470–72.   29. Ibid., pp. 486–87.   30. Ibid., p. 472.

Three days later, Jefferson wrote from Monticello to Bernard McMahon that after the delivery of the papers to Clark, he took them to Philadelphia, where he intended to take measures "for immediate publication."[31]

That not all the papers relating to the expedition were in Lewis' trunks is suggested by a letter written by Jonathan Clark to his brother George Rogers, dated Louisville, February 3, 1810, in which he reported that William was leaving Washington for Philadelphia, "in search of some of the papers, that he hoped had been sent there, by Governor Lewis—a part of the journals etc. of the trip to the Western oceans, had been sent to him [Clark?] but not the whole."[32]

As has been noted, four years before this letter was written, Jefferson had turned over the records of the expedition to Lewis, who had taken most of them back to St. Louis—but not all, for apparently he had left some in Philadelphia. At the time of his death, as seen from the inventory, Lewis had most of the papers, and in 1810 Clark was in search of the rest. We have no way of knowing whether he had in his possession the journal published here. All we can say is that the records were already scattered.

Even though Clark did succeed in collecting all the material—and the mass of it must have daunted even a man who had faced down a band of hostile Sioux—Clark realized that he must have help if the history was ever to be written. Now it had become something more than ink on paper; it was to be a monument to a shared experience with a departed comrade. After several rebuffs in his search for a collaborator, he turned to Nicholas Biddle.

Biddle, whose name was and still is almost synonymous with Philadelphia, was a young lawyer and literary dilettante. In the future he would leave a mark on American history as a diplomat and as Andrew Jackson's great antagonist. On March 17, 1810, after some hesitation, he agreed to undertake the task of writing the history of the expedition, and he promised to do all in his power to bring it to completion.[33] This meant, first of all, that Biddle had to acquire from Clark all the documents on which he would depend in writing the history. From this time on, Clark wrote often and continued to send him additional material as it came to hand.

To assist Biddle in organizing and integrating the scientific data, Clark had enlisted the help of Benjamin Smith Barton (see above, p. xxii). On May 22, 1810, Clark wrote to him from Louisville that he had been with Biddle at Fincastle and received from him "a Copy of such part of my journal as I had Copied from the Original, which I hope with the assistance of the specimins and what information the young gentleman who will hand you this letter (Mr. George Shannon) Can give you."[34]

This letter may refer to the copy he made of the River Journal after September 23, 1805 (see pp. 154–55 n.), but this is by no means certain, for the phrase "I had Copied" might refer to a copy made by some other person. At any rate, Clark had given Biddle a part of the original journal which, it is my belief, is printed here, and Biddle was handing on at least some of it to Barton.

In January of the next year Clark wrote to Biddle from St. Louis and sent him "some rough notes which I made at the Mandans the 1st year of my tour . . . A Copy of these notes were sent to Mr. Jefferson from the Mandans &c." (see pp. xxv–xxvi).

These two letters give us the last faint trace of the journals here published. To sum up: we know that Jefferson had these journals, the three notebook journals, and a copy of the Mandan notes in

31. Ibid., pp. 488–89.
32. This letter of Jonathan Clark in the Wisconsin Historical Society Collections is referred to by Jackson, p. 486 n.
33. Jackson, p. 496.
34. Ibid., pp. 548–49.

1805. We know that when Lewis came to Washington in 1806, he brought with him the morocco-bound notebooks that contained the record of the trip from Fort Mandan to the Pacific and return. We know that Jefferson examined them, and I interpret Jefferson's phrase "we left the papers in their hands" to mean that he returned the morocco-bound notebooks and the other journals and papers just mentioned. We know that when Clark arrived in Washington after Lewis' death, all the papers in Lewis' trunks including the morocco-bound notebooks were turned over to him. We do not know whether this journal was in the trunks or whether Clark had brought it with him from St. Louis. We do know that when the River Journal came into Biddle's hands, he dated it consecutively—both the rough notes up to September 23, 1804, and the clean copy after that date. After Biddle was through with the River Journal and the Mandan notes, he probably turned them over to Clark. It is impossible to determine under what circumstances the River Journal was combined with the Dubois Journal which, I believe, was sent from Fort Mandan to Louisville in 1805. Either Clark or some other person brought them together and wrapped them up in a copy of the *National Intelligencer*. One hundred and fifty years later the packet was discovered in an attic in St. Paul.

Here, then, in 1811, the trail ends, for in the correspondence concerning the publication of the history of the expedition and the disposal of the journals there is nothing to isolate this journal from the mass of material, most of which found its way into the collections of the American Philosophical Society in Philadelphia.

When this journal was discovered in St. Paul, I hoped that some inquiry into the life of General Hammond, in whose papers the packet was discovered, and an examination of his other papers, might yield some clue as to their whereabouts from 1811 until their discovery. A report of the effort made to find some solution to the puzzle is, I think, due the reader.

In the trial held in the United States District Court in Minneapolis in December 1953 over the question of ownership of the documents, there was no firm evidence brought out in the examination of witnesses that the family of General Hammond or his heirs ever knew of their existence. Indeed, it was on the initiative of one of the heirs to the estate of the General's daughter that the papers were turned over to the Minnesota Historical Society, with the alleged verbal understanding that after an inventory had been made, they should remain with the Society. No one seemed to have known that such an historical treasure as these documents was in the St. Paul attic, buried in the papers of the General, who had died in 1890. Had the heirs known that such was the case, it is doubtful that they would have initiated steps to have their grandfather's papers transferred to the Society. When the curator sorted out the Hammond papers and came upon the packet containing the journal, she noted that it looked as if it had not been disturbed for years. When she testified in the trial, she pointed out, however, that three small pieces of paper that were later found to be part of the journal were not found in the packet but were loose among the other papers.

Fortunately, in most cases where a collection of documents such as these is discovered, their origin and their history can be traced. There is usually some information from one source or another that will answer the question of how the owner acquired the papers, and the approximate time when they came into his hands. Starting with such data, it is usually possible to trace them back to their origin. In this case, however, there was no such information.

Because of the possibility that some connection between the Clark family and the Hammonds might have existed, the logical place to begin the investigation seemed to be Louisville. Members of the Clark family had lived there for years, and General Hammond and his wife, Sophia Hammond, had also resided there. There was also the possibility that the collection of manuscript material in the

Filson Club in Louisville might contain something useful. In Louisville I learned that the General's wife was the daughter of one Nathaniel Wolfe, who had come there in 1838 and began the practice of law. In 1864 General Hammond had been relieved of his duties on General Sherman's staff because of illness. He came to Louisville and married Sophia Wolfe, whose father died in 1865. Perhaps there had been some connection between the Clark and the Wolfe families; some property belonging to the Clark family may have been purchased by Wolfe, and these documents in some way or other may have come into General Hammond's possession when he married Wolfe's daughter. I could find no record of such an exchange of property. It is, of course, impossible to say that Wolfe, a prominent lawyer in Louisville, had no contact with the Clarks, or that some piece of furniture belonging to the Clarks did not at some time or other become the property of the Wolfe–Hammonds. But the collection in the Filson Club contained nothing that would even remotely connect the two families. Nor did I find anything in the Draper Collection of the Wisconsin Historical Society, in the Missouri Historical Society in St. Louis, or in other collections containing Clark papers that referred in any way to the Wolfe family. The trail hopefully begun in Louisville and elsewhere faded into mere conjecture.

There is only one time, so far as is now known, when General Hammond ever saw or handled any documents that Clark may have written. In the trial in Minneapolis, Oliver Wendell Holmes of the National Archives, in direct charge of the papers of the Indian Bureau, presented evidence on this point. His testimony deserves some mention here.

Until his death in 1838, Clark continued to direct Indian relations west of the Mississippi, first as principal agent for the Louisiana Territory, then Superintendent for the Western District and finally as Superintendent of the Central District. Following his death, the office and presumably all of its papers were moved first to St. Joseph, Missouri, then to Atchison, Kansas, and finally, in 1869, to Lawrence, Kansas. In 1878, the government decided to close out the superintendency and bring its papers to Washington. General Hammond, who was for a brief period an inspector in the Indian Bureau, was instructed to proceed to Lawrence, examine, classify, and arrange the official papers, make an inventory of them and box them up and send them to Washington. In the inventory that was presented as an exhibit in the trial, there are a few papers going back to the Clark period and an item described as "one bundle of old maps" and another of "old bills and papers" dated 1830 and 1833.

The presence of a bundle of old maps seemed significant, for in 1924 a bundle of such maps was transferred from the Indian Bureau to the Library of Congress. In this packet Miss Annie Heloise Abel discovered the map which she assumed was the Evans Map, which Clark took up the Missouri in 1804 and which is referred to in the footnotes accompanying this text as the Indian Office Map. Without going into the provenance of the map, Mr. Holmes merely referred to it to give some support to his argument that this map was in the bundle listed by Hammond, and if such a Clark document was included, the present journal might well have been among the papers found by Hammond in Lawrence, Kansas in 1878.

There is nothing in the Hammond papers that would support this conclusion. The diary kept by the General for the period records his trip to Kansas and the execution of orders given him by the Indian Bureau. The official papers were boxed, an inventory of their contents was taken, and the lot sent to Washington. There is not the slightest hint that Hammond ever saw the Clark journal that was found among his papers in St. Paul.

With all due respect to Mr. Holmes' solid and scholarly research, made in an effort to solve this puzzle, it must be admitted that the evidence is far too tenuous to support any conclusions. It is my hope, and I know that I share it with all those who are interested in the history of the American frontier, that further research and perhaps some fortunate discovery of new material will solve this fascinating problem.

However, we have this journal, a valuable addition to our knowledge of an American odyssey which captured the attention and imagination of the American people as they looked westward and wondered what lay beyond the farthest horizon. Across the span of years, these documents enlist us with those men who fought their great protagonist, the Missouri, pouring its flood down "through a vast and unknown barbarism." We feel Clark's excitement when for the first time he looked upon the wide sweep of the plains, and with him our minds reach out to the mountains that lie far to the west. In these days of our narrowed world, it is good to go with him into a new great land, known then only to the Indian and the few fur traders who had penetrated its fastnesses.

ꙮ *A Note on the Text* ꙮ

IN TRANSCRIBING THIS JOURNAL, I have tried to present the text in as readable a form as possible, and at the same time to preserve its authenticity. These are field notes or copies of field notes, and an examination of the facsimile of each document published in this volume will give the reader an idea of its character that no transcript could possibly reproduce. The interlineations, the blots, and the corrections tell their own story.

Clark's spelling and punctuation have been faithfully reproduced. No liberties have been taken in transcribing these documents, except that I have without annotation brought down the interlineations into their proper position in the text and have omitted words crossed out by Clark, unless they help convey his meaning more completely or reflect some difficulty he was having in the wording of his entry. In such cases I have enclosed the deleted words between the symbols < >. Conjectural emendations are within the usual square brackets. Clark underlined many words, perhaps for emphasis, perhaps out of habit. I have not reproduced such underlining in the text. A date for each document, from Document 13 on, was inserted by a hand other than Clark's or Lewis', and when it occurs it is printed in large type above the document. The importance of these dates is discussed in the Introduction. Whenever there is an entry in Lewis' hand or in the hand of any other identifiable person, I have noted it in the text.

Some of the documents are small fragments bearing no date. Each fragment has been given a number that follows the number of the document with which it belongs. Throughout the annotation I have referred to the *Original Journals of the Lewis and Clark Expedition,* edited by Reuben Gold Thwaites, as the Notebook Journals, and all citations to them as Thw., volume, page. To facilitate comparison of the two journals, I have followed Thwaites in dividing the journal into the same sections he used for the Notebook Journals from May 14, 1804, through April 7, 1805, using the same headings.

I. THE DUBOIS JOURNAL

December 13, 1803, to May 14, 1804

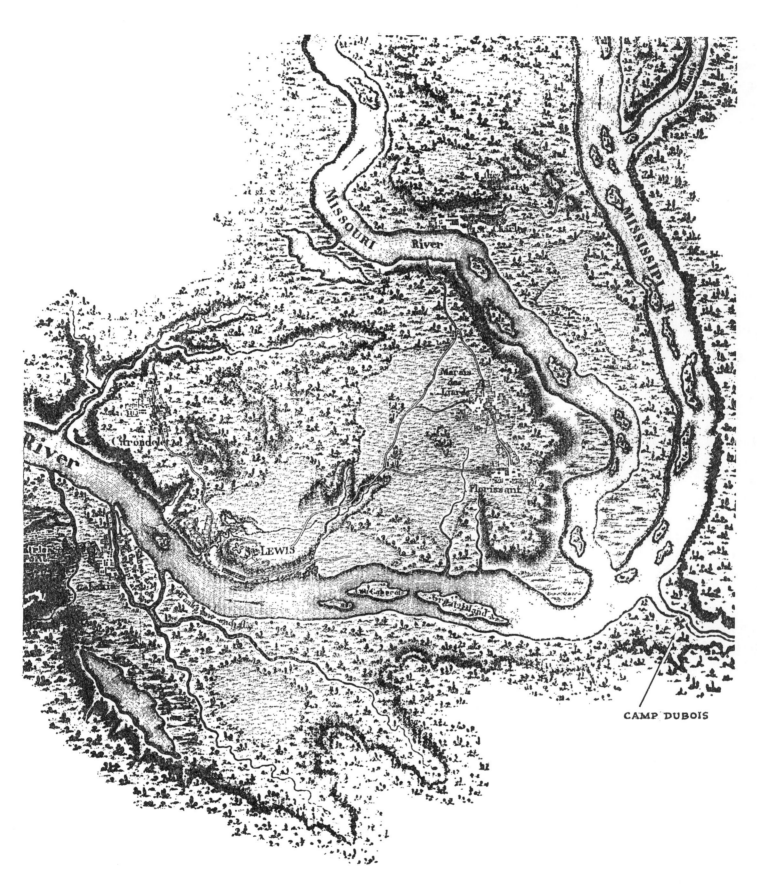

The junction of the Mississippi and Missouri rivers. From the map made in 1796 by General Victor Collot, published in his *Voyage dans l'Amérique Septentrionale*. The site of Camp Dubois is marked X. Scale: approximately 2 miles to the inch.

Tuesday on the [Dec.] 13ᵗʰ [1803] fixed on a place to build huts¹ Set the Men to Clearing land & Cutting Logs—a hard wind all day—flying Clouds, Sent to the Neighbourhood, Some Indians pass.

Wednesday—14ᵗʰ Continued to Cut Logs, Sent out into the Neghbrhood yesterday, Some Indians passed, wind Continue to blow hard river riseing—

Thursday—15ᵗʰ I cut a road to the prairy 2490 yards East Commenc the Cabins one Indian Came with Meat, 2 men Pass to dy hunters [k]illed Some grouse Snow

Friday—16ᵗʰ Continue to raise Cabins, Sent off C Floyd² to Koho [Cahokia] with Letters for Capt Lewis to put in the post office &c Several boats pass down to day a Pierogue Came to, a Mr Saml Greffeth³ good farmer who Lives 9 Miles up the Missouries & a Mr Charles [?] Gilbert⁴ a Trader in Salt The winds high to day—Cloudy rais one Cabin at night I write a Speach &c.&c.

S[aturday] 17ᵗʰ a Cold fine morning Towok [Took] equal allitudes

A M.. [38] ᵐ38 – 45   P.M [3]2 – ᵐ20 – 41
do   3[8] 41 – 59   " [3]2 – 21 – 46
do   3[8] 43 – 1   " [3]2 – 23 – 45

$$32° - 47' - 45''⁵$$

Missed the altidude at 12 oClock with the quadrent

Sunday 18ᵗʰ Clear Morning Took the Me[ridian] altitude of the Suns Lowr Limb with the Sextent found it to be 56° – 15′ – 22″. The Chronoter too Slow about 24′ – 20″—I also took the Median Altitude of the Suns Lowr limb with the quadt and foun 52° – 57ᵐ – 0 the errour of the instrument is 1° – 20′ – 00″ + ad +

$$\text{Lat} = 38° - 21' - 36''. \quad 1/10$$
$$\text{Qudt} = 38 - 31 - 57. \quad 1/10$$

I took the altitude of the ☉ L.L with the Sext: the 18 Decr and Calculated the Lattidude of River Dubuy [Dubois] i e—38° – 21′ – 36″ 1/10

also 19ᵗʰ and made it	38 – 23 – 8 – Dark [?] day	
also 3ᵈ January 1804 do	38 – 21 – 35	
also 4 do do do	38 – 21 – 6	2/10

76 – 44 – 14   2/10
76   43 – 11   1/10

Diffn   2 │ 1 – 3 – 1/10

38 – 22 – 31 – 5/10+
38 – 21 – 35   7/10

38 – 22 – 7.   2/10

True Lattidud⁶

[*The following appears written along the edge of the second page of the MS:*]
Left Fort Masacre [Fort Massac]⁷ the 13ᵗʰ of Novr 1803 at 4 oClock with an at [*Sentence incomplete*]

1. Camp Dubois. The site of the winter quarters had been determined before the party arrived there Dec. 12, 1803. In a letter to Jefferson from Cahokia, Dec. 19, 1803, Lewis wrote, "Capt. Clark continued his route [up the Mississippi] with the party to the river Dubois (distant from St. Louis 18 Miles) in order to erect Cabins for our winter residence at that place (provided it answered the description we had received of it) or otherwise to establish himself on a more eligible one as near it as possible" (Lewis to Jefferson, Cahokia, Dec. 19, 1803; Jackson, p. 147).

Clark, who continued to keep the journal Lewis had begun when he left Pittsburgh with the keelboat in Aug. 1803, wrote his last entry Dec. 12: "I came to the mouth of a little River Called Wood River, . . . The hunders which I had sent out to examine the Country in Deferent derections, returned with Turkeys & Opossoms and informed me the country was butifull and had great appearance of Gaim." In *The Journals of Captain Meriwether Lewis and Sergeant John Ordway*, Wisconsin Historical Society, *Collections*, 22 (Madison, 1916), 75–76; hereafter cited as the *Ohio Journal*. The Dubois Journal begins Dec. 13, 1803.

On the map drawn by Clark sometime in the winter of 1803–04 (Doc. 4), the mouth of the Dubois (Wood) River is placed below the junction of the Mississippi and Missouri, and is so located in this journal and in the Gass Journal (Patrick Gass, *Gass's Journal of the Lewis and Clark Expedition*, Chicago, 1904, p. [1]; hereafter cited as *Gass*). Today the mouth of this stream is 4½ miles above the confluence of the two rivers. During the past 150 years, the Missouri has shifted its course southward: in all probability the site of Camp Dubois is buried beneath the mud on the Missouri side. See U.S.G.S. Map, *Alton Quadrangle*, 1934.

The keelboat was anchored in the Dubois, and during the winter was drawn up on shore. From the Clark map, it is impossible to tell with certainty on which side of the Dubois the camp was located. The markings on the map suggest that it was on the south bank. John Reynolds, in his *Pioneer History of Illinois* (Chicago, 1887), p. 356, places the camp on the south bank: "The exploring party consisting of thirty four men, camped in the American Bottom, not far from the Mississippi, below the mouth of the Wood River."

In a letter to his brother-in-law, Major William Croghan (Clark to Croghan, River a Dubois, Jan. 15, 1804), Clark gave the following description of the country around the camp:

I have not been from my camp to any house since my arrival here. . . . My situation is as Comfortable as Could be expected in the woods, & on the frontiers; the Country back of me is butifull beyond description; a rich bottom well timbered, from one to three mile wide, from the river to a Prarie; which runs nearly parrilal to the river from about three miles above me, to Kasskasskia and is from three to 7 [7 written over 9] mile's wide, with gradual rises and Several Streams of running water, and good Mill Seats. This Prarie has Settlements on its edges from Kahokia [to] within three miles of this place.

The Missouri which mouths imediately opposet me <is a large turbalent> is the river we intend assending as soon as the weather will permit— This Great river which seems to dispute the preemininence with the Mississippi, coms in at right angles from the West, and forces its great sheets of muddy Ice (which is now running) against the Eastern bank (Jackson, p. 164.)

Extending from the Dubois River southward to the Kaskaskia was the region that Clark describes as "butifull beyond description." In this very fertile region the French had settled, and after the Revolution came a flood of Americans, to give it the name American Bottom. The first newcomers settled around Kaskaskia; after the Indian danger lessened, following Wayne's victory, others ventured further northward. By 1803–04, farms were numerous both above and below the Dubois. Some of the names appearing in the journal were those of farmers in the neighborhood who found a market for their produce at Camp Dubois. (See Reynolds, pp. 131, 201 ff.)

2. The names of most of the members of the expedition who left St. Louis in May 1804 are mentioned in this journal. There are also many lists of men made by Clark for one purpose or another—some apparently for roll calls, and others for special details. Opposite the names in some of the lists, the reader will note a word or two by Clark on the character of the men under his command. In his plans for manning the keelboat and the two pirogues, Clark listed the men many times.

Since biographies of the party, as far as they are known, are given by Thwaites, Coues, Wheeler, and others, it has seemed unnecessary to give them here. Rather, the editor has given the roster of the officers and men when the party left Camp Dubois. In the first list are the names of those who were permanent members of the party and who made the trip to the Pacific and return. In the second list are those who for one reason or another did not complete the trip. The names of this last group will be noted as they appear in the Notebook Journal. (See Reuben Gold Thwaites, ed., *Original Journals of the Lewis and Clark Expedition*, 8 vols. New York, 1904–05, hereafter cited as Thw.; Elliott Coues, *History of the Expedition . . . of Lewis and Clark*, 4 vols. New York, 1893, *1*, 253–60, hereafter cited as Coues, *History*; Olin D. Wheeler, *The Trail of Lewis and Clark*, 2 vols. New York, 1926, *1*, 54–135; Jackson, pp. 369–73.)

Captain Meriwether Lewis
Captain William Clark
York, Captain Clark's servant
George Drouillard, interpreter
John Ordway, sergeant
Nathaniel Pryor, sergeant

Privates
William Bratton
John Collins
John Colter
Pierre Cruzatte
Joseph Field
Reuben Field
Robert Frazer
Patrick Gass
George Gibson
Silas Goodrich
Hugh Hall
Thomas Proctor Howard
Francis Labiche
Hugh McNeal
John Potts
George Shannon
John Shields
John B. Thompson
William Werner
Joseph Whitehouse
Alexander Willard
Richard Windsor
Peter Wiser

The following did not complete the trip:

Sergeant John Floyd, died, Aug. 20, 1804. Patrick Gass appointed in his place.
Corporal Richard Warfington
John Boley
John Dame
John Robertson—sent back, June 12, 1804 (infra, pp. 33, 55 n.).
Ebenezer Tuttle
Isaac White
John Newman—courtmartialed for insubordination and sent back to St. Louis in April 1805.
Moses B. Reed—courtmartialed for desertion and sent back to St. Louis in April 1805.

3. Mr. Samuel Griffith. On the map of the region made by Clark (Doc. 4), his farm was located on the Spanish side of the Mississippi, on the narrow neck of land separating the Mississippi from the Missouri. From the map, it would appear that his farm was some ten miles from Clark's camp. Samuel Griffith came from New York and was settled by 1795. He was appointed ensign in the Territorial Militia of Louisiana in 1806. (See Clarence E. Carter, ed., *Territorial Papers of the United States, 13*, 547, hereafter cited as Carter, *Terr. Paprs*). He is listed as a captain in the Third Regiment of the Missouri Territorial Militia. (See Louis Houck, *History of Missouri*, 3 vols. Chicago, 1908, *2*, 100; *3*, 104, 111; hereafter cited as Houck, *Missouri*.)

4. I am unable to identify this person.

5. I have interpolated the figure "3" before the "8" in the column under "A M" and before the figure "2" in the "P M" column. On the next day, Clark gave the latitude as 38° 22′7″—a difference of six degrees from that recorded here.

6. Calculations based on the U.S.G.S. Map, *Alton Quadrangle*, give the present location of the mouth of the Wood (Dubois) River as latitude, 38°51′42″ N., longitude; 90°7′54″ W.

7. Fort Massac, on the north bank of the Ohio. The keelboat arrived there Nov. 11, 1803. In 1803 the fort was garrisoned by one company of infantry—three officers, 74 men (A.S.P.: *Military Affairs, 1*, 175). Here George Drewyer (Drouillard) was engaged as interpreter for the expedition (*Ohio Journal*, p. 47). The name "Fort Massacre" was in common use at the time (Reynolds, p. 53).

Monday 19ᵗʰ Der 1803

Took the altitude of S L Limb with the Sextt   found it 56° – 15' – 22" – also with the quaderant   found it 52° – 57' – 0"

the ex of quadt is   The Waggons Came with provisions this evening   Floyd returned with a Letter from Cap Lewis[8] one from S.S[9] and Sundery papers—an ax & a Flat Saw to be returned.

Tuesday 20ᵗʰ Decr

I Detain the waggons to haul logs for my building & Took the altitude of the Sun by both enstruments   found ☉ L L by Sextt was 56° – 9' – 7" –   by quaterent ☉ U L 54° . 10' – 0"   the exon of qudt is 1° – 20' – 0"   hauled Logs to day with the Comosaries Teem   men move into ther huts this eveninge. Chronometer has <Slew> stoped. last night   I wound her up at 12 to day as usial and She now goes   a hard frosty morning.

Wednesday 21ˢᵗ Decr   Cloudy Day   the Waggoner charged me three Dollars for his Services yesterday, Send out Shields & Floyd to hunt to day, they Kill 7 Turkeys   verry fat, I commence puting up the Logs for my huts to day   Water fall verry fast

[*Drawn on the reverse side of the document is a map by Clark of the junction of the Ohio and Mississippi rivers. On November 15, 1803, Lewis entered in his journal the following:* "Capt. Clark made a partial survey of the point [junction of the Ohio and the Mississippi] and ascertained by the Circumferenter and and [sic] projection that the width of the Ohio from*

	yards
the point was	*1274*
The Missippi	*1435*
and the width of them both from those observed	
points on their respective banks was	*2002*"[1]

The following are the notations made in Clark's hand explaining the map:]

From the Point of the Mississippi & Ohio 25 poles from the highest Land on the Sand point—From thence to A Signal on the opposit Side of the Ohio is N. 30 1/2ᵈ E 149 poles & 32 po: & 7/10 to the bank—From the Said beginning up the Ohio N 52 1/2° W 115 po: to a ——   Thence to the aforesaid Signal on the opposit Side of the Ohio is N, 68°, E—

From the Said Beginning Cross the Mississippi to a Signal is S 33° E— From Said point up the Mississippi is S 74° W 117 po: (to a Bluff of Sand opposit the Lower point of an Island)   From thence to the Said Signal is S 56° E—(To the upper point of Island is S 53 W, to Lower point is S 15 E)   From the Said point or begn: to the point on the West Side of the Mississippi is S 75° E—   From Said Point to a forked Tree on the East Side of the Mississippi Standing on the banke is S 77° E 700 poles (from thence to the high Land about 500 poles—

From the Signal on the East Side of the Ohio to a forked Tree on the bank below is S 66° E—   To the Point on the W Side of the Miss: below is S 55° E—   To the upper (house) or Signal is S 16° E Passing the lower point of the Sand Bar makeing from the Island above

From the highest part of the point along the high land up the Miss: is S 48° W 4 po: 14 Links, S 72 W. 144 po: S 13 W. 8 po: to the river where the bank Caves in. N 85" E 46 poles to the Willows, where the Bank sease to Cave in in the Course of the 3d observation

(The Course of the bank on the Spa: [Spanish] Side of the Miss: from the upper house Down is nearly S 85° E. abt 2 1/2 miles, & S 80 E about 450 yards to the lower point—Capt L) [*End of entry in Clark's hand*]

8. In this letter from Cahokia, Dec. 17, 1803, Lewis advised Clark that Drouillard had arrived with eight men from Tennessee. Among them was a house joiner and a blacksmith. He informed Clark that one Hennebury would supply him with a whipsaw, that corn could be obtained from Morrison's farm, and that he was forwarding a letter addressed to Clark that he had picked up in St. Louis. He added that he would be at Camp Dubois soon (Thw. 7, 288; Jackson, p. 144).

9. I am unable to identify S.S.

1. *Ohio Journal*, p. 48.

2. During the fall and winter of 1794–95, Lewis was with the troops under the command of General Daniel Morgan, who had been sent out to western Pennsylvania to suppress the Whiskey Rebellion. A cantonment for this force was set up 14 miles from Pittsburgh. There were protests from the inhabitants of the surrounding countryside over the marauding of the undisciplined soldiery. (See John Bakeless, *Lewis and Clark,* New York 1947, pp. 55–59; Charles M. Wilson, *Meriwether Lewis,* New York, 1934, p. 25; and Leland D. Baldwin, *Whiskey Rebels,* Pittsburgh, 1939.) This is apparently a rough draft made by Lewis at the request of one McFarlane, to be used in seeking indemnity for property damage.

[*The following entry is written in reverse order on the end of the manuscript and is in Lewis' hand:*]

Andrew Mc Farlane having informed me that he was about to make application to the general government <for> to be remunerated—for certain losses he sustained on his farm by the troops which were <stationed> cantoned on it under the comd of Genl Mor[gan] during the fall and winter 1794 [4 written over 5] and spring 1795 and being myself present during the whole of that period—I am induced to give the following statement <of facts which fell within the perview of my own observation> to be used by him as he may think most expedient[2]

[*End of entry in Lewis' hand*]

At Kaskaskais
The 3d Decr
<Sexion not> right

42°	− 27′	− 0″
21	− 13	− 30
	2	− 37 − refraction T: 1,—
21	− 10	− 53 1 − 4° F 6
		− 30
	16	− 17 Semideameter p 2 +
	8	+ Parallax T: 3 +
21	− 27	− 18 Suns Center
90		
67	− 32	− 42
22	− 2	− 7 Decklination
45	30	· 35

Kaskaskia   3d Decr

58°	− 33′	− 00″
29	− 16	− 30
	1	− 43 − refraction Ta: (1)
29	− 14	− 47
	16	− 17 + ☉ Diameter p: 2
	8	+ Parallax Ta 3
29	− 31	− 12
90		
60	− 28	− 48
22	− 2	− 7 Decklination
38	· 26	41
1	20	
39	− 46	− 41

At Kohokia
Lattitude as
worked by my
Self is
Degrees 38 − 6′ − 58″ N −
The Mouth Plate Crek
above Fort Charters [Chartres] is
Degrees 37° − 55′ − 36″ N.

At M: Missoureis
the 19th Decr

Sexton

$2 | 56° - 9 - 7''$

28 − 41 − 33   1/10

1 − 47 − 0−

_____

28 − 2 − 46 − 1/10

16 − 18 − 9/10 +

8

_____

28 . 19 − 13 +

8 − 49 −

_____

28 10 − 24

90

_____

61 − 49   36

23   25 − 28

_____

38   23 − 8   Differ with yesterday

54 seconds

Latidude

Qd^{ed}

1' − 32''

38

_____

54 Seconds | 54°   10' − 00''

27 − 5 − 0

1 − 47 −

_____

27 − 3 − 13

16 − 18 − 9 − Differ 4' 21'' − 9/10

_____

26 − 46 − 54 − 1

8 +

_____

26 − 47   2   1/10

1 − 20   +

_____

28   7   2: 1/10

90

_____

61 − 52 − 57   9/10

55.   32'' 8/10   23 − 25 − 28

11 − 27: 2   _____

1 − 9   38 − 27 − 29   9/10

_____

8

Differ from yesterday 3' − 18'' less

1.9   4 . 27   2/10   38   25 − 24

1 − 9. |4 − 32   38 − 6 − 58

_____   _____   _____

3   18   2/10   2   16   18 − 26

3

_____

15 − 26[3]

[*The following is in Lewis' hand:*]

Blaize Cenas[4]

H Baker   95 − 12th [?] Wharton, Lawler.[5] [*End of entry in Lewis' hand.*]
*The following is written across the end of the document in an unidenti-
fied hand:*]

Louisville November 26th 1803

Sir,

Pr

Thos Lisbet   Blacksmith,

Kaskaskies

Sent   42° ☉ 27 − 0''

Qdt <43   45>

58° − 33 − 00''

3. These calculations appear to be the result of Clark's effort to master the use of the
sextant.

4. A Mr. Blaze Cenas was in the crowd that
met the keelboat a few miles below Pittsburgh. Lewis had reason for getting his name.
He was allowed to fire off Lewis' air gun, and
caused considerable excitement by wounding
one of the spectators (*Ohio Journal*, p. 31).

5. I have been unable to identify these persons.

6. The creek here referred to is the River Dubois, in which the keelboat was anchored. See entry for Tuesday, Feb. 7, 1804 (infra, p. 27). On Clark's sketch map (Doc. 4) this river was drawn in and labeled "a Dubois." On the south bank and near the stream's mouth, he put a small triangle that may signify the location of the camp.

7. Pry or prize: a lever. Clark uses it here to mean a prop or wedge.

8. The only members of the party mentioned by Clark in the journal before the arrival of the eight men from Tennessee are Floyd and Shields. Pryor is mentioned by Lewis in his journal of the trip down the Ohio (*Ohio Journal*, pp. 27, 62).

Lewis was instructed by the Secretary of War, General Dearborn, to call on Captain Daniel Bissell at Fort Massac, and Captains Amos Stoddard and Russell Bissell at Kaskaskia for non-commissioned officers and privates, the total not to exceed twelve. An interpreter was to be engaged for $300 a year. The men selected were to be "good men who understand rowing a boat to go with Capt. Lewis as far up the River [Missouri] as they can go & return with certainity before the ice will obstruct the passage of the river" (Dearborn to Bissell and Stoddard, July 2, 1803, Jackson, pp. 103–04). Since the party did not enter the Missouri until late in the fall, Dearborn's instructions were not followed.

In a letter to Clark, Cincinnati, Sept. 28, 1803, Lewis wrote:

"I here had the pleasure of recieving yours of the 21st of August & the 11th of Septr. I am much pleased with the measures you have taken relative to the engaging the men you mention, as men of that discription only will answer our purposes. . . . I have two young men with me whom I have taken on trial and have not yet engaged them, but conditionally only, tho' I think they will answer tolerably well; there are a party of soldiers, 6 or 8 in number, now at Massac waiting my arrival. they were scelected from the troops in the State of Tennessee by Majr MacRea, perhaps most of these will answer; I am also authorized to select by voluntary engagement any men from the Companys of Capts R1. and D1. Bissel's and Stoddart's now occupying the posts of Massac and Kaskaskias; from these I think we shall be enabled to form our party without much difficulty. . . ." (Thw., 7, 272; Jackson, p. 125 and n.)

In a letter, Lewis to Clark, St. Louis, May 2, 1804, the latter was instructed that, in making out receipt rolls, he was "to commence with those inlisted in Kentucky from the dates of their inlistments, all others from the 1st of January 1804" (Thw., 7, 299; Jackson, p. 178). In the Draft of Receipt for Compensation (Thw., 7, 360–61), the names of the men whose enlistments began before Jan. 1, 1804, are as follows: Sergeants Charles Floyd, Nathaniel Pryor; Privates William Bratton, John Colter, Joseph Field, Reuben Field, George Gibson, George Shannon, John Shields.

Thursday 22nd Decr 1803

a verry great Sleat this morning, the river Covered with running Ice, and falls verry fast   15 Inches last night   the boat a ground in the Creek,[6] I had pries[7] fixed along to Support the boat, and all the heavy articles taken out in front & Center and Sto[r]ed under a guard on the bank—mist of rain, which prevents our doeing much to our huts to day, at 3 oClock Drewyer & 8 men 2 horses arrive from Tennessee, those men are not such I was told was in readiness at Tennessee for this Comd &c &c.[8]   recved a Letter from Cap Lewis also one from Mr Gratiot[9] offering a horse and his Services to Cap L; & my self in any way

Friday 23rd December 1803

a raney Day   continue to put up my huts   the men much fatigued <puting up> Carrying logs, I Send to Mr Morrisons[1] farm for a Teem & Corn, which arivd about 3 oClock, a raney Deggreeable day   Mr Griffeth Came down from his farm with a Load of Turnips &c as a present to me, Drewyear Came home to day after a <long> hunt, he Killed three Deer, & left them in the Woods, the Ice run to day   Several Deleaway pass   a chief whome I saw at Greenville Treaty,[2] I gave him a bottle of Whiskey, the water falls fast, the boat supt by Skids. I set the Detachment latterly arrived to build them a hut

Satturday 24th Decr

Cloudy morning, I purchase a Cargo of Turnips for 3/ a bushel of Mr Grereffeth, men Continue to put up & Cover the necessary huts, Drewyear returned with 3 Deer & 5 Turkeys   I send Shields with Mr Griffeth to purchase me Some butter   on the other Side of the river is the folks, finish Covering our huts this evening—two French Perogues pass up the river to day, and peregoue with black guard[3] Americans, passed down the river, The Indian Come in with a Deer this evening   a French man whome passed up to day told me that a man of abt 30 years of age well acquainted with the Missoures for 8 years, wished to go with me, but was afraid that the Comdt Should Know of it   his name is Lackduer Besernnet [?][4]

Christmas 25th Decr

I was wakened by a Christmas discharge & found that Some of the party had got Drunk <2 fought,> the men frolicked and hunted all day, Snow this morning, Ice run all day, Several Turkey Killed   Shields returned with a cheese & 4 lb butter, Three Indians come to day to take Christmas with us, I gave them a bottle of Whiskey and they went off after informing me that a great talk had been held and that all the nations were going to war against the Ozous [Osage?] in 3 months, one informed me that a English man 16 ms from here told him that the Americans had the Countrey and no one was allowed to trade &c   I ixplaind the <thing> Intention of Govmt to him, and the Caus of the possession, Drewyear Says he will go with us, at the rate ofd and will go to Massac to Settle his matters.[5]

December 26th Monday

—a Cloudy day   one of my party Killed 7 Turkeys last night at roost—continue working at the huts—The Ice run, This day is moderate, two men Willard & Corpl Roberson Came home to day at about 11 oClock, Corpl. White house & York Comce [commenced] sawing with the Whip Saws—nothing material—

December 27th Tuesday

—a fair Day   I put out Blankets goods &c &c to dry and Stored them in the Store room apparently in good order <I> nearly finish My Chimney to day   missed my observation—at abt 3 oClock to day three frenchmen in a Pierogue Came down pursuing a

Swan which they had wounded Some distance above, the Swan swan [swam] as fast as they Could row thier Pierogue and I thought rather gained on the pieroge as they passed—they Cought it 2 m below. I send home the Cart & oxen, Sent out Drewyer to hunt to day, early he returned Late with a Buck, he Saw three Bar on the other side of the Prarie

28 Decr   a Cloudy day   no Ice in the river, nothing remarkable to day —Drewyer Kill a Deer & the Indn Kill another

29th   Snow this morning   Cloudey & wet all day, finish my hut and write 2 Letters one to G.H.[6] & one to Col Anderson[7] & rain at night

30th Decr   Snow in the morning   I move into my hut, Cloudy morning. Colter Kill a Deer & a turkey, Drewyer & Serjt Odway set out for Kohokia, I arrange the guards on a new plan, wrote to Cap Lewis

In the list of expenditures of the expedition incurred up to April 1805, the names of these men are listed as receiving enlistment bounties in 1803. Jackson infers, I think correctly, that they are the nine young men from Kentucky mentioned by Biddle. Of these Shannon and Colter were probably picked up by Lewis on his journey down the Ohio and the others at Louisville or possibly Fort Massac (Thw., 7, 360–61; Jackson, p. 431 n.). Other names appear in this journal after the arrival of these men, but it is impossible to determine when they arrived. In a letter to Clark from Cahokia, Dec. 17, 1803, Lewis states that George Drouillard had arrived with the Tennesseans, and expresses the same dissatisfaction with them, as does Clark (Thw., 7, 288; Jackson, p. 144). George Drouillard, the French interpreter and hunter, was engaged at Fort Massac on Nov. 11, 1803 (*Ohio Journal*, p. 47).

9. Charles Gratiot was an important figure in St. Louis in 1803. He had moved there from Cahokia in 1781. He was present at the transfer of Louisiana to the United States, March 9, 1804, and signed the articles of cession along with Captain Lewis. His wife was the sister of Pierre and Auguste Chouteau (Houck, *Missouri*, 2, 11, 362 ff.; *D.A.B.*, 7, 503–04). Even before the French cession of Louisiana to the United States the arrival of the Americans foreshadowed an entirely new situation with which the leaders in the fur trade in St. Louis—the Chouteaus, Gratiot, and others—must cope. From now on they show an interest in all that goes on at Camp Dubois and a desire to render every assistance to the party. Gratiot supplied goods for the expedition and accompanied Captain Lewis and the party to St. Charles where on May 20, 1804, they met Clark, who had left Dubois with the keelboat and pirogues a week earlier. See infra, p. 43; Thw., *1*, 22; *Glimpses of the Past*, Missouri Historical Society, *8*, nos. 7–9, pp. 93–95; John Francis McDermott, *Old Cahokia* (St. Louis, 1949), pp. 190–94.

1. William Morrison of Kaskaskia was one of the leading merchants and landowners in the region (Jackson, pp. 144–45 n.; Nasatir, 2, passim; Reynolds, pp. 160 ff.). Morrison's farm was near the junction of the Mississippi and the Missouri and close to Camp Dubois (*The Missouri Gazette*, Feb. 3, 1809).

2. Lewis and Clark were both with General Anthony Wayne in 1793–94 on his invasion of the Indian country north of the Ohio, and Clark was with the column that met and defeated the Indians at Fallen Timbers on Aug. 20, 1794. After a year of negotiations, the Indians north of the Ohio and those further to the northwest signed the Treaty of Fort Greenville on Aug. 3, 1795, surrendering all claims to approximately two-thirds of the present state of Ohio and parts of Indiana and Illinois. This entry places Clark at Fort Greenville when the treaty was signed.

3. It is not entirely clear whether the river referred to here is the Mississippi or the Mis-

souri. In the Dubois Journal, Clark commonly uses the name Missouri when he notes the passing of craft up and down that stream; therefore, I believe that here he is referring to the Mississippi. I have no way of knowing who the "blackguard Americans" were. Clark may have been angered by the appearance of these interlopers just at the time that he and Lewis were trying to establish good relations with the authorities in St. Louis and with the Indians. The rumor was going the rounds among the Indians "that the Americans had the country and no one was allowed to trade." See the entry for the next day, Dec. 25. Clark undoubtedly knew of such rumors and perhaps suspected that these "blackguards" were circulating them.

4. The French names Ladouceur and Bissonette are both common in St. Louis. It is impossible to determine whether or not Clark is attempting to transcribe these names. A Louis Bissonette had a daughter named Angelica, who married a Ladouceur (Frederic L. Billon, *Annals of St. Louis in Its Territorial Days,* St. Louis, 1888, p. 427).

5. Lewis wrote to Clark (Cahokia, Dec. 17, 1803), "I have offered him [Drouillard] 25$ pr Month so long as he may chuise to continue with us" (Jackson, p. 144; Thw., 7, 288). In the text, I have retained without notation Clark's spelling of Drouillard, "Drewyer."

6. These initials probably stood for George Hancock of Fincastle, Virginia. His daughter, Julia, was engaged to Clark at the time. They were married in 1808.

7. Colonel Richard Clough Anderson, Revolutionary soldier and one of the early settlers of Louisville, Kentucky. His first wife was a sister of William Clark. (See *D.A.B., 1,* 270–71.)

Saty 31st of Decr   I Issued certain [order?] & prohibited a Certain Ramey from Selling Liqor to the Party,[8] Several things Killed to day. Colter Oddawey Willard Teakens [Leakins?][9] Hall & Collins Drunk. began to snow at Dark and Continued untill 9 oClock   Cloudy to day

January 1st 1804   Snow about an inch deep   Cloudy to day, a woman Come forward wishing to wash and doe Such things as may be necessary for the Detachmt   Several men Come from the Countrey to See us & Shoot with the men, they bring Sugare &c to trade, I purchase Sugar 6 lb at 1/6 per pound, I put up a Dollar to be Shot for, the two best Shots to win   Gibson best   the Country people won the dollar— (R [Reed?] & Ws. [Wiser, Windsor?] Drunk)   a Perogue Passed loaded with Salt & Dry goods. Jos: Vaun[1] offers to let the Contrator have Beef at 4$ pd. [produce?] or 3 $ 50 Cents in money, Pokers hake, the Nut is [*one word illegible*] a plant growing in the ponds with a large broad leaf, stem is [in] the middle of the leaf   in french Volies[2]   Three men Mr. Leebice[3] Blacksmith &c, one man offers to sell port at [*space*] apply to Hannerberry,[4] the blacksmith has traveled far to the North, & Visited the Man'd [Mandans] [*one word illegible*] on Missouris, a quiet people 6 day fr[om] [*one word illegible*] or Red river & that the M: [Missouri River] is about 150 yds over at this nation

January 2nd   Snow last night, <rain> a mist to day   Cap Whitesides[5] Came to See me & his Son, and some countrey people, Serjt Odderway return & bring me Some papers from Capt Lewis, who is [in] Kohokia on business of importance to the enterprise, the party verry merry this evenig. Mr Whitesides says a no. of young men in his Neghborhood wishes to accompany Capt Lewis & myself on the Expdts   Cap L. allso sent me a Letter from Capt Amos Stoddard which mentions his aptnt to the Comd of upper Louisiane, & to take possession of St. Louis &c[6]

Tuesday Jany 3rd 1804   a Verry Cold blustering day   <the> [*one word illegible*] is Doneyan & Co: Thermometer one oClock in the open air   the <quicksilver> Mercuria fell to 21 D. below the freezing point, I took the altitude of the suns L.L. and made it 57° 16 0 N by the Sexton [Sextant]   all the after part of the Day the wind so high that the View up the Missourie appeared Dredfull, as the wind blew off the Sand with fury as to Almost darken that part of the atmespear   this added to agutation of the water apd truly gloomy   Comy [Commissary] kiled a Beef &c at 3 oClock the q.s or murcy fell to 22 D. below feesing

| at 4 | do | —do | do— | 27 1/2 ditto | } in the air |
| at 5 | do | —do | do— | 30—or (O) | |

the wind violent all Day from N.NW. & NW.

The Americans are Settled up the Mississippi for 56 miles [*blot*] as high up a[s] the Sandy river from thence across to the Missouries river   a Salt works is establish[ed] on a Small river 30 miles up the river 10 miles from the Mississippi   I am told that an old french fort was once built on the opsd side of the river from me, and that Some remains of the clearing is yet to be seen, this must be the fort which was built in the year 1724 by M. de Bourgmot the Comdt[7]

The first Settlement made in this quarter was made 1679. de la Salle at [*space*] then Called Crevecoeur[8]

arkansas was settled by 10 F. men in 1685[9]

8. This man, who may have been one of the "blackguard Americans," had apparently set up a whiskey shop in the neighborhood (Bakeless, p. 106). A Matthew Ramey claimed land in the St. Louis district by making a camp on the Des Peres River in 1803 (A.S.P.: *Public Lands, 2,* 549). A William Ramy was signer of a memorial from the St. Charles district to the President, 1806 (Carter, *Terr. Paprs. 13,* 485).

9. Teakens, Leakens, or Leekens was finally discharged (infra, p. 27; Bakeless, p. 106).

1. I am unable to identify this person.

2. The French name for this water plant was *Graine de Volaille* or *Pois de Shicorat.* The Chippewas called it *Wab-bis-sa-pin* or Swan Root. The seed-vessel or "nut" was used by the Indians for food. The botanical name is *Nelumbo Lutea.* (See Lewis, "Botanical Notes," Thw., *6,* 137–38; Elijah H. Criswell, *Lewis and Clark: Linguistic Pioneers,* University of Missouri Studies, *15,* no. 2, Columbia, Mo., 1940, cvii.) The "Pokers hake" of Clark may be his rendition of the Kickapoo word for this plant, *Po-kish-a-co-mah.*

3. Lewis to Clark, Cahokia, Dec. 17, 1803: "Among the party from Tennessee is a blacksmith and a House joiner" (Jackson, p. 144; Thw., *7,* 288). It is impossible to tell from Clark's entry whether Mr. Leebice and the blacksmith are one and the same person. Because of Clark's erratic spelling, it is uncertain whether this man is Francis Labiche, who enlisted May 16, 1804, as a private (Thw., *7,* 360). He served as one of the bowmen on the keelboat. The other bowman was Cruzatte. Both of these men had spent two winters at the mouth of the Nodaway River, 450 miles up the Missouri (Thw., *1,* 34, 72, 37; *7,* 21). While the party was at Fort Mandan during the winter of 1804–05, a Gros Ventre chief, in talking to Charles MacKenzie of the Northwest Company, said, "There are only two sensible men among them [the Lewis and Clark party] the worker in iron and the mender of guns" (L. R. Masson, *Les Bourgeois de la Compagnie du Nord-ouest,* 2 vols. Quebec, 1889–90, *1,* 330). The mender of guns was clearly Shields, who probably was also the blacksmith (Thw., *3,* 304; *4,* 193). It is impossible to say with finality that the worker in iron was Francis Labiche.

4. A Patrick Heneberry was one of the earliest settlers in Six Mile Prairie above St. Louis on the Illinois side (Reynolds, p. 280). He was employed by Morrison from 1799 to 1805 (Jackson, pp. 144–45 and n.).

5. Captain William Whiteside. The Whiteside family was originally from North Carolina, and had migrated first to Kentucky and then to Illinois in 1793. Captain William, who had fought at King's Mountain, was the leader of the clan. He settled at New Design between Kaskaskia and Cahokia and built a fort there which was known as Whiteside's

Station. He was the leader in a number of forays against the Indians in the region around Cahokia. On one of these he and his son were wounded. He was later colonel of an Illinois militia regiment (Reynolds, pp. 185–90).

6. Captain Amos Stoddard was then in command of a company of the regiment of artillery. He was the officer detailed to conduct the ceremony of transferring Upper Louisiana from the Spanish officials to the United States representatives (Francis B. Heitman, *Historical Register and Dictionary of the United States Army*, *1*, 51, 928). Captain Stoddard, Lewis, and Clark were the only official representatives of the government of the United States in the St. Louis area during the winter and spring of 1804. When Lewis left with the party of exploration in May 1804, he appointed Stoddard as his agent in St. Louis. The correspondence of Stoddard is in the Missouri Historical Society. See *Glimpses of the Past*, Mo. Hist. Soc., *2*, nos. 6–10 and Jackson, passim.

7. Clark was misinformed. Fort Orleans, established in 1723 by Etienne de Bourgmont, French commandant of the Missouri, was located 250 miles up the Missouri. The fort at the mouth of the Missouri and opposite Clark's camp on the Dubois was Fort Don Carlos, completed by 1768 (Nasatir, *1*, 70; James B. Musick, *St. Louis as a Fortified Town*, St. Louis, 1941, pp. 14–15 and plates; Charles E. Peterson, *Colonial St. Louis*, St. Louis, 1949, p. 51). Fort Don Carlos proved useless in controlling the fur trade up the Missouri. The English traders and war parties of Indians used the Des Moines and portaged over to the heads of the Grand River, which entered the Missouri 240 miles from its mouth. The fort was abandoned ca. 1780.

8. Fort Crèvecoeur in the Illinois was built by La Salle in 1680: Francis Parkman, *La Salle and the Discovery of the Great West* (Boston, 1898), pp. 180–81.

9. Clark must refer to the six men Tonty left at the Arkansas villages in 1686.

1. Fort Prudhomme was established in 1682 at the third Chickasaw Bluff (near modern Natchez): Parkman, *La Salle*, pp. 297–98.

2. I am unable to locate the settlement here referred to.

3. There are lead and zinc deposits in this area near the mouths of the Cumberland and Tennessee rivers. The large island mentioned here is probably Cumberland Island, about ten miles up the Ohio River from the mouth of the Tennessee. A creek now known as Caney Creek comes in opposite this island. On this creek galena was discovered. The diggings were known in the frontier period as the "Old Silver Mines." The silver sheen of galena ore probably was the reason they were so named. The "15 m[iles] N." suggests the Sheridan mining area, 15 miles N.E., where

a fort was built by the F—at Prud-homme, or Chick: Bluffs in the year 1722[1]

Assumption

A Settlement was on an Island above the Ohio with an armed schooner in 1743—[2]

D. [Drouillard?] Says that about 7 m from the mouth of the Tennessee up the first Creek opposit the Island, and at the edge of the Canons, [?] near [?] S. [?] of Nalla [?]—<and> is a Lead mine   he also says that about 15 M N. is a Mine of Ore white and Deep [?] Black,[3]
Flag the word of the [*one word illegible*]
but one heart
Explain the Pond & fishing place above Waubash
[*The following figures are written between the entries for December 31 and January 1. They are written at right angles to the entries.*]

$$12$$
$$3$$
$$70 \mid 480 \mid 7$$

[*The following list of names[4] is written across the bottom of the manucript:*]

Floyd—	√	Odderway	√	x Boyley	
Shields—	√	Whitehouse—	√	x Leakens	√
Bratten—		√ Robertson—	√	Worrington	
Newmon—		Mc Neal		Worner	
R. Fields—		Goodrich		Thompson	
J. Fields—		o Windser—		Howard	
G Shannon—		Reed—		√ Potts	
Pryor—		√ Wiser		Collins	√
x Gibson—	√	Gess—		Frasure	
√ Colter—	√	x Willard	√	√ Hall	√

[*The following list is in the lower left-hand corner of the leaf containing the map:*]

Odway	.	. Robertson	x	Reid	.
. White house	.	Gass	.	Boy ley	x
. M. Neal	.	. Winser	.	Wiser	.
. Good rich	. —	Willard	x	Seekins	x

(about 3 will be sick)

[*The following list is on the right-hand side of the leaf containing the map; it is written sideways:*]

x Frasure [*one word illegible*] Corpls—	Thompson	Collins Black gard
	Potts	Worner
Howard—never Drinks water	Cpl Warrington	x Hall. Drink

[*The following list is on the bottom of the leaf containing the map:*]

Boat[5]
19 rowers
2 Interpts

3 of our pty
4 Extra
———
28
———
5 in perogue
1 Extra
———
6
———
5 in perogue
1 Extra
———
6
———
40

[The following list is on the bottom of the leaf containing the map:]

5 Intps & ourselves [?]
6 French
9 old party
10 Soldiers
10 do, if w x tng [?]
———
40

10
6
7
1
———
24

22	40		
8	24	7 · 7	36
6	16		20
4	8	4 1 +	16
40	8		12
			4 Extra Man *[one word illegible]*

zinc, the "white" ore and galena, the "black" ore, are found. I am indebted to Dr. Willard Jillson of Frankfort, Kentucky, for the information essential in clearing up this obscure passage.

4. These rosters and others found on pp. 32–33 were probably made up as roll calls.

5. As the figures in this list show, Clark was uncertain as to just how many men would comprise the party. He was evidently trying to determine the number to be assigned to the keelboat and to the two pirogues that would make up the flotilla of exploration. He returned to this problem a few days later. See infra, pp. 20, 21.

6. I am unable to identify this person.

3d Jany 1804   Excessive Cold after Sunset

Wed: Jany 4th   a Cold Clear morning, the river Covered with Ice from the Missoure, the Mississippi above frozed across, the Wind from the West, The Thermometer this morning at 19° below freesing, Continue Cold & Clear all day, I took the altd of S.L. L. and found it to be 57° . 27′ . 15″ N   purchase 12 lb Tallow for 6/ of Whitesides, who Sold the Beef to the Com: [Commissary] at 3$ pr Hw   Several Countrey people here to day—at 4 oClock the Murcuria of the Thmtr in a corner of a warm room was 20 D. above (o)—Worner & Potts fight after Dark without my Knowledge & the Corpl head of the mess left the hut & Suffered them to bruse themselves much, he has no authority, the other Part of the Detachment verry merry at night

2 $\lfloor 57°$. 27′ − 15″		the 4th Jany 1804
28 − 43 − 37 − 5/10		T
1 − 44 −		refraction (1)
28 . 41 − 53 5/10		P
16 − 19 3/10	+ Sun: Damt (3)	
3 −	+	
28 − 58 − 20 − 8/10		ent
8 − 49 −		E Ens
28 − 49 − 31. 8/10		
90		
61 − 10 − 28 − 2/10		
22 − 49 − 22		☉ Declena
Dgt 38 − 21 − 6. 2/10		

Thursday 5th Jany   the Creek rose Considerably last night   the river full of Ice, and the wind which blows from the West blows it to this Shore, a Madderate day, I suffer some men to assist Higgins[6] to raise his hut. Two men whome I sent to hunt grouse returned with a part of a hog which they found hung up in the woods & brought it in a[s] bear meat. I took the altitude of ☉ U. L. with the quaderent and made it 55° − 41′ − 30″ N. Errer of instrmt 1° − 13′ − 0″ +

5th Jany 1804

2 $\lfloor 55°$ − 40′ − 30″	☉ L L	
27 − 50 − 15	altitude of ☉ up limb	
1 − 48	refraction (T.1)	
48 − 27		
16 − 19 −	☉ Demeter (p 3)	
32 − 8		
8	+ Parallax (T 3)	
★ 27 − 32 16	The Suns Center	
Declination		
★(27 . 32 . 16		
1 17 − 0	+ E. E	
28 − 49 − 16		
90		
61 − 10 − 44		
22 − 43 − 31	Declination	

The Latd with Qude = 38 − 27 − 13 on the 5th Jany 1804.

I visited the boat frequently this day under apprehen[s]ion of the Creek which is now riseing washing the earth from the foot of the pries which is fixed under.

Jany 6ᵗʰ   I was up last night at 12 to right the Boat   the banks were Caveing in, which made it necessary to fix the pries frequently, this morning early I fixed the pries, and large peece of the bank sliped in, which obliged all hands to go down & make all secure   I order in those men who had fought got Drunk & neglected Duty to go and build a hut for a Wo[man] who promises to wash & Sow &c   I Spoke to the men on the Subject of my order, ⊙ U L with quadt to day is 1° 1′ − 1″ ad +   A hog was found in the Prairie by Some men [and] they Skined [it]   I send out Shields to enquire in the neighbourhood whoes hog it was & inform me. Thermometer at 12 oClock 31 above o. at 4 oCk at 30° abov. o.

7. From this passage it is clear that Clark had begun work on some sort of map ". . . for the purpose of Correcting from the information I may get of the Countrey to the NW" Since he had no personal knowledge of this region, he had to depend on such information and upon any maps that came his way. Lewis began seeking information and maps as soon as he arrived in Cahokia on Dec. 7, 1803. At Cahokia he met John Hay, postmaster of that place, who was to be of great service in supplying information. Hay had been as far north as the Assiniboin River and was familiar with the Red River country and the Upper Missouri (infra, p. 25 n.). Since the Louisiana Territory had not as yet been formally transferred to the U.S., it was important that Lewis meet the Spanish authorities at St. Louis and learn from them what they knew about the land. Lewis reported to Jefferson that, accompanied by Hay and a Mr. Jarrot as interpreters, he crossed the river to St. Louis, where they met Don Carlos de Hault Delassus, Governor of Upper Louisiana (Lewis to Jefferson, Cahokia, Dec. 19 and Dec. 28, 1803, Jackson, pp. 145–55). Later Lewis met Antoine Soulard, the Surveyor-General, who showed him a map of the Missouri River from its mouth to the Osage and up that river to its source. Soulard eventually produced two other maps. One was a map of Upper Louisiana, probably the map of the Upper Missouri and Mississippi, or a copy thereof, drawn by Soulard in 1795. A copy of this map with annotations by Clark is in the Coe Collection in the Yale University Library. Thwaites reproduced it in the Atlas of the Notebook Journals (Thw., 8, map 2). The third map was one of the Missouri as far north as the Mandans. This was probably a map made by James Mackay, whom Clark would soon meet at Camp Dubois. No one in or around St. Louis could give Clark more accurate and complete information concerning the Missouri River than this Scotsman, who had visited the Mandan villages on the Upper Missouri as early as 1787. He was then in the employ of English traders, whose post on the Qu'Appelle River lay 150 miles northwest of the Mandans. In 1793 he transferred his activities to St. Louis; two years later he headed the expedition of the Missouri Company of St. Louis, commissioned by the Spanish authorities there, to open trade with the Indian tribes along the upper river. Mackay and his party established winter quarters north of the Platte. In the following year John Evans, Mackay's lieutenant, got as far upriver as the Mandans. On the return of the party to St. Louis in 1796 or early 1797, a map made by Mackay was turned over to the authorities (Nasatir, 1, 96–108). This, or a copy of it, was the map given Lewis by Soulard. At least two other copies of this map can be identified. On Nov. 13, 1803, Clark's friend, William Henry Harrison, Governor of Indiana Territory, wrote from Vincennes that he was sending a map (Harrison to Clark, Vincennes, Nov. 13, 1803, Jackson, p. 135). The letter was addressed to the two captains "on their way up the Mississippi supposed to be at Cahokia." Our knowledge

6th Jan. the banks about the Boat Continue to Cave in, which causes great attention in me to prevent the Boats getting injered by any one part falling more than another—the Sawyears come on to day better than usial, Whitehouse & Reed, agree better than they did last week—or in other Words Re[ad] saws better from practice.

7th Satdy Jany—Some rain last night, a thow [thaw] and Some rain to day. The boat give me much trouble, [as] the banks are Continaly Slipping in on each Side which looses the pries, up last night and frequent thro the rain today attending the boat, I drew a Map for the purpose of Correcting from the information which I may get of the Countrey to the N W[7]

Sunday 8th Janry   Rained moderately all last night, a butifull Morning a few large Sheets of thin Ice running this morning, Send out Colter & George [Drouillard] to the head of the Deboues [Dubois] R. to hunt—the Wind rose from the S W at 10 oClock. Took the Meridian altitude of ☉ L L with Sext. made it 59° – 22′ – 52″ N,—a French man & his famly Came to see me to day   I trade with them for Onions, & gave Tin [?] &c This man made complaint that he had lost a Hogg—Some Hog meat had been brought in as before mentioned, as the men whome brought it in are absent, I postpone the inquirey untill tomorrow   I Lay down to sleep, to make up for the want of rest, Clouded up at 1/2 past 2 oClock the Wind chifted to the N W, moderate. R Field Killed a Deer to day, this is the first of his turning out—

Mon. 9th Jany—Some Snow last night, a hard Wind this morning from W, N W, river Rises with large Sheets of Ice out of Mississippi, the morning is fair (the man Ramey gives me much trouble)   I took Collins & went to the place he found a Hog skined & Hung up, the Crows had devoured the meet, Killed Prary fowl and Went across a Prary to a 2nd Bank where I discovered an Indian Fortification,[8] near the Second bank I attempted to cross a Bond [Pond] of about 400 yds Wide on the Ice & Broke in   this fortress is 9 Mouns forming a Circle   two of them is about 7 foot above the leavel of the plain on the edge of the first bank and 2 M from the Woods & about the Same distance from the main high land, about this place I found great quantities of Earthern ware & flints— about 1/2 M. N. is a Grave on an Eminince   I returned before Sun Set, and found that my feet, which were wet had frozed to my Shoes, which rendured precaution necessary to prevent a frost bite, the Wind from the W, across the Sand Islands in the Mouth of the Missouras, raised Such a dust that I could not See in that derection, the Ice Continue to run & river rise Slowly—exceeding Cold day

Tuesday 10th   a fine day, the river rose 6 Inches last night, the Creek also rises & Boat nearly afloat   I am verry unwell all day, owing I believe to the Ducking & excessive Cold which I underwent yesterday, at 1 oClock Joseph Fields returned & crossed the River between the Sheets of floating Ice with Some risque, his excuse for Staying so long on the Mississippi were that the Ice run so thick in the Missourie where he was 30 miles up that there was no crossing, he Says that the people is greatly in favour of the Americans, Cap. Mackey has Just returned from Surveying of some lands up the Missouras, which has been lately granted   he says "a boutifull Countrey presents it self on the route he went & returned."[9] Three miles to the first settlements from this place in a West direction.[1] I feel unwell to day

Wednesday 11ᵗʰ Jany. I was unwell last night   Slept but little, A fine morning, the river still riseing, The Missourie runs with fine Ice, the Boat is afloat, one man McNeal <lost> out last night, he Sepperated from the hunting party about 7 miles from this place, he returnd this evening. Sjt Ordday was also lost all night   at 1 oClock the wind blew strong from the West and turned Couled & Cloudy this afternoon, I am a good deel indisposed.

Thursday 12ᵗʰ Jany 1804   My Chimney got on fire last night, a fair morning, the wind from the S West, the river Continue to rise moderatly, I took Maridinal altitude of Suns Lower Limb with Sextent and made it 59° . 31′ – 52″. N   the error of Enstrument as usial   river Continue to rise with large sheets of ice running against the Ice atached to the bank with great force, the Boat is a float, and in perfect order

Friday 13ᵗʰ January   Sent N Pryor with Letters &c to Cap Lewis a[t] Kohokia   the river rise, a fall of Snow last night, the Missourie is riseing and runs with Ice   A Cloudy & warm day, I am better &c   a fine rain in the evening ⊙

Satturday 14ᵗʰ January   A Snow fall last night of about an Inch [and a] half   The river <Still riseing> falling and running with Ice, A fair Sun shineery morning—the party Caught 14 Rabits to day & 7 yesterday. a Cold afternoon. the Mississippi is Closed with Ice.

Sunday 15ᵗʰ Jany   river falling & runs still with Ice, I took the M altitude of ⊙ L L. & made it 60° – 33′ – 50″ N, at Sun Set Maj Rumsay[2] the Comsy arrived with Some provisions in a waggon Mr Todd,[3] Seven or Eight men followd the Waggon Intoxicated from the Whiskey   they receced [received] of R— [Ramey] on the way out of the barrel which was for the Party. I ordered a Gill to each Man   a Cold night   the Wag: in passing the Lowe[r] Prarie which was covrd with Ice Suft [Sufficiently] Strong to bear the teem but not the waggon which caused it to be dift [difficult] to pass

Monday 16ᵗʰ Jany   this Morning Maj. R [Rumsey] observed that he brought 2 trunks of Goods, and asked pirmition to Sell them to the Citizens for Provisions and the Mens Coon Skins, I accented to the plan, and agreed he might untill other Arrangements, after the Arrival of Capt Lewis—I settled with the Contractor for what has been furnished to this day and find him Due the Party 30 gills of Whiskey which he payed,—and 750 rats [rations] of Soap candles & vinager, for which he gave his Due bills, the Party made up a Shooting match with the Country people for a pr [pair of] Leagens, Reuben Fields made the best Shot, next one went & the [one word illegible] was Shields R, F[ields] Colter &, Mr Prior returned at 8 oClock in the evening with a letter from Capt Lewis[4] (Lent Colter 3/ lent George 3/) and one from Louisville & 3 news papers which Capt Lewis had Sent me—also a file & 3 plain Bits Whip Saw file

Tuesday 17ᵗʰ Jany   A Verry Cold morning   at 7 oClock the Thermometer in the air fell 8° below, o, the wind from the N W, a Stiff Breeze   Ice run greatly out of Missouras—at 9 oClock the Thermometer 6ᵈ below o—at 10 oClock 3ᵈ below o at 12 oClock at o. at 1 oClock 1° above o. at 2 oClock 1 1/2° above o. 3 oClock at o.[5]

that this was a Mackay map, and that it was sent by Harrison, rests on a discovery made by Miss Annie Heloise Abel in 1916, of a map in the Office of Indian Affairs, among the papers of the Western Superintendency of which Clark was later the head. On the back of the map in Harrison's hand is the address to Lewis and Clark "on a voyage up the Mississippi." The names on the map are in French and correspond to the names set down in Mackay's Table of Distances, which he turned over to his superiors when he returned to St. Louis. Clark translated Mackay's names of streams and islands into English. Undoubtedly Clark had this map from Harrison before him when he made his entry for Jan. 7, 1804.

Another Mackay map was soon to be on its way to Clark: on Jan. 13, 1804, Jefferson wrote to Lewis from Washington that he was sending a map by Evans (Thw., 7, 291; Jackson, p. 163). That Jefferson ascribed the map to Evans, Mackay's lieutenant, is of no significance. Miss Abel mistakenly concluded that the map which she found in the Indian Office was the one mentioned by Jefferson, overlooking the address in Harrison's hand mentioned above.

We can conclude that Clark had three maps on Jan. 7, 1804: the Soulard Map of Upper Louisiana, the Mackay Map given Lewis by Soulard, and the Mackay Map sent him by Harrison. Later he received (in all probability) the so-called Evans Map sent by Jefferson. In my annotation, I have referred to the map sent by Harrison as the Indian Office Map. I believe Clark took this map upstream with him: his handwriting on the map establishes this conclusion. Three days after this entry Mackay visited Clark at Camp Dubois. Although there is nothing in the entry for Jan. 10 (supra p. 16) to indicate what took place at the meeting, no doubt Clark had many questions to ask of this knowledgeable Scotsman.

8. From Clark's description, it would appear that he had come upon a northern group of the Cahokia mounds. These were northwest of Cahokia and near enough for Clark to reach. Three railroads have built their tracks through the site so that the mounds have long been obliterated. A field diagram of the ten mounds is given by D. I. Bushnell in "The Cahokia and Surrounding Mound Groups," *Papers of the Peabody Museum, 3*, no. 1 (Cambridge, Mass., 1904), 5–20.

9. Supra, p. 16 n.

1. Perhaps the small settlement at the junction of Coldwater Creek with the Missouri. See Clark's Map, Doc. 4.

2. Major Nathan Rumsey was the agent of Elijah G. Galusha, the contractor for army rations in the St. Louis area (Jackson, p. 168, n.).

3. There were several farmers by the name of Todd who had settled in the American

Bottom south of Clark's camp. Reynolds (*Pioneer History of Illinois,* pp. 201, 425), mentions three of them, Edward, Thomas, and William, any one of whom might have been the "Mr Todd" referred to here. I do not believe the Todd mentioned here was a part of the well-known family of Col. John Todd, prominent in Illinois affairs. Andrew Todd, the fur trader and associate of John Hay (infra p. 25 n.), died in 1796.

4. The covering for this letter was used for the July 7–8, 1804, entries (infra, p. 74–75, and Doc. 29).

5. The entry for Jan. 17 is written over the following:
> Provision
> Whiskey M
> My st
> My Helth
> The Mens—pt
> R. Field
> Hays Paper on Passes
> Maps
> B——

at 4 oClock the Thermometer was 1 1/2° below 0. at 5 the Ther: was at 3° below 0,—at 9 oClock 6° below 0, A Verry Cold night; the Missouris has fallen to day about 6 Inches, runs with Ice—Ice from shore 20 yds in the river is 5 1/2 Inches Thick—

Wednesday 18ᵗʰ Jany, a Cloudy Morning with moderate breaze from the N W. b[y] W   The river run with Ice, At 8 oClock the Thromtr Stood at 1° below 0,—9 oClock 1ᵈ ab[ove] 0, at 10 oClock 2° abov 0, at 11 oClock rose to 4° above 0, <at 12 oClock> and Snow beg[an] to Snow, at 12 oClock The Thermt at 2 above 0. Snow, about 1 Inch   at 1 oClock 2 abov 0,—at 2 o Clock 1 abov 0, <Snow Stoped> and left off Snowing—

Thursday 19ᵗʰ Jany   Some Snow fell last night, a Cloudy morning, the river continues to fall, a[nd] Some Ice running, at 8 oClock this morning the Thermormeter Stood at 13° above 0, the Wind moderate from the N W, at 9 oClock 15° abov 0, at 10 oClock 16° above 0, at 11 oClock 16° above 0, at 12 o'clock 19° above 0, at 1 oClock 17° abo 0, at 2 oClock at 15 1/2°—abov 0, at 3 oClock at 13° abov 0, at 4 o'Clock 11° abov 0, at 5 oClock 10 1/2 abov 0,—Gibson Killed 3 Deer & Colter 3 Turkey, Shields 4 Turkey, Worne[r] & Thompson 14 rabits—

Friday 20ᵗʰ 1804 Jany—a verry cold night, river Still falling <some> no Ice running out of the Missouries, The wind this morning from N W— the Thermometer at 7 oClock stood at 5° below 0, at 8 oClock 7° below 0, at 9 oClock 4° below 0, at 10 oClock 2° below 0, at 11 oClock 2° above 0, at 12 oClock 4° abov—Took the M Altitude of ☉ L L with Sext: & made it 62° – 30′ – 45″ N (Cromt. too fast 1ʰ – 26′ – 10″) at 1 oClock the Thmt. Stood at 6° above 0, at 2 oClock the Them at 8° above 0, The river Mississipi raised & some [of] the Ice formed above the Missouris broke Loose & floted down, this Ice is 9 Inches Thick. <no Ice flotes down the> at 3 oClock 11 abov 0, (Cloudy) at 4 oClock at 8° abov 0, at 5 oClock 7 1/2 abov 0,—Cloudy, many Grous[e] Caught to Day & Hall Caught 14 Rabits—

		mls	months	days
1804	From Du bois to the Manden Nation 1500 miles at 10 Mls pr Day will be 150 days Viz: May June, July Augt & Sept.—	1500 in	5 –	5
	From Do. at 12 mls pr day 125 days Viz: May June July Augt & 5 days in Septr		– 4 –	5
1st Winter	From Mandens to the rock Mountains is 12° <say> is 12° [*sic*] W. at 41 mls [to a degree of longitude] Say 900 miles at 10 pr Day is 90 Days, Viz: Sept. Oct. Novr & 4 Dy	900 in	3 –	0
	From Same at 12 Miles pr Day 65 Days Septr Octr & 19 of Novr		2 –	15
	From the Mountains to the Ocean in Longttd 123° W say 10° at 41 miles to a degree of Longtd add the windings 650 Miles at 10 Miles will take 650 in May June and July . . , [85?] Days		3 –	0

6. In his letter to Croghan, Jan. 15, 1804, Clark wrote that he was collecting information "so as we may make just Calculations before we start." With the information from Mackay and others, he could set down, with some confidence, the first figures in his calculations, "from Du bois to the Manden Nation 1500 miles." From then on it was guesswork. The Soulard Map (Thw., *8*, map 2), a copy of which Clark had at the time, shows the Missouri River flowing almost due east from the Rocky Mountains before turning southeastward above the mouth of the Platte. This is a complete distortion, for the river, heading in southwestern Montana, flows north for more than 200 miles before turning eastward. Not until it passes the mouth of the Yellowstone does it turn southeastward. However, with Mackay's information and a copy of the Indian Office Map, which he had received from Harrison before the copy Jefferson was sending reached him, Clark would know that the reach of the Missouri from Camp Dubois to the Mandans was generally northward instead of westward, as on the Soulard Map.

Whatever may have been the extent of his information at the time he drew this chart, Clark must have believed that the river flowed straight eastward from the mountains to some point not far above the Mandans. This is clear from the fact that he counted degrees of longitude straight west in getting his estimate of the distance. "From Mandens to the rock Mountains is 12° W at 41 mls" [to a degree]. This works out to about 500 miles. Clark apparently felt that if he added 400

From the Same place at 12 mls 54 days, May & June ....   2 – 0

Days

The time to the Ocean @ 10m pr Day ....   11 – 0

The Time @ 12 ms pr day ....   8 – 20 days

1805

(Delay 15 days)
Returning from the Ocean to the river 650 miles @ 10 ms pr Day is 65 days Viz: 15 in August, Septr 20 in Octr ....   650 M – 2 – 5

do—Viz <to Mandans 900> in 65 Days M at 12m pr Day 54 Day [4 written over 5] 15 July, Augt 9 in Septr ....   1 – 24

ditto to the Mandens @ 20 ms pr Day 45 Days Septr Octr ....   900 ....   1 – 21

ditto to the mouth Nov & Dec @ ...   2 – 0

Returning to the Mandan @ 10 pr   3 – 26

do   do   at 12 ... do   3 – 15

	Months to Mandans	Months to Mountains	Months to Ocean	Time	[one word illegible] winter &c	Total Time	
at 👉10	5 – 0^D	3 – 0^D	2 – 0	5 – 28	15 months [5 written over 6] – 28 Day		Total going out
at 👉12	4 – 5	2 – 15	2 – 0	5 – 12	14	2 [2 written over 22]	

<Total   30   0 going out>

Return   at 10 or 12 miles

2 – 0 – 1 – 15 – 2 – 5 = 0 – 0 – 5   25 Total returning (say to Decr 1805–)[6]

Total   19 – 27 at 12 Miles pr Day progression

Total   21 – 23 at 10 Miles pr Day progression

miles to this it would be enough: "say 900 miles." As it turned out, the expedition covered over 1,500 miles before it stood at the top of the watershed (Thw., *6*, 61–64). In his estimate of the distance from the continental divide to the ocean, he counted off 10 degrees of longitude, 410 miles, added "the winding," and put down 650 miles. The error here was not too great. The actual distance traversed

<If 36 men including Drewyer>
<Big boat 24   12>

25>

2 of us
1 sevt
2 Intprs =   5
If we take 37 men

The Boat of 25 men

    1 Pierogue   6
    1   do –   6
              ——
               37
              ——

If the party to connst of

30 men

    Boat of 24 men
    1 Periogue of 6—
    ————————————
               30
    ————————————

If the Party to consits of 25

    Men all in the Boat of 20 ores
    ————————————

        If 40 men

Boat of   26
1 Peroque   8
1   do –   6
          ==
           40
          ==

        If 50 men

Boat 26 men
1 Perog: 10
1 do   7
1 do –   7
          ——
           50

Those Numbers will Depend
on the probabillity of an
oppisition from roving parties of Bad
Indians which it is probable
may be on the [*blot*] R. [?][7]

as examples are necessary

Supposeing the party to Consist of 2 Intpers 4 Non Comd officers and
21 Men and the rules to be observed is Strictly Such as Cap. L & C shall
from time establish, and a Violiation or Disobediance Shall be Subject to
Such punishments as Derected by the articles of War, in like Cases and
Such other punishments, as Shall be inflected by the sentence of a court
Martial which <shall> are to be formed in the following manner, Viz;
one Intptr   A sergt to act as president, and at least 1 N Comd officer &
5 privates members   The Court to Consist of not less then 7 members,
<in Capital offenses and> at other times when Convenient one of the
Capts will preside at the Court in that Case the Court will have an addition to their number of a Presdt <who will have 2 votes> (but in all
Cases Capt L. & C doe reserve to themselves the right [of] rud[u]cing N C
officers at will of inflicting such punishment as they may thing [think]
right agreeable to Law, at any time which from the nature of the offence
& the good of the Service require it)   This Court will act agreeable to
the rules and regulations of the Articles of War and Such others as may
be established by the Said Cp L. & C. from time to time.[8]

by the party was 834 miles. For the whole distance from Camp Dubois to the Pacific,
Clark's estimate of 3,050 miles was nearly a
thousand miles too low; the actual mileage
was 3,958 miles (Thw., *6, 67*).

It should be noted that in estimating how
long it would take to get to the Pacific and
back, Clark allowed for no rest periods, nor
for the time-consuming councils with the Indians. Out of the 165 days taken to reach the
Mandan villages, for instance, 37 days were
spent in camp and council with the natives.
It is clear from the chart that Clark did not
intend to winter with the Mandans but push
on, and winter (1804–05) far upstream close
to the divide. Having reached the ocean in
June or July 1805, Clark intended that the
party tarry there for only 15 days and then
head for home. As it turned out, over five
months of the winter of 1804–05 were spent
with the Mandans, and the second winter,
1805–06, was spent at the mouth of the Columbia, where the party stayed for four and
one-half months.

If one checks the Notebook Journals for
the days when the party was actually on the
move, it turns out that 376 days were used
in going from Camp Dubois to the Pacific.
With the current of the Missouri to speed
them on after they had crossed the divide,
the party made the trip from the Pacific home
in 186 days traveling time. In all, 562 days
traveling time were consumed by the round
trip, or approximately 19 months, about the
time that Clark estimated for the whole trip.
The actual elapsed time, from May 13, 1804,
to Sept. 23, 1806, was about 29 months. These
estimates reflect the careful thought Clark
gave to this problem, with the information he
had to go on at the time he made these calculations.

7. See supra, p. 32.

8. During this winter, Clark was busy organizing the party and establishing military
discipline. This rough draft of a plan for setting up courts-martial suggests the early need
for disciplinary measures in dealing with the
untamed recruits. From this time on, courts-
martial were a common occurrence.

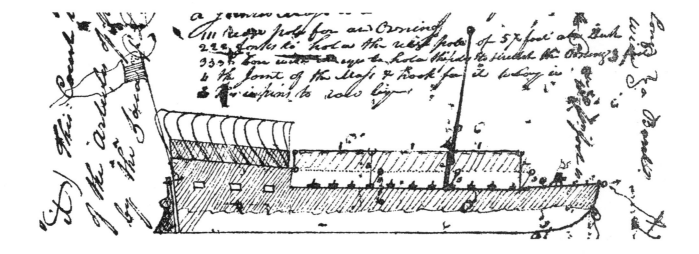

[Key to Drawing]

a Jointed Mast to let down of 32 feet long
1 1 1 Ridge poles for an orning
2 2 2 forks to hold the ridge pole of 5 1/2 foot abv Deck
3 3 3 Base [?] with a eye to hold the poles to stretch the orning 3 feet
4 the Joint of the Mast & hook for it to Lay in
T[hole] is pins to row by

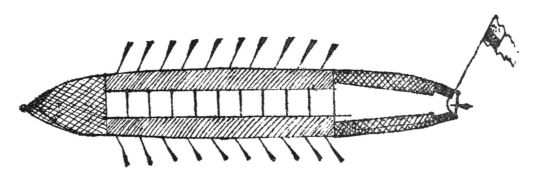

Clark's drawings of the Keelboat, Side Elevation, and Deck Plan. See Document 7.

	Boat 31 feet in Hold	Inches	
2 men takes up 3 feet	do 14 do on Cabn	32 Long	a Bench [?][9]
	do 8 – 4″ wide	22 wide	

Lockers, must be 2 foot [?] – 6 In wide	
do – & – 31 feet Long	156 foot of Plank a [one word illegible]
do about – 1 – 6 Deep	pr foot is

Lockers on the Cabin – 14 – 0 – long	
do Wide 3 – 0 – wide	84 feet
do _____ 3 – 0 – Deep	

9. During the winter and early spring, the crew made lockers and benches for the keelboat (infra, p. 27). These are Clark's directions for building them and an estimate of materials required.

Ends & Divisions &c &c &c   60
    300
Calculate 1 for Season[ing] &   75
<6>
4
wast[e]   375

Defined the Word Sense

It is a faculty of the Soul, whereby it perceived external Objects, By means of the impressions they make on certain organs of the body. These organs are Commonly reconed 5, viz: the Eyes, wherby we see objects; the ear, which enables us to hear sounds; the nose, by which we receive the Ideas of different smells; the Palate, By which we judge of tastes; and the skin, which enables us to feel the different, forms, hardness, or Softness of bodies.[1]

1. I have no explanation for this passage, which appears to be a copy-book exercise. Perhaps it indicates an effort on the part of Clark to improve his prose and spelling.

2. One of the most important tasks was the collection of supplies and the preparation of them for the journey. This is the first of many entries in the journal which give lists of provisions to be stowed away in the keelboat and the two pirogues.

3. Doc. 28 may have been used as a cover for Lewis' answer to this letter (infra, p. 72).

Satturday 21ˢᵗ 1804   The Snow this morning <at the camp> [?] is about 2 1/2 Inches Deep, & Snowing fast, The Thermometer Stood at 7° abov o, at 8 oClock, & wind from the NE, The river running with Ice and falling a little, at 9 oClock the Thermtr at 7° abv o,—at 10 oClk The Thmtr 7° abov o, at 11 oClock 10° abov o, & Snow's—at 12 oClock 10° abv o, <Snow> or fine Hails increas, at 1 oClock 10° abov o, at 5 oClock 17° abov o, [one word illegible] haileing fine hail,

Sunday 22ⁿᵈ Jany 1804   Snow all <night> the last night, and Snows this morning, the debth is 5 3/4 Inches: The Thermometer Stands at 9 oClock this morning in the Open Air at 11° abov o,—, at 12 oClock rose to 14° abov o, and Stoped Snowing   wind Easterly   at 3 oClock 13° abo o, riv nearly Clear of Ice,

Smunday [Monday] 23ʳᵈ Jany 1804   a Cloudy morning but little Ice runs to day   The Thermtr at 8 oClock 11° abo o, at 12 oClock Stood at 10° abov o, (I pen an Ordr to Corpl) at 3 oClock 17° abo o, in the evening the wind raised [?] and Shifted to the North   caught 14 rabits & Killed 2 Deer—

Tuesday 24ᵗʰ   a Butifull morning   Clear Sunshine   the wi[n]ds ligh[t] from the NW, the Thermometer at 9 oClock Stood at 4° abo o, (I take fesick)   at 10 oClock 8° abv o, wind West, at 12 oClock—14° abo o, at 3 oClock 11° abov o, Smone [Some] Small pieces of Ice running   Sick to day [one word illegible]

Wednesday 25ᵗʰ Jany   a verry Clear mone Shiney night   a fair morning, last night was a verry Cold one   (I was Sick all night. The branch[es] of [the] Trees and the Small groth ar[e] Gilded with Ice from the frost of last night which affords one of the most magnificent appearances in nature, the river began to Smoke at 8 oClock and the Thermometer Stood at 2° below o, at 9 oClock at o, at 10 oClock at 5° abov o, at 11 oClock 12° abv o, at 12 oClock 16° abov o, at 1 oClock 18° abov o, at 2 oClock 19° abo o, at 3 oClock 16 abov o, wind from W N W—Sick—2 Deer Killed to day &c

Thursday 26ᵗʰ Jany 1804   a Cloudy warm Day   I am verry unwell all day, Gibson Killed two Deer, R. field one, the men Kill Racoons [one word illegible]   Rabits &c in great quantity, verry little Ice running to day   the fessic I took yesterday work to day. The men make a Sled to haul wood   one man Stay out to night (Winser)   I direct a Slay to be built to haul things from the Countrey &

Jy 26ᵗʰ

To Stow away in the Boat[2]

Kegs	In	I	
45 for pok	18 long	10 Thick	
50 for flour	24 "—	15.	"
18—Whisky	15. –	12	"
7	Corn		
120			

Friday 27ᵗʰ Jany 1804. a Cloudy Morning   some Snow, this Morning I am verry unwell, to day at 1 oClock 28 abov o, (I send off How[a]rd express to day to Cap Lewis at Koho: [Cahokia] with a Letter[3] <I am some better,> Winser who was out Last night returned   he Killed a Deer &

Turkey—Gibson Killed 1 [1 written over 8] Deer to day, Collons [Collins] one near camp

Saty 28ᵗʰ Jany 1804   a Cloudy morning   verry cold wind from the N W Some floating Ice in the River at 9 oClock 5° above 0, Snows at 10 oClock 8° abov 0, at 11 oClock 10° abov 0, <Shine> Sun Shines, 3 french men from Paraie De Soue⁴ called   at 12 oClock 12° abov 0, at 1 oClock 14' abv 0, Mr Bagley⁵ came with Potatos fowls &—I trade him   Mr Cummins⁶ Came with Meel [?] & Brandy from Contractor   at 2 oClock 18° abov 0, Mr Anty Coxe⁷ called to Day to inqure after his horses, at 3 oClock 20° above 0,—4 oClock 18° abov 0, Some womin came to day at 6 oClock 14° abov 0, Porter all frosed & several bottles broke, I Deliver out 12 flints & some Canstr Pow[d]er to hunders.

Sunday 29ᵗʰ Jany   a butifull morning   the river rise a little   no Ice The Thermometer at 9 oClock Stood at 16° above 0, at 11 oClock 22° abov 0, at 12 oClock 24° abov 0, Took the alltiude of Suns Lowr Limb. 66° – 50' – 30" – E.E. 5° – at 3 oClock 28° above 0, at 4 oClock 26° abov 0, at 5 oClock 23° abov 0, – Shields Killed a Deer to day, Express returned from Koho [Cahokia]: brought a Letter from Capt Lewis, & 4 other from Kenty, 8 bottles of wine some Durant [?] & files

Monday 30ᵗʰ Jany 1804   a Cloudy morning, Some Snow   send out 10 hunters to day <to> in three parties, at 9 oClock The Thermotr stood at 22° abov 0, a little wind from N.   at 10 oClock 24° abov 0, cleared up & Sun Shown   stoped Snowing, but little Ice running this morng—at 11 oClock 25° abov 0, at 12 oClock 25° abov 0, Took M alt of Suns L.L. 67° – 22' – 52" – Er[ror] of In[s]trument 6' –, at 1 oClock 25° abov 0, at 2 oClock 26° abov 0, Reed Killed a Deer & wild Cat, Cloudy, 3 men cross the river to day, at 3 oClock 28° abov 0, at 4 oClock 27° abov 0, at 8 oClock 16° abv 0, about Sun Set Capt Lewis <return> arrived accompanied by Mr J. Hay⁸ & Mr Jo Hays⁹ of Kohokia—   The hunters killed 5 Deer to day—

Tuesday 31ˢᵗ Jany   a fair morning   the Trees guilded with ice   at 7 oClock the Thermometer Stood at 7 oClock 10° below 0,

4. Portage des Sioux? A small village at the old "Sioux carrying place" between the Mississippi and Missouri rivers. François Saucier and his brother Mathieu established this settlement in 1799 (at the instance of the Spanish government) to ward off possible encroachments of the Americans across the Mississippi. This village was at the Missouri end of the portage which cut across the narrow neck of land separating the two rivers. (See Houck, *Missouri*, 2, 88–89; McDermott, p. 51; Illinois Historical Society, *Cahokia Records*, 2, 626–27.)

5. A Rev. David Badgley and his family arrived from Hardy County, Virginia and settled in American Bottom in 1797 (Reynolds, pp. 201, 259, 236–37, 280).

6. A Cummings was settled below the camp on Six Mile Prairie (Reynolds, p. 357).

7. I am unable to identify this person.

8. One of the first persons Lewis met when he arrived at Cahokia on Dec. 7, 1803, was John Hay, the local postmaster. He was born in Detroit in 1769, the son of John Hay, a native of Pennsylvania. In 1783 he entered the employ of the Northwest Company and was sent out with a party to the Assiniboin country. He came to Cahokia where, with Todd, whom he had met on the Assiniboin, he set up a store. The Hay-Todd concern traded into the Indian country to the north and west. In 1799 the Governor of the Northwest Territory, Arthur St. Clair, appointed him clerk of court and treasurer of St. Clair County. In 1814 he left Cahokia and settled in Belleville on the Missouri. He headed a party of Cahokia citizens who were present at the ceremony of cession when the United States took over Upper Louisiana on March 9, 1804 (Reynolds, pp. 225–29).

Hay accompanied Lewis on his visit to Colonel Delassus, Governor of Upper Louisiana, and Soulard, Surveyor-General. Hay acted as interpreter and was instrumental in persuading these officials to allow Lewis to copy three maps. (See supra, p. 16 n.). At the same time, Lewis received from Hay a copy of the Mackay-Evans journal of a trip up the Missouri, which Hay promised to translate. Hay also promised to turn over to Lewis his journal of a trip from Michilimackinac to the Assiniboin River (Thw., *1*, 4–6).

9. John Hays was born in New York City in 1770. At an early age he entered the employ of the Hudson's Bay Company and was sent to Mackinaw. His services with the company took him to the Lake of the Woods, the Upper Mississippi, and the Red River. In 1793 he settled at Cahokia, where he was employed by Hay and Todd. After the dissolution of this company, he set up as an independent operator, trading with Prairie du Chien. From 1798 to 1818 he was sheriff of St. Clair County. He was appointed Indian agent to the Potawatomi in 1822. (See Reynolds, pp. 223–24. Reynolds is incorrect in stating that John Hays was postmaster at

Cahokia. Lewis says that John Hay held that office.) The visit of these two Cahokians, Hay and Hays, is important, for both of them had first-hand knowledge of the country to the north: trade routes, the Indians, and the extent to which the English had encroached on what had been Spanish territory and was soon to become American (Thw., *1,* 4–6).

Jany 31ˢᵗ   at 9 oClock some Ice running this morning, my head akes much, I went up the river with Cap Lewis & Gentlem[en]   at 12 oClock 24° abv 0, at 2 oClock 28° abv 0, at 4 oClock 28° abv 0, Mr. Whitesides & Chittele[1] crossed from the opposit Side of the Mississippi—at 9 oClock P M 15° abov 0, wind SW. by W—took Latts [?]

Wednesday 1ˢᵗ Feby 1804   a Cloudy morning & warm wind from the S.W,   I rode out 6 miles on Mr Hays horse   am verry sick, wind was verry high at 1 oClock, a warm Day, all the good[s] put out & aired   I am very unwell

Thurday 2ⁿᵈ Feby   Mrs Hays & Hay set out for Kohokia, Cap Lewis & my self accompanyed them one mile, & then went to Mr & [*space*] Kanes[2] and returned to Dinner, verry sick   wind high from SW

Friday 3ᵈ   I am verry unwell all day, take medicine without pain   Thawing Day

Satturday 4   Discharge Leakens for theift with a Small Correction   a warm Day   some rain last night, in the Evening the River Covered with large Sheetes of Ice from both rivers, the River & Creek rised Suffecent to take the boat up the Creek some distance   moderate day   I am verry sick   wild fowl pass

Sonday 5ᵗʰ Feby   Still Sick, The french Man Wife &c came to See us to day   Mrs Cane als   Hanley[3] sent us some Butter & milk, river riseing & Covered with Small Ice. Ct L send out Shields to get walnut Bark for pills,[4] fowl pass

Monday 6ᵗʰ Fby   a fair day   Snow nearly gone, Some Ice Still runing Sick take Walnut pills, Winser killed a Badger. My P[ills] work &c   great numbers of wild fowl flying Northerly. Swans in great number, river began to fall   Thompson return from Kohokia

Tuesday 7ᵗʰ   some rain last night, Rain this morning, the [river] falling 8 Inches. Sergt Odway returned from Kohokia @ 2 oClock   rain Incres a little, The Creek or River a Dubois raisin fast, Swept off a canoo belonging to a Maumies Indian from out its mouth. if the present fresh continue a fiew days, the water passing down this small river [the Dubois] will Wash off all that immence quantity of mud which has filled up its mouth for 300 yards by the Missourie Oze [Ooze] or mud

Wednesday 8ᵗʰ Feby 1804   a Cloudy morning   some rain, and snow   a Great raft of Ice Come Down the Creek to day, the river rises & some running Ice, a man arrived from Mr Hay at Koho, [Cahokia] with letters & an Invitation to 2 balls at St Louis

Thursday 9ᵗʰ   a fine morning   river still rise & Ice pass down the greater part out of the Missouras.[5]

Wednesday 21ˢᵗ March 1804   I returned to Camp at Wood river down the Missouri from St Charles in a Boat from the Platte river, Cap Lewis & my self Mr Choteau & Gratiot & went to stop 110 [?] Kickpo from going to war against the Osages & [*one word illegible*] W—.[6] River Rise

Thursday 22ᵈ   Set the workmen to work about the Boat, sent a man to

1. This is probably Dr. Hanson Catlett of Eddyville, Kentucky, whose name is also spelled by Clark as Callay, Catlate, and Catlet (infra, pp. 29, 37, 38). The Secretary of War, in a letter to Captain Stoddard in St. Louis, suggested that if Dr. Catlett were in the vicinity and were willing to serve as doctor for the garrison, he should be engaged as a surgeon's mate. He was so commissioned (Dearborn to Stoddard, Washington, Feb. 15, 1804; National Archives, War Department, *Military Book,* no. 2, 1803–06; Heitman, p. 290).

2. I am unable to identify this person.

3. A Samuel Hanley lived in Randolph County, Kaskaskia Land District, Indiana Territory, having settled there prior to 1788 (A.S.P.: *Public Lands, 2,* 163; Carter, *Terr. Paprs, 7,* 595; Reynolds, pp. 424–25).

4. Walnut bark appears in the old pharmacopeias but not in recent ones. The 1808 edition of *The London Medical Dictionary, 1,* 843, under "juglands," states that the shells are astringent, an ointment of leaves boiled in lard is a useful application to hemorrhoids and old ulcers, and that the bark and catkins are strongly emetic. Dr. Frank B. Queen, Professor of Pathology at the University of Oregon Medical School, to whom I am indebted for the above, suggests that in 1804 it was probably used as a mild purgative.

5. The journal is interrupted at this point. Both Lewis and Clark went down to St. Louis. On March 10, 1804, the formal transfer of Louisiana from France to the United States was made. Lewis signed the official instrument of cession. In a letter of March 17, 1804, to General Dearborn, Captain Stoddard (the official representative of the United States at the cession) reported that he had inspected the fortifications around St. Louis in the company of Captains Lewis and Clark (*Glimpses of the Past,* Mo. Hist. Soc., 2, 94).

6. Jean Pierre Chouteau and his half-brother, René Auguste, were then the two most powerful and influential figures in St. Louis. From the beginning of the town in 1794, they had engaged in the fur trade, particularly with the Osage. This tribe, of whom it was said, "There are no nations in these territories who are not at war with the Osages," was at the moment in danger of an attack (Trudeau to Carondelet, St. Louis, April 10, 1793, in Nasatir, *1,* 172). The St. Louis traders had no intention of allowing this, for it might impair their valuable trade with this tribe.

examine if the Indians had recrossed home. butifull weath[er]   Missourie river rise

Friday 23rd   The man returned, with a Lette[r] from Mr Souier [?] the Comdr of Passage Desous [Portage des Sioux] informing me that the <Ind> Kickapoos has gone home, good weath[er]   the ice continu[es] to rise—10 Inch[e]s to day & 8 last night

Saty 24   I sent Newman with Letters to Koho [Cahokia] & to Cap Lewis at St Louis, fair weather   river rise fast

Sunday 25th   a fair morning   river rose 14 Inch last night, the men find numbers of Bee Trees, & take great quantities of honey, at 11 oClock 24 Sauekees came pass from St Louis, and asked for Provisions   I ordered them 75 lb Beef, 25 lb flour, & 50 lb meal—Guterge [Goodrich] returned with Eggs & [one word illegible], Willard brought in 10 pr Hinges George Shannon Caught 3 large Cat fish—The musquetors are verry bad this evening. Newman return with Letters & Papers from St Louis ancore

Monday the 26th of March 1804, a verry smokey day   I had Corn parched to make parched meal, Workmen all at work prepareing the Boat, I visit the Indian Camps, In one Camp found 3 Squaws & 3 young ones, another 1 girl & a boy   in a 3rd Simon Gertey & two other famileys[7] Gertey has the Rhumertism Verry bad   those Indians visit me in their turn, & as usial ask for Something   I give them flour &c   Several Fish Caught to day, the Mississippi R Continu to rise & discharge great quantity of form [foam?] &c

Tuesday 27th   rain last night verry hard with thunder, a Cloudy morning. one man Sick to Day   all hands parching Corn &c   Some Delaways pass down to St Louis (Simon Gerty)   river continue to rise   beating at two morters parched Corn. "I am unwell"

Wednesday 28th   a Cloudy morning, all hands at work prepareing for the voyage up the Missourie. Cap Louis [*sic*] arrived at 4 oClock from St Louis

Thursday 29th   Rained last night   a violent wind from the N this morng with rain, Some hail   we have a trial of John Shields. John Colter & R Frasure which take up the greater part of the day,[8] in the evening we walk to Higgens   a blustering day all day, the blacksmiths return with part of their work finished, river continue to rise, cloudy Day

<Wedny> Friday 30th of March 1804. a fair Day   I write engagements & Capt Lewis write   I loaded [?] a small pr of Pistols to prevent [?] the consignments [?] which may arrive. this evenging in enforcing our regluation. not to do injury[9] Prior [?] is verry sick   I sent out R Fields to kill a squirel to make him Soup   I red the orders on Parade this evening   J. Sh [Shields]: & J. Co. [Colter] asked the forgiveness &c & promised to doe better in future. the other prisoners were dismissed &c

Satturday 31st of March   a fine morning   Sent over two men to the Island to see about a horse which was seen in distress <at> there, Majr Runsey arrived

Sunday   a fair morning   Mr Dr Catlaty [Catlett's] Boat arrived with provisions, & we sent down a Cannoo for the Docr who intended to come by Land, The French Man & his Wife came on a visit to day, a Draft for Squads, &c &c the [*one word illegible*] bo Dr Catlates Boat arrived with provisions, Cap Lewis went to St Louis with Dr Catlate [Catlett] on business, a Northern Light seen [*one word illegible*] at about 10 oClock frequently changing color, appearing as various [?] in the atmuspier

Monday 2nd of April   Mr Hays & Amdol[1] arrive from Koho: by Land in the evening Majr Garrou[2] Boat come up on his way to Prarie de chaine [Chien] loaded with provisions &c, for sale at that place, a cleaning to Day   three men Sick   all mess arranged, & men makeing Parched Meal   those Gentlemen Stay with me all night, I send down Willard to St Louis—

Tuesday 3rd   I wrote a letter to Mr John Campbell,[3] of Prarie De chaine by Mr Hay & the Gentlemen bound to [t]hat place, those Gentlemen set out at sun rise, I have meal made & the flour Packed & repacked, also some porkie [?] packed in barrels, a Windey Day   Capt Lewis returned with Dr Catlate [Catlett]   wind blew verry hard all night. Some rain

7. Simon Girty was, in the words of one writer, "more cordially hated by western Americans than any other man" (Temple Bodley, *George Rogers Clark*, New York, 1926, p. 57). His biographer states that "it is now known that he [Girty] had not at any time after 1796 and before the War of 1812 . . . been in the United States—not once had he crossed the Detroit River. He was indeed too much disabled from his infirmities to have undertaken the journey" (C. W. Butterfield, *History of the Girtys*, Cincinnati, 1890, p. 307). However, there were rumors in the West that he had appeared at various times and places south of the border. That he desired to visit his friends and relatives in the United States at this time is apparent in a letter dated Amherstburg, Nov. 11, 1804, to his brother, John Turner, who at the time was living on the Monongahela four miles below Pittsburgh (Draper MSS 12 U 13, in the Wisconsin Historical Society). In this letter, Girty reported that he was living with his children and was in perfect health. "I cannot give any further intellegenc[e]," he continued, "concerning the affairs of me and my family I will lik[e]wise crave you to send me an account of the times with you or wether I might be safe to goe see you or not as I should be Quite happy to see you once Before my Departure to an other Region from which no traveller Returns." No evidence has been found that he made any journey into the Pittsburgh area, which would indeed have been dangerous. A trip along the Maumee-Wabash route to the Mississippi in company with one of the many parties of Indians who were constantly going over it would have been safe enough.

After the transfer of Upper Louisiana to the United States on March 10, 1804, there was a great influx of Indians into the St. Louis area. Captain Amos Stoddard, who had taken control from the Spanish-French authorities, reported that the Indians "crowd here by hundreds to see their new father and to hear his words . . . if the customary presents be denied or suspended, they will commit depredations or murders on the Inhabitants. As yet I have only furnished them with provisions . . . Capt Lewis has furnished them Whiskey and Tobacco" (Stoddard to Claiborne, St. Louis, March 26, 1804, *Glimpses of the Past*, Mo. Hist. Soc., 2, 98). Under such conditions, Girty would be safe with a party of Delawares. The editor has no explanation for Clark's matter-of-fact comment on meeting this man, whom every Kentuckian regarded as "the great renegade, the white savage."

8. "Tried Several men for misconduct" (Thw., *1*, 4).

9. This rather cryptic passage apparently refers to Clark's preparations to prevent any of the men under his command from stealing any of the stores about to arrive at the camp.

1. I am unable to identify this person.

2. This man is Nicholas Jarrot, whom

Lewis met at Kaskaskia just after his arrival in Dec. 1803 (supra, p. 16 n.). Reynolds refers to him as Nicholas Jerrot, a French emigré who settled in Cahokia in 1794. His boat plied between Cahokia and Prairie du Chien in the fur trade with the Indians of the Upper Mississippi. Pike found him at Prairie du Chien in April 1806 (Elliott Coues, ed., *The Expeditions of Zebulon Montgomery Pike, 1805–1807*, 3 vols. New York, 1895, *1*, 206; hereafter cited as Coues, *Pike*). Although Clark spelled his name "Garrou," this man is not to be confused with Joseph Garreau, an *engagé* of the Missouri Company in 1794–95, who had a reputation for corruption and double-dealing among the fur traders. He is mentioned in the Notebook Journal as being at Fort Mandan in 1805 and with the Arikara in 1806 (Thw., *1*, 272; *5*, 355).

3. John Campbell had been active in the fur trade at Prairie du Chien as early as 1790. In Dec. 1807, he was made Indian Agent. In 1808, he was killed in a duel with Redford Crawford (Peter Lawrence Scanlon, *Prairie du Chien*, Menasha, Wis., 1937, pp. 77, 170–71).

4. As early as 1790, the Crawfords were established as traders at Prairie du Chien, where they were associated with Robert Dickson (Scanlon, p. 77). In a letter (Stoddard to Dearborn, St. Louis, June 3, 1804, *Glimpses of the Past*, Mo. Hist. Soc., *2*, 110; Jackson, pp. 196–97), Stoddard wrote, "A few weeks before he [Lewis] left . . . , he intrusted an Indian trader, by name of Crawford, with a parole or speech addressed to the Ayowas [Iowas] and Scioux who dwell on the banks of the river Demoine."

5. I am unable to identify the persons whose initials appear here.

6. In a letter to his mother in Connecticut, Stoddard told her of a dinner and ball he gave to repay all the courtesies shown him by the inhabitants. The affair was given at Stoddard's house and cost $622.75. He hoped he would be remunerated by the government for this outlay (Stoddard to Mrs. Samuel Benham, *Glimpses of the Past*, Mo. Hist. Soc., *2*, 113).

Wednesday 4th   all day Packing Provision   Setled account with the Contractor for all the Issues [?] to the first of the month & what Provisions he had furnished   hard wind and rain last night, Mr Crawford[4] sent his Canoo by to [*tear*] a Speach to the Seioux & Ioway Indians

Thursday 5th   Thunder & lightning last night   wrote the Speaches to the Aiyous [?] & Seioux [?] & Ioways, Several country people came to Day to pay a visit, Men and Wimmin, the wind is violiently hard from the W N W all day   river Still rise, Send by Mr Crawford Some queries reletive to the Indians, and Vocabulary also some instructions &c the Contractors Boat return to St Louis. the [wind] Shift to the North at Sun Set & Cold, Banks fall in

Friday 6th   a cloudy Day   river fall 10 Inches, the Bark Canoo set out for Mackenaeck, [Mackinac]   give out Knives Tomahawkes &c &c to the men, Sgt Pryor Still Sick, Several countery people Came to Camp to day at one oClock the wind bley [blew] hard from the N W, in this Countery the wind <which> points for rain & snow is from S.E, to, N E, the fair weather winds S W & West, clear and Cold from the N W & North, wind seldom blows from the South—at about 9 oClock P M began to Snow and Continued a Short time, wind blew hard from the N West   I write to S G [?] & F T [?],[5] give order &c &c

Satturday 7th   Set out at 7 oClock in a Canoo with Cap Lewis my servant York & one man at 1/2 past 10 arrived at St Louis. Dressed & Dined with Capt Stoddard & about 50 Gentlemen, A Ball succeeded, which lasted untill 9 oClock on Sunday   no business to day[6]

Monday 9th & Tuesday 10th, Wednesday 11, attending to Sunderey stores &c

Thursday 12th   Set out from St Louis at 6 oClock a m in Majr Rumseys boat &c

Friday 13th   arrived at Camp at 10 oClock A.M. all is well
   [*The following is in an unknown hand:*]
                  Leave Cahoke 8 o'c
                  Arrive at Kaskas[kia]—fine [?] d y
Leave Caho. 8 O'C Thursday moring—and arive at Kas <by way of the American bottom> 6 O'C Friday evening—leave Kas. Saturd—8 O'C—arrive St Ginevieve 12 O'C same day—leave St Genevieve 1 O'C P m. same Day, arrive Cape Girardeau monday <morning> 12 O'C—Leave Cape Girardeau 2 O'C—arrive at New Madrid 12 O'C Wednesday—[*End of entry in an unknown hand*]
   [*The following is in Lewis' hand:*]
on their return leave New Madrid Thursday 6 O Clock A.M Friday 6 O clock P.M. leave Cape Girardeau 6 oclk. A M. Saturday arrive at St. Genevie Sunday 6 oC P.M leave it at 7. same day and arive at Kaskaskias at 9 P.M. on the same day—leave Kaskaskias at 6 A.M. on Monday and arrive on Tuesday 5 Oclock P.M. at Cahokia—[*End of entry in Lewis' hand*]

4175 Complete rations		
@ 14 1/2 Cents—		605-37 1/2
5555 Ration of flour		
at 4 1/2 cents		231-97 1/2

25 Cask Corn @ 50 cents		12-50
12 do Salt 3$—		36—
100 G. Whiskey 128 cents		128-00
10 bus Corn fo I.—[Indians?]		50-00
20 G Whiskey do—		25-00
58 Keggs—50 cents		29-0
4000 rats pork @ 4 1/2 cents—		180-0
45 Keggs 1$—		45-0
15 do— @ 75 cts—		11-0
5 ditto @ 1$—		5-0
		1304-48

7. See Thw., *1*, 15, Detachment Orders, May 4, 1804, and Bakeless, pp. 106–07. Here in brief form is Clark's estimate of some of the men under his command. The task of disciplining the party was Clark's, and these brief notations suggest some of the difficulties encountered in dealing with these tough Kentucky and Tennessee frontiersmen.

740 lbs   Pork bone extracted   11
603 lbs   of Bone   70
————   ————
137   difference   770
                                   70
                                   ————
                                   7
210   80
  65   70 lb
————
145   11 Hogs of porkc at
          21 flour
          [*one word illegible*] had 14 flour Kegs
          & 5, 10 Gal Kegs Empty

50 Kegs in the Boat
21 of which is filled with flour
11   do   of Poark
 4   do by Mr E. of flour
36 ready by tuesday morning
         the; 3d of April
     (55 flour Keggs in) Pork Kegs they will way
              about 80
                  14 [*one word illegible*]
                  ————
               94
<Each Barrel of Pork>
       Poerogue of 8 Tuns

No Man is to absent himself from Camp <with> on any pretence What ever without permission from the Comdgn offcier present, under the pain of punishment agreeable to the rules & articles of War for Disobedience of Orders, the guard Shall Strictly attend to former Orders without the Smallest Variation[7]

S. [Shannon? Shields?] opposed order & Has threttened Od—
[Ordway's] Life   wishes to return
Wa[rner]—& P. [Potts? Pryor?] fought
F. [Fields? Frazier? Floyd?] & W H. [Whitehouse?] do
N. [Newman] & Co—[Colter? Collins?] do
Co—[Colter? Collins?] lo[aded] his gun to Shute S.O. [Sergeant Ordway?]
     —& Disobyed Orders
Wor[ner]
R. F[ields] was in a mistake & repents
Gib. [Gibson] Lost his Tomahawk
Wh—[Whitehouse] wishes to return
Fr[azer]   do   do   has don bad

Kansas ⎤
Otoes ⎟ 1
Parnees ⎟
Republican ⎦

———————

Mahar—2

———————

Poncaras ⎤ −3
Rickerie ⎦
Sous—4

———————

Loup ⎤ 5
Chayon ⎦
Mandans &c   6

5
18 men
1
1
1
1

1
25
1
1

1
1
4

	32
Cp L	8
C	40
D	
I	
y	5
22	
4	26
8	
1	9
1	40

22 − 6   [6 written over 4] − 4
7 − 1 −
29   7

26
−3
15 Howard 13
2 of us & york
1 Interpeter
G Drewyer
C. Floyd
N Pryor
R. Fields
Jo Fields
J. Shields
J. Shannon
J Gibson
J Colter
J Bratten
5 Newmon
4 J Odderway
3 Gass
8 Robertson
− Goodrich
6 McNeel
11 − Wiser
9 Bole eye
− Willard
10 Reed
− Whitehouse
1 Wenser
− Woverington
2 Thompson
7 Worner

Whitehouse
Willard
Potts
Colter

1
2
3
4
5
6
7
8
9
10

32

12 Potts ————————— 11
13 Collens ————————— 12
– Frasure —————————
14 +–+ Hale —————————

9

Floyd√	x	Odeway	11			Newmon
Pryor	x	Wnser	2			Robertson
Fields√	x	Gass	3			Willard
Bratten√	x	Newmon	4			Hale
Shields	x	Thompson	5			
Shannon	x	Warner	6			Hale +
Colter√	x	Howard	7			Potts
Gibson	x	McNeel	8			Goodrich
	–	Robertson	9	x		*Frasure
	–	Boleye	10	x		x Worthyton
	x	Reed	11			Boleye
	x	Willard	12			
	x	Wiser	13			10
	x	Collins –	14			
	x	Hale				
		Potts				Hale
		Goodrich				Potts
		√Worthington				Goodrich
		√Whitehouse				
		√Frasure				

R Worthington ⎫
Robertson   ⎬ to return[8]
Boleye   ⎭
Frasure
Bratton
Colter
Collins
Floyd
Fields
Fields
Goodrich
Gass
Gebson
Howard
Hale
Newmon
McNeil
Potts
Shields
Shannon

Wortheyton
White house
Frasure
Boley

Odeway
Reed
Pryor

Thompson

Whitehouse
Willard
Warner
Wesir
Wenser

8. The first mention in this journal of the plan to send back a party to St. Louis at some time during the journey up the Missouri. No party was sent back until the keelboat returned in the spring of 1805. Corporal Worthington [Warfington] commanded the return party. Frasure [Frazer] went with the exploring party to the Pacific (infra, p. 157 n.). Robertson was probably sent back in June shortly after the party left Camp Dubois (infra, p. 55 n.).

9. I am unable to identify this person.

1. Wolpard (Woodford, Woodfard, Woolfort) was probably Adam Woodford, whose boat plied between St. Louis and Louisville. On the return of the expedition to St. Louis in 1806, Clark forwarded to Louisville "in care of Mr. Wolpards" a large box of specimens and a small box of papers (Thw., *6*, 279).

In a memorandum in Lewis' hand in the Missouri Historical Society, dated April 1804, there is the following: "The contractor will take Woodfards wiskey @ 1 Dol. pr. Gal. I think we cannot take more provisions than the quantity sent. M. Lewis" There is added in Clark's hand, "5 bar. Wiskey Wolpard has that qty in store." In a petition from St. Louis to Jefferson signed July 4, 1806, the name of Frederick Woolford of the Ste. Geneviève District appears (Carter, *Terr. Paprs, 13*, 554; Jackson, pp. 176 n. and 349 n.).

Journal

The 13th of April 1804   at 10 oClock I arrived in Maj. Rumseys boat from St Louis, with Sundery articles for our Voyage, a Cloudy day   I hoist a Flag Staff, After part of the day fair, river falling   I give out to the men Lead, Powder, & an extra gill of Whiskey—5$ of Cap Lew at St Louis

Satturday 14th 1804   a fair Day   wind high from the [*space*]   I sent Reed to St Louis with a letter & some [*one word illegible*] &c   Locks to be mended, lent Majr Runsey 12$—paid Reed 10$ took out of bag 8$ in all 30$ out of bag to day—a Gentleman from winchester by the name of McLain[9] Came to Camp bound on land hunting, I had finished off and packed up to day in part of my store of Provisions—
Received of Majr Runsey

14 flour Kegs		
19 Pork Kegs	14th Apl	13 Bags of Parched Meal of 2 bus: each
537 lb Salt		9 do Common Meal of NC— do
		11 do & 3 barrels of N:Corn Huled do
		3 do: & 30—1/2 do—of Flour—do
		7 Barrels of Salt of 2 1/2 Bushels
		each _____ do

Sunday 15th of April, a fair morning   Sent out Shields with Mr. McLaine to the head of Wood River. Settled with Mrs Cane for all to this day & paid 12/c—Clouded up at 12 oClock   the wind from the S. W   blew verey hard   a Boat pass up the <Missouris> Mississippi under Sail at 1 oClock—Several men out to day Hunting & visiting. Mr Wolpards[1] Boat came up to day at 2 oClock under Sail, Left St Louis at 8 oClock A.M. Some Shooting at a mark

(31 candles)

Monday 16th   a fair Morning   Some rain last night & hard wind from the S. W.
by W.   Packed away

1 Bag Candle wick	1 Keg of Hogs Lard
2 Boxes of candles	1 bag of Coffee 50 lbs
" one pail Soap	2 do Sugar—
44 Kegs of Pork packed lb 3115	1 do Beens.—
6 Half barrels of pork do 590	7 bags of Biscuit
	4 Barrels of Biscuit

Several men confined for Drunkness to day, wind verry hard.

Tuesday 17th   Reed came from St Louis at 45 M after 10 oClock with Letters for me from Col. Anderson   I sent out 4 men to hunt a horse to Send to Cap. Lewis, out all day without finding him   making a Mast fixing orning & packing Pork to day   The after part of this day Cool Completed packing fifty Kegs of Pork & roled & filled them with brine, also packed one Bar: Meal & one bu Parched [corn] of an inferior quality. (out of the bag 10$)

Wednesday 18th April 1804. a fair morning. Newmon Killed a Black Lune [Loon]. Vegetation appears to be suppriseingly rapid for a few days past, R F killed a Muskrat   Several of the inhabitents came to Camp to day. Majr Runseys boat fall down one mile to river [Mississippi?]   Came to carry to the Salt works, I send Sergt Floyd & G. Shannon with two horses to Capt Lewis at St Louis, at 3 oClock Capt Louis [Lewis] arrive. The wind from the S.E. rained the greater Part of <last> this night.

Thursday 19th A rainy morning   Slept late, Thunder and lightning at 1 oClock, men Shoot at a mark, rain at 2   Settled with Majr Rumsey &c   rain continued

Friday 20th   rain last night & this morning. the river fall slo[w]ly. I have my Sword, Durk &c fixed   rain all day, assort Papers &c   dark Sultrey weather (took out of the Bag 32$ &c   Some Thunder.

Satturday 21th   rain all last night slowley   a Cloudy morning   some rain   river raised last night 12 Inches   at three oClock A Cannon was herd up the Missouris, Soon after Mr Choteau arrived with 22 Indians,[2] we Saluted them and after Staying one [H]Our, Cap Lewis & myself Set out with them to St Louis, where we arrived before night.

Sundy, Mon: & Tuesday, at St Louis

Wednesday 25   At 1/2 past 12 Set out for Camp, and arrved at night in a Perogue

Thursday 26. Mr Hay arrived, river falls,

Friday 27   prepareing to pack up Indians goods

Satturday 28   Mr Hay packing up[3]   all hands at work prepareing. Several Country men Came to Win my mens money, in doing So lost all they had, with them. river fall

	Pork		
N°	1. 64.		2203
	2. 68.		
	3. 94.		
	4. 68.	<33 ·· >	
	5. 75.	34. 90.	
	6. 69.	35. 90.	
	7. 68.	36. 90.	
	8. 68.	37. 68.	
	9. 68.	38. 68.	
	10. 69.	39. 68.	
	11. 68.	40. 68.	
	12. [space]	41. 68.	
	13. 68.	42. 68.	
	14. 68.	43. 68.	
	15. 68.	44. 68.	
	16. 68.	45. 68.	
	17. 68.	46. 90.	
	18. 68.	47. 100.	
	19. 68.	48. 100.	
	20. 68.	49. 100.	
	21. 68.	50. 100.	
	22. 68.		
	23. 68.	[lbs] 3605	
	24. 68.	12. 100	
	25. 68.		
	26. 68.	3,705	

2. See supra, p. 27 n.

3. Hay had made many trips up the Mississippi on trading ventures among the northern tribes. He would be an expert in packing the Indian trade goods the party was taking along and directing their loading into the keelboat. This apparently was what he was doing in the crowded days before the party set out. He would hardly be packing up goods for his own annual trip up the Mississippi to Prairie du Chien: his headquarters and store were at Cahokia.

```
27. 68.                                                              lb [?]
28. 68.                                    in 44 in Pork Kegs   3115
29. 68.                                    do 6    do    do      590
30. 68.
31. 68.
32. 68.                                          in all [?]    ‾‾‾‾
33. 90.                                                        3705
────────
2,203
                              24
            over   33      25
```

Sunday 29ᵗʰ of April 1804, Mr Hay still packing up goods, Some Kikapoo Chiefs come down, Wolpards Boat arrive from St Charles, River Still fall

Monday 30   a fair day   all hands at work   Mr Hay nearly finish packing up goods [*one word illegible*]   Mr McClain arrive. River Still fall

Tuesday 31ˢᵗ   Some fog this morning   Several Country people arive   I attempt to <heel the boat>

Wednesday 2ⁿᵈ May   Mr Hay, Wolpard &[c] leave Camp to St Louis at 12 oClock   several Drunk   Heel the boat.

Thursday 3ᵗʰ   I write letters to Sundy Gentlemen by Mr Choteau some wind, rive[r] falling   worked at Boat   hauled her up & examined the bottom, Mr Lousa [Lisa]⁴ & other arrive   also Sergt Floyd from St Louis with Letters to me. Majr Rumsey was polite enough to examine all my provisions   Several Kegs of Pork he Condemed.

Friday 4ᵗʰ   a rainey Day, much Shooting   Several Boats pass down to day—the river riseing a little   I send two men to St Louis with letters Maps   Salt & [*one word illegible*]

Satturday 5ᵗʰ   a Cloudy day   rains at different times   a Sauckee Chief with 8 or 10 arrive & Stay all night   2 Perogue[s] of Kickapoos return from St Louis. I gave [them?] 4 1/2 gals Whisky & some Tobacco.

Sunday 6ᵗʰ   Several of the Countrey people In Camp Shooting with the party   all git beet and lose their money   a fair Day

Monday 7ᵗʰ   I Load the Boat all day, a fair Day   Mr Rumsey Ride a public horse to St Louis   a fair day   Sent Sjt Ordway with a perogue to St Louis after Colter arrived express & [*one word illegible*] with a Hors & Tallow.

Tuesday 8ᵗʰ of May   Load the Boat & one perogue to Day. verry hot day, after Loading the Boat Maned her with 20 oares & went [to] the middle of the River & up the Mississippi a feiw miles, took the different courses of the Rive[r]s in the point, Returned & found Doct. Catlet at Camp.

Wednesday 9ᵗʰ   a fair Day   warm. I move the party into tents   Mr Rumsey & Several other men arrive, Dr Catlet Set out late for St Louis. the others Soon after, I send to the Missouras Water for drinking water, it being much cooler than the Mississippi which Keeps possession of about 1/4 of the bead [bed] or Channel

Thursday 10ᵗʰ   Some rain last night   Cloudy morning verry hot, in the after part of the day, I continued to fix Tents Covering, Adjust the Load &c   order every man to have 100 Balls for ther Rifles & 2 lb of Buck Shot for those with Mussquets &c

Friday 11ᵗʰ   a warm morning   I write all day in the evengn   about 4 oClock a Violent gust from the NW by W, [*one word illegible*]   the [*one word illegible*] up the Creek some distance, Seven french arrive with Drewyer⁵   I send Drewyer and the horses to St Louis

4. Manuel Lisa is described by Chittenden as "the most active and indefatigable trader St. Louis ever produced" (Hiram M. Chittenden, *History of the American Fur Trade of the Far West*, 3 vols. New York, 1902, *1*, 129). He had arrived in St. Louis from Vincennes only five years before this entry. This newcomer had challenged the power of the group led by the Chouteaus, which had controlled the fur trade of the Missouri from the establishment of St. Louis in 1764. Lisa's interest in the expedition and the information he might obtain from it must have been intense. Upon their return in September 1806, Lisa was ready to act upon any information Lewis and Clark brought back about the country beyond the Mandans. By the spring of 1807, he led his first expedition up the Missouri and its tributary, the Yellowstone. At the junction of this river with the Big Horn, he established Fort Lisa. Here he was in a position to exploit a new fur trading area—the region which Clark had traversed on his return down the Yellowstone. When Lisa returned to St. Louis, he organized the St. Louis Missouri River Fur Company, in 1808–09. From that time on until his death in 1820, he was the leader in the fur trade on the Missouri from the Mandans to the base of the Rocky Mountains. He could not have been a welcome visitor at Camp Dubois. Lewis believed that Lisa was responsible for a petition (critical of Lewis) which had been sent to the newly-appointed American governor of Louisiana, General Claiborne. In a letter to Clark, dated St. Louis, May 6, 1804, Lewis wrote, "Damn Manuel [Lisa] and triply damn Mr. B. [Benoit? See infra, pp. 62 n., 78]. They give me more vexation and trouble than their lives are worth—" (original in the Missouri Historical Society, St. Louis; Jackson, p. 180).

In any case, Lisa could have been of little help in furnishing information, if he had any, to the two captains, for he spoke Spanish and found it very difficult to communicate in either French or English (Chittenden, *1*, 126–36; Nasatir, *2*, passim).

5. Since Clark consistently spells Drouillard "Drewyer," I shall adopt his spelling hereafter without further notation. Three days before the party set out, Drewyer arrived with seven *engagés* who had been hired as boatmen to accompany the party. For a comment on the number and names of these men, see infra, pp. 69–70.

6. "I refur to the Comsnt of my Journal No. 1." In Jefferson's instructions to Lewis, June 20, 1803, he wrote, "Your observations are to be taken with great pains & accuracy, to be entered distinctly, & intelligibly for others as well as yourself, . . . Several copies of these, as well as your other notes, should be made at leisure times & put into the care of the most trustworthy of your attendants, to guard, by multiplying them, against the accidental losses to which they will be exposed" (Jefferson to Lewis, Washington, June 20, 1803, Thw., 7, 248; Jackson, p. 62). Jefferson was intent on making sure that the written records of the expedition were not lost. If one set were lost, other records might be retained. On May 14, 1804, the date of departure, Clark commenced "my Journal," written in a notebook designated as Codex A (Thw., *1*, 16 n.; plate opp. p. 16). At the same time he continued the daily entries in this journal. Thus, Clark kept two journals, the Notebook Journal and this one. When he had filled his first Notebook, by Aug. 15, 1804, he began the second, Codex B (Thw., *1*, 110). On Oct. 2, 1804, he began the third, Codex C (Thw., *1*, 178). This Notebook continues to April 7, 1805, when the party was ready to leave Fort Mandan for the mountains. These three are the first of the notebooks of the expedition, May 14, 1804 to Sept. 25, 1806. These are the notebooks transcribed and edited by Thwaites. The journal printed here ends with the entry of April 3, 1805, "we Shall pack up today and Set out tomorrow" (infra, p. 185).

This journal is written on separate sheets of paper of various sizes. From their nature the editor believes that many of them were written on the keelboat while it was proceeding up the Missouri. The constant emendations support this opinion. Furthermore, Clark notes in the journal that on July 14, 1804, his notes blew overboard, which obliged him "to refur to the Journals of [the] Serjeants" (infra, p. 77; see also the Introduction).

Sat: 12th   Doct Catlet Set out at 11 oClock   rain all the evening, I still arrangeing the Stores &c.

Sunday 13   a rainey Day   a frenchman arrive Soon after Hall from St Louis with Letters from Capt Lewis   I send out to enquire for Rumsey &c

Monday 14th   a Cloudy morning   fixing for a Start   Some provisions on examination is found to be wet   rain at 9 oClock   Many of the Neighbours Came from the Countrey Mail and feeMail   rained the greater part of the day, I set out at 4 oClock to the head of the first Island in the Missourie 6 Miles and incamped, on the Island   rained. I refur to the Comsmt of my Journal N° 1.[6]

II. THE RIVER JOURNAL

May 14, 1804, to April 3, 1805

FROM THE DUBOIS TO THE PLATTE:
MAY 14, 1804–JULY 22, 1804

May the 14th 1804—Monday [*Second entry for May 14*]
Set out from Camp River a Dubois at 4 oClock P.M. and proceded up the Missouris under Sail to the first Island in the Missourie and Camped on the upper point opposit a Creek on the South Side below a ledge of lime-stone rock Called Colewater,[2] made 4 1/2 miles, the Party Consisted of 2 Self one frenchman [Drouillard?] and 22 Men in the Boat of 20 ores, 1 Serjt & 7 french in a large Perogue, a Corp and 6 Soldiers[3] in a large Pe-rogue.[4] a Cloudy rainey day. Wind from the NE.   men in high Spirits

Tuesday 15—rained all last night and this Morning untill 7 oClock, all our fire extinguished, Some Provisions on the top of the Perogus wet, I sent two men to the Countrey to hunt, & proceed on at 9 oClock, and pro-ceeded on 9 Miles and Camped at a Mr Pip:[er's] Landing just below a Coal Bank on the South Side[5]   the prarie Comes within 1/4 of a Mile of the river on the N. Side   I sent to the Setlements in this Pairie & pur-chased fowls &c   one of the Perogus are not Sufficently maned to Keep up.

★Course Distance and time assending the Missouri River
Tuesday May the 15th 1804

Course	Distance mls	Time h m	Remarks & refurences★
West	1—0	0—25	to point on Stbd Side, passed the [*one word illegible*] of the Island High Lands on the Larbord Side
N. 18° W—	2—0	1—5	⎰ to a pt on Stb: Side opposit an
N. 11 W—	2—1/2	20.	⎱ Island (2) a Sand Bar in the Midlle a pot [point?] Stbd Side
N 20 W—	1—1/2	1—40	Point on the Larboard Side passed an Island (3)
S 10 W—	1—1/2	0—50	Point on the Starboard (4)
S 22 W.	1—0	1—0	to Point on Stbd Side passed an Island near the middle of the River (5)
	9—1/2	6—20	

Refurences from the 15th of May   (2) a large Island to the Starboard, (3) passed a Small Island in the bend to the Starbord, opposit Passage De Soux and with[in] 1 1/2 miles of the Mississippi,[6] observed a number of gosselins on the edge of the river   many passing down, Strong water & wind from the N E— (4) Passed a Place Lbord Called the Plattes, a flat rock projecting from the foot of A hill, where there is a farm, (5) pass an small Isld: near the Center of the river, run on Several logs this after noon, Camped at Mr Pipers Landing.

Wednesday May 16th
A fair Morning, Set out at 5 oClock   passed the Coal hill (call by the natives Carboneau)   this hill appears to Contain great quantytes of Coal, and also ore of a rich appearance haveing greatly the resemblance of Silver[7]   arrived Opposit St Charles at 12 oClock, this Village is at the foot of a Hill from which it takes its real name Peeteete Coete [Petite Côte] or the little hill, it contains about 100 indefferent houses, and abo[u]t 450 Inhabetents principally french, those people appear pore and extreemly kind,[8] the Countrey around I am told is butifull. inter spursed with Praries & timber alturnatly and has a number of American Settlers   Took equal altituds with Sextion m a 68° – 37' – 30"   Dined with the Comdr & Mr Ducetes [Duquette] family[9]

1. Beginning with Document 13 there is written above the first entry a notation giv-ing the dates of the entries in the document, set off thus:

These notations are not in Clark's hand; I believe that they are in the handwriting of Nicholas Biddle. See the Introduction, p. xxi.

2. Coldwater Creek. Cantonment Belle Fontaine was established in 1805 near its mouth.

3. The count of 40 made by Clark in this entry did not include Lewis, who had not yet joined the party. The words "2 self" probably mean Clark and his servant, York. This count does not correspond with that found in the Detachment Order of May 26 (Thw., *1*, 30–31). In the list of that date there are 41 names, and to it must be added the two captains and their servant, bringing the count to 44. This figure, however, appears incorrect when com-pared with the count made two months later at the mouth of the Platte. For a further dis-cussion of the number and composition of the party see *infra*, p. 69 n.

4. One of these pirogues had started out from Pittsburgh with the keelboat, the other had been purchased by Lewis on his way down the Ohio (*Ohio Journal*, pp. 35–39).

5. A James Piper is listed as claiming 800 arpents of land on the Missouri in the St. Charles district under a transfer dated Dec. 5, 1804 (A.S.P.: *Public Lands*, 2, 634, 689).

6. The little village of Portage des Sioux on the Mississippi took its name from a trail that crossed the narrow neck of land between the two rivers. Clark is apparently referring to the point where the trail comes down to the Missouri. See Doc. 4, Map.

7. This was probably a lead mine.

8. This village, the earliest and most im-portant settlement on the north bank of the Missouri River, had been called Les Petites Côtes and later Village des Côtes and finally St. Charles. A number of Americans had set-tled in the neighborhood on grants made to them by the Spanish authorities (A.S.P.: *Pub-lic Lands*, 2, 463–728; Houck, *Missouri*, 2, 79).

9. François Duquette was born in Canada in 1774. He came first to Ste. Geneviève and then in 1796 to St. Charles. He owned con-siderable land under Spanish grants in St. Charles and in the district and operated one of the grist mills in town (Houck, *Missouri*, 2, 85, 257; A.S.P.: *Public Lands*, 2, 168, 689, 690, 700).

1. The men here referred to were William Werner and Hugh Hall, "absent last night without leave," and John Collins, absent without leave and "behaving in an unbecoming manner at the ball last night and for Speaking in a language after his return to camp tending to bring into disrespect the orders of the Commanding Officer." All three were convicted and sentenced to lashing (Orderly Book, St. Charles, May 17, 1804, Thw., *1*, 19–21).

2. The wife of M. Duquette was Marie Louise Beauvais, daughter of Vidal Beauvais of Ste. Geneviève (Houck, *Missouri, 2,* 85).

3. This is probably Matthew Lyon, a Kentucky trader who had sublet the army contractorship for this area to Rumsey in 1802–03 (Jackson, p. 168 n.).

4. Lauriesme, Lauremus (Thw., *1,* 21). This could be Clark's spelling of Lorimier. Louis Lorimier was commandant at Cape Girardeau. (See Houck, *Missouri, 2,* 171–81; Lewis, *Ohio Journal,* p. 59 n.). He is listed as sub-agent in the Indian Department as L. Laurimier (Letter, Pierre Chouteau to Wilkinson, St. Louis, April 12, 1806, in Nasatir, 2, 771).

5. In the Notebook Journal (Thw., *1,* 21) the words, "loaded with whiskey Hats &c &c" are added.

A M 7° = 55' – 6"	P M – 4" = 4' – 35"
7 = 57 – 35	4 = 6 – 0
7 = 58 – 49	4 = 6 – 19 ★

★Course Distance and time assending the Missouris the 16th of May last 1804

Course	Distance	Time	remarks &c
South—	2–0	1–5	to pt L: Side opsd a Cole bank after passing the head of the Sd Island, and
S 85 W—	7–0	3–25	a Drift wood abov to the Center of St Charles. (1)

(1) Passed an Island on the L side just above the bank one just above, two small ones oposit under the St Shore, one on Lb Side below St Charles, arrived at this place at 12 oClock   a fine Day

Thursday the 17th 1804   a fine Day   3 men Confined for misconduct, I had a Court Martial & punishment[1]   Several Indians, who informed me that the Saukees [Sauk] had lately Crossed to war against the Osage Nation   Som aplications, I took equal altitudes   Made the M a. to be 84° – 39' – 15"

A M 8° – 35 – 40	P M 3 – 23 – 24
– 37 – 50	– 24 – 50
– 38 – 20	– 25 – 50

Measured the Missouras at this place and made it 720 yards wide, in Banks. a Boat came up this evening, I punished Hall agreeable to his Sentence in part, a fine after noon; Suped with Mr Ducett an agreeable man more agreeable Lady,[2] this Gentleman has a Delightfull Situation & garden.

Friday May the 18th 1804 a fine morning   took equal altitude and made it 97° – 42' – 37"   M.A——

A M. 9 = 9ᵐ – 51"	P M. 2 = 49' – 24"
9 = 10 – 16	2 = 50 – 50
9 = 11 – 34	2 = 51 – 10

I had the Boat & Pierogue reloded So as to Cause them to be heavyer in bow than a sturn   recved of Mr Lyon[3] 136 lb Tobacco on act of Mr Choteau   Gave out tin Cups & 3 Knives to the French hands, Mr Lauriesme[4] [Lorimier] returned from the Kickapoo Town to day   [He] delayed a Short time & Set out for St Louis, I sent George Drewyer with Mr Lauriesmus to St Louis & wrote to Cap Lewis   Mr Ducete made me a present of river Catts & Some Herbs   our french hands bring me eggs milk &c &c to day   The wind hard from the S.W.   Two Keel Boats came up to this place to day from Kentucky[5]

Satturday May the 19th 1804   a Violent Wind last night from the W.S W, Suckceeded by rain with [which] lasted som hours, a Cloudy morning   Many persons Came to the boat to day   I took equal altitudes. Mar time 76° – 33' – 7"

A M— 8 = 12' – 50"	P M— 3 = 45 – 59
8 = 14 – 9	3 = 46 – 22
8 = 15 – 30	3 = 47 – 41

I heard of my Brothers illness to day which has given me much concurn,[6] I settle with the men and take receipts for Pay up to the 1st of Decr next,[7] I am invited to a ball in the Village, let Several of the men[8] go,—R Fields Kill a Deer[9] George Drewyear returned with a hundred Dollars, he lost

Sunday 20th May

a Cloudy morning   rained and a hard wind last night, I continue to write Rolls, Send 20 men to Church to day   one man Sick   Capt Lewis and Several Gentlemen arrive from St Louis thro a violent Shoure of rain,[1] the most of the party go to the Church.

Monday 21st May

Dine with Mr Ducete & Set out from St Charles at three oClock after getting every matter arranged, proceeded on under a jentle Breese, at one mile a violent rain with Wind from the S.W.   we landed at the upper point of the first Island on the Stbd Side & Camped, Soon after it commenced raining & continud the greater part of the night, 3 french men got leave to return to Town, and return early   (refur to fig:, 2.)

25th refured to fig: 2. | Left St Charles May 21th 1804: Steered N: 15° W 1 3/4 Ms N 52° W to the upper point of the Island and Camped Dureing a rain which had been falling half an hour, opposit this Isd coms in a Small creek on the St Sd and at the head one on the Ld Side   rains powerfully.

Tuesday May 22nd

Delayed a Short time for the three french men who returned and we Set out at 6 oClock   a Cloudy morning   rained Violently hard last night   Saw Several people on the bank to day & passed several small farms, Capt Lewis walk on Shore a little &c   passed a Camp of Kickapoo Indians, & incamped in the Mouth of a Small Creek in a large Bend on the Stbd Side.

The Courses & Distances of this day is as follows Viz

S 60° W. 3 miles—Passed the upper point of the Isd on which we lay last night to a pt L: Sd.

S:43° W. 4 miles—this course passes a pt on Lbd Sd and this an Island in the Mid: R: to a pt St Sd.

West. 3 1/2 Miles—psd the Mo: of Bonom [Bonhomme] Creek[2] Lbd Sd pt 1 1/2 ms an Isd in Mid: R: to pt on Sbd Sd abov

S. 75° W. 7 1/2 miles—psd a pt on Lbd round an Isd bend to the N: 2 Sm:

Total 18   Isd opsd one nearest the Larboard Side to the pt in the Cent. to Stb opposit the lower pt of Tavn [Tavern] Isld: and at the mouth of Osage Woman river[3]

Wednesday May 23rd   8 Indians Kick: [Kickapoo] Came to Camp with Meat we recvd their pesents of 3 Deer & gave them Whisky:

Set out early   run on a log: under water and Detained one hour   proceeded on [one word illegible] the Same Course of last night (2 miles) passed the mouth of a creek on the Sbd Side called Woman of Osage River[4] about 30 yds over, abounding in fish, Stoped one hour where their was maney people assembled to see us,[5] halted at an endented part of a Rock which juted over the water, Called by the french the tavern which is a cave 40 yds long with the river 4 feet Deep & about 20 feet high, this is a place the India[ns] and french Pay omage to, many names are wrote up on the rock   Mine among others,[6] at one mile above this rock coms in a small Creek called Tavern Creek, abov one other Small

6. The two brothers of William Clark, Generals Jonathan Clark and George Rogers Clark, were living in Louisville. In the biographies and papers of the two there is no mention of any serious illness at this time.

7. In the Draft of Receipt for Compensation, the last date of enlistment for those in the party when it left St. Charles is May 16, 1804 (Thw., 7, 360). A rough form of the draft of receipt but not filled out is given following the entry for May 24. (See infra, p. 44.)

8. One of the men, Whitehouse, has the following entry for May 18: "passed the evening verry agreeable dancing with the french ladies, etc." (Thw., 7, 31).

9. Game was plentiful along the river. On June 30, 1804, Clark noted that "Deer [were] to be Seen in every direction and their tracks are as plenty as Hogs on a farm" (infra, p. 64). Each day Drouillard, usually accompanied by the best hunters in the party, left the camp in the morning and rode along the shore to hunt meat for the party. The deer were killed, carried down to the shore, and picked up when the keelboat and pirogues came along. When possible, some of the venison was jerked—cut in long, thin slices and dried in the sun. A half pound of venison and bear oil or fat mixed with parched corn was considered an adequate ration (Nasatir, 1, 37).

As they ascended the stream, buffalo signs were seen (June 6, Thw., 1, p. 41). Clark shot the first elk one month out from the starting point (July 14). By then they were passing through the high plains, where not only deer but elk, antelope, and buffalo were plentiful. There, too, following the herds, was the lobo wolf of the plains. "I killed an imence large yellow Wolf" (infra, p. 82). Between May 19 and July 22, the hunters had brought in 77 deer, 11 bear, and 1 elk. Later, as the reader will note, antelope and buffalo were added to the food supply. The profusion of game on the banks of the river was a source of constant remark. These men, hunters all, knew that back from the stream and for thousands of miles to the west, the plains and the streams that crossed them must be teeming with wild life. Lewis, in his letter to his mother written at Fort Mandan, reflected the wonder of the party at this hunters' paradise (Thw., 7, 311; Jackson, pp. 222–25).

1. The party consisted of Captain Lewis, Captain Amos Stoddard, Lieutenants Stephen Worrell and Clarence Mulford; Messrs. Chouteau, Gratiot, Delauny, Labbadie, Rankin, and Dr. Antoine Saugrain (Thw., 1, 22).

2. On the Indian Office Map, an island, not the river, is called I. au Bonhomme, Good Man's Island. The river is so named in the Perrin du Lac Map of 1802. See also the sketch map, Doc. 15. It is called Bonhomme Creek on the Missouri River Commission Map of 1892–95, plate II. These maps are hereafter referred to as M.R.C. Maps.

Clark made small sketch maps of this portion of the river between the Osage River and the mouths of the two Charitons. Over these maps are the entries of June 4 (Doc. 17) and June 5 (Doc. 18).

3. The Little Femme Osage River (M.R.C. Map, plate II.

4. This is the Femme Osage River (idem).

5. The people referred to here lived in a small settlement of 30 or 40 families, mostly American. Daniel Boone settled here in 1797, and Whitehouse in his journal refers to it as "boons Settlement." Later, Boone moved upstream to La Charette (Thw., 7, 31; Houck, *Missouri*, 2, 93–94).

6. Ordway in his journal calls this "Corn tavern," which suggests that it may have been used as a cache by the fur traders (*Journal of. . . . John Ordway*, Wisconsin Historical Society, *Collections*, 22, Madison, 1916, 80, hereafter cited as *Ordway*). In the Notebook Journal, Clark does not mention putting his name on the rock (Thw., *1*, 27).

7. The term "drifts" was used to describe masses of driftwood brought down by the current of the river and lodged against some obstruction. These barriers, called by the French *embarras*, often extended upriver for some distance and were extremely difficult to pass.

Creek, camped at 6 oClock/ after expirencing great dificulty in passing Some Drifts/ on the Stb Side,[7] examined the Mens arms   found all in good order except the Detachment of Solds in the Perogue—R Field Killed a Deer.

Thursday May the 24th 1804   Set out early   passed a Small Isd in the midlle of the river, opposit the on the Lbd Side is projecting Rock of 1/2 a mile in extent against which the Current runs, this place is called the Devils race grounds, above this coms in a Small Creek called the little quiver, a Sand Island on the Stbd Side, passed Several Islands & 2 creeks, on the Stbd Side a Small Island on the Lbd Side above we wer verry near loseing our Boat in Toeing   She Struck the Sands/ which is continerly roaling/ <& turns> the Violence of the Current was so great that the Toe roap Broke, the Boat turned Broadside, as the Current Washed the Sand from under her   She wheeled & lodged on the bank below as often as three times, before we got her in Deep water, nothing Saved her but [*sentence unfinished.*]

[*The following is a rough draft in Clark's hand of a form intended for use in listing terms of service and pay for members of the party:*]

We the Subscribes do acknowledge to have received of Capt <following> Several Sums <ammunted> Mentioned against our respective names, <and due us> in Liew of Cloathing and rations not Drawn, and Due us for the respective periods herein expressed—for which we have Signed triplicate receipts this 19th of May 1804 St Charles—

Names	Commencement of Service	Term paid for Mon Day	Day & Mo Dollars	Amt reived Do Cts	Signer Names	Witness

[*There are two entries for May 23 and May 24. As these are written in two separate documents, No. 13 and No. 14, they have been left in that form.*]

May 23rd   Course of last night S: 75 W   Continued 2 miles to the Said
point St Side   passed the upper Point of the Island   Thence S 52° W.
7 Miles to a pt on St Sd passing Tavern Island [and] two small Isd in a
bend to the St: side   the mo: [mouth] of Oge [Osage] Womans River at
1 m: the Cave called the Tavern, Lbd Side at 5 m: Situated in the Clift,
opposit a Small Island on the Stbd Side/ R. & Js: (Fields came in) with
many people, passed the Tavern Cave, Cap Lewis assended the hill
which has [a] peninsulis projecting in raged points to the river, and was
near falling from a Peninsuler   hard water all Day   Saved himself by
the assistance of his Knife, passed a Creek 15 yds wide at 1 mile called
creek of the Tavern on the Lbd Side, camped opposit the pt which the
Last course was to. one man sick.

May 24th   Set out early, Killed a Deer last night. examined the mens
arms, & Saw that all was prepared for action., passed an sm [small] Island
in the M.R, [Main River?] opposit a hard place of water called the Devill
rac[e] grown[d]. S 63° W 4 miles to a point on the Sd: Starboard Side N
68 W to a point on Lbd Side 3 Ms: Passd a Small Willow Island on the
Lbd Side to the point of a Is^d L'Side—S 75° W to a point on Stbd Side 3
Miles, Passed the upper point of the Island. Crossed and in a verry bad
place we got our Boat a ground & She Bocke the Toe Roap & turned the
Sand, bring [?] [one word illegible] the in Wheeling three times, got off
returned to the head of the aforesaid Island, and Came up under a falling Bank. hard water   this place being the worst I ever Saw, I call it the
retregrade bend. Camped at an old house.

$$\begin{array}{r} 4 \\ 3 \\ 2 \\ 3 \\ \hline 12 \end{array}$$

8. On the Indian Office Map this stream is labelled "a Dubois" and below this, "Dubois's River." (Houck, *2*, 73 n.).

9. The St. Johns River, found on both the Indian Office Map and Clark's map, is not mentioned in any of the journals, or in Clark's "Summary of Rivers and Creeks" (Thw., *6*, 56). Ordway, Gass, and Floyd give the name St. Johns to the village La Charette across the river from the mouth of this stream (*Ordway*, p. 81). The wording of both the Notebook Journal and this journal is here obscure. The R. La freeau, called *la poceau* in the Notebook Journal, may be the St. Johns.

1. Daniel Boone moved to this place from "boons settlement" downstream (supra, p. 44 n.). It is not certain whether he had settled at La Charette when the expedition passed (Houck, *Missouri*, 2, 94). This little village was the last white settlement the explorers were to see until their return, Sept. 19, 1806 (Thw., *5*, 389). At La Charette the party met Regis Loisel "imediately down from Seeder [Cedar] Isld. Situated in the Country of the Sciox 400 Leagues up he gave us a good Deel of information" (Thw., *1*, 29).

A meeting with Loisel would be one of great importance to the explorers, for next to Mackay, this man should have been in a position to give more detailed information than any other person. He was a partner in the Missouri Fur Company, organized in St. Louis in 1796 and in 1804 operating under the name of Clamorgan, Loisel, and Co. When Loisel met Clark he was returning from the fort he had built on the Île aux Cèdres about 100 miles above the mouth of the White River and over 1,200 miles up the Missouri. He had wintered there with his partner, Tabeau, in 1803–04, and left him in charge when he started for St. Louis. His other associate, Jean Vallé, was established farther upstream at the mouth of the Cheyenne River. Another partner of Loisel, Hugh Héné, had for some years been with the Tetons (infra, p. 153 n.; p. 181 n.; see also Nasatir, *1*, 114–15). The fact that such an important meeting was not recorded by Clark in these notes, but noted with some detail in his Notebook Journal, is some evidence that the two accounts were being made at the same time.

2. In the Notebook Journals in Philadelphia, there are here interpolations in Biddle's handwriting. Thwaites, in his transcription, identified these interpolations as Biddle's. The name of Beef Island is a case in point. Evans, Mackay, and Clark call this island Beef Island or Île au Boeuf. Biddle wrote in Buffalo Island (Thw., *1*, 29). Coues copied it from Biddle's *History of the Expedition under the Command of Captains Lewis and Clark*, and Thwaites used Biddle's interpolation in the Notebook Journal.

25 May

Set out early   Course West to a Point on Sbd Side   at 2 Miles passd a Willow Isd in a Bend to the Lb a creek called Wood rivr Lbd Side[8] N 57 W. to a pt on the Sd Side 3 Miles passed the Mouth of a creek St Side Called Le quiver, this Same course continued to a Point Ld Side 2 1/2 Miles further. opposit a Isd on Sd Side Passed a creek Called R. La freeau[9] at the W. N20° W 2 miles   To a Small french Village called La Charatt of five families only,[1] <this is the sett> in the bend to the Starbord   This is the <only> Last Settlement of Whites, an Island opposit

May 26th 1804. Set out at 7 oClock after a hard rain & wind, & proceed on verry well under Sale. Wind from the ENE S50° W 3 1/2 ms to a point opposit the mouth of Beef Island & River on the Lbd Side, N 80° W 2 1/2 miles to point on the Lbd Side, passed Beef Isd on Sbd Side Beef Creek on the Back of the Isd.[2] N 88 W. 3 1/2 Ms to pt to St Side above the upper point of Beef Island N. 82° W 1 1/2 miles to pt St Side, N 37° W 5 1/2 miles to a Point on the Lbd Side an Island on the Starbd Side, passed a willow Island and a Creek called Sheppards R,[3] on the Lbd Side about, passed 2 willow Islands on the Lbd Side in a Bend N 60 W. 2 M to a point on the St Side passed an Isd on the St Sd <N 71° W. 3 M: to a pt on Ld Side passed a> of the said Isd   The wind favourable to day we made 18 miles   a Cloud rais[ed] & wind & rain Closed the Day

Sunday May 27th   as we were Setting out this morning two Canoos loaded with Bever elk Deer Skins & Buffalow Robes, from the Mahars [Omaha] nation, they inform that they left that place 2 months, a gentle Breese from the S E, N:71 W. 3 miles to a point on the Labd Side opposit the lower point of [space] Island, passed a willow Island on the L. sd opposit the upper Point of the Isd   we Camped on last night   S 82° W 6 ms to a pt on Lbd Side   passed the lower pt of a Isd   Passed 4 casieux [cajeux][4] 3 from Grand Osage one from the Parnees [Pawnees]. Passed two Isd on the S Side a Creek of 20 yds Wide on the Lb Side near the upper point, this Creek is Called Ash Creek N. 74° W 1 1/2 miles to pt on Lbd Sd nearly opst the upper pt of the big Island called [space] Isle, on the stbd side back of this Isd Coms in Otter R.[5] & two other Creeks, S 70° W. 5 m: to a pt on St Sd opposit Gasconnade River passing a pt on Lbd Side   we camped on an Isd in the mouth of Gasconade R, this river is 157 yards wide   a butifull stream of clear water. 19' foot Deep   Hills on the lower Side

Monday 28th May
rained hard all the last night   Some wind from the S W, one Deer Killed to day, one Man fell in with Six Indians hunting, onloaded the perogue, & found Several articles Wet, Some Tobacco Spoiled. river begin to rise

Tuesday 29th May   Sent out hunters, got a morning obsvtn and one at 12 oClock, rained last night, the river rises fast   The Musquetors are verry bad, Load the pierogue

May 29th 180[4]   Set out from the mouth of the Gasconnade, where we took obsvern   I left a Perogue for a man lost in the woods, [Whitehouse] Course N. 54 W 2 m to a point Lb Side   Passed the Isd on which we camped, river still rised, water verry muddey N 78° W 2 ms to a pt on Lb Side   passed two willow Islands first smaller and a creek on Lbd called Deer Creek one oposit the Point St Side and incamped on the Lb Side rain all night

[*The following four lines are written in pencil:*]
Form [?] the tents together gro [?] along the Bank [?] N: 76 W 25 Poles S 26 W, to the point above—S 19° to the pot below the River

 From the pole on the Bank to the upper point is S 11 [?] E to the lower point is [?] S L L S 42 1/2 East to the pole at the Lower Side

	Gasconnade 157 yds 28 1/2 poles Wide			
below the mouth of Gascond	35	do	do	193
above do do	38 1/2	do	do	215.

Course of the River gasconnade is S 20° W—River up N 70° W   The River Down N 29° E

$$
\begin{array}{r}
2 \\
4 \\
2 \\
2 \\
\hline
13
\end{array}
$$

3. The French word *berger,* shepherd, is preserved in the present names of Big and Little Berger Creek, Berger Bottom, and the town of Berger (M.R.C. map, plate IV.

4. A *cajeu* was a small raft made by lashing two canoes together.

5. Sometimes called Rivière à la loutre (as given on the Indian Office Map).

6. This was Whitehouse's first adventure, the discovery of a cave near the river. "I went a 100 yards under ground had no light in my hand if I had, I should have gone further their was a Small Spring in it. it is the most remarkable cave I ever Saw" (Thw., 7, 32).

7. The Notebook Journal calls this Rush Creek (Thw., *1*, 36).

8. There is no entry in this journal for May 31. On that day the party met a cajeu loaded with peltry. In the Notebook Journal (Thw., *1*, 36–37), Clark reports that the party met a cajeu from the Grand Osage River. The crew, consisting of a Frenchman, an Indian, and a squaw, had letters from one of Chouteau's men who had been sent to the Osage. Chouteau was informed in the letters that the Osage had burned his letter and had stated that they did not believe that the Americans had taken possession of Louisiana and that they would not trade with St. Louis. Whitehouse, Ordway, Gass, and Floyd all mention this encounter in their journals.

9. These two men set out from St. Charles with the four horses that were to accompany the party the whole distance to the Mandans, 1,600 miles upstream. Drewyer, usually with one or two companions, left the party each morning to hunt. The meat was packed on the horses and taken down to the river bank to be picked up by the party when it came up.

May 30ᵗʰ Wednesday, Set out at 7 oClock after a heavy rain, rained all last night, a little after Dark last night Several guns were herd below, I expect the French men firing for Whitehous who was lost in the woods.⁶

2

2

3

4

Course West 2 M. to a pt Lbd Side opsd an Isld   a Cave on the St Side Called Monbrains Tavern, a Creek above, S. 80° W 2 ms to pt Lb Side passed an Isd on the St Side, a Sand bar & Creek Called rest Creek⁷ on the Lb Side—Rain hard, S 78. W 3 mls to pt on Lbd Side psd a willow Isd in Mid: R. a willow Island S. 66° W, 4 ms to a pt Lbd Side, opposit the mouth of a Small River called Miry River of about 80 yds wide a Willow Isd in the River, a large Isd above S 4 [*one word illegible*] W 6 Ms to a pt on Lbd Side, passed a Isd in the Mid: came to in the mouth of a Creek Lbd Side yds wide called [*space*] one on St Side of 60 yds wide called little Miry at 2 mls   Passed a Creek of 15 yds wide on the Lbd Side at 14 miles Called Grindstone Creek & incamped in the Mouth, Low land on both Sides of the river & creek⁸

2

2

3

4
—
11

June 1ˢᵗ Friday 1804   Set out early, the Same Course S 48° W of Wednesday contd 4 mls passed the mouth of Little Miry on the Stb & <Bear Creek on the Larbd at 6 ms this Creek is about 25 yds wide,> A [?] high rich Land on the Lb Side, S. 45° W to an Island opposit a hill on the S. sd 6 ms   this Isd is on the Lbd   passed the Mo. of Bear creek 25 yds wide at 2 ms & three Small Isd, Some Swift water and banks falling in Wind a head from the West, S 39° W 3 Ms to the Pt above the mouth of Osage River Larb Side, Camped   fell a number of Trees in the Point to take observation   a fair after noon, Set up untill 1 oClock to take Som observations &c

4

3

6

7

6

June 2ⁿᵈ—Took the Dist. of Son & moon &c &c   I measured the Osage & Missourie at this place made ther width as follows, the Missoure 875 yd wide   The Osage R 397 yds wide, the distance between the 2 rivers 80 poles up is 40 ps   Took equal altitudes & Mredian altitude also—and made them [*space*]   I assended the hill in the point 80 ps from the pt found it about 1 [1 written over 2]oo foot high, on the top is 2 graves, or mouns, a Delightfull prospect from this hill which Comds both rivers Drewyer & Shields came to the opposit Side to day at Sunset⁹ we sent across & brought them over, they had been absent 7 [7 written over 8] Days   Swam many creeks, much worsted. they informed us

2

6

[*Written across the above entry is* Carsuex—Raft.]
[*Written in reverse below entry for May 30:*] that the Country on both Sides of Muddy river to the hill called by the french [*space*] 3 ms below

this place a Small Prarie below the hill, 4 Deer Killed to day   I assend a
hill & after measuring the river &c &c &c

1. Sgt. Ordway, who was the helmsman of the keelboat, ran too close to the shore and the mast was broken by an overhanging tree. Hence the name, Mast Creek (Thw., *1*, 39; *Ordway*, p. 82).

2. Just beyond this island the party passed the future site of the present capital of Missouri, Jefferson City, on the south bank. Just beyond and on the north side is the mouth of Cedar Creek.

3. There are no nightingales in North America. Coues suggests that Clark heard a cardinal or redbird, the "Virginia Nightingale;" it might have been a mockingbird (Thw., *1*, 39 n.).

4. This point is not named in the Notebook Journal (Thw., *1*, 38–39). Floyd mentions it as "Batue De Charr, a prarie on the S Sid" (Thw., *7*, 8). The hornbeam or yoke elm was called *charme* by the French.

5. Some of the French *engagés* had been up the Missouri before, notably Labiche and Cruzatte. They were a great source of information.

June Sunday 3rd 1804

the fore part of the day fair   I attempted to take equal alltitudes, & M Altitudes, but was dis apointed   the Clouds obsured the Sun, took the D. of o & c: Capt Lewis & George Drewyer went out & Killed a Deer, We Set out at 5 oClock P M   cloudy & rain/, West 2 the mo. [?] of Murrow [Moreau] Creek lb Sd Mls to a pt St Side Keeping along the Lbd Side 1 ms, passed the mouth of a creek on Lbd Side 3 ms, I call Cupboard, Creek, mouth behind a rock which projects into the river, camped in the mouth of the Creek aforesaid, at the mouth of this Creek I saw much fresh sign of Indians, haveing crossed   2 Deer Killed to day. I have a verry sore Throat, <great> & am Tormented with Musquetors & Small ticks.

June 4th 1804 Monday, a fair Day   sent out 3 hunters, our mast broke by the boat running under a tree[1]   Passed an Island on Stbd Side on which grow Seede[r] a Creek at [*space*] miles on Starbd Sd[2]   Course N 30° W 4 Ms to pt on St Side below 2d Isd passed a Creek on Lbd Side 15 yd wide, I call Nightingale Creek. this Bird Sang all last night and is the first of the kind I ever herd, below this creek and the last.[3] Passed a Small Isd on the Stbd N. 25—W. 3 ms to a pt on St Sd   passed a Sm. Isd on St Sd and Seeder Creek on the same side 20 yds wide passed a Creek on Lbd Sd 20 yd wide, I call Mast Creek, this is a Short Creek, fine land above & below the mouth. Jentle rise of about 50 foot, Delightfull Timber of Oake ash walnut hickory &c &c   wind from N W. by W. N. 58° W. 7 1/2 ms passed a Creek Called Zon car on the Lb Side, N 75 W 3 ml to a pt S. Sd called Batue a De charm,[4] a plain on the hill opposit. I got out & walked on the L Sd thro a Charming Bottom of rich Land about one mile   then I assended a hill of about 170 foot on the top of which is a moun[d]. and about 100 acres of Land of Dead timber on this hill   one of the party[5] says he has found Lead ore a verry extensive Cave under this hill next the river, the Land on the top is fine, This is a very bad part of the river Seven Deer Killed to day by our hunters—one of the horses is snaged, the other lost his shous to day   the Bottom on the St Side to day is covered with rushes, not verry good   the high land Batue a Decharm coms [*one word illegible*] to the bank on the Labd Side and good 2d rate land

June 5th Tuesday, Jurked the Vennison Killed Yesterday, after seting over the Scouting Party or hunder[s] of 3 men   Set out at 6 oClock Course N 57° W to a pt on S. Sd 5 ms passed a Creek on L sd I call Lead C of 10 yds   passed one on the S. Called Lit: good womans Creek about 20 yds wide[6]   Passed a Willow Isd a Butifull Prarie approaching near the river above Lead C & extends to the Mine river in a westerley Derection, passed the Mouth of the Creek of the Big Rock 15 yds Wide at 4 ms on the Lbd Sd at 11 oClock brought [to?] a caissie [cajeu] in which was 2 men, from 80 League up the Kansias River, where the[y] wintered and caught a great qty of Beever but unfortunately lost it by the burning of the plains, the Kansas Nation hunted on the Missourie last winter and are now persueing the Buffalow in the Plains, passed a Projecting Rock called the Manitou a Painting[7] from this Deavel to the Pt on the Lbd Side N 23° W 7 1/2 ms   The same course passed a lage Is 2 1/2 ms on the Lbd Side Creek cld Manitou about 40 yds wide,[8] a Sand bar in the middle of River   passed up between the sand & L. Shore one Mile to a Small Creek 10 yds wide,/ I call Sand C/. We run on the Sand and was obliged to return to the Stard Side, I am verry unwell with a slight feever from a bad cold caught three days ago at the Grand so' [Osage ?] R— passed a Small Willow Isd on S. Side, a large one in the Middle of the river, York swam to the Isd to pick greens, and swam back with his greens, the Boat Drew too much water to cross the quick Sands which intervened, She Draws 4 foot water, a fair wind   our mast being broke by accidence provented our takeing the advantage of it   passed—the lower point of a large Island, opposit the current devides between <three> 4 Small Isds on the St Side. we found the water excessively hard for 12 miles as we were oblged to pass up the center of the Current between two of the Isds & round the heads of the other 2   the Current setting imediately against the points which was choked up with Drift for a mile—Above those Isd on the St Side   we camped altogeth[er]   our Hunter or Spy Discovered the sign of a war party of abt 10 men[9]

6. There are two streams of this name flowing into the Missouri from the north, mentioned in both the Notebook Journal and this journal: Little Goodwoman's Creek and, farther upstream, Goodwoman's River, marked on the Indian Office Map as *R. à la bonne femme.* See infra, p. 44.

7. Clark made a sketch of this Indian painting of the Manitou. See Doc. 19, Facs. In the Notebook Journal, he made a more elaborate drawing (Thw., *1,* 40).

8. On the Indian Office Map this stream is called *R. petit manitou.* Farther upstream there is the Manitou River or the Big Manitou of Mackay's Table of Distances. The map carries no name for the latter stream. See infra, p. 52.

9. In the Notebook Journal Clark added that this war party was probably Sauk, traditional enemies of the Osage (Thw., *1,* 41).

1. Evans and Mackay identify this creek as *"R. a la roche percee."*

2. Mackay, in his Table of Distances, calls this *R. de la Petite Saline.* These salines were important on the frontier and were one of the first resources to be exploited. Ordway writes that "Salt has been made their &c" (*Ordway,* p. 83). These salines or salt springs would be known to the *engagés,* hence the word "Information" in parentheses.

3. In his Notebook Journal (Thw., *1,* 42), Clark wrote a description of this: "Several Courious paintings and carving on the projecting rock of Limestone inlade with white red & blue flint, of verry good quallity, the Indians have taken of this flint great quantities." In this journal, Clark's drawing shows the Manitou, the buffalo, and the Indian, for the Manitou had the power to bring the buffalo to the Indian (Doc. 19, Facs.). Ordway called the creek by the limestone cliff the Big Devil Creek, perhaps to distinguish it from the little Manitou, which had been passed (*Ordway,* p. 84).

4. See supra, p. 51 and n.

Wednesday the 6th of June 1804.

Mended our Mast this morning and Set out at 7 oClock, under a jentle Braise from the S,E by S   N 28° W 3 1/2 miles to a hill on St Sd pass:g the N: belge [bulge] of the Island Called Split Rock Island, the river rose last night a foot, the Countery about this Isd is delightfull   large rush bottom of rushes below on the St Side   N 49° W, 1 1/2 Ms to the mouth of Split rock <Creek> River yds wide[1] on the Starboard Side opod the pt of a Isd: passed a place in the projecting rock Called the hole   thro' the rock, a <Small> round Cave pass thro the Pt of rock's   west 1 1/2 ml to a pt on Std Sd opposit a clift of rocks abt 200 foot   N 31.W. 4 ms 1/2 to a pt on L: Side   passed Saline Creek on the L. Side a large Salt Lick & Spring 9 ml up the Creek, one bushel of water will make 7 lb of good Salt   (Information)[2]   Took Meridian altitude of ☉ Limb. 37° 6' 0" equat to [space] of Lattidude on this Creek, so great a no of Salt Springs are on it that the water is brackish   N 51° W to a Belge of an Isd on the S. Sd at 3 ms. Passed a Willow Isd in Middle, Some wind in the after part of to day from the S E, (the Banks are falling in greatly in this part of the river) as also is one Side or the other in all the Course, we assended on the North Side of the Isd and finding that the perogues Could not Keep up Camped 2 hs by Sun: on the Sd Sd   the land below this is good.

Thursday 7th of June 1804   Set out early   passed the head of the Isd from the Isd <to a pt on Lbd Side> N. 61° W. to the mouth of a Creek Called big monetu on St Sd 4 1/2 Ms psd a Sand bar in the river, Som Buffalow sign   sent out George Drewyer & Newmon to hunt <them> Capt Lewis and 6 men went to a Lick up this Creek on the right Side over 2 ms & 2 other[s] not far above   the water runs out of the bank & not verry strong. 3 to 500 g for a bushel.

S 88° W. 2 Miles to a pt on Lbd Side, high bluff on the Stbd Side, Monitou Creek is 30 yds Wide at the mouth, passed a painted part of a Projecting rock[3]   we found ther a Den of rattle Snakes, Killed 3   proceeded and passed, S 81° W 4 Ms to a pt on S. Side   passed an Island in the Middle of the river, S. 87° W. to a pt of high land on the L. S: pass:'g over the Middle of a Willow Island, Ms 3 1/2   proceed on 1/2 a mile on this Course a[nd] Camped at the mouth of Good Womans river on the S.S. about 35 yds wide & navagable som Dt[4]   our hunters brought in 3 bear this evening—& infd that the Countery between this R. & the Monitou R is rich and well watered, Capt Lewis went out an hour this evening

June 8th Friday

Set out at Day light   proceeded on the Course of last night S 87° W 3 ms   passed a Willow Island, from the Point of last Course S 81° W. 3 ms to a pt on S. S: passd a [space] Isd in the middle of the river, passd a run on the Ld S: above a pt of rocks 3 mls on which there is a number of Deer Licks, N 88° W. 3 Ms to a pt L S: N. 83° W 2 Ms to the Mo of Mine River, psd an Isd—This river is 90 yards wide & navagable for Perogues about 90 Ms. I went out on the L S. about 4 ms below this R. and found the Countery for one mile back good Land and well watered   the hills not high with a gentle assent from the river, well timbered with oake, walnit Hickory ash, &c. the land Still further back becoms thin and open, with Black & rasp Berries, and Still further back the Plains Commence, The french inform that Lead ore is found on this river in Several places, it heads up between the Osagees & Kansas River the right hand folk [fork] passes in a Short distance of the Missouris at the antient Little Osages Village   our hunter Killed, 2 Deer, after Staying one hour at the Mouth of this River, Capt Lewis went out & proceeded on one Mile & came in, he fount the land in the point high and fine   Course N. 64° W 1 Ml to a pt on S.S. N. 80° W to the Lower pot of a Id on L.S. passed a <large> small Isd in the M: R. At (3 Ms) met 3 men on a Caussee [Cajeu] from R Dis Soux, above <The Mahar> [Omaha] Nation loaded with fur.[5] <N 39 W 3 1/2 Ms to pt on S.S. opsd a Prarie>   Camped on the Lower point of an Id L.S. called the Mills, here I found Kegs an[d] Pummey stone, and a place that fur or Skins had been burred [buried] by the hunters   our Hunters Killed 5 Deer, Some rain, the Countrey on S.S. is verry fine

9th of June Satterday   Set out early, water verry Swift   got fast on a log, detained us 1/4 hour   Hard rain last night. N 39° W 3 1/2 Ms to a pt on the S.S. opposit the Commencement of the 1st Prarie, Called Prarie of the Arrows, the river at this place about 300 yds Wide   passed a Small Creek, Arrow Creek 8 yds wide L. Sd   the Current exceedingly Strong N 34°: E 2 Ms to the Belg [bulge] of a Small Island Situated on the L.S. Passed the Mo: of Arrow Creek N 83° W 1 1/2 Ms to a pt on L.S. <of High Land> opposit Black bird C[reek] small   passed the head of the Isd & a small Willow one to the L.S.   (⊙ Merdn altd back obsvn 37—00'—00—N. 39° W 2 [2 written over 1 1/2] to a pt <on S.S.> of High Land on the L. Side opst a pt on St S. river about 350 yds wide at this pt a Wind from the S. at 4 oClock, (Handson Sutn [Situation?]) on the High pt a prarie & Small Lake below   N 32° E 3 1/2 Ms to a pt on L.S. passed an Isld. in the Mid River   in passing up on the S.S. opsd the Isd the Sturn of the boat Struck a log which was not proceiveable   the Curt Struck her bow and turn the boat against Some drift & Snags which [were] below with great force: This was a disagreeable and Dangerous Situation, particularly as immens large trees were Drifting down and we lay imediately in their Course,—Some of our men being prepared for all Sitiuations leaped into the water Swam ashore with a roap, and fixed themselves in Such Situations, that the boat was off in a fiew minits, I can Say with Confidence that our party is not inferior to any that was ever on the waters of the Missoppie[6] we crossed to the Island and Camped, our hunters lay on the S.S. <Gibson verry nearly>   the wind from the S.W.   the river continue to rise Slowly   Current excessive rapid—The Countrey on the S.S. high bottom & delightfull land   that on the L.S. is up land or hills of from 50 to 100 foot higher than the bottom & a thinly wooded. Countrey,. Lands tolerably Good: Comminced raining at 5 oClock and continued by intervales the greater part of the night. We discovered that one of our French hands had a Conpt[7] [Complaint?]———We commsd Doctering. I hope the Success in this case, usial to an [Sentence incomplete]

[The figures below are inserted below the journal entry for June 8th:]

3
3
2
3 1/4
18
9
10
10
18
15 1/2
―――――
83 3/4
4

5. Clark recorded in the Notebook Journal (Thw., 1, 44) that this party had been out for twelve months and had "made about 900$ in pelts & furs. they were out of Provisions and out of Powder."

6. Clark's commendation of his men is not found in the Notebook Journal (Thw., 1, 44-45). The name "Missoppie," in Clark's telegraphic style, may mean both the Missouri and the Mississippi.

7. The word "complaint" was commonly used at this time to mean any chronic disorder. In this case Clark is probably referring to a venereal disease (Thw., 1, 279). The party was well equipped to treat such cases (Thw., 7, 236).

17
13
───────
117 3/4
5
17 1/2
12 1/2
14
14
12
───────
192 3/4
24
───────
216
5
───────
221

June 10ᵗʰ Sunday 1804   Some rain last night   We set out early   Saw a number of Goslings this morning, Continued on the Course of last night, thence N. 8: E 2 1/2 ms to a pt on the L.S.   passed a part of the River that the banks are falling in takeing with them large trees of Cotton woods which is the common groth in the Bottoms Subject to the flud North 1 Ml along the L. Side <N. 23° W to the Mo: of Chareton> N. 40° W. 1 ms along the L, S. opposit the two Charletons [Charitons] on the N. Side, those rivers mouth near together, the 1ˢᵗ 40 yds. wide the next 90 yds Wide and navagable Some distance in the Countrey, the land below is high & not verry good. Came to and took Mdnl altd on Sons U.L. back obsvn with the octant   made it 37° – 12′ – 00″, delayed 1 1/2 Hour. N. 70° W 1/2 of a ml along the L. Sd—S 60° W 1/2 m. on L.S. the Same Course to the Pt S.S. 1 1/2 Ms   We halted and Capt Lewis Killed a Buck   the Current is excessiveley Swift about this place   N. 80° W. 3 Ms to [*hole in MS*] a pt on S.S.   passed a Isd Called Sheeco Is-lan[d]⁸   wind from the N W   Camped in a prarie on the L.S, Capt Lewis & my self Walked out 3 Ms   found the country roling open & rich, with plenty of water, great qts of Deer   I discovered a Plumb which grows on bushes the hight of Hasle, [Hazel] those plumbs Are in great numbers, the bushes beare Verry full, about double the Sise of the wild plumb. Called the Osage Plumb. & am told they are finely flavoured

11 June Monday—as the wind blew all this day from the N, W. which was imedeately a head we could not Stur, but took the advantage of the Delay and Dried our wet articles examined provisions and Cleaned arms, my Cold is yet verry bad—the river beginning to fall   our hunters killed two Deer, G Drewrey killed 2 Bear in the Prareie to day, men verry lively Danceing & Singing &c⁹

12ᵗʰ of June, Tuesday   We Set out early, passed thro: a verry bad bend N.25° W. 3 1/2 to a pt L.S.   N. 70° W. 2 1/2 ms to a pt on S. S.   passed a Sand bar—N 60° W 3 1/ ms to a pt on S.S.   passed Plumb. C at 1/2 a ml on L.S. and halted to Dine, and 2 Caussease [Cajeux] Came Down from the Soux nation, we found in the party an old man who had been with the Soux 20 years & had great influence [*hole in MS*] with them, we provld [prevailed] on this old man   Mr [*tear*] Duriaur [Dorion] to return with us, with a view to get Some of the Soux Chiefs to go to the U.S.   purchased 300b of Voyagers Grece @ 5$ cwt a pd   made Some ex-changes & purchases of Mockersons & found it Late & concluded to in-camp. Those people inform that no Indians are on the river,¹ The Coun-trey on each Side of the river is good²

13ᵗʰ June Wednesday, we Set out early   passed a verry round bend to L.S.
<Papers for the \ passed two Creeks 1 ml apt [apart] Called Creeks
\Secretary at War/ of the round Bend, between those Creeks Stbd S.
is a butifull Prarie, in which the antient Missourie Indians had a village, at this place 300 of them were killed by the Saukees   Passed the antient Missouries villages on right,³ a fair day. . Course N 40° W 2 1/2 pt L S., S 29° W 3 ms pt S.S., This nation once the most Noumerous is now al-most extinct, about 30 of them, liveing with Otteaus on the R. Platt, the remainder all distroyed, took altd of S. U L with qdt which gave   N 28 W. 1 1/2 ms to pt S. [S written over L] S.   Passed some Charming land, I have not Seen any high hils above Charleton [Chariton River] and the hils below for Several days Cannot to [be] turmed hills but high Land, not exceeding 100 above the high water mark   N 30° W, to a pt L.S. 2 Ms passed a verry bad Sand bar, where the boat was nearly turning &

8. Coues and Thwaites give the name as *chicot,* the French word for "stump."

9. The French hands could be counted on for a song and a dance after camp was made and the men had eaten. Chittenden wrote of them that "they cheered up the weary com-pany as martial music does the tired soldier" (Chittenden, *1,* 57 n.).

1. This party was in the employ of Regis Loisel (see supra, p. 46 n.). Pierre Dorion, who had been employed by Loisel as an inter-preter at the post on the Île aux Cèdres, was persuaded to join the expedition as interpre-ter (Annie Heloise Abel, *Tabeau's Narrative,* Norman, Okla., 1939, p. 213 n.; A.S.P.: *Pub-lic Lands, 8,* 118). A lively account of old Dorion and his numerous progeny is given in Washington Irving's *Astoria, 1,* 196–97, and in Coues, *History, 1,* 21 n. Clark pur-chased from this party 300 pounds of voya-geur's grease.

2. Whitehouse wrote in his journal for this day that one of the men belonging to Cap-tain Stoddard's artillery company in St. Louis had been sent back with this party. A Cor-poral Robertson is mentioned by Clark on Dec. 26, 1803, in the Dubois Journal (supra, pp. 8, 12, 33), and on April 1, 1804, he is listed as a private (Thw., *1,* 13). In the company book of Stoddard's company, a Corporal John Robinson is listed (Jackson, p. 373 n.). This is probably the same man sent back to St. Louis. Six soldiers had been assigned to the party: they were not regarded as permanent mem-bers of the party and were to be sent back whenever the commanders deemed it expedi-ent. In the Detachment Orders of May 26, 1804, Corporal Warfington and the five pri-vates under his command are listed: Robert-son's name does not appear (Thw., *1,* 31).

3. Neither Evans nor Mackay place any "antient Missouries villages" below the mouth of the Grand River. They both locate such villages above the Grand, which are also noted by Clark (infra, p. 57). Evidently, if Clark is correct, the villages of this tribe were below as well as above the mouth of the Grand River.

4. The Grand River parallels the Chariton. Clark is confused here when he says it passes the Chariton. The Grand River was one of the common routes taken by the war parties of Iowa, Sauk, and Fox, who lived along the Des Moines and raided the Osage and the Missouri. The English traders who were on the Des Moines by 1793 caused the Spanish authorities great concern because of their influence over these Indians and the ease with which they could approach the lower Missouri.

5. This "place of Snakes" is given in the Notebook Journal (Thw., *1*, 48) as Snake Bluff. Mackay calls this *Wachanton ou Endroit du Serpent.* With slight variation in spelling, the same name appears on both the Indian Office and Perrin du Lac maps.

6. The Notebook Journal entry (Thw., *1*, 48) omits this recognition of the quality of the men under Clark's command.

7. In the Notebook Journal (Thw., *1*, 48) Clark says that they were detained two hours in an attempt to persuade one of this party to go with them to the Platte where the Pawnee villages were. Ordway says the party consisted of four Frenchmen; Floyd, of three Frenchmen and a Negro.

8. This is probably the Wakenda Creek on the M.R.C. Map, plate XI. A modification of the name Wachanton is found on the Indian Office and Perrin du Lac maps and in Mackay's Table.

9. Drewyer's story about the snake that gobbled like a turkey is expanded in the Notebook Journal. Drewyer had heard the Indians mention such a creature and one of the French hands supported him (Thw., *1*, 48).

fastening in the quick Sand and came too in the mouth of Grand R.S.S. this River is about 120 yards wide and navagable for Perogues a great distance, it heads with the River Dumoine [Des Moines] <St Peters> passing the river Carlton. [Chariton][4] a Butifull open Prarie Coms to the river below its mouth, we landed and walked to the hills which is abt 1/2 a mile. the Lower prarie over flows. the hunters killd a Bare & Dere, this is a butifull plain   the Prarie rich & extensive, Took Some Looner observations which Kept Cap L. & my self up untill half past 11 oClock.

14th June, Thursday   We Set out at 6 oClock after a thick fog   proceeded on verry well   S. 33. W 2 Ms to the lower pt of an Isld S.S. S. 60° W thro a narrow 1 ml channel to a Small prarie S. S. opposit this Isd on L.L. is a butifull high Plain. from the Isd S. 70° W. to a pt L.S. 2 1/2 ms just below a piece of High Land on the S.S. Called the place of Snakes,[5] passed the worst place I have Seen on L.S. a Sand bar makeing out 2/3 Cross the river   Sand collecting &c forming Bars and Bars washg a way, the boat Stuck and turned, She was near oversetting   We saved her by Some extrodany exertions of our party (ever ready to inconture and [all?] fatigues for the premotion of the enterprise,[6] I went out to walk on the Sand Beech, & killed a Deer & Turkey, during the time I was from the boat a Caussee [Cajeau] came too from the Pania [Pawnee] nation loaded with furs[7]   We gave them Some whiskey & Tobacco. & Settled Some desputes & parted   S. 5 E. 3 Ms to pt on S.S. passed a creek S.S. 25 yds wd called Snake Creek[8] or [*space*]   passed a bad Sand bar S.S. which we were obliged to run great Sesque [risk] of Loseing both Boat & men, Camped above, G Drewyer tels of a remarkable Snake inhabiting a Small lake 5 Ms below which gobbles like a Turkey & may be hurd Several miles, This snake is of emence [?] size.[9]

[*The following figures are written above the entry for June 10:*]

    2 1/2
    1
    2
    1
    1
    1
    2
    ____
    12

15ᵗʰ June Friday 1804, we Set out early   proceeded on about 1 ml and the Boat turned on a Sawyer which was near doeing her great damage, the river is riseing fast & the water exceedingly Swift,. S. 35° W 2 ms alg. S.S. S 50° W. 1 1/2 ml to a pt on L.S.   passed a Prarie & Creek on the L.S   S. 51° W 2 1/2 ml to a pt on S.S.   psd a Small Willow Island, S. 8w to pt L. S. 3/4 of a Ml   psd the Lower pts of 2 Isd S. 80° W. 2 Ms to the upr pt of an Isd on S.S.   passed thro a verry bad part of the river, the wost moveing Sands I ever Saw, the Current So Strong that the ours and Sales under a Stiff breese Cld not Stem it, we were oblged to use a toe rope, under a bank constantly falling, S. 5° W 2.Ms to a pt on S.S.   psd along a Isd on the left, to the lowr pt of one Still on the left   S 12° W 1 1/2 Ms to a pt S.S. opsd the antient Village of the little Osage   passd a bad Sand bar on which we Stuck for a Short time   this is said to be the worst part of the river and Camped [*one word illegible*] opsd the bend in which the antient Villages of the little Osarge & Missouries,[1] the lower or first of those villagies (L. Osages) is Situated in Butifull Plain at the foot of Some riseing land, in front of their Villges next the river is a butifull bottom Plain in which they raised their Corn &c   back of the Village the high Prarie extends back to the Osarge River, about 3 ms above & in view   the Missouries nation resided under the protection of the Osarges after their nation was riducd by the Saukees [Sauk] below, thos[e] built their Village in the Same low Prarie and lived there many years, the war was so hot & both nations becom So reduced that the Little Osage & a fiew of the Missoures Moved & built a Villge 5 ms near the Grand Osage, the rest of the Missoures went and took protection under the Otteaus [Oto] on Platt river

16ᵗʰ June Satterday   Set out at 7 oClock   Proceed on N. 68° W. 2 1/2 Ms   passed a Isd close on the S.S. at the lower point   Drewer & Willard had Camped & had with them 2 bear & 2 Deer   we took in the meat & proceeded on. Some rain this morning   West 2 Ms pass an Isd on S.S. & prarie, to a Belge [Bulge] of Snag Isd. L.S. a butifull extensive Prarie on S.S.   Hills at about 9 Ms distant. Mr Mackey has Laid down the rems [remains] of an old fort in this Prarie which I cannot find[2]   S 85° W. 1 Ml along the Isd L.S.—S 61° W alg L.S. 1 ml   S 30° W, 3, Ms to pt S.S. opsd an Isd & head of the last   S 40° W 1 Ml S.S.   Passed a verry bad place where the Sand was moving constantly, I walked on Shore obsd fine high Bottom land on S.S.   camped late this evening.

1. See supra, p. 55 n.

2. Fort Orleans, established in 1723 by Etienne de Bourgmont (Nasatir, *1*, 20). Biddle (*1*, 49–50) cites Lewis and Clark as referring, in an entry for June 13, 1804, to a French fort on an island opposite a plain between two creeks called the Round Bend Creeks. This would place the fort about 5 miles downstream from the Grand River or about 17 miles upstream from the two Chariton Rivers. Biddle has Lewis and Clark citing Du Pratz as a source of their information in placing the fort in this location. Coues (*History*, *1*, 23–24) copied Biddle almost verbatim, but added a footnote in which he berates Lewis and Clark for distorting Du Pratz. He then follows Du Pratz and Biddle in placing the fort on an island. He points out that this island is in reality above what is called Malta Bend on the Missouri Commission Map. Though Coues does not name it, this island can be identified as Wakenda or Cranberry Island (M.R.C. Map, plate XI. This would place the fort approximately 52 miles above the Chariton River.

Both the Notebook Journal (Thw., *1, 50*) and this journal report Clark looking for the fort on June 16, 1804: ". . . we came to on the S.S. in a Prarie at the place where Mr. Mackey lais down a old french fort . . ." There is no mention of Du Pratz in either the Notebook Journal or this journal. There is no indication that the fort was located on an island: in fact, they both designate very clearly that, according to Mackay, the location was on a prairie on the starboard or north side. According to the courses and distances of the Notebook Journal and this journal, the editor computes that Clark expected to find the fort approximately 45 miles upstream from the Chariton River, or on what is called the Wakenda Prairie opposite Malta Bend (M.R.C. Map, plate XI). Fort Orleans, however, is not mentioned in anything of Mackay's authorship accessible to the editor. Trudeau does not mention it in his journal. It is, however, to be found on both the Indian Office and Perrin du Lac maps. It is located on these maps on the starboard or north side: "vieux fort." The location of the fort would correspond roughly to that of the Notebook Journal and this journal. Clark's "Summary of Rivers and Creeks" (Thw., *6*, 57) places Fort Orleans 16 miles above the "Two Charliton Rivers." This would be comparable to Biddle. Every source has the fort close by an ancient village of the Missouris.

The chief source of confusion seems to arise from the fact that there were two ancient villages of the Missouris. One village was located in the approximate vicinity of the fort as it is placed in Biddle's text. Both the Notebook Journal and this journal agree on an ancient village at this point. The second village was located about where the fort is placed in the Notebook Journal and this journal, though on opposite sides of the river. This fact can explain Clark's mistake in summarizing (Thw., *6*, 57) and placing the fort in the vicinity of the lower village. Biddle undoubtedly used Clark's "Summary"—and placed greater credence in this than the journals. He also apparently was following Du Pratz, along with the Notebook Journal, and interjected Du Pratz's name in the text to give added reason for his changing the location of the fort and the day the expedition passed it. Coues realized that on June 15 the expedition actually passed the location given by Mackay, and he realized that the fort was misplaced in the Biddle version. However, he assumed the captains were at fault, never questioning the veracity of Biddle's text. In so doing, he placed the fort upon an island, though this journal clearly states that it was supposed to be on a prairie on the starboard or north side of the river. In his map (ca. 1728) Dumont de Montigny places the fort correctly on the north (starboard) side of the Missouri and above Malta Bend (Nasatir, *1*, plate opp. 14).

The phrasing of this sentence, "Mr Mackey has Laid down the rems [remains] of an old fort . . . ," strongly suggests that Clark was looking at his map, which he usually referred to as the Evans Map. In this case he appears to recognize that Mackay had actually drawn it. See the discussion on this point, supra, pp. 16–17 n. The Notebook Journal uses the same verb, "lais down."

58

June 17 [7 written over 8]. 1804   Rope walk Camp[3]
The Current of the River at this place is a Stick will float 48 poles 6 feet
in the rapidest part in 23 Seconds, further out is 34, Still further 65 – 74 –
78 – 82 are the Trials we have made.

June 17th Sunday 1804   Cloudy   Wind, S. E.   Set out early S. 65° W 1
Ml   Came too to Make ores, and a Cord for a Toe Rope[4]   all this day
imployed in getting out ores, & makeing for the use of the Boat [a tow
rope] out of a large Cable rope which we have, G Drewyer Came up
[with] a Bear & 2 Deer, also a fine horse which he found in the woods,
Supposed to have been left by Some war party from the osages, The
Ticks are numerous and large and have been trousom [troublesome] all
the way and the Musquetors are begining to be verry troublesome, My
Cold Continues verry bad   the French higherlens [hirelings] Complain
for the want of Provisions, Saying they are accustomed to eat 5 & 6 times
a Day, they are roughly rebuked for their presumption,[5] the Country
about abounds in Bear Deer & Elk and [on] the S.S. the lands are well
timbered and rich for 2 Ms to a butifull Prarie which risies into hills abt
8 or 9 Ms back—on the L.S a, Prarie coms on the bank which is high and
contines back   rich & well watered as far & Light [?]

June 18th Monday   Some raind last night, Sent out 6 Hunters <last>
to day across the R: they Killed 5 Deer & Cotte [Caught] a Bear verry fat
we continue to repare our ropes & make oars all day, heavy rain all the
fore pt of the day, the party Drying meat & greesing themselves,[3] Several
men with the Disentary, and two thirds of them with ulsers or Boils,
Some with 8 or 10 of those Tumers[7]   Mesquetors verry bad   we finish
our Cords & oars this evening   Men in Spirits

$$
\begin{array}{r}
3 \\
1\ 1/2 \\
1\ 1/2 \\
4 - \\
3 - \\
\hline
13
\end{array}
$$

June 19th Tuesday   raind last night   arranged everry thing and Set out
8 oCk   wind in favor from the S.E.   Course N. 87° W 3 Ms to up pt of
a Is on S.S. [blot] S. 80° W. 1 1/2 pt L. Sd   psd up pt Isd on S. S.—hard
water. S. 70° W 1 1/2 Ml along the L.S., high rich bottom   S. 58° W 4
1/2 pt S.S.   Passed an Isd Close on the L.S. & 3 Sand bars   S. 68 W. 3
Ms pt S.S.   pass Tabbo Creek 15 yds wide on L S. opsd a Small Isd[8]   we
passed thro between 2 Isds by Clearing away Drift wood, passed the
Lower pt of the Isd of Pant[h]ers S.S. formed by a narrow Channel   S.
83° W. 4 [4 written over 3] ms   Plenty of Goose & Rasp buries on the
banks, passed a verry bad point of rocks of 1/2 a mile   oblige to Draw
the Boat up by a rope, Camped opposit a Lake at 2 ms distant on the L.S.
this lake is large and is a place of great resort for Deer and fowls of
everry kind   the bottom low & covered with rushes

June 20th Wednesday 1804   Set out after a heavy Shour of rain and proc-
ceeded on the Same Course of yesterday S. 83° W 3 Ms   passed Some
Sand Isds in the bend to the L.S. bad water   a large Creek on the S.S.
called Tiger Creek   a willow and a low Isd above S.S., S 42° W. 1 m alg
L.S.   wind S.W. hard, Some high land on L.S.   S 46° W 2 Ms to P: L.S.
psd the head of the Isd   S. 51° W, 1 1/2 ml pt L.S. opsd an Isd and
large Butifull Prarie called Sauke Prarie,[9] pass hard water, Saw Pilicans

3. The alteration of the date from June 18
to 17 is not in Clark's hand but in that of
Biddle, who dated each document (see Introduction, p. xxi). Thus, we have two entries
dated the 17th: the first, dated the 18th in
Clark's hand and then changed by Biddle to
the 17th; the second, dated in Clark's hand
the 17th. In the Notebook Journal (Thw., *1*,
51), Clark does not mention that he named
this camp site Ropewalk Camp, where a new
rope was made out of materials that Captain Lewis brought from Pittsburgh. Whitehouse calls the camp Rope Walk Camp
(Thw., *7, 36*).

4. Long oars called sweeps were used when
sails could not move the boat upstream. If the
boat could not be rowed, poles were used. A
line of men was formed on both sides of the
boat, facing the stern. The first man in each
line set his pole into the bed of the river and
walked aft. He was followed by the second
and so on. As each man reached the stern, he
withdrew his pole, turned and walked forward to take his turn again in the line. If the
current was still too strong to move the boat,
then towing (cordeling) was used.

5. This difficulty with the *engagés* is not
mentioned in the Notebook Journal (Thw., *1*,
51).

6. Buffalo tallow, plastered on the exposed
parts of the body, was some protection against
insects. On June 12, Clark had purchased
from Loisel's patron three hundred pounds
of such grease, called voyageur's grease (supra, p. 55 and infra. p. 62). "Muscatoe Cur-
tains" were included in the list of supplies
made out by Captain Lewis for the expedition (Thw., *7, 234*). Ordway notes that such
nets or biers were issued "to sleep in" (*Ordway*, p. 87).

7. From the middle of June through July
and August, Clark refers again and again to
what he calls, "ulsers, Boils and Tumers."
Perhaps these boils were due to mosquito
bites that became infected. It is unlikely that
the diet of venison and parched corn would
result in these eruptions, for the men were
used to such fare. The good spirits of the men
apparently rose above such minor difficulties.

8. There is some confusion here. In the
Notebook Journal (Thw., *1, 53*), Clark states
that the party passed the mouths of both
Tabbo Creek and Tiger River on June 19.
The Journals of Gass and Ordway and these
notes place the date as June 20. If these notes
were used in preparation of the Notebook
Journal, the question arises as to why the
mistake was made. The M.R.C. Map, plate
XII, gives the name Tabo Creek. Coues (*History*, *1*, 27–28 n.) suggests that the name
should be Tabeau, "a personal name of a
Canadian who was hereabouts." This suggestion would probably refer to Pierre-An-
toine Tabeau, the associate of Clamorgan
and Loisel and author of the narrative of
Loisel's expedition to the Upper Missouri.

However, Miss Abel, editor of the Loisel narrative, refers to a Pedro Tabo at Florissant and a Pedro Tibo at St. Charles (Abel, p. 42 n.). Either of these two (assuming there were two and not variant spellings of the same name) may have given his name to this stream.

9. Called *Prairie des Sakias* on the Indian Office Map.

1. Clark's theory that the drinking of Missouri River water caused the men to perspire more than usual is not mentioned in the Notebook Journal (Thw., *1*, 53). The humidity and the excessive heat of the Lower Missouri Valley in June, which the men had to endure as they fought their way against the current of the river, was reason enough. There was plenty of mud in the river water; the next day Clark records a half wine glass of mud to a pint of water.

2. The "very high spirits" of the men resulted in a good deal of horseplay. In the Notebook Journal, Clark does not mention that the sand-throwing was in fun but says that York came near "loseing an eye" (Thw., *1*, 53).

3. The names of these two streams have given editors much difficulty. On the Perrin du Lac Map, they are called *de l'Eau Bleue;* The Indian Office Map has *L Eau Bleu;* the Notebook Journal, *Eue-bert;* Floyd, *Duebau;* Ordway, *Eue bow;* Gass, *Du Beau* and *Du Bois.* On Clark's map this stream is called *Bau Meaux.* In this journal there is the only statement that the streams were "called Eue-beux after a french man" whose name was presumedly Herbert or Hubert. Among the *mémoires* sent to Paris between 1716–19 by the French authorities in Louisiana was one by a Hubert, giving information as to the Missouri River as far north as the Arikara (Nasatir, *1*, 12). Geronimo, or Guillaume, Hébert was a signer of two petitions sent to the Spanish authorities in 1801 (ibid., *2*, 645, 651).

on a Sand bar   S. 70° W along L.S.   passd Isd 3/4 Ml   Swift water, one remarkable circumstance in the water of this River is a free use of it will create prespreation, the Swet run off our men in a stream when th[ey] row hard,[1] York verry near loseing his Eyes by one of the men throwing Sand at him in fun & recved into his eyes[2]—passed Some bad water. S. 25° W 1 1/2 Ml pt on the S. side, we came to at 1/2 a Ml on the lower point of a Willow Isd S.S. in View of a Sand bar on both sides of the Isd <of> over which the water riffleed and rowed like a great fall, We took Some Luner observations of the Moon & Stars   Set up untill one oClock   the Musquetors verry troublesome   our flank Guard or Hunters have not been with us for two nights, We saw them to day at the Mouth of the Tiger R, the lands on the L.S. is verry fine & well timbered near the river and appears equally good on the other side but not so high

21st June Thursday 1804   River raised 3 Inches last night after our bow man Peter Crusat a half Mahar [Omaha] Indian examined round this Small Isd for the best water, we Set out determined to assd [ascend] on the North Side, and Sometimes rowing Poleing & Drawing up with a Strong Rope we assended without wheeling or receiving any damage more than breakeing one of my S. [Starboard?] Windows, and looseing Some oars which were swong under the Windows

The Course of last night S. 25 W 1 Ml   psd the lower point of a large Island on the L.S. behind which is two Creeks   this Isd & Creeks are Called Eue-beux after a french man,[3] The water we Drink, or the Common water of the Missourie at this time, contains half a Comon Wine Glass of ooze or mud to every pint—S. 77° W, 2 1/2 Mls alg: S.S.   psd the hd of the Isd & Small one in midl   N. 30° East 1 1/2 Ms   psd a Counter Current on the L.S.   Pass Lower pt of a Isd Close on the L.S. North alg L.S. 1 ml   Some wind from the S.S.E. at 3 oClock   N. 18° W. 1/2 Ml L.S.   N. 84° W 1/2 Ml   S. 80° W 3/4 Ml along L.S.   passed Several Small willow Isd on the L.S. High Land on the <L> S.S   S. 35° W 3/4 Ml alg L.S, pass 2 Isd Small on the right. S. 14° W 2 Ms to pt S.S. Came to at the last mentioned point   Two me[n] Sent out to hunt this after noon   Came in with a Deer, at Sun Set   The ellement had every appearance of wind, The hunters informed me that the high Countery on the S.S. is of a good quallity, and well timbd   The High lands on the L. Side is equally good   The bottom land on this river is alike 1st low and covd with Cotton wood & willows Subject to over flow   the 2nd is higher groth Cotton Walnut ash Melberry Linn [Linden] & Sycomore

1

2 1/2

1

1

———

6

22ⁿᵈ June Friday   after a violent gust of wind accompanied with rain from the West, which commenced at Day brake, and lasted about one hour, we Set out under a gentle Breeze from the NW. and proceeded on S. 14° W. 2 1/2 Ms to pt on L.S.   Ord[way] Killed a goose, S 25° W 3 Ms to a pt on S.S.   psd snags and Swift water on the S.S.—S. 66° W: 1/2 a ml on S pt   N 60 W 4 1/2 ml to pt L.S.   passed a large Isd on the S.S.— (Farenthiers [Fahrenheit] Thermomete[r] at 3 oClock P,M, 87ᵈ which is 11ᵈ above Summer heat) and one [island] on the L.S. opposit against which there is a handsom Prarie of high Bottom & up Land, Capt Lewis went out in this Prarie & walked Several miles, Come to opposit the mouth of a large Creek on the S. S. Called River of the Fire Prarie[4] at the mouth of this creek the party on Shore Shields & Collins was camped waiting for our arrival & inform that they Passd thro: Some fine Lands, and well watered   G D. [Drouillard] Killed a fine Bear to day

23ʳᵈ June Satturday   Some wind this morning from the NW.   Set out at 7 oC   proceeded on N. 70ᵈ W 2 Ms to an Isd Close on the S.S.   I went on Shore & walked up thro: a rich bottom for about Six miles, Killed a Deer & much fatigued   N. 75 E. to a point in a bend L.S. 1 1/2 the river fell 8 Inches last night.

Sunday June 24ᵗʰ   set out at 1/2 after six continuing the course on the Lard side N. 80. E 1/4 of a mile to point Lard. N. 55 1/4 of a mile to point Lard Due west to a point Stard 3 miles good water
(I joined the Boat theis morning with a fat Bear & two Deer, last evining I struck the river about 6 miles (by land) abov the Boat, and finding it too late to get to the Boat, and the wind blowing So hard Down the river that She could not assend, I concluded to Camp, altho I had nothing but my hunting Dress, & the Musquitors Ticks & Knats verry troublesom, I concl[ude]d to hunt on a Willow Isd Situated close under the Shore, in Crossing from an Island, I got mired, and was obliged to Crawl out, a disegreeable Situation <for> & a Deverting one of any one who Could have Seen me after I got out, all Covered with mud. I went to my Camp & [s]craped off the Mud and washed my Clothes, and fired off my gun which was answered by George Drewyer who was in persute of me & came up at Dark   we feasted of meet & water the latter we made great use of being much fatigued & thirsty—The meet which hung up near the water <attracted> [*one word illegible*] a large Snake made Several attempts to get to it and was so Detirmined that I Killed him in his attempt, the Snake appeared to make to that part of the meet which Contained the milk of a Doe,[5] On this part of the River I observe great quantites of Bear Sign, they are after Mulbiries which are in great quantities)   Water [*sic*] N 85ᵈ W. 4 1/2 Ms to a pt on L Side, Came to above the mouth of a Creek on the L.S. abt 20 yds Wide Called Hay Cabbin Creek   Latd of this place is 38° – 37' – 5″ North—Capt Lewis took Sergt Floyd and walked on Shore, George Drewyer Killed 2 Deer   R Fields Killed a Deer Dureing the time we wer Jurking the meet I brought in,[6] West 1/2 ml along the L.S.
   S 21° W. 3 ms to a pt on the S.S.   pass a Creek on the S.S. just above Some rocks Some distance from Shore   1 of Thise Creek is Called Sharriton—Cartie,[7] a Prarie on the L.S. near the river. Capt Lewis Killed a Deer, & Collins 3. <Drewr 2 to day>   emence number of Deer on both Sides of the river, We pass between two Sand bars at head of which we had to raise the boat 8 Inches to get her over, Camped at the Lower point of a Isd on the L S.   the Party in high Spirits.

4. Fire Prairie is marked on the Indian Office Map, in Mackay's Table of Distances, and in Truteau's *Journal* (*A.H.R. 19, 303*). On Perrin du Lac's Map, the stream that came in opposite the prairie is called the *R. du Feu*. On Clark's Map the river is Fire Prairie River.

5. Clark's account of this adventure in this journal is much more detailed than his reference to it in the Notebook Journal (Thw., *1*, 56–57).

6. Because of the extremely hot weather, it was necessary to jerk the meat as soon as it was brought to camp. The word *jerk* is from the South American word *charqui*, probably of Indian origin, taken over by the Spaniards and brought north with them to the Indians of the plains.

7. Coues and Thwaites give this as *Charretins écarté*, a creek that is separated (*écarté*) just above its mouth. *Ecarté* may also be translated as "lonely, remote." The party had passed the two Charitons ninety miles downstream. Since this creek is also named Sharriton (Chariton?), the adjective *écarté* may well mean "distant" or "remote."

8. The Notebook Journal calls this Bennet's Creek (Thw., *1*, 58). Nearly a month later, July 14, and nearly 200 miles upstream, Clark notes: "an old fort where Mr. Bennet of St. Louis winttered." (infra, p. 78, and Thw., *1*, 78). Clark's "Labeenie" and "Mr. Bennet" are probably one and the same and refer to François N. Benoit, the son-in-law of Charles Sanguinet. Both of these men, along with other important fur traders in St. Louis, attempted to break the monopoly of the Chouteaus and others over the Missouri River trade. In a petition to Salcedo, Governor at New Orleans, dated June 4, 1802, these men asked that this monopoly be broken up and that the former general liberty of trade be restored (supra, p. 37 n. Nasatir, *2*, 677–80).

9. On the Indian Office Map which Clark had with him, this stream is called the *L Eau Bleu* or the Blue Water River. It is now called the Blue River and flows through the eastern section of Kansas City. Perrin du Lac's Map of 1802 calls it the *R. de l'Eau Bleue* and gives the same name to the longer river which flows into the Kansas River in the east-central section of the present state of Kansas. The M.R.C. Map, 1892–95, plate XIV. gives the name Big Blue River to the smaller stream. Thwaites and Coues appear to have consulted these maps, and to have identified it as the Big Blue River without pointing out that this stream should not be confused with the Kansas tributary.

1. Clark's "Parrot-quetes" is the Carolina parakeet, the only member of the parrot family whose range extended this far north. Its "emence" numbers did not save it from the same fate as the passenger pigeon—total extinction.

2. This apparently is a rough draft of a bill issued to Loisel's patron, whom the party met on June 12 (supra, p. 55 and n.), for 300 pounds of voyageur's grease at $5 per cwt. This amount must have been included in the $81.16 paid by the government to the estate of Regis Loisel in April 1805 ("Financial Records of the Expenses of the Lewis and Clark Expedition," in Jackson, pp. 424, 430 n.).

Monday June 25th a heavy fog Detain us about an hour Set out passed the Isd on a course from the last point S 49d: W. 3 Ms to a point on the S.S. S 55° W 1/2 Ml S.S. a Coal—Bank on the opposit or L.S. Side, this bank appears to Contain great quantity of excellente Coal, the wind from N.W a Small Creek Called Coal or (Charboned) [Charbon] N 50° W to the pt, L.S. 3 1/2 miles Hard water & logs, Bank falling in, Passed a Small Creek L.S. Called Labeenie[8] a Prarie is Situated on the S.S. a Short Distance from the river, which contains great quantities of Wild apples of the Size of the Common apple, the French say is well flavered when ripe, which is the time the leaves begin to fall N 70° W 1/2 Ml along the right Side of a Willow Isd Situated on the L. Side S. 80° W 1/2 Ml L.S. S 55° W. 1/2 Ml to Pt of Smal Isd L.S. S 15° W 1/2 Ml L.S.–S. 2° E 2 Ml pt on Lbd S. / here I will only remark that the Deer in the Morning & evening are feeding in great numbers on the banks of the River, they feed on young willow, and amuse themselves running on the open beeches or points We have hard water this afternoon round the heads of Small Islds on the L. Side below a Small High Prarie S. 48° W. 2 Ms pt S.S. passd a small Isd on which we Camped The party on Shore did not join us to day, or have we Seen or her [heard] of them river falling fast about 8 Inches in 24 hours, the Hills on the L.S. this evening higher than usial about 160 or 180 feet. the lands appear of a Simalier to those passed

Tuesday June 26th We Set out early wind from the S.W. on the Course of last night S 62° W 1/2 Ml on S.S. an Island on the L: Side S 80° W 1/2 Ml S.S, passed the mouth of a Small river called Blue Water river (in french R. La Bleúe)[9] this River heads with the Mine river in a divideing ridge between the Kancis & Osage Rivers N 87° W, 1 Ml S.S. N 85° W 3 Ms to point on the L. Side Mdn altd 38 – 32′ – 15″ N high land on L.S. abt 90 foot. high jutting over the riv[er] S 80 W. 1/2 Ml L.S. S. 37° W 2 1/2 Ms to pt S. S. psd a large Dangerous Counter Current on the S.S. above Some rocks a Small willow Isd in the bend to the L.S. Killed a large rattle Snake emence number of Parrot-quetes[1] S 58° W 1 Ml alg S.S. our Party on shor cam in Killed 7 Deer, & 3 from the boat N 54 W. 1/2 Ml to a pt L.S. at mouth of the Kansas River Camped a pt opposit the Kansas river

[*The following is in Lewis' hand. The entry for June 25 and 26 is written over it.*]

Grand River June 12th 1804

Sir,

I have purchased from Mr Louiselle's Pattroon three hundred pounds of voyager's grease for which I am to pay by [*End of passage in Lewis' hand*][2]

at the Mouth of the River Kansas

June 26: 27″ 28 & 29ᵗʰ——

This river is 366 Miles above the mouth of Missourie   it is in Lattitude 38° 31′ 13″ North   it is 230 yds wide at its mouth & wider above from the point up the Missourie for about 3 ms N. 21° W, Down the Middle of the Missourie is S. 32° E, up the upper bank of the Kansais, is S. 54° E the river turns to the East above a pt of high land, well Situated for a fort & in view of the Missourie one mile up & on the upper Side,[3] the width of the Missourie at this place is about 500 yds   Missourie Water weighs 78. The Kansais weghs 72   river Muss raised in the time at the Kanseis 2 foot and began to fall.

The wood land on each Side of the Mouth of this river is extensive and of a good quallity as far as our hunters was back, but badly watered with Springs, only two being Seen by them

Some punishment of two men Hall & Collins for takeing whiskey out of the Barrel last night   agreeable to the sentences of a Court Mtl of the party. who we have always found verry ready to punish Such Crimes[4]— Many Deer Killed to day

[*The entry for June 26, 27, 28, & 29 is superinscribed on the following memorandum, which appears to be a rough draft of an order for the regulation of the camp set up at this time at the mouth of the Kansas River:*]
Allarm post or order of Battle
arms to be Situated & the Duty &c
Messes of men under a Serjiant who is to
detail for every day one man of his squad to Cook &c
who shall have the management of the provisions
dureing that day or issue, each Days rations must
be divided &c &c
Order of encampment, Tents, fires & Duty
Signals &c &c
S 81 W to pt
pased an [*one word illegible*] S.S. 5 Ms

3. Since the party was to camp here for several days, the men were put to work erecting a breastwork of timber and brush six feet high (Thw., *1*, 59; *Ordway*, p. 89). Whitehouse in his journal writes that this temporary breastwork was built "Least the Savages would Attempt Comeing in the Night . . . I was Informd by one of our Men that traded Up the River that 300 Warriers lives in One Village Up the River About 50 leagues" (Thw., 7, 39).

4. Collins was charged "with getting drunk on his post this Morning out of whiskey put under his charge as Sentinal, and for Suffering Hugh Hall to draw whiskey out of the Said Barrel intended for the party." Hall was charged with the taking of whiskey from the barrel "stored on the Bank." Both were found guilty. Collins received one hundred lashes and Hall fifty (Orderly Book, Kansas River, June 29, 1804, Thw., *1*, 61–62). This punishment was probably not as severe as the account indicates. Certainly, a hundred lashes on the bare back administered by a cat-o'-nine-tails would have impaired a man's usefulness for days. From the comment that there was a readiness to punish such crimes, it might be inferred that the men lined up armed with ramrods from their guns or switches, and the culprit was made to run the gauntlet. However, it is more likely that the stealing of whiskey warranted the most severe punishment in the eyes of the men. The supply was limited, and they looked forward to a dram after the day's struggle with the Missouri.

5. Beginning with this entry, Clark changed his method of recording the day's course and distance. From the beginning of this journal on May 14, he had often recorded them within the descriptive material of each entry. From this point on, the course and distance are at the beginning or the end of the day's entry, with numerals in the appropriate places of the text to identify the point where the course and distance were taken. In the documents themselves there is evidence that he left space below the intended day's entry for this record. In some cases, the course and distance are crowded in because he did not leave enough room. It has been suggested by Robert Metzdorf that Clark recorded these on a slate while the keelboat was moving upstream and then later transferred them to this journal. This is quite possible and would account for the crowding; a set of slates was among the supplies of the party (Thw., 7, 232, 240).

From an examination of the originals of the Notebook Journals it is clear that Clark copied the course and distances from this journal into the Notebook Journals, for in them they are neatly listed at the beginning or end of each day's entry without any overwriting, crossing out, or interlineations.

6. On the Indian Office Map, this stream is marked *petite rive platte*. Beside it Clark wrote, "Little Shole River."

7. This comment on the provisions is not given in the Notebook Journal (Thw., *1*, 62).

8. Slaky: muddy, miry.

9. This stream is not named on Clark's Map. The M.R.C. Map, plate XV. gives several small unnamed streams, any one of which might be Biscuit Creek.

29ᵗʰ of June 1804,[5] Set out from the Kansas river 1/2 past 4 oClock, proceeded on   passed a ④ small run on the L.S. at 1/2 mile   a (1) Island on the S.S. at 1 1/2 Ml   Hills above the upr pt of Isd L.S.   a large Sand bar in the middle. Passed a verry bad place of water, the Sturn of the Boat Struck a moveing Sand & turned within 6 Inches of a large Sawyer, if the Boat had Struck the Sawyer, her Bow must have been Knocked off & in Course She must hav Sunk in the Deep water below   Came to & camped on the S.S. late in the eveninge.

Course & Distance June 29: referunces
N 21d   W. 3 1/2 Ms to a pt on L.S: passed a Pt on L.S. and the Lower Pt
            of an Isd L.S.
(1) N 18° W. 3/4   on L S. opsd head of Isd
S. 79° W 3   ms to a pt on S.S.
            ——————
            7 1/4

30ᵗʰ June, Set out verry early this morng   Saw a verry large wolf [*space*] on the Sand bar this morning walking near a gange of Turkeys (1) at 10 miles above the Kansis   passed the mouth of a Small river call the (Petete Plate) or the little Shole river,[6] this river is about 70 [70 written over 80] yds Wide and has Several rapids & falls, well calculatd for mills, the land on this river is Said to be Roaling, Killed 2 Deer Bucks swinging [swimming] the river   the wind from the S.W.   here we opened the Bag of Bread given us by [*space*] which we found verry good, our Bacon which was given us by [*space*] we examined and found Sound and good   some of that purchased in the Illinois Spoiled, <I found> a relish of this old bacon this morning was verry agreeable,[7] Deer to be Seen in every direction and their tracks are as plenty as Hogs about a farm, our hunts Killed 9 Deer to day   the land below the last river is good, that above between the two rivers which is near together is slaik'y[8] and bad on the N. Side, the other Side is good land, Landed on the L.S. below an Isd called Demond [Diamond] Island

Course Distance & refurrencees June 30ᵗʰ
N. 20ᵈ W 2 Ms to pt L.S.   Boat wheeled
N. 30ᵈ W 1/2 Ml on L.S.—High land on the S.S.
S. 64° W. 2 1/2 Ms to pt on S.S.   passed Litte River Platt. ①
West. [*space*] 1 Ml on S.S.   a small Creek on L.S.
N. 60° W 4 Ml to a pt on the L.S.
            ——————
            10

July 1ᵗʰ 1804, last night one of the Sentenals Changed [Challenged] either a man or Beast, which run off, all prepared for action, Set out early   passed the Demond Isd   pass a Small Creek on the L.S.   as this Creek is without name we Call it BisCuit Creek[9]   Brackfast on the upper point of a Sand beech, The river still falling a little   a verry warm Day. I took some Medison last night which has worked me very much   party all in helth except Boils—

[*The following is from Doc. 24, inserted here in its proper place:*]

passed a Sand bar in the river above the Isd covered for a ml with Drift Wood, Came to   Capt Lewis took Medn altitude & we delayed three hours, the day being excessively hot, Turkeys are plenty on the Shore, <Some of the men> G. Drewyer inform that he [he written over they] Saw Pue Canns [pecan] Trees on S.S. yesterday   great quantities of raspburies an Grapes, ② pass a Creek on the L.S. called Remore (Tree

Frog) Creek,[1] an Isd above in the Mid: and <a Pond on> 2 Willow Isds on the S.S. all of the Same name; The two Willow Isds has been made within 3 years & the Main Chanl runs now on the L S. of the large Island where there was no runing wate[r] at low water from this Island   the range of Hills up the river to the N,W, pass a run on the L.S. a Butifull extensive Prarie, Two Islands just above Called (Isles des Parques) or Field Islands, those Islands are, one of our French hands tels me that the French intended to Settle here once & brought their Cows and put them on those Islands, Mr Mackey Says the first village of the Kanseis was a little above this Island & made use of as fields,[2] no trace of any thing of that Kind remains to be Seen on the Isds   fine Land on the L Side, Hills near the river all day, Camped on the lower pot of 1st Isd

[one word illegible] July 1
N. 62°: W. 1 1/2 Ml to S.S. Side of an Island (Demond I)
N. 40° W. 1/4 Ml on S.S. of the Isd 1 [1 written over 2] Sand Isd on Left
N. 28° W. 3/4 Ml to pt on L.S.   passed the upper point of Isd
N. 45. W. 3 1/2 Mils to a pt on S.S.   cours Cond to tree in ops prary on
    the Ld S.

[End of Doc. 24]

Course Distance and refurrences (by Ltte) July 1.
——— 6 Mls on the course's of this morning—N. 32ᵈ W. 1 1/2 Ms to a pt
on the L. Side. N 14ᵈ W. to the right side of an Isd
N 58 W. 2 1/2 Ms to pt L S.   passed a Creek on L. S. ② passed the
    head of the Isd
N. 42 W. 1 [1 written over 2] 1/2 Ms to a pt on S.S.
N. 72 [?] / W 7 [blot] Ml to North Side of a Island ③ Creek L.S.
N. 22 E   13   and a Butifull extensive Prarie [?]
                 ————
         North
           16   13   High and dry
                     10
                      7
                    ————
                     30

1. The French word *rémora* means a sucking fish. The English word "remora" is the name given to a salt-water fish. Therefore, it is safe to assume that the name is here applied to the common sucker of inland waters. The editor has no explanation for Clark's translation of this French word as "tree frog." The French *grenouille*, frog, is too different from *rémora* for even Clark to misspell it. Coues identifies this as Nine Mile Creek (*History, 1,* 36).

2. This entry suggests that Clark had with him something more than the Mackay Map (supra, p. 58 n.). The phrase "Mr. Mackey says" is substantially repeated in the entry for September 14, 1804, when Clark wrote that he was looking for an old volcano, "Said to be in this neighbourhood by McKey" (infra, p. 138). From these two passages it seems clear that Clark had both Mackay's Table of Distances and his journal of his expedition up the Missouri in 1795–96. In a letter to Jefferson from Cahokia, Dec. 28, 1803, Lewis wrote, "I have also obtained Ivins's [Evans'] and Mac Kay's journal up the Missouri, it is in French & is at present in the hands of Mr. Hay who has promised to translate it for me" (Jackson, p. 155 n.).

3. Clark's use of nautical terms, starboard side (S.S.) and larboard side (L.S.) has caused some confusion among editors of the journals of the expedition. Ordway says this creek was on the south and the editor of his journal, Dr. Quaife, on checking with the Notebook Journal, concluded that Clark's entry "S.S." meant the south side instead of the starboard side (*Ordway*, 91 n.; Thw., *1*, 64).

4. Whitehouse in his journal recorded that the "Boat Swong the [men] Exerted them selves mighty well" (Thw., *7*, 39).

5. Fort Cavagnolle. After the destruction or abandonment of Fort Orleans, about 1743, this post was set up "to protect the Trade of this [Kansas] nation in the valley of the Kansas." (*Floyd*, in Thw., *7*, 15). In 1758, Kerlérec, then Governor of Louisiana, reported that the fort consisted "of a circle of piles which encloses some bad cabins and huts. The officer there commands seven to eight garrisoned soldiers and some traders" (Report of Kerlérec, Governor of Louisiana, to Vaudreuil, Governor of Canada, Dec. 12, 1758, quoted in Nasatir, *1*, 52).

July the 2ⁿᵈ 1804   Set out verry early this morning   passd on the Left of the Isles des parques   High butifull Situation, on the L S. the land indifferent lands   a Creek coms in on the S.S. Called parques, all at once the river became Crowded with drift that it was dangerous to cross   this I Suppose was from the caveing in of the banks at [t]he head of some Island above, ③ passed a Creek on the L.S. called Turquie or Turkey Creek[3]   passed a verry bad Sand bar on the L, S.   the 20 oars & Poals could with much dificuilty Stem the Current,[4] passed a large Island on the S.S. Called by the Inds Wau-car-ba War-con-da or the Bear Medison Island, at 12 oClock came to on the Island and put in a mast, detained four hours, exceedingly hot, wind in. forepart of the day from the S.E. George Drewyer informs that the Lands he pass through yesterday & to day on the S.S. was generally Verry fine   he Saw two Springs of fresh water near the Island, Deer sign has become so Common it is hardly necessary to mention them, we Camped after dark on the S.S. opposit the 1ˢᵗ old Village of the Kanzas which was Situated in a Valley between two points of high land, on the river back of their village commenced an extensive Prarie <the French> a large Island in front which appears to have made on that Side and thrown the Current of the river against the place the Village formerly Stood, and washes away the bank in that part. The french formerly had a Fort at this place, to protect the trade of this nation, the Situation appears to be a verry ellegable one for a Town,[5] the valley rich & extensive, with a Small Brook Meanding [meandering] through it and one part of the bank affording yet a good Landing for Boats   The High Lands above the Fere [Fire ?] river on each Side of the Missourey appear to approach each other much nearer than below that plain, being from 3 to 6 miles between them, to the Kansas, above that place from 3 to 5 mls apart and higher Some places being 160 or 180 feet   the river not So wide   We made a Mast of Cotton wood, <yesterday> to day in the Course of the evening & night it turned of a butifull red colour

N. 22° E w 1 1/4 Ms to a pt on the L S. in a bend ①

N. 10° W 2 1/4 Ms to a pt of a little Isd on the S.S.   passed the head of ② Isd ② a Creek L.S

N. 34° E 1 1/2 to a pt on L.S.   psd   passed Turkey Creek L. S. ③

N. 10° W. 1/2 Ml on the L.S.   high land on the S.S.

N. 48 W. 1 1/4 ml on Lbd S. <opsd Lower pt> of an Isd ④ on S.S.

S 50 W.—[space] To the old village of the Kansas on L.S.   pass a Bulge of Isd

N. [?] 78 W 1/2 of a Ml to a Pt on S.S.   psd 2 runs on S.S.

S. 81° W 2 1/4 Mls to a pt on the S.S.   passed the head of the Island near opsd pt

N. 82° W 2 Mls to a pt on the S.S.   passed verry Swift water, & Camped.

<u>10 1/4</u>

N. 53. W. 1 Ml alg. S.S.

N 50 W 1/4 Ml alg. S.S.

N. 18 E 1 Ml to pt on L. [?] S opsd an Isd   N. 40° E to Low pt of Island 1 1/4 Ml

July 3ʳᵈ 1804   Set out verry early this Morning and proceeded on under a gentle Breeze from the South   passed two Islands one a Small Willow Island on the L.S. ①   The other a large Island Called Cow I. (Isle Vache), this Island is large, opposit to the head on the S.S. is a ② large Pond, a Bad Sand bar on the S.S.   we attemptd without Success, & was oblige to Cross back,   I saw a White horse on the L.S. in view of the upper point of the Island, ③   passed a large Sand bar at the S. point, w[e] halted to day about a mile above the Island and found a horse, which had been lost by the Indians, verry fat and jentle, Sent him on to join the others which was ahead on the L S at this place, the french had a tradeing house, for to trade with the Kanzes on a high bottom on the L.S. near the hills which is Prarie   proceeded on round a large Sand bar on the L.S. & Camped (opposit a large Sand bar in the middle of the river). on the L.S. a Butifull Small Stream passes back of the trading house, before mentioned

[*The entry for July 3, 1804, is written over the following figures:*]

```
     17.11
       20    [?]
  6 | 351
       58          [one figure illegible]
     17.16—3
       20
  6 | 356
     59·33
       4
     59·37
```

July 4th Wednesday 1804, Set out early   passed the mouth of a Beyeau [bayou] leading from a Lake on the S.S.[6] this Lake is large and was once the bend of the River, it reaches Parrelel for Several miles, Came to on the L.S. to Dine & rest a Short time, a Snake bit Jo: Fields on the Side of his foot which swelled much   apply Barks to the wound, pass a Creek on the L.S. about 15 yards wide cuming out of an extensive Prarie   as this Creek has no name, and this day is the 4th of July, we name this Independance us. [U.S.] Creek[7] above this Creek the wood land is about 200 yards, back of those wood is an extensive Prarie open and high, which may be Seen six or seven [miles ?] below—Saw great Nos of Goslins to day nearly grown, the last Mentioned prarie I call Jo Fields Snake Prarie, Capt Lewis walked on Shore & Saw a large moun[d]. & 3 roads leading [to it ?]   We Camped in this plain   one of the most butifull Plains I ever Saw, open & butifully diversified with hills & vallies all presenting themselves to the river[8] covered with grass and a few scattering   a handsom creek meandering thro trees at this place the Kansan Inds formerly lived, and had a verry large Town   I passed a creek ④ observed Springs braking out of the bank, a good Situation for a fort on a hill at the upper part[9]

July 3d 1804[1]
N 53° W. 1 Miles along the L. Side
N 50 W. 1/4 Ml   do   do
N. 18° E 1 Ml to a pt on the L.S. opsd two Islands, one Small near the
      point ①
N. 32° W 3/4 to Pt on left side of the Island
N. 10° W 1/2 Ml to pt on L.S.
N. 60° W 1/4 Ml to W. Pt on Isd L.S.
N. 78 W. 1/2 Ml to pt on L.S. opposed the head of the Is to a pond on
      S.S. ②
S. 56°: W 2 1/4 Ml to Pt on L. [?] S. of the Missourie
N. 50 W. 1 Ml on the S.S.
N 45 E 3 ms to a pt on L.S.   passed Several Sand bars ③
N. 12 E—1/2 Ml on L. Side round a Sand bar & Camped
II

6. In the southern states, the term "bayou" meant the overflow of a river or lake, a back-water.

7. In the Notebook Journal (Thw., 1, 66–67), Clark called this creek "4th of July Creek" and a creek passed later in the day was named "Creek Independence" which in his Courses and Distances is called "creek of the Kansies old Village" (infra, p. 68). It appears that Clark straightened out this confusion when he wrote the day's entry in the Notebook Journal. On his map he lists only Independence Creek.

8. Ordway's description is so similar in wording that it is worth noting: "we camped in the pla[i]ns one of the most beautiful places I ever saw in my life, open and beautifully Diversified with hills and vallies all presenting themselves to the River" (Ordway, p. 92).

9. In this journal there is no report of any celebration of Independence Day. However, in the Notebook Journal (Thw., 1, 67), Clark recorded that "we closed the [day] by a Descharge from our bow piece [swivel gun], an extra Gill of whiskey."

1. The courses and distances for July 3 and 4 are written over the following memorandum that was probably jotted down at some earlier time:

      Lock
      Moles
      Vests
      Seeds
      presen of [*one word illegible*]
      4 Cartrges Boxes
      ring

2. See supra, n. 7.

July 4th 1804

N. 70° W. 1 Ml on L. S. S, pd a Pond

S. 45 W. 3 Ms Pt L. S. <L pond> a sm Isd L.S

N. 75 W. 1/4 Ml on S. S.

N. 40° W 6 Ms to pt S.S. opsd Pr [Prairie?]

N. 12° E. 2 3/4 [3/4 written over 1/2] Mls to L.S.   psd Sm. Isd L.S. ②

N 10 E 2 to a pt S.S. opsd ③

Passed a Creek L.S. called creek of the Kansies old Vilg of 30 yds wide[2] and camped where the old village was on the L.S.   the point.

The Plains of this countrey are covered with a Leek green Grass, well calculated for the sweetest and most norushing hay—interspersed with cops [copses] of trees, Spreding ther lofty branchs over Pools Springs or Brooks of fine water. Groops of Shrubs covered with the most delecious froot is to be seen in every derection, and nature appears to have exerted herself to butify the Senery by the variety of flours <raiseing> Delecately and highly flavered raised above the Grass, which strikes & profumes the Sensation, and amuses the mind   throws it into Conjecterng the cause of So magnificent a Senerey [*several words illegible*] in a country situated far removed from the Sivilised world to be enjoyed by nothing but the Buffalo Elk Deer & Bear in which it abounds & [*two words torn*] Savage Indians[3]

The names of the french Ingishees [*engagés*], or Hirilens [hirelings]

———

1	Battist de Shone. Patrn Perogue [Baptist Deschamps]	
★2	Joseph Le bartee [Liberty?]	
3.	Lasones [Baptist La Jeunesse]	
4	Paul Preemau [Paul Primaut]	in
5	Chalo	Perogue
6	E. Cann	
7	Roie	
8	Charls Cougee	

—————

★ J, Le bartee   [Liberty]
Rivee   [Rivet]   } in the large Boat

—————
—————

Pieter Crousatt   half Indian
William La Beice [Biche] Mallat   [Matelot?]   } bow men
3 Sergts & 23 [3 written over 2] men for the boat   < Good
George Drewyer. Hunter & 4 Horses   Bowmen >
1 Corpl & 4 Privates in a Perogu to be Sent back from Plate river
Mr Dueron [Dorion] inteptr for the Sues
Capt. Lewis my self & York
in all 46 men July 4th   4 horses & a dog[4]

3. This description is written on one side of a small fragment, torn from a notebook of the size of those carried by the party. In Clark's entry for July 4 in the Notebook Journal (Thw., *1*, 67) is the following description: "the Prairie had a most butiful appearance Hills & Vallies interspsd with Coops of Timber gave a pleasing diversity to the Scenery." Perhaps the longer description given in this journal was written first and condensed for the Notebook Journal. Clark seldom wrote as he did here, and the contrast with his usual matter-of-fact descriptions is marked. There is no doubt that he was deeply moved by this, his first real view of the plains.

4. By Clark's own figures here, the total should be 47 instead of 46 men on July 4, 1804. The three sergeants were Floyd (died Aug. 20, 1804), Ordway, and Pryor. The 23 men were Bratton, Collins, Colter, J. Field, R. Field, Frazer, Gass (made sergeant after Floyd's death), Gibson, Goodrich, Hall, Howard, McNeal, Newman, Potts, Read, Shannon, Shields, Thompson, Werner, Whitehouse, Willard, Windsor, and Wiser. The two bowmen, Pierre Cruzatte and Francis Labiche, are listed separately, making a total of 28. Add to this one corporal and four privates. When the party set out, Corporal Warfington commanded a squad of five, including Robert Frazer. He, however, became a member of the party of discovery (Thw., *1*, 184). This gives a total of 33 men. Drouillard, Dorion, York, and the two captains bring the number to 38. According to the list given here there were nine French hands: Le Bartee is counted twice. This would give a total of 47 for the party. However, this figure is open to some question, for there is still some confusion in the names and number of French *engagés* with the party.

Below I have prepared three lists of the French hands. The first is the one Lewis recorded in his Orderly Book as the Detachment Order of May 26, 1804, shortly after the party left Camp Dubois; the second is Clark's list given here; the third is a list of those to whom wages were paid in the summer and fall of 1805 on their return to St. Louis. This last is taken from the accounts of Lewis' expenses through 1805, found in Jackson's collection of documents relating to the expedition, pp. 419–31.

It is now possible to list the following ten *engagés* as being with the expedition on July 4:

1. Baptist Dechamps—patron
2. Etienne Mabbauf (Malboeuf)
3. Paul Primaut (Preemau, premor)
4. Baptist La Jeunesse (Lageuness, Lasoness, Lajeuness)
5. Peter Roi (Roie)
6. François Rivet (Rivee, Rives, Reevey)
7. E. Cann (Carrn, Carr, Cane)
8. Joseph Le Bartee (La Liberty, Jo Barter)
9. Peter Pinaut (Charles Pineau?)
10. Charls Caugee

Etienne Malboeuf (Mabbauf) is on Lewis' list of May 26, 1804. In the Financial Records of the Expedition a warrant is listed as issued on Oct. 4, 1805, for wages due to B. La Jeunesse and E. Malboeuf (Jackson, p. 422). Presumably these two men had returned to St. Louis from Fort Mandan. I believe Clark overlooked Malboeuf in making out his July 4 roster. The names of Charles Hebert and Joseph Collin are not found in Clark's list or in the list of wages paid, nor do their names appear anywhere in the journals of the expedition. In Clark's list the name Charlo might have been applied to Pinaut. If these assumptions are correct, the roster on July 4, 1804, was 48 men, four horses, and a dog.

Lewis' List of May 26, 1804	Clark's List of July 4, 1804	Names in Lewis' Expense Accounts through 1805
1. Baptist Dechamps, patroon.	Baptist de Shone	B. Deschamp
2. Etienne Mabbauf		E. Malboeuf
3. Paul Primaut	Paul Preemau. Paul *premor* (Thw., *1*, 218, Nov. 6, 1804).	
4. Baptist La Jeunesse	Lasoness, Laguness (Thw., *1*, 218, Nov. 6, 1804).	B. Lajeuness
5. Peter Pinaut	Charlo (?)	Charles Pineau
6. Peter Roi	Roie	
7. Francis Rivet	Rivee. Revey, Rives (*Ordway*, p. 167, 187.) Reevey (Thw., *5*, 350).	Francis Rivet
8.	E. Cann. He is listed as Cane (infra, p. 118) as Carrn and Carr (Thw., *1*, 109, 121).	
9.	J. Le Bartee. (La Liberty, Jo Barter) The story of his desertion in August 1804 is told in all the journals.	
10.	Charles Cougee	
11. Charles Hebert		
12. Joseph Collin		

July the 5th 1804   Set out verry early this Morning, swam the horse across the river, proceeded on for two miles under the bank where the old Kansas town formerly stood (say in 1724)[5]   The Cause of those people moveing from this place I cannot learn, but naterally conclude that War has reduced their nation & compelled them to retire further into the Plains with a view of defending themselves & opposeing their enemey more effectually on hors back/   I neglected to mention yesterday that the Lake on the S.S. was large   say 3/4 ml wide & 7 or 8 long   one creek & Several brooks running into it from the hills, It contains Great quantities of sun fish & Gosling's from which we gave it the name,/ passed Some verry bad Sand bars Situated parrelel to each other, ① the Boat turned three times once on the Plat of a drift wood. She recved no <damage> proceiviable damage, we came to for Dinner at a Beever house, Cap Lewis's Dog [Scannon][6] went in & drove them out. the high Lands on the L.S. is open, a few trees scattering ②   passed a Small Creek on the L.S in the ls bend to the left I call <Reas Creek> yellow oakey [ochre] creek from <the number from about a> a bank of that mineral just above. we camped on the L.S. under a high bank   Latd 39° – 25' – 41″ north[7]

Course & Distance July 5th 1804
N 35° E 1 ml on the S.S. opposit the old village of Kanzes
S. 56° E 2 ml to the L. point a Large Eddey on the L.S. and a bad Sand bar
East—1 ml on L.S.   a Sand bar in middle &c &c ① Boat turned 3.
N. 18° W. 2 Mls to a pt on S.S. opsd a Prarie   psd a creek L.S. ②
N 1 Ml on S.S.
S. 70° E 3 Ml to a pt of Willow on the L S.   wind from SE

———
10

on the banks of this river I observe great quants of Grapes, berries & roses   Deer is not So plenty in this three days past as they were below that. Elks are plenty about those Praries. Some Buffalow Sign.

July 5 to July 6 to

6th July Friday. We Set out early this morning & Proceeded on/   the river falls Slowly/   wind S.W/   passed a sand bar in 1st bend to the right ①   passed a Small Island at the S. pt   a verry warm day/   worthy of remark that the water of this river or some other cause, I think that the most Probable throws out a greater preposn of Swet than I could Suppose could pass thro: the humane body   Those men that do not work at all will wet a shirt in a Few minits & those who work, [the sweat] will run off in streams/   opposit the 3rd point passed a Prarie on the S.S. Called Reeveys Prarie/   from a man of that name being Killed in it[8] opposit this Prarie the river is Confined in a verry narrow Space Crowded on S.S. by emence [?] Sands which were moveing and dificult to pass. the huntr Sent in 3 Deer Jurked   on the 4th point of to day is a Small Island & a Sand bar 2 miles out in the river, this is Called the Grand Bend, or Grande de Tour,[9] I walked on this Sand bar   found it a light Sand intersperced with Small Pebbles of various Kinds, also pit coal of an excellent quallity was lodged on the Sand, We camped on the L.S at a s[ize?]able creek   a whiper will perched on the boat for a short time, I gave his name to the creek

Course Distance & refurences July 6. 1804
N. 58° E. 1 Ml on the L. Side opposit a Sand bar in the river
North 3 Ms to a pt on S.S. an Isd: ① (N45 E. thro the Chanel)

5. In the Notebook Journal there is the additional information that de Bourgmont, the commandant at Fort Orleans, visited the Kansas Indians in 1724 (Thw., *1*, 67). Clark was correct in his information (Nasatir, *1*, 21).

6. Scannon (or Scamon or Semon) was a Newfoundland for which Lewis paid $20. He accompanied the party to the Pacific. Clark writes that the Indians were much astonished at "my black Servant [York] & the Segassity of Capt Lewis's Dog" (Thw., *2*, 366).

7. The entry for July 5 is so similar in wording to that of Ordway for the same date that there is little doubt that one was used in writing the other. Ordway, however, does not refer to the dog, Scannon (*Ordway*, pp. 91–92). The Notebook Journal (Thw., *1*, 67–68) is enough different from Ordway to warrant the conclusion that Clark gave him the entries from this journal to copy, and then wrote the entry in the Notebook Journal later.

8. The Notebook Journal does not give the origin of the name "Reevey's Prairie." Ordway (p. 93 and n.) calls it "Reevey's or St. Michel's prarie" and gives the same information as found here. It has been noted that the Ordway journal often follows very closely the wording of this journal.

9. This has been identified as the bend in the Missouri upon which the present city of St. Joseph, Missouri is located. This bend should not be confused with the Grand Detour, 750 miles upstream and marked on all the early maps. None of the maps used by Clark has this St. Joseph Bend marked. However, Truteau in his journal notes it (Truteau's *Journal, A.H.R., 19*, 304).

1. The entry for July 6 is written over the following:

    Capt William Clark
    River Dubois
    Pvt Howard.

N. 10° W 1/4 on S.S. an Isd

S. 76. E 1/2 Ml on S.S. to the head of the Island, a Pad [*sic*] Batteue [bad bar?]

S. 60° E 1 3/4 Ml to a pt on the L.S.   (Willows)

N. 70° E 1 1/2 Ml along a Sand bar on the L.S. opposit a Prarie ②

N 50° W 1 ml on the L.P.   Passed a bad Sand

West 3 Ms to a pt on the S.S. a Small Island ③ & Sand bar

    12

(N 6) 4 E)

<N. 40l E 2 ml on the S.S.>

<N. 75° E 2 ml to pt on the / L.S.>[1]

7th of July Satturday 1804   Set out early   passed Some verry swift water
on the L.S. which compelled us to Draw up by the Cord. [to cordelle] a
verry warm morning, passed a butifull Prarie[2] on the right Side which
extends back, those Praries has much the appearance from the river of
farms, Divided by narrow Strips of woods   those Strips of timber grows
along the runs which rise on the hill & pass to the river   a Cleft above,
one man sick (Frasure)[3] struck with the Sun, Saw a large rat on the Side
of the bank, Killed a wolf on the Bank   passed ② a verry narrow part
of the river, all confined within 200 yards, a yellow bank above, passed a
small willow Island on the S. point, (in Low water those Small Willow
Islands are joined to the Sand bars makeing out from the Points) a pond
on the S.S near the prarie we passed yesterday in which G D. [Drouil-
lard] Saw Several young Swans/   we Came to and Camped on the L.S.
the two men sent out last evening with the horses did not Join us this
evening agreeable to orders—a hard wind with Some rain from the N E
<Dark> at 7 oClock which lasted half an hour, with thunder & light-
ning   river fall a little

Course Distance & reffurrences July the 7th
N. 40° E 2 ms on the L. point <round> over the Sand bar
N 76° E 3 [3 written over 2] ms to the pt on the L.S.   passed Sand bars
N 50° E 1 3/4 [3/4 written over 2] ms to a Prarie in the bend to the S.S.
      ① St Mickles Pro: [St Michael's Prairie]
N 30° W 1 [one figure illegible] ml on the L.S.   a Bluff on S.S.   Hunts
      Sent in 2 Deer
N 76° W 1/4 ml on L.S.
S 66° E 2 ml to pt on S.S. from which a Sand bar makes
N 74° W 1 1/2 on the S. Side opposit a yellow Clift river abt 200 yds wide
      ②
N. 45° E 1/2 ml on S.S.   a pt of a Willow Island ③
N. 70 E 2 ms to a pt on L S.—a Sand bar puts out
    —
    14

8th of July Sunday   Set out early this morning, the sick man [Frazer]
much better, Serjt Oddeway was waiting at a Creek[4] on the L.S. below
an Island, passed ① two Island on the S.S. and came to at the upper
point, G Drewyer went out   R. Fields & Guterich, [Goodrich] five men
Sick to day with a violent Head ake &c and Several with Boils, we appoint a cook to each mess to take charge of the Provisions. in Serjt Pryor
= Collens   in Sjt Ordway's Werner   in Sergt Floyd's Thompson,[5] [two
words illegible]   The french men Killed a young Deer on the Bank, ②
passed up a narrow channel of about 80 or 100 yds wide about 5 miles to
the mouth of Nadawa [Nodaway] River[6] which coms in to this Channel
from the N W. and is abt 70 yards wide at its mouth [space] feet Deep
and has a jentle Current, Perogues can navagate this river near its head,
which is between the Missourie & the Grand River, passed up the gut 3/4
of a mile to the river at the head of the river Island & camped   opposit
the head of this Island is another nearest the <Larboard Shore,> Middle R   this Island Nadawa is the largest I have seen, formed by a Channel washing into the Nadawa river.—"8. or 10 000 acres"

Course Distance & Reffurs 8th July.
N. 28° E 1 ml on the L pt a Sand bar
N. 10° W. 1 1/2 to the Lower point of a Island [Little Nodaway Island]
    on the S.S.
N 25° W. 3 ml to a pt on the L.S.   passed the Isd & one on the side ①

2. St. Michul [St. Michael's] Prairie (Thw.,
1, 69).

3. The sick man, Frazer, was keeping a journal in accordance with Jefferson's instructions
that as many of the men as possible should
be urged to keep one. On his return to St.
Louis he made arrangements for publishing
it. He wrote a prospectus for his forthcoming
work which, in manuscript form, is in the
Wisconsin Historical Collections. However,
the journal was never printed, and the MS
has never been found (Thw., *1*, xxiv, lv,
lxxxv n.; see Jackson, p. 346 n.).
Mrs. Maud A. Wilson of Trenton, Illinois,
who is a great-granddaughter of Robert
Frazer, has written this editor that there is a
tradition in the Frazer family that when her
great-grandfather returned to St. Louis, he
gave his journal to a Frenchman to take to
France for publication. After some time, he
sent for Frazer and told him the journal was
lost at sea in a storm. Whatever credence can
be given to the Frenchman and his story, it
adds only another speculation as to the fate
of the Frazer journal.

4. Ordway says of this stream, "my Captain
he named it Ordway Creek" (*Ordway*, p. 93).
Clark makes no reference to this incident in
this journal nor is Ordway Creek mentioned
in the Notebook Journal nor found on
Clark's map. Ordway was obviously proud of
this recognition by his captain and it is re-
grettable that Clark apparently forgot or did
not choose to put Ordway's name on the map.

5. The Detachment Order of July 8 in Captain Lewis' Orderly Book gives in detail the
regulations laid down (Thw., *1*, 71–72). There
were no men enlisted as cooks in the army at
this time. The men were divided into messes,
with one man appointed in charge of each
mess. Provisions were issued to him and he
was "to receive, cook and to take charge" of
the food issued. Those detailed were to cook
"for their several messes in due time, and in
such a manner as is most wholesome and best
calculated to afford the greatest proportion
of nutriment; in their mode of cooking they
are to exercise their own judgment." For this
service these men were relieved of guard duty
and camp chores. The French *engagés* formed
a mess by themselves.

6. On the Indian Office Map this stream is
called "Riv Nadawa, Mandan River." Whitehouse, whose prose is of a special kind, recorded that "a bear apeared but coul⁴ not be
Shot   Made his Alopement" (Thw., *7*, 41).

7. The entry for July 8 is written over the
following, which is in Lewis' hand.
> Capn Wm Clark
> River Dubois
> Pryor

N. 56 W. 1 1/2 ms to the Lower point of an Island [Big Nodaway Island]
     ② S 30 W. up the Chnl
West—1/4 mile on Left of the Island
S 10° W.—1/4 ml to a pt on S. Shore.
N. 25° W. 1/4 ml to pt on Isld
N. 40° W. 1/4 ml to the bend on S.S.
N. 70 W 1/2 ml to a bend on the S.S.
S 70. W 1/4 ml to a bend in the Island.
N 82 W 1/2 ml to a   do in   Isld
N 42 W. [*one figure illegible*] ml to a   do do   S. Side—
S 50 W 1/2 ml to   do in   do
                8 1/4
S 15° W: 1/4 to a bend of Isd. 30
S 80 W 1/4 to the head of Isle
               1/2
              12
10
N. 65 W 1/4 ml to a bend on Isld
N. 18 W 1/4 ml to a bend S.S.
N 38 W 1/2 ml to a bend S S
S. 20° W 1/2 ml to a pt   a Isd opsd the Nadawa R.
S 15. W [*one figure illegible*] to a bend of Isd
S 80 W 11 1/4

                         59   22
                         25. 41
                       13 – 41[7]

July the 9th Monday 1804   sent one man back to the mouth of the
<creek> River to <brand> mark a tree, to let the party on Shore See
that the Boat had passed the river,[8] Set out <at Si> early   passed ① the
head of the Island Situated in the Middle of the river   a sand bar at the
head, ② passed the mouth of creek or Bayou on the S.S. leading from a
large Pond of about three miles in length,[9] at 8 oClock it commenced
raining, the wind changed from NE. to S.W. ③ at 6 miles   passed the
mouth of a Small Creek on the L.S. called Monters Creek, the river at
this place is wide with a Sand bar in the Middle, passed a place on the
L.S. about 2 miles above the Creek, where Several french men camped
two years to hunt[1]—④ passed a Island on the S S. of the river in a bend,
opsd a high Land on the L.S.   wind Shifted to the N.W. in the evining,
opsd this Island, and on the L.S. Loup or Wolf River Coms in, this river
is about 60 yards Wide, but little water running at the mouth, this river
heads with the waters of the Kanzas, and has a perogue navigation Some
distance, It abounds with Beaver, camped opposit the head of the Island
on the L.S.   Saw a fire on the S.S.   Supposed the four flankers, to be
theire, Sent a perogue for them, the Patroon & Bowman of the Perogue
French, they returned & informed, that when they approached the fire,
it was put out, which caused them to return, this report causd us to look
out Suppose ing a pty of Soux going to war, firierd the bow piec[e] to allarm & put on their guard the men on Shore   every thing in readiness
for Defence.

Course Distance & Reffurencies for July the 9th
S. 60°: W. 1 1/2 ms to the upper point of an Island in the River ①—
    passed the mouth of a Gut from a pond ② S.S.
S. 20° W. 3 1/2 ms to a point on the S.S.   passed a Sand bar and point on
    L.S.—(rains).
N 82 W 3 1/2 ms to a point on the L S. Side, psd a Sand bar, a Small
    Creek on the L.S. ③
N. 68° W 5 1/2 ms to a point on the L.S. ④   passed a Island on the S.S.—
    Just below the pt pass Wolf R ⑤

  14

July 10th Tuesday   Set out this morning with a view to Land near the
fire   Seen last night, & recornetre, but soon discovered that <the> our
men were at the fire, they were a sleep early last evening, and from the
course of the wind which blew hard, thei [i written over y] r yells were
not hea[r]d by party in the perogue, a mistake altogether,—. proceeded
on, passed [tear] Prarie on the upper Side of Woolf River, at 4 miles
passed ① a Small L S Creek Called [hole] R. Pape[2]   this Creek is about
15 yds Wide—and called after a Spanierd who killed himself at th[e]—
mouth. ② Dined on an Island Called de Selamen [Solomon's?] and delayed 3 hours, and proceeded on, opposit this Isld on the L.S. is a ③ butifull Bottom Prarie whuch will Contain about 2000 acres of Land covered with wild rye & wild Potatoes, great numbers of Goslings on the
Banks & in the Ponds near the river, Capt Lewis Killed two this evening,
we came to & camped for the night. at a point on the S.S. opposit a yellow
clay clift.—our men all getting well but much fatigued, the river is on a
Stand nether rise nor fall, The bottom on the S.S. is verry extensive &
thick. the Hills or high land is near the river on the L.S. and but thinly
timbered, Back of those hills is open plains.

Course Distance & Reffrs July 10th
N. 80° W. 3 1/4 ms to the Starboard Point passed a Sand Bar

8. Bratton (*Ordway*, p. 94). As we shall see,
it was a wise precaution to let the flanking
party on shore know that the boats had
passed a certain point. Further upstream a
man was lost for days because he thought the
party had passed him while he was hunting
on shore. In his effort to catch up with the
boats that were still behind him, he walked
until he was exhausted (infra, p. 136).

9. "as our flanking party saw great numbers of Pike in this Pond, I have laid it down
with that name anex'd" (Thw., *1*, 72). The
name does not appear on the Clark map.

1. In the Notebook Journal (Thw., *1*, 72),
Clark writes, "about two mile above is some
Cabins where our Bowman & Several frenchmen Campd two years ago." "Our Bowman"
must refer to either Pierre Cruzatte or Francis
Labiche. See supra, p. 69 and n. Ordway
wrote that the Frenchmen came "for to hunt
& raise corn, etc." (p. 94). Floyd added that,
"Seve[r]al French faileys had Setled and
made Corn Some Years ago   Stayed two years
the Indians came Freckentley to See them and
was verry frendly" (Thw., 7, 16).

2. Pappie Creek, in the Notebook Journal
(Thw., *1*, 73). Whitehouse, whose journal is
always full of surprises, has nothing about the
tragedy of the Spaniard, but wrote "whare
[we] Stopd to take breakfast the willd Rice
was pleanty Groeing on the bank of the
River, Straberyes, Rosies, Red and White"
(Thw., 7, 41).

3. The present Big Nemaha River.

4. The men must have found these fruits a welcome addition to their diet of meat and parched meal. Ordway wrote on July 19, "we gathered a quantity of cherries at noon time & put in to the Whiskey barrel" (*Ordway*, p. 99).

5. Willard was courtmartialed and charged with "Lying down and Sleeping on his post whilst Sentinal, on the Night of the 11th Instant." He admitted lying down but said he did not sleep. He was found guilty on both charges and sentenced to 100 lashes to be administered in four equal installments (Lewis, Orderly Book, July 12, 1804; Thw., *1*, 76).

N. 19. E 3 1/2 ms to a point on the L S. passed a creek ①
North 3/4 ml to Lower point of an Island ②
S. 80° W. 3/4 ml to a pt on the Left side of the Island opsd a prarie ③
N. 50° W. 1 1/4 ml to a pt on the P.: L. S passed a bad Sand bar
N. 83° W. 2 ml to a pt S.S.— —

—————————
10 Miles   S. 66 – W

July 9 to 13th

July 11th Wednesday, Set out early   proceeded on   passed a Willow ① Island in a bend to the S.S.   Sent out Dreweyer & Jo: Fields to hunt, Back of this Island a creek coms in on the S.S. called by the Indians Little Tarkio Creek   I went on Shore above this Island on the S.S.   found the bottom Subject for overflow wet and verry thickly interwoven with grape vines—proceeded on at about 1/2 a miles from the river about 3 ms and observed fresh Sign of a horse, I prosuud the track, with an expectation of finding a Camp of Indians on the river, when I got to the river, I saw a horse on the beech, this horse as appears was left last winter by Some hunting party, probable the Othoeuz [Oto], I joined the Boat on the Sand Island Situated opposit the mouth of Ne. Ma.har River,[3] this river Coms in on the L.S. is about 80 yds Wide and navagable for Perogues Some Distance up   the Praries commence above the mouth and Continus on both Sides of this R   Drewyer killed 6 Deer to day   J. Field one   Several hunters sent out up the Ne Mahar R

Course Distance & reffurence July 11th 1804
N 30 W 3 mls to <a point on the L S above> the head of a Small willow
        <prarie, & opposit a> ① Island on the S.S. in a bend—
N 86° West 3 ms pssg. [?] a point on the S.S. to the South Side of a Sand
        Island opsd a Ne-Mahar ②

—————————
6

July 12th Thursday   Som hunters out on the S.S.   those on the L.S. did not return last night, our object in delaying here is to tak some observations and rest the men who are much fatigued   made Sundery observations, after an early Brackfast I took five men and went up the River Ne Ma har about three miles, to an open leavel part of an emence prarie, at the Mouth of a small Creek on the Lower Side, I went on Shore, & passed thro the plain   passed Several noles to the top of a high artificial noal from the top of this noal I had an emence, extensive & pleaseing prospect, of the countrey around, I could see the meandering of the Little River [Nemaha] for [*hole*] at least 10 miles winding thro a meadow of 15 or 20000 acres of high [*hole*] bottom land covered with Grass about 4 1/2 feet high, the high lands which rose irregularly, & were toped with mounds or antent graves which is to me a Strong evidence of this Countrey haveing been thickly settled,—. This River is about 80 yards wide with a gentle Current and heads up near the Parnee [Pawnee] Village on River Blue a branch of Kansas, a little timbered land near the mouth for 1 mile above, only a fiew Trees, and thickets of plumbs cheres &c are seen on its banks   the creeks & little reveens makeing into the river have also some timber—I got grapes on the bank nearly ripe, observed great quantities, of Grapes, plums crab apls and a wild Cherry, Growing like Comn Wild Cherry only larger & grows on a small bush,[4] on the side of a sand stone clift 1/2 ml up & on Lower Side   I marked my name & day of the month near an Indian mark or Image of animals & a boat   Tried Willard for sleeping on his post,[5] our hunters killed some deer, Saw elk & buffalow.

My notes of the 13th of July by a most unfortunate accident blew over Board in a Storm in the morning of the 14th obliges me to refur to the <notes> Journals of Serjeants, and my own recollection [of] the accurrences Courses Distance &c of that day—[6] last night a violent Storm from the N.N.E.— ① passed Tar-ki-o River, at 2 miles   a chanl running into this river 3 ms abov forms St Josephs Isld. Passed an elegt Prarie in the 1st bend to the left. Conta[in]ing a grass resmlg Timothy, with Seed like flax, ② passed a Island in a bend to the S.S. at 12 ms   I walked on Shore S.S. lands, low & overflows, Killed two Goslings nearly Grown, Sailed under a Wind from the South all day, Camped on a Sand Island on the L. pt opposit a high & extensiv Prarie, on the S.S. the Hills about 4 or 5 ml off, this Plain appears extensive,[7] great appearance of a Storm from the North W. [?]. this evening verry agreeable the wind Still from the South ———

Course Distance & reffurrence July 13 1804

N. 8° E 1 Ml to Pt on S.S. passed the Sand Island

N. 28 E 3 1/2 Ml to pt on L.S. psd Tar-ki o R. [*one letter illegible*] St Joseps Isd L.S. ①

S. 70° W 3 Ms to pt on S.S. opsd a Prarie ②

N 46° W 1 1/2 Ms on the S. point opsd the Prarie & a Hill L.S

N. 30° W 1 1/2 Ms to a pt on L.S.

N. 45° W 4 1/2 Ms to a pt on L.S. passd a Island & Sand bar ③

N. 6 [6 written over 7]6 W 3 1/2 Ms to a pt on S.S.

N. 8 W. 2 Ms to a pt on L.S. leaving a Sand Island on which we camped to the left, on this Island I lost my notes, in a storm.[8]

———
20

Course Distance and Reffurrence July 14th 1804

N 70° W. 2 Ms to a pt on S.S.   pass an Isld Small on S.S. ①   a violent Storm from N.E.

N. 20° W. 2 Ms to a pt on L.S.   wind from N.W. by N.

N. 30° W 1 Ml on the L: S.

N. 50° W 2 1/2 Ms to the Lower point of an Island

N. 87. W. 1 1/2 to a second point of same Island on Lad side of the same

———
9

a little above the lower point of this island a creek falls in on the Stard. called by the Maha Neesh-nah-ba-to-na—[9]   this is a considerable creek   is as large as the mine river, and runs parallel with the Missouri through much the greater portion of it's course

July the 14th Satturday   Some hard shours of rain accompaned with Some wind detained us untill about 7 oClock, we then Set out and proceeded on about a mile a[nd] th[e] atmispere became Suddenly darkened by a blak & dismal looking Cloud, we wer in a Situation, near the upper point of a Sd Isd & the opsd Shore falling in   in this Situation a Violent Storm of Wint from the N, E/ passing over an Open plain, Struck the boat nearly <broad Side>, Starboard quatering, & blowing down the Current/   the exerssions of all our men who were out in an instant, aded to <the> a Strong Cable and anchor was scrcely sufficent to Keep the boat from being. thrown up on the Sand Island, <the Storm> and dashed to pieces   the Waves dasthed over on the Side next to The wind the lockers which was covered with Tarpoling prevented the[m] coming into the Boat untill the Boat was creaned [careened] on the side from the Wind   in this Situation we continued about 40 minits, the two perogues about a quater of a mile above, one of them in a Similer Situation with

6. It is clear that Clark wrote this on July 14, describing the storm that struck the flotilla shortly after they left camp that morning. The part written from the sergeants' journals and from "my own recollection" begins with the words "passed Tarkio," continues through the courses, distances, and references, and ends with the words, "in a storm." It is surprisingly detailed and suggests that either the sheet containing the courses and distances was not lost or someone else was also keeping a record. None of the published journals of Ordway, Gass, Floyd, or Whitehouse shows that Clark used them in preparing this entry. It seems to me that the whole incident supports the contention that this journal, written on loose sheets of paper, was the first recording of each day's journey and that this was enlarged upon when Clark had time to write in his Notebook Journal.

7. Whitehouse calls this "Hurican prarie" (Thw., 7, 42).

8. This entry is written over a notation made by Clark [?] four months before. The margin is cut off, leaving only parts of sentences as follows:

	from the Osagies Nation with.
Append	twenty odd of the Natives or chiefs
Ordway	of the Nation with him [Sa]iled
from	[?] dowen the Mississippi [*space*]
Camp	bound to St Louis and 3 guns fired
F J	ers of rain
	Showers of Rain all that night

This incident refers to the arrival in St. Louis in April 1804 of Chouteau and Gratiot, after their trip up the Missouri in March to stop the Kickapoo from going to war with the Osage (supra, p. 27). Clark noted their return in his entry for April 21 (supra, p. 35). Therefore this fragment must have been written on or near this date.

9. Mackay calls this stream the "Rivre Nichinibatone." The Indian Office Map names it "*R. Channaille de Baton*, Cane River & Channel." The present name is the Nishnabotna River.

1. The description of this storm in the Notebook Journal is a revised account with some explanatory words and phrases added. The experience of the men in the two pirogues is more circumstantial in this journal. In the Notebook Journal, Clark makes no reference to his notes blowing overboard (Thw., *1*, 78). I have rearranged the entries for July 13–14 to clear up the confusion in the document itself. By examining the facsimile of Doc. 31, the reader can note the changes made.

2. Supra, p. 62.

3. Barren lands. In Kentucky, the term "barren" was applied to really fertile land in the carboniferous limestone formation (Criswell, p. 11; see also *O.E.D.*, *1*, 681).

4. The last sentence is written at right angle to the entry of July 15.

the Boat, the other under the charge of George Gibson in a much better position, with her Ster[n] faceing the wind, this Storm Suddenly Seased, & 1 minit the river was as Smoth as glass, the wind Shifted to the S.E and we Set Sail, and proceeded on   passed[1] 1 <an> a Small Island on the S.S. and Dined—R: Fields who has charge of the horses &c. on Shore did not join us last night—. passed a old fort where Mr Bennet[2] of St Louis winttered 2 years & traded with the Otteaus [Oto] & Panies/ [Pawnee] on the S.S. 1 ml abov the little Island, I went out on the L.S. and observed two Elk on a Sand in the river, in attempting to get near those elk obseved one near us   I shot one. continued on Shore & thro the bottom which was extensive, Some Small Praries, and a peponce [preponderance] of high rich & well timbered bottom, in the Glades I saw wild Timothy, lams quarter Cuckle bur & rich weed, on the edges Plumbs of different kinds Grapes, and Goose berries, Camped on the L.S.   Ruben Fields and Gulrich [Goodrich] joined the Party   two men unwell, one a Felin on his finger, river fall

Course Distance and reffurrences July 15th 1804
N. 30° W. 3 1/2 Ms to a pt of a willow Isld on the L.S.   psd the Isld on
    S.S. ①

[The following is in Lewis' hand:]

S. 75. W. 1/4 mile to a Lard point of the same Island the boat passed to
    lard of
<N 89>   Isd   the hill here projects to the river—
N. 89. W. 1/4 to a lard pt on the same island—the hills here leave the
    river
N. 88 W. 1/4 to a point on Lard main shore opposite a sand bar, took
    merd. Altd ⊙ L L
due. W. 1 1/4 mile to a pt <Lard.> stardd oposite which the hills again
    touch the river
N. 45 W. 1 1/2 mile to the mouth of Little Ni ma-haw on the Lard. in a
    bend oposite the lower point of a large sand bar—
N. 30 E 1 1/2 to a point on lard. a deep bend to the right below this point
N. 30 W. 1/2 to pt Lard.
N. 15. 3/4 to a pt of an Island. due E. from this about three miles is a
    large pond

——————————— *[End of entry in Lewis' hand]*

July 15th Sunday 1804. a heavy fog this morning which Detained us untill 7 oClock, put Drewyer Sgt Floyd on Shore, at 9 I took two men and went on Shore, with a view to Kill Some elk, passed thro open plains, and barroney lands[3]   Crossed three butifull Small Streams of water, Saw great quantity of Cherres, Plums, Grapes & Berries of Difft Kinds, the lands Generally of a good quallity, on the Streams the wood <grasey> escapes the fire, at about 7 miles I Struck the river at the mouth Ne ma ha Creek about 40 yds wide, near this Creek on a high part of the Plains I had a extensive View of the river & Countrey on both Sides. on S. a contnuation of the plain as far as I could See, on the N. a bottom Prarie of about 5 Ms wide & 18 to 20 long, hills back of this Plain. I swam across the Creek and waited for the Boat about three miles above, we camped opsd an Island.[4]

July 16ᵗʰ 1804 Monday   Set out verry early and proceeded on the Side
of a Prarie   passd the head of the Island opsd which we Camped last
night, ① passed a Small Willow Island off the L. point, hills make near
the river   ② passed a large Island <on the> nearest the L.S. below the
pt a small willow Isd   also one on the Side   this large Island is called
fair Sun   the wind favourable from the South. Boat run <a sho> on a
Sawyer, ④ pass a place on the L.S. where the hill abt 20 acres has sliped
into the river lately Just above passed under a clift of Sand Stone L.S. a
number of Burds Nests in the holes & crivises of this rock which Continus 2 miles, ⑤ passed a willow Island in a Deep bend to the S.S.   river
2 mile wide at this place, not[e] deed [dead?] Snags across, passed the
Lower point of a Island called Isle Chauvin⁵ Situated on the L. Point
opposit an extensive Prarie on the L. S., This prarie I call Ball pated
Prarie from the range ball [bald] hills, at from 3 to 6 miles from the river
as far as my sight will extend, we camped in a point of woods opsd the
Isd on S.S. in a bend.

Course Distance & reffurrences July 16ᵗʰ 1804.⁶

1 N. 70° W 1/2 Ml to a point on the Left of the Island, opsd to which we
  Camped last N[ight]

2. N 35° W 1 1/2 Ms to a Bend to the L.S. in a prarie opsd the head of the
  Island

3. N 30 E 1 ms to the lower point of a willow Isld opps L. Pt ①

4 N. 40 W 1/4 Ml up the Sd Willow Island—The high lands near the
  river L.S.

5. N 30 W. 2 Ms to a pt sd of sm. Isd—on S.S. psd a pt on the L.S at 3/4
  psd the Small Isd—

7. N 35 W 1/2 ml to a L. S. of a Small Willow Island, in the pt of the
  large Isd psd a Small Willow Isd ③

6. N 15 E 1 1/2 ml to the lower pt of a Isd Called Good Sun   psd a Small
  Isd at the Lowr Point ②

8. N 15° W 3/4 to a pt of on the <s Small Island>, L.S. high lands 3/4
  of a ml on L.S.   land open

9. N. 38 W. 3/4 To a pt <of the Isd> on the left side of the Isd   psd
  over a Sml Sd Isd on L.S.

10. N. 54 W. 3/4 To Lower pt of a sml Wil. Isld on the Side of the large
  Isd

11. N. 38 W 3/4 To a pt on L.S. [one word illegible] is the Sand Island
  took altd of ☉ L.L. 40° − 20′ − 12″ N.

N. 52 W 1/2 To a pt of the Island   high land below or or [sic] near the
  riv

13. N. 50° W 1 1/4 miles To a pt on L.S. above the head of the Island
  high land at this point— ④

N. 58° W. 2 Miles To a pt on the S.S. north on the S. Point 1/4 Ml
  Wind from S. purpn [one word illegible]: Clift of Sand Stone
  on L.S.

15 N 40° E 6 miles to a upr Pt of wood on the bend on the Stbd Side
  ───
   20

  Some high Ball [Bald] hills at about 4 miles from the river on
  the S.S.   passd a Sand bar, from the S. Sd ⑤ a Willow Island in
  S. bend, 4 Praries on L. Side & camped in the upper point of a
  wood, in a prarie.

<N. 40 E>
<N. 28 W>
<N. 21 W>

5. In Mackay's Table of Distances, this is
called Bald Island. The French word, *chauve*,
bald or bald-pated, may be the origin of the
Chauvin given by Clark. However, on the In-
dian Office Map the name given is *Isle
Chauvin* and following this, Chauvin's Island.
A Jacques Chauvin was certified to a claim of
1,063 arpents of land on the Missouri in the
St. Louis district on May 17, 1800 (A.S.P.:
Public Lands, 2, 464).

6. The long list of courses and distances for
this day gives the reader some idea of the
twisting character of the river. In a single
day, over a course of 20 miles, the direction of
the keelboat was changed 15 times from north
to north by east or north by west, in one case
58 degrees. Chittenden has called it "a winding staircase," like a snake coiling and uncoil-
ing its length of over three thousand miles
(Chittenden, 2, 764).

7. The party had passed the mouth of the stream several days before (supra, p. 77). The course of this creek parallels the Missouri, so by riding eastward, Lewis would strike its upper reaches.

July 17th Tuesday, river fall 3 Inches   we concluded to <Stay> lay by to day to fix the Longitude, and get the Cromometer right, (She run down Day before yesterday), Several men out hunting to day   Capt Lewis rode out to Neesh-nah-ba-to na Creek[7] which passes thro. the Prarie (on which there is some few trees) within [space] mile of the Missoureis, wind from the S E.   Several of the party have tumers of different Kinds some of which is verry troublesom and dificuilty to cure. I took a meridian altitude (43° . 27°) which made the Lattitude of this place 40°—27'—6"— 4/10 North.—(The Ball Hills <run> bear N 25° W for 30 ms   The bend on L.S. passing the Isd on the right Side is N. 28° W. 4 Ms)   Took equal altitudes

		h m	
Took Suns Azmuth Comps <Crom>		7 – 50 – 8	
	h m s		
Sextnt & time 1st	5 – 53 – 10	" – 15 – 28	A M
	altitude	" – 52 – 55	
	28° – 51' – 45"		

moon

* obsd	☽ an Spica	* Star West		
H Time	Distance	Azmuth	4 – 4 – 38	
8 – 53 – 11——41° – 50 – 00			" – 6 – 3	P M
		N 85° W	" – 7 – 24	
" – 59 – 0——41 – 53 – 15				
			Altd 69° – 36" – 00"	
9 – 2 – 58——41 – 54 – 0		2nd Time		
		h m		
" – 5 – 49——41 – 55 – 0		– 5 – 59 – 20"		
" – 8 – 2——41 – 56 – 0		altitude		
		26 – 35 – 30		
" – 15 – 24——41 – 57 – 0				
		Comps a zc		
" – 21 – 10——41 – 58 – 0				
		N. 84° W.		
" – 25 – 18——42 – 0 – 0				

tried a part of the Comn pt [Common Point?] of the Current in 40 Seconds   the water runs 50 fathem 30"—20" in places
Cap Lewers returned, Saw Some hand som Countery, the Creek near the high land is rapid and nearly as muddy as the river, & rising   Gutrich [Goodrich] caught two verry fat Cat fish   G Drewyer Killed 3 deer, & R Fields one, a puff of wind brought Swarms of Musquitors, which disapeared in two hours, blown off by a continuation of the same brees.
    altd   North Star   Cromometer too Slow 6Mts – 51s. 6/10 to day
  Time
(10 – 23m – 18s—81° – 9' – 15"   July 17)

July 18th Wednesday   a fair morning   the river falling fast, Set out at Sunrise under a gentle Breeze from S.E by S. at 3 miles   passed the head of the Island on L.S. called by the French Chauve or bald pate ① opsd the middle of this Island the Creek on L.S. is within 300 yds of the river. back of this Island the lower point of ② another Island in the bend to the L.S.   passed large Sand bar making out from each point with many channels passing through them, "Current runs 50 fathm in 41 seconds" but little timber on either side of the river, except the Isds & points which are low wet & covered with lofty trees, cotton wood mulberry Elm

&c &c   passed the head of a long Island in high water at this time no water passes thro: the Channel ③ opposit the Lower point of a Island on the L.S. pass the Island and opsd the point ④ above & on the L.S. the hills come to the river, This Hill has Sliped into the river for about 3/4 of a mile, and leaves a Bluff of considerable hight back of it   this Hill is about 200 foot high compsd of Sand Stone intermingled with Iron ore of an inferior quallity on a bed of Soft Slate Stone.

Course Distance & Rifferes July 18th 1804.

N. 28° W. 3 3/4 Ms to Curve in the bend to the L.S.   passing Bend of the Island on L.S.   Several Sand bars on Left   the Creek nea[r] ①

S 28° W. 3 3/4 Ms to a pt on the S.S.   Psd the head of the Island on the L.S.   one behind this ②

S 32° W.—1/2 Ml on S. pt   passed a Sand bar, a long Island on the L.S. in high water

S 88 W.—1/4 Ml on Do. a Sand bar to the left   wind from the S.W. hard

N 55 W.—1/4 Ml on do   do do   do—

N. 48 W. 2 1/2 Ms to a pt on L.S.   psd a Sand bar <or an Island> L.S.

N. 64 W. 2 [2 written over 3] 1/2 Ms to a pt place where water runs out to form the Isd on S.S.   passed the <head> of the Island ② and Lower pt of a Isd L.S. ③

N 50 W 3 [3 written over 5] Ms to a pt on S.S. opsd a red bank on L.S. Iron ore ④

N. 18° E 1 1/2 Ms to a pt on L.S.   opsd a Small Island in the middle of the river   Camped ⑤

18

We passed a verry bad Sand bar ④ a little above the hill and incmpd on the L.S. opposit a Small Island in the river, Saw a Dog this evening[8] appeared to be nearly Starved to death, he must have been left by Some party of Hunters   we gave him some meet, he would not come near, G Drewrer brought in 2 Deer this evening

of no consequence 3   July 19th[9]   after breakfast which was on rosted ribs of a Deer and a little Coffee I walked on Shore intending only to Keep up with the Boat, Soon after I got on Shore, Saw Some fresh elk sign, which I was induced to prosue those animals by their track to the hills   after assending and passing thro a narrow Strip of wood Land, Came Suddenly into an open and bound less prarie, I say bound less because I could not See the extent of the plain in any Derection, the timber appeared to be confined to the River Creeks & Small <Creek> branches, this Prarie was Covered with grass about 18 Inches or 2 feat high and contained little of any thing else, except as before mentioned on the River Creeks &c   This prospect was so Sudden & entertaining that I forgot the object of my prosute and turned my attention to the variety which presented themselves to my view   after continueing. on this rise for Some minits, I deturmined to make my course to a line of woods to S.E.   I found in this wood a butifull Streem of running water, in prosuing it down Several others Joined it and at 3 miles fell into the river between 2 clifts, I went up & under one clift of dark rich clay for 1/2 ml above this a clay bank which had Sliped in her[e] I found Sand Stone containing Iron ore, this ore appears to be enbeded under the clay just above the water[1]

8. The party was on the lookout for Indians. The stray dog mentioned here appeared important to Floyd, for he supposed the Indians had lost it: "this is the first Sine of Indians we have Saw" (Thw., 7, 19).

9. In this journal there are two entries for July 19. The second of these entries corresponds with the one of that date in the Notebook Journal (Thw., 1, 84–85). This first one, which gives Clark's impression of the "open and boundless prarie" when suddenly he saw it spread out before him, he omitted from the Notebook Journal. The modest comment "of no consequence" is in Clark's hand, but it is impossible to tell whether it was written at the time or later.

1. The entries for July 18 and 19 are written over the following in Lewis' hand:
Capt William Clark
River Dubois
Pr Serg Floyd
Note send your letters down if possible by Monday evening M. L.

2. *Four de tourte,* pie oven.

3. At this point Clark inserted his courses and distances, followed by the rest of the entry for the day.

4. There must have been many good-natured jokes passed around in the naming of various points on the journey. This helped to keep the men in good spirits. The consumption, two months out from St. Louis, of the last of the butter must have been a memorable occasion. Such good names as Biscuit, Nightingale, Whippoorwill, and No Preserves Creeks, and many others, have unfortunately been lost and do not appear on any map.

5. The mouth of the Platte was some 40 miles upstream.

6. *L'eau qui pleure* (now the Weeping Water Creek) on the Indian Office Map.

7. At the end of this day's entry in the Notebook Journal (Thw., *1,* 85–86) Clark wrote, "It is worthey of observation to mention that our Party has been much healthier on the Voyage than parties of the same number in other Situation. Tumers [boils] have been troublesom to them all."

July 19th Thursday 1804 [*Second entry for July 19*]
Set out early   pass between 2 Islands one in Mid: & the other L.S. opsd wher Prarie aproaches the river S.S.   This place is called the Bakers oven or in french four le tourtere[2] pass   Some[3]

Course Distance & Reffers
North 1/4 ml to the Lower pt of a Isd on L.S. called Bakers oven ①
N 10° W 1 1/4 Ms to a pt on the L.S.   bad Sand bars   psd the 2 Isds ①
N 45° W 1 Ml ② on the L. Side   Sand bar on S.S.
N. 85° W 2 Ml S.S. opsd high land ② — a Sand bar on the S. Side in a bend
N 82 W. 3/4 Ml to the mouth of a Creek in a bend on L. side Above a Clift
N. 13 W 2 1/2 Ml to Pt L.S. psd a Sliped in bank ③ a Isd on the S.S.   a run L.S.
N. 54° W 3 ms to pt on S.S.   passd Some Clifts, passed a willow Isld in Midl a Deep bend to the L.S.   a large Sand bar on L.S. ④
———
10 3/4

high lands 4 1/2 ms above the Isds on the L.S. forming a Clift to the river of yellow earth, on the top a Prarie, passd many a bad Sand bar in this distance, & the river wide & Shallow, above this Clift 2 Small butiffull runs Come from the Plains & fall into the river, a Deer lick on the first, above those two Creeks, I found in my walk on Shore Some Iron ore in a bank which had Sliped in to the river about 3/4 ml above the Creeks, I took a cercquite around & found that those two runs mentioned contained some a good proporion of wood Surrounded by a Plain, with grass about 18 Inchs high, Capt Lewis walked on Shore after Dinner) in the first bend to the right above those Runs passed a Small Island opsd is a Sand bar   I call this Island Butter Island, as at this place we mad use of the last of our butter,[4] as we approach this Great River Platt[5] the Sand bars are much more noumerous than they were, and the quick & roleing Sands much more dangerous, where the Praries aproach the river it is verry wide, the banks of those Plains being much easier to undermine and fall than the wood land   passed ④ a willow Island situated near the middle of the river, a sand bar on the S.S. and a Deep bend to the L S. camped on the right side of the Willow Island—W. Bratten hunting on the L. S Swam to the Island. Hunters Drewyer killed 2 Deer, Saw great numbers of young gees. The river Still falling a little   Sand bars thick always in view.

July 20th Friday 1804, a fog this morning and verry Cool   George Drewyer Sick   proceed on over a Sand bar, Bratten Swam the river to get his gun & Clothes left last night   psd a large willow Isd on the L.S. ①   passed the mouth of l'Eau que pleure the English of what is the water which cry's[6]   this Creek is about 20 yards wide falls into the river above a Clift of brown Clay L.S. opposit a willow Island, at this Creek I went on shore   took R Fields with me and went up this Creek Several miles & crossed thro: the plains to the river above with the view of finding Elk, we walked all day through those praries without Seeing any, I killed an emence large yellow Wolf—The Countrey throu which we walked after leaveing the Creek was good Land covered with Grass enterspersed with Groves & Scattering timber near and about the heads of Branches[7]

Course Distance & Reffns   July 20th 1804

N. 18° E 3 ml to a Pt L.S.   psd a Willow Island on S.S.   a Creek on L S. ①

[*The following is in Lewis' hand:*]

<N. 48 W. 2 1/2 M. to pt Sard oposite to a deep bend and prarie on the
  Stard   oposite this pt to the right of it is the upper point of a
  small Is. with a large sand bar below it   the Is. is seperated by
  a narrow chal from L.S.>

N. 48. E. 2 1/2 m. to a pt on Std side of an Island. oposite the upper pt of
  a 2nd Island which is devided from it by a narrow Channel   a
  deep bend to Sd side of this small Island— —

[*End of entry in Lewis' hand*]

N. 5. W 3 m. to Lard point of an Isd

Due N. 6. M, to the point of an Isld on Lard side of the same.

N. 18 W 3 1/2 Ms to a Point on the L.S.   high land psd the hd of Isld
  a large Sand bar on the L.S. on Which there was two Swans

18

Capt Lewis tried to kill one of them without Suckeess, Camped
above the bar on the L.S.   a verry agreeable Breeze all night
Serjt Pryor & Jo: Fields brought in two Deer   river still falling. a large Spring 3/4 ml below Camp

<N. 22, W. 3 ms to a pt L.S. opsd a pt of high Land psd Pigeon C. S.S.
N. 28° W ms to a pt Starboard S passed. [*space*] & over a Willow pt on
the L S. and a pt of high land L S ①>[8]

8. The entry for July 20 is written over the
following:
    Jeffersonville   May 4th   25   1804
    Captain William Clark
    Kahokia or
    Mail   some-where on the
    Missoria's

83

9. Now there were 600 miles of river behind them, and two months of labor against its unrelenting current. Ahead of them lay a thousand miles' journey before winter came and the party built its winter quarters among the Mandans. Because of the gradual shoaling of the channel as the little flotilla proceeded, it was soon necessary to transfer some of the cargo from the keelboat to one of the pirogues, thereby causing a change in plans (infra, p. 139). The party had met no Indians on the way, save a few Kickapoos at the very outset. The villages of the Kansas stood empty, for their inhabitants were all out on the plains hunting the buffalo. From now on, there would be Indians—Oto, Pawnee, Omaha, and the Teton Sioux. The last, always a threat to earlier parties, had to be met and dealt with. There were councils to be held with these tribes, for Jefferson had been very explicit on this point. These many councils (which Clark did not consider when, in his camp on the Dubois, he estimated times and distances: supra, pp. 19–20) delayed the party so that it was November before they reached the Mandan villages. Clark's hope that the party could reach the base of the Rocky Mountains before winter had, perforce, to be abandoned.

The Platte, which a later traveler described as "but a drain for the melting snows of the mountains," was unlike any of the tributaries of the Missouri that the explorers had passed. Not until they reached the Yellowstone, 1,300 miles away, were they to encounter such a large river. The journals contain a full description of the Platte's wide entrance and its swift current—"a very Strong Streame" wrote Whitehouse, "it Baks the Missiry over" (Thw., 7, 43). Geographers call such a stream a "braided river."

1. Francis Labiche or Pierre Cruzatte. (See supra, p. 75 n.).

2. This name is on the Indian Office Map.

July 21st Satturday, Set out verry early and a Gentle Breeze from the S.E proceeded on verry well, passed a ① Willow Island L.S. opsd a bad Sand bar   passed Some high land covered with Timber, in this Hill is Semented rock & Limestone   the water runs out and forms Several little Islands in ② high water on the S.S.   a large Sand bar on the S.S. above and opposit the wooded High Land, at about 7 oClock the wind Seased and it Commenced raining   passed many Sand bars opposit or in the Mouth of the Great River Plate[9]   this river which is much more rapid than the Missourie has thrown out imence quantities of Sand forming large Sand Banks at its mouth and forced the Missourie close under the S.S.   the Sands of this river Comes roleing down with the Current which is Crowded with Sand bars and not 5 feet water at any place across its mouth, the Rapidity of the Current of this river which is greater than that of the Missourie, its width at the Mouth across the bars is about 3/4 of a mile, higher up I am told by one of the bowmen[1] that he was 2 winters on this river above and that it does not rise <four> 7 feet, but Spreds over 3 miles at Some places, Capt Lewis & my self went up Some Distance & Crossed   found it Shallow. This river does not rise over 6 or 7 feet

Course Distance & Reffurences July 21st 1804

N. 22° W. 3 1/2 ms to pt S.S. opposit a point of high land on the L.S.

N. 28 W. 6 1/2 ms ⎰ to a pt on S.S. psd a pt of willows   a Willow Isd ①
on L.S. & a high pt on the L.S.   passed <Sand bar
in the river on a Island large on> the L.S. Sm cr
Small Channel ②

N. 39° W. 3 1/2 miles to a pt on S.S. <just Below opposit> the R. Plate.

13 1/2   psd a pt high land Covd with wood L.S.   a Sand bar near the S.S.   a large Sand bar

N. 8° W 2 ⎰ Ms to a point L.S.   the Junction of the Missr & Platt Rivers
―――   a Verry extensive View of the river   pass many Sand bars in
15   every direction thrown out by the Plate R which runs East

N. 10° W. 4   The Same Course Continud up the Missourie to a Pt L S
―――
19   —[space] Miles passed a Sand bar on the S.S.   wind N.
Proceeded on   passed the mouth of Papillion or Butter fly Creek[2] 3 miles on the L.S.

a large Sand bar opposit on that Side   Camped above this bar on L.S. great number of wolves about us all night   R. Fields killed a Deer hard wind N.W.   cold

[*The following is a fragment, on the margin of which is the date,* 21st *July (1804). The handwriting is that of Lewis.*][3]

by a boiling motion or ebolition of it's [the Platte's] waters occasioned no doubt <from> by the roling and irregular motion of the sand <it is be> of which its bed is entirely composed   the particles of this sand <is driven in large bodies> being remarkably small and light <are> it is easily boied up <and and by the water> and is hurried by <in large> this impetuous <current in> torrent <sometimes in> large masses from place to place in with irristable forse, collecting and forming sand-bars in the course of a few hours <and> which as suddenly disapated <them> to form others <one> and give place <to the> perhaps to the deepest channel of the river. where it [the Platte] enters the Missouri it's superior force <drives the> changes and directs the courant of that river against it's northern bank where it is compressed within a channel less than one third of the width it <just> had just before occupied*. <and> it dose not <then> furnish the missouri with it's colouring matter as has been asserted by some, but it throws into it immence quantities of sand and gives a celerity to it's courant of <of> which it abates but little untill it's junction with the Mississippy. the water of this river is turbid at all seasons of the year but <was> is by no means as much so as that of the Missourie. The sediment it deposits, consists of very fine particles of white sand while that of the Missoury is composed principally of a dark rich loam—in much greater quantity

[*There follows an entry in Lewis' hand, dated July 21, as noted above.*]

21st July   <we made some many experiments to determin the velocity of the courant of the Missoure in different parts> from the experiments and observations we were enabled to make with rispect to the comparative velocities of the courants of the rivers Missouri Mississippi Missouri and Plat <it the following result is> it results that a vessel will float in the Mississippi about below the <mouths> entrance of the Missouri at the rate of four miles an hour. in the Missouri from the it's junction with the Mississippi to the entrance of the Osage river from 5 1/2 to 6 from thence to the mouth of the Kanzas from 6 1/2 to 7. from thence to the Platte 5 1/2 while the Plat <may safely b> is at least 8.—The Missouri above the junction of the river plat is equal to about 3 1/2 miles an hour as far as the mouth of the Chyenne where its courant still abates <to about 3 miles an hour> and becomes equal to about three miles an hour   from information it dose not increase it's volocity for [*Sentence incomplete*]

July 22nd Sunday   Set out verry early with a view of getting Some timbered land & a good Situation to take equil altitudes in time   proceeded on nearly a North 15d W <Course> 7 Ms to a pt S.S. opposit Some high Lands on L.S. above the upper point of a long willow Island in the middle of the river   6 Deer killed to Day   we deturmined to Stay here 4 or 5 days to take & make obsvts & refresh our men   also to Send Despatches back to govement—Wind hard N.W.   Cold.[4]

Cours & Distance
Above the Platt
N. 15° W. 10 Miles to
a point on Sarboord
Side, where we Campd
to delay a few
days—
    W Clark

3. This fragment, in Lewis' handwriting, is a rough draft of his description of the entrance of the Platte into the Missouri, given in his "Summary View of Rivers and Creeks, Etc." (Thw., *6*, 38–39). Lewis completed and revised the "Summary View" at Fort Mandan during the winter of 1804–05 (Thw., *6*, 29 n.). However, it would appear that this rough draft was written while the party was at the mouth of the Platte, since the date, July 21, 1804, appears on the margin and again for the day's entry. The preceding part of the description, which begins here with the words "by a boiling motion," is found in the "Summary" and is as follows:

"Thirty two miles higher up, and distant 630 miles from the confluence of the Missouri and Mississippi, the great river Platte disembogues on the S. [south] side. The steady, regular, and incessant velocity of this stream, is perhaps unequaled by any on ea[r]th; notwithstanding it's great rapidity the surface of the water continues smooth, except when occasionally interrupted—" (Thw., *6*, 38).

This is followed in the "Summary" by a rewrite of Lewis' rough draft given here.

4. Part of the entry for July 21 is written over the following:
        Genl. W. Johnson P M
          Vincennes
      Captn William Clark
      St Louis
        I T
Attention
Jn Hay Esqr
Post Mastr Cahokia

3 | 632

210—2/3

The distance assending the
Missourie from the mouth
each Day &c &c miles

21 from the mouth to St Charles

3 1/4

18

9

10

10

18

15 1/2

104 3/4 To the Gascennade
river. N. S.S.

4 ⎫
17 ⎬ 34
13 ⎭

138 3/4 Great Osarge River South S.

5 ⎫
17 1/2 |
12 ⎬ 63 1/2
14 |
14 ⎭

201 3/4 To the Mine River S.S.

12 ⎫ 25
13 ⎭

226 3/4 To the two Rivers of
Charlton N S.

10 ⎫ 19
9 ⎭

245 3/4 old Missourie Village
N. Side

9

254 1/4 To the Grand River
North Side

8 ⎫
12 |
10 |
17 1/2 |
6 3/4 |
7 1/2 ⎬ 110 Miles from Grd
10 1/2 R. to Kansas
3 1/2 |
11 1/2 |
13 |
9 3/4 ⎭

364 [4 written over 6] 1/4
To the Kansas River
South Side

```
 7  ⎤
10  ⎥
12  ⎥
11 1/2  ⎬ 67
11 1/4  ⎥
15  ⎦
```

431 To the 2d old Village
    of the Kansas

```
433  ⎤
10  ⎥
12  ⎬ 48
14  ⎥
12 1/4  ⎦
```

479 To the Nordaway R: N S.

```
14  ⎤
10  ⎬ 30
 6  ⎦
```

510 1/4 To Grd Ne Ma har R. S.S.

```
20 1/2  ⎤
 9 1/2  ⎥
 9 3/4  ⎬ 0 1/2
20 1/4  ⎦
```

570 1/4 Bald pated Prarie N.S.

```
18  ⎤
10 3/4  ⎥
18  ⎬
14 1/2  ⎦
```

630 T: the Great River Platt
    South Side

```
  2
 ────
    635
  4
  6
 ────
```

642 To the Camp of Observation
    above the R. Platt on
    the right Side

P M		A.M.
h m		
3 − 51 − 56″		8 . 0 . 49
" − 52 − 14		" . 2 . 9
" − 53 − 45		" . 3 . 38

```
altd   72 − 49 − 00
    53   642   12
        53
       ────
       112
       106
       ────
         6
```

The Lattitude of River Debous 38° 55′ 19″ 6/10 N. and Longtd 89° 57′
    45″ W of Greenich

The do—of the gasconade River 38° 44′ 35″ N. & Longtd about 91ᵈ 16″
    00′ W.

The do of the Great Osage River 38° 31′ 6″ N. & Longtd about 91ᵈ 38′.
    W.

5. The place selected for the camp (called White Catfish Camp) was ten miles above the mouth of the Platte. The two captains decided to stop here a few days in order to hold a council with the Oto, whose villages were nearby. All the Indians along the river, including this tribe, had been disturbed by the news that the United States now possessed the country west of the Mississippi. Many of them traded with the Northwest and the Hudson's Bay companies, and the representatives of these companies lost no time in spreading the rumor that their new masters were going to close down the trade. Councils must be held with the chiefs of the tribes "to let them know of the Change of Government the wishes of our government to Cultivate friendship with them, the Objects of our journy and to present them with a flag and Some Small presents" (Thw., *1*, 88).

The do of th[e] mouth of Kansis 39ᵈ 5′ 25″ North
The do of Nordaway river—39. 55. 56.   do
The do of the Bald pated Prarie 40. 27. 6.   do
The do of Camp above River Plate—41. 3. 19—N.

22ⁿᵈ of July 1804   Completlly arranged our Camp, posted a two Sentinals So as to completely guard the Camp, formd bowers for the men &c &c   Course from R Plate N 15ᵈ W. 10 Ms⁵   [*This is Clark's second entry for July 22.*]

FROM THE PLATTE TO THE VERMILION:
JULY 23, 1804—AUGUST 24, 1804

6. Cruzatte is not described in the Note-book Journal as a half-breed.

7. While in camp at the Dubois in January, Clark had started a map "for the purpose of Correcting from the information which I may get of the Country to the N.W." (supra, p. 16). He had apparently added to this map as the party moved upstream and took the opportunity at the camp to start making a copy. Three days later he wrote, "the Wind blew verry hard all Day . . . which incomoded me verry much in my tent, and as I could not Draw in the Boat was obliged [to] combat with the Musqutr under a Shade in the woods." Clark made small sketch maps of portions of the lower river, three of which appear in this journal (Documents 15, 17, 18). He may have made many others; these were preserved because portions of his journal were written over them. Thwaites found 50 detailed maps described by him as made "for the most part by Clark while on the trip," which illustrate the greater part of the journey both going and returning. These were reproduced by Thwaites in the *Atlas* of his edition of the Notebook Journals (Thw., *8*, plates 3–53). The originals are now in the Coe Collection in the Yale University Library. The first of these maps begins with Fort Charles, 80 miles above the Big Sioux River. Thwaites was in error, for he confused Fort Charles with St. Charles, which is only 25 miles from St. Louis (Thw., *8*, plate 5). These maps, of small sections of the route, continue all the way to the Pacific and, on the return, as far as the mouth of the Yellowstone. They differ from the sketch maps in this journal, noted above, for they are much more carefully drawn and in greater detail. Whether the maps given in Thwaites were drawn from rough sketch maps which were later discarded, we have no way of knowing. A map of the river from Camp Dubois to the Mandans was completed by Clark during the winter of 1804–05, and sent downriver when the keelboat left for St. Louis in April 1805. A hand-tracing of this map is reproduced in Coues, *History, 4;* a photo-reproduction of a copy of the lost original may be found in Sara Jones Tucker, *Indian Villages of the Illinois Country*, part 1 (Springfield, 1942); a somewhat later version by the same cartographer, Nicholas King, is in Carl I. Wheat, *Mapping the Transmississippi West* (San Francisco, 1958–61), *2*, 36–37.

8. Clark was preparing his map of the Missouri up to the Platte to send back by one of the pirogues. This move had been planned from the outset. Lewis was also busy preparing reports to send to Jefferson (infra, p. 106).

9. The date notation by Biddle does not head this document but is placed above the entry for July 24.

1. On the Indian Office Map, this river is drawn in but not named. On the Perrin du Lac Map the name *R. Corne du Cerf* is given.

Camp 10 Ms above the river Plate Monday July the 23rd a fair morning—Sent out a party of 5 men to look to timber for ores, two other parties to hunt   at 11 oClock Sent, G. Drewyer & Pete Crusett [Cruzatte] 1/2 Indn[6] to the otteaus [Oto's] Village about 18 Ms West of our Camp, to envite the Chiefs & principal men of that nation to come & talk with us &c &c, also the panis [Pawnee] if they Should meet with any of that nation (also on the S. side of the Plate 30 Ms higher up (at this Season of the year all the Indians in this quater are in the Plains hunting the Buffalow   from some signs seen by our hunter and the Praries being on fire <ner> in the derection of the Village induce a belief that the nation have returned to get green Corn) raised a flag staff   put out Some provisions which got wet in the french Perogue to sun & Dry. I commenced Copying my map of the river[7] to Send to the Presdt of the U S. by the Return of a pty of Soldiers, from Illinois[8]   five Deer Killed—one man a bad riseing on his left breast. Wind from the N.W.

Equal altitudes taken at this place the two following days Viz:

		h	m	s	
July 22nd Sunday A M		8.	53.	53	
		".	55.	20	
		".	56.	48	
			given altitude		
	h	m	s		
P M	2.	58.	37	}	
	3.	0.	0		
	3.	1.	28		
	92d	. 37'.	0.		
	h	m	s		
A M	7	. 33	. 32	}	
	"	. 34	. 55		
	"	. 36	. 22	}	July 26th
P M	4	. 15	. 22	}	
	"	. 16	. 51		
	"	. 18	. 14	}	

July 22. to 27[9]

White Catfish Camp 24th of July Tuesday. a fair morning   the wind rose with the Sun & blows hard from the S.   thos Southerley Breezes are Dry Cool & refreshing, the Northerley Breezes which is more frequent is much Cooler, and moist, I continue my Drawing. Cap Lewis also ingaged prepareing Some paper to send back, one of the men cought a white Catfish, the eyes Small & tale resembling that of a Dolfin.

White Catfish Camp 25th of July Wednesday. Several hunters Sent out. at 2 oClock the Two men Sent to the Otteauz [Oto] Village returned and informed that no Indians were at the Town, they Saw Some fresh Sign near that place which they persued, but Could not find them, they having taken precausions to Conceal the Rout which they went out from the Village—the Inds of the Missouries being at War with one & the other or other Indians, move in large bodies and Sometimes the whole nation Continue to camp together on their hunting pls   Those men inform that they passed thro a open Plain all the way to the Town a feiw Trees excepted on the water courses—they Cross the papillion or the Butterfly Creek within a feiw miles of Camp and near the Village a handsm [handsome] river of 100 yards Wide Called the Corné de chearf [Corne du Cerf] or the Elkhorn,[1] which mouths below the Town in the Plate N.

Side   Wind from the S.E.   2 Dee[r] & a Turkey Killed to Day   Several grous Seen in the Prarie

Whit[e] Catfish Camp 26ᵗʰ of July. Thursday. the Wind blew verry hard all Day from the South with Clouds of Sand which incomoded me verry much in my tent, and as I could not Draw in the Boat was obliged [to] combat with the Musqutr under a Shade in the woods—. I opened the Breast of a man   the discharge gave him ease &c.   5 beaver Caught near Camp—. only I Deer Killed to day. The Countrey back from Camp on the S.S. is a bottom of about 5 ms wide   one half the Distn timber, the other high bottom Prarie, the opsd Side a high Hill about 170 foot rock foundation. timbered back & below. a Prarie

2. Quaife, the editor of the Ordway Journal, identifies this spot as the site of the present city of Omaha (*Ordway*, p. 101 n.).

3. This stream, which enters the Missouri on the starboard side, is a few miles above Council Bluffs, Iowa. Today this stream is known as Pigeon Creek (*Ordway*, p. 102 n.).

Course Distance and reffurence July 27th

North 1 1/2 miles to a Willow point on the L.S.
West 2 do to Sand pt on S.S. opsd a pond L.S.
N. 10° E 3 do to a point of <high Land on> the L.S.   passd a large Sand bar in the river
N. 8. W 4 do to a pt on S.S. opposit a high part of the Prarie
N. 54 E 4 1/2 miles to a coops of wood in a bend to the L.S.   passed a Pt

15

on S.S. opposit the commencement of this Course   I went out on the L.S. at Some riseing land, and found about 200 acres of Land imediately on the river covored with Mouns of Dift hight's & Shapes. a pond back & low land all round—a Beyou above

White Catfish
Camp July 27th Friday, Charged [loaded] the Boat & Perogue after a small Shower of rain, conpleted our ores & poles, crossed over the two horses, with a view of their going on the S W. Side of the Missouri and Set out at Half past 1 oClock   proceeded on verry well under a gentle Breeze, passed a high Island of high wood land on the L. Side just above Camp, this Island is formed by a pond Supplied by great number of Springs from this hill, this Pond has 2 out lets, & when the river is high the water passes thro the Pond, passed a Sand Island in the 2nd bend to the right. Camped in a bend to the <right> L.S. in Som woods,[2] I took R. Fields & walked on Shore & Killed a Deer, and did not get to the Boat untill after night   a butifull Breeze from the N W. this evening which would have been verry agreeable had the musquitors been tolerably pacifick, but they were rageing all night, some about the Sise of house flais [flies ?]

July 28th Satturday   Set out this morning early, the wind blou fron the N.W. by N.   a Dark Smokey Morning, Some rain at 1 Ml   passed a Bluff on the S.S. it being the first high land approachng the river above the Nodaway, a Island and Creek S.S. just abov this creek I call <Bald> Indian Knob[3] G. Drewyer Came with a Dee[r] & informs he heard fireing to the S.W.   I walked on Shore on the S.S.   found some good Prarie out from the S. pt   The High Lands approach the river 1st bend to left   The party on Shore brought in a a Missouri Indian who resides with the Otteauz, this Indian & 2 others were Hunting in the Prarie their Camp is about 4 miles off. This Indian informs that his Nation is in the Plains hunting the Buffalow, the party with which he is encamped is about 20 familey Hunting the Elk, we landed on S.S. below an Island

Course Distance & reffurence's the 28th of July 1804 Satturday

S 82° E 1 mile on the L. Side to pt of a Sand bar L.S
N. 10° W. 1/2 ml on the L.S.   the high land approaches the river on S.S.
{ this is the first place the high land has touched the river above
{ the Nordaway. nearest 3 ms
N. 30° W. 1/2 m on L.S.
N. 77° W 3 m to a point on the L.S.   passed a Island & creek on S.S abov Bluffs
N. 6 [6 written over 7]o W 3 ms to a pt on S.S.   psd the Isd S.S. <& opsd the old Otteaus village> L.S

[*The following is in Lewis' hand:*]

N.   "   " 3/4 m.   the same course continued—

N. 63 E. 2 m. to a pt Lardd opposite to a small <willow> island from

<u>   10. 3/4   </u>   which it is divided by a cannel of [*space*]

                   yards in width

[*End of entry in Lewis' hand*]

                1st course the 29th July

                North 3/4 of a mile on L.S Isld ①

                N. 80° W 1/2 ms to a pt on L.S opsd Bowyer Riv ②

                <N. 85. W 2 ms. to a wood> in a bend L.S High Land

                North 3/4 to pt on S.S.

July 29th Sunday   We Sent one frenchman. le Liberty[4] & the Indian to the Camp to envite the party to meet us at the next bend of High Land on the L.S. a Dark morning   wind from the W.N.W.   rained all last night—Set out at 5 oClock &, proceeded on   passed the Island, opposit this Island on the S.S the Creek called Indian Knob Creek which mouths Several miles on a Direct line below, is within 20 feet of the Missouri & about 5 feet higher

—— The 4 courses of the 29th to come in here

N. 11° E. 3 1/2 miles to an object in the bend Stard Shore (4)

N. 70° W. 2 1/2 Miles to a pt of wood on the S.S.   Saw two black eagles

S. 82 W. 2 miles to a point of timber on the L.S. below a Clean High

         Prarie

S. 8   1   proceeded on 1/2 mile & camped on the S.S.——

       <u>12</u>

Caught three large cat fish to day verry fat   one of them nearly white those Cat are So plenty that they may be caught in any part of this river but few fish of any other Kind——

(4) at the commencement of this course passed much fallen timber apparently the ravages of a dreadfull haricane which had passed obliquely across the river from N.W. to S.E. about twelve months since. many trees were broken off near the ground the trunks of which were sound and four feet in diameter.

     Willard lost his gun in Bowyer R.   R. Fields Dive & brought it up

     All the Wood Land on this part of the Missouries appear to be Confined to the Points & Islands.

     Boyers River[5] is about provably [probably] 25 yds Wide, Willard near loseing his Gun in this river, two men Sick & Sevral with Boils, a Cold Day   Wind from the N W.   Som rain the fore part of the Day.

[*The following figures are scattered through the last paragraph:*]

10	10
15	15
10	10
<u>12</u>	<u>1</u>
<u>47 3/4</u>	<u>36</u>
32	32
80	66

                                   8 [*one figure illegible*]

4. This is Le Bartee, whose name is on the July 4 list of the party that Clark made when the party was encamped at the mouth of the Platte (supra, p. 69). This is the first mention of him in the journals (Thw., *1*, 93). Ordway calls him Jo Barter (p. 102 and n.).

5. This stream is on the Indian Office Map, where it is labeled Boyer's River and *d a Voyer*. Mackay's Table of Distances calls it Boyer River.

6. See supra, p. 90 n.

7. Here, some 25 miles above the site of the present city of Council Bluffs and on the west bank of the Missouri, the party held its first Indian Council, July 31 to Aug. 3. Ordway was as impressed with the beauty of the spot as Clark, and noted that "it is the Smothest & prittyset place for a town I ever Saw" (*Ordway*, p. 103). This is the "Handsom Prarie" of the Notebook Journal, to which the two captains gave the name Council Bluff, where they held their council with the Oto (infra, pp. 95–97; Thw., *1*, 98).

8. The French is *blaireau*.

9. The first mention of Floyd's illness. On the next day Floyd himself wrote in his Journal, "I am verry Sick and Has ben for Somtime but have Recoverd my helth again" (Thw., *7*, 22). On the following day, Ordway mentioned Floyd's sickness (*Ordway*, p. 104). Not until Aug. 19 does Clark mention it in the Notebook Journal (Thw., *1*, 114).

July the 30ᵗʰ Monday   Set out early & proceeded on West 3 3/4 mls passd one pt to the L.S and one to the S.S. to a Clear open Prarie on the L.S. which is on a rise of about 70 feet higher than the bottom which is also a prarie covered with high grass Plumbs Grape Vine & Hezel—both forming a Bluff to the River, the Lower Prarie is above high water mark at the foot of the riseing ground & below the High Bluff   we came to in a grove of timber and formed a Camp   raised a flag Pole, and deturmend to waite for the Ottu Indians—The White Horse which we I found below Died last night, after posting out the guards &c &c Sent out 4 men to hunt. I am ingaged in [*space*] and Drawing off my courses to accompany the map Drawn at White Catfish Camp,⁶ Capt Lewis and my Self walked in the Prarie on the top of the Bluff and observed the most butifull prospects imagionable, this Prarie is covered with grass about 10 or 12 Inchs high, (Land rich)   rises about 1/2 [1/2 written over 1] a mile back Something higher. and is a Plain as fur as can be seen, under those high Lands next the river is butifull Bottom interspersed with Groves of timber,⁷ the River may be Seen for a great Distance both above & below Meandering thro: the plains between two ranges of High land which appear to be from 4 to 20 ms apart, each bend of the river forming a point which Contains tall timber, principally Willow Cotton wood some Mulberry elm sycamore & ash   the groves contain walnit coffee nut & oake in addition & Hickory & Lynn [Linden]   Jo. Fields Killed Brarow [Badger]⁸ or as the Ponie [Pawnee] call it Cho car tooch, this animale burrows in the ground & feeds on Bugs and flesh principally the little Dogs of the Prarie, also Something of vegetable kind   his Shape & size is like that of a Beever, his head Mouth &c is like a Dog with its ears cut off, his tale and hair like that of a Ground hog   Something longer and lighter, his internals like a Hogs, his Skin thick & loose, white & hair short under its belly, of the Species of the Bear, and it has a white Streake from its nose to its Sholders, the Toe nails of its fore feet which is large is 1. Inch and 3/4 qtr long and those of his hind feet which is much Smaller is 3/4 long. Short legs, raseing himself just above the ground when in motion We have this animale Skined and stuffed   Jo & R. fields Killed som Deer at a Distance and Came in for a horse to bring them in, they have not returned this evening, a gred number of Swans in a pond above L.S. [opposite] to our Camp. Serjt Floyd verry unwell   a bad Cold &c.⁹ Several men with Boils, great Qts of Catfish   G. D [George Drouillard] Cought one Small Beever alive. Som Turkey & Gees Killed to day. arms & all things in order. a fair evining, and Cool.

July 31ˢᵗ Tuesday   a fair Day   3 hunters out this morning   G. Drewyer Killed a verry fat Buck one Inch fat on the ribs   Merdn altd Latd is. 41ᵈ 18' 0" 5/10—North. R & Jo: Fields returned at 10 oClock   the[y] Killed 3 Deer, and lost the horses, cought a small Beever which is already taim, Several men out hunting the horses without Sucees, The Ottoes not yet arrived, I complete the copy of the Courses &c. &c.   Musqueters verry troubleson

August the 1ˢᵗ 1804   a fair morning, Sent out two men after the horses & one back to examine if the Indians have been there, [*space*] Beever Cought last night, the air is cool and pleaseng

	azmth	altd
Comp.	N. 86ᵈ E.	68ᵈ 47' 15"

Equal altitudes. & magnitu.   Azmoth

Time	m	s		h.	m	s.
= A.M.	7 – 52	. 55	p.m	3 – 50 – 42		
"	– 54 – 20			" – 52 – 3		
"	– 54	47		" – 53 – 31		

Prepared the Pipe of Peace   verry flashey. wind rose at 10 oClock and blowed from the W.S.W. very pleasent all day   Several men geathering grapes &c two men after the horses which Strayed the night before last. those Praries produce the current blue common in the U.S.   the Goose Berry Common in the U.S,   two Kind of Honeysuckle, the Bush which I have Seen in Kentucky, with a paile Pink flower, also one which grow in Clusters about 4 or 5 feet high bearing a Short flour in clusters of the like colour. the leaves single

This being my birth day I order'd a Saddle of fat vennison, an Elk fleece & a Bevartail to be cooked and a Desert of Cheries, Plumbs, Raspberres currents and grapes of a Supr qualtity.[1]

3 Deer & an Elk Killed to day   The Indians not yit arrived. a Cool fine eveninge Musquetors verry troublesom, the Praries Contain Cheres, Apple, Grapes, Currents, Raspburry, Gooseberry Hastlenuts and a great vairety of Plants & flours not common to the U S.   What a field for a Botents [botanist] and a natirless [naturalist]

August 2nd 1804 wind from the S E G: Dreweey returned with the horses & one Doe Elk   the countrey thro which he passed is like what we See from the Bluff above Camp   three men out Hunting one Beaver caught this morning. at Sunset 6 chiefs and their warries [warriors] of the Ottos, and Missoures,[2] with a french man by the name of Far fonge,[3] we <Spoke> Shook hands and gave them Some Tobacco & Provisions, they Sent us Water Millions   Three verry large & fat Bucks Killed to day   the wind continued hard from the S.E.—the 4 qtr of one Buck weigh'd 147 lb 1 1/2 Inch fat on the ribs

August 3rd Friday   prepare a Small preas[en]t for those Indians and hold a Councul Delivered a Speech & made 8 6 chief[4] [blot] gave a fiew preasents and, a Smoke a Dram, Some Powder & Ball [blot]—the man we <lef> Sent not yet come up, [La Bartie] Those people express great Satisfa[ct]ion at the Speech Delivered they are no oreters, big, open Counternances, ottoes large Missor [Missouri] Small at 4 oClock Set out under a gentle Breeze from the S.E proceeded on N. 5 d E 5 Ms Passed a Pt on the S.S. and round a large-Sand bar on the L.S. and Camped above, below a great number of Snags quet [quite?] across the river, The Musquetors more numerous than I ever Saw them, all in Spirrits, we had Some rough Convasation G. Dr. [Drouillard] about boys.

1. Clark was thirty-four. This little celebration is not mentioned in the Notebook Journal (Thw., *1*, 96) or in any of the journals of the men. The term "fleece" was usually applied to the meat taken from both sides of the hump of a buffalo. This apparently applies to the fat meat lying on the shoulders of an elk. This passage is modestly inserted between the lines in writing so fine as to be almost illegible.

2. After more than a week of waiting the chiefs and their followers came in from the plains. The Missouri, who had lived downriver and who had been so decimated by their enemies and by smallpox, had come up and joined forces with their friends, the Oto. Both tribes were small and weak and were in constant danger from the more powerful tribes around them, particularly the Pawnee.

3. The Notebook Journal (Thw., *1*, 97) has the name as Mr. Fairfong. He was interpreter for the Oto and lived with them (infra, p. 110). I am unable to identify this person. Jackson suggests that Fairfong may have gone downriver after the Oto council and reported to Chouteau in St. Louis that the party had reached the Platte. Chouteau then sent the news to Jefferson (Jackson, pp. 216–17 n., 219 n.). See the Introduction.

4. This brief notation concerning the giving of medals to the chiefs is enlarged upon by Clark farther on, in the entry for Aug. 3.

5. Clark's conjecture that the various Indian tribes he listed "once formed 3 great Nations" is erroneous. Hodge states that the Osage, Kansas, Ponca, Omaha, and Quapaw at one time formed an associated group—the Dhegiha—of Siouan stock (F. W. Hodge, ed., *Handbook of American Indians,* 2 vols. Washington, 1907–10, 2, 119, hereafter cited as Hodge). The Missouri, Iowa, and Oto were another traditionally associated group of the Siouan family—the Chiwere (ibid., p. 164–65).

The second "great nation" of Clark, the Pawnee, Loup, Republican, and the Arikara is also incorrect. There was a Pawnee confederacy (ibid., p. 214) composed of the Grand Pawnee or the Chaui, the Republican or Kitkehahki, who lived on the Republican River, the Tapage or Pitahauerat, and the Loup or Skidi. This last group had been associated with the Arikara, whom Clark gives as the fourth tribe of the "great nation." By the time Lewis and Clark encountered them, they had parted from the Skidi and were located between the Grand and Cannonball rivers, over 700 miles farther upstream (ibid., 1, 83–84).

As to the third "great nation," the Mandan, Cheyenne, and Gros Ventre, there is again nothing to support Clark's theory. The Mandan were closely associated at this time with the Gros Ventre of the Missouri or Hidatsa (ibid., pp. 508, 796–98). There appears to have been no association of these two tribes with the Cheyenne.

Clark also lists a fourth nation, "The tribes of the Soux all retain the same name." Here Clark is on safe ground, for Dorion, who had lived with the Sioux for 25 years, could enlighten him. There were eight bands of the Sioux, and they did constitute a "nation," the Dakota (ibid., 2, 579).

6. One of the four tribes of the Pawnee Confederacy, called by the fur traders the Republican Indians because their range was along the river of that name, which flows through southern Nebraska and east-central Kansas where it joins the Kansas River.

7. See infra, note 3.

8. Some of these medals have been found in various places near the route taken by the party. They were hollow and made of silver. On the obverse side was a profile of Jefferson with the legend, "Th. Jefferson President of the United States, A.D. 1801." On the reverse side there were clasped hands, a crossed pipe, a battle-ax, and the words, "Peace and Friendship" (Wheeler, 2, 123–24). These medals were of various grades. The grade given to a chief depended on his importance. Clark's wording, "made 1 Great Chief," means that he conferred on the chief of the Oto a medal of the first rank. See Clark's list of Oto and Missouri chiefs given farther on in the entry for Aug. 3. In the list of supplies made by Clark when the goods were being packed at Dubois, there are three large medals and 71 of smaller sizes (Thw., 6, 276).

[The following are the speeches and notes made by Clark at the council with the Oto:]

The Osage & Kansies are the Same language
the Ottoes & Mahars [Omaha] Speek many words of the Osarge language
The Ottos, Aiaways [Iowa], & Missouries Speake the Same language
the Panies [Pawnee] & Recreries [Arikara] Speak the Same language also
        the Loups & repub. [Republican]
the Mahar, & Poncarar [Ponca] the Same Language
The Cheaun [Cheyenne], Mandin & Grovanter [Gros Ventre] the Same

The Probibility is that those defferant tribes have once formed <one> 3 great nats.[5] Viz: the Missouries, Osarge, Kanzes, Ottoes, Mahars, & Poncaras & arauaies [Iowa]   one nation.
The Panies, Loups, Republican,[6] Recrerces the 2nd
The Mandans Cheeons, & Grovanters the 3rd
T[he] tribes of the Soux all retain the name 4th

It is possible that the <Mandain>, Mahar & Poncarear may have been a Distinct nation, as they only Speek Some words of the osage. which have the Same Signification
25 Day to St Ta fee [Santa Fe] S. of W. Cross the heads of Arkansas around the head of Kanzies River[7]

after Delivering a Speech informing thos Children of ours of the Change which had taken place, the wishes of our government to Cultivate friendship & good understanding, the method of had [*sic*] good advice & Some Directions, we made <8> 1 Great Chief to [of] the [Oto, We-ar-ruge-nar, Little Thief] who was not present, to whom we adressed the Speech & Sent some presents a Meadele[8] & flag, we Made 2 second Chiefs one for the Missouris & another for the Ottos (those two tribes are nearly equal 170 each) and 4 principal men, to thos principal men to thos we gave a Small Comtn [Commission] to each man to whom w[e] gave authority, a preasn of br. Clt [breech clout] Gart[erin]g Paint & a medl or Contn [Commission]   a Small Coms [Commission] was delivered for the whole[9]

each Chief & principal man delivered a Speech acknowledging ther approbation to what they had heard and promised to prosue the good advice and Caustion, they were happy [with?] <ther> new fathers who gave good advice & to be Depended on   all Concluded by asking a little Powder. & a Drop of milk. [whiskey]

  186 – 64
 1434 – 5
  108
———————
1728 – 69

I answered those speeches   gave them 50 balls one Canuter [Canister] of Powder & a Dram—after Cap Lewis Shot his air gun a few times which astonished the nativs,[1] we Set Sail. recved from thos people water millions &—

The Cheifs & Principal men of the ottoes & Missoures made by M L. & W C
the 3rd August 1804

Viz.	Indian Names	Tribe	English signification
1.	We-ar-ruge-nar	Ottoe	Little Thief
2. {	Shingo-ton go	Otto	Big horse
{	We tha a	Missouree	Hospatallity

	Shon-Guss-can	Ottoe[2]
	Wau-pe-ur	Miss
3[d]	Au-ho-ning ga	M
	Ba Za con ja	Ottoes
	Au-ho-ne-ga	Miss

from this place I am told by Mr Fauforg the interpeter that it will take a man 25 Days to go to St a fee [Santa Fe], pass the heads of Arkansas, round the Kansas head, across some mountains from the top of which the City may be seen   the Spaniards have envited those Indians & the Panies [Pawnee] to trade with them & some french & a few indians are gorn from the Panias to that city this summer—[3]

The Situation of this place which we Call Council Bluff which is handsom ellevated   a Spot well Calculated for a Tradeing establishment, the Bank high & leavel on top well calculated for a fort to command the Countrey and river   the low bottom above high water & well situated under the Command of the Hill for Houses to trade with the natives[4]   a butifull Plain both abov and below   at no other bend on either side does the High land touch the river for Some distance up, as I am told.

those Bluffs afford good Clay for Brick, a great quantity on the 3 points one opsd one abov & one below.—the Situation I am informed is, within 1 Days march of the Ottoes, 1 1/2 of the Panias, 2 of the Mahars, & 2 1/2 of the Loups Villages, also Convenient to the roveing Bands of Soux, Those people are now at war with each other, an establishment here would bring about peace and be the means of keeping of it.[5]

9. These "commissions" were printed forms, to be issued to Indian chiefs who showed that they were friendly to their new rulers, the United States. They were filled out with the names of the chief and the tribe. The chief was to acknowledge the authority of the United States and promise to live in peace. All citizens of the United States were charged to treat the said chief and his tribe in a friendly manner, for they were under the protection of the United States. The smaller and weaker tribes probably felt that it would do no harm to have such a paper. Several of these blank forms have been preserved. A copy of one is found in Thw., *1*, 113 n. (infra, p. 150 n.).

1. This is the first appearance of Lewis' prized air gun since it was used to astonish the natives at Marietta, Ohio (supra, p. 7 n.). On that occasion the demonstration nearly ended in tragedy. We have no record from the Indians as to whether they were much impressed.

There were two types of air guns available at the time, one with the compressed air stored in a ball-shaped reservoir beneath the barrel, the other with the reservoir in the butt of the gun. Such guns were being made in the United States and in England and Germany.

2. In the Notebook Journal (Thw., *1*, 98), Shon-Guss-can is translated as White Horse.

3. Santa Fe, and the trade that might be opened with that distant outpost, were involved in Jefferson's thinking as he considered the possibilities growing out of the Lewis and Clark exploration. In his instructions to Lewis of June 20, 1803, he urged Lewis to get information as to the Rio Grande and its distance from the Missouri (Thw., 7, 249–50; Jackson, p. 63).

This was undoubtedly in Lewis' mind when, on his way down the Ohio, he wrote to the President from Cincinnati on Oct. 3, 1803: "I have concluded to make a tour this winter on horse back of some hundred miles through the most interesting portion of the country adjoining my winter establishment; perhaps it may be up the Canceze [Kansas] River and toward Santafee, at all events it will bee on the South Side of the Missouri" (Thw., 7, 279; Jackson, p. 131). This daring scheme of Lewis was immediately vetoed by Jefferson. In his letter to Lewis, dated Washington, Nov. 16, 1803, the President strongly advised the Captain not to enter the Missouri until spring and added, "you must not undertake the winter excursion which you propose in yours of Oct. 3. Such an excursion . . . would, by an accident to you hazard, our main object. . . . The object of your mission is single, the direct water communication from sea to sea formed by the bed of the Missouri & perhaps the Oregon" (Thw., 7, 282; Jackson, p. 137).

Jefferson went on to say that other expeditions were contemplated, one up the Red River and down the Arkansas, another along the tributaries of the Platte, and a third, an exploration of the Des Moines and St. Peters rivers. These plans of Jefferson matured in the William Dunbar expedition to the Washita in 1805–06, the expedition up the Red, led by Thomas Freeman in 1806, and Zebulon Pike's exploration of the Upper Mississippi in 1805–06 and his journey up the Arkansas in 1806–07.

In Lewis' "Summary of Rivers and Creeks" compiled at Fort Mandan in the winter of 1804–05 (Thw., *6*, 40), the Platte was described as "passing the heads of the Arkansas at no great distance from Santa Fee." Clark laid down a route on his map from the Platte to Santa Fe.

The traders at St. Louis were eager to use the lower portion of the Missouri and its tributaries to get to the southwest. The expedition was only a few miles from home on its return when it met a large boat going upstream. A former army officer, one Captain McClellan, was in charge. He told the two captains that he was on his way to the Platte, and from there he intended to follow the route "to the confines of New Spain," where he hoped to open trade with Santa Fe (Thw., *5*, 387). For further information on McClellan, see Chittenden, *1*, 160–63.

4. This spot, which the explorers named Council Bluff, is not to be confused with the site of the present city of that name located on the east bank of the Missouri several miles downstream (supra, p. 94 n.). In Clark's plan for the defense of the west, made after his arrival at Fort Mandan (infra, p. 188), Council Bluff was one of the locations selected by him as a site for a fort and trading house. Fifteen years later, in 1819, Col. Henry Atkinson established a fort there that bore his name. In his opinion this was "the most desirable outpost on the continent." However, it was abandoned in 1827 as no longer important in the defense of the frontier (*The Story of Fort Atkinson*, Washington County Historical Society, Fort Calhoun, Nebraska, n.d.).

5. The above is written over the following rough draft of a pay roll:

a/c	Term of Service Charged		Pay per Month		Amount of Pay		Bounty recd
	Months	Days	Drs	Cents	Dollars	Cents	

Cash recevd in Lieu of Clothing & Provisions		Total Amount Received		Remarks
Dolls	Cts	Dolls	cents	

Augt 3ᵈ   Camped on the upper point of a large Sand bar L.S.   Misqu-
ters verry bad. Some place near Conncile Bluff will be the most proper
place for a tradeing establishment, for maney of the nations, the distance
is to the Ottoes one Days, Ponies [Pawnees] 1 1/2 days, to the Mahar, 2
days, to Loups 2 Days & a half 16 or 1800 men [?]—and convenient for
Some <Republicans are also> bands of the Sues[6]

[*The following line that is crossed out is in Clark's hand:*]
                                                    St Louis
<Your letter of the 7ᵗʰ of Feby I recved With great pleasure>

                                                Aug 3 to 6

Course Distance & Reffurance August 4ᵗʰ Satturday, 1804
S. 80° W. 1 1/2 Ml to an old Tradeing house on the L.S.   passed a Sand
        pt Makeing from S. pt ① bad ps
N. 25 W. 2 1/4 mls to a Willow pt on the L.S.   passed a large Sand bar
        ② psd a Creek on L.S. ③
S. 70. W. 1 3/4 Ms to a Willow point on S.S.   passed maney Snags. opsd
        a Creek of the Ponds L.S.
N. 24 W. 2 1/2 Ms to a Willow point on L.S.   passed a Sand from S.
        Point
N. 24 W. 3 1/2 Ms to a Copse of willows in a bend L.S.   willow pt on the
        S.S. opsd a <Smooth Plain,> river verry wide & shallow
S. 84 E. 3 1/2 Mls to a point Lard side passing a <Stard> pot on Stard
        side. Wind E. due
        ———
        15

        1/2
        3 1/4
        4 1/2
        1 1/4
        2 1/4
        ———
        12

The high land is Some distanc from the river on both Sides and at this
place is <not within 20 miles of> apt [approximately?] 10 or 12 Miles a
part, the tops of the high land on the S.S. appiair to contain <more timber that [*one word illegible*] on the Larboard Side, the willow is low &
not so plenty as below.>

August 4ᵗʰ   at 7 oClock the heavens darkened and a violent wind from
the N W. suckceeded which lasted about <half> an hour, with a little
rain. Set out this morning early thro a narrow part of the whole Channel
Confined in some parts between the ① Sand on one Side & the bank on
the other (which is washing in) within 200 yards, this Chanl Crowded
with Snags. at 1 1/2 m: passed an old tradeing house L.S. where one of
our Crew passed 2 years P. C. [Pierre Cruzatte] tradeing with the Mahar
[Omaha]; & Ponies [Pawnee],—[7] above 1 ml a ③ Creek Coms in opsd a
large bad ② Sand bar   this ③ Creek is the outlett of 3 ponds, which
recved ther water from the Smaller Streams running from the hills on
the L.S, Great qts of Gees, passed in the next bend L.S. an out let to the
Pond, Butifull bottom Prarie on both Sides of the river, Pumuy Stone is
found on the Sides of the river of various Sizes. Wind a head. Reed the
man who went back to the Camp of last night for his Knife has not Come
up this evening—[8] we camped at <the> a pt on the L. S. at a Beaver
house. 1 Buck Killed to daye.

6. This is a second entry for Aug. 3.

7. This old trading house may be the one
established by Mackay when he led his expedition up the Missouri in the summer of
1795. By October he had reached the villages
of the Oto. Near their villages, he built a
house and left some traders there, while he
continued up the river to the Omaha villages
where he built a fort, Fort Charles (infra, p.
107), and remained there that winter (Nasatir, *1*, 97–108; *2*, 460–64). This entry places
Cruzatte with the Mackay expedition, or at
the fort, sometime after 1795. If so, he was a
very valuable man to have along, for his
knowledge of the river, the Indians, and the
previous trading ventures would have been
invaluable.

8. Nor did he come back until captured
and brought back as a prisoner. See infra, pp.
100, 107–08.

9. The *R. des Soldats* of the Indian Office Map.

1. The desertion of Read was the most serious breach of discipline the party was to encounter on the whole trip. Rigorous measures had to be taken and an example made, or the success of the expedition would be imperiled. Read, according to Sergeant Floyd, went back "to Git his Knife [Aug. 4] which he Had Left at the Camp the Boat went on and He Did not Return, that night nor the next day nor Night, pon examining his nap-Sack we found that he had taken his Cloas and all His powder and Balles, and had hid them out that night and had made that an excuse to Desarte from us with out aney Just Case. . . . we expect he will make for the ottoe town . . . not mor than 2 days Jorney from whare he Run away from us" (Thw., 7, 24).

August 5th Set out early wind from N E. Great appearance of Wind & rain, (I have remarked that I have not heard much thunder in this Countrey) <lightning is Common as in other Countries> a verry large Snake was Killed to day called the Bull Snake, his Colour Some thing like a rattle Snake Something lighter—the bends of the river to day is washing away the banks, haveing nothing to oppose the turbelance of the [river] when Confined by large hard sand Points, forceing this Current against the bends—the Soil of the entire bottom between the high land, being the mud or ooze of the river of some former period mixed with Sand & clay easely Melts and slips, or washies into the river the mud mixes with the water & the sand collects on the points Camped on the S.S.—I went on on Shore S.S. this evening Saw Some turkeys and in persueing them Struck the river 12 miles below the place by water I went out, I think the Peninsul is about 370 yards across subjuct to overflow, & washes into numerous Channels, Great quantites of Graps ripe & of three Defurent Kind Some large & fine. I Killed a Turkey, and made Camp in the night, musqutors verry troublesom—Reed the man who went back for his Knife has not yet joined us———

Courses & Distance of Aug 5th Sunday

S. 60° E. 1 1/2 across a large Sand bar to a point on M Stbd Shore below a large willow Island on S. Bend

N. 20 W. 3/4 Ms to a pt above a Sand bar on the opsd the upper pt of the Island, (much Beaver Sign)

N. 34 W 3 1/4 Ms to a pt on the L.S. passed one on the L.S.

North 3/4 m. to a pt on the right of a Sand Island. making from the L. Pt

S. 45 W. <to> 2 1/4 Ms to a 3 Small trees in a Bend L.S. passi'g over a Sand point S.S.

N. 45 W 4 1/2 Ms to a point on S.S. the High land Grat Distance from the R

North 1 1/4 on the S.S. to a pt of Sand bar—opsd a falling in bank river narrow

N. 70 E. 1/4 on the S. Sand bar

S. 30 E. 2 Ms to the pt of a Sand bar makeing out from the L. point the same continued 1/2 miles Psd a Sand in the Md

N. 45 E. 2 1/2 [*Beginning of handwriting of Lewis:*] to the <mouth>
————
20 1/2

lower point of an Island close to Stard Shore it behind this Island on the Stard side that the Soldier's river disimbogues itself [*End of entry by Lewis*]

August 6th Monday 1804 at 12 oClock last night a violent Storm of wind & rain from the N.W. one Perogue (Bapteest Le Joness [La Jeunesse] Patroon) lost her colours Set out early & proceeded on passed a large Island on the S.S. back of this Island Rivie de Soldiert come in on the S.S.—the Solder's [Soldier's][9] river is about the Sise of Nodaway 20 yd wide at the mouth, passed two remarkable places, where the River had once <river> Passed———[*one word illegible*] We have every reason to belive that one man has Deserted Moses B: Reed he has been absent three Days and one french man [La Bartie] we Sent to the Indian Camps has not joined us, we have reasons to beleve he lost himself in attempting to join us at the Councel Bluff—we are deturmend to Send back 4 men to take reede Dead or alive,[1] also hunt La Liberty and to meet us at the Mahar [Omaha] nation as Soon as the order is executed.

Course Distance reffurence. 6th Augt Monday 1804

N. 30° E 1 Ml to a pt on the L.S. the Island opposit and about opsd Soldier's River

N. 15 E 3 1/2 Ms to pt in a bend S S below <these the> a chanl of the river lately filled up   passed a Sand bar below making from pt below the upr pt of R. ① This Island is Seperated from the L.S by a Chanl of 40 yds.   Swift Crt

West 1 mile to a pt of woods above a large Sand bar Makeing out from the L. poent.

West 1 1/2 Ms to a pt on L.S. Willows

S. 55 W. 3 1/2 Ms to a pt of Willows on the S.S.   the lands naked & within 3 Ms of the R. Ld [Larboard]

N. 10 W. 1/2 on the S. pt   a Sand bar in the Middle

N. 18. E 3 mile passing over a Sand bar on L.S. to a pt on the Same Side.

North 1 1/2 Ml to a pt on the S.S.

N. 18. W 1/2 on the Sand bar. from the pt

East 3 <1/2> to a pt Willows making from the L. point   psd a place of snags

N 16. E 1 1/2 Ms to a pt on the S.S.   an old bed of the River S.S. but fiew <no> Snakes on this part of the river

⎯⎯⎯⎯
20 1/2

August 7th Tuesday   last night about 8 oClock a Storm of wind from the N.W. which last 3/4 of an hour   Mosquetors more troublesom last night than I ever saw them, Set out late this morning   wind N.

Course Dis

North 2 ms to a pt of Willows on the L.S. opposit, Saw 10 Pelicans flying

N. 25. W. 1/2 Ml on the L point   N. 45 W. 1/2 Ml on the L. point of a Sand bar

N 45 W. 1 Ml to the point of a Sand bar makeing out from the L pt

S 12 E 2 1/2 Ml to the do—do [ditto, refers to line above, "L. pt of a Sand Bar"] from the St. Point   Win fair—

S. 70 E.—1/2 ml to the Willows on the S.S.   G. Drewyer, R. Fields, W. Bratten & Wm Labuse [La Biche], sent after Reed Deserted, La Liberty absent & a Speech to the ottoes with a view to get a feew of their Chief to the Mahars to make a peace between them, Sent Some Tobacco, Wampon, and Speech   als[o] gave pointed orders to the party in writeing

N. 36 W. 2 1/2 Ms to a pt of Willows on the L S.   a large Sand [bar?] makeing out from it—

N. 73. W. 3 Ms to a pt of Willows S.S.   I went out and discovered that two Bayoues run thro the point & Cutit [Cut it] into Island, which I call Detachment Islands as from this bend We detached Dreweys R. Fields Bratten & Labeccue [Labiche]   no game of any Kind

N. 83° E 2 1/2 Ms to a pt of Cotton wood, passing over a Sand bar from the Said point

N. 32. W. 1 1/2 Ms to a Sand point makeing out from the S. point

N. 12 E 1/2 M to the willows on the S.S. and camped[2]

⎯⎯⎯⎯
16

　　　　leav
suger 60 = 150
salem [?] 110 = 300
⎯⎯⎯⎯
450

2. The entries for Aug. 6 and 7 are written over the following:
Jeffersonville I.T. Feb 9th
　　　　　　　　　　　　　25
　　　Capt William Clark
　　　　　near
　　　Cahokia

By
Mail

3. This was John Dame, who was sent back to St. Louis with the party from Fort Mandan in April 1805 (*Ordway,* p. 107 and n.).

4. The Little Sioux River. This is one of Clark's more bizarre efforts at spelling the word Sioux. On his map, drawn when the expedition returned in 1806, he had not yet achieved success. Ordway, in his entry for Aug. 8, spells it "Cueox."

5. The Sioux name for stone. The Little Sioux, called the First River of the Sioux in Mackay's Table of Distances (Nasatir, 2, 489), and *petite Rive Des Sioux* on the Indian Office Map, was a part of an important trade route that led from the Missouri up the Little Sioux to its headwaters, thence to the Upper Des Moines and down that river to the Mississippi.

6. This lake, in northern Iowa close to the Minnesota line, was in 1857 the scene of the massacre of some 30 settlers who had taken up land on this exposed frontier. Their attackers were a renegade band of Wahpekute Sioux, who had returned to their lands from which they had been excluded by treaty in 1851 (Hodge, 2, 902–03).

Course Distance & reffurenc August the 8th Wednsday 1804
N. 20° E 2 miles to the pt of a Sand Isld from the S S.   the river narrow
      & choked up with Snags ①
S. 50 E 2 Mls to a pt of Willows on the L.S.   Dame[3] Killed a Pelican
East—1/2 mile on the Side of Sand Island from the L. pt
North 1 1/2 ms to the mouth of little Rivers De <Peux> Cucoux
      [Sioux].[4] S.S. ②
N. 70° W. 2 Ms to the Lower point of an Island/ on the [*space in MS*]
      no ③ water,
N. 20 W. 1 Ml to a pt on the right Side of the Island
N. 52 W. 7 Ms to a pt of high wood in a bend to the L.S.   passed the Isd
     ——
     16
          at 1/4 of a Ml on the point of which was great numbers of
          Peli[c]an   river wide & Shoal. <Cap Lewis took Medr altd>
Half altitide of ⊙[s] below Little S. river S.S
h   m
8. – 26. 59
8 – 28. 29
8 – 30. .8
   —————
   altitude
   —————
   d   m   "
   80 – 14 – 15   1 1/2 Ms below Littl. R. de Sous

    I walked on Shore with one man Collins,—the bottoms Covered with very [*Sentence incomplete*]   Collin Killed an elk, I fired 4 times at one & have reasons to think I kiled him but could not find him, The Misqutors were So troublesom and thick Musqutors in the Plains that I could not Keep them out of my eyes, with a bush. in my absens Capt Lewis Killed a Pelican on Pelicans Island, at which place maney Hundreds had collected, they left 3 fish which was fresh and very good, we camped on the S.S. in a streght part of the river———

    August the 8th 1804   Set out this morning at the usial time at about 2 miles ①   passed a part of the river so choked up with Snags that we found a little dificult to get thro' with Safty, the wind as usial from the N W.   one of the Soldiers Killed a Pelican on the Sand Isd   passed the mouth of little ② River de Cucoux on the S.S.   this river is about 80 yards wide & navagable for Pirogus Some distance & runs parrelel to the Missourie   it coms in from the River from the N E,   it contains great Quantitys of fish Common to the Countrey. two miles above is ③ an Island   the Channel formerly run on the right <but that side is now nearly filled up> with Sand   many hundreds of pelicans on this Island —we call it Pelican Island   Capt Lewis Killed one   this river Soux Called by the Sueoux Ea-Neah Wau-de-pon.[5] is Stone R heads in three Leagues of the river Demoin, and passes thro a Lake about 20 legues in sircfs [circumference] which is also within 5 Leagus of the Demoin, this lake at one place is confined by two rocks within a narrow Space <also> this lake of Different wedth, with many small Islands, from the Lake to the Mahars about <60 or 70 miles>. F[rench] leagus distant 4 Days march to the Dog Plains [Prairie du Chien] 90 leagues, one Principal branch of the Demoin is called Cat river, the Lake which this river Litt Souex heads in is Called Despree [d'Esprit][6]
Cap Lewis took Merdn altitude and made the Lattetude. 41[d] – 42' – 34. 3/10 North. altd of Sun ⊙ – 56[d] – 9' – 00" –

Course distance & reffurence the 9th of August Thursday

N. 30° E 2 1/2 Ms to the pt of a Sand bar on the L. Side   Wind fair

N. 32. W. 1 Ml to the pt of High Woods on the L. Side

N. 22° W. 2 1/2 Ms to a Pt of high woods on S. S.—a large Sand bar makeing out from it

N. 15° W. 2 Ms to a pt of High land, L. S opsd to which the River latterly run, & a Circut of 5 Leagues has been cut off. the old channel is Ponds & Isds

[*The following is in Lewis' hand:*]

N 15. W. <2. M. across a large Sand bar to a point of woods> on Lard
Shore, this is opposite to the cut point. 6 leagues arround

N. 46. W. 1 1/2 M to willow point on stard Side

N. 35° W. 2 M.—S S.   the river now came gradually arround to the E. of
north. no point appearing

N. 60° E. 2 1/2 miles, to a willow point on Lard side—

N. 44 W. 3 1/2 miles to point Stard. Shore.
<u>   </u>

17 [7 written over 5] 1/2
                  <N. 60 W 1 3/4 to a pt of> Sand L.S.

2 1/2

3 1/2   [*End of entry in Lewis' hand*]

5
<u>   </u>
11

1 1/2
<u>   </u>
12 1/2

Aug 9th to 12

9th Augt Thursday 1804   The fog of this morning detained us untill 1/2
passed 7 oClock at which time we left our moreing and proceeded on under a gentle Breeze from the S.E,[7]   I went on Shore   found the Land
the Same as yesterday   Killed a Turkey. and camped on the L.S.   great
deel of Beaver Sign to day   one Beaver Cought   Musquetors worse this
evening than ever I have Seen them.

August 10th

Course Distance and remarks 10th of August 1804 Friday.

                                        d 3/4

N. 60° W. 2 ms to a pt of Sand making from the L. point

S. 80° W. 1/2 Ml on the [*sic*] to a Drift wood. This place is called Coupe
a Jarche[8]   a place where the river cut through and shortend
the River Sevl mls

South 18° E, 2 1/2 Ms to som snags near some Willows on the S.S.   passd
the High <land> wood on L.S. in this Co's at 1 ml

S. 20° W. 2 1/2 ms to a <Black> Burnt Stump on the the Bank in the
bend to L.S. at which place I was yesterday at this place within
3/4 of a mile & round the bends 13 ms

West 3 1/2 Ms to two Cotton wood trees at the Mouth of a Small Creek
in a bend to the L.S.   near the high land a <Bluff> clift &c 1
ml above.

N. 40 W. 1. 1/2 ms to a Clift of yellow Sant Stone on the L.S.   this is the
first high land which touches the river above Councel
Bluff, (this Clift is one mile only

N. 52° W. 1 1/2 ms to the pt of a Saand barr from the S. point   passed
the Clift on the L.S.

7. Whenever possible, sails were used on
the keelboat and the pirogues, to the great
relief of the men. Whitehouse wrote for this
day, "the Wind blew South had Good Sailing
for better than 14 Miles" (Thw., 7, 49).

8. *Coupe à Jarche* or Jacques' Cut, where
the river cut through a bend. However the
French *coupe-jarret* means a cut-throat, a
name which might have been given by the
French *engagés* to this place.

9. Both Thwaites and Quaife quote the description by Brackenridge of the ferocious chief, who appears to have once gotten hold of some arsenic and used it upon anyone who displeased him (H. M. Brackenridge, *Views of Louisiana . . . Journal of a Voyage up the Missouri in 1811,* Pittsburgh, 1814, pp. 229–30). It is said that he was buried mounted on his horse in the mound described by Clark (Thw., *1,* 106 n.; *Ordway,* p. 108 n.). The white flag bound in red, white, and blue may have been hoisted on this hill as a signal to the Omaha with whom the captains were about to hold a council.

N. 79° E 3 Ms to a pt of Small willows on the L.S. passing the high timber on S S. at 1 ml   wind hard from the S.W.

N. 29 E 1/2 of a mile on the L. point, the boat run on a log & detained us 10 minits

North 1 1/2 ml to the pt of a Sand bar makeing out from the L. point

N 68° W. 3/4 ms on the L. point   a sand bar makeing out from this Course.

N. 85° W. 2 1/2 Ms to the Lower point of a willow Island off the S. point —Black bird the late king of the Mahars Toom or inclosed grave on the top of a high round Hill of about 300 feet in the Prarie L.S.   bore west about 4 miles. (Musqutos bad)

22 1/4

August 11ᵗʰ Satturday 1804   about day this morning a hard wind from the N.W. followed by rain, we landed at the foot of the hill on which Black Bird The late King of the mahar⁹ who Died 4 years ago & 400 of his nation with the Small pox was burred ① and went up and fixed a white flag bound with Blue white & Read on the Grave which was about 12 foot Base & circueller, on the top of a Penecal [Pinnacle] about 300 foot above the water of the river, from the top of this hill may be Seen the bends or meanderings of the river for 60 or 70 miles round & all the County   around the base of this high land is a Soft Sand Stone Bluff of about 40 or 150 foot, the Crooked, passed a Creek Called Waieu Con di peeché C or bad God creek of bad spirits on the L.S.   above the Bluff on this Creek the Mahars had the Small pox & <400 of them Died> 4 years ago, Lattitude 42ᵈ 1′ 3″ 8/10 taken on the Point above the Creek. the river is verry crooked, we are now within 3/4 of a mile of the river at a place we Shall not get around to untill tomorrow noon—   We are 3 Legues from the Mahars by land and the great quty Beaver sign induce a belief that those people do not hunt much.

Course & Dis Augt 11ᵗʰ

S. 52° W. 1/2 ml on the Sand point S.S of the Sand Island   Wind N.W

N. 25 W. 2 Ms to a pt of low willows from a L. pt passing over a Sand bar. from the Sd pt psd the Isd

N 72 W. 2 1/3 Ms to A pt. on the S. S.   Willows opposit the high land which the, pt of high land which the Maha King was bured Capt Louis [sic] and my self went up, & fixed a whit Flag on the grave   A wind & rain Strike in from S.

N. 24 W. 1/2 Ml on the Side of the willows S.S. a Sand bar   passed a Creek on the L.S. called

Wau con di peeche
Great Spirrit is bad

S. 81. E 2 3/4 Ms to the begining of a pt of willows on the L.S. at the comemcment of this Course is a Small channel passing about half way thro a Prarie from a bend to the L.S. within 3/4 a mile and [space] miles round the point   The Flag bore S. 12ᵈ E.

N. 84° E. 6 Ms to the high wood above, a Prarie in the bend on S.S   the river wide & Shallow. the wood is opsd a pt

N. 22° E 2 1/4 Ms to a pt of willows on the L.S.

North. 1 3/4 Ms to a cotton tree in a bend to the S.S. haveing passd a Sand pt from the L. Side & camped on the L.S.   Cap Lewis Killed a Duck

N 45: W 1 1/2 Ml to a Sand Pt on the L. Side. a number of Blue crains

17 1/2   flying over

I have observed a number of places where the river has changd its Bead
at different times

Time & Dist the Moon & Sun

h – m – s		d ′ ″	
1 —13. 45—		73 – 6	45
" —16. 48—		73 – 6 –	0
" —18. 39—		73 – 6 –	0
" – 20 – 55—		73 – 7.	45
" – 22 – 25—		73 – 8.	30
" – 24 – 24—		73 – 9.	30
" – 25 – 45—		73 – 9.	30
d″– 27 – 43—		73 – 10 –	45
" 29 – 33—		73 – 11 –	30
" 31 – 30—		73 – 12 –	0

1. On the margin of Doc. 42, in the lower left-hand corner, is a profile drawn in red. Although there is no certainty that Clark drew the picture, the fact that he wrote the fourth line of his courses and distances on this page in red suggests that he used the same red crayon to draw the little sketch. In the list of supplies there is no red ink, but two "creyons" are listed (Thw., 7, 232). The position of the profile on the page suggests that it was made while Clark was writing the course and distances and before he finished his entries. The remainder of the entry is written over the sketch.

The subject is obviously a boy. There are no Indian characteristics about the face. Perhaps it is one of the French *engagés*. This little portrait, and one of a man smoking a pipe, Doc. 58, are, as far as I know, the only ones found in the Lewis and Clark material. We do not know who the subject is, nor are we certain as to the artist.

2. See infra, pp. 139 n., 144 n.

12ᵗʰ August Sunday 1804   a South wind   we Set out early   the river wider than usial, and Shallow, at 12 we halted in a bend to the left to take the Meridian altitude & Dine, & sent one man across where we took Dinner yesterday to Step off the Distance across [the] Isthmus, he made it 974 yards, and the bend around is 18 3/4 miles above this bend about 4 miles. a yellow & Brown Bluff Commeces and Continus 3 or 4 miles on the L.S.   this Bluff has Some Sand Stone, Some rich Black mole [mold] mixed with yellow Clay, a fiew Red Ceeder on the tope, which is <about>, from 20 to 150 foot high   the hill Still riseing back, I think may be estemated at 200 foot   on the top is timber, the wind for a few hours this evening was hard and from the S.E.   In the evening about 5 oClock Cap L. & my self wen on Shore to Shoot a Prarie wolf which was barking at us as we passed   [*Continued after entry for August 12*]

Course Distance August 12ᵗʰ & Reffurences
N. 45° W. 1 1/2 to a pt of willows on the L. Side
S. 42. W. 1/2 Ml on the point of a Sand bar from the L.S.   the river is wide here
S. 22. E. 2 1/4 Ms to the pt makeing out from the L.S.   passed the timber on the L.S. at 1/2 m.
N. 78. W. 3 1/2 Ms to the pt of willows on the L.S.   wind favourable from the South   [*Written in red ink or chalk in Clark's hand*]
S 68. W. 2 1/2 ms to the upper pt of of [*sic*]   Some Cotton trees in the bend to L.S.   at this place the Isthmus is only 973 yd wide or from one bend to the other & 18 3/4 Miles around   the Mahar Kings grave is S. 18° 2 about 1/2 miles   Took Medn altd 59° 8' – 0"—
N 49ᵈ W. 4 1/2 Ms to a pt on the L.S. opposit a Bluff, haveing passed a Sand point makeig out on S.S. at 1 Ml & one from the L.S. at 2 1/2 Mls—
N. 12 W. 3 Ms to a pt on the S.S.   a Red Ceeder Bluff of about 200 feet high on the L.S.
N. 46. E. 2 3/4 to a pt of <willows> on the L.S.   a <Sand bar makeing out> sand Island[1]
_____
20 1/4
and Camped on the Sand Island, the Musquetors verry troublesom, both Cap Lewis & myself are much ingaged <we> preparing despatches to Send back by the Perogue which will return as Soon as those despatches are ready.[2] (broke a faverate De[c]anter)
This Prarie Wolf Barked like a large fest [feist] and is not much larger, the Beaver is verry plenty, not with Standing we are almost in Sight of the Mahar Town—Cought a verry Large Catfish this morning, prepared the Indian present which we intend given to the Mahars   P. Wiser Apt Cook to Serjt Floyds Squad from to day

L [?]	50		6
	283		1 1/4
	19:3/4		3/4
	8		[*one figure illegible*]
	_____		_____
	28		
	2		17—
40			
8			

13th of August. Munday 1804. Set out this morning at Day light the usial time and proceeded on under a gentle Breeze from the S.E. passed the Island &c

N. 66^d W. 2 3/4 mls to pt of low willows on the S.S. a Sand bar makeing out from it

N. 11. W. 5 1/4 Ms to a pt of cotton wood on the bend to the S.S. passing over <1 1/2 ms to> the pt of a Sand bar from the S S. & one from the L. Side,. Wind fair

S 44° W, 2 1/2 Mls to a point on the S.S. to a Willow Isd on S. point and[3] opsd to which Mr Mackey had a Small fort in which he traded withe the Mahars the winter 95 & 96 & call the place Fort Charles[4]

West 3/4

N. 50. W. 1 <3/4> Mls to a Point of high woods below the mo. of a beayuw from a Pond in a Bend to the L.S.

N. 20 E 2 1/4 Ml to a pt of Willows on the L.S. passed a Creek on which the Mahar village is Situated at 1 1/2 Ml a Sand bar on the S.S. & one on the L.S. Passed the Willow Island on the S.S. Wind hard

North 1/4 of a ml on the Sand bar L.S.

N. 69. W. 2 1/2 ms to the upper pt of Cotton wood in a Bend to the L.S. opsd a lage Island, he[re] We Came too Formed a Camp on the Sand L.S. & Despatched Sgt Oddeway Peter Crousett. &

_____
14"

3 men to the Village[5] of the Mahars, 1 league for the nation to Come and talk with us on tomorrow, the S. E. wind Continues high, we take Some Luni observations and go From this Fish Camp the River is N 55^d West as far as can be Seen, the Sand bar only changeing the Derection of the Current the Hills leave the river on the L. Side

14th of August at 12 oClock the Party Sent yesterday to the Towns returned, and informed that they could not find any Indians, they had not returned from hunting the Buffalow in the Praries, wind Shifted to the N W. our party Sent after the Deserter and to the Otteau towns, have not Came up as yet

The Situation of this Village, now in ruin Siround[ed] by enunbl [innumerable] poste of grave[s] The ravage of the Small Pox 4 years ago they follow the Buf: and tend no corn[6]

August 15th Wednesday I took ten men & went out to Beaver Dam across a Creek about a mile S W from Camp. and with a Branch Drag caught 318. fish, of the following Kind i'e Pike, Samon, Bass, Pirch, Red horse, Small cat, & a Kind of Perch called on the Ohio Silverfish I aslo Caught the Srimp which is Common to the Lower part of the Mississippi, in this Creek & in the Beaver Pond is emince beads of Mustles verry large & fat—in my absence Capt Lewis Send the Souex interptr [Dorion] & a party to a Smoke which appeared to rise at no great distance to the north with a view to find Some Band of that nation, they returned and informed that the [fires] had been made Some time by Some Small party, and the hard wind of to day had set the Prarie on fire from Some high trees, which was left burning all well, Party from Ottoes not come up.[7]

3. There are many such confused entries in Clark's courses and distances. I present this detailed example as evidence that Clark took down his data in these rough notes and then copied them in the Notebook Journal, correcting whatever mistakes he had made in the original. The reader will note that the entry "S 44 W, 2½ Mls to a point on the S.S." is followed by the words "to a Willow Isd on S. point and." These words should follow the entry "W ¾." In the Notebook Journal Clark copied this, changing it slightly to read, "West ¾ of a mile to the Pt. of Willow Isd. on the S. point" (Thw., *1*, 109).

4. After establishing a trading house at the Oto villages in 1795 (supra, p. 99 n.), Mackay's next stop was at the Omaha villages, some 80 miles upstream. Here, in Nov. 1795, he built Fort Charles as a base from which to continue his trip to the Mandans.

5. Mackay, in his Table of Distances, described the village of the Omaha as on the south or larboard side of the Missouri. This would be about eight miles above Fort Charles. He wrote that the "village is situated in a beautiful Prairie near the foot of the hills a league from the Missouri. There is a small river that flows near to the village" (Nasatir, *2*, 489).

6. By Aug. 14, Clark had filled part one of the Notebook Journal which he had been keeping at the same time as this journal, and began part two (Thw., *1*, 110 n.).

7. The entries for Aug. 14 and 15 are written over the following in Clark's hand:
Capt Meriwether Lewis
St. Louis
Pr Mons Vansee Gutaru
I will thank you to send the letter derected to [*one word illegible*] & Smiley to the post office to go by the next mail

8. A division of the Hidatsa, who are a division of the Minitari (infra, p. 170 n.).

9. In lists such as this, Clark used the letters N.S. and S.S. to mean north side and south side. In both of his journals, he stuck to the nautical terms, larboard side, L.S., and starboard side, S.S.

42.15.13
42.12.10—

3. 3

1.31

42. .13.41

From the Mahars to the White River 80 Leagus
/ to the Chion [Cheyenne] R.   150   "
to the Rukarees [Arikara] –   250   "

then to the Mandins   10

thenc to the Wattesoons[8]   3 – to Mu

[*five letters illegible*] tun 3

Lake Dasepere Mad Lake [Lake d'Esprit]
the head of the Little Souix River
Ottoes returned to
the Village 4th of
august, the Panies the
15th of August.
Louisiana <Lark Smy> Fish Camp on a Sand bar 3 ms N.E of the Mahars Town Augt

16th 1804   a verry cool morning   the winds as usial from the N W. Capt Lewis with 12 [?] men went out to the Creek & Pond & Caught about 800 fine fish with a Bush Drag of the following kind i'e 79 Pike, 8 Salmon, 1 Rock, 1 flat Back, 127 Buffalow & read Horse, 4 Bass & 490 Cat, with many Small & large Silver fish,—I had a mast made & fixed to day The Party Sent to the Ottoes not yet arrived. the wind Shifted around to the S E.   the night's are Cool & a Breeze rises after generally; sometimes before night which Blows off the Musquitoes cools the atmospere.

28.49	7.70.15	70
13.41	70	5
15 8	10510	3510
	17.3	6

17th August 1804. a fine morning   Wind from the S.E.   I will here annex the Latds & Distances of the Different notable placies. from the River Dubois or mouth up:
To St Charles Village on the N. side—21 Miles by water—in Lattitude 38° 54′ 39″ North

" the mouth of the Gasconade. S. do—104—"   do—38. 44. 35   "
" the mouth of the Great Osarge. S." – 138—"   do—38. 31. 6— "
" the mo. of Mine River—S.   "—201—————————————
" the mo. of the 2 Charltons R: N."   226—————————————
" the mo. of Grand River on the N. side ⎤   254—in Lattitude
" just above the old Missouries Village ⎦   38° 47.54 North
" the Mo: of the Kanzies River S. Sd   366—" do   39. 5.25   "
" the Pt [?]: above the Demont Island——   "—do——39. 9.38   "
" creek Independance below the plain ⎤
where the Kanzes had ther 2d Village S.S. ⎦ 433—"—do——39.25.42. "
" the Mo. of Nodawa River N.S.—   481—"—do——39.39.22   "
" the mo: of Grand Ne ma har R. S.S.   511—"—do——39.55.56   "
" Isd opsd the Bald Pated Prarie—N.S.   570—"—do   40.27. 7. "
" the Mo: of River Platt—   S.S.   632—"—"——————————
" the White Catfish Camp 10 ms abov—   642—"—do—   41. 3.19. "
" Council Bluff (with the Ottoes) S.S.   682—"—do   41.17.—. "
" Mo. of the Little Siouex River N.S.   766—"—do—   41.42.34   "
" Camp Opsd the Mahars Village S.S.   86[6 written over 7]4[4 written over 0]
          —"—do   42.13.41. "[9]

The Longitudes are not yet calculated, We must be at this time about 99° 45″. 00′ ″ West of Greenwich——I collected a grass much resembling wheet with a grain like Rye, much fuller of grain, one like Rye & one like Barly Grass Small, a Grass like Timothey except Seed which is on branches. from the main Stalk——Late this evening one of the party Sent after the deserters returned & joined us, he left the party 3 miles back, they cought both Deserters, one of them La liberty [La Bartie], got away from them, the Great Chief & 2nd Chief of the Ottoes accompanied the Party with a view to bring about a Piece between themselves & the Mahar   a great missfotune that the Mahars have not returned from the hunt——Sent & fired the Prarie near Camp to bring in the Mahars & Souex if any are near. a Cool evening   2 Beever Cought

18th August 1804. a fine morning, despatched Jo. Fields for the Party from the Ottoes, whom did not come up last night   Wind from the S.E. in the after Part of the Day   *Panies[1] (returned from their hunt, the 12th of august) the Party arrived, we had a Short talk after which we gave them Provisions to eate & proceeded to the trial of Reed, he confessed, & we Sentenced <to run> him only to run the Ganetlet four times thro: the Detachment & party, and not to be considered in the future as one of the Permonant Party, after the Puni[s]hment of about 500 [?] Lashes,[2] at night we had Some talk with the Chiefs about the Cause of War between them and the Mahars. posponed the further consultation untill tomorrow. had a Dance which lasted untill 11 oClock, the Close of Cap Lewis Birthday.[3] a fine evening   wind S.E

[*This entry in Lewis' hand*]

<N. 5 N. 52. W. 7. Miles to a point of high woods on Stard and having passed the lower point of Pellican Island 1/4 of a mile, to which the last course was taken>[4]

[*End of entry in Lewis' hand*]

36   <Children>
45
45
‾‾‾
126   <Ottoes & Missouries>
         <you do [*one word illegible*]>
My Father, I am Sorry that the first man I brought:—
1 – Frenchman——
2 Great Chiefs of the Ottoes—
2 Second Chifs of the Missouries—
5 Wariors, accompanied the Party Sent to the Towns, in [*one word illegible*]
Fields Will: Bratten G Drewyer & W Labieche.

19th of August Sunday 1804   a fine morning   wind from the S.E   I prepd a preasent for the Chiefs & Warriers., the main Chief Brack fast with us naked; & beged for a Sunglass.—at 10 oClock we assembled the Chiefs & Warriers and under an owning [awning] and delivered a Speech, explanitary of the one Sent to this Nation from the Council Bluff, &c &c——
         Roloje[5]   Francis [?] Durwain [?]
1 Children[6]   When we Sent the 4 men to your towns, we expected to see & speake with the Mahas by the time you would arrive and to <make> Lay the foundation of a peace between you and them. The Spech of Peteet Villeu Littl Theif, If you think right and can waite untill all our warriers Come from the Buffalows hunt, we Can then tell you who is

1. The Oto returned from their hunt, but the Panies (Pawnees) were not at the council. It is clear from the asterisk Clark put by the word "Panies" that in going over the entry later he detected his mistake. Dorion was left behind with instructions to meet them and talk peace with them (Thw., *1*, 131–32).

2. The trial and punishment of Read, described in greater detail in the Notebook Journal (Thw., *1*, 112), was as follows: "proceeded to the trial of Reed, he confessed that he 'Deserted & stold a public Rifle Shotpouch Powder & Ball' and requested we would be as favourable with him as we Could consistantly with our Oathes—which we were and only Sentenced him to run the Gantlet four times through the Party & that each man with 9 Switchies Should punish him and for him not to be considered in future as one of the Party."
   The Indian chiefs were present, and it is clear that they did not like the performance, and asked that the man be pardoned. Clark told them that punishment was necessary and explained to the chiefs "the Customs of our Countrey." Ordway wrote that the chiefs were "verry Sorrey etc" (*Ordway*, p. 111).
   Although Clark wrote that the Indians were satisfied with his explanation, it is doubtful that they were. To beat a man of one's own tribe was unthinkable, for it violated the Indian belief in the dignity of a fellow tribesman. They tortured their enemies, but even then they respected courage in their adversary when he was put to the stake.
   Le Bartee, who was captured with Read, got away from the party before it got back to camp. The party heard no more of him. Since he was a French hired hand and not an enlisted man, no further efforts were made to apprehend him.

3. Lewis was thirty years old, four years younger than Clark.

4. This entry of course and distance (in Lewis' hand) was made on Aug. 8, when the party passed an island they named Pelican Island because of the great number of pelicans found there. It is copied in the courses and distances for Aug. 8 (supra, p. 102; Thw., *1*, 104).

5. See infra, p. 112.

6. The following is the only report we have of the proceedings in the council with the Oto and Missouri that includes the speeches of the chiefs. These were the first tribes the party had met on their way up the Missouri, and this was the first council of many that the explorers were to hold on their way west. Clark continued his attempts to record the speeches made by the chiefs of the various tribes.

7. This man is called Francis Labiche in detachment orders and throughout both journals. There was no other Labiche with the party.

8. The Oto and Missouri chiefs returned for another council with the Americans, saying they feared that the Pawnee and Omaha would attack them. The Missouri had been stealing horses, and two of the thieves had been killed by the Omaha. The two captains apparently could do little about this, and rebuked the chiefs for using the Omaha affair as an excuse to get some more presents and whiskey. Clark wrote in the Notebook Journal that he "rebuked them verry roughly for haveing in object goods and not peace with their neighbours" (Thw., *1*, 113).

9. Good soldier that he was, Floyd tried to keep his journal as long as he could. His final entry was made on Aug. 18 at which time he must have been very ill. In the entries for Aug. 19 and 20 in this journal, Clark gave a few details not found in the other journals. There was York's attentiveness, the attention of Clark who sat up with Floyd "the greater part of the night," and the effort the next day to assuage the sick man's pain by stopping on shore and preparing a warm bath, which was never used, for the man died before they could get him to it.

our men of Consequence—My fathers always lived together with the father of the B [*one letter illegible*] & we always live with the Big horse ——all the men here are the Suns of Chief and will be glad to get Something from the hands of their fathers.——My father always directed me to be friendly with the white people, I have always done So and went often to the french,/ give my party pieces of Paper [Commissions] & we will be glad—The names—
a Meddel to Car. ka pá há or Crow's head
a Comsi or Cfte Sar ná no ne or Iron Eyes   a Ottoe & says he is Brave
    "   Née Swor un ja   Big ax   a Ottoe approves.
    "   Star gra hun ja. Big blue Eyes a Ottoe <approves> Delivers up his comtn. [Commission]
    "   Ne ca sa wa—Black Cat a Missouris   approves the Council & he wants paper for his men at home, he after wards came & petitioned for his Paper.
    "   War – sar shá co—Brave Man   aproves
The Speach of the Big Horse   I went to hunt Buffalow   I heard your word and I returned, I and all my men with me will attend to your words —you want to make peace with all, I want to make peace also, the young me[n] when they want to go to war where is the goods you give me to keep them at home, if you give me Some Whisky to give a Drop to my men at home   I came here naked and must return home naked. if I have Something to give the young men I can prevent their going to war. you want to make peace with all, It is good   we want Something to give my men at home. I am a pore man, and cant quiet without means, a Spoon ful of your milk [Whiskey] will qui[e]t all
2ᵈ Speech of the Little Thief   I want Mr Faufon & Mr La bieche to make a piece with the panies & Loups. I want William to go & make a piece with the Loups, he can Speake english & will doe will [well] to go.— refused that William La biech⁷ shall accompany Faufon

Augt 17 to 25

Those people were not well Satisfied with the Presents given them, they were much Surprised at the air gun and Several curiosities which wer Shown them none more than the magnet, those people became extreemly troublesom to us begging Whisky & little articles.⁸ Sergt Floyd was taken violently bad with the Beliou[s] Cholick and is dagerously ill we attempt in vain to releive him, I am much concerned for his Situation —we could get nothing to Stay on his Stomach a moment [*one word illegible*]   appear exosting fast in him   every man is attentive to him <york pr> lly [York principally ?]

20ᵗʰ August Monday   after giveing faufon [Fairfong] Some goods the Indians a Canister of whiskey, we Set out under a gentle Breeze from the S.E   Shields went with the horses—I am Dull & heavy been up the greater Part of last night with Sergt Floyd, who is as bad as he can be to live   the motion [?] of his bowels having changed &c &c is the cause of his violent attack &c &c⁹

Course N. 56ᵈ W. 3 mls to a pt of Willows on the Island S.S
North 3/4 of a mile on the left of the Said Island—N 72ᵈ E 2 1/4 mls to the upper pt of the Island   N 18° E. 2 1/2 miles to the lower point of an Island on the S.S.   passed some Sand bars in the river   North 3 1/2 miles to a Bluff on the S.S. and the first above the old Ayauwa Village on

the S.S.   we Came to [to] make a warm bath for Sergt Floyd hopeing it would brace him a little, before we could get him in to this bath he expired, with a great deel of composure, haveing Said to me before his death that he was going away and wished me to write a letter—we <took> Buried him to the top of a high round hill over looking the river & Countrey for a great distance   Situated just below a Small river without a name to which we name & call Floyds river, the Bluff Sergts Floyds Bluff—[1] we burried him with all the honors of War, and fixed a ceeder post at his head with his name Title & Day of the month and year Capt Lewis read the funeral Services over him after paying everry respect to the Body of this desceased man (who had at all times given us proofs of his impatiality sincurity to ourselves and good will to Serve his Countrey)   we returned to the Boat & proceeded to the mouth of the little river 30 yd wide & Camped   a butifull evening

21st August Tuesday   we Set out verry early this morning under a gentle Breeze from the S.E   course S. 82° E 3 mls to the upper pt of a Bluff on the S.S.   passed Willow Creek and Some rock <above> below the mouth of the Seouex [the Big Sioux] river on the Starboard Side   those Clifts are about 170 fee[t] high, this river heads with the St peters [Minnesota River] and is navagable 75 Leagues (by the act of Mr Durien [Dorion]) to a fall of near 200[2] for [from], 2 large & som small Pitch[e]s. below the falls on the <left> right a Creek coms in on which <all> the red pipe Stone is percured, & in the praries about, a place of Peace with all nations.[3] South 1 1/4 Miles to the lower pt of a sand & willow Island in the Middle of the river   S. 48 W 1 3/4 Miles to the head of the Said Island, passing Sand bars thro which the water passes the whole <rout> Course   River Shalow & wide   Wind blow's hard   <North> West 2 Mls to a high wood on the L S., passed a large Sand bar from S.S.   river wide   N 36° W. 4 ms to a Beyau above wher the Mahars had a village in the bend to the L.S.   a Sand bar on S.S. & one in the midde   a large Island on the S.S. on which we Saw 4 wolves, one man out Hunting Shannon[4]   N. 18 E 2 ms to a Pt of willows on the L.S.   Wind verry hard from the S.E.

Latd 42° 28′ 49″ 6/10 north. this Countrey has a great Sameness but little timber—

N. 22° W. 3/4 on the L.S. opsd to which the R. Sieuix is within 2 miles on the S.S.—S 50′ W. 1/4 ml on L.S.

S 28 W. 2 ml to willow pt on the S.S.   S 78 W. 1/2 on the Sand bar to the L.S.

N. 12 W. 2 ms to a Willow Pt [blot] the L. Side   pass Sand bars

S. 60 W 1 3/4 mls to on the Sand bar on the L.S.   exme &   Give Sjt Pryor Sg. Floyds things except shot p.[ouch] & tomk. [tomahawk]

South 2 1/2 ms to low willows on S.S. and incamped on the L.S.   one man out [until ?] 12 with the horses

———————

22 3/4

22nd of August <Friday> Wednesday 1804   Set out early   wind from the South. G. Shannon joined the Boat last night. course this morning is S 47d [two figures illegible] W. 1 1/4 on the S. point West 1 1/4 ml to the commencement of a Bluff on the L.S.   the High land near the river for some distance below. This Bluff contain Pyrites alum, copperass & a kind Markesites Capt [Lewis] was near being Poisened by the Smell in pounding this substanc[5] also a clear Soft Substanc which <will mold and become pliant like wax> I belv to be Arsenic or cobalt.

Dr. Frank B. Queen of the Medical School of the University of Oregon suggests that Clark's phrase, "the motion [?] of his bowels having changed," showed that the diarrhea had stopped and that the last stage of peritonitis, paralysis of the bowels, had set in. Floyd's death, then, was unquestionably due to a ruptured appendix.

1. This stream still retains the name Clark gave it. It empties into the Missouri at Sioux City, Iowa. The whole bluff was named Floyd's Bluff, but the end farther upstream was named Sergeant's Bluff.

2. The figure given in the Notebook Journal is 20 feet (Thw., *1*, 115). However, the total height of the falls is 90 feet.

3. This was a very important route of Indian travel. The trail led up the Big Sioux to the falls where the city of Sioux Falls, South Dakota, now stands. From there it led up Split Rock Creek and its tributary, Red Pipestone Creek, to the famous pipestone quarry in southwestern Minnesota. To this spot came the Indians from many tribes to obtain the soft red stone, catlinite, from which pipes were made.

4. "Hunting Shannon" became a familiar task for the party all the way to the Pacific and back. The young seventeen-year-old had a genius for getting lost.

5. A term applied to white iron pyrites (iron disulphide), usually containing arsenic.

6. The explorers were hard put to think up names for the hundreds of small streams and islands. Trivial incidents often suggested names: the mast of the keelboat broke, hence "Mast Creek"; the party used up the last of the butter they had purchased before starting out, hence, "Butter Island." In the entry for Aug. 19 (supra, p. 109) Clark wrote down three words. Whether all three came to him in his sleep we do not know, but as he notes here, one did. He appears to have thought that perhaps this was no way to select names, for he has crossed out the reference to his dream. In the Notebook Journal the name "Roloje" appears as "A name I learned last night" (Thw., *1*, 117). Unfortunately the name has not been preserved. It is now Iowa Creek (*Ordway*, p. 114 n.).

7. Patrick Gass was elected to the post of sergeant left vacant by Floyd's death. He received the highest number of votes cast, 19 (Thw., *1*, 117).

8. This was the party's first buffalo—they had reached the buffalo country. There had been signs, but Joe Field, now one of the best hunters in the party, had downed one. It was a huge bull, and Ordway wrote that it took Lewis, himself, and ten other members of the party to drag the carcass down to the boat. "We pickled down our Buffelow meat & jerked the venison. the Sand blew so thick. . . . we could not see across the River" (*Ordway*, p. 115).

I observe great Quantity of Cops ans [Copperas] or cobalt and alim pure & Straters of white & brown earth of 6 Inch thick. a creek coms in above. the Bluffs on which there is great quantites of those minerals This Creek I call Roloje[6] a <name given me last night in my sleep,> at those allem [alum] banks Shelds joined in with two Deer—

Course N. 18° W. 2 1/2 ms to a point High wood on the L.S.   passed the creek & a Sand bar

N. 56° W. 5 1/2 ms to a <Bluff> on the L.S.   Clift opsd a pt on the S.S. passed Sand bars on both Sides of the river ②

N 54° E 2 Mls to a pt of Sand on the L.S. opsd to which the Souix R. is near the Missou and 3 or 4 ms east at which place this river comes out of the high Countrey

N 48 W. 6 1/2 to a Single tree in <the prarie> a butiful large Prarie [*one word illegible*] Pl. on the S.S.   passed a Pt of Sand on the S.S.   2 sand bars in the River wide   this Said Course continued to the upper tree of Some woods   Camped on the S.S.   a

————
19

great Deel of Elk Sign fresh   Capt Lewis took a dost of salts this evening to carry off the effects of /arsenec/ or cobalt which he was trying to find out the real quallity ②   passed a Clift of Rock much impregnaled with alum, containing also a great quantity of cobalt——ordered a vote of the men for a Sergeant of the three highest numbers a choice to be made [*two words illegible*] Gass Bratton & Gibson—Gass[7] is worth remark, that my Ink after standing in the pot 3 or four days Soaks up & becons thick

23rd August <Satturday> Thursday 1804 Set out this morning verry early, the two men R. Fields & Shannon did not come up last night, I went out and Killed a fine Buck, J. Fields killed a Buffalow, 2 Elk Swam by the boat whilst I was out and was not killed, many guns fired at it   R. Fields Came up with the horses & brought two Deer, Collins killed a Small doe, Several Prarie wolves seen   Course West 4 Mls to the mouth of a Small run between two Bluffs of yellow clay   North 3 1/4 miles to the upper pt of Some timber in the bend to L.S. near where R. [J ?] fields killed the Buffalow   passed the pt of High Land on S.S. at 1/4 of a mile, Capt Lewis went out with 8 men & brought the buffalow to the river at this bend,[8] C. Lewis Killed a goose, wind blew hard <I am obliged to make the next Corses Short on ackount> of the flying Sands which rasies like a Cloud of Smoke from the Bars when the wind <rises> Blows, the Sand being fine and containing a breat [great] perpotion of earth and when it lights it sticks to every thing it touches   at this time the grass is white   S 48° W 3 miles to a point of willows on the S.S. haveing passed the Sand Island L.S.   camped on the L S above the Island   Saw an elk Standing on a sand bar. Shields Shot it thro' the neck

————
10 1/4

24th August <Sunday> Friday 1804. Some rain last night & this morning, we Set out at the usial time and proceeded on the Same course of last night   Continued S. 48° W. 2 1/4 Mls to the Commencement of a Blue Clay Bliff on L Sd about 180 or 190 feet high   West under <ruged> rugged Bluffs 1 3/4 ms passing Several Small Dreens, [Drains], falling into the river <thees> those Bluffs has been lately on fire and is yet verry Hott, great appearance of Coal, & imence quantities of Cobalt in Side of that part of the Bluff which sliped in, on the Sides of the hill

9. The buffalo berry, the *graisse du boeuf* of the French *engagés*.

[The following, Documents 44 and 45, are fragments and are inserted here in their proper places.]

great quantities of a Kind of Current or froot resembling the Current in appearance   much richer and finer flavd grows on a Srub resembling a Damsen and is now fine and makes a Delightfull Tang[9]   above this Bluff I took my Servent and a french boy I have and walked on Shore   I killed a Deer which York Packed on his back   In the evening I killed two Buck Elk and wounded two others which I could not persue by the Blood as my ball was So Small to bleed them well, my boys each Shot an elk—it was late and I crossed a Point   Struck the river above and halted the boat and 12 men went out brought in the Meat   all the after part of to day it rained   we are all wet. Capt Lewis and my self Concluded to visit a High Hill Situated in an emence Plain three Leagues N. 20° W. from the mouth of White Stone river, this hill appears to be of a conic form and by all the different nations in this quater is Supposed to be a place of Deavels or

1. This stream appears to have had many names. The name on the Indian Office Map which Clark had with him is the Renville, which Clark misread as the Kenville. The Indians called it the Washisha, the White Earth, the White Stone, or the Smoky Earth, perhaps from the smoking bluffs nearby (Coues, *History, 1*, 84). Ordway called it "Little Peoples River" (*Ordway*, p. 116). On his return journey, Clark called it the Redstone (Thw., 5, 374), which is more like its present name, the Vermilion River. It is a short stream issuing from prairie lakes in Clay County, South Dakota.

that they ② are in human form with remarkable large heads; and about 18 inches high   that they <remarkably> are very watchfull and ar armed with sharp arrows with which they can kill at a great distance; they are said to kill all persons who are so hardy as to attempt to approach the hill; they <have a> state that tradition informs them that ma[n]y indians have suffered by these little pèople and among others that three Maha men fell a sacrifice to their murceyless fury not meany years since—so much do the Mahas Souix and Ottoes and other neighbouring nations believe this fable <that they> no consideration is sufficient to induce them to approach this hill.

*[Part of the Courses and Distances for August 24th are found
in the entry for that date. They are continued here.]*

S 82 [?] W 4 { Due N. 2. m. from a willow point at the upper part of a
bluff Lard. to a willow point on the same side, the river
leaves the Lard Bluff at the commencement of this course

N. 15. E. 1 1/4 M. to a point on Stard

N. 10. E 1/4 M. to an object in the bend Stard   extensive sand bar on
the Sard. side

N. 45. W. 1 1/2 to the lower point of small willow Island.

W. 1 1/4 M. to the upper point of a sandbar connected with the Island ①

S. 40. W 2 1/2 to a willow point Stard. shore

11 1/2

881
21
―――
902 3/4
12 1/4
―――
91 [*one figure illegible*]

*[A fragment, Document 45, is inserted here referring to the Kenville
or Whitestone River. See Notebook Journal (Thw., 1, 118–19).]*

about the center of this Sand Island the river of white Stone (as Called
by Mr Evins [*one word illegible*]   Kenvill R.[1] falls in on the
Stard Side [?]   it appear to be about 25 or 30 yards Wide; at
the mouth of this river 10 Indians had latterly Cross. Supposed
be be Soues, the part of a band which are at war with the mahars, This Soues nation are divided into bands Som 100 to 500
men in a band   at peace with each other, ther Interest & preju-
dices different, for instance one band the most envetterate en-
imy of the Mahars, all the other Bands in the greatest harmony
<withich> with that nation and even go with thim to War,
those Soues, follow the Buffalow, & Kill them on foot, they
pack their Dogs, which carry ther Bedn [burden]

FROM THE VERMILION TO THE TETON:
AUGUST 25, 1804—SEPTEMBER 24, 1804

2. This is the E. Cann in the list of the French *engagés* set down in this Journal on July 4 (supra, p. 69). He is called Carr in the Notebook Journal (Thw., *1*, 121). The dog, Scannon, was along, too.

3. Gained the summit (*O.E.D., 8,* 712).

Augt 25ᵗʰ Satturday 1804   This morning Capt Lewis & my Self G D. Sjt Ouderway Shields J. Fields colter Bratten Cane² Labeeche corpl Wovington Frasure & York Set out to Visit this mountain of eval Spirits, we Set out from the mouth of the White Stone Creek, at 8 oClock, at 4 miles cross the Creek in an open plain, at 7 ms the dog gave out & we Sent him back to the Creek   at 12 oClock we rose³ the hill   Some time before we got to the hill we obsevd great numbers of Birds hovering about the top of this Mound   when I got on the top those Birds flw off. I discovered that they wer Catechig [Catching] a kind of flying ant which were in great numbers abought the top of this hill, those insects lit on our hats & necks, Several of them bit me verry Shart [Sharp?] on the neck, near the top of this nole I observed three holes which I Supposed to be Prarie Wolves or Brarous [Badgers], which are numerous in those Plains. this hill is about 70 foot high in an emince Prarie or leavel plain from the top I could not observe any woods except in the Missourie Points and a few Scattering trees on the three Rivers in view. i e the Soues River below, the River Jacque [James River] above & the one we have   3 have crossed   from the top of this Mound we observed Several large gangus of Buffalow & Elk feeding   upwards of 800 in number   Capt Lewis being much fatigued and verry thursty obliged us to go to the neares water which we Could See, which was the [*one word illegible*] Creek at right angles from the Course we came out, and we got water in three miles in the Creek above whre the beaver had damed it up   after a Delay of about one hour & a half we Set out for our boat, Cross the Creek three times wast deep, passing down an ellgent bottom of about a mile in width bordered by a ridge of about 50 feet from the top of which it was leavel to the river, we proceeded on by a circular Dercetion to the place we Crossed this Creek going out where we delayed for the men to rest themselves about 40 minits in a small grove   here we got Great quantites of the best largest grapes I ever tasted, Some Blue Currents still on the bushes, and two kind of Plumbs, one the Common wild Plumb. the other a large Yellow Plumb. growing on a Small bush, this blumb is about double the Size of the Common and Deliscously fla-voured—Those plains are leavel without much water and no timber all the timber on the Stone [White Stone] River would not thickly timber 100 acres of land—we returned to the boat at Sunset, my servent nearly exosted with heat thurst and fatigue, he being fat and un accustomed to walk as fast as I went was the cause—[4] We Set fire to the Praries in two Places to let the Sous know we were on the river and as a Signal for them to Come to the river above, our Party in the Boat & one Perogue undr the Comd of Sergt Pryor answered us by fireing a prarie near them. we proceeded on to the place we Camped last night, and as it began to rain and verry dark, we concluded to Stay all night, our boys prepared us a Supper of jurked mee[t] and two Prarie Larks (which are about the Size of a Pegeon) and Peculier to this country) and on a Buffalow roabe we Slept verry well   in the Morning we proceeded on and joined the boat at 6 Miles, they had camped & were Jurking an Elk & 5 Deer which R. Fields & Shannon had brough in. from the Mound to the Hill. S.S. mo: of R. Soues S 70° E. to the opsd Hills S. 45° E. and to the woods near River au Jacque [James River] is West—

4. Good sightseers that they were, the party had to visit the hill where, as the Indians told them, there were little men, 18 inches high, with big heads. It was a hard climb under the hot August sun; Lewis and the dog dropped out, but the rest reached the top. There were no little men, but they did see several holes in the ground (*Ordway*, p. 116).

On the way down, Clark complained that York was unable to keep up because he was fat. He has been pictured as a tall, power-fully built Negro by such artists as Russell and Paxson. After all the exertions of the trip up the Missouri this far, York should have been able to keep up. Brief as it is, I believe that this is the only description of the appearance of Clark's body servant. The hill is now called Spirit Mound and is in Clay County, Nebraska.

5. The formal order appointing Patrick Gass sergeant is given in Lewis' Orderly Book, Aug. 26, 1804 (Thw., *1*, 125).

6. The news "Shannon is lost again" must have been passed around. When Shields and J. Fields later reported that they could not find him, Clark wrote in the Notebook Journal (Thw., *1*, 127), "This man not being a first rate Hunter, we deturmined to Send one man in pursute of him with some Provisions." Since the party was getting into Sioux country, this was a serious matter. This time Shannon was lost for more than two weeks.

7. This stream is called the *Riv qui courre,* Rapid River, on the Indian Office Map. The party arrived at its mouth on Sept. 4 (infra, p. 132). The modern name of this river is the Niobrara.

92 1/2

Augt 25ᵗʰ Satturday   [*Second entry for August 25*] ⑩   wind S E   The Boat under Serjt Pryor after drying some goods which got wet in the french Perogue & jurking the meet killed yesterday Set out at 12 oClock and proceeded on Six miles and Camped on the L.S.   passd a Bluff of blue earth at 3 miles and a large Sand Island in a bend to the S.S. at 5 miles, R Fields brought in 5 Deer, G Shannon an Elk this eveng: rain

[*The entry for August 25 is written over the following figures:*]

12

[Blot in Ms.] 4 3/4

  1 [*one figure illegible*]

  1 [*one figure illegible*] 1/4

10 1/2

  7

  9

    1/2

                L

Course, Destance & Reffurence august 25ᵗʰ 1804 at 3 oClock Murcky 86
      abo 0,

S. 72° W. 1 Ml the S.S. opposit a <Bluff> of Blue earth on the L.S.

West 1/2 Ml on the S.S. opposite the Bluff, the River verry narrow

N. 22. E 3 Ms to a pt of high willows on the L.S. opposit a Sand Isd in a
    bend

N. 40. W. 1 Ml on the L.S. opsd an Island afore said

S. 86. W 1/2 on the L.S. to a point of willows, where the Boat lay
        sinc last night Sunset.

    Miles 6

26ᵗʰ August Sunday 1804   arrived at the boat at 9 oClock A.M.   Set out at 10 oClock after Jurking the meet & Cutting the Elk skins for a Toe Roap. and proceeded, leaveing G Drew[yer] & Shannon to hunt the horses, at <9 miles> the river verry full of Sand bars and Wide   Course S 66° W. 2 Mls to a Sand bar Makeing out from the S.S.   N. 82° W: 7 Mls to a pt of willows S S   passd a Island & large Sand bar on both sides river wide and a Clift of White earth on the L.S of 2 ms in length to a point of Willows on the S.S opposit arch Creek   above the Mouth of this Creek a Chief of the Maha nataton displeased with the Conduct of Black bird the main Chief came to this place and built a Town which was called by his name Petite Arch [Arc] (or Little Bow)   this Town was at the foot of a Hill in a handsom Plain fronting the river and Contained about 100 huts & 200 men, the remains of this tribe Since the Death of Petete arch has joined the remaining part of the nation   This Creek is Small—we apt Pat Gass Sergeant Vice Floyd Dicesed, Geathered great quantity of Grapes & three Kinds of Plumbs, one yellow round, & one ovel, & the Common wild Plumb. Misquetors bad to night—I have apt you [*Sentence incomplete*]⁵

    9

27ᵗʰ August Monday, this morning the Morning Star was observed to be verry large, G Drewyer Came up and informed that he could neither find Shannon or the horses, he had walked all night—we Sent Shields & J. Fields back to look for Shannon⁶ & the horses and to Come up with us on the river above at the grand Calumet or River KaCure [Qui Courre]⁷ & we Set out under a Gentle Breeze from the S.E.   proceeded on passed a

Bluff at 7 Mls Several mile in extent of white Clay or Marl or Chalk, under this bank we discovered Large Stone resembling lime incrusted with a Substance like Glass which I take to be Cabolt, also ore, three Mls above this Bluff we Set the Prarie on fire, to let the Soues know we wished to see them   at two oClock <we landed>   an Indian Swam to the Perogue, we landed & two other Came   they were boys, they informed us that the Souex were Camped near, on the R Jacke [James] one Maha boy informed us his nation was gone to make a peace with the Pania's [Pawnee] we <proceed>   Send Sjt Pryor & a frenchman with the Interptr Mr Durion to the Camp to see & invite their great Chieff to Come and Counsel with us at the Calumet Bluffs [*space*]   Mile abov on L.S.—we proceed on 1 1/2 Miles farther & Camped S.S.   N. 73 W. 7 mls to the upper pt of Calx or Chalk Bluffs on L.S.   passd a large Sand bar on L.S. & 2 on S S.   North 3 mls to a tree in the bend to S.S.   W. 2 1/2 m to the mouth of rive Jacque[8] S.S. the Sisze of R S [*three letters illegible*]   S. 80 W. 1 1/2 on the Side of a large mud bar on the S.S. and camped.

14

28th August Tuesday, 1804   The wind blew hard last night   one Indian stayed with us all night, Set out under a Stiff Breze from S and proceedd on   passe a Willow Island at two miles   Several Sand bars   the river here is wide & shallow   full of sand bars—The High land appear to be getting nearer to each other   passed a Bluff containing Some white earth on the L.S.   below this Bluff for some mile the Plain rises gradually to the hight of the Bluff which is 70 or 80 foot, here the Indian boy left us for his Camp—Capt Lewis & my Self much indisposed—I think from the Homney [Hominy] w[e] Substitute in place of bread,[9] (or Plumbs)   We proceeded on about 3 Miles higher and Camped below the Calumet Bluff in a Plain on the L.S. to waite the return of Sergt Pryor & Mr Durioun [Dorion] who we Sent to the Soues Camp from the mouth of R: Jacque [James River], before we landed the French rund a Snag thro: their Perogue, and like to have Sunk, We had her on loaded, from an examonation found that this Perogue was unfit for Serivce, & Detur-mined to Send her back by the Party intended to send back and take their Perogue,[1] accordingly Changed the loads, Some of the loading was wet   wind blows hard from the South. J Shields & J. Fields joined   they did not overtake Shannon with the horses who is a head of us.

1st <The> Polsey   ⎫
2 White Crain   ⎪
3 Litle Bowl   ⎬   Bou Rouley [Bois Brulé] gangue [gang][2]
4 red hand   ⎭

Cours Dist. &

S. 76° W. 4 [4 written over 3] 1/2 Mls to the lower part of a Bluff of white earth on the S.S haveing passd Several large Sand bars on each Side of the water.

S. 60. W. 4 Mls to the low part of the Calumet Bluff on the L.S. having pass a point on east Side & Several Sand bars

8 [8 written over 7] 1/2

29th August Wednesday 1804—   rained last night and Some this morn-ing   verry cloudy   Set Some men to work to make a Toe rope of Elk Skin, and my self to write, Sent one man to pursue Shannon a head with Some provisions, I am much engaged writing a Speech

8. The James River. The present city of Yankton, South Dakota, is situated near its mouth. The council with the Sioux was held across the river from present-day Yankton.

9. When the Indian chiefs arrived, they were given some of this hominy. "our Cap-tains Sent them over Some lyed corn & To-bacco &c." (*Ordway*, p. 119).

1. See infra, p. 139.

2. These were Yankton Sioux. Clark con-fused this division of the Sioux with the Bois Brulé, a division of the Teton Sioux, which the party met on Sept. 24 (infra, p. 146).

3. Old Dorion had lived for 25 years with the Sioux. On his return with the exploration party he found one of his many progeny, Pierre Jr., with the Yankton. Later, this son joined the overland party of the Astorians; he was killed by the Indians on the Columbia River (Thw., *1*, 128 n.).

4. This was the party's first sight of the *tipi,* the Plains Indians' lodge.

at 4 oClock Sergt Pryor & Mr Durion the Soues interpeter with about 70 Soues arrived on the opposit Side of the river   we Sent over for them, who came over   Mr D. & his Son[3] who was tradeing with the Indians came over   Mr Durion informed that three Chiefs were of the Party, we Sent over Serjt Pryor with young Mr Durion, Se[n]d Kettles for the Indians to cook the meat they Killed on the way from thir Camp (2 Elk & 6 Deer) a bout a bucket of Corn & 2 twists of Tobacco to Smoke intending to Speak to them tomorrow—   G. Drewyer Killed a Deer—   Sergt Pryor informs that when he approached the Indian Camp they Came to meet the[m] Supposeing Cap Lewis or my self to be of the party intending to take us in a roabe to their Camp—   he approached the Camp which was handsum made of Buffalow Skins Painted different Colour, their Camps formed of a Conic form Containing about 12 or 15 persons each and 40 in number,[4] on the River Jacque [James] of 100 yds wide & Deep Containing but little wood, They had a fat dog Cooked as a feest; for them, and a Snug aptmt for them to lodge   on their march they passed thro plains covd with game &c. &c. &c.

125   64:64

30th August Thursday 1804   a Foggeie morning   I am much engagd after Brackfast   we sent Mr Doroun in a Perogue to the other side i'e' L S. for the Chiefs and [w?]arriers of the Soues, he returned at 10 oClock with the Chiefs, at 12 oClock I finished and we delivered a Speech to the Indians expressive of the wishes of our government and explaining of what would be good for themselves, after delivering the Speech we made one grand Chief   1 2ᵈ Chief and three third chiefs and deliverd to each a few articles and a Small present to the whole   the grand Chief a Parole [Commission], Some Wampom & a flag in addition to his present, they with Drew and we retired to dinner, Mr Durions Sun much displeased that he could not dine with Cap Lewis and my Self—   the number of Soues present is about 70 men—   Dressed in Buffalow roabes, a fiew fusees [Hudson's Bay guns], Bows and arrows, and verry much deckerated with porcupine quills, a Society of which only four remains is present, this Society has made a vow never to giv[e] back let what will happen, out of 22 only 4 remains, those are Stout likely men who Stay by them selves, fond of mirth and assume a degree of Superiority—, the air gun astonished them verry much   after night a circle was forrm around 3 fires and those Indians danced untill late,[5] the Chiefs looked on with great dignity   much pleased with what they had, we retired late and went to bead. wind hard from the South.

31st of August Friday   rose early   a fair Day—   a curios Society among this nation worthey of remark, i'e' formed of their active deturmined young men, with a vow never to give back, let the danger or deficuelty be what it may, in war parties they always go forward, without Screening themselves behind trees or any thing else, to this vow they Strictly adheer dureing their Lives, an Instance of it, is last winter on a march   in Crossing the Missourei a hole was in the ice imediately in their course which might easily be avoided by going around, the fore most man went on and was drowned, the others were caught by their party and draged around— in a battle with the Crow de curbo [Corbeau] Indians out of 22 of this Society 18 was killed, the remaining four was draged off by their friends, and are now here—   they assocate together Camp together and are merry fellows, <to become one of the Society> This Custom the Souex learned of the de Carbours [Crow] inhabiting the Cout Noie or Black mountain [Black Hills]   all the Chiefs Delivered a Speech agreeing to what we Said &c &c & beged which I answered from my notes. We made or gave a certificate to two Brav man the attendants of the Great Chief gav them Some tobacco and prepared a Commission for Mr Darion [Dorion] to make a peace with all the <Chief> nations in the neighbourhood Mahas [Omaha], Porncares [Ponca], Panei [Pawnee], Loups, Ottoes and Missouries—   &c to take to the President Some [of?] the Gt Cheifs of of each nations who would accompy him   allso to do certain other things, and wrot Instructions—   gave him a flag and Some cloaths— the Chiefs Sent all their young men home, and they stayed for Mr Dorion—   in the evening late we gave the Comsn [Commissions] & Instruction to Mr Durion & he recved them with pleasa [pleasure?], & promised to do all which was necessary. I took a Vocabulary of the Seoex language, and a fiew answers to Some queries I put to Mr Pitte [Pierre] Dorion respecting the War No. [Number] Situation Trad &c &c of that people which is divided into 20 tribes possessing Sepperate interest   they are numerous between 2 & 3000 men, divided into 20 tribes who view their interests

5. Both Ordway and Whitehouse give lively and vivid accounts of this performance (*Ordway*, pp. 119–20; Thw., 7, 54–55).

as defferent   Som bands at War with Nations which other bands are at peace—   This nation call themselves—Dar co tar [Dakota?]. The french call them Souex   Their language is not perculiar to themselves as has been Stated, a great many words is the Same with the Mahas, Ponckais [Ponca], Osarge, Kanzies &c   clearly proves to me those people had the Same Oregean [Origin]—   this nations inhabit the Red river of Hudson bay, St Peter [Minnesota River] Missippi, Demoin R. Jacque & on the Missourie   they are at War with 20 nations, and at piece with 8 only— they recved their trade from the British except a a few on the Missourie, they furnish Beaver Martain [Marten] Loues [Loups: wolves] orter [otter], Pekon [Picou: Lynx] Bear and Deer and have forty Traders at least among them. The names of the Different bands of this nation are———

1st Che cher ree or Bois ruley [Brulé] (the present band) Inhabit the Souex. Jacque & Demoin Rivers———

2nd Ho in de bor to or poles. they live on the head of the Suouex River ———

3rd Me Ma car jo (or make fence on the river.) the Countrey near the Big bend of the Missouri.

4th Sou on te ton (People of the Prarie)   they rove North of the Missourie in the Praries above.

5th Wau pa coo do (Beeds [?])   they live near the Prarie de chaine [Prairie du Chien] on the Mississippi—

6th Te tar ton (or Village of Prare) on the waters of the Mississippi above Prare de Chain (or Dog Prarie)

7th Ne was tar ton (Big Water Town) on the Mississippi above the mouth of the St Peters River.

8th Wau pa to (Leaf Nation). 10 Leagues up St Peters

9th Cas car ba (White man) 35 Lgs up St Peters

10 Mi ac cu op si ba (Cut Bank) reside on the head of St Peters river

11 Sou on—on St Peters in the Praries

12th Se si toons—40 Leagues up St Peters.

The names of the othe[r] tribes I could not get in. [*Doc. 49 continued below after the speeches in Doc. 50.*]

"31ˢᵗ August 1804" Speeches[6]

at 8 oClock the chiefs and warriers met us in council all with thier pipes with the stems presented towards us, after a Silence of abt [*space*] The great Chief Dressed himself in his fine cloathes[7] and two warriers in the uniform and armer of thier Nation Stood on his left with a War Club & Speer each, & Dressed in feathurs.

The Shake hand 1ˢᵗ Chief

Spoke My Father. I am glad to here the word of my G.F. [Grandfather, the President of the U.S.] and all my warriers and men about me are also glad.

My Father—now I see my two fathers th[e] Children, of my great father, & what you have said I believe and all my people do believe also—

My Father—We are verry glad you would take pitty on them this Day, we are pore and have no powder and ball.

My Father—We are verry Sorry our women are naked and all our children, no peticoats or cloathes.—

My Father—You do not want me to Stop the boats going up if we See,[8] I wish a man out of your boat to bring about a peace, betew [between] all the Indians, & he can do so. [Dorion]

My Father—Litsten to what I say   I had an English medal when I went to see them, I went to the Spanioreads   they give me a meadel and Some goods, I wish you would do the Same for my people.—

My Father—I have your word   I am glad of it & as soon as the Ice is don running I will go down & take with me, Some great men of the other bands of the Soues—

My Father.—I will be glad to See My Grand Father but our Women has got no Cloathes and we have no Powder & Ball, take pity on us this day.

My Father—I want to listen and observe wath [what] you say, we want our old friend (Mr Durion) to Stay with us and bring the Indians with my Self down this Spring.

My Father—I open[e]d my ears and all my yound men and we wish you to let Mr Durion Stay, and a perogue for to take us down in the Spring.

The Speach of the

White Crain [Crane] Mar to se ree 2ᵈ Chief

My Father's listen to my word, I am a young man and do not intend to talk much, but will say a few words.

My Father—my father was a Chief, and you have made me a Chief   I now think I am a chief agreeable to your word as I am a young man and inexperienced, cannot say much   What the Great Chief has Said is as much as I could say.——

Par nar ne Ar par be Struck by the Pana [Pawnee] 3ᵈ Chief

My father's I cant Speek much   I will Speek a little to you

My fathers—ther's the Chiefs you have made high, we will obey them, as also my young men, the Pipe I hold in my hand is the pipe of my father, I am pore as you See, take pity on me   I believe what you have Said

My fathers—You think the great meadel you gave My great Chief pleases me and the small one you gave me gives me the heart to go with him to See my Great father. What the Great Chief has Said is all I could Say. I am young and Cant Speek.

A Warrier by name Tar ro mo nee spoke

My father—I am verry glad you have made this man our great Chief, the British & Spaniards have acknowledged him before but never cloathed him. you have Cloathed him, he is going to see our Great father, We do not wish to spear [spare ?] him but he must go and see his great father

My Father's My great Chief must go and See his Gd father, give him some of your milk [Whiskey] to speek to his young men,

6. On two separate sheets from which the following is transcribed, Clark jotted down, as best he could, the speeches of the chiefs. Clark's handwriting is hurried and consequently it may be assumed that he made these notes while the council was in progress. In the Notebook Journal he wrote only a single paragraph summarizing the speeches (Thw., *I*, 131). On the other hand, Ordway, in his journal, recorded in much greater detail the words of each speaker. He too must have been at the council and made notes. Perhaps Clark turned over to Ordway the document here printed to assist him in preparing his excellent account of the proceedings. In comparing Clark's notes with the report of Ordway, the reader will recognize the latter's skill as a narrator (*Ordway*, pp. 119–23).

A comparison of the list of names of the chiefs as put down by Clark with that of Ordway illustrates the difficulty the party found in transliterating the Indian names. However, the effort was made, for the government was anxious to obtain as much information as possible of the leaders of the various tribes.

Clark's List	*Ordway's List*
Shake Hand	Weucha
White Crane, Mar–to–ree	Matthuga
Struck by the Pania,	Pandanapappya
Par–nar–ne–Ar–par–oe	
The Half Man—Ar–la–we–char–chi	Anckasweekachappa
A Warrior—Tar–ro–mo–nee	Meadatuncka

7. The "fine cloathes" given to the head chief were "a red laced coat & a fine cocked hat & red feather & an american flag & a white Shirt &c. all of which he was much pleased with" (*Ordway*, p. 120).

8. The traders going up the Missouri were in constant trouble with the Sioux, who stopped them and robbed them of their goods. There was an implied threat in the chief's words, and in those of another chief who spoke later (*infra*, p. 126).

9. Clark here computed that there were 160 leagues or 480 miles to travel before the party reached the Mandan villages. At this place, they were 1,140 miles from the mouth of the Missouri.

My father. our people are naked, we wish a trader to Stop among us, I would be verry glad our two fathers would give us some powder and ball and some Milk with the flag.
Speech of
Ar ca we char chi the half Man 3ᵈ Chief
My fathr's I do not Speak verry well, I am a pore man and
My Fathr's I was on[c]e a Chief boy now I am a man and a chief of som note.
My Fathr's—I am glad you have made my old Chief a fine and great man, I have been a great warrier but now I here your words, I will berry my hatchet and be at peace with all & go with my Great Chief to see my great father.
My fath—s. When I was a young man I went to the Spaniards to see ther fassion, [Fashion] I like you[r] talk and will pursue you[r] advice, since you have given me a medal. I will tell you the talk of the Spaniards
My Father's—I am glad my Grand father has sent you to see the read [red ?] people on this river, and that he has given us a flag large and handsom the shade of which we can sit under—
My Fathr's—We want one thing for our nation very much we have no trader, and often in want of good[s]
My Fathers—I am glad as well as all around me to here your word, and we open our ears, and I think our old Frend Mr Durion can open the ears of the other bands of Soux. but I fear those nations above will not open their ears, and you cannot I fear open them—.
My Fathers. You tell us that you wish us to make peace with the Ottoes & M. [Missouri] You have given 5 Medles I wish you to give 5 Kigz [Kegs ?] with them—
My Fathers.—My horses are pore running the Buffalow give us Some powder and ball to hunt with, and leave old Mr Durion with us to Get us a trader
My Father.—The Spaniards did not keep the Medal of the T[o]ken of our Great Chief when they gave him one You have Dressed him and I like it I am pore & take pitey on me—.
My fathers—I am glad you have put heart in our great Chief he can now Speak with confidence, I will support him in all your Councils—after all the chief presented the pipe to us
The Half man rose & spoke as follows wds.
My father—What you have Said is well, but you have not given <me a paper> any thing to the attendants of the Great Chiefs—after which [Sentence unfinished.]
from White river to the Isd of Ceder in the Great Bend of the Missourie Called the Grand detour is about 30 Leajus [Leagues]
from thence to Mo: of the Chien [Cheyenne] R:

1 [1st Village ?] Aricaras is ab. ———————	28	do
& To R au Narrow [Moreau?] S.S. ———————	25	do
To the upper Aricaras Village ———————	64	Lgs
to the Mandins ———————	10	
to the Wanutaries ———————	3	do

160 [leagues]⁹
3
480 [miles]
1140
1620

126

1142   White R.
   6
   9 1/4
  26 1/4
─────────
1180 1/2
   30
─────────
1214

In the evening late we gave Mr Dorion a bottle of whiskey and himself with the Chiefs crossed the river and Camped on the opposit bank[1] soon after a violent Wind from the N W. accompanied with rain

1. Dorion left the party at this point. As we shall see, his services as interpreter were missed when the party met the Brulé Sioux three weeks later (infra, p. 148 n.). He agreed to "Stay and Collect the Chiefs from as Many Bands of Soux as he coud this fall & bring about a peace between the suoex and their neighbours &c. &c. &c." (Thw., *1*, 131).

[*August 31 continued:*] The Distance of the Sun and moon
Sun and Moon the moon West

Time   Distance
H. M S.   d   ′   ″
11—12—18   _____   41. 51—00
11—14—23   _____   " —48—00
" —15—49   _____   " —46—00
" —16. 42   _____   " —45. 30
" —17. 52   _____   " —46. 30
" —19. 32   _____   ". 46. 30

2. Clark tried to clear up this confused entry in his Notebook Journal by writing the following: "and some land with bows [boughs] and evident marks of being made 24 [feet] above water" (Thw., *1*, 134).

3. Another week passed before Shannon was found.

4. This "antient fortification" which Clark, following Jefferson's instructions, measured, described, and mapped, was nothing but piles of sand caused by the high winds of the plains. The French accompanying the party told him there were numbers of these "fortifications" along the river. In Doc. 51, Clark made a rough sketch of these fortifications which he enlarged and perfected later. See Thw., *1*, plate facing p. 136.

September 1ˢᵗ Satturday 1804   Mr Durion left his Kettle which we gave him, which we Sent to him and Set out under a gentle Breeze from the South (raind half the last night,) proceeded on— pass Calumet Bluff of a \<redish\> yallowish read & a brownish white Hard clay, this Bluff is about 170 or 180 foot high   here the high lands aproach the river on each Side with a jentle assent, opsd the Bluff   a large Island Covered with timber is Situated close to the L.S.   we passed the Island opposit which the high land approach [approach *written over one illegible word*] the river on both Side (river ros 3 Inchs last night)   passed a large Island covered with wood on the L.S.   Some rain, cloudy all day—   the river wide & Hils close on each Side, Came to before night to go & See a Beaver house which is 1 1/2 Miles to the L.S. of the riv   Cap Lewis & my self with two men went to See this house which was represented as high & situated in a Small pond. we could not find the pond. Drewyer Killed a Buck Elk, it is not necessary to mention fish as we catch them at any place on the river, Camped at the lower point of Bonhomme Island———

Course Distance & reffurence Septr 1ˢᵗ 1804

N 88° W. 4 Mile to a high point of the Bluff on the S.S. haveing passed an Island on the ① L.S. & Several Sand bars

S. 75. W. 2 to the low point of \<Land\> a large Island on the S.S. passd a pt on the L.S. and a Sand bar, \<on the\>

S 68. W 4 Ml to a \<tree\> pt on the L.S. haveing passed the upr pt of the Isd \<a pt\> on the S S and som high banks 24 fee[t] abov the water, with [*one word illegible*] & clare [clear] eviden[ce] of the land being made² als[o] a tree, [?] a Sand bar above Isd

S 80 W 5 m to a tree on an Isld call Bonom [Bonhomme] on the S. S.
————— haveing passed 1 pt on the S.S.   a Deep bend & a San & willow
16   Bar on the L.S.   water rose 3 Inches last night

2ⁿᵈ of Sept. Sunday 1804—   Set out early & proceeded on   passed the Island & Came too above below a yellow Bluff on the S.S.   the Wind being hard from the N.W.   verry Cold   Some rain all day   much Thunder & lightning   G Drweyer R. Fields Howard & Newmon Killed four fat Elk on the Isld   we had them Jurked & the Skins Stretched to Cover the Perogues   water riseing, I observe Bear grass & Rhue, in the Sides of the hills   at Sunset the [wind] luled and cleared up cool—   Aired the meet   all in high Spirits—   Shannon & the man Sent after him has not yet joined us—³

Course Distance & reffurence Sept 2ˢᵗ 1804

N 75 W. 3 ml to the lower part of a antient fortification on the L. Side in a bend, passed over a prarie on the Island   This fortification ①

N. 45. W. 1 Ml on the L. pt passing the head of the Island at 3/4 a Mile a bluff of yello   clay on S.S.   Hills at a Distc High on L S

miles 4

2 Sepr description of a antient fortification⁴

① From the river on the top of the antient fortification at this the 12 foot high 75 feet Base first Course from the river is S 76° W 96 yards. S 84° W. 54 yds   at this angle a kind of ravilene [ravelin] covering a Saleport [Sallyport], bearing East N 69 W widing [Winding?] 300 yds passed a gate way at 280 yds the bank lower & forming a right angle of 30 yards—   two wings or mounds runing from a high nold [knoll] to the West of the Call [?] way one 30 yards back of the other covering the gate (at this place the mound is 15 feet 8 Inches higher than the plain forming a Glassee [glacis] outwards & 105 feet base   N. 32 W. 56 yards N. 20 W. 73 yards   this part of the work is about 12 feet high, leavel & about 16 feet wide on the top)   at the experation of this course a low irregular work in a Direction to the river, out Side of which is serveral ovel mounds of about 16 feet high and at the inir part of the gouge [gorge] a Deep whole across the gouge   N. 32. W 96 yds to the Commencment of a wall of about 8 feet high   N. 81° W. 533 yards to a Deep pond 73 yds in Deameeter, and 200 yards further to a Saleport, where there is evident marks of its being covered, the same course contined 1030 yards to the river bottom.

One half of the first part of the Fortification is washed into the river, a Second line, has run from the Northrn extremity parrelel with the river (as it appears to have run at that time N. 55 W. this of different hith from 4 to 10 feet—   The high land is about 3 ml from this fortress, and rise to Small mountains Say from 3 to 400 feet   the high land on the opposit or North Side of the Missourie is 110 feet forming a yellow Clay bluff to the water and is leavel back as fur as can be Seen. I am informed by the intepertes & french, that they have Seen, numbes of those fortifications in different parts of this cty. [country] pirtcularly on the Platt Kansies and the North of this place on the river Jacque. two Small fortifications is on the Arc Creek on the upper side 1ᵗ 1/4 of a mile up & the 2ᵈ 1/4 higher, nearly square   each angle 100 yards

& 7th[5]

3ʳᵈ September Monday 1804   Set out at Sun rise, verry Cold morning clear and but little wind from the N W.   we proceeded on, the river wide, took an obsivation below Plumb Creek which mouths on the S S. this Creek is Small & coms in between [*one word illegible*] 2 white banks, Great quantities of Plumbs of a most delisious flavour, I have collected the Seed of 3 Kinds which I intend to Send to my brother, also Som grapes of a Superior quallity large & well flavoured, the river is riseing a little, Several wild goats seen in the Plains they are wild & fleet[6]   Elk & Buffalow is verry plenty, Scercely any timber in the Countrey except a little on the river in the Points. Saw Some Signs of the 2 men who are a head, Colter has not over taken Shannon   Camped on the L.S. at the edge of a Plain—

Course Distance and reffurences 3ʳᵈ <Aug> Septr

West 1/2 Mile on the Point on the L.S.   a Bluff of yellow clay opsd
S. 35° W. 3 ml to the upper pt of Some wood at the foot of the high land
    in a bend on the L.S.   passed a large Sand bar 400 yds wide on
    L.S. & a pt and Sand bar makeing out from the S.S.—
West 5 1/2 Mls passed a pt & a Deep bend on the S.S. and a large Sand
    bar from the L.S to an Object in the bend to L.S. near the Hill
S. 45. W. 1 Ml on the S.S. to the mouth of Plumb Creek passing under a
    white bank resembling Chalk, a Sand bar on L.S.
South 5 Miles to a pt on the S.S. pasing a pt on the L.S. & a Sand L S.
————but little timber in this countrey—   the hills on the S S. high
    15   at the end of this course

4ᵗʰ of September Tusday 1804. a verry cold wind from South E. by S. we Set out early   proceeded on to the mouth of a Small creek in the bend to the L.S. Called <Sand> white line [lime] [*two words illegible*] at 1 1/2 miles furthr passed the mouth of a White paint Crᵗ[7] R au platte

5. The figure is in Biddle's hand. As has been noted in the Introduction, this dating was placed at the head of each document. In this case, however, it does not apear above the first entry of Sept. 1, 1804.

6. This is the first mention, in any of the journals, of the antelope. The French called it *cabri,* young goat, kid. Later, Clark prepared a specimen, "bones and all," which was intended for shipment to Washington (*Ordway,* p. 131).

7. In this journal and the Notebook Journal, the name is given as *R. au Platte* or White Paint Creek. In the sketch map of this portion of the Missouri, this double name appears (Thw., *8,* Map 5). No such name is given in Mackay's Table of Distances or on any other map.

or about 25 yd same side called, I walked on the top of the hill forming a Cliff Covd with red ceeder an extensive view from this hill, at 3 Miles from the Creek the high land jut the river forming a Bluff of Bluish Clay Continue 1 1/2 miles came to at the mouth of qui courre (rapid) [Niobrara] this river Comes roleing its Sands whuch (is corse) into the Missoures from the S W by W. this river is 152 yards across the water and not exeeding 4 feet Deep it does not rise high when it Does it Spreds over a large Surface, and is not navagable it has a Great many Small Islands & Sand bars, I went up this river 3 miles to the Spot the Panis [Pawnee] once had a large village on the upper Side in a butifull extensive Plain riseing gradialy from the river I fel into a Buffalow road joined the boat late at night at the Pania Island.

Course Distance and refference the 4th of September 1804—
S. 5 W 1 1/2 miles to the Mouth of a Creek on the L.S. th below a Ceede[r] Clift
S. 35 W 1 1/2 Mls to the mo: of a Creek on L.S. passing under a Red Ceeder <Bluff> clift
N West 3 mls to the upr pt of a wood on the L.S. opsd a Bluff of bluwish Clay, several sand bars L.S.
N. 72. W 1 1/4 ml to a mound on the L. Side bluff on the L.S. Several Sand bars in the river
West 3/4 ml to the mo: of river que courre on the L.S. ③ hills leave the river S S.
_____
8

5th September 1804 Wednesday, Set out early the wind blew hard from the South as it has for Some Days past, we Set up a juny [jury] Mast & Sailed,[8] I saw a large gangue of Turkeys, also Grous seen Passed a large Island of about 3 miles long in the Middle of the River opposit the head of this Island the Poncarre [Ponca] River Coms in to the Missouree on the L.S.— the S.S is a Clift under which great numbers of springs run out of mineral water, Saw Several wild goats [Antelope] on the Clift & Deer with black tales,— Sent Shields & Gibson to the Poncar Towns, which is Situated on the Ponca river on the lower side about two miles from its mouth in an open butifull Plain, at this time this nation is out hunting the biffalow they raise no corn or Beens, Gibson Killed a Buffalow in the Town, The two men which has been absent several Days is [*Sentence continued after the following:*]

Course Distance & reffurence the 5th of <aug> September
N: 85° W. 2 Mls to a willow pt S.S. <under a bluff opsd a> a <Bluff> Clift on the L.S. opsd
N. 35° W 3 Mls to a pt on the Clift to S.S a large Island Call Pania Is. in the middle opsd
N. 58 W 3 1/2 Ml to a <pt on the Clift> creek on the S.S passed the head of the [island] at 1 mile & Sand bars making from it the mouth of Ponia [Ponca] river opposit
West 3 1/3 mls to the lower pt of a large Island
N. 70 W. 1 3/4 Mile on the right of the Isd to the head. pass a Willow Isd
_____ & Sand bar
13 3/4

ahead, we came to on the upper pt of a large Island at 3 oClock to make a mast   Sent out Some hinters on the Island (which I call no preserve Island, at this place we used the last of our Preserves)   They killed 3 bucks, & two Elk which we jurked—.

6th <August> Septr Thursday 1804, a Storm this morning from the N W. at day light which lasted a fiew minits, Set out after the Storm was over and proceeded on   a hard wind ahead   passed the [island] which is seperated from the S. Side by a narrow Channel. the morning is verry Cold.

course W. 1 1/2 Ml to a pt of wood on the Starboard Side opsd a Bluff
N. 85 W 7 Ml psd a pt on the S.S. at 1 1/2 mls above which is large Sand
     bars, on the L.S. high Clifts of Blue & redish Soft rock, Colter
     joined us at this clift—   Camped on S. Side before night   no
     timbering

    8 1/2

in reach ahead, R. Fields killed 2 Deer   Saw Buffalow, & Goats this eve-ning, the river riseing a little

7th September Friday 1804. a verry Cold morning   Set out at Day light
N. 60° W. 3 Mls to the pt of a Bluff on the S.S. opsd a pt on the L.S. be-
    low [w]hich there is a Sand bar
West 2 1/2 Mls to aTree in the bend to the L.S near a mountain which
    is round formg a point on the riseing 70 feet higher than the
    high land   from its Shape & Situation resembles a cupeblow
    [Cupola]   passed 2 small Islds on the S.S.—near the foot of
    this high Nole we discovered a Village of an annamale the
    french Call the Prarie Dog which burrow in the grown & with
    the rattle Snake and Killed one & Caught one Dog alive[9]
    caught in a whole 2 frogs
N. 60 W. to the Bluff near the hole Killed a Dark Rattle Snake with a
    P[rairie] do[g] in him

    5 1/2

9. The business of capturing a live prairie dog required the efforts of the whole party. Every available kettle was used to bring water up from the river to flood out the animal. Five barrels of water were poured into the burrow. Finally, after working all the after-noon—only 5½ miles were made upstream that day—they "Caught one Dog a live" (Thw., 1, 141–42). Whether this was the same animal that was sent downstream in the keel-boat from Fort Mandan the following April, I have no way of knowing. That particular prairie dog's odyssey is a story in itself: from Fort Mandan to Pierre Chouteau in St. Louis, from him to General Claiborne in New Or-leans, from the General by sea to Norfolk, Virginia, and thence to Jefferson at Monti-cello. Jefferson finally found a home for the traveler in Charles Wilson Peale's natural his-tory museum in Philadelphia. The lengthy correspondence concerning the prairie dog and his traveling companions, a prairie hen and four magpies, may be found in the Jeffer-son Papers in the Library of Congress, and in Jackson, pp. 235 ff.

1. Jean Baptiste Truteau was sent up the Missouri in June 1794 by the newly organized Company of Explorers of the Upper Missouri, which had been authorized by the Spanish authorities at New Orleans and St. Louis. The Lieutenant-Governor, Zenon Trudeau, appointed Truteau to head the expedition, and instructed him to go up to the Mandans and to record all information concerning the river and the Indian tribes he met. At the Mandans, he was to build a fort, establish trade, and lay down regulations for its conduct. He was also instructed to urge the Indians to stop trading with the British, and he was to promise them that the trade up the Missouri from St. Louis would be extended and enlarged. The interest of the St. Louis authorities concerning a route from the Missouri over the mountains to the Pacific is reflected in Truteau's instructions to inquire as to the distance by river to the sources of the Missouri.

This expedition was turned back by the hostile Teton Sioux, so that Truteau did not reach his destination, the Mandan villages. In November 1794, he built for himself and his men a trading post, called Pania House, some 25 miles above the mouth of the Ponca River, where he wintered, 1794–95. There is some doubt that he spent the winter of 1795–96 there, so that Clark's figure "96" may be incorrect (Nasatir, *1*, 84–93). This spot has been identified as seven miles above the Tower, described by Clark as a mountain "resembling a cupeblow" (*Entry for Sept.* 5). See *South Dakota Historical Collections, 7* (1914), 414 n.

There is some confusion over the similarity of the names of Zenon Trudeau, Lieutenant-Governor at St. Louis, who organized the expedition, and Jean Baptiste Truteau, who led it. Jefferson, in a letter to Lewis (Washington, Nov. 16, 1803, Thw., 7, 281; Jackson, p. 138), wrote that he was sending him extracts from the Truteau Journal. Clark confuses the names and refers to "Trodow's" instead of Truteau's house.

2. Beginning with the word "halted," and continuing to the words "river fallinge," the entry is not in Clark's hand. After comparing the handwriting of this passage with that of Whitehouse, whose journal is in the Ayer Collection in the Newberry Library in Chicago, I believe this entry was made by Whitehouse.

[*September 7 entry continued:*] The Village of those little dogs is under the ground a conisiderable distance   we dig under 6 feet this rich hard clay without getting to their Lodges   some of their wholes we <po throw> put in 5 barrels of water without driving them out, we caught one by the waters forceing him out. ther mouth resemble the rabit, head longer, legs short, & toe nails long   ther tail like a g[round] Squirel which they Shake and make chattering noise   ther eyes like a dog, their colour is Gray and Skin contains Soft fur

8th of September 1804 Satturday. Set out early and proceeded on under a gentle breese from the S.E.   at 3 mls passed the place where Trodow[1] wintered one winter [17]96 <below the mouth of a creek on the L.S. at> N. 35 W. 7 Ml to a pt L.S. opsd Trodos house situated in a wood on S S. no [number] of rabits.

N. 88 W 10 Miles to a pont of woods Sbd shore. 1. mile above the commencement of this course, the lower point of a willow Island commences, this Island 1 1/4 in length; in the center of the river a small sand Island at its upper extremity. x high bluff on

――――
17

Lard begining at the upper point of the Island—   much higher hills than usual appear to the <West> N, distant about [*one figure illegible*] miles, recently birnt—   three small islands commence five miles from the commencement of this course and continue about two miles lying on the Stard side of the main chanl   here met with six buffaloe bulls of which we killed two—   1 1/2 miles further an Island on the Lard [bord] about m[ile] in lengh   came too at the lower point of this island and encamped, jerked the meet we had taken today consisting of two Buffaloe, one large buck Elk 1 Elk fawn, three fawn deer, three turkies & a Fox squierel

I went out to day on the S.S with a view to find Some of the little dogs, and Coats [goats], traveled over a riged [ridged ?] and mountanious Countrey without water & riseing to 5 or 600 hundred feet, Islands & Sands interveneing prevt my getting to the boat untill after night, in my absent Cap. Lewis killed a Buffalow, I saw Greid many Buffalow. & white wolves. (Sailed all day)

9th <Aug> Septembr Sunday, Set out at Sunrise and proceeded on passed the Island   Several gangus of Buffalow on the Sides of the hils on the L.S.[2]   halted on the L. Side   took breakfast. Capt Clark walked on Shore, we proceeded on N. 34. w. 3 miles to 2nd point of an Isl L.S. a creek came in opposite lower point on N. S.   passed the Island   Several Sand bars above, &c a willow Isl on L.S.   halted on S.S. at 12 o.C. for m. observation, above the mouth of a Small creek which came in close below a grove of cottonwood Timber.—

N. 40. W. 2 1/2 miles to upper point of the grove of cottonwood. Several Sand bars above the willow Isl at the bend of the river. the current verry rapid: N. 83. W. 3 3/4, to a point of woods on Starbord Side. passed Several Sand bars above the willow Isl   passed a high Bluff on L.S. about 100 feet high & of a dark coullour, we took dinner at the mo. of a Small Creek which came in btetween the Bluff, passed 2 more Small runs in the Same Bluff. G. Drewyer killed & put on bord the pearogue one Buck & 2 fauns. N. 36. w. 4. miles to lower point of wood on L. Side in bend. N 36 w. to pt S.S. opposite a willow Isl on S.S.   Several Sand bars above. &c. R. Fields came to the Boat   had killed one Buffalow. passed red ceeder on the edge of the hills on bouth Sides of the river but most on the bluff on L S.   passed a handsome round knob on the hill on L. St little abo[ve] passed a Smll creek in bend at lower end of a Sand bar. L.S. and camped on a Sand bar. Capt Clak came in, Y.—k [York] killed a buffalow near the Boat by the derections of the master [?], Capt Lewis wint out with R Fields & each killed a buffalow, a fair Day wind from the S E   Lattide 43° 11. . N.   Capt. Clark did not get a Goat or a black taile deer the objects of his pursuite. river fallinge [*End of passage in Whitehouse's (?) hand*]

10th September Monday   a Cloudy morning   Set out early under a gentle Breeze from the S E.   passed two Small Islands one on the L.S. & the other on the S.S. both in the first Course   at 10 1/2 miles passed the lower pt of Ceder Island[3] Situated in a bend to the L.S.   this Island is about 2 miles long Covered with red Ceder, the river is verry Shallow opsd this Island—   below the Island on the top of a ridge we found a back bone with the most of the entire laying [?] <in> Connected for 45 feet   those bones are petrified   Som teeth & ribs also Connected.[4] at 3 mls abov ceder I passed a large Island on the S.S.   to this Island Several <Islas> Elk Swam above this Island on the <L.S.> Midle is Situated 2 Islands small one above the other, those Islands are Called Mud Islands and camped on the upper Island of the, 3 Buffalow 1 Elk &c Killed to day, river falling.

3. This particular island, called Cedar Island by Clark, is not to be confused with an island of the same name further upstream, where Regis Loisel had his trading house (infra, p. 144).

4. For years, Jefferson had been interested in acquiring the skeleton of a mammoth. On his way down the Ohio in the late summer of 1803, Lewis had tried to satisfy Jefferson's longing for mammoth bones. In a letter from Cincinnati, dated Oct. 3, 1803 (Thw., 7, 274–79: Jackson, pp. 126–31), Lewis reported that he had visited the Big Bone Lick on the Kentucky side of the Ohio and viewed the collection of mammoth bones uncovered there by a Cincinnati doctor. On the way to the Pacific and back the two captains looked for more bones.

In the Notebook Journal Clark reported that this specimen was "the backbone of a fish, 45 feet long tapering to a tale" (Thw., 1, 144). Whitehouse reported "a ruck of bones . . . which appeared to be the Bones of a monstrous large fish" (Thw., 7, 57). Gass wrote that part of these bones were sent to Washington (*Journal,* p. 30). Quaife suggests that the fish was probably a fossil reptile. In any event, the party came up with some bones for Jefferson and a tale that any fisherman would approve.

5. The meat and hides of the cows were superior to those of the bulls. Later, when buffalo hides took the place of fur peltry in the trade, the hides of the buffalo cows brought the highest prices. This was one reason for the rapid destruction of the herds in the 1860s and '70s.

6. The concern of the party as to the fate of George Shannon was ended. He had failed to return to camp on Aug. 26. He was ahead of the boat, pushing on, believing the boat had passed him. The story told here is substantially the same as in the other journals.

There is, however, one puzzling phrase, both in this journal and the Notebook Journal (Thw., *1*, 145, and infra, p. 138). In the Notebook Journal, Clark wrote that "he [Shannon] became weak and feable deturmined to lay by and waite for a tradeing boat, which is expected, Keeping one horse for the last resorse, thus a man had like to have Starved to death in a land of Plenty for the want of Bullitts or Something to kill his meat." Ordway reported that Shannon "was returning down the river in hopes to meet some other Boat" (*Ordway*, p. 129). In this journal on Sept. 15th, Clark wrote that the party passed the spot "where Shannon lived on grapes waiting for Mr Clintens boat Supposeing we had went on." I have been unable to identify any Mr. Clinten among the traders on the Missouri. Furthermore, there is nothing in any other journal referring to "a tradeing boat, which is expected." Jackson has suggested that Clinten is perhaps one Charles Courtin, a trader on the river. He notes that references to a Coartong or Coutau in the journals of the party on their return in 1806 may refer to Courtin. Other allied documents give Corton, Couteau, and Courtean. It is possible, knowing Clark's spelling, that Clinten was Courtin (Jackson, p. 437 n.).

Course Distance & reffurence Septr 10th 1804.

North. 5 Mls to a Small Island in a bend to S.S. undr a bluff of hard black earth, passd a Isd on the L.S.

N. 65 W. 2 Ml to a pt on L.S.   passed the Islands on each side

N. 80 W 1/2 Mile on the L. Side, (a ① fish bones found on the top of a hill Petrefied 45 longier [?] in form

S 80 W 3 Ml to Ceder Island in <the middle> L.S of this passed Sand bars

N. 70 W. 8 1/2 Mls to the lower pt of an Island in a bend to the L.S. haveing passed Ceder Island ② and a large Island on the S S <This Island is covered with Ceders> covered with timber ③ & many Sand bars   water Shallow.

N. 35° W. 1 Ml to the Lower pt of a 2ᵈ Isd Seprtd from the first by a nar-

now Channel (one remarkable circumstance is — $\frac{19^{ths}}{20}$ of the buffalow seen is Bulls, <but> the Inds Kill the Cows.—5

_____

20

St [?] P.— a large Salt Spring of remarkable Salt water much frequented by Buffalow, Some Smaller Springs on the Side of the hill above less salt, the water exesiv Salt, and is 1 1/2 miles from the river on the S. W. or L.S. opposit Ceder Island—

Course Distance & Reffurenceis the 11th of September

N. 35° W. 4 1/2 Mls to the lower pt of a Island, haveing passed the Isld on which we [camped ?] & a large Sand bar from the upr pt

N. 70° W. 2 Mls to the head of the Island on the L.S. of it

N. 45. W. 3 Mls to a pt on the L.S. below an Island. ①

N. 50. W. 2 Mls to the upper pt of an Isd on the L.S.   passed one on the L.S. ops to which L.S. opsd at 1/4 of ml is a Village of littl dogs

West. 4 1/2 Mls to a pt on the S.S.   passed an Island on the S S. just above the last. Several Sand bars.

_____

16

we came too at the mouth of a Creek on the L.S. at Dark in a heavy Shower of rain, it continud to rain the greater part of the night, with a hard wind from the N W cold————

Septr 11th Tuesday 1804   Set out early   a cloudy morning   the river verry wide from one hill to the other, with many Sand bars   passed the Isd on which we lay at a mile   passed three Isds one on the L.S. (1/4 of a mile from it on the L.S. a village of little Dogs. I Killed four, this village is 800 yards wide & 970 yd long on a jentle Slope of a hill in a plain, those animals are noumerous)   the other two Islands are on the S.S. the river is verry Shallow & wide, the [boat ?] got a ground Several times— The man G Shannon, who who left us with the horses above the Mahar village, and beleeving us to be a head pushed on as long as he Could, joined us. he Shot away what fiew Bullets he had with him, and in a plentifull Countrey like to have Starvd. he was 12 Days without provision, subsisting on Grapes at the Same [time ?]   the Buffalow, would come within 30 yards of his Camp, one of his horses gave out & he lift him before his last billuts were consumed—6, I saw 3 large Spoted foxes to day a black tailed Deer, & Killed a Buck elk & 2 Deer, one othr Elk 2 Deer & a Porkipine Killed to day   at 12 oClock it became cloudy and rained all the after noon, & night.

Course Distance &c. 12th of Septr 1804.

N. 45° W. 4 Miles to a point of woods on the L.S.   passed an Isd Troublesom Island[7] in the middle of the river   at the upper pt of this Island the river was so crouded with sand bars that we found great dificulty in getting the boat over, She turned on the sand 4 times and was verry near turning over. we camped on the L.S. near a village of Prarie Dogs   some rain all day to day & Cold—   I walked on Shore   Saw Several foxes Several villages of Prarie dogs, and a number of Grouse

Septr 12th [13?] Wednesday 1804   Set out early   a Dark Cloudy morning wind from the N W. cold   passed, (a village of Little Squirals or Prarie dogs opsd Camp on the N. Side.)

Course Distance & remarks 13th Septr Thursday 1804

N. 45° E 1 1/2 Ml on the L.S.   wind N W. a Sand bar makeing out   a Dark raining morning. G D. [Drewyer?] caught 4 remk by large Bever

N. 30 E 1 Ml on the L.S.   verry Cold day or morning   Hills high S.S.

N. 60. W. 1 Ml on the L.Side to the Commencment of the black Bluffs[8]

N. 64° W 2 3/4 to a wood on the L.S. passing under a Bluff L.S. and Sand bars all along on the S.S.

North 1 3/4 Ml to a pt of high Land on the S.S.   pass Sand bars on both Sides/   rains

N. 10 W 4 [4 written over 3] Ml to the lower pt of a timber on S.S. passing under a Bluff S.S.   passing a large Sand Island on the L.S.
_____ & Sand bars and camped under a Bluff on the S.S.   Musquitors
12   verry bad, wors than I have seen them, qts [quantities] of mud wash into the rivr from a Small rain

[*The course and distances for September 13, 1804, are written over a sketch map of some portion of the river. Since there are no names on the map, it is impossible to identify the location.*]

7. The Notebook Journal (Thw., *1*, 145) does not give this name to the island. Ordway records the name, with an account of the difficulty encountered at this point; the boat, caught on the sandbar, nearly capsized—hence the name.

8. In the Notebook Journal, Clark wrote, "a Bluff of Slate & Coal" instead of "black Bluffs."

9. Supra, p. 65 and n.

1. At this time of the year, the antelope was getting a fresh set of horns. Unlike the deer or the elk, the antelope does not shed his horns completely, only the outer casing. The remainder is soft and pulpy until the hardening process is complete.

2. The jackrabbit of the plains.

3. Ordway and Whitehouse both report that this creek was named Shannon Creek. The name, however, was not retained. It is now Ball Creek (*Ordway,* p. 131 n.).

4. Mackay, in his Table of Distances, describes this river as "shallow and rapid, on the south bank. [of the Missouri] Takes its waters in the country far away to the S.W." (Nasatir, 2, 490). Whitehouse called it "a handsom river and a handsom country."

Septr 14ᵗʰ Friday 1804   Course Dists & rifur.

Set out early   proceeded on   passed Several Sand bars   water wide & Shallow   N. 68° W. 2 3/4 [3/4 written over 1/2] mls to a pt of high Land on the L.S.   passed a round Island on the S S.— Caught 3 beaver last night, Some drizzeley rain   cloudy & Disagreeable and Som hard Showers, I walked on Shore with a view to find an old Volcano Said to be in this neghbourhood by Mr Mc Key⁹   I was Some distance out   could not See any signs of a Volcanoe, I killed a Goat, which is peculur to this Countrey about the hite of a Grown Deer Shorter, its horns coms out imedeately abov its eyes   broad 1 short prong the other arched & soft¹ the Color is a light gray with black behind its ears, white round its neck, no beard, his Sides & belly white, and around its taile which is Small & white and Down [to] its hams, actively made   his brains on the back of its head, his noisterals large, his eyes like a Sheep   only 2 hoofs on each foot, no a[n]telrs (more like the antelope or gazella of Africa than any other Specis of Goat). Shields Killed a Hare weighing 6 1/2 lb: verry pore, the head narrow and its ears 3 Inches wide and 6 [inches] long, from the end of the fore [foot ?] to the end of the hind foot is 2 feet 11 Inch. hite 1 foot 1 3/4   its tail long & thick white, clearly the mountain Hare of Europe,² a rainy evening   all wett   The Soil of those Plains washes down into the flats, with the Smallest rain & disolves & mixes with the water. We see back from the river high hills is a leavel plain, evidently the remains of mountains, what mud washed into the river within those few days has made it verry mudy, passed two Small creeks on the L.S. & camped below a 3ʳᵈ on the L.S.   rained all evening

S. 70° W. 2 1/2 Ml to an object on the pt on the L.S.   passed the Mo[uth] of a run L.S.

N. 4 W. 2 1/2 Mls to the Mo of a Small Creek in the bend to the L.S.

N. 10 E 1 1/4 Ml to the Mo. of a Creek on the L.S., passed a bad Sand bar.

9 0/4

Pass

Course Distance & reffurence 15ᵗʰ Septr Satturday

N. 50° E 2 Mls to point of White River on the L.S.   above is a handsom Situation for a town more timber than usial above the Riv passed Several Sand

N. 26 E. 1 1/2 Ml to a pt on the L.S.   a Bluff on the S.S.

N. 10 W. 1/2 Ml on the L.S. to a Bluff. of Black Slate

N. 30 W. 2 Mls to the <upper> Lower pt of an Island, on the L.S. this Island is covered with ceeders ② & Cald Rabit Isd

North 2 Mls to the Mouth of a Creek on the L.S a Point of high land opposit. under which we camped, I Killed Elk & Deer to day. White River is about 400 yds Wide & like this R. [the Missouri]

9

September the 15ᵗʰ Satturday 1804   Set out early   passed the Mouth of a [Creek?] on the L S. where Shannon lived on grapes waiting for Mr Clintens [?] boat Supposeing we had went on,³ Capt Lewis and my Self halted at the mouth of White River⁴ & wend up a Short   Crossed &c   this river is about 400 yards, the water Confined within 150 yards, the Current regularly Swift, much resembling the Missourie, Sand bars makeing out from the points, Some Islands   we Sent up two men to <travs> go up this river one Day and Meet us to morrow   we proceeded on   passed a Small Island Covered with ceder timber, & great number of rabits, no game except rabits, and Camped on the S.S. opposit a large Creek, on which there is more wood than usial on Creeks in this quaterr   this creek raised 14 feet last rain   I Killed a Buck elk & a Deer.

September 16th Sunday,[5] we proceeded on 1 1/4 Miles and Camped <for the> on the L. Side in a butifull Plain Surounded with timber in which we Saw Severall Der, we delayed here for the purpose of Drying the articles which were wet & the cloathes. [and] to Load the Perogue which we had intended to send back finding the water too Shoal Deturmind to take on the Perogue[6]   also to make Some observations for Longitude &c. the two men G. & R. F [Goodrich? Gass? and Reuben Field?] joined us and informed "that the river as far as they were up had much the appearance of the river about the Mouth, but little timber and that chiefly elm [Cottonwood], the up land near between this river & the White river is fine, Great numbers of Goats, Deer of three kinds, Buffalow, & wolves, & Barking Squrels, The fallow Deer, Cloudy, all day[7] Cleaning out the boat   examinig & Drying the goods, & loading the Perogue, I killed 2 Deer   Capt Lewis one & a Buffalow, one Buffalow & five other Deer Killed.[8] I observed Pine Burs & Burch Sticks in the Drift wood up White river which Coms in on the L.S.   imedeately in the point is a butifull Situation for a town   3 Gentle rises, & more timber about the mouth of this river than usial   and Camped in some Timber round a plain   Grea numbers of plumbs near Camp, a Village of Barking Squirels near.

N. 72° E. 1 1/4 [4 written over 2] to a pt on the L.S.

1 1/4 [4 written over 2]

from this date———   refer to the Book No 2[9]

5. In the Notebook Journal, Thwaites has inserted a fragment, listed by Coues as Codex Ba, containing entries written by Lewis for Sept. 16–17. For the same two days, Clark recorded his entries in both this and his Notebook Journal. This lends some support to the suggestion that has been made that Lewis was also keeping a journal, for at the end of this fragment are the words, "This is a part of No. 2." There is no way of knowing whether this refers to part two of the journal Clark was keeping in the notebooks, or to one kept by Lewis (Thw., *1*, 150–51, 152–54).

6. The party was having increasing difficulty in getting the keelboat upstream: at this season of the year, the level of the water in the Missouri goes down. More sandbars and shoal water were encountered (supra, p. 84). The captains were confronted by a problem: from the beginning of the expedition (supra, p. 33) they had intended to send one of the pirogues back to St. Louis. Jefferson was careful to instruct Lewis to avail himself of every opportunity for sending back information as to the progress of the party. In his instructions to Lewis, June 20, 1803, (Thw., 7, 251; Jackson, pp. 64–65), the President wrote:

As far up the Missouri as the white settlements extend, an intercourse will probably be found to exist between them & . . . St. Louis. . . . further up the river, the traders may furnish a conveyance for letters. Beyond that you may perhaps be able to engage Indians to bring letters for the government to Cahokia or Kaskaskia. . . . Avail yourself of these means to communicate to us, at seasonable intervals, a copy of your journals, notes & observations of every kind . . .

Apparently Lewis and Clark had met no one with whom they could trust such a valuable communication, and had long since decided that they would turn one of the pirogues around, man it with soldiers, and send it downriver. The condition of the river prevented the carrying out of such a plan. The keelboat was in trouble, so part of its load had to be transferred to the pirogue previously destined for St. Louis (Thw., *1*, 149, 150; *Ordway*, p. 132).

The importance of this change of plan, as it is related to the character of the documents transcribed in the journal and their provenance, will be discussed further on (infra, p. 144 n.; see also the Introduction).

7. The nights were getting colder now, and Clark issued flannel shirts to the men (Thw., *1*, 149).

8. The buffalo killed were so thin that the hunters probably took only the brains, marrow bones, and hides. The hides were used to cover one of the pirogues to protect the baggage (Thw., *1*, 149). The brains were used to soften the hides and to make them more flexible after they were dried and scraped.

9. Infra, p. 144 and n.

1. In the Notebook Journal, Lewis recorded what he saw and did on this excursion. His description of stalking the wary antelope is excellent (Thw., *1*, 152–54).

2. A magpie. After seeing many of these birds, Clark apparently gave up the idea that this was a peculiar kind of crow and wrote in the Notebook Journal, "The Corvos or magpye is verry Common in this quarter" (Thw., *1*, 181).

3. The blacktail deer.

4. From Clark's description I do not think that this was a coyote, an animal considerably larger than any fox. In the Notebook Journal he wrote that it "Burrows in the ground" (Thw., *1*, 155). Coyotes do not live in burrows. I believe that what Clark killed was a swift fox, a plains fox now very rare. I have seen a specimen of this animal similar to Clark's description in Wyoming, where it is called simply a "swift." For a list identifying the animals and birds mentioned in the journals, see Jackson, pp. 291–98.

Above White river

17th of Septr Monday 1804 Dried all those articles which had got wet by the last rain, a fine day Capt Lewis went hunting with a vew to see the Countrey & its productions,[1] he was out all Day Killed a Buffalow & a remarkable bird of the Spicies of Corvus, long tail of a greenish Purple, varigated a Beek like a crow white round its neck comeing to a point on its back, its belley white feet like a Hawk abt the size of a large Pigeon[2] Capt Lewis returned at Dark. I took the Meridian & equal altitudes to day made the Lattitude. [*space*]

Colter Killed a Goat, & a Curious Kind of Deer, a Darker grey than Common the hair longer & finer, the ears verry large & long a Small resepitical under its eye its tail round and white to near the end which is black & like a cow in every other respect like a Deer, except it runs like a goat. large.[3]

The hunters brought in 8 fallow Deer & 5 Common Deer to day, Great numbers of Buffalow in the Praries, also a light Coloured woolf Covered with hair & corse fur, also a Small wolf with a large bushey tail— Some Goats of a Different Kind Seen to day,— great many Plumbs, rabits, Porcupines & barking Squirels, Capt Lewis Killed a rattle Snake in a village of the Squerel's and Saw a Hair to day. Wind from the S.W. we finished Drying our Provisions some of which was wet and spoiled, I Killed a Prarie wolf to day Septr 18 about the Sise of a Gray fox with a bushey tail the head and ears like a Fox wolf, and barks like a Small Dog— The annimale which we have taken for this Fox is this wolf, we have seen no Foxes.[4]

18th Septr Tuesday Set out early wind from the N W. Modrt our boat being much litened goes much better than usial
Course N. 45° E 1 Ml to the lower point of a Island ①
N. 25° E. 3 Ml to a pt on the L.S. passed the Isd at 1 Ml & some Sand
        bars makeing from it a Creek opsd on S.S.
N. 14° E 1 1/2 Mls to a point of willows on the L.S.
N. 10 W. 1 1/2 Mls to a point of wood on the L.S. hard wind
N. 22 W 1 Ml to a pt of wood on the L.S. and Came to at 5 oClock to
        ——— jurke the meat killed to day. and what was collected from
    N. 8
        what was Killed yesterday, i e 10 Deer to Day 4 & a Elk yesterday a cole night for the Season

Septr 19th Wednesday 1804, Set out early. a Cool morning clear & still
Course N. 50° W. 3 Ml to a pt of wood on the S.S. a Bluff on the L.S.
        opposit. here Commences a butifull Countrey on both Sides of
        the river
North 4 Miles to the mouth of a River S.S. ①—
N. 30. W. 2 1/2 Miles to the upper pt of the Island S.S. <in the middle
        of the river> ②
N. 43° W 2 on the L.S. Passd a creek ③
N. 54° W. 3 Ml <on the> to a pt of wood on the S.S.
N. 70 W. 5 Mls to a Bluff on the L.S. passed a creek ④
West 3 1/2 Miles to some timber on the L.S. passed a creek ⑤ Camped.

    23 miles

① & ② passed a large Island Situated nearest the S.S. 1/2 a mile from the Lower pt of this Island, the 1st of the 3 rivers mouths which is about 35 yards wide, running from the N.E. one mile above the 2nd Comes in this is Small not more that [than] 15 yards wide   a Short Distance above a 3ᵈ comes in scattering its waters thro a bottom. I walked on Shore to See this great Pass of the Sioux and Calumet ground,⁵ found it a handsom Situation, and Saw the remains of their camps on the 2ᵈ river, for many years passed— ③ passed a creek on the L.S. 15 yds wide   we ④ passed a Creek 20 yds wide   ⑤ passed a Creek 20 yd wide on the L.S.   I call night C[reek] as I did not get to it untill late at night, above the mouth of this Creek we camped, the wind being favourable, for the boat I Killed a fat Buffalow Cow, and a fat Buck elk, york my servent Killed a Buck, the Hunte[r]s Killed 4 Deer, & the boat crew Killed 2 Buffalow Swiming the river, handsom Countrey of Plains, I saw many trovs [droves ?] of Buffalow & a Gangue of 30 or 40 Elk and othr Scattering elk. &c   a fine evening   I hurt my hands & feet last night——

September the 20ᵗʰ Thursday 1804   Detchd 3 men across the Big bend. Called th Grand de Tour)⁶ with the horse, to stay and hunt & jurk provisions untill we get around   ① passed a Island on the S.S.   the river Crouded with Sand bars,

The Course
N. 50° W. 3 1/4 miles to the upper Point of an Island on the S.S. about
    2 Ml long
North 4 Mls to a pt on th L.S.   passed one on the S.S. abov the Island—
N. 10° W. 1 1/2 Mls to a pt of wood on the L.S.—
N. 22° W. 3 Mls to the L.S.
N. 60 W. 2 Mls to a Small timber on the L.S.—
West 3 Mls to a wood on L S.
S. 73. W. 3 1/2 Mls to a pt of wood on L.S.—
South 4 miles to a tree on L.S.   passed a Island ① situated on the L.S.
    this Island is Small with a large Sand [bar?]
S. 74 E 3 1/2 Miles to a point of wood on the L.S.   pass Sands & Gd [?]
S. 56. E 3 1/2 to a pt on the S.S. opsd a high hill on the L.S. [space] ② &
S. 28. E. 2 Mls to a ceder hill on the L.S in a bend opposit the Gorge of
    this bend where the river is only 1 1/4 mile across & 30 Miles
    around, the hills high with some low land—   This Day is re-
    fured to ① ④ & for farth[er] expranation
    ———
33 1/4

5. In the Notebook Journal, Clark added, "those rivers is the place that all nations who meet are at peace with each other, called the Seoux pass of the 3 rivers" (Thw., *1*, 156). On the Indian Office Map this place is labeled, "Portage des Sioux, The Sioux carrying place." The three rivers are the modern Crow, Elm, and Campbell creeks, on the Lower Brulé Indian Reservation in South Dakota. From this point, the Indian route led across the James to the Upper Big Sioux River and thence to the heads of both the Minnesota and Red rivers.

6. This big bend in the river, or Grand Detour, is described in all the journals and found on the maps. In the Soulard Map (Thw., *8*, Plate 2) a huge loop was drawn in, 20 miles across at its narrowest point and about 100 miles long. The Indian Office Map has it drawn correctly. Truteau reported that the river makes a loop of ten leagues, and that the distance across the neck of the loop was under two miles. Clark put it at 2,000 yards or about 1¼ miles (infra, p. 142). A sketch map of the Grand Detour is drawn over the entry for Sept. 21. (See Doc. 56.)

7. Ordway and Gass called this stream Tyler's Creek, and Clark labeled it as such on his map. Its present name is Medicine Creek.

8. The current of the Missouri cut under its soft banks and great masses of soil and rock slid into the river, carrying with it cottonwoods growing along the stream. This was a constant danger to all boats tied up near the shore. When steamboating began on the upper river, there were instances of such large boats being completely wrecked.

20   20

September   1804.   Thursday (Continued
[hole] N W. extremity of this bend   passed Small Island on the L.S.
opposit the upper Point of this Solitary Island Came too to [one word illegible] at the mouth of a Small run on the S.S. & Newmon & Tomson picked up Some Salt mixed with the Sand in the run, Such as the ottoes Indians Collect on the Sands of the Corn de Cerf [Elkhorn] R. & make use of,[7] Camped on a Sand bar on the S.S. above the Island—   I went out to examine the portage which I found quit[e] Short 2000 Yards only, the Prarie below & Sides of the hills containing great quantites of the Prickly Piar which nearly ruined my feet, I saw a hare, & I beleve he run into a hole, he run on a hill & disapeared, I saw on this hill several holes. I saw Several Goats Elk Ders &c & Buffalow in every Derection feeding. R. Fields Killed a Deer & 2 Goats   one a feemale, which differs from the male as to Size being Something Smaller, Small straight horns without any black about the neck   Camped late

21st of September 1804 Friday 1804, last night or reather this morng at a half past one oClock the Sand bar on which we Camped began to give way, which allarmed the Sergt on guard & the noise waked me, I got up and by the light of the moon observed that the Sand was giving away both above & belong [below] and would Swallow our Perogues in a few minits, ordered all hands on board and pushed off   we had not got to the opposit Shore before pt of our Camp fel into the river.[8] we proceeded on to the Gorge of the bend & brackfast, the Distance of this bend around is 30 miles, and 1 1/4 miles thro:, the high lands extends to the gauge [gorge] and is about 2000 feet   the plain in the bend as also the two opposit Sides abov & below is delightfull plains with graduel assents from the river in which there is at this time Great number of Buffalow Elk & Goats feedg   The Course from the gauge on the L.S. is S. 70 W. 4 1/2 Miles to the pt of ceder Timbir on the L.S.   pass Sands. worthy of remark the cat fish not So plenty abov white river & fish much smaller than usial, Great nunbers of Brant & plover, also goat and black tail Deer.
N. 50° W. 2 1/2 passed a Willow Island on the L.S.   a large Creek
        Called Tylors <Creek> R. at 1 1/2 ml about 40 yds wide
        above the Island on L.S.   [This entry, for September 21, 1804,
        is written over a sketch map of the Big Bend of the Missouri.]
6.t fowd [?] W [?] 7
West 4 1/2 Mls to a pt of wood on the L.S. pass Sand bars & Shoal wat[er]
        the river here is wide nearly a mile in width—   Camped on the

11 1/2
        S.S. below the Mock Island, after passing a number of Stones of
        Different Sises on the Shore of the Same Side, hunte[r]s Killed
        a Deer, Bever, and a <black> white wolf and a Turkey, Saw
        many goats and Elk to day——

[This fragment, giving the mileage from the mouth of the Missouri to the Big Bend, is in Clark's hand:]

			Miles				
From River Dubois. to St Charles———			21	in Latitude	38°	54′	39″
from	Do–..	to the Mouth of Gasconade	104	do . . .	38.	45.	35.
do	do—	to the Mouth of Osarge R:	138.	do.	38.	31.	16
do	do	Mine river on the South.	201.	do.	————		
do	do	to Grand R. on the N. Side	254.	do.	38.	47.	54
do	do	to Kanzies R on the South.	366.	do.	39.	5.	25
do	do	to Creek indepenanc at the Kanzies old village South	433.	do.	39.	25.	42
do	do	Nodaway River. N Side.	481.	do.	39.	39.	22.
do	do	Nemahar R. S. Side	511.	do.	39.	55.	56
do	do	Bald pated Prarie N. Side	570	do.	40.	27.	7.
do	do	the mo. of the Great River Plate on the South Side	632	do abt	41.	00.	0.

from the mouth of Missourie river to the Councel Bluffs opsd the Ottoes	682	in Latd	41° 17′ 0″
to Little Sieoux River on N Side..	766.	do.	41. 42. 34.
to Mahar village . . . S. Side 3 ms off R.	864.	do	42. 13. 41.
to Mouth of the Great River Souex 3 miles west of Floyds river on N. Sd	880.	do	42. 23. 49.
to Mo. of River Jacque on the N. Sd	970.	do.	42. 53. 13
to Mo. of River que Curre or the rapid river on the South Side	1020.	do	————
to no preserves Island 5 miles North of the Poncaries Village on the little river Pania on the S. Side—	1037.	do	————
to White River on the L.S. is . . .	1142.	d.	
" Grand de Touit [Tour] or Big bend	1283	do.	44. 11. 33. 3/10

[End of Document 57; return to Doc. 56.]

9. For years the St. Louis traders had expended money and lives attempting to open up a safe and profitable trade with the tribes of the Upper Missouri. The barrier of the Teton Sioux, whom Lewis and Clark were about to encounter, had prevented peaceable intercourse. In 1800, Loisel and his partner, Clamorgan, had renewed the effort. Loisel had obtained from the Spanish authorities a land grant to Cedar Island and had built a fort there. As has been noted, Lewis and Clark met Loisel on May 25, 1804, coming downriver from his fort (supra, p. 46 n.).

1. On one side of Doc. 56 are the entries for Sept. 20–23, 1804. On the verso is the address to General Jonathan Clark, William's brother. "Those scripts," as Clark called them, are the entries of this journal for the period May 13 to Sept. 23. They were sealed up and addressed to Jonathan. The folds of the document, the position of the inscription, the location of the seal, and the tear in the upper left-hand corner leave no doubt in my mind that this packet of notes was made on or about Sept. 23.

On Sept. 16 (supra, p. 139 n.), the two captains abandoned the plan to send dispatches downstream by one of the pirogues. Because of the shoaling of the river, it was necessary to retain all three craft and redistribute the loads. Since a pirogue could not be released, the next best hope was to meet a boat headed for St. Louis. There is evidence that such a boat was expected (Thw., *1*, 145). When Shannon was lost, Clark recorded that he was waiting for "Mr. Clinten's boat" (supra, p. 138 and n.). We do not know how Clark knew of an expected boat or who Mr. Clinten was. In any event, Clark had prepared a packet for his brother, but when the expected boat failed to appear, he took "those scripts" up to Fort Mandan. The reader will note, following the words "all those scripts," Clark wrote, "& draw from my Journal at some other time." It seems clear that he is here referring to his Notebook Journal, and that he will draw from it whatever information he might need of the journey up to this point. The reader will also note that Clark begins Doc. 58 with the heading "A Continuation of Notes taken assending the Missourie in 1804—by W. Clark." Furthermore, there are two new entries for Sept. 22 and 23, similar to but not identical with those of the same dates that he has sealed up. The importance of the change in the character of this journal after this date and its relevance to the problem of the provenance of these documents is discussed in the Introduction.

22^(nd) September. Satturday 1804——
a thick fog this morning untill 7 oClock which detained us, Saw Some old tracks of the Indians on the S.S.   proceeded on— one French man with a abscess on his thigh which pains him verry much for 10 or 12 Days a butifull Plain on both Sides   low high land under which there is a number of lage Stone, we See great numbes of Buffalow feeding   S. 72° W. 5 miles to a pt on the S.S. opsd a High Bluff   passed under a Bluff L.S.   altitude at opsd the Lower pt of 1^(st) Isd of the 3 Sisters with Sexton 92° 50″ – 0″   Oct 89° – 47′ – 0″——— 1 The Lattitude produced from those obsevations is 44° 11′ 33″ 4/10 North.

West 1 mile on the S.S. a bottom Commences on the L. at the end of the
    course
N. 38. W. 4 1/2 miles to a point of timber on the S.S. opposit Ceeder
    Island on which Louselle winterd 1803⁹   passed a Small Island
    at one & 1/2 Miles, and a large Island 3 miles long above Called
    the 3 Sisters situated near the L.S.   opposit this Island a large
    Creek Coms in on the L.S
N. 30° W. 3 Miles to a pt on the S.S.   passed Ceeder Island in the Mid-
    dle of the river nearly in the form of a Dimond— ② the main
    Current on the L. Side Louisells <Hous> fort of ceder op it
    70 foot squar on the L.S. on the South Side of about the middle
    a number of Indian camps, all the Cotton wood Cut down to
    feed their horses.
Louisells Fort is 23 yards Squa[re]   each room is 20 feet Square and Sub
    Divided
Thenometer <112> abv 0
N. 22 E 2 1/2 Mls to the lower point of a timber on the S.S. below Cabid
———
 16   [Cabri] Islan (or Goat Isd). I walked out on the L. Side this
    evening & Killed a Deer, Camped late, great number of large
    Stone Some distance out from the Shore   Camped on the S.S.
    at the end of this Course—   The hunter Came in, Complain of
    their Mockersons being burnt out by the Salts on the hills
    they killed only 1 Deer———

23^(rd) Septr Sunday 1804   (days and nights equal)   Set out early unde[r] a gentle Breeze from the S E N. 46° W 3 3/4 Miles to the mo: of a creek on the S.S.   passd a pt on the L.S.   <passed> ① a Small Island opsd in the bend to the S.S.   This Island is Called goat Island, ① this Creek is 10 yards wide, passed bad Sand bars— S. 46° W. 2 3/4 Mls   a wood at a Spring in the bend to the L.S.   Saw the prarie a fire behind us near the head of Ceder Island L.S. N. 80° 4 1/2 to the lower pt of Elk Island [*space*] pass 2 Willow Islands [*two words illegible*]   I saw this morning 12 of those Black & white birds of the corvus Spicies [*magpies*].——Capt Lewis went out to hund on the Island   a great number of Buffalow in Sight [*space*]   I must Seal up all those scripts & draw from my Journal at some other time¹

                             Wm Clark   Cpt

Genl Jona Clark
    of
    Kentucky
                    Sept 20^(th)
To the 22^(nd) of Septr 1804
To the Care of Genl Jona Clark
    near Louisville Kty
To be opened by Capt W. Clark
or Capt: Meriwether Lewis

A continuation of Notes taken assending the Missourie in 1804— by W. Clark

to 26 [Biddle's addition]

Satturday the 22ⁿᵈ of September 1804—²

A Thick fog this morning detained us untill 7 oClock, The plains on both Sides of the River is butifull and assends gradually from the river; Noumerous herds of Buffalow to be Seen in every derections. ① Took the altitude of the Sun & found the Lattitude to be 44°—11′—33″—N— ② passed a Small Island on the L. S— and one on the S.S— imediately above, & about 3 m: long, on the L.S. opposit this Island a Creek of about 15 yds wide mouthes, Called the Creek of the 3 Sisters ③ passed Cedar Island 1 1/2 M. long & 1 M. wide Situated a little above the last and nearest the S.S— near the upper part of this Island on its S. Side a Tradeing fort is Situated built of cedar— by a Mr Louiselle of St Louis, for the purpose of Tradeing with the Teton Bands of Soues (or "Sieux") about this Fort I saw numbers of Indians Temporary Lodges, & horse Stables, all of them round and to a point at top,³ I observed also numbers of Cotton Trees fallen for the purpose of feeding their horses on the Bark of the limbs of those trees which is said to be excellent food for the horses— we came too on the S.S. below a Small Island called Goat Island, passed a no: of large round Stones, som distance in the river as also in the Sides of the hills,— I walked on the Shore this evening and Killed a verry large Deer— our hunters Killed 2 Deer & a Beaver, they Complain of the Mineral quallites of the high land distroying their Mockersons—.

Course Distance & rufferences 22ᵈ Sept

S. 72° W. 5 Miles to a pt on the S.S— passing under a high Bluff on the L.S— ①

West. 1 Mile on the S.S—to the commencement of a bottom on the L.S.

N. 38° W. 4 1/2 Miles to a pt of timber on the S.S. opsd Cedar Isd passed 2 Isds & a Creek opsd L.S. ②

N. 30° W. 3 Miles to a pt on the S.S— passed Ceder Island & Louisells Fort— ③

N 22° E. 2 1/2 Miles to Some timber on the L.S—opposite a Small Island call Goad Isd—

———
16

Sunday the 23ʳᵈ September 1804

Set out under a gentle breeze from the S.E— ① passed Goat Island Situated in a bend to the S.S— above passed a Small Creek 12 yards wide on the S.S.— we observed a great Smoke to the S W. which is an Indian Signal of their haveing discovered us, I walked on Shore and observed great numbers of Buffalows, ② passed 2 Small Willow Islands with large Sand bars makeing from thier upper points ③ passed Elk Island Situated near the L.S. about 2 1/2 Mls long & 3/4 wide, Covered with Cotton wood, a red berry Called by the French "grue de buff,"⁴ Grapes &c. the river is wide Streight & contains a great numbr of Sand bars, ④ passed a Small Creek on the S.S. 16 yds wide I call Reubens Cr— R. Fields was the first who found it—⁵ Came too & Camped on the S.S. in a Wood, Soon after we landed three Soues boys Swam across to us, those boys informed us that a Band of Sieux called the Tetons of 80 Lodges wer Camped near the mouth of the next River, and 60 Lodges more a Short distance above them,⁶ they had that day Set the praries on

2. In the preceding document (56) Clark made entries for Sept. 22 and 23. They are brief, and Sept. 23 has no list of courses and distances. The two entries for the same dates which follow are more detailed and courses and distances are given for Sept. 23. It appears that these were made after the "scripts" were sealed up.

3. Ordway gives the following excellent description of this typical Missouri river fur-trading post (*Ordway*, p. 135):

it was all built up [of] Ceeder and picketed in with ceeder about 65 or 70 feet Square with a Sentery Box in 2 angles corners the pickets is 13½ feet high above Ground. the Tradeing house is 45½ by 32½ feet. divided into four equal apartments one for Merchantise one for a common hall. one for peltery &c. 2 peltery presses. this Tradeing house is built of ceeder high and covered with hughn [hewed] guttered ceeder, in the winter they cover them over with Buffaloe hides which answer a Good purpose. the chimneys built with Stone Clay & Wood their is Indian camps for a large distance about this place, where the Souix Indians came to Trade with Mr Louisells.

4. *Graisse du boeuf (graisse du buffle)*, the buffalo berry (Thw., *6*, 155, 158).

5. As in most cases where a stream was named after one of the men, the name is not found in Clark's list of rivers and creeks or on his map. It is now known as East Medicine Knoll River (Thw., *1*, 162).

6. These were Bois Brulé, a subdivision of the Teton Sioux and one of the eight main subdivisions of that tribe. This band turned out to be far more hostile than the Yankton Sioux that the party had met a month before and with whom they had held a council (supra, pp. 121–26).

On the arrival of the party at the mouth of the Teton River, the Brulé were ready with "their bows Strung and guns Cocked." The courage of Clark, who was on shore with a few men, and the sight of the men on the keelboat with guns leveled, dissuaded the Indians from immediate attack. The next two days were taken up with ceremony. A few miles up the river was another band of Brulé; if the party could be delayed long enough, reinforcements might arrive. When this help did not come, the Indians renewed their hostile posture, for they were determined to prevent the party from going any further. Ordway wrote in his journal that the Indians declared "we might return back with what we had or remain with them, but we could not go up the Missouri any further, about 200 Indians were then on the bank. Some had firearms. Some had Spears. Some had a kind of cutlashes, and all the rest had Bows and steel or Iron pointed arrows" (*Ordway*, p. 142). Again, a show of force by the party was enough, and the party proceeded on its way upstream. Later the party met the other band of Brulé who offered no resistance. This encounter with the Brulé was the most serious Indian threat that the expedition had to face on its journey to the Pacific and return. In previous years these Indians had blocked most attempts of trading parties to go up the Missouri, and they were to continue to be a source of trouble for years to come.

7. In the Notebook Journal, Clark wrote that this particular island was named Good Humored Island (Thw., *1*, 163).

8. Truteau, in his Description (Nasatir, *2*, 378), noted that the Indians called this stream Tranquil Water; the French, the Little Missouri. On the Indian Office Map it is named the Little Missouri. Neither of these names nor the name Teton, given to it by Clark, has remained. The present name is the Bad River. Opposite its mouth is the city of Pierre, South Dakota.

fire to let those camps Know of our approach— we gave those boys two twists of Tobacco to carry to their Chiefs & Warriors to Smoke, with derections to tell them that we wished to Speak to them tomorrow, <near> at the mouth of the next river— Capt Lewis walked on Shore, R F. Killed a She Goat or Cabbra."

Course distance & refferens 23rd Septr

N. 46° W. 3 3/4 Miles to the mouth of Smoke Creek in a bend S.S. passed Goat Isd of Sand ①

N. 46° W. 1 3/4 Miles to a coaps of woods at a Spring in a bend to the L.S.

N. 80° W. 4 1/2 Miles to the lower pt of a Island   passed 2 Small Islands, & sand bars   2   3

N. 85° W. 5—Miles to a pt on the L. S—   passd the upper pt of Elk Isd at 2 1/2 Miles—   3

West 5 Miles to a pt on the S.S—below a Creek L.S—   pass'd one on the S.S—   4

_____
26

Course & Distance & refferan 24th Sept

N. 80° W. 3 Miles to a point on the Starboard Side, river wide   passed a Creek L.S.

West 2 1/2 Miles to the S. Side of an Island Situated near the L. Shore ①

West 4 Miles to a point on the S.S—   passed the Island. on the L.S. ①

S. 85° W 4. Miles to the mouth of Teton River on the L.S.   Several Inds ②

_____
13 1/2

Monday the 24th of September 1804

a fair Morning   Set out early, wind from the East, passed the mouth of a Creek on the L.S. Called Creek in high water. passed a large ① Island on the L.S. about 2 1/2 Miles long on which Colter had Camped & Killed 4 Elk. the wind from the S.E.— we prepared Some Clothes a fieu Medals for the Chiefs of the Teton band of Sioux we expected to meet at the next River—   Much Stone on the S.S. of the River, we Saw one hare to day—   our Perogues Called at the Island for the Elk, Soon after we passed the Island Colter ran up the bank & reported that the Sioux had taken his horse, we soon after Saw five indians on the bank, who expressed a wish to come on board, we informed them we were friends, and wished to Continue so, we were not abraid any Indians—   Some of their young Men had Stolen a horse sent by their Great Father to their great Chief, and we Should not Speak to them any more untill the horse was returned to us again—   passed a Island about 1 1/2 M. long on which we Saw maney elk & Buffalow,[7] we Came too off the Mouth of a Small river, The Teton of the burnt woods [Bois Brulé] is Camped 2 Miles up this river, this river we Call Teton is 70 Yds wide and coms in on the S W Side—[8]   I went on Shore and Smoked with a Chief, Called Buffalow Medison, who Came to See us here. The Chief said he Knew nothing of the horse &c &c. I informed them we would [c]all the grand Chiefs in Council tomorrow, all continued on board all night—

FROM THE TETON TO THE MANDANS:
SEPTEMBER 25, 1804—OCTOBER 26, 1804

9. The difficulty in dealing with the hostile Teton Sioux was increased by inadequacy of communication. Old Dorion, who spoke Sioux, had been left behind. In the Notebook Journal, Clark refers to two interpreters (Thw., *1*, 165); further on he wrote that he "gave our Mahar inteptr" some gifts for a group of Omaha squaws held captive by the Sioux. Peter Cruzatte, who could speak Omaha, was with the party (Thw., *1*, 170). It would appear that the Tetons spoke to the Omaha interpreter, who spoke in Omaha to Cruzatte, who translated into English. This may be one of the reasons why the speeches made by the Indians in council are not given in any detail.

1. One of a group of young warriors who policed the camp, maintained order, and organized the band when on a buffalo hunt (Hodge, *2*, 614).

2. In the Notebook Journal, Clark explained why this island was so named—"as we were in bad humer" (Thw., *1*, 165).

3. In the Notebook Journal, Clark wrote that the "Smokeables" were "Bawe roley" (*bois roulé*) or rolled wood, a name given by the French for the tobacco of the Indians. This was a mixture of scrapings of bark and roots from red willow, dogwood, sumac, and other shrubs. The general name applied to this mixture was Kinnikinnick (Thw., *1*, 166 n.; Hodge, *1*, 692).

25th of September 1804 off Teton River

a fair Morning   the wind from the S.E.   raised a Flagg Staff and formed an orning & Shade on a Sand bar in the Mouth of Teton R to Council under, the greater portion of the party to Continue on board— about 11 oClock the 1st & 2d Chief arrived, we gave them to eat; they gave us some meat, (we discover our interpeter do not speak the language well)[9] at 12 oClock the Councill Commenced & after Smokeing agreeable to the usial custom C.L. [Captain Lewis] Delivered a written Speech to them, I some explinations &c   all our party Paraded, gave a Medal to the grand Chief an Indian Un-ton gar-sar bar, or Black Buffalow— 2° Torto-h[h written over p]on-gar, Partezon (Bad fellow)   the 3d Tar-ton-gar-wa-ker, Buffalow medison—   we invited those Chiefs & a Soldier[1] on board our boat, and Showed them many curiorsites, which they were much Surprised, we gave they 1/2 a wine glass of whiskey which they appeared to be exceedingly fond off   they took up an empty bottle, Smelted it, and made maney simple jestures, and Soon began to be troublesom   the 2d Chief effecting Drunkness as a cloak for his vilenous intintions (as I found after wards,) realed or fell about the boat, I went in a perogue with those Chief who left the boat with great reluctians, my object was to reconsile them and leave them on shore, as Soon as I landed 3 of their young men Seased the Cable of the Perogue, one Soldiar Huged the mast <which was> and the 2d Cheif was exceedingly insolent both in words and justures to me declarieng I should no go off, Saying he had not recived presents suffient from us—<his> I attemped to passify <him> but it had a contrary effect for his insults became So personal and his intentions evident to do me injury, I Drew my sword at this motion Capt Louis ordered all in th[e] boat under arms, and <ordered all hands under arms> the fiew men that was with me haveing previously taken up their guns with a full deturmination to defend me if possible—   The grand Chief then took hold of the Cable & Sent all the young men off, the Soldier got out of the perogue and the 2nd Chief walked off to the Party at about 20 yards back, all of which had their bows Strung & guns Cocked—   I then spoke in verry positive terms to them all, <but> principaly addressing my self to the 1st Chiief, who let the roape go and walked to the Indian party about, 100—   I again offered my hand to the 1st Chief who refused it—   (all this time the Indians were pointing ther arrows blank—   I proceeded to the perogue and pushed off and had not proceeded far before the 1st & 3r Chief & 2 principal men walked into the water and requested to go on board, I took them in and we proceeded on abot a Mile, and anchored near a Small Island, I call this Island Bad humered Island[2]

26 N S pt

N. 28. W. 4 1/2 Miles to a pt on L.S.

26th of Septr   set out early and proceeded on—   the river lined with indians   came too & anchored by the particular request of the Chiefs to let their Womin & Boys see the Boat, and Suffer them to Show us some friendship—   great membes [numbers ?] of men womin & Children on the bank viewing us—   Those people are Spritely   Small legs ille looking set men perticularly, they grease & Black themselves when they dress, make use of Hawks feathers about thier heads, cover with a Roab each   a polecat Skin to hold their Smokeables,[3] fond of Dress, Badly armed. ther women appear verry well, few Teeth, High Cheek [bones] Dress in Skin Peticoats, & a Roabe with the flesh Side out and harey ends turned back over their Sholdes, and look well—   they doe all the Laborious work, and I may say are perfect Slaves to thier husbans who frequently have Several wives— Cap Lewis & 5 men went on Shore with the Chiefs, who appeared to wish to become friendly   they requested us to remain one night & see them dance &c.— in the evening I walked on Shore, and Saw Several Mahar Womin & Boys in a lodge & was told they were Prisones lately taken in a battle in which they Killed a number & took 48 prisoners—[4]   I advised the Chiefs to make a peace with that nation and give up the Prisoners, if they intended to follow the words of their great father   they promised that they would do so—   I was in Several Lodges neetly formed, those lodges are about 15 to 20 feet Diametr Stretched on Poles like a Sugar Loaf, made of Buffalow Skins Dressed about 5 oClock I was approached by 10 well Dressed young men with a neet Buffalow Roab which they Set down before me & requested me to get in   they carried me to ther Council Tents forming 3/4 circle & set me down betwn 2 Chefs where <they had> about 70 men were Seated in a circle, in front of the Chief   6 feet Square was cleared & the pipe of peace raised on forks & Sticks, under which was Swans down <spred> Scattered, the Flags of Spane[5] & the one we gave them yesterday was Displayed   a large fire was made o [o written over i]n which a Dog was Cooked, & in the center about 400 lb of Buffalow meat which they gave us,— Soon after, I took my seat the young men went to the boat & brought Cap Lewis in the Same way & placed him by me   Soon after an old man rose & Spoke approveing what we had done.

4. Whitehouse wrote that "they killed 65 men and took 25 women prisoners. they took the 65 of the Mahars sculps and had them hung on Small poles, which ther women held in their hands when they danced" (Thw., 7, 64).

5. Perhaps by displaying the Spanish as well as the American flag, the Tetons wished to inform their guests that the transfer of their allegiance from the Great White Father in Madrid to his successor in Washington had not been consummated as far as they were concerned.

6. Whitehouse, who was along, wrote, "they gave us different kinds of victules to eat. Some of it I never Saw the like before" (Thw., 7, 64).

7. This tactic of the Sioux is not mentioned in the Notebook Journal.

8. Several of these printed commissions that were not used have been preserved. A copy of one is found in Thw., *1*, 113. The commission issued to Wah-cha-Pa is now in the Huntington Library in San Marino, California. This chief's name is inserted and it is signed by the two captains. It is the only commission filled in and signed that has been preserved. A facsimile of this commission is found in Bakeless, opposite p. 83. See also Jackson, pp. 209–10.

9. In the confusion and excitement the rumor started that the Omaha were attacking (Thw., *1*, 170).

They form thier Camp in a circle form. requesting us to take pitty on them &c. answered—

The great Chief then rose in great state and Spoke to the Same purpos and with solemnity took up the pipe of peace and pointed it to the heavens, the 4 quartrs and the earth, he made Som devestation [Dissertation?], & presented the Stem to us to us to Smoke, after Smokieng & a Short Harrang to his people we were requested to take the meat, and the Flesh of the Dog gavin us to eat—[6] We Smoked untill Dark, at which time all was cleared away & a large fire made in the Center, Several men with Tamborens highly Decorated with Der & Cabra [antelope] Hoofs to make them rattle, assembled and began to Sing & Beat— The women Came forward highly decerated with the scalps & Tropies of war of their fathes Husbands & realations, and Danced the war Dance, which they done with great chearfulness untill 12 oClock, when we informed the Cheif we intended return on bord, (they offered us women, which we did not except)[7] 4 Chiefs accompanied us to the boat and staid all night— Those people have a Description of Men which they Call Soldiars, those men attend to the police of the Band, correct all vices &c. I saw one to day whip 2 Squars who appeared to have fallen out, when the Soldier approached all appeared [to] give way and flee <with> at night they Keep 4 or 5 men at different distances walking around their Camp Singing the acursenes [occurrences] of the night all in Spirits this evening wind hard from the S E

I saw 25 squars & Boys taken 13 days ago in a battle with the Mahars, in which they destroyed 40 Lodges, Killed 75 men & boys, & took 48 prisones which they promised us Should be delivered to Mr Durion now with the Yankton [*two words illegible*], we gave our Mahar interpeter a few alls [awls ?] &c. &c. to give those retched Prisonis, I saw Homney [Hominy] of <wild> ground Potatos a Spoon of the Big Horn animal [Rocky Mountain sheep] which will hold 2 quarts

27th of Septr 1804— The Bank as usial lined with Sioux, gave th 2 principal Chiefs a blanket & a peck of Corn each, Capt Lewis accompanied the chiefs to their Lodges, they informed us that a great part of their nation had not arrived, & would arrive to night and requested us to Delay one Day longer, that thay might See us

I rote a letter to Mr Durion, & prepared Some Commissions & a Meadel. & Sent to Captain Lewis— at 2 oClock Capt Lewus returnd with 4 chiefs & a Brave man named War-cha pa—[8] (when a[ny] of thos people Die they pierce ther flesh with arrows above & below ther elbows as a testimony of ther greif) after a delay of half an hour I went with them on Shore, they left the boat with reluctiance (we Suspect they are treacherous and [we] are at all times guarded & on our guard) They again offered me a Young woman and wish me to take her & not Dispise them, I wavered [?] [dismissed ?] the Subject, at Dark the Dance began as usial and performed as last night womin with ther Husbands & relations cloths, arms scalps on poles &c. &c. Capt Lewis joined me & we continued untill about 11 oClock and 2 Cheif accompaned us to the boat I with 2 Cheifs was in a Perogue going on board, by bad Stearing the parogue Struk the Cable with Such force as to brake it near the anchor (Cap Lewis and 3 or 4 men on Shore, I had all hands up and was Compelled to Land— the Chief got allarmed & allarmed the Indians the 1 Chief & about 200 men Came down in great hast armd and for action, and found it was false,[9] <they> about 20 of them Camped on Shore all night— this allarm Cap Lewis as well as my self viewed as the Signal of their intentions, one half on guard, our misfortune of loseing our anchor obliged us to lay under a falling in bank much exposed to the accomplishment of the hostile intentions of those Tetons (who we had every reason to believe from ther Conduct intended to make an attempt to stop our progress & if possible rob us— Peter Crusat who Spoke Mahar came in the night and informed me that the Mahar Prisoners told him that the Tetons intended to Stop us— We Shew'd but little signs of a knowledge of there intentions

28th of Septr 1804 Friday   I made maney attempts in defferent ways to find our anchor without sukess [success], the Sand had covered her up, we Deturmined to proceed on to Day— and after Brackfast we with great Dificuelty got the Chiefs out of the boat, and when we were about setting out the Class Called the soldiars took possession of the Cable— the 1t Chief who was still on board and intended to go a Short distance up with us, was informed that the men Set on the Cable, he went out and told Capt Lewis who was at the Bow, thy wanted tobacco   The 2° Chief Demanded a flag & Tobacco which we refused to give, Stateing proper reasons to them for it, after much rangleing, we gave a <twist> carrot of Tobacco to the 1st Cheif and he to the men & jurked the Cable from them & [we] proceeded on under a Breeze from the S E.   we took in the 3rd Chief who was Sitting on a Sand bar 2 miles above— he told us the Rope was held by order of the 2d Chief who was a Double Spoken man— Soon after we Saw a man rideing full speed up the bank, we brought him on board, & he proved to be the Sun of the 3d Cheif, by him we Sent a talk to the nation, explanitory of our hoisting the red flag under the white, if they were for peace stay at home and doe as we had Derected them and if they were for war or deturmined to attempt to Stop us, we were ready to defend our Selves (as I had before Said)— We Substituted large Stones in place of an Anchor, we came to at a Small Sand bar in the middle of the river and Stayed all night— I am verry unwell I think for the want of Sleep—

Course & Distane 28th of Sept

N. 33° W. 3 M. to the exty [extremity] of a Sand bar on the L.S.   passed
          a willow Isd L. S
S. 80° W. 3 M. to a bend on the S.S. at a wood opsd some high land L.S.

6

Capt W. Clarks Notes Continued. as first taken—[1]

29th of September Satturday 1804— Set out early Some bad Sand bars, at 9 oClock we observed the 2d Chief with 2 men and Squais on Shore, they wished to go up with us as far as the other part of their band, which would meet us on the river above not far Distant we refused to let one more come on board Stateing Suffient reasons, observd they would walk on Shore to the place we intended to Camp, offered us women we objected and told them we Should not Speake to another teton except the one on board with us, who might go on Shore when ever he pleased, those Indians proceeded on untill late in the evening when the Chief requested that the Perogue might put him across the river which we agreed to— Saw numbers of Elk on the Sand bars to day, passed an old Ricara [Aricara] Village at the mouth of a Creek without timber[2] we Stayed all night on the Side of a Sand bar 1/2 a Mile from the Shore.

Course & Distanc &c.

South 60° W. 2 Miles to a point on the S.S.
N. 80° W. 1 1/4 M. to a tree on the L.S.
N. 16° E. 2 1/2 M. to a point on the S.S.
N. 80° W. 1 3/4 m. to the mouth of a Creek L.S.
N. 45° E. 2 M. to a point on the L.S.
N. 25° E. 1 1/2 M. to a Willow Island.

30th of September Sunday 1804 had not proceeded far before we discovered an Indian running after us, he requstd to go with us to the Ricaras [Arikara], we refused to take him, I discovered at a great Distanc a great number of men women & children decending a hill towards the river above which the Chief with us told us was the other Band, Some rain & hard wind at about 10 oClock we anchored opposit the Camps of this band and told them we took them by the hand, and Sent to each Chief a carrot of Tobacco & Some to the principal men and farth[er] Said that after Staying with the band below 2 days to See them we had been badly treated and Should not land again, as we had not time to Delay— refured then to Mr Durion for a full account of us, and an explination of what had been Said,[3] they appeard anxioes for us to eat with them and observed they were friendly we apoligised & proceeded on under a Double reafed Sale— the Chief on board threw out to those that ran up Small pieces of Tobacco & told them to go back and open thier ears, We Saw great number of white guls— refresh the party with whiskey, in the evening we saw 2 Indians at a Distance, The boat [tear] turned [tear] by accident & was nearly filling and rocked verry much, allarmed the Indian Chief on board who ran and hid himself, we landed & the Indian express a wish to return, we gave him a Blanket Knife & some tobacco and advised him to keep his men away, we camped on a Sand bar. verry Cold & windy—

Course & Distance

N. 30. W. 3 M. to the upper point of Some woods S.S.
N. 80° W 1 1/2 m on the S.S.—
N. 64° W. 3 M. to a Bush on the L.S.
N. 46° W. 1 1/2 M. on the L.S.
N. 10° W. 3 m to a pt on the S.S. passed the 2nd Band of Tetons,
North 2 M. to a tree on the S.S.
N. 24° W. 4 M. to a point on the L.S.
N. 50° W. 2 1/2 M to the Lower point of Pania Island.

1. This document, unlike any other in this journal, is written on both sides of a large sheet of paper, made up of smaller ones pasted together. It is closely written with hardly any corrections. It could not possibly have been written in the field. The heading in Clark's hand, "Captain W. Clarks Notes Continued. as first taken," indicates that they were copied from notes made in the field. The importance of this document in the determination of the provenance of this journal is discussed in the Introduction.

2. Clark named this No Timber Creek (Thw., *1*, 172).

3. Here Clark seems to imply that Dorion was with the party when it met with the Tetons. The Notebook Journal clears up this confusion. In it he wrote, "referred them to Mr. Durion for a full account of us and to here our Talk Sent by him to the Tetons" (Thw., *1*, 173).

1ˢᵗ of October Monday 1804.[4] The wind blew hard from the S.E. all last night, Set out early   passed a large Island in the middle of the river opposit this Island the Ricaras lived in 2 Villages on the S W. Side,[5] about 2 Miles above the upper point of the Island   the Chyenne River coms in on the L.S. and is about 400 yards wide dischargeing but little water for a R. of its size, the current jentle, and navagable, to the Black mountains [Black Hills] we haule the Boat over a Sand bar, River wide & Shoal, pass'd a Creek at 5 mls we Call Sentinal Creek, a Small one above, but little timber about this river, the hills not so high as usial, the upper Creek I call lookout Creek, Camped on a Sand bar, opposit a Tradeing house, where a Mr V [V written over Leb]alles & 2 men had some fiew goods to trade with the Sioux, a boy came to us, This Mr Vallie informd us he wintered last winter 300 Leagus up the Chyenne River under the Black mountains,[6] he sais the River is rapid and bad to navagate, it forks 100 Leagus up   the N. fork enters the Black mountain 40 Leagues above the forks[7]   The Countrey like that on the Missouri less timber more cedar, the Coal Mns [Mts] or Black M. is high and some parts retain Snow all Summer, covered with timber principally pine, Great number of goats and a kind of anamal with verry large horns about the Size of a Small Elk,[8] White Bear [Grizzly]   no bever on the chien [Cheyenne] great numbers in the Mountains, The Chyenne Nation has about 300 Lodges   hunt the Buffalow, Steel horses from the Spanish Settlements, which they doe in 1 month—   the chanal of this River is Corse gravel, Those mountains is inhabited also by the white booted Turkeys   worthy of remark that the Grouse or Prarie hen is Booted, the Toes of their feet so constructed as to walk on the Snow, and the Tail Short with 2 long stiff feathers in the Middle.

Course & Distance

N. 80° W. 3 m. to the upper point of Pania Island.
N. 70° W. 2 M. to the Mouth of Chyenne River L.S.
N. 16° W 2 1/2 Miles to a point on the L.S.
N. 50° E. 4 M. to willows on the L.S.   passed 2 Creek.
S. 53° E. 4 1/2 M to a pt on the S.S, psd a Bluff L.S.

2ⁿᵈ of October Tuesday 1804, Mr Vallie Came on board, Lat. 44° 19'. 36. N. we observed Some Indians on a hill on the S.S.   one came to the river & fired off his gun and asked us to come [hole] [as ?] he wish us to go to his Camp near at hand   we refused, passed a large Island on the S.S., here we expected the Tetons would attempt to Stop us, and prepared for action, &c   opposit this Island on the L.S. a small Creek comes in, w[e] call this Caution Island, camped on a Sand bar 1/2 a mile from the main Shore   the wind hard from the N W. cold, the current of the river less rapid, & retains less sediment than below.

Course & Distance

S. 70° E 2 1/2. M. to a wood on the L.S.— S. 80° E 1 1/2 M. on the L.S.—
N 62° E. 2 M on the L.S.   N. 15° E 4 M. to the L.S. of an Island Situated
    near the S.S.—   N. 28. E. 2 M to the upper pt of the Sand bar
    abov the Island.

3ʳᵈ of October Wednesday 1804   The N W. wind blew verry hard all night with Some rain, we Set out early, at 12 examoned our Stores & goods, Several bags Cut by the Mice and Corn scattered, Some of our Cloth also cut by them also papers &c &c   at 1 oClock an Indian Came to the Bank S.S, with a turkey on his back   4 other soon joined him Some rain, Saw Brant & white guls flying Southerly

4. Although there is no mention of it in this journal, Clark began on Oct. 1 to write entries in the third notebook of the Notebook Journal. Coues calls this "the Mandan Codex." Unlike the two marbled-cover notebooks in which the trip thus far is recorded, this has a cover of brown leather. At the same time Clark continued to make entries in the second notebook for Oct. 1 and 2. Thus for these two dates there are entries in both notebooks. On Oct. 3 the second notebook was filled and from then on the journal continues in the third notebook, through April 7, 1805, when the party left Fort Mandan for the west (Thw., *1*, 174 n., 178 n.; *7*, 415).

5. Nine years before, Truteau had found the Arikara living in these villages (Nasatir, *2*, 379). While he was with them, they abandoned this spot to move farther upstream, to be near their friends and allies, the Mandans. In 1796 there were 500 warriors there. Their constant wars with other tribes, particularly the Teton Sioux, and the ravages of smallpox reduced their number and resulted in considerable consolidation of their scattered villages. They were much more sedentary than many of their neighbors, raising corn, which they exchanged for peltry and meat with the Cheyenne and the other Plains tribes (Hodge, *1*, 83–86).

6. One of the many small traders, licensed or unlicensed, found on the Missouri. Clark, in the Notebook Journal, called him Mr. Jon [Jean] Vallee. He was probably connected with the Vallé family, prominent in Ste. Geneviève. The young Frenchman with Vallé who had first hailed the party was recognized by one of the *engagés* (Ordway, p. 145; Nasatir, *1*, 111; Thw., *1*, 175–76).

7. This fork is the present Belle Fourche River.

8. The Notebook Journal describes this animal as having large circular horns—obviously the Rocky Mountain sheep (Thw., *1*, 176).

9. As the party continued upstream, the shoaling of the river made it increasingly difficult to get the keelboat over the sandbars. The decision not to send back one of the pirogues made it possible to transfer some of the stores from the keelboat (supra, p. 139) and thus get it upriver as far as the Mandans.

1. Gass, in his journal, notes that this Indian was told that the party was not a trading party and that "we had seen his chief and told him all we had to say" (Gass, p. 44). The chief referred to was probably one of the Teton Sioux. To the Indians, the appearance of the keelboat and the two pirogues meant the arrival of trade goods. If the white man's party were strong, there would be trade; if it were weak, there was the possibility of plunder. The Tetons had to be convinced that the party was not a trading party and that it was strong enough and resolute enough to defend itself.

2. Named on the Indian Office Map *I bonne esperance*. There is some confusion here, for on this Map, an island several miles downstream is labeled as "I[sle] & village." The only island with a village was La-hoo-catt, which, according to the journal, was encountered after Good Hope Island was passed. This confusion was quite natural, for the names of islands and other locations are crowded together on the map.

3. The reading in this journal is La-hoo-call. As Clark sometimes did not cross his t's, the spelling La-hoo-catt found in Thwaites (*1*, 179) is probably correct.

4. This creek, which was not named by Clark, is called Teed Creek by Ordway (p. 146) and by Whitehouse (Thw., 7, 66), and Teel Creek by Gass (p. 44).

5. This stream, not named by Clark, is called Hidden Creek by Gass (p. 59) and by Whitehouse (Thw., 7, 67). Quaife, in his annotation of the Ordway journal, clears up the confusion concerning the creeks passed that day. Ordway called this stream White Goat Creek. He did not note the creek called White Brant Creek by Clark, but both Whitehouse (Thw., 7, 67) and Gass (p. 45) called this stream White Goat Creek. Quaife goes on to point out that Coues, in his efforts to reconcile discrepancies in the journals, added to the confusion. The White Brant Creek of Clark is the White Goat Creek of Gass and Whitehouse; the White Goat Creek of Ordway is the Hidden Creek of Gass and Whitehouse (*Ordway*, p. 146 n.).

6. In comparing this journal with the Notebook Journal, the editor has noted the similarities and differences between the two texts. This passage is typical. In the Notebook Journal (Thw., *1*, 181) Clark wrote, "passed a Village of about 80 neet Lodges covered with earth and picketed around, those loges are Spicious [spacious] of an Octagon form as close together as they can possibly be placed

Course & Distance

N. 50° E. 2 1/2 M. to a wood L.S.   N. 54° E 2, M. to a tree in a bend S.S.
N. 2 M to a point of high lands on the L.S.   N. 22° W. 1/2 M. on the
      L.S. under a Bluff (sand bars so Common, impossible to Describe them)—9

4th of October Thursday—the Wind blew all night from the N W. Some rain   we were obliged to drop down 3 miles to get a Channel Sufficient Deep to pass   Several Indians on the bank, call'd to us frequently to Land, one gave 3 yels & Sciped a Ball before us, we payed no attention to them, while at Brackfast one Swam across to us, beged for Powder, we gave him a Small piece of Tobacco & put him over on a Sand bar,1 passed a large Island in the middle of the river Good hope I.2 Passed a small Creek L.S.   Camped on a Sand bar at the upper point of an Island on which is the remains of an old ricara Village fortified Called La hoo call3   It was circular, this Village appears to have been deserted about 5 or 6 years, 17 houses yet remain, the Island contains but little timber, the evening verry cold and wood Surce [scarce], make use of Drift wood

Course & Distance

N. 18° W. 8 1/2 M. to a point on the S.S.—   passed Good hope Island
      N. 12°
E. 1 1/2 M. on the S.S.   passd a Creek L.S4 N. 45° E. 2 M. on the S.
      point passed Le hoo calls Island—

5th of October Friday 1804   Frost this morning, Set out early   passed a Small Creek on the L.S.   saw 3 Tetons on the S.S.   they beged Some Tobacco, We proceed on   passed a Creek on the S.S.5   I saw a white brant in a gangue on the Sand bar   Saw a large herd of Cabra or antelopes Swiming the River, we Killed four of them   passed a Small Island on the L.S.   a large Creek on the L.S at the head of the Island   White Brant Creek, I walked on the Island which is covered with wild rye, I Killed a Buck & a Small wolf this evening, Clear pleasant evening, Camped on a mud bar S.S.   refreshd the men with whiskey.

Course Distance &c

N 63° E 1 1/2 Miles to high land on the L.S.   East 3 m. to a pt of Timber on the L.S.   passed a Creek L.S.   N. 80° E. 1 1/2 M to a tree in a bend to S.S.   N. 36° W. 2 M. to a pt of high Land on the L.S.   passed a Creek on the S.S.   N. 50° W. 3 m. to a pt on the S.S.   N. 17° W. 3 to a tree on the S.S.   passed an Island and Creek L.S.   N. 16° E 6 M. to a point on the L.S. opposit a willow Isd

6th of October Satturday 1804   Cold Wind from the N.   Saw many large round Stones near the middle of the River   passed an old Ricara village of 80 Lodges Picketed in those lodges in nearly an octagon form, 20 to 60 feet Diameter   Specious [Spacious] covered with earth and as close as they can stand, a number of Skin Canoes in the huts, we found Squashes of 3 different Kinds growing in the Village   Shields Killed an Elk close by—6   The Magpy is common here, we Camped off the Mouth of Otter Creek on the S.S.7   this Creek is 22 yds. wide & heads near the R. Jacque,—contains much water.

and appear to have been inhabited last Spring, from the Canoes of Skins Mats buckits &c found in the lodges, we are of oppinion they were the recrereis [Arikara] We found Squashes of 3 Different Kinds growing in the Village, one of our men Killed an Elk close by this Village."

In my opinion, the preceding passage is based on this journal. The passage in the Notebook Journal is more detailed and is less telegraphic in style. The last sentence in the above passage is identical in both journals, except that Shields in the Notebook Journal becomes "one of our men," not an uncommon change.

From a close examination of the two passages, it seems clear to this editor that the entry in the Notebook Journal is a rewrite of this journal's entry. Such comparisons can be made throughout the major portion of this journal.

7. On the Indian Office Map, this is the Rivière à la loutre, the Otter River, which comes in on the north or starboard side. It is so noted in the Notebook Journal (Thw., *1*, 181). The letters S.S. in Clark's recording always mean the starboard side, and not the south side. Ordway and Gass state that the river comes in on the south side. Whitehouse uses S.S. and probably means the south side, for he uses the compass directions consistently. This brings up the question of how much of the other men's journals was taken from Clark's recording. Quaife's footnote in the Ordway Journal states that all the journals, including Clark's, were wrong. This is not the case. Clark, as noted above, placed it correctly (*Ordway*, pp. 147–48 n.).

8. This is the present Moreau or Owl River, which flows through the Cheyenne Indian Reservation in Dewey County, South Dakota. On close examination of the small maps 8 and 9 in Thw., *8, Atlas,* one can make out the word "orrow" and the upper part of another letter not legible. There is then a possibility that this stream may have already been named the "Morrow" or Moreau. In his list of estimated distances from the Cheyenne River, Clark wrote *R. au Narrow,* perhaps his spelling of Moreau (supra, p. 126).

Before reaching the mouth of this river, both Ordway and Gass noted a stream coming in on the north or starboard side, to which they gave no name, although Ordway leaves a blank space after the words, "passed a creek on N S called [*space*]." Whitehouse, however, called it Goodrich Creek, after one of the members of the party. Clark does not mention it here or in the Notebook Journal, nor is it to be found on his map (Thw., *1,* 182; *7,* 67; *Ordway,* p. 147; *Gass,* p. 45).

9. The Notebook Journal records that these two Indians were members of the "Beiffs De Medesons (*Buffles des Médecins*) Lodge" (Thw., *1,* 182). This designation of the "Buffalo of the Medicine Men" is perhaps explained by Hodge's comment that "the buffalo was supposed to be the instructor of doctors who dealt with the treatment of wounds, teaching them in dreams where to find healing plants and the manner of their use" (Hodge, *1,* 170).

1. This is probably the present Blue Blanket Island. Coues (*History,* pp. 156–57) suggests that the next island upstream, unnamed by Clark, is the present Blue Blanket Island. However, an examination of the M.R.C. Map shows Coues to have been mistaken.

2. No name is given to this creek in either of the Clark journals. Ordway, Whitehouse, and Gass call it Slate Run. The reader will note that throughout the journals of the men, names are given to islands and streams which do not appear in the Clark journals. The men perhaps found some amusement and satisfaction in recording such names as came to mind. Perhaps in some cases the French, more familiar with the river, suggested names. In any event, they do not appear in the journals of Clark or on his map. The present name of this creek is Bellman Creek.

3. This river is not found on the Indian Office Map. On the small map of this portion of the Missouri in Thw., *8,* no. 9, it is labeled the *R. au Carn* (carne: carrion?). Both this journal and the Notebook Journal give it the Arikara name, the We-tar-hoo. Its present name is the Grand River. Gass, Ordway, and Whitehouse make no mention of this stream. It is impossible to say whether they overlooked it or, as Quaife suggests, they confused it with the Ma-ro-pa, two miles farther upstream (*Ordway,* p. 148, n.).

4. The Notebook Journal (Thw., *1,* 183) notes this river as follows: "passed a Small

Course & Distance &c.

N. 4° E 8 m. to a wood pt on the L.S.   N. 8° W. 1 M. on the L.S.   N. 32° W 3 m. to a pt on the S.S.   N. 40d W 2 M. to Otter Creek S.S.

7th of October Sunday 1804   frost last night, passed a River 90 yds wide the Ricaras Call Sur-war-kar-ne[8]   all the water of this river runs in a chanel of 20 yards, the Current appears jentle, I walked up this River a mile, Saw the tracks of white bear, verry large, also a old Ricara village partly burnt, fortified   about 60 Lodges built in the Same form of those passed yesterday, many Canoes & Baskets about the huts—   about 10 oClock we saw 2 Indians on the S.S.   they asked [*one word illegible*] for Something to eat & told us they were Tetons of the band we left below on ther way to the Ricaras   we gave them meat &c[9]   wind hard from the Soath, passed a large open Island covered with grass and wild rye, I walked on the Isd & 4 men   they Killed a Braroe [Badger] & a Black tale Doe with a black breast the largest Deer I ever saw, the great numbers of Grous on it, we call it Grous Island, Camped opposit the Island near the S. Side.

Course Distanc & reffurence

N. 42° W. 2 M. to the Mouth of Sur-war-kar-ne river L.S.   N. 30° E. 3 1/2 miles to a Bend S.S.   N 30° W. 2 M. to a pt of high land L.S.   N. 35° W. 7 M. on the L.S.   N. 10° W. 1 M. on the L.S. to a pt—   N. 80° W. 3 M. to the left Side of Grous Island[1]   N. 45° W. 1 M. to the head of So Isd   West 2 1/2 M to a point on the main S.S.   high open [*hole*] lands on both Sides.

8th of October Monday 1804. a cool Morning   wind from the N.W. passed the Mouth of a Small Creek on the L.S.[2] about 2 1/2 Miles above the Isd   Passed the Mouth of a River on the L.S. called by the Ricaries We-tar-hoo.[3] this river is 120 yards wide, the water Confined within 20 yards, throws out mud with little Sand, great quanties of red Berries, resembling Currents near the Mouth of this river   Latd 45° 39'—5' N. this river heads in the 1t Black Mountain, 2 Miles higher up passed a Small River on the L.S. Called Maropa 25 yards wide chocked up with mud—[4]   our hunters discovered a Ricara village on an Island a fiew miles above   we passed the 1t Ricara Village about the center of the Island, in presence of Great numbers of Spectators and Camped above the Island on the L.S. at the foot of Some high land. Mr Gravotine [Graveline] a French man joined us as an interpeter)[5]   The Island on which 1t Ricara Village is Situated, is about 3 miles long Seperated from the Main L. Side by a Narrow Deep Channel, those Indians Cultivate on the Island Corn Beens Simmins Simnels, Squashes, Tobacco &c &c   after Landing Capt Lewis with Mr. Gravelin and 3 men went to the Village, I formd a Camp on Shore with the Perogue crew & guard, with the Boat at anchor, Capt Lewis returned late, a french man and a Spaniard accompanied him[6]

Course Distance &c

N. 70 ° W. 2 M. to a Tree in a bend to the L.S.   passed a Small Creek L.S.   N. 10° W 1 M. to a point on the S.S.   N 15° E 2 1/2 M. to the mouth of We terhoo River in a Bend to the L.S.   N. 40° E 1 M. on the L.S.   N. 30 E 1 M to the mouth of Maropa River on the L.S.   N. 15° E 1 M. to the lower point of an Island North 3 1/2 M to a pt on the L.S   passed the 1s Ricara V. & the Island river 25 yards wide Called Rear par [Rampart?] or Beaver Dam R: this river Ma-ro-pa is entirely chocked up with mud." The bracketed word [Ma-ro-pa] suggests that Biddle, in going over the Notebook Journal now in the American Philosophical Society, might have inserted the word Ma-ro-pa, getting it from the Gass Journal (p. 46, or from Clark's sketch map, Thw., *8,* no. 9). The Indian Office Map has only the word *"Riviere"* for this stream. At its mouth is the site of the Grand River Indian Agency, which Thwaites mistakenly placed at the mouth of the Grand River (Thw., *1,* 183 n.). The present name is Oak Creek. Just north of the mouth of this stream, the present boundary separating South from North Dakota cuts across the Missouri River (*Ordway,* 148 n.).

5. This is the first contact of the party with the Arikara. This tribe, which later gave so much trouble to American traders, had long been in contact with the French coming up from St. Louis. As early as 1734, they had been visited by a French trader. In 1793, Garreau, who was with the D'Eglise expedition, remained with this tribe. Jean Baptiste Truteau, who led the first major expedition up the Missouri under Spanish auspices in 1794, wintered with them and was with them as late as 1796. Mackay and Evans, who made the next important effort of the Spanish to reach the Mandans and so block off the British from the Upper Missouri, were with the Arikara in 1795. After the failure of this effort, trade by small parties continued. In 1802 and again in 1804, Regis Loisel, accompanied by Pierre Antoine Tabeau, made trading expeditions upriver. The Lewis and Clark party met Loisel returning to St. Louis shortly after they set out (supra, p. 46 n.). Tabeau was left with the Arikara, where he met the party. With him was Joseph Graveline. He was used as an interpreter, and continued with the party on to the Mandans. On Nov. 6, 1804, Graveline, two of the French hands, and two boys left the Mandans for the Arikara (infra, p. 174). He returned in February 1805 with letters from Tabeau (infra, p. 184). He remained with the party until April 1805, when he was selected to act as pilot of the keelboat on its return journey to St. Louis. Lewis described him as "an honest, discrete man and an excellent boat-man" (Thw., *1,* 283). He was later employed by the Indian Department as Resident among the Arikara. Tabeau went into the employ of the Canadian companies after 1804. (See Nasatir, *1,* 28, 114; *2,* 771.)

6. On this date, Robert Frazer, who had enlisted on Jan. 1, 1804, was selected as one of the Corps of Northwestern Discovery (Thw., *1,* 184). Not all the men who had enlisted before the party set out were included in the permanent party; some were sent back (infra, p. 185).

7. Pierre Antoine Tabeau, mentioned earlier in this journal, was a partner of Loisel. When the latter went down to St. Louis in the spring of 1804, he left Tabeau in charge of their trading post at Cedar Island. He was not there when the party passed the island two weeks earlier (supra, p. 145). They found him here at the Arikara villages with his associate, Graveline. Since both could speak Arikara and Sioux, the party now had competent interpreters. These men were of great assistance to the Americans during the winter and spring of 1804–05.

8. This is the first mention in the journals of the "bull boat" of the Upper Missouri Indians.

9. The question of which Arikara chief accompanied the party to the Mandans would be of slight importance were it not that it has some bearing on the question of whether the Notebook Journals were sent downstream in April 1805. A year had passed since that date, and it would be nine months before the party got back to St. Louis from the Pacific. On April 11, 1806, however, Jefferson was writing a speech addressed to "My friends & children of the Ricara nation." He wrote that it would give him ". . . a great pleasure to see your beloved chief* arrive here on a visit." Apparently he was as confused as is this editor, for after the word "chief" he indicated his perplexity by putting an asterisk. At the head of this rough draft (the fair text has not been located) he wrote, "Piaketo, Eagle's Feather," crossed this out and wrote, "Toone, Whippoorwill," crossed it out and finally wrote "Arketarnawhar, chief of the town." Since this last was not crossed out, he seems to have decided that this was the chief's name (Jackson, p. 306).

When one turns to the Notebook Journal and this journal, one discovers the source of all the confusion. In the Notebook Journal for Oct. 9, 1804, and in this journal for Oct. 10. Clark listed the names of the three chiefs of the Arikara. The first chief, Ka-ha-wiss-assa, Lightning Raven, does not appear again in either journal but is listed in Clark's notes of the council with the Arikara (Thw., 7, 303). The second and third chiefs, Po-casse, Hay (called Lassel in the Notebook Journal, 1, 187) and Pia-he-to, Eagle's Feather, appear in both journals. Both of them had creeks named after them by Clark. In both journals Clark wrote that on Oct. 12, the three came on board the keelboat. After some palaver, two of them took their leave. In the Notebook Journal, Clark wrote that "the third proceeded on with us to the Mandens by name." This is followed by a blank space in the manuscript apparently to be filled in later when Clark learned his name (Thw., 1, 188). Four days later, the name of the chief, Ar-he-tar-nar-shan, Chief of the Town, was recorded in both journals (Thw., 1, 195; infra, p. 161). This may not have been the man's real name, for all three men were chiefs of towns and could be so designated. To add to the confusion, Clark wrote, in his entry in the Notebook Journal for Oct. 20, that "the Chief with Too ne tels me that na-

9th of October [October written over Aug] Tuesday 1804   a windey night   Some rain, and the [wind] continued So high & cold We could not Speek in council with the Indians, we gave them Some Tobacco and informed them we would Speek tomorrow, all the grand Chiefs visited us to day also Mr Taboe,[7] a trader from St Louis—   Many Canoes of a single Buffalow Skin made in the form of a Bowl carrying generally 3 and Sometimes 5 & 6 men,[8] those Canoes, ride the highest Waves—   the Indians much astonished at my Black Servent and Call him the big Medison, this nation never Saw a black man before, the wind verry high, I saw at Several times to day 3 squars in single Skin Buffalow Canoes loaded with meat Cross the River, at the time the waves were as high as I ever Saw them in the Missouri—

10th of October 1804   at 11 oClock the wind Shifted from S.E to N.W Mr Taboe visited us—   we hear that Some jealousy exists as to the Cheefs to be made—   at 1 oclock the Cheifs all assembled under an orning near the Boat, and under the American Flag. we Delivered a Similar Speech to those delivered the Ottoes & Sioux, made three Cheifs one for each village and gave them Clothes & flags—   1s Chief is name Ka-ha-wiss assa lighting ravin   2d Chief Po-casse (Hay) & the 3rd Pia-he to or Eagles Feather—[9]   after the Council was over we Shot the air gun, which astonished them, & they all <Departed> left us, <we> I observed 2 Sioux in the Council   one of them I had seen below, they Came to interceed with the Ricaras to Stop us as we were told—   the Inds much astonished at my black Servent, who, made him self more turrible in thier view than I wished him to Doe as I am told telling them that before I caught him he was wild & lived upon people, young children was verry good eating   showed them his strength &c. &c.—[1]   Those Indians are not fond of Licquer of any kind—

11th of October Thursday 1804   wind S.E.   at 11 oClock met the 1s Chief in Council, he Thanked us for what we had given him & his people promised to attend to our advice, and Said the road was open for us and no one dar shut it &c. &c. we took him and one Chief on board and Set out, on our way took in the 2d Chief at the Mo of a Small Creek, and Came too off the 2d village which is 3 miles above the Island, we walked up with the 2 & 3 Chiefs to their villages which is Situated on each Side of a Small Creek, the[y] gave us Something to eat in thier way, after conversations on various Subjects & Bearieng [on] the civilities of those people who are both pore & dirtey we informed the Chiefs we would here what they had to Say tomorrow and returned on board about 10 oClock P M. Those people gave us to eat corn & Beans, a large well flavoured Been which they rob the Mice of in the Plains and is verry nurishing— all tranquillity—

12th of October Friday   after Brackfast we joined the Chiefs & Indians on the bank who wer waiting for us, and proceeded to the 1st village and Lodge of the Pocasse, This man Spok at Some lengths, to the sam[e] purpote [purport ?] of the 1s Chief, & Declareing his intentions of visiting his great father, Some Doubts as to his Safty in Passing the Sioux, requested us to take a Chief of their nation and make a good peace with the Mandan for them, that they Knew that they were the Cause of the war by Killing the 2 Mandan Chiefs—   this Chief & people gave us about 7 bushels of corn, Some Tobacco of thier own make, and Seed Legins & a Robe   We proceeded to the 3rd Chiefs village which is the largest, after the usial Serimoney of Eating Smokg &c he Spoke to near the Same amount of the last Chief, & more pleasently, he gave us 10 bushels of corn, some Beens & Simmins, after he had Spoken, and [I] gave Some Sketches of the Power & Magnitude of Our Countrey, we returned to our Boat, I have the rhumetism on my neck [*blot*] the Chiefs accompanied us on board, w[e] gave them Some Sugar Salt and a Sun Glass each, and after eating a little they returned on Shore leaveing one to accompany us to the Mandans, and we Set out viewed by men womin & children of each village   proceeded on about 9 1/2 miles and camped on the S S. clear & cold— The Ricaras Are about 500 men Mr Taboe say 600   able to bear arms, and the remains of ten different tribes of Panias reduced by the Small Pox & wares [wars] with the Sioux, they are tall stout men corsily featured, their womin Small & industerous raise great quantites of corn beans &c also Tobacco for the men to Smoke, they collect all the wood and doe the Drudgery comnon amongst Savages— Their language is so corrupted that many lodges of the Same village with dificuelty to under stand all that each other Say— They are Dirty, Kind, pore, & extravegent; possessing natural pride, no begers, rcive what is given them with pleasure, Thier houses are close to gether & Towns inclosed with Pickets, thier Lodges are 30 to 40 feet in Diameeter covered with earth or Neet Poles Set end wise resting on 4 forks [and] Supporting Beems Set in a Square form near the center, and lower about 5 feet high   other forks all around Supt strong Beems, from 8 to 10 of those with a opening at top of about 5 to 6 feet Square, on the Poles which pass to the top, Small Willow & grass is put across to support the earth—[2] The Sioux exchange, Some merchndze of Small value which they get from Mr Caneron [Cameron] of St Peters[3] for Corn &c and have great influence over this people   treat them roughly and keep them in continual dread— The Ricaras are at war with the Crow Indians and Mandans— &c &c— The Ricaras, have a custom Similar to the Sioux in maney instances, they think they cannot Show a Sufficient acknowledgement without [giving ?] to their guest handsom squars and think they are despised if they are not recvd

The Sioux followed us with women two days   we put them off. the Ricarries we put off dureing the time we were near their village— 2 were Sent by a man to follow us, and overtook us this evening, we Still procisted in a refusial—[4] The Dress of the Ricara men is Simpally a pr of Mockersons & Legins, a flap, and a Buffalow Robe— Their Hair is long and lais [lays] loose   their arms & ears are decerated with trinkets

The womin Dress Mockersons & Legins & Skirt of the Skin of the Cabre or Antelope, long fringed & [*one word illegible*] to the fringes & with sleaves, verry white, and Roabes— all were Dressed to be without hare in the summer   Those people make large Beeds of Diferrent colours, out of glass or Beeds of Dift colors, verry ingeniously

Course & Deistance &c.

N. 45° E. 2 M. To the Mouth of a Creek between the two upper Ricara villages S. 75. E. 1 1/2 M. to a Point on the L.S.   N 45° E 2 M to a pt of wood L.S.   N. 45° E 2 M. to a pt of wood on the L S   N. 20° W. 2 1/2 M to a pt on the L.S.   N. 8° W 1 1/2 M. to a pt on the L S   river narrow and large wooded points

13ᵗʰ of October Saturday 1804. Newmon confined for Mutinous expressions,[5] proceeded on   passed a camp of Sioux on the S.S.   those people did not Speak to us. passed a Creek on the S.S. 18 miles above the Ricaras I call Stone Ido[l] Creek,[6] this Creek heads in a Small lake at no great distance, near what there is a Stone to which the Indians asscribe great

tion lived" (Thw., *1*, 200). This looks as if there were two Arikara on board, the chief and one Toone. In the next day's entry he refers to him again as "Too ne is a whipperwill the Cheif of the Ricares." How Jefferson knew that Too ne was called a "whipperwill" is a mystery, for Thwaites bracketed off this word as being inserted by Biddle or someone else. This editorial practice is followed consistently by him (Thw., *1*, 11 n.). Too ne, or Whippoorwill, does not appear in this journal or in the notes made at the council with the Arikara found in Thw., 7, 303–05. Since Jefferson used all the variants of the Arikara chief's name, it is, I believe, clear that he had at least the Notebook Journal before him. See the Introduction for a comment on this point.

1. In the Notebook Journal, the effect of York upon the Indians is recorded thus: "Those Indians wer much astonished at my Servent, they never Saw a black man before, all flocked around him & examind him from top to toe, he Carried on the joke and made himself more turribal than we wished him to doe." In this journal, York's yarn that "young children was verry good eating" terrified his hearers. Nothing could have been more repulsive to these Indians than such a practice, for the love and devotion which the Indian bestowed on his children was a characteristic noted by all observers. Cannibalism was practiced occasionally, but only in case of extreme starvation or as a ritualistic practice, such as eating a portion of the heart of a brave enemy in order to give courage and strength to the victor. No wonder York "made himself more turribal" and was admonished by his master. York undoubtedly furnished much amusement to the men, but was often a problem for his master (Thw., *1*, 186).

2. This description of an Arikara house is more complete than that found in the Notebook Journal (Thw., *1*, 188–89). Gass gives the most complete description (p. 61).

3. Murdoch Cameron's trading post was on Lac qui Parle near the head of the St. Peters River. Zebulon Pike, on his expedition up the Mississippi River in 1806, met Cameron on the shore of Lake Pepin. Pike recorded that the trader had violated his license by selling liquor to the Indians. He and his partner, Rollet, "have been the occasion of great confusion and of much injury to the other traders" (Coues, *Pike*, *1*, 202, 204). The Englishman, Featherstonehaugh, described him as "an enterprising, sagacious Scotchman who had amassed a good deal of property by trafficking with the Indians" (*A Canoe Voyage up the Minnay Sotor*, 2 vols. London, 1847, *1*, 314–15).

Lewis and Clark had good reason to believe that Cameron was the cause of much of the unrest among the Indians on the Upper Missouri. The Teton Sioux, with whom the party had had such difficulty (supra, pp. 146–51), were supplied with arms and ammunition by the Sisseton and Yankton Sioux, who got them from Cameron. With these weapons, the Tetons became the terror of the upper river. This barter made them independent of all trade coming up the Missouri, but "furnished them with the means, not only of distressing and plundering the traders of the Missouri, but also, of plundering and massacreing the defenceless savages of the Missouri, from the mouth of the river Platte to the Minitares, and west to the Rocky mountains." Lewis urged that this trade be cut off until such time as the government was able to establish military control over the area (Thw., *1*, 275; *6*, 45, 89, 95–96).

4. Gass notes that the Indian and two squaws "remained with us all night" (p. 49).

5. This was a serious matter. As the hardships of travel and the Indian menace mounted, rigid discipline had to be maintained at all costs. Newman was tried "by 9 of his Peers they did 'Centence him 75 Lashes'" (Thw., *1*, 191–93). Ordway and Gass were both on the jury. Ordway makes the briefest reference to it. Neither Gass nor Whitehouse records the event. As Quaife points out, their silence is eloquent, for it was a grim business (*Ordway*, p. 153 n.).

Newman was "Disbanded [from] the party" (Thw., *1*, 191) and acted as a laborer thereafter. He was sent back to St. Louis with the keelboat in April 1805. While at Fort Mandan during the winter and on his return to St. Louis, the man did everything possible to redeem himself in the eyes of his captains and his comrades. He begged to remain with the party, but was denied. Lewis, however, in his letter to the Secretary of War after the return of the party, had words of praise for Newman's conduct: "he exerted himself, on every occasion, to become useful. This disposition induced him to expose himself too much to the intense cold of that climate [Fort Mandan] and on a hunting excursion, he had his hands and feet severely frozen, with which he suffered extreme pain, for some weeks." Lewis went on to report that during the voyage of the keelboat to St. Louis, "he was extremely serviceable as a hunter" and the safety of the boat and its crew was at times dependent on his personal exertions, for he was "a man of uncommon activity and great bodily strength." Because of his exemplary conduct, Lewis urged that he be given one third of the gratuity awarded to Baptiste Le Page, who took Newman's place (Lewis to Henry Dearborn, Secretary of War, Washington, Jan. 15, 1807, Thw., *7*, 355–58; Jackson, pp. 364–73 and n.).

6. Quaife identifies this stream as the present Spring, or Hermaphrodite, Creek (*Ordway*, p. 152 n.).

virtue &c. &c.[7] at 21 Miles passed a Creek 15 yds wide on the L.S   I call Pocasse, we observed great quantites of grapes, a fine Breez from the S E camped on the L.S.   Som rain thus evening, we formed a Court Martial of 7 of our party to Try Newmon, they Senteenced him 75 Lashes and banishment from the party—   The river narrow   current jentle & wood plenty on the Bottoms   the up land is as usial open devercified plains, generally rich & leavel.

Course & Distance

N. 60° W. 3 M. to a pt on the S. S.   N. 40° W. 2 M. to a point of timber on the L.S.   N. 10° W. 2 m to a point on L.S.   N. 53° W. 1 1/2 M to a point on the S.S.   North 2 M to a point on the L.S. opposit a Creek on the L.S.   N. 18° E. 3 Miles to the upper point of Some timber on the S.S. & camped

14th of October Sunday 1804   Some rain last night   we Set out in the rain which continued all day   passed a Creek on the L.S. Piaheto 15 yds Wide,[8] halted on a Sand bar and had the punishmt inflicted on New-mon, which caused the indian Chieif to cry untill the thing was ex-plained to him   Camped opposit an antient fortification which is on the L.S., when I explained to the Chief the Cause of Whipping N— he ob-served that examples were necessary & that he him self had made them by death, but his nation never whiped even from thier bearth.[9]

Courses & Distance

S. 70° W. 3 M to a <point on the L.S.> Bend on the L.S.   N. 63° W 2 M. to a point on the S.S.   passed a Creek L.S

N. 30° W. 1 1/2 to a Tree on the L.S.   N 40° E. 1 1/2 to Some trees on the S.S.

N 60° W 3 m to <Some trees> a pt on the L S   N. 70° 3 m to a point on the S.S.—   passed an antient fortification.

15th of October   Rained all last night, passed a Ricara hunting camp on the S.S. & halted at another on the L. S, Several from the 1t Camp visited us and gave meat as also those of the Camp we halted at, we gave them fish hooks Some beeds &c as we proceeded on we Saw a number of indians on both Sides all day, Saw L.S some Curious Nnobs high and much the resemblance of a heped [hipped?] rough house, we halted at a Camp of 10 Lodges of Ricaras on the S.S., we visited thier Lodges & were friendly recved by all—   their women fond of our men—&c[1]

Course Distance

West 2 1/2 M to a Creek on the L.S.   North 4 M. to a wood point on the L. S.   N 34° W. 3 1/2 M. to a pt S.S.   <passed an old Chyenne village on the L.S. below a Creek> on the L.S.   a Camp of Ricaras on the S.S.

16th of October Tuesday 1804   Some rain this Morning   2 Squars verry anxious to accompany us   we Set [out] with our Chief on Board by name Ar he tar nar shan (or Chief of the Town)[2] a little above our Camp on the L.S. passed an old Shyenne Village, which appears to have been serounded with a wall of earth; this is the retreat & first Stand of this nation after being reduced by the Sioux and drove from their Coun-trey on the heads of red River [deprived] of Levenispice[3] where they cultivated the lands—[4]   passed a Creek I call So-harch or Girl Creek L.S. 2 miles higher passed Woman Crreek [sic] or Char-part   passed an Is-land Situated in a bend to the S.S. at the lower point of this Island a

7. Here is a tale that any good traveler from Herodotus on would have recorded. In his Notebook Journal, Clark gives it in detail: "those People have a curious Tradition of those Stones, one was a man in Love, one a Girl whose parents would not let [them] marry, the Dog went to morn with them   all turned to Stone gradually, commenceing at the feet. Those people fed on grapes untill they turned, & the woman has a bunch of grapes yet in her hand." The stones were lo-cated on an open prairie, and the Arikara, whenever they passed, paid reverence to them and made votive offerings. There is no indi-cation that any of the party visited this shrine, for they were anxious to reach the Mandans before winter set in. Earlier in the voyage upriver, such a point of interest would not have been overlooked. However, it was raining, and the sentence of Newman had to be carried out (Thw., 1, 191).

8. Named after the Arikara chief, Pia-he-to, Eagle's Feather (Thw., 1, 193).

9. The reaction of the Arikara chief is un-derstandable. To whip a man was an insult to his manhood; death was preferable.

1. "Those people are much pleased with my black Servent. Their womin verry fond of carressing our men &c." (Thw., 1, 194).

2. Supra, p. 158 n.

3. The only reading of this obscure passage that this editor can suggest is that the Chey-enne were driven from the Red River and de-prived of their living space.

4. At the beginning of the 18th century, the Cheyenne were living in what is now northern Minnesota. Following repeated in-cursions of the Sioux, who were being pressed westward by the more formidable and better armed Chippewa, the Cheyenne moved across the Red River and settled along a fork of that river which still bears their name, the Shey-enne River in North Dakota. Under Sioux attacks, they retreated still farther westward, making a stand against their enemies at the place noted here. Driven from there, they finally established themselves in the Black Hills and to the south and west. Part of the tribe moved south to the Arkansas and its upper tributaries, in what is now eastern Col-orado and western Kansas. This group, who came to be called the Southern Cheyenne, allied themselves with the Arapaho. Those who remained north of the Platte, the North-ern Cheyenne, finally allied themselves with the Sioux. In the last bitter struggle between the Army of the Plains and the Sioux that culminated in the battle of the Little Big Horn and the decimation of Custer's com-mand, these Northern Cheyenne fought alongside of their former enemies.

5. In the Notebook Journal (Thw., *1*, 195), Clark wrote that this island was called Carp Island by Evans. The Indian Office Map has the label, *I & R au Carpe*. This river is probably the War-re-con-nee of Clark, the present Big Beaver Creek.

6. In the Notebook Journal, commenting on the "many extraordinary Stories," Clark writes that they were all "about Turtles, Snakes, &c. and the power of a perticeler rock or Cove on the next river which informs of every thing none of those I think worth while mentioning" (Thw., *1*, 197).

7. In the Notebook Journal (Thw., *1*, 198), Clark wrote that these two men were in Graveline's employ. They had gone up the river in a canoe belonging to Graveline to hunt near the Mandans, who had robbed them of their guns and peltry. When they met Lewis and Clark, they asked that they be permitted to accompany the party up to the Mandans in the hope that they might recover their property. Their identity cannot be determined. Quaife suggested that they were François Rivet and Phillipe Degie (*Ordway*, p. 191 n.). Here he is following Thwaites, who noted that this pair were the two French hunters mentioned by Clark in the Notebook Journal as being on the keelboat when it left Fort Mandan in April 1805 to return to St. Louis. But Rivet could not have been one of the two men met on October 18, 1804, for he had been with the party from the outset (supra, p. 69). Degie cannot be identified, unless one is willing to agree that one "Greenyea," who was with Rivet at Fort Mandan on Aug. 21, 1806, is Thwaites' "Degie." Clark's spelling is not as bad as that (Thw., *6*, pp. 349–50).

Creek comes in Called Kee-tooch Sar-kar-nar or the place of Beaver above the Island a Small River on the Same S. Side Called War-re-con-nee Elk shed thier horns, this river is 35 yards wide & heads near the River au Jacque, Carp Island[5] wind hard a head from the N W. Saw great numbers of goats or Antelope on Shore, Capt Lewis one man & the Ricara Chief walked on Shore, in the evening I discovered a number of Indians on each Side and goats [antelope] in the river or Swiming & on Sand bars, when I came near Saw the boys in the water Swiming amongst the goats & Killing them with Sticks, and then hauling them to the Shore those on Shore Kept them in the water, I saw 58 Killed in this way and on the Shore, the hunter with Cap Lewis Shot 3 goats I came too and camped above the Ricara Camp on the L.S. Several Indians visited us duereing the night Some with meat, Sang and were merry all night.——

Cours & Distance 16 [October, 1804]

North 4 M to a point on the S.S. passed 2 Creeks L.S. N. 10° E 6 M. to the upper pt of some timber on the L.S. opsd a Creek haveing passed an Isld on the S.S a Creek at its lower point N. 1/2 a m. on the L. Side N. 30° W 1 M on the L. point N. 38° W. 3 M. to a point on the S.S.—

17th of October 1804 Wind S.W. I walked on Shore with the Ricara Chief and an Intepreter, the[y] told me maney extraodinary Stories,[6] I Killed 3 Dear & a Elk, the Chief Killed a Deer and our hunters Killed 4 Deer, in my absence the wind rose so high that the Boat lay too all Day; Latd 46° 23′ 57″ N. I caught a Small uncommon whiperwell we observe emence herds of Goats, or Antelopes flocking down from the N E Side & Swiming the River, the Chief tels me those animals winter in the Black Mountain, and in the fall return to those mounts from every quarter, and in the Spring disperse in the planes, those emence herds we See all of which is on the N E Side of the River is on their way to the mountain, and in the Spring they will be as noumeroes on their return (some gangus [gangs] winter on the Missouri) camped on the L.S.

Course Distance &c.

N. 10° E. 1 1/2 M to a pt on the L.S. N. 1/2 a M on the L.S.
N. 10° W. 1/2 a M. on the L.S. N 33° W. 3 1/2 M. to Some wood on the L.S.

18th of October 1804. at 6 miles passed the Mouth of La Bullet or Cannon Ball River on the L. Side about 140 yards Wide, and heads near the Black Mountains above the mouth of this River, in and at the foot of the Bluff, and in the water is a number of round Stones, resembling Shells and Cannon balls of Different Sises, and of excellent grit for Grindstons— the Bluff continues for about a Mile, The water of this River is confined within 40 yards— we met 2 french men in a Canoe, who informed us they wer trapping near the Mandans and were robed of the 4 Traps, & part of their Skins and several other articles, by Indians he took to be Mandans those men return with us,[7] Saw emence numbers of Goats all Day S.S. our hunters Kill Sevral passed a large Creek Called Che wah or fish Creek on the S.S. 28 yds wide, passed a Small Creek at 2 M on the L.S. Camped on the L.S. Saw a no of Buffalow, & in one gangue 248 Elk our hunters Killed 6 Deer & 4 Elk this evening, The Countrey is leavel and fine Some high Short hills, and ridges at a Distance, Bottoms fine and Partially timbered with Cotton wood principally Some ash & Elm.

Course Distance &c

N. 50° W. 3 m. to Cannon ball River L.S.   N. 20° W. 2 M to a pt of wood on the S.S. passing Can Ball Bluff L.S.   North 2 1/2 m to a pt of wood on the L.S.   N. 15° W. 1/2 m on the L.S. opsd a Creek. N. 10° E. 2 1/2 to a point on S S   passd a Small Creek L.S.   N. 20° E. 3 m to a point of wood on the L.S.

19th of October Friday 1804. Set out early under a gentle Breeze from the S.E.   more timber than Common in the bottoms   passed a large Pond on the S.S.   I walked out on the high land L. Side and observed great numbers of Buffalows, I counted in view at one time 52 gangues of Buffalow & 3 of Elk, besides Deer & goats &c   all the Streems falling from the hills or high lands so brackish that the water can't be Drank without effecting the person making use of it as Globesalts [Glauber's Salts]—, I saw in my walk Several remarkable high conocal hills, one 90 feet, one 60 and others Smaller—   the Indian Chief Say that the Callemet Bird[8] live in the hollows of those hills, which holes are made by the water passing from the top &c &c   I also Saw an old Village fortified Situated on the top of a high Point, which the Ricarra Chief tels me were Mandans, we Camped on the L.S.   I Killed a Deer & Saw Swans &c   our hunters Killed 4 Elk and 6 Deer to Day—

Course Distance &c.

N. 60° W. 2 1/2 m. to a pt on the S.S.   passed a Creek S.S.   N. 40° W. 2 M to Some wood in a bend to the L.S.   N 10° E. 1 1/2 m to a pt on the L S.   N. 20° W. 2 M. to a tree in the bend S.S.   N. 83° W. 3 M to the point S.S.   N. 44° W. 1 M. to a Willow pt on the L.S. opsd a Lake S.S.   N. 30° W. 2 M. to a tree in bend S.S.   N. 80° W. 3 m. to a pt on the S S.

20th of October 1804   wind from the S E, I walked out to view those remarkable places pointed out by Evens, and continud all day   Saw an old Village of the Mandans below the Chess chi ter R. [Heart River] appear to have been fortified above the village on the Same L.S. is a coal bank where we Campd   passed a small Creek on the S.S. and an Island on the L.S covered with Willows Small Cotton[wood]   the Countery which I passed this day is Delightfull, Timber in the bottoms, Saw great nos of Buffalow Elk Goats & Deer   as we were in want of them I Killed 3 Deer, our hunters 10 Deer and wounded a White Bear,[9] I saw Several fresh tracks of that animal double the sise of the largest track I ever Saw, great numbers of wolves, those animals follow the buffalow and devour, those that die or are Killed, and those too fat or pore to Keep up with the gangue

Course Distance &c.

N. 30° W. 2 M to some timber in a bend to the S.S. at a Creek, N. 10° W. 1 M on the S. S.   N. 54° W. 3 M to a pt on the L.S   N. 2 miles to some trees in a bend to the S.S. opposit an Island   N. 70° W 2 M. to a point on the S.S.   passed the Island   N. 50° W 2 M. to the upper part of a Coal Bluff L S.   pass an old Mandan V[illage] L S

21t of October Sunday 1804   a verry Cold night   wind hard from the N.E.   Some rain in the night which feesed as it fell, at Day began to Snow and continued all the fore part of the day,[1] at 1/4 of a mile passed the Mouth of Chess-che tar (or Heart) River L.S. 38 yards wide,[2] this river heads near Turtle mountain with Knife River   on this River is a

8. Thwaites identifies the "Callemet Bird" as the golden eagle, whose tail feathers were used to decorate the calumet pipes used on ceremonial occasions (Thw., *1*, 199 n.).

9. The silver tip, or grizzly, bear.

1. The party had been delayed on its long journey up the Missouri by accidents of one kind and another, numerous Indian councils, and, toward the end of September, by low water. The hope expressed by Clark in January 1804, that the party would reach the base of the "rock Mountains" before winter set in, had long since been abandoned (supra, p. 19). Winter was near; winter quarters must be built near the Mandan villages, provisions must be obtained from the Mandans and from hunters sent out by the party. There was no time to lose. The Great Divide of the Rockies was still 1,700 miles westward by river and trail.

2. Just before reaching the mouth of the Heart River, the party passed the future site of Fort Abraham Lincoln. From this fort, Custer and the Seventh Cavalry set out on the ill-fated march that ended on the Little Big Horn in June 1876.

3. The single tree on the open plain marked the spot where the Sun Dance took place. This ceremony, common among all Plains Indians, was held sometime during the summer and continued for about a week. Although the practice of self-torture, mentioned here by Clark was only a part of the ritual, it has come to be looked upon by the white man as the only important feature of the ceremony. Nevertheless, there were days of fasting and days of dancing, full of symbolism and performed according to long-established tradition. "The Sun Dance," writes Hodge (2, 651–52) "was not only the greatest ceremony of the Plains tribes, but was a condition of their existence. More than any other ceremony or occasion, it furnished the tribe the opportunity for the expression of emotion in rhythm, and was the occasion of the tribe becoming closely united." The Indians knew that the sun rules the plains—something that the white man has not yet fully learned.

4. Notwithstanding the cold weather, the Tetons "had not an article of clothing except their breech-clouts" (*Gass*, p. 52).

5. Supra, p. 162 n.

6. With 1,600 miles of river behind them, the first leg of their journey was nearly completed, and their first (revised) objective attained. The oncoming winter precluded any farther advance.

7. These Indians had already moved westward and in 1804 were living farther up the Missouri, on the Knife River. The Mandans called them the Minitari, "those who had crossed the water," referring to their crossing the Missouri 40 years before Clark made this entry. The French called them the *Gros Ventre* or Big Bellies. They were also called the Hidatsa. The Mah-har-ha (Amahami) were another division that had become a part of this group. (See infra p. 169 n.; Hodge, *1*, 47, 508, 547–49.)

8. This was the first contact with the Mandan, who had known of the party's progress upriver for some time. Their great chief and his party had come down to meet them. This tribe first settled on the lower reaches of the Missouri after they left their earlier homes east of the Mississippi. In the 18th century, they moved upstream and established themselves near the mouth of the Heart River, where the party found them. Clark estimated there were around a thousand of them settled in three villages along the Missouri. Part of their subsistence came from raising corn, beans, and squash, which they used for trade with the Plains Indians and with the fur traders. Their supply of buffalo was always uncertain, for they were weak and their hunting parties out on the plains were continually harried by their more powerful neighbors.

Among many others, George Catlin believed that the Mandans were descended from the Welsh. The curious notion that some Indian tribe in North America was descended from a party of Welshmen, who were supposed to have come here in the 12th century,

Smothe Stone which the Indians have great fath in & consult the Stone on all great occasions which they say Marks or simblems [symbol + emblems] are left on the Stone of what is to <pass> take place &c an old Mandan Village above the mouth of this Little River, I saw a Single tree in the open Plains which the Mandans formerly paid great Devotion to run Cords thro their flesh & tie themselves to the tree to make them brave,[3] passed an old Village on a Small run on the L.S. one on the bank L. and Camped, I Killed a fat Buffalow this evening— Little gun all my hunting [?]

Course Distance &c

S 80° E 2 Mi. to bend on S.S. 2ᵈ Vig [Village?] passed Chess-che-tar River N. 16° W. 1 1/2 M. to a wood S.S. N. 40° W 3 1/2 M. to a pt on the S.S. River wider & more Sand than common.

22ⁿᵈ of October 1804 last night at about 1 oClock I was violently attacked with Rhumetism in my neck, which was so violently [ill] I could not move, Cap L applied a hot stone raped in flannel which gave temperry ease, we passed a War party of Tetons on their way as we Supposed to the Mandans of 12 men on the L.S.[4] we gave them nothing and refused to put them across the river, passed 2 old Villages at the mouth of a large Creek L.S and a Small Island at the head of which is a bad place, an old Village on the S.S. and the upper of the 6 Villages the Mandans occupied about 25 years ago this village was entirely cut off by the Sioux & one of the others nearly, the Small Pox distroyed great Numbers

Cours & Distance

N. 50° W. 3 m to a pt on the S.S. N 34° W. 3 m. to the Lower pt of an Island on the L.S. N. 34° W 3 to a pt on L.S passed a Bad riffle old vig [village] S S &c N. 1 m to a pt on the L.S, N. 24° W. 2 m to a pt on the S.S.—

23ʳᵈ of October 1804 Some Snow, passed 5 Lodges of fortified the place the two french men were robed[5] Those are the hunting Camps of the Mandans, who has latterly left them. we camped on the L.S.

Course Distance &c

N. 45° E. 2 M. bend S.S. N. 18° W 1 1/2 m to a High land L.S. N. 65° W. 3 m to a tree in a bend to the L.S. N 33° W 2 1/2 m. to a pt on the L.S. N. 18° W. 1 m. on the L.S. N 45° W. 3 M. to a point on the S.S.—

24ᵗʰ of October[6] Cloudy Some little Snow (my Rhumetism Contine, not so bad as the 2 last days,) a butufull Countrey on both sides, bottoms covered with wood, we See no game to day, passed an old [village ?] of a Band of Mi ni tarres Called Mah har ha where they lived 40 year ago on the L.S.[7] Came too on an Island Caused by the river cutting through a narrow point 7 years ago, on this Island we wer visited by the grand Chief of the Mandans a 2ᵈ Chief and Some other, who wer Camped on the Island,[8] those Chief met our Ricarra Chief with great corduallity, & smoked together Cap Lewis Visited the camps 5 Lodgs, and proceeded on & camped near a 2ᵈ Camp of Mandans on the S.S. nearly opposit the old Ricara & Manden Village which the Ricarras abandoned in the year 1789

Course & Distance &c

N. 20° W 1 1/2 m to a pt on the S.S.   N. 10° W. 2 m. to a pt on the L.S. opsd to new Mandan Island—   Cut point—   N. 34° W. 2 m to S S.   N. 64° W 2 m to a point of high land on which the Mandans & after them the Ricaras formrley lived.

"Course and Distance &c the 25 of October

N. 30° W. 3 M. to a pt on the L.S.   pass old Ricara village. ① W. 1 m on the L.S.   S. 80° W. 1 M on the L.S.   S. 60° W 2 M. to a pt on the L S opsd the old mandan Villages ②. S 30° W 2 m. to a tree on the L.S.   S. 33° W. 2 m. to a point on the S.S. opsd a hill.

Course Distance &c 26ᵗʰ of October

N. 45° W 1 m. bend L.S.   N. 70° W 1 m. to a pt S.S.—   S 26° W. 2 m. to a camp of Mandans L.S.—   West 1 m 1 S.—   N. 27° W. 3 miles to [a point ?] L.S. [where] Fort Mandan stands[9]   passed Bluff L   N. 55° W. 1 m. to a pt on L.S.   S. 60° W. 2 M to the 1st Mandan village on the L S

was derived from Welsh bardic writings. Amateur anthropologists and romantics were looking for Indians somewhat lighter in hue than their copper-colored neighbors, and who spoke a tongue as difficult as the Welsh. Catlin satisfied himself, if no one else, that the Mandans were indeed the Welsh Indians. Neither the Mandans nor the Welsh were consulted. See G. Catlin, *North American Indians* (New York, 1841), pp. 259–61.

9. In this journal, the course and distances for Oct. 25 and 26 precede the entries for those two days. In the entry for Oct. 26 are the words "Fort Mandan stands," which refer to the collection of log huts in which the party spent the winter. Since the building of Fort Mandan did not begin until early November, these words were written in sometime later. The Notebook Journal has the fort placed on "a point" (Thw., *1*, 207).

1. Menard. It was unfortunate that the two captains did not have an opportunity to meet this man. From all accounts, he had gained much information through his contact with the tribes farther west and through his journeys as a free trader. In 1790, Jacques D'Eglise found him living with the Mandans, where he had been for 14 years. Jean Baptiste Truteau, on his expedition up the Missouri in 1796, noted that Menard gave him accurate information about the Yellowstone River some 300 miles beyond Fort Mandan. Truteau describes him as dependable, "frank, and honest" (Nasatir, *1*, 82, 304, 332).

David Thompson refers to a French Canadian named Manoah, whom he met on his visit to the Mandan villages in 1797–98. From the following description, it seems reasonably certain that Menard and Manoah were one and the same: "We paid a visit to Manoah, a french canadian, who had resided many years with these people; he was a handsome man, with a native woman, fair and graceful, for his wife, they had no children; he was in every respect as a Native. He was an intelligent man, but completely a Frenchman, brave, gay, and boastfull." Thompson goes on to say that his boastfulness resulted in his death. He was with a party that was attacked by enemies. On his return to the village, "he praised his own courage and conduct and spoke with some contempt of the courage of those with him, which they did not in the least deserve and for which he was shot" (J. B. Tyrrell, ed., *David Thompson's Narrative of His Explorations in Western America*, Toronto, 1916, p. 230, hereafter cited as Thompson, *Narrative*).

Alexander Henry, in his journal, says that "old Menard was pillaged and murdered by three Assiniboines in 1803 on his way to the Missouri" (Elliott Coues, ed., *New Light on the Early History of the Greater Northwest*, 3 vols. New York, 1897, *1*, 311–12, hereafter cited as Coues, *New Light*). This corroborates the account in this journal and the Notebook Journal (Thw., *1*, 205). Thompson wrote his *Narrative* some 30 years after the event. However, there is the possibility that the Mandans did not tell all they knew.

2. The British establishments referred to here were along the Assiniboine River, just above the Souris River that joins the Assiniboine from the south. When Clark made this entry, there were three British posts in this area: Brandon House of the Hudson's Bay Company, Fort Assiniboine of the Northwest Company, and Fort Souris of the X.Y. Company. This latter company was in the process of merging with the Northwest Company.

The route from the Assiniboin to the Mandans, Arikara, and Gros Ventre villages along the Missouri had been in use for some time. James Mackay had used it in 1787 on his journey from Fort Espérance on the Qu'Appelle River, a branch of the Assiniboine. He was probably the first white man to come in contact with the Mandans. From then on the trade developed. In 1795 Evans reported that the Northwest Company had set up a fort at the Arikara village nearest the Mandans in 1792. In 1797 David Thompson, then in the employ of the Northwest Company, made the journey to obtain information as to the route and the trading prospects. His journal gives the first detailed description of the "Assiniboin Road." He reported that the journey might be made in ten days in good weather, provided the parties were not waylaid by the Assiniboin or Sioux, who were a constant threat to traders (David A. Stewart, *Early Assiniboin Trading Posts of the Souris Mouth Group, 1785–1832*, Historical and Scientific Society of Manitoba Transactions, no. 5, new series, July 1930; Nasatir, *1*, 94–95, 540; Thompson, *Narrative*, pp. 209–37; infra, pp. 178–79 n.).

3. Hugh McCracken was a free trader to whom credit had been extended by the Northwest Company at Fort Assiniboine. David Thompson in his *Narrative* (p. 209) lists him as one of the party who set out from Fort Assiniboine in November 1797. He describes him as "a good hearted Irishman who had been often to the [Mandan] villages, and resided there for weeks and months." This man was with Alexander Henry on his visit to the Mandans in 1806. Henry refers to him as "an old Irishman formerly belonging to the artillery" (Coues, *New Light*, *1*, 304). Clark was to use him later as a messenger to deliver a letter to the Northwest Company agent at Fort Assiniboine (infra, p. 172).

4. Three corn mills are listed among the articles purchased for the party (Thw., 7, 238–39). Ordway wrote that one was given to the Arikara on Oct. 11 (*Ordway*, p. 151). No mention of this is to be found in the other journals. The second was given to the Mandans (infra, p. 169). The third was cached near the mouth of the Marias River on June 11, 1805 (Thw., 7, 99). Alexander Henry saw what was left of the mill given to the Mandans when he visited them in 1806. "I saw the remains of an excellent large corn mill which the foolish fellows had demolished to barb their arrows; the largest piece of it which they could not break or work up into any weapon was fixed to a wooden handle, and used to pound marrow bones to make grease" (Coues, *New Light*, *1*, 329).

25th of October Thursday 1804   a Gentle Breeze from the S.E by E passed an ① old Village on a high Plain where the Mandans onced lived & after they lef the Village & moved higher the Ricaras took possession & live untill 1799 when they abandaned it & flew from the just revenge of the Mandans, a verry extensive Bottom above the Village about the Center of which ② the Mandans lived in 2 villages on the L.S, but little timber—   Several parties of Indians on each Side of the River going up— in vew in everry directions—   we are informed that the Sioux has latterly taken horses from the Big Bellies or Mi ni tarees and on their way homardwards th[ey] fell in with the assinniboins who Killed them and took the horses & a frenchman Menari[1] who resided with the Mandans for 20 years past was Killed a feiw days ago on his way from the Britishment astablishments on the assiniboin River, 150 miles N. of this place, to the Mandans by the assiniboin Indians—[2]   we were frequently Called to by parties of Indians & requested to land & talk, passed a verry bad place & Camped on a point S S. opposit a high hill   Several Indians Visit us this evening, the Sun of the late great Chief of the Mandans who had 2 of his fingers off and appeared to be pearced in many places   on inqureing the reason, was informed that, that it was a testimony of their greif for Deceased freinds, they frequently Cut off Sevral fingers & pierced themselves in Different parts, a Mark of Savage effection, Wind hard from the S W.   verry Cold   R Fields with a Rhumetism in his Neck   one man R. [Read?] in his hips   My Self much better, Those Indians appear to have similar Customs with the Ricaras, they Dress the Same   more mild in ther language & justurs [gestures?] &c. &c.

26th of October 1804 [4 written over 5]   Wind from the S.E   We Set the Ricara Chief on Shore with Some Mandans, Many on each Side Veiwing of us, we took in 2 Chiefs, (Coal) and Big Man) and halted a fiew Minits at their Camps, on the L.S. fortified in thier way, here we Saw a trader from the Ossinniboin River Called McCracken,[3] this man arrived 9 day ago with goods to trade for horses & Roabs   one other Man with him—   we Camped on the L. Side a Short distance below the 1st Mandan village on the L.S.   many men women & Children flocked down to See us—, Capt Lewis walked to the village with the Chief and interpeters, my Rheumetism incrissing prevented me from going also, and we had Deturmened that both would not leave the boat at the Same time untill we Knew the Disposition of the Nativs, Some Cheif visited me & I smoked with them,— they appeared delighted with the Steel Mill[4] which we were obliged to use, also with my black Servent, Capt Lewis returned late—

AT THE MANDANS:
OCTOBER 27, 1804–APRIL 3, 1805

27th of October Satturday 1804   we Set out early and Came too at the
village on the L.S. where we delayed a few minits, I walked to a Chiefs
Logg & Smoked with them, but could not eat, which did displease them
a little, here I met with a Mr Jessomme, who had lived in this Nation 13
years, I got him to interpet & he proceedd on with us   we proceeded on
to a central point opposit the Knife River, & formed a Camp on the
L.S. above the 2d Mandan village & opsd the Mah-har-ha [Minitari] village—

Mah hars village

and raised a flag staff— Capt Lewis & the Intepeters walked down to the 2ᵈ Village of Mandans, & returned in about an hour, we Sent 3 Carrotes of tobacco to the other villages & enviting them to come down and council with us tomorrow,— we endeaver to precure Some Knowledge of the principal Chiefs of the Different Nations &c— will to give my ideas as to the impression thais man [Jessaume] makes on me is a cunin artfull an insonce [insolent?] ar— [?] he tels me he was once empld by my brother in the Illinois & of his description I concive as a Spye upon the British of Michillinacknac & St Joseph,[5] we think he may be made use full to us & do employ him as an interpeter— no. of Indians bring their wives &c. to the camps of our party on Shore &c.

Course distance &c

West 2 M. to a bend on the L.S.   passed a Coal bank on the L.S.
N. 10° W. 2 M to a wood on the S.S.   passed the 2ᵈ Mandan V. on the S.S. to the place we counciled & Stayed untill the 1ˢ Nov.—

Cours & Distance up the Missouri abov the Mandans

N. 12° W. 3 M. to a Bluff 30 feet high above the wooded bottom L.Side
N. 20° W. 2 M. to a tree under a Bluff of about 20 feet high on the S.S.
N. 30° W. 1 1/2 M. to a pt of the Same Bluff 30 feet high in which is Coal
N. 45° W. 1 1/2 M. to the lower point of an Island, the current on the L.S.

28ᵗʰ of October 1804   the wind So hard from the S.W. We could not meet the Indians in Councils, those who visited us we sent to the nearest village, Consulted the Black Cat M[andan] Cheif[6] about the Cheifs of the Different Villages, who gave his Oppinion to us.

29ᵗʰ of October 1804   a fine morning   after Brackfast we were Visited by the Old Chief of the Big Bellies or Me ne tar res,[7] this Man has Given his power to his Son who is now on a war party against th Snake Indians who inhait [inhabit] the Rockey Mountains, the S W wind verry high— we met in Council under an orning and our Sales stretched round to keep out as much wind as possible & Delivered a long speach similar to what had been Said to the nations below, the old Chief was restless before the Speech was half ended, observed his Camp was exposed & could wait no longer &c   at the Conclusion of the Speach we mentioned the Ricaras & requested them to make a peace & Smok out of the Sacred Stem with their Chief which I introduced and gave him the pipe of peace to hand around, they all smoked with eagerness out of the pipe held by the Ricara Chief Ar-ke-tar-na-shar[8]   we mentioned our hands that were to be discharged here, also the roberrey commited on th 2 french men below, & requested them to answere us tomorrow, gave the Chief Small preasents and a fiew presents for each village   Shot the air gun which both surprised and astonished the nativs, and Soon dispersed— our Ricara Chief Came told me he wished to return to his Nation tomorrow I put him off & Said we would send a talk by him after the Chiefs had spoken to us— we gave a Steel mill to the Mandans which was verry pleasing to them
The Chief who recved Medals to Day are as follows viz—
in Council

5. René Jessaume (Gissom, Jussom, Jissom, Jessiaume, Grousseaume) was a free trader who had lived with the Mandans for 15 years. He obtained the goods for this trade on credit from the Northwest Company posts on the Assiniboine River. In the spring of 1793, David Monin, the clerk who had been left in charge of Pine Fort on the Assiniboine, set out for the Mandan villages with Jessaume and two other free traders. They reached the Mandans, where it would appear Jessaume and one other remained. Monin and the other free trader set out on their return to Pine Fort, and were killed by a war party of Sioux (Diary of John MacDonell, in Charles M. Gates, *Five Fur Traders of the Northwest*, Minneapolis, 1933, p. 112). Jessaume served as an interpreter with David Thompson on his trip to the Missouri in 1797–98. Thompson describes him as one who spoke Mandan fluently, and was acquainted with their customs and manners. Indeed, from all accounts, he participated in their religious rites and ceremonies whenever such association would increase his standing among the natives. See Thompson, *Narrative*, p. 234–35, and the Charles MacKenzie Narrative in Masson, *1*, 376–82. His wife was a Mandan woman and he had one child who is described by Ordway as "tollerable white" (*Ordway*, p. 159).

This entry of Clark, which appears in no other journal, adds something to our information concerning the man. Because of the general agreement by the white traders as to the shifty character of Jessaume, his story that he had been used by Clark's brother, George Rogers Clark, as a spy on the British must be taken with a grain of salt. Perhaps he was trying to get into the good graces of the two captains. However, there is the possibility that he might have been in the Illinois country during Clark's campaign in the West.

That dour old Scot, Alexander Henry, probably reflects the general reputation that Jessaume had acquired. "He retains the outward appearance of a Christian, but his principles as far as I could observe, are much worse than those of a Mandane; he is possessed of every superstition natural to those people, nor is he different in every mean, dirty trick they have acquired from intercourse with the set of scoundrels who visit these parts" (Coues, *New Light, 1*, 333).

Jessaume had been involved in difficulties from another quarter. In 1796 the Spanish authorities in St. Louis had dispatched James Mackay up the Missouri to report on the activities of the English along the upper river, and to warn them away from the region now the property of the King of Spain. When Evans, Mackay's lieutenant, arrived at the Mandan villages in October 1796, he found Jessaume and other free traders from the Northwest Company's Assiniboine post in possession. Backed by that company, and fearful that his remaining trade goods would be confiscated, Jessaume instigated a plot to murder Evans. This was foiled by friendly Mandans, and Jessaume set out for the Assiniboin, leaving Evans in possession. As soon as the latter departed, however, Jessaume and the other free traders returned and the threat of the

Spaniards from the south ended (see the extracts from the Evans Journal for 1796, in Nasatir, *2*, 496–97).

When the Lewis and Clark party got back to the Mandan villages in 1806 on their return from the Pacific, Jessaume accompanied the Mandan chief, She-he-ke, or Big White, on his visit to Washington. "he [Jessaume] informed us . . . that the big white Chief would go if we would take his wife & Son & Jessoms wife and 2 children [which] we wer[e] obliged to agree to do" (Thw., *5*, 343).

6. In the Notebook Journal, Black Cat, or Poss-cap-sa-hee, was called by Clark the Grand Chief of the Mandans as well as the principal chief of the upper Mandan village (Thw., *1*, 209, 256). During the winter, the two captains were in constant touch with him and appeared to have had great confidence in him. "This man," wrote Lewis, "possesses more integrety, firmness, inteligence and perspicuety of mind than any indian I have met with in this quarter, and I think with a little management he may be made a usefull agent in furthering the views of our government" (ibid., 256).

7. This is the expedition's first real contact with the Minitari or Gros Ventre. These Indians lived in villages on the Knife River, which enters the Missouri some seven or eight miles above the site chosen by the two captains for their winter quarters. Hodge notes that these were Hidatsa, a division of the Gros Ventre, and are to be distinguished from the Atsina, who lived farther west and were also called Gros Ventre. The latter were associated with the Blackfeet (Hodge, *1*, 508; *2*, 570).

There was always the possibility that the traders of the two competing British companies might succeed in fomenting trouble between the Minitari and their neighbors, the Mandan and the Arikara. However, the constant threat of the Sioux made possible some sort of alliance among the three nations. This was one of the objectives of Lewis and Clark in bringing together the chiefs of the three tribes. It was hoped that such an alliance would counteract the influence of the British traders. However, no permanent peace was achieved and by the time the party returned from the Pacific, the old quarrels had been renewed.

8. *Supra*, p. 158 n.

1ᵗ Mandan village Ma-too-ton ka—

    1ᵗ Chief Sha-ha-ka Big White)⁹ 2ⁿᵈ Ka-goh-ha-me little Crow

2   do village Roop lar-nee   1ᵗ grand Chief Poss-cop-sa-he Black Cat—
                                      2ᵈ Chief Car-gar-no-mok-she. raven man Chief.

Mah. har-ha village   1ᵗ Chief Ta-tuck-co pin re has, white Buffalow skin unfolded

Little Minetarre village   1ᵗ Chief Omp-se-ha-ra. Black Mockerson.
                                       2ᵈ Chief Oh-harh   little Fox.

The Grand village of Minetarres, The One Eye is the principal chief and he is out on a hunting party.[1] we send

9. She-he-ke (Coyote) was called Big White, *Le Gros Blanc,* by the traders because he resembled a heavily-tanned white man. This principal chief of the lower village of the Mandans was fat, good-natured, and talkative. The two captains found him friendly and ready to assist them in making peace among the three tribes. On the expedition's return from the Pacific in 1806, Big White was persuaded to go with the party downriver (Thw., *5,* 353) and thence to Washington for a visit with President Jefferson, who entertained him at Monticello. A portrait of him was made in Philadelphia, and is now in the possession of the American Philosophical Society of Philadelphia. (See reproduction in *Ordway,* p. 181.) Big White returned to St. Louis, and in May 1807 set out with his family and a party under the command of Nathaniel Pryor, now an ensign, for his home. The party was stopped by the Arikara and forced to turn back. It was not until 1809 that She-he-ke got back to his village. His stories of what he had seen and done during his visit in the East were regarded by the Mandans as just another evidence of the well-known boastfulness of a man whom they did not regard as a great warrior. Later, he was killed in a fight with the Sioux when he went out to watch his tribe drive off an attacking party (Hodge, *2,* 518–19).

1. Although Le Borgne, or One Eye, "the Grand Chief of the Minitari" (Thw., *1,* 212), had a bad reputation in some quarters (*Ordway,* p. 186 n.), the Northwest trader from the Assiniboin, Charles MacKenzie, found him friendly and useful. MacKenzie notes in his journal that on his trips to the Minitari he stayed in One Eye's lodge. The Cheyenne actually thought that MacKenzie was his son. The influence of this chief was important to the Northwest Company in its effort to set up trade with the Crow farther west, for One Eye had adopted the Crow chief, Red Calf, as his son (Masson, *1,* 345).

Lewis and Clark were aware of the importance of this man and his association with the British traders. On the return of the expedition from the Pacific, they stopped at One Eye's village and presented him with their swivel gun, "and told him when he fired this gun to remember the words of his great father which we had given him. this gun had anounced the words of his great father to all the nations which we had seen &c. &c." It was hoped that this ceremony and gift would "ingratiate him more Strongly in our favour" (Thw., 5, 342–43). It is doubtful that he was much influenced. MacKenzie records that "Le Borgne said a great deal in favour of the [Northwest] Company, but he did not praise the Americans" (Masson, *1,* 345).

2. In Clark's list of Minitari chiefs who were at the council there is the name of "Caltar-co ta—cherry (grows [growing] on a bush) old chief" (Thw., *1*, 213). This is the only chief whose name approximates "the Grape" who carried presents to One Eye.

3. In the Notebook Journal there are further details concerning this incident. The boy was a half-breed and "Those ignerent people say this boy was Saved by the Great Medison Speret because he was white." However, it was a green buffalo skin that saved him, thrown over him by his mother "who perhaps had more fore Sight for the pertection of her Son, and [l]ess for herself than those who escaped the flame" (Thw., *1*, 211).

4. The rumor going about that the Northwest Company intended to establish a fort near the mouth of the Knife River may have led Lewis and Clark to consider building their fort in that vicinity (Thw., *6*, 52). However, as wood was scarce and game above this point not as plentiful as below, they concluded that a location here was not feasible. Gass wrote that Lewis led this reconnaissance, but Ordway supports the entry of Clark in this journal and in the Notebook Journal (*Gass*, p. 55; *Ordway*, p. 160; Thw., *1*, 213).

5. Under the heading "Indian Speeches and Data," published in the appendix of Thwaites' edition of the Notebook Journals, there are notes, taken by Clark on loose sheets of paper, of the Oct. 11 meeting with the Arikara and of this council with the Mandan and Arikara chiefs on Oct. 31 (Thw., *7*, 303–06). These are probably the ones referred to here. In this journal, the speech of the great chief of the Mandans, Pose-cop-sa-he (Black Cat), is not as detailed as in the notes made by Clark, presumably at the council, or as found in the Notebook Journal (Thw., *1*, 214). In both, the chief told of the disappointment of his people, who were out hunting and found, when they came in for the council, that there were no presents for them. He added that "I am not so much so but my village are."

6. The two captains had not been at the Mandans very long before they were aware of the influence of the British traders on the Indians around them. This influence might well be great enough to prevent the assertion of the authority of the United States, and to retard the development of American trade in that area. Furthermore, the task of getting the three tribes to agree on any peaceful arrangement was being made more difficult. Murdock Cameron of the Hudson's Bay Company had channeled part of the trade through his friends, the Teton Sioux, to his post on the St. Peters River. To the north, the posts of the Northwest Company had for several years used the route from the Assiniboine River to the Mandans, and were busy diverting some of the trade of the Minitari, Assiniboin, and the Crow which would have gone through the Sioux to Cameron.
The party had been at the Mandans less than two weeks when Lewis dispatched by

by the Grape[2] all the articles for this grand Chief and all the Village what goods was intended for that Village— The Prarie got on fire and went with Such Violenc & Speed as to Catch a man & woman & burn them to Death, Several escapd among other a Small boy who was Saved by getting under a green Buffalow Skin, this boy was half white, & the Indians say all white flesh is medisan, they say the grass was not burnt where the boy sat &c. &c.[3] this fire passed us at 8 oClock and lookd truly tremendious.

30th of October Tuesday 1804 many Indian Chief visit us to day. I went in th[e] Perogue to the Island 7 miles above to look out a proper place for to winter, it being near the tim[e] the riv[er] begins to run at this place, and the Countrey after a few leagues high[er ?] is Said to be barron of timber, I found no place soutable, & we concluded to drop down to th next point below & build a fort to winter in[4] the Party Danced which Delited the <savages> Indians.

31s of October Wednesday 1804 The main Chief of the Mandans Sent 2 Cheifs for <us> to envite us to Come to his Lodge, and here what he has to say I with 2 interpetes walked down, and with great cerimony was Seated on a Robe by the Side of the Cheif; he threw a Robe highly decorated over my Sholders, and after smokeing a pipe with the old men in the circle, the Chief Spoke "he belived all we had told him, and that peace would be genl [general] which not only gave himself Satisfaction but all his people; they now could hunt without fear & thier women could work in the fields without looking every moment for the ememey, as to the Ricaras addressing himself to the Chief with me you know we do not wish war with your nation, you have brought it on your selves, that man Pointing to the 2d Chief and those 2 young warriers will go with you & Smoke in the pipe of peace with the Ricaras— I will let you see my father addressing me that we wish to be at peace with all and do not make war up on any— he continud to Speak in this stile (refer to notes)[5] he delivered 2 of the Traps to me which was taken from the french men, gave me 2 bushels of Corn, I answered the Speech which appeared to give general satisfaction—and returned to the boat, In th evening the Chief Visited us Dressed in his new Suit, & delayed untill late the men Dancd untill 10 oClock which was common with them wrote to the N W Copanys agent on the Ossinniboin River by a Mr Mc-Crackin.[6]

1 November 1804 Visited by Several Chiefs of the lower Village who requested we would call on them &c. Spoke to the Same Purpote [Purport] with the Grand Chief.[7] we Set out in the evening & I with the Party droped down to the place we intended to winter & Cap Lewis is called at the Village 3 miles above &c. &c.

2nd Novr 1804 Friday— Capt Lewis returned to the Village & I fixed on a place for to build a fort and Set to work[8] Capt Lewis returned in the eveng with 11 bushels of Corn, the Ricarre Chief Set out for his Village accompanied by several mandans—

3rd of November Satturday 1804 wind hard from the west Commence building our Cabins, Dispatched 6 hunters in a perogue Down the River to hunt, Discharged the french hands,[9] Mr Jessomme his squar & child moved to camp, the little Crow loaded his squar with meat for us also a Roabe, we gave the Squar an ax & &c. Caught 2 bever near Camp

McCracken a letter to Charles Chaboillez, the Northwest Company's *bourgeois* at Fort Assiniboine. This letter stated that he and Clark had been commissioned by the government of the United States to explore the Missouri and the western parts of the continent, "with a view to the promotion of general science." Lewis went on to say that as winter was imminent, the party had fortified itself to remain near the Mandans until spring. The party desired to cultivate the good will of all well-disposed persons and, in accordance with the liberal policy of the United States, would permit them to come and go and afford them protection. In conclusion Lewis asked Chaboillez to give him any information about the country that "you might conceive of utility to mankind." A copy of the passport issued by the British chargé d'affaires in Washington was enclosed with this letter. The letter was signed by both Lewis and Clark (Thw., 7, 307–08; Jackson, pp. 213–14).

7. The Mandans were concerned as to where the Americans would decide to locate their fort. The two captains had been upstream and had not found a suitable location. She-he-ke, Big White, the chief of the first village, asked, "are you going to stay abov or below [during] this Cold [season]?" Lewis told him that since there was no proper place upstream, they intended to drop downstream a few miles. She-he-ke expressed disappointment at this, saying that it would be too far to send corn from his village. The dependence of both the Americans and the Mandans on the available supply of Indian corn is well expressed in his words, "if we eat, you shall eat, if we Starve you must Starve also" (Thw., 7, 306).

Meat would be in short supply before winter was over, for the buffalo were both scattered and poor in flesh. There also was always the danger of running into Sioux hunting parties out on the plains.

8. The site finally decided upon was on the east bank of the Missouri, four miles below the Mandan villages and six miles below the Knife River, according to Clark's "Summary of Rivers and Creeks" (Thw., 6, 61). Here was a place well supplied with cottonwood, the only wood of sufficient size available for building. Ordway noted that it "will Split Tollorable well, and as their is no other building timber in this bottom we expect to Split punchin to cover the huts with" (*Ordway*, p. 162). The illustration (given in Gass' journal) of the men building the huts suggests some of the difficulty in using the cottonwood, which is without any straight grain. (See Wheeler, 1, 207.) Ordway noted that the cottonwood "will rive well So that we are in hopes to make enofe to cover our buildings. but afterwards found it difficult and Gave up the Idea" (ibid., p. 164). The cracks between the logs were stuffed with rags, grass, and mortar, and the whole was covered with a thick coat of earth. The party might have done better to copy the winter lodges of the Mandan and Gros Ventre, which would have

been more easily constructed, warmer, and more comfortable. Nevertheless, the labor of some 40 men over a period of about three weeks resulted in a fort that was defensible and reasonably comfortable. Such an experienced westerner as François-Antoine Larocque, who arrived from the Northwest Company's post on the Assiniboin just about the time that the fort was completed, approved. "Arrived at Ft. Mandan, being the name the Americans give to their Fort which is constructed in a triangular form, ranges of houses making two sides, and a range of amazing long pickets, the front. The whole is made so strong as to be almost cannonball proof. The two ranges of houses do not join one another, but are joined by a piece of fortification made in the form of a demi circle that can defend two sides of the Fort, on top of which they keep a sentry all night; the lower parts of that building serves as a store. A sentinel is likewise kept all day walking in the Fort" (The Larocque Missouri Journal, in Masson, 1, 307–08).

Lewis and Clark were military men, and their fortifications had to be constructed according to the principles of military engineering, irrespective of the building materials available. Furthermore, such a formidable post would impress the Indians and the traders.

9. To the entry for Nov. 3, 1804, in the Notebook Journal, there has been added the following: "The Frenchmen 9 engaged thus far now returning—but 2 or 3 volunteered to remain with us the winter which they did, & in the Spring left us" (Thw., 1, 217). This passage is in the hand of Biddle, who freely interpolated into the Notebook Journal information received from Clark in 1810–11 while he was preparing his history of the expedition.

There were nine Frenchmen "engaged thus far" at Fort Mandan in April 1805. They were the nine *engagés* listed in Clark's roster made at the mouth of the Platte on July 4, 1804, plus Malboeuf whom he overlooked. Le Bartee deserted after the list was made bringing the count back to nine (supra, p. 95). The Frenchmen Cruzatte and Labiche were enlisted men and not *engagés*. Baptiste Le Page, who was with the Mandans when the party arrived, enlisted on Nov. 2, the day before this entry.

1. The name Toussaint Charbonneau appears in the Journal of John McDonnell of the Northwest Company, who set out in the spring of 1793 from the Lachine Rapids above Montreal for the company's posts on the Assiniboine River (The Diary of John McDonnell, in Gates, *Five Fur Traders*). After his arrival at the company post, Fort Espérance on the Qu'Appelle River, a branch of the Assiniboine, he sent out a party on Nov. 6, 1793, with supplies for Pine Fort, farther downstream. In that party was Charbonneau (Masson, *1*, 285). In 1832, Maximilian of Wied said that Charbonneau had lived with the Gros Ventre for 37 years (Wheeler, *1*, 131). That would place him in the country in 1793. Whether or not he came up from Montreal with McDonnell's brigade in that year is impossible to determine. In Clark's letter to Charbonneau, Aug. 20, 1806, wherein Clark made his offer to establish the Frenchman and his family on a farm in Illinois, he wrote, "If you wish to visit your friends in Montreall I will let you have a horse" (Thw., 7, 329; Jackson, p. 315).

In November 1804, Larocque, with a party from Fort Assiniboine heading for the Mandan villages, inquired at the Gros Ventre villages for Charbonneau, "it being his usual place of residence," and was told that he was at the Mandans "with some Americans." The next day Larocque met Lewis with Charbonneau and Jessaume (Masson, *1*, 302–03). The two captains permitted Charbonneau to assist Larocque as interpreter during his stay with the Gros Ventre. When the party returned from the Pacific, Charbonneau remained again with the Gros Ventre—although he wanted to go to Washington as interpreter for the Gros Ventre chiefs, but they refused to go. Clark offered to take him to the Illinois country; he refused, saying there was no chance for him there, and he must continue to live his life among the Indians (Thw., 5, 344). He lived with them until his death, about 1837–38 (Wheeler, *1*, 130–34).

Lewis refers to him as "a man of no peculiar merit; was useful as an interpreter only, in which capacity he discharged his duties in good faith" (Thw., 7, 359). Clark, on the other hand, appears to have formed a real attachment to him. After the party had left Charbonneau at the Gros Ventre villages and started downstream for St. Louis, Clark sent him a letter from the Arikara village. In it Clark renewed his offer to provide a farm for Charbonneau, and said that if he brought his son Baptiste with him, Clark would educate him and treat him as his own child. "You have," wrote Clark, "been a long time with me and have conducted your Self in Such a manner as to gain my friendship, your woman who accompanied you that long dangerous and fatigueing rout to the Pacific Ocean and back, diserved a greater reward for her attention and services on that rout than we had in our power to give her at the Mandans" (Clark to Charbonneau, Aug. 20, 1806, Thw., 7, 329; Jackson, p. 315).

Sacajawea, one of Charbonneau's wives, was the mother of Baptiste—"my little dancing boy" as Clark called him—and both went

4th of Nov.   a french man by Name Chabonah,[1] who Speaks the Big Belley language visit us, he wished to hire & informed us his 2 Squars were Snake [Shoshoni] Indians, we enga[ge] him to go on with us and take one of his wives to interpet the Snake language   The Indians Horses & Dogs live in the same Lodge with themselves

6th of Nov.   Mr. Gravolin our Ricara Interpreter & 2 of our french hands & 2 boys Set out in a Canoe for the Ricaras   Mr Gravelli[n] is to accompany the Ricaras Chiefs to the City of Washington in the Spring,[2] Great numbers of Geese pass to the South which is a certain approach of ice—

13th   The Ice begin to run   we move into our hut, visited by the Grand Chief of the Mandans, and Che chark Lagru [*la grue*, the crane]. a Cheif of the Assinneboins & 7 men of that Nation, I smoked with them and gave the Chief a Cord & a Carrot of Tobacco—   this Nation rove in the Plains above this and trade with the British Companys on the Ossinneboin River, they are Divided into several bands, the decendants of the Sioux & speak nearly their language   a bad disposed Set & Can rais [raise] about 1000 men in the 3 bands near this place, they trade with the nations of this neighbourhood for horses corn &c[3]   Snow all Day   Cap. L. at the village.

[*From this date, November 6, 1804, through to the end of the journal on April 3, 1805, the entries are few and there are many breaks. Events that took place over a number of days are crowded into one entry. The reader should refer to the Notebook Journal (Thw., 1, 235–79) for the continuing record of this period.*]

The most pressing task was to supply the party with meat. Hunting expeditions were sent out in the bitter cold of a Dakota winter, when at times the thermometer registered 40° below zero. On such ventures out onto the storm-swept plain, the men endured great hardships. Frostbites were common. Since the game had moved away from the immediate vicinity, it was necessary to go downriver, in one case 30 miles, and camp for several days in the open. Sleds were built at the fort to bring in the meat, and horses had to be shod so that they might travel over the ice. In one instance 2,400 pounds of meat were brought back to the fort. At that season of the year, the game was so poor and thin that it was scarcely worth bringing in. Either Lewis or Clark went out on such expeditions, and the Notebook Journal was kept by the one remaining at the fort. Corn and beans were traded from the Indians, who received in return battleaxes, knives, and other ironware, fashioned out of scrap by the blacksmiths, who were busy all winter supplying such articles for this very important barter.

The urgent task of getting the fort built before winter set in required the efforts of all hands. Consequently the keelboat and the pirogues had been neglected and were now frozen fast in the river. Only with great effort were they freed and drawn up on shore.

There were constant alarms and excursions. A war party of Sioux attacked a hunting party and made off with some of the meat and a few horses. The Mandans, who were as much in need of buffalo as the American party, were out on the plains. Some were killed by hostile Indians, some froze to death, and others came in with frozen feet and hands.

There were constant rumors. Charbonneau came back from the Gros Ventre villages and reported that One Eye, their great chief, was talking against the Americans and that the Hudson's Bay man was encouraging him. He also had heard that the Northwest Company was planning to

with the expedition to the Pacific. She has become an almost legendary figure, through the efforts of romanticists. She was a Shoshoni who had been captured when a child and sold to Charbonneau when she was fourteen. Her child, Baptiste, or "Pomp," as Clark called him, was born on Feb. 11, 1805, while the party was in winter quarters at the Mandans. After the return of the party, Charbonneau, Sacajawea, Baptiste, and two other children of Charbonneau arrived in St. Louis, where Clark provided for Baptiste's education. Sometime later Prince Paul of Württemberg, who was on a visit to the United States, took Baptiste back with him to Germany. He did not return until about 1829. Later he served as guide and interpreter for Western travelers (Bakeless, pp. 438–39; Grace Hebard, *Saca-jawea,* Glendale, California, 1933, pp. 118–27).

2. The Notebook Journal gives more detail. "Mr. Jo Gravelin our ricare interpreter Paul premor [Paul Primaut]—Laguness [La Jeunesse] & 2 french Boys, who Came with us, Set out in a Small perogue, on their return to the recare nation & the Illinois" (Thw., *1,* 218). With the departure of these four, the number of *engagés* who came all the way up the Missouri with the party was reduced from nine to six. In Feb. 1805, Graveline returned with two Frenchmen. There is no way of knowing whether they were those mentioned above or not.

3. This is the party's first contact with the Assiniboin. This tribe, who were of Siouan stock and whose language differed only slightly from their Sioux neighbors, ranged from the Saskatchewan River across the Assiniboin and down to the Missouri and its tributary, the Milk River. They had been driven westward from the area north of Lake Superior to the Lake of the Woods, thence to Lake Winipeg, some 50 years before Lewis and Clark found them on the northern plains. By that time, they were wholly dependent on the buffalo, bartering pemmican for trade goods with the English posts and for corn from the Mandans, Gros Ventre, and Arikara. They were inveterate enemies of the Sioux and preyed on the weaker tribes on the Missouri (Hodge, *1,* 102–05). Lewis calls them "vicious . . . pay little respect to their engagements, great Drunkards" (Thw., *6,* 104).

build a fort at the Gros Ventre villages. Several Gros Ventre appeared and told the two captains that they had not dared to come to Fort Mandan for fear the Americans would kill them. The uneasiness of the Indians finally subsided somewhat; the snow and cold prevented any serious trouble among the tribes, who were all suspicious of each other. One Eye finally paid a visit to the fort, and was received with great ceremony. Two guns were fired in his honor, and he was presented with a flag, a medal, a gorget, and a scarlet shirt.

The two Northwest Company men, Larocque and MacKenzie, were frequent visitors, and their relations with the two captains were, on the whole, pleasant enough. However, they could not have failed to apprehend that this expedition was the first step in the extension of American power into the regions to the west, and that such a thrust would jeopardize their future prospects of controlling the fur trade of this great unexploited area where, as MacKenzie put it, "beaver were as numerous in their [the Indians'] rivers as buffalo and other large animals were in their plains" (Masson, 1, 341). Here, then, in the remote Mandan villages on the upper Missouri, the interests of trade and empire clashed as they had 60 years before on the upper Ohio.

There were no outward signs of conflict. However, in addition to the rumors floating about, there was more concrete evidence. On one of his visits to the fort, Larocque requested that he be permitted to go along with the expedition on their journey to the Pacific. His request was promptly turned down (Thw., 1, 252). Some weeks later, Charbonneau returned from the Gros Ventre villages loaded down with presents given him by Chaboillez, the bourgeois in charge of the Assiniboin district. Clark immediately suspected that their interpreter, who had been hired to accompany the party, had been corrupted. He was not far from the truth, for a few days later, Charbonneau told the two captains that he would not go with the party if he were required to work or stand guard. He further stipulated that he be permitted to leave the party at any time if any member displeased him, and that he be allowed to take his trade goods with him. To all intents and purposes, Charbonneau was to take the place of Larocque, who had been turned down. The interpreter was promptly discharged, and Graveline was to take his place (Ordway, p. 186). Later, however, Charbonneau changed his mind, requested reinstatement, and admitted that his conduct had been wrong and that in his simplicity he had done a foolish thing. On March 18, he was enlisted as a permanent member of the party (Thw., 1, 269, 271, 274–75). His term of service began with the date of the departure of the party from Fort Mandan, April 7, 1805. There is no mention of the Charbonneau affair in this journal.

These intrigues and rumors made it abundantly clear that in this newly acquired and remote area, the authority of the United States was contested by both Indian and white. Only a military force could subdue the hostile Sioux, thwart the machinations of the English traders, and impose some sort of peace among the warring tribes. The extension of the American fur trade into this region and the opening up of a transcontinental route to the Pacific depended upon the establishment of American control of the whole length of the Missouri River.

Sometime during the winter at Fort Mandan, Clark prepared a chart (Document 60, infra p. 188) which, I believe, is the first plan for the defense of the Far West—all that vast area from the Arkansas on the south to the Great Falls of the Missouri on the north and from the Mississippi westward to the Upper Missouri. Not only were forts to be established and garrisoned by Federal troops, but also government trading houses *set up, under the law of 1796 that created the Factory System. As a military frontier policy actually developed, posts were established at most of the locations designated by Clark: Fort Leavenworth in eastern Kansas, Fort Osage on the Missouri River, Fort Smith and Fort Gibson in the Arkansas area, Fort Atkinson at Council Bluff, Fort Crawford at Prairie du Chien, Fort Snelling at the junction of the St. Peters with the Mississippi and, much later, Fort Buford at the mouth of the Yellowstone.*

Another task that took up some of Clark's time was the completion of his map of that portion of the Missouri already traversed, and a projection westward based upon information gathered by him and other members of the party (Thw., 1, 239, 244, 266). This map was sent along with the other papers dispatched downriver in April 1805.]

4. The leader of the party was George Henderson (Thw., *1*, 232). They had come down from Brandon House, the Hudson's Bay post on the Assiniboine (*Ordway*, pp. 168–69).

5. The arrival of the English traders of the two competing companies from their posts on the Assiniboine added to the difficulties of the Americans. The two captains had striven to bring about peace among the Mandans, Gros Ventre, and Arikara so that they could use their combined strength against the Sioux and the Assiniboin. These tribes must trade for guns and ammunition if they were to defend themselves against their enemies. The exploring party had little to trade, and could only promise that the traders from St. Louis would in time reach their villages. "It is true," MacKenzie quoted the Mandans as saying, "they [the Americans] have ammunition, but they prefer throwing it away idly than sparing a shot of it to a poor Mandane" (Masson, *1*, 330). Here, however, were the English, with whom they had traded for years and who, through the Sioux and Assiniboin, could keep them in a constant state of anxiety and by spreading rumors cause dissension among them.

We are fortunate in having the journals of both François Antoine Larocque and Charles MacKenzie, the leaders of the seven-man party that left the Northwest Company post, Fort Assiniboine, on Nov. 11, 1804 (Masson, *1*, 299–313, 327–93). They stayed at the Gros Ventre village, only a few miles from Fort Mandan, and met and talked with Lewis and Clark many times and were in constant contact with the Indians with whom they were carrying on trade.

Their journals give the reader the only known record of the activities of the exploring party by anyone not a part of it. Their comments must be discounted somewhat, for they were far from unprejudiced observers, knowing as they did that the arrival of the Americans was but the first step in the extension of American authority and trade into the northern part of the Louisiana Purchase. Eventually American traders would arrive to channel the trade down the Missouri and away from the posts on the Assiniboine and St. Peters rivers.

On the very day of their first meeting with the Northwesters, Lewis and Clark complained to Larocque and MacKenzie that their interpreter, one Baptiste Lafrance, had been making unfavorable comments as to the intentions of the Americans, and warned them of "the Consequences if they did not put a Stop to unfavourable & ill founded assursions &c. &c. (Thw., *1*, 227). Larocque was also told by the captains that there was a rumor that he intended to give flags and medals to the Indians. He was forbidden to do so, as such things were regarded "as the sacred emblems of the attachment of the Indians to their country. As I had neither flags nor medals, I ran no risk of disobeying those orders; of which I assured them" (Masson, *1*, 304).

19th of November 1804   our hunters return with 32 Deerr, 12 Elk & a Buffalow   Ice ran which detained the huntes much   Cap Lewis visit the Me ne tar rees, the 25th and returned the 27th of Nov. with 2 Chiefs &c. &c. and told me that 2 Clerks & 5 men of the N W Company & several of the hudsons Bay Company[4] had arrived with goods to trade with the indians   a Mr La Roche & Mc Kenzey[5] are the Clerks   (Distanc 150 Miles across)[6]

30th of Nov.   an Indian Cheif Came and informed us that five Men of the Mandans Nation was on a hunting party to the S W, distance about Eight Leagues, they were Surprised   one man Killed two wounded and nine horses taken, Severale others men wer on hunting partes & were to have returned Several days ago & had not yet returned, & that they expected to be attacked by an army of Sioux   I took 23 men and went to the Village determined to collect the warriers of the Different Villages and meet the Sioux—   The village not expecting Such Strong aid in So Short a time was a little alarmed of the formable appearance of my party—   The principal Cheifs met me at 200 yards Distance from the Town, and envited me to his Lodge. I told the Nation the Cause of Comeing &. was to assist in Chastiseing the enimies of my Dutifull Children—   I requested [the] great Cheif to repeat the circumstance of the Sioux attack as it realy happined which he did—   I told them to Send runners to the other villages & assemble the warriers & we Would go and Chastize the Sioux for Spilling the Blood of my Dutifull Children— after a Conversation of a few Minits amongst themselves, a Cheif Said that they now Saw that what we had told them was the trooth and we were ready to protect them and Kill those who did not listen to our Councils (and after a long Speech) he concluded   said the Sious who Spilt our Blood is gorn home—   The Snow is deep and it is Cold, our horses Cannot Travel thro the plains in pursute—   If you will go and conduct us in the Spring after the Snow is gorn, we will assemble all the warriers & Brave men in all the villages and go with you". I answered the Speach at Some length, explained to them their Situation declareing our intentions of Defending them at any time dureing the time we Should Stay in ther nieghbourhood, explained the Situation of the Ricaras & told them not to get angrey with them untill they were Certain of their haveing violated the treaty &c. &c.[7] I crossed the River on the Ice and returned to the fort

MacKenzie's opinion of Lewis was unfavorable: he "could not make himself agreable to us. He could speak fluently and learnedly on all subjects, but his inveterate disposition against the British stained, at least in our eyes, all his eloquence." On the other hand, "Captain Clarke was equally well informed, but his conversation was always pleasant, for he seemed to dislike giving offence unnecessarily" (ibid., p. 336).

The Americans assured the traders that they would not be molested in their traffic with the Indians unless they violated the regulations laid down by the United States. However, it was clear that they were not the Spanish, whose feeble and intermittent efforts to assert control over the Upper Missouri had been disregarded by the English. Lewis and Clark informed them that the American government might establish a factory (government-operated trading post) similar to the one at Detroit, which would undersell the two English companies and by such means keep the Indians quiet.

In spite of tension and suspicion on both sides, there were pleasant visits to the fort and favors extended. Clark took care of Larocque's horses, keeping them with his own when it was feared the Assiniboin might run them off; the gunsmith with the American party repaired Larocque's gun, and Lewis fixed his compass. Larocque seems to have been less antagonistic to his hosts than Mac-Kenzie, whose journal is full of acid comments.

6. The distance from the Northwest Company post on the Assiniboine River to the Mandan villages. In the Preliminary Memoranda at the beginning of the first volume of the Notebook Journals, Thwaites included a memorandum written by Lewis containing information given him by John Hay (supra, p. 16 n.). This gives the distances on the trading route from the Otter Tail River in modern Minnesota to the Assiniboine River. It is followed by a section written by Clark headed "The Course from the Fort Mandan to the Fort Chaboillez's [Fort Assiniboine] on the Assinna Boin is North 150 miles." Then follows a table of distances and a small sketch map of the route (Thw., *1*, 4–6).

7. The speech of the chief and Clark's reply are given at greater length in the Notebook Journal. The rumor had gotten about among the Mandans that some Arikara were with the Sioux attacking party. This disturbed them; Lewis and Clark, who had been trying to bring peace between the two tribes, went to some length to calm their fears. "You know that the Seeaux have great influence over the ricarees, and perhaps have led Some of them astray." Clark went on to say that the Arikara were dependent on the Sioux for guns and ammunition, and that it was good policy for them to keep on as good terms as possible with the Sioux until they found other means of obtaining supplies. It is quite possible that the English traders were responsible for these rumors (Thw., *1*, 230–32).

[Document 65 inserted here]

⚜ Document 65 ⚜

8. This supplementary entry for Nov. 30 is written on one side of a large sheet, taking up about one half of the space. This large sheet had been used to seal up the notes Clark made during the winter of 1803–04 at the Dubois River. For further discussion of this document, as it relates to the problem of the provenance of this journal, see the Introduction, pp. xvi–xvii.

9. This probably refers to the young Mandan chief. Whenever possible the Indians recovered their dead after a fight and carried them to their lodges for burial. The speech of the dying chief is not given in the Notebook Journal.

<We Promiss>[8] [November] 30th in the morning early a Indian Came to the river opposit & requ[e]sted to be brought over, that he had Some thing to Say from his nation we Sent for him, and after he had Smoked— he Said he thought the river was frosed across here & expected to Cross on the ice—   7 or 8 Mandans out hunting in a S.W; Derection from this place about 8 Leagues, after they had made their hunt and on their return was attackted by a large Party of Seaux, one of the party a young Chief was Killed 2 wounded & 9 horses taken, the men who made their escape Say the one half of the party who attacked them was Panias [Pawnee]—   The two Panias who Came here a fiew days ago was imediately Sent home, for fear of their being [hole] [p]ut to death by the party Defeated—   Tw [hole] [of t]he attacting party was Known to be Panies. The man who was killed mentioned that after he was wounded, <men> that he had been at war & been wounded, "this day I shall die like a man before my Enimies, ! tell my father that I died bravely, and do not greive for me—

4 of the Big bellies who were Camped near thos missing, and Serching for him[9] in their Camps above—   no one Dare to go to the ground where the battle was for fear of the Sioux being noumerous—.

1t Decr   a young Cheif arrived   7 chiens [Cheyenne] Came to the Village with a pipe & the 3 Ricares who Came here a fiew days ago & Sent off yesterday have returned and Say that the Sieaux & ricares are camped together

[On the verso of Document 65 is the following address, written diagonally across the large sheet:]

General Jonathan Clark
Near Louisville Kentucky

[In the lower right hand corner in reverse is the notation:]

Notes at Wood River
in 1803–4

[In the center above the address and in reverse is the word "Nothing."]

3
21
2
—
26   [End of Document 65]

180

♒ *Document 64* ♒

2ᵈ of Decr 1804   Visited by Several Mandan Cheifs and 4 Chyannes Inds who Came with a pipe to the Mandans, Sent a Speech to ther Nation a flag & Some tobacco, also written a Speech to the Ricaras & Sioux, informe them what they might depend on if they would not open their ears, &c. &c.[1]

at Fort Mandan

7ᵗʰ [*space*] of December 1804, we were informed by a Chief that great numbers of Buffalow were on the hills near us   Cap Lewis with a party went out & Killed 11   three in view of our fort, The weather so excesive Cold & wolves plenty, we only saved 5 of them, I with a party turned out on the 8ᵗʰ and found the Buffalow at 7 ms distant   Killed 8 & a Deer, I returned with 2 Cows leaving men with remaining meat—   Several men badly frost bit—   The Themormeter. Stood this morning at 44ᵈ below Breizing [Freezing]. Capt Lewis went out 9ᵗʰ & Stayed all night out Killed 9 buffalow—   maney of the Buffalow Killed were So meager that they not fit for use—   Collected by the ade of Some horses the best of the meat   in fact all we could save from wolves &c.   I went on a hunting party the 14 & 15 of Decr—   much Snow verry cold 52° below freesinge. N W. & H Bay Clerks Visit us on the 16ᵗʰ[2]   also Mr Hainey,[3] Cold Tem: 74° below freesing———

I visit the Mandans on the 1ˢ of January   Capt Lewis the 2ⁿᵈ

10ᵗʰ of January 1805   This morning a boy of 13 years of age Came to the fort with his feet frozed, having Stayed out all night without fire, with no other Covering than a Small Robe goat skin leagens & a pr Buffalow Skin mockersons—   The Murcery Stood at 72° below the freesing point—   Several others Stayed out all night not in the least hurt, This boy lost his Toes only———

3ʳᵈ of February 1805   our provisions of meat being nearly exersted I concluded to Decend the River on the Ice & hunt, I [I written over we] Set out with about <8> 16 men 3 horses & 2 Slays   Decended nearly 60 miles Killed & loaded the horses back, & made 2 pens which we filed with meat, & returned on the 13ᵗʰ[4]   we Killed 40 Deer, 3 Bulls 19 [9 written over 6] Elk, maney So meager that they were unfit for use

1. On this day a letter was sent to Tabeau and Graveline at the Arikara villages downriver. There was danger of hostilities breaking out between the Arikara and the Mandans, in spite of previous peace councils, and the two captains wanted to know what was going on. The Frenchmen were instructed to tell the Arikara what course the Americans would take "if the Rickores & Seauex did not follow our Derections and be at peace with the nations which we had addopted" (Thw., *1*, 233).

2. On Dec. 16, 1804, the Americans received from Chaboillez a reply to their letter of Oct. 31 (supra, p. 173 n.). In it the Northwest Company *bourgeois* "expressed a great anxiety to Serve us in anything in his power" (Thw., *1*, 238).

3. Hugh Heney (Hainey, Hany, Henney, Héné, Ené). In Lewis' report, "The Ethnology of the Eastern Indians," Heney is described as the only trader among the Miniconjou, a division of the Teton Sioux, who lived on the Missouri near the mouth of the Cheyenne River (Thw., *6*, 97).

In June 1800, a Monsieur Héné, one of the agents of Clamorgan, Loisel, and Company of St. Louis, led a trading expedition up the Missouri. It was believed that this expedition had been waylaid by the British traders and Héné murdered. However, this rumor was false and Héné returned safely to St. Louis. On July 6, 1801, he and Loisel entered into a *Convention de Commerce* to trade with the nations of the Upper Missouri, which he signed as Hugh Heney. After the consolidation of the Northwest Company with its rival the X.Y. Company in 1804, Heney became a clerk in the Upper Red River division along with Larocque and Mac-Kenzie (Nasatir, *1*, 112–14; *2*, 622, 628, 636; Masson, *1*, 402).

Larocque made the following entry in his journal on Dec. 14, 1804: "Returned after dark and found Mr. Heney who was just arrived from Fort Assiniboin . . . He brought a letter from Mr. Chaboillez which altered my plan as to going to the Fort [Assiniboine] so that I will now pass the winter here." On Dec. 16, he recorded that he and Heney had returned to Fort Mandan (Masson, *1*, 307).

Lewis and Clark found Heney to be intelligent and cooperative, and from him they got information as to the country both to the east and west of the Missouri (infra, p. 184 n. See also letter, Lewis to Jefferson, Fort Mandan, March 5, 1805: Jackson, pp. 220–21 and n.). On the return of the expedition from the Pacific, Clark, who was then descending the Yellowstone, sent Sergeant Pryor ahead with three men on July 23, 1806. They were to go to the Mandan villages and make contact with Heney. If he were not there, Pryor was to go to Fort Assiniboine and there deliver a letter from Clark addressed to Heney. Pryor and his men ran into difficulties, for the Crow stole all their horses, and they had to return with the letter undelivered. In his letter Clark wrote that he placed perfect reliance on Heney, and enlisted his aid in persuading some of the Teton chiefs to go to Washington, Heney accompanying them. Clark also assured him that if he wanted the office of Indian Agent among the Sioux, he would have "our wormest intersessions in your behalf with our government."

Jackson points out that this letter, in Clark's hand and signed by him, must have been written by Lewis, for it is characteristically his style, and that this is a copy. This conclusion is adequately supported by the entry, in the Notebook Journal for July 1, 1806 (Thw., 5, 179). On that date this letter was written. Two days later the two captains parted, Lewis for the Missouri River and Clark for the Yellowstone. Not until Aug. 12 were they reunited, at the junction of the two rivers. Clark carried this letter with him, probably signed by both men. Before he dispatched Sergeant Pryor on July 23 with it for delivery to Heney at the Mandans, he dated it July 20 "on the River Rochejhone" and made this copy (Thw., 5, 282–86; Jackson, p. 313 n.).

4. On Feb. 11, Clark entered in the Notebook Journal: "about five Oclock this evening one of the wives of Charbono [Sacajawea] was delivered of a fine boy" (Thw., 1, 257–58).

[*The following is in Lewis' hand:*]
Preperation for Lunar Calculation[5]
Feby 23rd 1805 Fort mandane   S this and
Latitude of the place of observation _____ 47° 21' 47"

5. In one of the Notebooks, Codex O, Lewis recorded his astronomical observations. On this fragment of paper are what seem to be the preliminary calculations for determining the longitude at Fort Mandan, made by him on Feb. 23, 1805 (Thw., *6*, 261–63; *7*, 420).

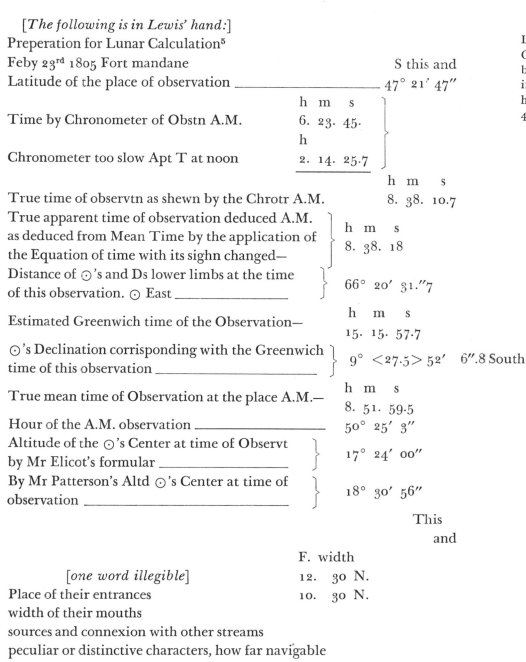

	h	m	s
Time by Chronometer of Obstn A.M.	6.	23.	45.
	h		
Chronometer too slow Apt T at noon	2.	14.	25.7

	h	m	s
True time of observtn as shewn by the Chrotr A.M.	8.	38.	10.7

True apparent time of observation deduced A.M.
as deduced from Mean Time by the application of   } 8. 38. 18 (h m s)
the Equation of time with its sighn changed—

Distance of ☉'s and Ds lower limbs at the time
of this observation. ☉ East _____ } 66° 20' 31."7

Estimated Greenwich time of the Observation— } 15. 15. 57.7 (h m s)

☉'s Declination corrisponding with the Greenwich }
time of this observation _____ } 9° <27.5> 52' 6".8 South

True mean time of Observation at the place A.M.— } 8. 51. 59.5 (h m s)

Hour of the A.M. observation _____ 50° 25' 3"

Altitude of the ☉'s Center at time of Observt }
by Mr Elicot's formular _____ } 17° 24' 00"

By Mr Patterson's Altd ☉'s Center at time of }
observation _____ } 18° 30' 56"

This
and

	F. width		
[*one word illegible*]	12.	30	N.
Place of their entrances	10.	30	N.

width of their mouths
sources and connexion with other streams
peculiar or distinctive characters, how far navigable
face and discription of the country through which they pass
how far
Salt river branch of the Republican alter to W.

This

N
an many
Lewis
oo

[*End of Doc. 35 in Lewis' hand*]

❧ Document 64 ❧

6. Clark had written Tabeau on Dec. 2, 1804, seeking information as to the rumors that the Arikara had broken their truce with the Mandans and that some of them had been seen with a Sioux war party (supra, pp. 180–81). The letter of Tabeau, brought to Fort Mandan by Graveline, not only assured the Americans that the Arikara were ready to join the Mandans against the Sioux, but had some words about the trouble-maker on the St. Peters River, Murdoch Cameron, who was inciting the Sioux (Thw., *1*, 267).

Because of this danger from the east, the two captains needed to know as much as possible about the country that lay between the Missouri and the Red and St. Peters rivers. The efforts of the Hudson's Bay traders and others in that region to get control of the Upper Missouri trade by supporting the Sioux against the Mandans, the Arikara, and Gros Ventre, might well block all efforts toward peace among these tribes. If these hostile traders had their way, the Sioux would act as middlemen for the trade, and the tribes on the Missouri would be subjected to the harsh demands of the Sioux and their backers. One hundred and fifty years before, the Iroquois had played the same role along the Mohawk.

Hugh Heney was one man to whom the Americans could turn for information. On Dec. 17, 1804, Clark recorded in the Notebook Journal, "We found Mr. Henny a Verry intelligent Man from whome we obtained Some Scetches of the Countrey between the Mississippi & Missouri, and Some Sketches from him, which he had obtained from the Indins. to the West of this place also the names and charecktors of the Seeaux &c." (Thw., *1*, 238).

A small map, made by Clark and found among the documents presented here, may well be a copy of one of the Heney sketches (Doc. 66). That this map is only a part of a larger one is apparent from the incomplete sentence in the upper margin, "and trade & Steel horses from the Spaniards." The courses of the rivers St. Peters, Red, and Sheyenne (Clark's "Chien") are inaccurately drawn. The Sheyenne River is placed too far to the south and the distance of one mile between it and the St. Peters is impossible. The courses of the Red and the Sheyenne in relation to one another are less distorted. The other rivers, the Big Sioux, the Jacque [James] and the War-re-con-ne are properly placed. The dotted line may indicate the trail from the Red and St. Peters rivers to the Arikara villages located about 35 miles below the mouth of the War-re-con-ne. However, it may be a boundary line. Lewis, in his "Ethnology of the Eastern Indians" (Thw., *6*, 93), defined the area east of the Mississippi as claimed jointly by the various bands of Sioux. The northern boundary was a line running between the heads of the Red and St. Peters rivers, and westward across the head of the Sioux and to the War-re-con-ne.

The other inscriptions on the map appear to be memoranda, perhaps jotted down as the map was being drawn. The chief, Ma-to-win-ka, is identifiable. He was chief of a band of Yanktonais Sioux, and is listed in Lewis'

14th [February, 1805]   Sent 4 men with the Horses shod & 2 Slays down for the meat I had left, 22 miles below those men were rushed on by 106 Sioux who robed them of 2 of their horses— & they returned

15th [February, 1805]   Capt Lewis with a party of men & 4 Indians went in pursute of the Sioux, the Indians returned the next Day & informed me that the Sioux had Burnt all my meat & gorn home (they Saw me but was afraid to attact me)   Capt Lewis returned the 21st with 2400 lb of meat, haveing Killed 36 Deer & 14 Elk, the Sioux burnt one of my meet houses, they did not find the other

26th of Feby 1805   Drew up the Boat & perogus, after cutting them out of the ice with great Dificuelty— & trouble

28th of February 1805 Thursday   Mr Gravilin 2 frenchmen and 2 Ricaras arrived from the Ricaras with letters from Mr Taboe &c. informing us of the Deturmination of the Ricaras to follow our councels— and the threts & intentions of the Sioux in Killing us whenever they again met us—   and that a party of Several bands were formeing to attacke the Mandans &c. &c.[6]

We informed the Mandans & others of this information & answered also the wish the Ricars had to live near them & fite the Sioux &c. &c. &c. despatched 16 Men 5 Miles abov to build 6 Canoes for the voyage, being Deturmend to Send back the Barge— on the [*space*] 9th of March we were Visited by the Grand Cheif of the Menetarres, to whome we gave a Medal & Some Clothes & a flag. Sent a French Man & a Indian with a letter to Mr Tabboe informing them the Ricarras of the <wish> desire the Mandans had to See them &c. &c.———
I visited the Mandans on the 20th & have the canoes taken to the River, ready to Decend to the fort when the River Clears, I return on the 21st and on my return I passed on the points of the high hills S. S. where I saw an emence quantity of Pumice Stone, and evident marks of the hills being on fire   I collected some Pumice Stone, burnt stone & hard earth and put them into a furnace, the hard earth melted and glazed the other two a part of which i,e. the Hard Clay became a Pumice-Stone, I also collected a Plant the root of which is a cure for the Bite of a mad dog & Snake which I shall Send—   Mr Haney (I think it grows in the Blue R Barrens <M—I> the Indians make large Beeds of Different colours—

22 of March 1805   Visited by the 2nd Cheif of the grand Village of the Minetarrees to whome we gave a Medal & Some Clothes acknowledging him as a 2d Chief, he Delayed all night, & Saw the men Dance, which is common amusement with the Men   he returned the 23rd with Mr La Rocque & Mc Kinsey two of the N W. Companys Clerks——— Some few drops of rain this evening for the first time this Winter   visited by many Indians to day———

25th of March 1805   prepareing to Set out   Saw Swan passing N E.

26th [of March 1805]   The ice broke up in Several places in the evenig broke away and was nearly takeing off our new Canoes   river rise a little

27th [of March 1805]   river choked up with ice opposit to us and broke off in the evengn

28th [of March 1805]   had all the canoes, the B & Perogus corked pitch [*blot*] & tined oover [*sic*] the Cotton Wood, which is win[d] Shaken (the Mandans feed their horses on the cotton wood Sticks in places of corn).

29th [of March 1805][7]   the ice Stoped running owing to Some obstickle abov   all prepareing to Set out but few Indians visit us to day   they are watching to catch the floating Buffalow which brake through the ice in crossing, those people are fond of those animals ta[i]nted and Catch great numbers every Spring

30th of March [1805]. The Ice is passing in great quantites, river ran a little, The Plains are on fire on both Sides of the river—   it is common for the indians to Set those Plains on fire near their village for the advantage of early Grass. for the hors & as an inducement to the Buffalow to visit them——

31t of March Monday 1805 . . Cloudy   Several gangus of Ducks and Geese pass up   not much ice floating. All the party in high Spirrits, but fiew nights pass without a Dance   they are [in] helth   the – v.n – 1 [venereal] which is common with the Indians and have been communicated to many of our party at this place—   those favores bieng easy acquired   all tranquille

April 1st 1805   we have Thunder lightning hail and rain to day   the first rain of note sinc the 15 of October last, I had the Boat Perogus & Canos put in the water, and expect to set off the boat with despatches   in her will go 6 Americans 3 frenchmen, and perhaps Several ricarra Chief[s] imedeately after we Shall assend in 2 perogus & 6 canoes, accompanied by 5 french who intends to assend a Short distance to trap the beavr which is in great abundance higher up[9]   our party will consist of one Interpeter & Hunter, one French man as an interpreter with his two wives[1] (this man Speaks Minetary to his wives who are Skiatars [?] or Snake Indians of the nations through which we Shall pass, and to act as interpretress thro him—   26 americans & french my servant and an Mandan Indian and provisions for 4 months——[2]

April the 2nd   a Cold rain day   we are writeing and prepareing dispatches all day—   I conclude to Send my journal to the President of the United States in its original State for his own perusal, untill I call for it or Some friend if I should not return, an[d] this Journal is from the 13th of May 1804 untill the 3rd of April 1805. wrote untill verry late at night but little time to devote to my freinds,[3] the river is falling fast.

3rd of April   we Shall pack up to day and Set out tomorrow.[4]

schedule of the Sioux as Mah-to-wy-ank-ka. Lewis noted that he was friendly to the whites and had great influence in his band and nation (Thw., *6*, 99).

The word "Saukee," as placed on the map, can have no geographical implication. The Sauk and Fox had their homes along the Wisconsin River. It is true that the Yanktonais Sioux were the only branch of the Sioux with whom the Sauk maintained friendly relations. This may account for their name on this map. It is difficult to determine whether the name of René Jessaume is written in Clark's hand. The editor can offer no explanation for its appearance. It is true that the Frenchman supplied Clark with information concerning the country surrounding Fort Mandan.

7. On the margin of this document, opposite the entry for March 29, is the profile of a man drawn in red crayon. Since one line of the entry near the drawing is in red, it can be assumed that Clark made the sketch. See also the drawing on Doc. 42, p. 106, and n.

8. The keelboat set out with ten men on board (*Ordway*, p. 191). This is substantiated by Clark's entry for April 7, when he referred to a letter from Tableau in which he said that he would board the boat at the Arikara villages with four Arikara chiefs. Clark added that this "addition will make the party in the boat 15 Strong" (Thw., *1*, 286).

The party of ten in the keelboat included Corporal Warfington and the four enlisted men who had been under his command since the start of the expedition: John Boley, John Dame, Ebenezer Tuttle, and Isaac White. With them and under his command were Moses B. Reed and John Newman. These two had been dropped from the permanent party, one for desertion and the other for insubordination. Of the French on the boat, there were Joseph Graveline as pilot and one other (Thw., *1*, 283). An Arikara chief who was lame was on board (*Ordway*, p. 190). This accounts for the ten passengers on the boat when it left Fort Mandan. The two Frenchmen who followed the keelboat cannot be identified. Thwaites says they were François Rivet and Phillipe Degie (Thw., *1*, 283 n.), and Quaife follows this interpretation (*Ordway*, p. 191 n.). This conclusion seems to be based on an entry of Clark's for Aug. 21, 1806, on the party's return. On the way downriver they met three Frenchmen who were on their way from the Arikara up to the Mandans. Clark wrote: "two of them Reeved & Greinyea wintered with us at the mandans in 1804" (Thw., 5, 349–50). This is not enough evidence to support the conclusion of the two editors. Because of Clark's erratic spelling, the whole thing becomes guesswork. Reeved may be Rivet, but who is Greenyea? One encounters such difficulties throughout Clark's journal. At the Mandans on the return of the party, Clark met one "Rokey who was one of our Engagees as high as the Mandans" (Thw., 5, 356). Who, of the list of *engagés*, is he? All that can be said is that four Frenchmen went downriver, Graveline and three others. That would leave five Frenchmen at the fort, of which we know that three (Clark says five) followed the party west for a short distance.

9. There were at least three Frenchmen who set out up the river apparently ahead of the party. On April 10, Lewis recorded that a party of three were overtaken. They intended to go up to the mouth of the Yellowstone to trap beaver, and to go along with the party for protection. However, when they got a few miles above the mouth of the Little Missouri, 30 miles from Fort Mandan, they decided to remain there (Thw., 1, 293). Lewis wrote that the party left them without any expectation of seeing them again. There is no further mention of them in the Notebook Journal. De Voto states that they were from either Tabeau's or Deschamps' party, but I can find no support for this statement (Bernard De Voto, *The Journals of Lewis and Clark,* Cambridge, 1953, p. 94 n.). Deschamps, who had been the *patron* of the French, joined the party at St. Louis and remained with it until it reached Fort Mandan. A Mandan set out with the party to show them the river, as he had been near its head. However, he turned back within two days.

1. Charbonneau took only one of his wives, Sacajawea, with him.

2. In all there were 33 in the party, excluding the Mandan who turned back. Twenty-six were Americans, including the two captains, York, three sergeants, and 20 enlisted men. The Frenchmen include the enlisted men, Cruzatte, Labiche, and Le Page; Drouillard, Charbonneau, Sacajawea, and her infant son completed the party. The dog, Scannon, who was included in Clark's July list made at the Platte, went along, too.

3. For a discussion of the dispatches and the journal Clark sent downriver in the keelboat, see the Introduction.

4. On April 7, 1805, the keelboat departed for St. Louis, and the party of exploration set out on its great adventure. More than a year before, in his winter quarters at the mouth of the Missouri, Clark had tried to answer the question, how long and how far? The answer lay ahead, for before them were 2,000 miles of river and trail to the Great Divide, and another thousand before they looked out on the fog-shrouded Pacific.

On the day the party left Fort Mandan, Lewis recorded in his journal his own feelings at that moment and what must have been, in one way or another, those of all the men under his command. "Our vessels consisted of six small canoes, and two large perogues. This little fleet altho' not quite so rispectable as those of Columbus or Capt. Cook, were still viewed by us with as much pleasure as those deservedly famed adventurers ever beheld theirs; and I dare say with quite as much anxiety for their safety and preservation. we were now about to penetrate a country at least two thousand miles in width, on which the foot of civilized man had never trodden; the good or evil it had in store for us was for experiment yet to determine, and these little vessells contained every article by which we were to expect to subsist or defend ourselves . . . enterta[in]ing as I do, the most confident hope of succeeding in a voyage which had formed a da[r]ling project of mine for the last ten years, I could but esteem this moment of my departure as among the most happy of my life. The party are in excellent health and sperits, zealously attached to the enterprise, and anxious to proceed; not a whisper or murmur of discontent to be heard among them, but all act in unison, and with the most perfect harmony. I took an early supper this evening and went to bed" (Thw., 1, 284–85).

The Distances of the following places as estimated from the mouth of the Missourie, with Lattitude anexed _____ 1806 [?][5]

To St Charles Situated to the North Side	21	miles in Lattitude	38°	54′	39″
" The mouth of Gasconade River S. S.	103.	ditto.	38°	44.	35.
" The mouth of Osarge River S. S.	137.	do . .	38.	31.	16
" The mouth of Grand River N. S.	252 . .	do . .	38.	47.	54
" The mouth of Kensas River. S. S.	364 . .	do . .	39.	5.	25.
" The mouth of Independence Creek S. S.	432 . .	do.	39.	25.	42
" The mouth of Nodawa River. N.S.	480 . .	do. . .	39.	39.	22
" The mouth of the Gd. Nemaha. R. S. S.	510 . .	do . .	39.	55.	55
" The Mouth of Bald pated prarie N.S.	509 . .	do. . .	40.	27.	7.
" The Mouth of River Platt S. Side.	630 . .	do . .	40.	54.	35.
" The Councel Bluff on the S. S.	680 . .	do . .	41.	17.	0.
" The mouth of the Little Seaus. R. N. S.	763 . .	do . .	41.	42.	34.
" The Camp opsd the Maha Village S. S.	866 . .	do . .	42.	13.	41.
" The mouth of Seaux River on the N. S.	882 . .	do . .	42.	23.	49.
" The mouth of River Jacque on the N. S.	974 . .	do . .	42.	53.	13.

5. This fragment, Document 66, has on its verso the small map referred to supra, p. 184 n. When compared with Clark's "Summary of Rivers and Creeks" (Thw., *6,* 56–59), this appears to be a condensation wherein only the more important places—mouths of the rivers, etc.—are listed. The list of distances continues in Document 67. On its verso is Clark's estimate of the military posts that should be established in the West. It is the first plan for the defense of the Indian Frontier and was elaborated by Calhoun when he was Secretary of War, 1817–25. See supra, p. 176.

	Miles	
To the mouth of the River Que courre S. Side (rapid) is	1020	in Latd
" The mouth of White River on the South Side	1148 do	
" The Island in the Grand de tortu or Big bend of the Missourie is	1200—do	
" The fort on the Island of Ceders is	1243 do	44° 11′ 33″
" The mouth of the Teton River on the So. Side	1280 do	_____
" The mouth of the Chien/ or Dog River. So. Side—	1327. do	44° 19′ 36″
" The mouth of the Sur-war-kar-na River So. Side	1407. do.	_____
" The mouth of the We-ter-hoó River So. Side	1432 do.	45. 39. 5
" The Ricara Villages. 3 on the S.S. _____	1440 do.	_____
" The River Boulet or Cannon Ball R.	1511 do—	46. 29. 00
" The River Chiss-che-tar & old Village. L.S.	1551. do	_____
" The 1ˢᵗ Village of the Mandens L.S.	1612 do.	_____
" Fort Mandan on the N. Side is	1609. do	47. 21. 47
" Knif River & Shoemans village S S—	1616—	
" The Mouth of Muddey Creek N S _____	1630.	

[*This table, dated 1805, must have been made at Fort Mandan. It is in Clark's hand.*]

1805— if Soldiers act as Boatmen & soldiers
The Number of Officers & Men for to protect the Indian trade and keep the Savages in peace with the U S. and each other

Names of elegable Situations of Establishments	Agents	Colonel	Majors	Captains	Loutents	Ensigns	Serjon Mates	Interpreters	Sergeants	Corporals	Musick	Privats	Total	Distance from each oth[er]
At St Louis ———	1	1	1	1	1	1	1	1	3	7	4	60	68	_____
at the Osarge, or Arkansaw	–	–	–	1	–	1	1	1	1	1	1	–45	48	_____
" the mouth of Kanzes—	–	–	–	–	1	–	1	1	1	2	1	–25	28	366
" the Counsel Bluff—	–	–	–	–	1	–	1	2	2	2	2	–30	36	316
" " Chien or Shar ha R—	–	–	–	1	1	1	1	3	4	4	4	–75	88	640
" " Rochejone river—	1	–	–	1		1	1	4	3	3	3	–45	54	500
" " Falls of Missourie—	–	–	–		1		1	2	1	1	1	–30	33	700
" " Head of Kanzes or Arkansas	–	–	–	1	1	1	1	2	4	4	4	–75	87	_____
on the Mississippi Prarie de Chien	1	–	–	1	1	1	1	2	4	4	4	–70	82	_____
St Peter or Falls of St Anthoney	–	–	–	–	1	–	1	1	2	2	2	–30	36	_____
do – do Sand Lake—	–	–	–	1	–	1	1	1	2	4	2	–40	48	
on the St Peters River	–	–	–	1	1	1	1	1	4	4	4	–75	82	
	3	1	1	8	9	8	12	22	32	32	32	600	700	

FACSIMILES
OF
DOCUMENTS

(continued overleaf)

#3.

Thursday 22nd Decr 1803

a verry great sleet this morning, the river covered with
running Ice, and falls verry fast 15 Inches last night
the boat aground in the Crick, I had pieces fixed along
to Support the boat and all the heavy articles taken out
in front & Center and Stored under a guard on the bank
a Mist of rain, which prevents our doing much to our
huts to day, at 3 oClock Drewyer & 8 Men, arrived from
Tennisee, those Men are not such I was told was in
readiness at Tennisee for this Corps, &c. recvd a Letter
from Cap Lewis also one from Mr Gratiot offering a horse
and his Services to Cap L & My self in any way

Friday 23td December 1803

a rainy Day, continue to put up My huts, the men
much fatigued Carrying logs, I send
to Mr Morrisons farm for a Team & Corn, which arived
about 3 oClock, a rainy Disagreeable day Mr
Griffith came down from his farm with a Load of
Turneps &c to me Drewyer came home to day
after a hunt, he killed three Deer, & left them
in the woods, the Ice run to day Several Delaways
a Cheif whome I saw at Greenville Treaty, I gave
him a bottle of Whiskey, the water falls fast the ba
luss by Shids, & set the Detachment totaly arived to build them a hut

Satturday 24th Decr Cloudy Morning, I purchase a Cargo of Turneps
for 3/ a bushel of Mr Griffeth, men Continue to put up & cover
the Necessary huts, Drewyer returned with 3 Deer & 5 Turkeys
I send Shields with Mr Griffeth to purchase me some butter
on the other Side of the river in the folks, finish Covering
our huts this evening — two French Perogues pass up the river
to day, and perogous with black guard Americans, passed down
the river, The Indian Come in with a Deer this evening
a French man whome passed up to day told me that a man of abt
30 years of age well acquainted with the Missouris for 8 years, wished
to go with me, but was afraid that the Comd. Should Know
of it his name is Lackduer Besinet

(continued overleaf)

Christmas 25th Decr.   I was wakened by a Christmas discharge &c found that
Some of the party had got Drunk & found, the Men frolicked and hunted
all day. Snow this morning, the rain all day Several Turkey killed
These returned with a Deer & 3 butter. three Indians Come to
day to take Christmas with us, I gave them a bottle of Whisky
and they Went off after informing me that a great talk had
been held and that all the nations were going to war against
the Ozous is 3 months, one informed me that a man 16 ms. from her
told them that the Americans had the Country and no one was
allowed to trade &c. I explain the thing to him, and the case
of the proposition, Drewyear Says he will go with us, at the rate of
and will go to Massac to settle his Matters

January 26th, Monday - a Cloudy day one of my party Killed 7 Turkeys
last night at roost - Continues working at the huts - The Ice
run. This day is moderate two Men Wiliard & Corpl. Roberts came
home to day at about 11 oClock, Corpl. White house & York Complt.
Sawing with the whip Saw - Nothing Material

December 27th, Tuesday — a fair Day I put out 8 Blankets, &c. &c to
dry and stored them in the Store room apparently in good order—
nearly finish My Chimney to day, Missed my observation - at abt.
3 oClock to day three frenchmen in a Pierogue Came down pursuing
a Swan which they had wounded some distance above, the Swan
swam as fast as they could row their Canoe and I thought
rather gained on the pieroge as they passed— they caught it below
below. I send home the Cart & oxen, Sent out Drewyer to hunt
to day early he returned late with a Buck, he Saw three Bear
on the other Side of the Prarie

28 Decr. a Cloudy day no Ice in the river, nothing
remarkable to day — Drewyer Kill a Deer & the Indn
Kill another

29th Snows this morning Cloudy & wd all day, finish
my hut and write 2 letters one to G. H. & one to Col Anderson
rain at night

30th Decr Snow in the morning I move into my hut, Cloudy
morning Colter Kill a Deer & a turkey, Drewyer & Lieut. Odway
set out for Koheskia, I arrange the guard on a new plan, wrote
to Capt. Lewis

31st

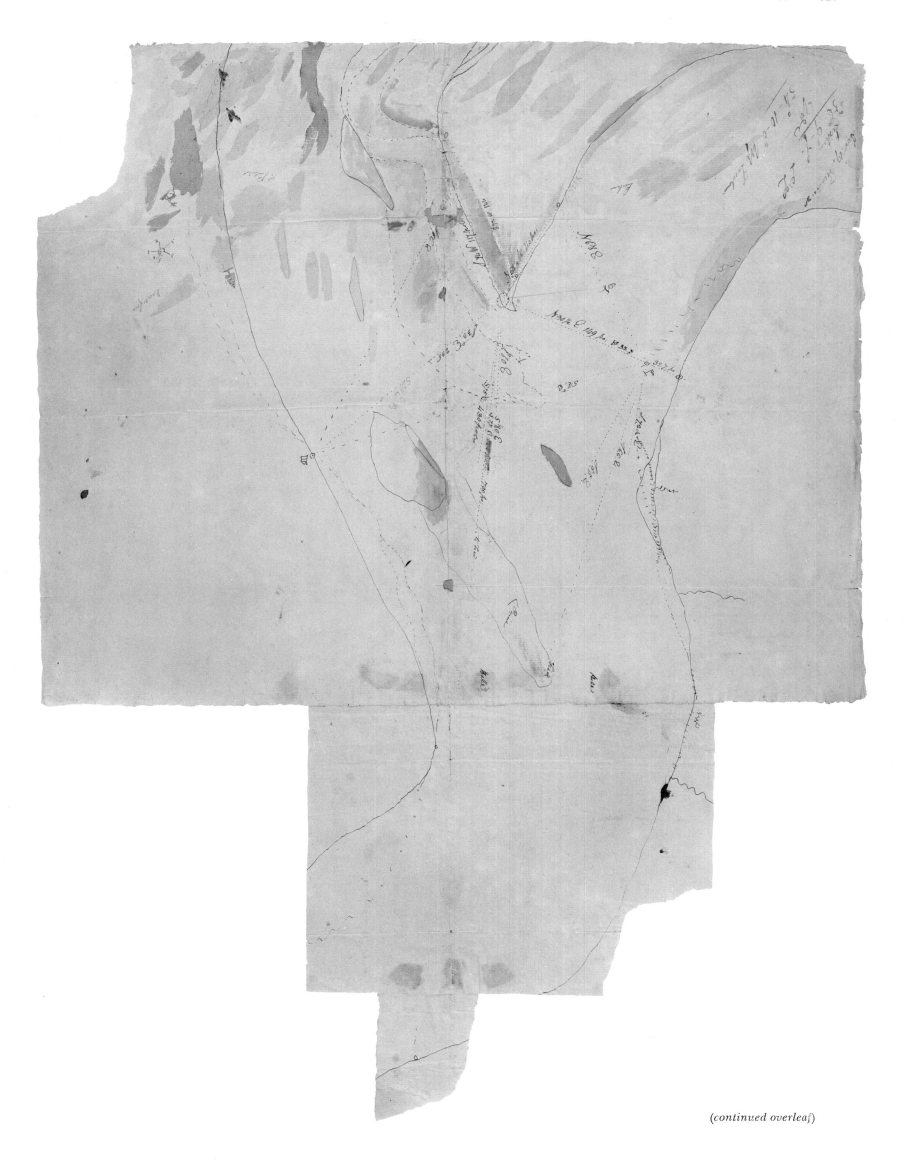

(*continued overleaf*)

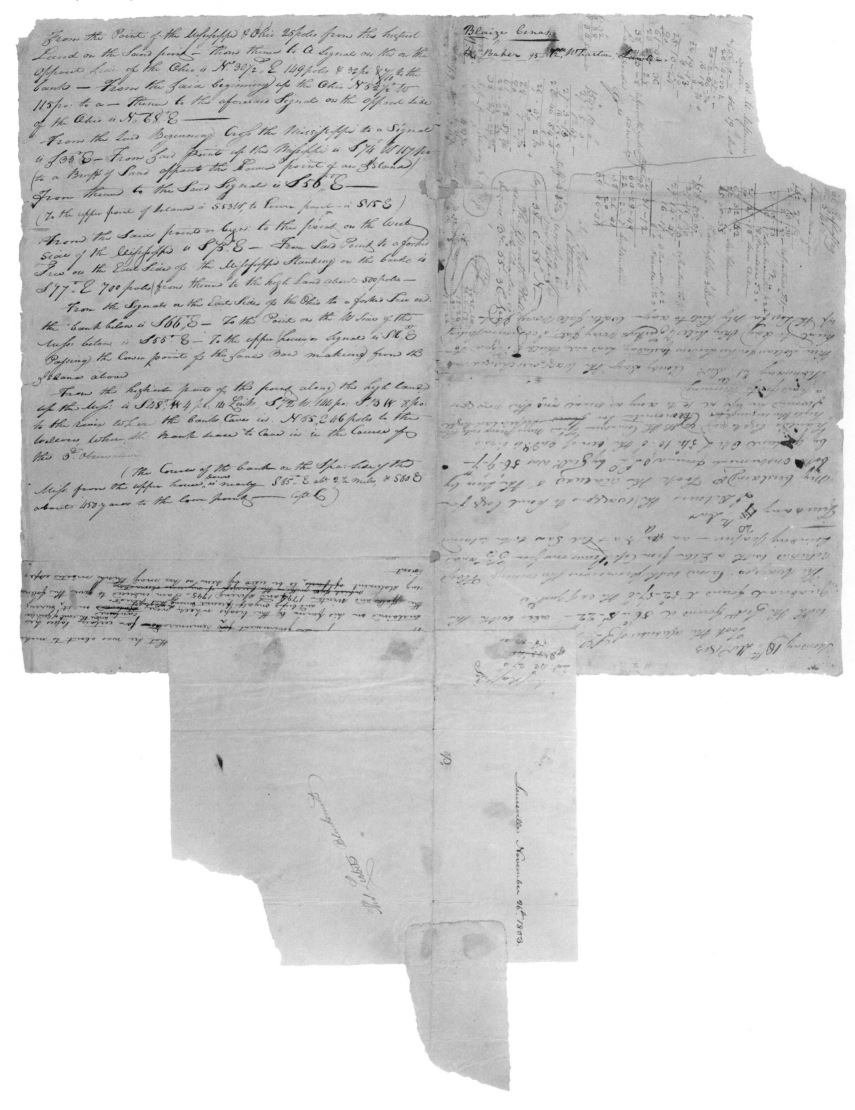

From the Point of the Mississippi & Ohio 25 poles from the highest
Land on the Sand point — Thence thence to a Signal on Hill on the
opposite side of the Ohio is N 30½ E 149 poles & 32 po & ⁴⁄₁₀ to the
banks — From the said beginning up the Ohio N 52½ W
115 po: to a — Thence to the aforesaid Signal on the opposite side
of the Ohio is N 68 E ———

From the said Beginning Cross the Mississippi to a Signal
is S 33 E — From said point of the Mississippi is S 74 W 147 po:
to a Bluff of Sand opposite the lower point of an Island)
From thence to the said Signal is S 56 E ———
(To the upper point of Island is S 53 W to Lower point is S 15 E)

From the Said point or bluff to the point on the West
side of the Mississippi is S 8 E — From said point to a forked
Tree on the East Side of the Mississippi Standing on the bank is
S 77 E 700 poles from thence to the high Land about 500 poles —

From the Signal on the East Side of the Ohio to a forked Tree on
the bank below is S 66 E — To the Point on the W Side of the
Miss below is S 55 E — To the upper house or Signal is S 56 E
Passing the lower point of the Sand Bar making from 13
Islands above

From the highest point of the point along the high land
up the Miss: is S 48 W 4 po: 14 Links S 70 W 144 po: S 3 W 8 po:
to the river where the banks Caves in N 85 246 poles to the
bellow where the Bank have to Cave in is in the Course of
the 3d Observation

(The Course of the bank on the Spa side of the
Miss from the upper house down is nearly S 55 E abt 2½ miles, & S 60 E
about 1450 yards to the lower point ——— opte C)

Blaize Cenas

Dr Baker 95 Mr Mc Wharton ...

(continued overleaf)

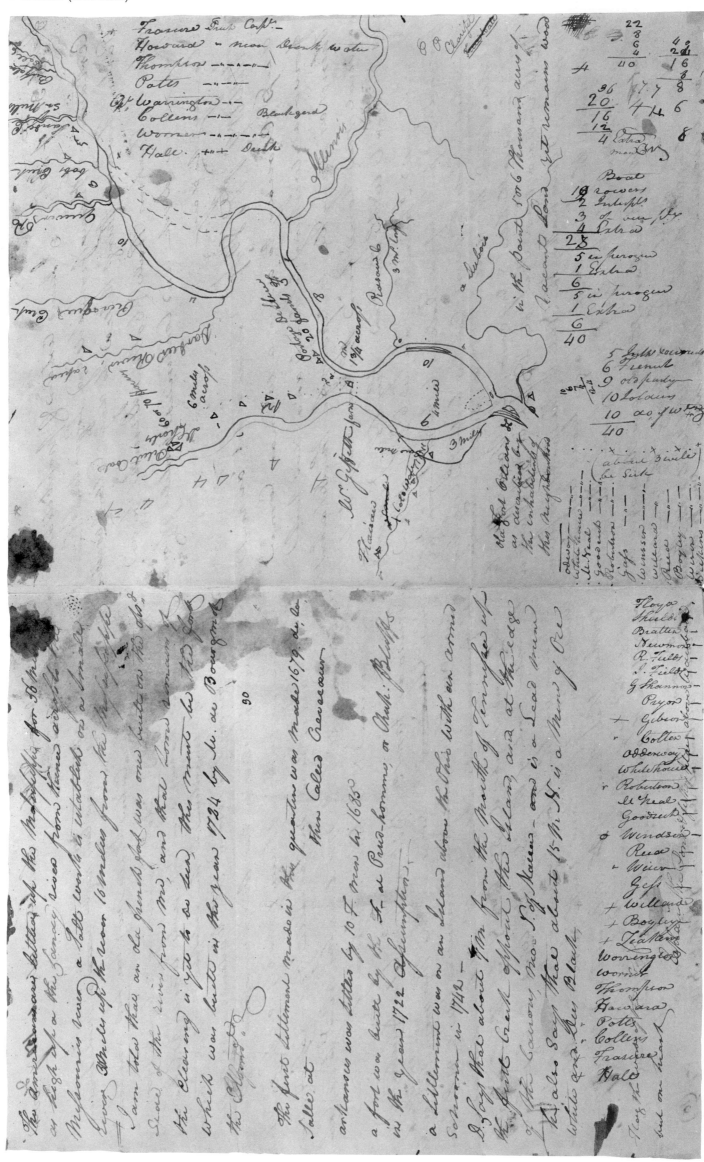

Say (10) 3ᵈ Janᵧ 1804

Excessive Cold after Sunset

Wed: Janᵧ 4ᵗʰ a Cold Clear morning, the river Covered with Ice from the Missourie, the Mississippi above froze across, the Wind from the West, the Thermometer this morning at 19° below freezing, Continue Cold & Clear all day, I took the altᵈ of S. L. L. and found it to be 57°. 27′. 15″. N″. purchase 12ᵗʰ Tallow for 6/ of Whiteside, who Sold the Beef to the Com: at 3 ₰ ℔. H″ Several Country people here to day — at 4 oClock the Murcurie of the Thmtʳ in a corner of a warm room was 20 D. above (0) —

Worner & Potts fight after Dark without my Knowledge & the Corp. head of the mess left the Post & Suffered them to bruse themselves much, he has no authority, the other Part of the detachment Voary Merry at Night

$$\begin{aligned}
2) \overline{57. 27 - 15} & \quad \text{the } 4^{th} \text{ Janᵧ 1804} \\
28 - 43 - 37 - 7/_{10} & \quad \text{refraction } 1\text{—}1 \\
\underline{1 - 44} & \\
28 . 41 - 53 \; 5/_{10} & \\
16 - 19 \; 3/_{10} & \quad + \text{ Sem: Diam } (3) \\
\underline{8 \; -- \; +} & \\
28 . 58 - 20 - 8/_{10} & \quad \text{Ɛ Em: w} \\
\underline{8 - 49} & \\
28 - 49 - 31 . 3/_{10} & \\
\underline{90 - .. - .. -} & + \\
61 - 10 - 28 - 2/_{10} & \quad \text{☉ Dulena:} \\
\underline{22 - 49 - 22} & \\
\text{Dᵍ } 38 - 21 - 6 \; 2/_{10} & \\
\end{aligned}$$

Thursday 5ᵗʰ Janᵧ the Creek rose Considerably last Night the river full of Ice, and the Wind which blows from the West blow it to this Shore, a moderate day, I suffer some men to apist Higgins to raise his hut, two men whome I sent to him grown returned with a part of a hog which they found hung up in the woods & brought it in a Bear meat, I took the altitude of ☉ W. L. with the Quadrant and made it 55° - 40′ - 30″ N. Ervr of Instrem. 1° - 13′ - 0″ + Quadᵗ

(continued overleaf)

Quad.   5th Jany 1804   55.54

2/55 - 40 - 30"   ⊙ L L   allow the ⊙ L L was obd
27 - 50 - 15 altitude of ⊙ up Limb   by quadrant 5th Jany
        1 - 48 - refraction (T.1)   27 - 50 - 15 altitude ⊙
      48 - 27   1 - 48 - refraction
      16 - 19 - ⊙ demeter (p3)   27 - 48 - 27
      32 - 8   16 - 19 + Diamet.
         8 + Parallax (T.3)   8 + Parallax
* 27 - 32 16 The Suns Center.   1 - 13 - ⊙ + Error End.
                                    29 - 19 - 54
62 - 27 - 44   90
22 - 43 - 31   Declination   60 - 43 - 56
39 - 43 + 13   22 - 43 - 31 - Diamet
    1 - 13 + 13 + Ex   * 27. 32. 16 + E.E.   29 - 19 - 34
39 - 44 - 26   1 17 - 0   29 - 32 - 16
39 - 30 - 13   28 - 49 - 16   60 - 27 - 44
                       90   22 - 43 - 31 -
The Lat with Qd =   61 - 10 - 44 Declination 37 - 34 - 13
                     22 - 43 - 31   on the 5 Jany 1804
                     38 - 27 - 13 on the 5 Jany 1804

I viewed the boat frequently this day under apprehension
of the Creek which is now rising washing the earth from
the foot of the piers which is fixed under

Jany 6th I was up late night at 12 to light the Boat
the banks were caveing in, which made it necessary
to fix the piers frequently, this morning early I fixed
the piers, and large Pew of the bank slipped in, which
obliged all hands to, go down & make all secure
I ordered those men who had fought god Drunk
& neglected Duty to go and build a hut for a Wo=
who promised to wash & Sew &c. I spoke to the men
on the subject of my order,   ⊙ L L with quad. to day was
is 1½' ad +   2/55 - 54 0"   Error of
a hog was found in the Praw   2 - 57 - 0   1 - 47
by some men as they observed   1 - 47 -   27 - 55 - 15
I send out Shields to enquire   55 - 13   16 - 19 +
in the neighbourhood whose hog   16 - 19   2 - 0 -
it was & inform me. Thermometer   39 - 54 +   30 - 10 - 40
at 12 oClock 31 above 0. at 4 oCk at 30° above 0. 37 - 44   Say (11)

day (11) The [trouble] about the Boat continues to [cave] in, which causes great attention in me to prevent the Boats getting injured by any one part [falling] more than another — the [Law]suit come on to day better than usual, Whitehouse & Reed agree better than they did last week, or in other words do fare better from [Probation].

[5th & 6th Jany] — Some rain last night, a thaw and some [snow] to day. The boat give me much trouble, & the banks are continualy sliping in on each [head] which tore the [fire], up last night and frequent this thro to day attending the boat. I drew a Map for the purpose of Correcting from the information which I may get of the Country to the N.W.

Sunday 8th Jany — Rained moderately all last night, a butifull Morning a few large sheets of Ice running this morning, Send out [Colter] & George to the head of the [Dubois] R. to hunt — The Wind rose from the S.W. at 10 Oclock, Took the Meredean altitude of o LL with [——] made it 59° — 22 — 52" N — a French man & his family came to see me to day I trade with them for Onions, & gave [——]. This man made Complaint that he had lost a Hogg — Some Hog meat had been brought in as before mentioned, as the men whome brought it in are absent, I postpone this inquirey untill tomorrow. I Lay down to sleep, to make up for the want of rest. Cloudd up at ½ past 2 Oclock. the wind chifted to the N.W. moderate. R Fields killed a Deer to day, this is the first of his turning out —

Mon. 9th Jany — Some snow last night, a hard wind this morning from W.N.W. river rises with large sheets of Ice out of Missisippi. the Morning is fair, the man Ramey gives me much trouble, I took Colter & went to the place he found a Hog [Skined] & Pung up, the Crow had [devoured] the meat, Killed Prarie fowl and Went across a Prary to a 2nd Bank where I [discovred] an Indian Fortification, near the [——] bank I attempted to cross a Bond of about 400 yds wide on the Ice, I Beleve in this fortress is 9 Mound forming a Circle two of these is about 7 foot above the leavel of the plain on the edge of the first bank and 2 m from the Woods & about the same distance from the near high land, about this place I found great quantities of Earthen ware & flints — about ¼ m N. E. a grave on an [eminence] I returned before Sun Set, and found that my feet which were wet had froze to my [shoes], which rendred [——] Necessary to prevent a [frost bite], the wind from N.W. across the [Sand] Islands in the Mouth of the Missouri raised such a dust that I would not be in that derection, the Ice continue to [——] & river rise slowly — [——] [——] Cold day

Tuesday 10th a fine day, the river rose 6 Inches last night, the Crak also [——] & Boats many afloat, I am very unwell all day, [owing] I beleve to the [Duckling] & [——] Cold which I underwent yesterday — at 10 Oclock Joseph Fields returned & Crosed the River between the Sheets of floating Ice with some [danger], his excuse for Staying so long was that [——]

(continued overleaf)

Mississippi river, that the Lee run to which is the Missouri where he was
30 miles up that there was no crossing; he says that the people is greatly
in favour of the Americans, Cap. Leakey has just returned from surveying & some lands up the Missouri, which has been lately granted
he says "a beautifull country presents its self" on the coast he went
& returned three miles, to the first settlement from this place
is a West direction. I feel unwell to day

Wednesday 11th Jany, I was unwell last night slept but little a fine
morning, the river still rising, the Missouri runs with fine Lee the
Boat is afloat, one man McNeil came out last night, he separated
from the hunting party about 7 miles from this place, he return
this evening & so the was at 10 oClock the wind blew strong from the
West, and turned cooler & cloudy this afternoon I am a good bit
indisposed

Thursday 12th Jany, 1804. My Chimney got a fire last night a fair morning, the
wind from the West, the river continue to rise moderately, I took Meridianal
altitude of Suns Lower Limb with Sextant and made it 57°-31-52. N M
error of instrument as usual, river continues to rise with large bodies of
ice running against the ice attached to the bank with great force, the Boat
is afloat and is perfect order

Friday 13th January, Sent N. Pryor with letters &c. to Capt. Lewis a Kahokia
the river rise, a fall of snow last night the Missouri is rising and
run with Ice & cloudy & warm day, I am better &c. a fine rain in
the evening

Saturday 14th January, a snow fell last night to about an inch deep
the river still rising and running with Ice, a fair sun shining
morning — the party caught caught 14 Rabets to day & 7 yesterday, a cold
afternoon. the Mississippi is closed with Ice.

Sunday 15th Jany. river falling & runs still with Ice, I took the M.
altitude of ☉ L. L. & made it 60-33-50 N, at Sun set Mss Ramsey
arrived with some provisions in a waggon of Mr. Todd two or eight men follow
the waggon Intoxicated from the Whiskey they drew of &c on the way out
of the barrel which was for the party, I ordered a Jill to each man
a cold night the Waggon passing the Prairie which was Cover'd with Ice left many to drive the
waggon which caused to be left for
Monday 16th Jany. this morning Mss. R observed that he brought
2 trunks of goods and asked permission to sell them to the settlers for
provisions and the Mira Coon skins, I assented to the plan and
agreed he might untill other arrangements after the arrival of Capt.
Lewis — I settled with the Contractor for what has been furnished to this day and
find him Due the Party 30 Jills of Whiskey which he payed — and 750 rat. of hog
Candles & vinegar, for which he gave his due bills, the party made up a
Shooting match with the Country people for a W. Leager, Ruben
made the best shot, next one Wint & the 3d was Shields R. F. Co
Gibson &c. Mr. Pryor returned at 8 oClock this evening with a
from Capt. Lewis (Sure Colter 3 & Geo. 3) and one from
News papers which Capt. Lewis had for me also a file of 3 plays
Tuesday 17th Jany a very cold morning at 9 oClock the Thermometer
air Ale 6 below, the wind from the N.W. a Stiff Breeze Ice
of Missouri at 9 oClock the Thermometer 6 below 0 at 10 oClock 3 below
at 12 oClock at 0. at 1 oClock 1 above 0, at 2 oClock 4 above 0, 3 oClock at 0.

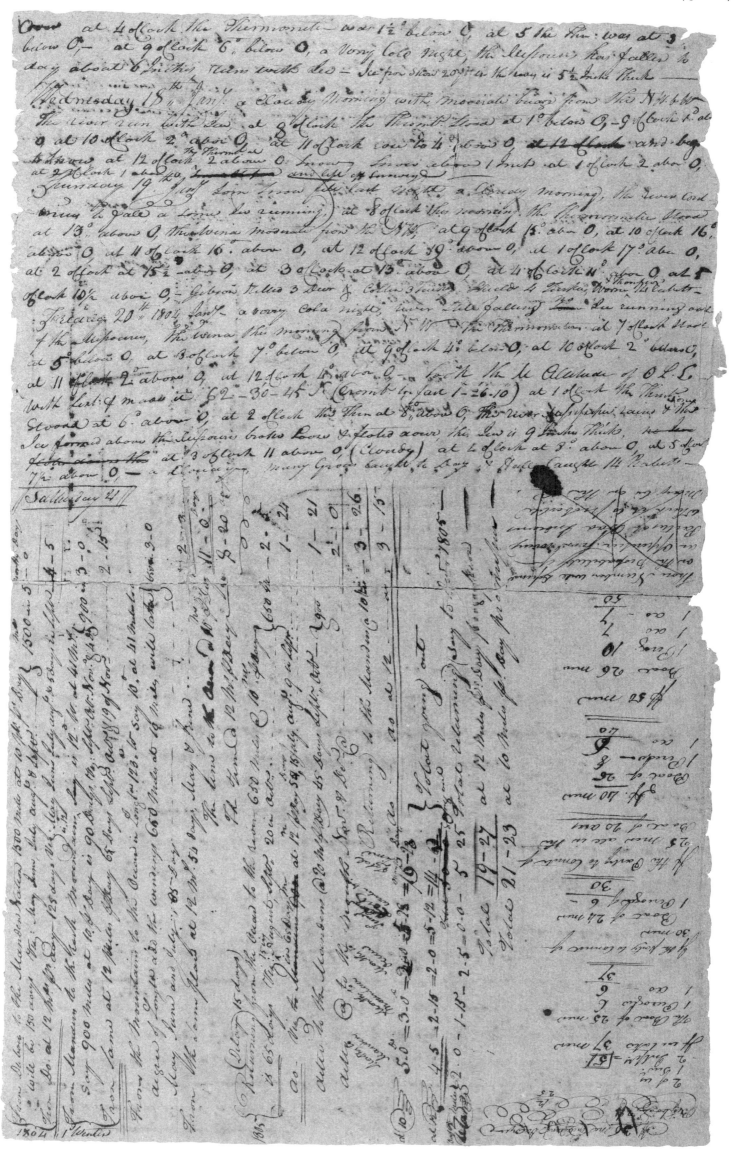

(continued overleaf)

as example or necessary

(Supposing) the Party to consist of 4 Non Com. Officers and 21 Men and the rules to be observed is Strictly Such as Cap L & C shall from time Establish, and a Violation or Disobedience shall be Subject to Such punishment as Directed by the articles of War, in like Case and Such Other punishments, as shall be inflicted by the Sentence of a Court Martial which are to be formed in the following Manner, Viz, one Inspector of Sec. to act as president and at least 1 N Com. Officers & 5 private Members the Court to Consist of not less than 7 Members, in Capital Offences and at Other times when Convenient one of the Cap[t]. will preside at the Court in that Case the Court will have an addition to their Number of a prsd. who will have 2 Votes but in all Cases, Col L & C the doe reserve to themselves the right reducing N Com Officer at will of inflicting such punishments as they may think right agreable to Law at any time which from the nature of the Offence & the good of the Service require it.) This Court will act agreable to the rules and regulations of the Articles of War and Such Others as may be established by the Said Col L & C from time to time.

Satturday 21st 1804 the Snow this morning is about 2½
Inches Deep, & Snowing fast, the Thermometer Stood at 7° above 0,
at 8 oclock, & Wind from the N E, the river running with Ice
and falling a little, at 9 oclock the Therm at 7° abov 0, – at 10 oclk
the Therm 7° abov 0, at 11 oclock 10° abov 0, & Snows – at 12 oclock 10° abov
0, or fair haile, the merias at 1 oclock 10° abov 0, at 5 oclock 17° abov 0, &
hailing & snow hail,

Sunday 22nd Jany 1804 Snow all the night last night, and Snows
this morning, the debth is 5½ Inches, the Thermometer Stands
at 9 oclock this morning in the Open Air at 11° abov 0, – at 12 oclock
rose to 14° abov 0 and Stoped Snowing wind Easterly at 3 oclock
13° abov 0, river nearly Clear of Ice

Monday 23rd Jany 1804 a Cloudy morning but little Ice runng
to day the Therm at 12 oclock Stood at 18° abov 0, (I Sun an Ordr
to Corpl) at 3 oclock 17° abov 0, in the evening the winds veered
and shifted to the North course Hunters & Killed a Deer.

Tuesday 24th a Beautyfull morning Clear Sunshine the wind lys from
the NW. the Thermometer at 9 oclock Stood at 4° abov 0 (Stake frozen)
at 10 oclock 8° abov 0, wind West, at 12 oclock 14° abov 0
at 3 oclock 11° abov 0, Snow Small peu of Ice running Deer to day

a Very Clear moon Shiny night
Wednesday 25th Jany a fair morning last night was a Very Cold one (I
warketh all night, the trees and the Small Groth ar Gilded with
Ice from the frost of last night Which affords one of the most
Magnificent appearances in nature the river began to Smoke
at 8 oclock and the Thermometer Stood at 2° belov 0 at 9 oclock
at 0, at 10 oclock at 5° abov 0, at 11 oclock 10° abov 0, at 12 oclock
16° abov 0, at 1 oclock 15° abov 0, at 2 oclock 19° abov 0 at 3 oclock 16
abov 0, wind from WNW Ice 2 Deer killed to day

Thursday 26th Jany 1804 a Cloudy warm Day I am very unwell all
day Gibson Killed two Deer, R field one, the men Kill Raccoon hir Rabits
&c in great quantity, very little Ice running to day the river Stood
yesterday work to day the men
make a Slea to haul wood
one man Stays out to night Warner I
derict a Sley to be built to haul
things from the Country & Jany 26th

To Stow away in the Boat
Kegs   In   I Th
45 for pork   18 long   10 Thick
56 fa flour   24   15
½ Corn   Whisky 15   12

Freeport 27th Jany: 1804. a Cloudey Morning Some Snow, this Morning
Mr Kitt unwell, to day at 1 oClock 28 abov 0, (I send off
Howard express to day to Cap. Lewis at Koho: with a Letter I am
Sore better, Winsor who was out Last night returned he killed
a Deer & Turkey — Gibson killed a Deer to day, Collons one near Camp

Saty. 28th. Jany: 1804 a Cloudey morning, verry Cold Wind from the N 88
Some floating Ice in the River at 9 oClock 5° abov 0 Snow at 10 oClock
8° abov 0, at 11 oClock 10° abov 0, the Sun Shone, 3 french Men from
Pavia below called at 12 oClock 12° abov 0, at 1 oClock 14°. abov 0,
Mr. Bagley Came with Potatos fowls &c — Mr. Cummin Came
with Meal & Brandy from Contractor at 2 oClock 18°. abov 0,
Mr. Anty Coxe called to day to inquire after his horses, at 3 oClock
20°. abov 0, 4 oClock 18°. abov 0, Some winsin Came to day at
6 oClock 14°. abov 0, Porter all froze & several bottles
broke, I delivered out 12 flents & Some Powder to hunters.

Sunday 29th. Jany a beutifule morning the river rise a little no Ice
the Thermometer at 8 oClock stood at 16°. abov 0, at 11 oClock 22
abov 0, at 12 oClock 24°. abov 0, Took an altitude of Suns
Lower Limb 66° 58' 30" D 2 S — at 3 oClock 24° abov 0,
at 4 oClock 26°. abov 0, at 5 oClock 23°. abov 0, Shields killed
a Deer to day, Express returned from Koho: brought a Letter from Capt. Lewis, & 4 other
from Shunly. 3 bottles of wine Some Durant & files

Monday 30th Jany 1804 a Cloudey morning, Some Snow send
out 10 hunters to day in three parties, at 9 oClock The Thermot.
stood at 22° abov 0, a little wind from N. at 10 oClock 24°. abov
0, stoped Snowing, but little Ice running this morng —
at 11 oClock 25°. abov 0, at 12 oClock 25°. abov 0, Took M. alt.
of Sun D 2 67° 22' 52" — Error Instrument 6 —, at 1 oClock 25
abov 0, at 2 oClock 26° abov 0 Reed killed a Deer & wild
Cat, Cloudey 3 men Cross the river to day, at 3 oClock
28°. abov 0, at 4 oClock 27° abov 0, at 5 oClock 16° abv
0 about sun set Capt. Lewis arrived accompanied by
Mr. J. Hay & Mr. Jo Hays of Kohokia — The hunters killed 5 Deer
to day

Tuesday 31st Jany. a fair morning the river Guarded with Ice
at 7 oClock the Thermometer stood at 7 oClock 10°. below 0,

9

Widnesday 8th Feby 1804 a Cloudy morning Some rain, and snow a Great raft of ice came Down the Creek to day, the river rising & running ice, a man arrive from Mr Hay at Koho, with Letters & an Invitation to 2 balls at St Louis

Thursday 9th a fine morning river still rise & ice pass down the greater part out of the Missouri

Wednesday 2th March 1804
    I returned to Camp at wood river down the Missouri from St Charles in a Boat from the Platte river, Cap Lewis & my self W Choteau & Gratiot & went to Stop 150 Kickpoo from going to war against the Osages & send W drouin in

Thursday 22d. set the workmen to work about the Boat, sent a man to examine if the Indians had recrossed home. butifull weather river rise   Missouri

Friday 23rd. the man returned, with a Letter from Mr. Soues the Comd. of Passage Desous, informing me that the Kickapoos was gorn home, good weather the river continue to rise — 10 Inches to day & 3 last night.

Saty. 24 Isent Newman with Letters to Koho. & to Cap Lewis at St Louis, fair weather river rise fast

Sunday 25th a fair morning river rose 14 Inch last night, the men find numbers of Bee Trees, & take great quantities of honey, at 11 oClock 24 Saukees Came pass from St Louis, and asked for Provisions I ordered them 75 lb. Beef, 25 lb flour. & 50 lb Meal — Gutereg returned with Log & Joe, Willard brought in 10 p. Hinges George Shannon Cought 3 large Cat fish — the Musquetors are verry bad this evening. Newman return with Letters & Papers. from St Louis.   (ancore)

(continued overleaf)

207

Jow[.], 0, Jany 31st at 9 oclock soon Jae running this morning, my head akes much, I went up the river with Cap[t] Lewis & Gratlion at 12 oclock 24° abv o at 2 oclock 28° abv o, at 4 oclock 28° abv o, Mr Whiteside & Chittete crossed from the opposit side of the Mississippi — at 9 oclock P.M. 15° abov o wind S.W. by W. look salts

Wiansday 1st Feby 1804 a Cloudy morning & worm wend from the S.W, I rode out 6 miles, an very sick, wind rose very high at 1 oclock, a worm Day, all the good put out & and I an very unwell

Thursday 2nd Feby Mrs Hays & Hay set out for Kohokia, Cap Lewes & my self accompanyed them one mile, I then went to Mr ___ & Kans and returned to Dinner, very sick, wind high from S.W.

Friday 3rd Ian very unwell all day, taked medicine without fair thawing Day
Saturday 4 discharge Jeakins for thift with a small Correction a worm Day, some rain last night, in the Evening the River Covered with large sheets of Ice from both river, the River & Creek rised sufficent to take the boat up the Creek some antena moderate day Ian very sick — wild foul pass

Monday 5th Feby still sick, the french man Wife &c Came to see us to day Mrs Cane albt Hanley sent us som Butter & milk, river rising & Covered with small Ice & send out Shields to get Walnut Bark for pills, foul pass

Monday 6th Feby a fair day snow nearly gone, som Ice still runing sick taked Walnut pills, winter killed a Badger. My R___ work &c great number of wild foul flying Northerly, Swans in great numbers, river began to fall Thompson return from Kohokia

Tuesday 7th some rain last night, Rain this morning, fell & inches, serg[t] Odway returned from Kohokia rain turns a little, the Creek or River a Dubois rains fast, swept off a Canoo belonging to a Maurice Indian from out of its mouth. if the present fresh continues a fiew days the water passing down this small river wile Wash off all that imence quantity of mud which has filled up its mouth for 300 yards by the Missouri &c o rivers ancore

Monday the 26th of March 1804 — a Norry Smoky day I had Corn parched to make parched Meal, Workmen all at work preparing the Meal, I went the Indian Camps, In one Camp found 3 squaws & 3 young ones, another 1 girl & a boy in a 3rd Simon Getty & two other familys Getty has the Rhumatism — very bad these Indians visit me in their turns, & as usual ask for something I give their flour & several just come to say the Missisippi R. continue to rise & discharge great quantity of Ice &c

Tuesday 27th — Rain last night very hard with thunder, a Cloudy morning our man Sick to day all hands parching Corn &c — Some Delawarys pass down to StLouis (Simon Getty) river continue to rise, two Mortes parched Corn "I am untell"

Wednesday 28th — a Cloudy morning, all hands at work prepareing for the voyage up the Missourie. Capt Lewis arriv'd at 4 oClock from StLouis

Thursday 29th — Rained last night a violent wind from NW this morning with rain Some hail we have a trial of John Shields, John Colter & R. Frasure which take up the greater part of the day in the evening We walk to Huggens a blustering day all day the blacksmith return with part of their work finished, river continue to rise, Cloudy day

Friday 30th of March 1804 a fair day I wrote engagements & Capt Lewis writes Darus a very good hand ont R. Fields to kill a squirel to make him Supper &c the order on Parade this evening &c &c ackia the Injuans &c & promised to do better in future, the other Pruseros were dismissed &

Saturday 31st of March a fine morning sent over two men to the Island to see about a horse which was seen in distress & there Maj. Rumsey arrived

Sunday a fair Morning Mr Cattaty Boat arrived with provision, I we sent down a Canoe for the Doct. who intended to come by land, The French issue & his wife came on a visit to day — a Draft for Squad, & Mr Cattaty Boat arrived with provision, Capt Lewis went to StLouis with Dr Cattatt on business, a Nothing little done at about 10 oclock, apparantly Changing Clear, appears no Sujurn — in the evening Major

Monday 2nd of April Mr Hays & Amsol arrive from Kiho, by land Garro Boat come up on his way to Prarie du chaine loaded with provision & for Sale at that place, a cleaning to day three men Sick all mess arranged, O men make me Parched Meal, those Gentlemen stayd with me all night, Send down Cattatt to StLouis —

Tuesday 3rd I wrote a letter to Mr. John Campbell, of Prarie du chaine by Mr Hay & the Gentlemen bound to that place, those Gentlemen set out at Sun rise, I have Meal made & the flour Packed & repacked, also Some parked in bariels a Windey Day Capt Lewis return with Dr Cattatt wind blew very hard all night, Some rain

Wednesday 4th all day Packing Provision Settled account with the Contractor for all the Issuet made &c, of the Month & what Provision he has furnishd hard wind and rain last night Mr Crawford lend his Canoe by to a thael to the Saline to Survey indians

Thursday 5th wrote the Speeches to the Ayou & Faiada Thunder & lightning last night & Loways, Several Country people came to day to pay a visit, men & wimin, the wind Westerly hard from the NW&W all day river still rise, Send by Mr Crawford Some querey relitive to the Indians, and Vocabulary also some instructions &c the Contractors Boat return to StLouis the Shift to the North at Sunset & Cold, Boats falls all fill'd

Friday 6th a Cloudy Day river fall 10 Inches, the Pork Canoe let out for Mackenach, given out knives Tomahawks &c &c to the men &c for your Zeile Sick, Several Country people came to camp to day at one Oclock the wind blew hard from the NW, in this Country the wind &c points for rain from SS to NE, the fair Weather Winds fly & West Clear and Cold from the NW & North, wind seldom blows from the South — at about 9 oClock P.M began to Snow and Continued a short time, wind blew hard from the NWest I return to StG & &c give orders &c &c

Saturday 7th set out at 7 oClock in a Canoe with Capt Lewis my Servant York & one man at ¼ past 10 arrivd at StLouis Dispd & Send with Capt Stoddard & about 50 gentlemen a Ball which lasted, which lasted untile 9 oClock on Sunday, no business to day

Monday 9th & Tuesday 10th, Wednesday 11th, attending to Sundry things &c Thursday 12th set out from StLouis all hands a got to their Quarters by Friday 13th arrivd at Camp at 10 oClock &c as usual &c

(continued overleaf)

209

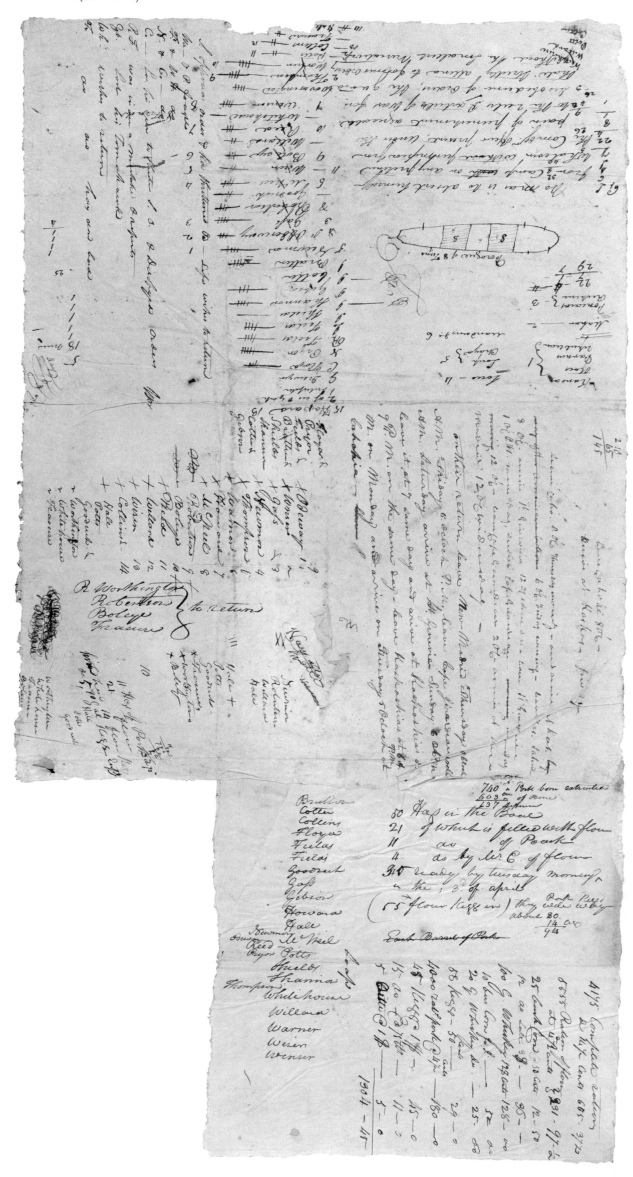

Journal

The 13th of April 1804 at 10 oclock I arrived in Majr. Rumsey's boat from Louis, with Sundry articles for our voyage, a Cloudy day I hoist a Flag Staff, After part of the day fair, river falling I give out to the men Lead Powder, & an extra gill of Whiskey —

5 $ of Cap Lew at St Louis

Saturday 14th 1804 a fair Day wind high from the I sent Reed to St Louis with a letter & some Scarlet &c Locks to be Mended.

Lent Majr. Rumsey 12 $ — paid Reed 10 $ took out of bag 8 $ in all 30 $ out of bag to day — a Gentleman from Winchester by the name of McLain came to Camp bound or land hunting, I had finished off ana packed up to day in part of my Stores of Provisions —

13 Bags of parched Meal of 2 bus: each
9 do. Common Meal of do — do
11 do & 3 barrels of N. Corn Huled do
3 do. & 30 ½ do. of Flour — do
7 Barrels of Salt of 2¼ bus bls: each — do

Received of Majr Rumsey
14 flour Kegs
19 Pork Kegs } 14 aprl.
537 Salt

Sunday 15th of April a fair Morning Sent out Shields with Mr. McLaine to the heads of Wood River. Settled with Mr Cane for all to this day & paid 12/c — Clouded up at 12 oclock the wind from the SW blew very hard a Boat pass up the Mississippi under Sail at 5 oclock — Several men out to day Hunting & Visiting. Mr Wolperts Boat came up to day at 2 oclock under Sail. Left St Louis at 8 oclock A.M. Some Shooting at a mark

31 Candles

MONDAY 16th a fair Morning Some rain last night & head wind from the S.W. by W. Packed away

1 Bag Candle wick
2 Boxes of Candles
in one part Soap

4 Kegs of Pork packed
6 Half barrels of pork do

1 Keg of Hogs Lard
1 bag of Coffee 50
2 do Sugar —
1 do Beens —
7 bags of Biscuit
4 Barrels of Biscuit

Several men Confined for Drunkness to day, wind verry hard.

Tuesday 17th Reed came from St Louis at 45 M after 10 oclock with Letters for me from Cr. Ambros — I sent out 4 men to hunt a horse to Send to Cap Lewis, out all day without finding him making a Mast fixing orning & packing Pork to day the after part of this day Cool

```
22.03
33 – .90
34 – .90
35 – .90
36 – .98
37 – .98
38 – .68
39 – .68
40 – .68
41 – .68
42 – .68
43 – .68
44 – .68
45 – .60
46 – .90
47 – 1.00
48 – 1.00
49 – 1.00
50 – 1.00
```

Completed packing
fifty Kegs of Pork, &
rolea & filled them

with brine, also packed one Bar: Meal, & one b⟨u⟩ Parched
of an inferior quallity.   (out of the bag 10 ℔

Wednesday 18th April 1804. a fair morning) Newman killed
a Black Bear. Vegetation appears to be supprising ly
rapid for a few days past, R.F. Killed a Musk rat.
Several of the inhabitents came to Camp to day. Maj.
Rumsey boat fall down one mile to river Dbow to Carry
to the Salt works. I Send Serjt. Floyd & G. Shannon with
two horses to Capt. Lewis at St. Louis, at Bo[...]k Capt.
Lewis arrive. the wind from the S.E. rained the greater
part of this night.,

Thursday 19th a rainy morning) Slept late, Thunder and
lightning at 6. oClocks, Men Shoot at a mark, rain al 2
Sellea with Maj. Rumsey   &c   rain continues

Friday 20th, rain last night & this morning) the river fall
Sloly I have my tools, Dunk &c fixed rain all day, afoot
Doshes & Dark Sultry weather (look out of the bag 32 ℔ &
some Thunder

Satturday 21 th rain all last night Sloaly a Cloudy
(Morning) Some rain river raised last night 12 Inchs, at
three oClock a Canirow Was herd up the Missouri, Loos with
M. Choteau arriver with 22 Indeans, & we Saluted them
and after Staying one hour, Capt Lewis & my Self Set out
with them to St Louis when arived before 3 Night.

Sundy, Mon: & Tuesday, at St Louis

Wednesday 25 at a past 12 Set out for Camp and arived
at night in a Pirogue

Thursday 26. Mr. Hay arived river falls,

Friday 27. preparing to pack up Indean goods
Satturday 28 Mr. Hay packing up all hands
at work preparing Several Country men Come
to bor my mens Money, in dowp So lost all
they had, with them. river fall
                                        Say on

Say on)

Sunday 29th of April 1804, M. Hay still packing
up goods, som Kickapoo Chiefs come down, Wolperts
Boat arrive from S Charles.   river still fall

Monday 30th, a fair day all hands at work
Mr. Hay nearly finish packing up goods (Kunst)
Mr. M'Clair arrive.   river still fall

Tuesday 31st som Fog this morning, Several Country
people arrive   I attempt to heel the boat

Wednesday 2nd May   M. Hay, Wolpard, & leave Camp to S Louis
at 9 oClock Several drunk   Heel the boat.

Thursday 3rd   I write letters to Sundy Gentlemen by Mr. Chotean
som wind, river falling worked at Boat hauled her
up & examined the bottom, Mr. Louca & others arrive also
Serj. Floyd from S Louis with letters to me.   Maj.
Rumsey was polite enough to examine all my provision
Several Kegs of Pork he Condemned

Friday 4th a rainy Day, much Shorting Several
Boats pass down to day — the river rising a teller
I send two men to S Louis with letters Maps Salt & Lime

Saturday 5th a Cloudy day rains at different times
a Saukee Chief with 8 or 10 arrive & stay all night
2 Perogus of Kickapoos return from S Louis. I gave 4 ½
gals Whiskey & Som Tobacco.

Sunday 6th Several of the Country people In Camp Shooting
with the party all git beate and lose their money   a fair Day

Monday 7th I Load the Boat all day, a fair Day Mr. Rumsey
ride a public horse to S Louis   a fair Day   Sent Ordway with
a perogus to S Louis after Cotten arrived Express, & tied with a Hors & Tallow.

(continued overleaf)

12

Tuesday 8th of May Load the Boat & our perogue to Day. Verry hot day, after Loading the Boat Maned her with 20 oars & went the meddle of the river & up the Mississippi a few miles, took the different Courses of the river in the point, returned & found Doct. Cattlet at Camp

Wednesday 9th a fair Day worm. I move the party into tents Mr. Ramsey & Several other men arrive, Dr. Cattlet set out late for St. Louis. the others soon after, I Send to the Missouras Water for Drenking water, it being much Cooler than the Mississippi which Keeps pofsefion of about ¼ of the bead or Channel

Thursday 10th som rain last night Cloudy morning verry hot, in the after part of the day, I continued to fix tents Covering, adjusrt the Load &c. order every man to have 100 Balls for their Rifles & 2 lb of Buck Shot for those with Musquets &c. F.

Friday 11th a worm morning I write all day on the every: about 4 oClock a violent gust from the N W by W, and the Galls up the Creek bore dutance, Seven french arrive with Drewyer. I send Drewyer and the horses to St Louis

Sat: 12th Dr. Cattlet set out at 11 oClock rain all the evening, I state arrangeing the Loons &c.

Sunday 13 a rainy Day a frenchman arrive, Soon after Hale from St Louis with Letters from Cap Lewis I send out to enquire for Ramsey &

Monday 14th a Cloudy morning fixing for a Start Some provision on examination is found to be wet rack at 9 oClock Many of the neighbours came from the Country Mail and perkeal rained the greater part of the day, I set out at 4 oClock to the head of the first Island in the Missourie 6 miles and incamped, on the Island rained. I refer to the Cours. of my Journal

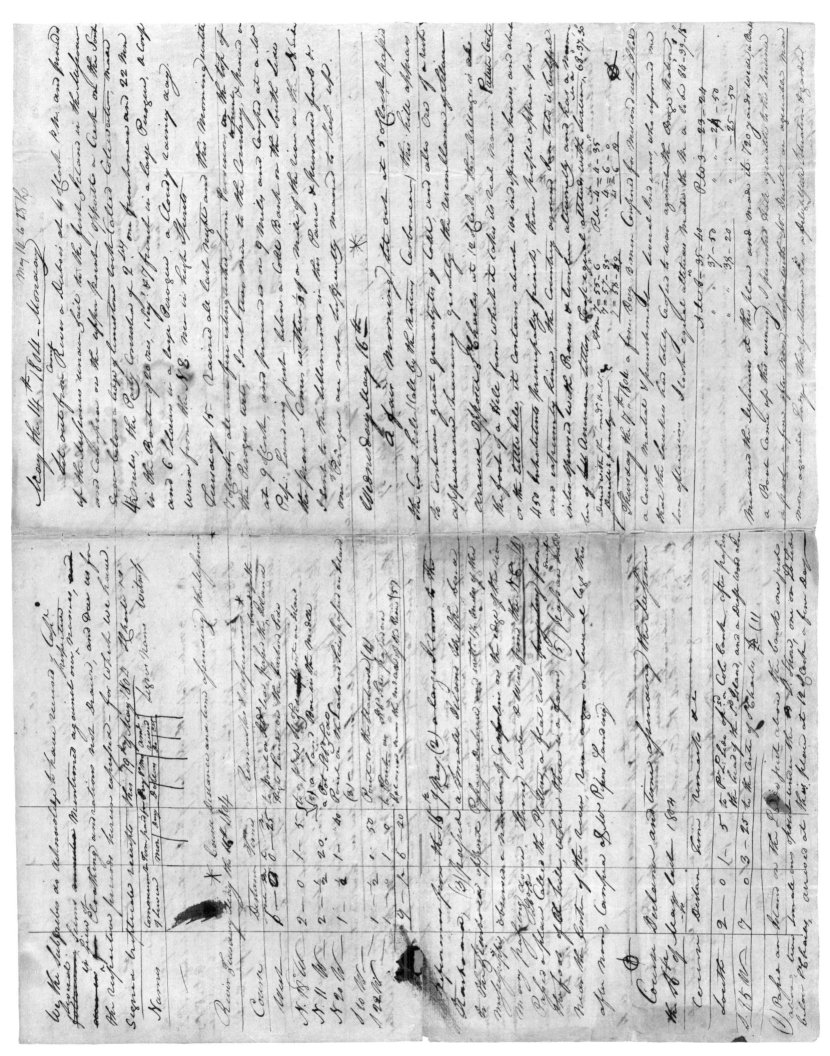

(continued overleaf)

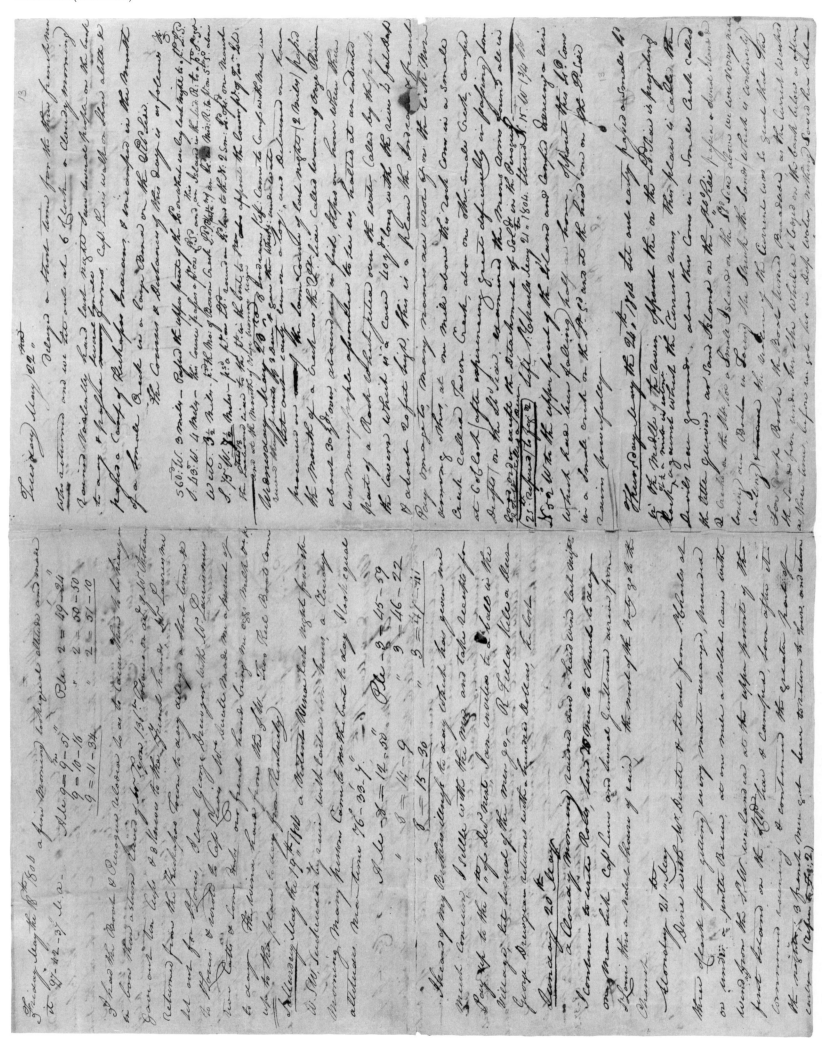

Doc No 14

May 23rd Course of last
Night S. 75 W Continued 2 miles to the
Said point & Side, passed the upper
Point of the Island... S.S.
then S 52 W. 7 Miles passing
Tavern Island two small Is.
in a line to the N. Side the Mo: of
Osa Womans River at 1 M: the Cave
called the Tavern Dr. Lewis at 4 M: Situated
in the Cliffs opposite a Small
Island on the S. of Side. R. & S.
Fields came in) with many
people, passed the Tavern
Cave, Capt Lewis' assended the
hill which has peninsula's
projecting into the in raged
points to the River, and was
near falling from a peninsula
(had escape all day)
saved himself by the asistance of
his Knife, passed a Creak 15 y. wide
at 1 Mile called Creek of the Tavern
on the Lb. Side, Camped opposite the p.
which the Last Course was to. our
men sick.

(*continued overleaf*)

May 26th Set out early, Killed a
Deer last night, examined the
mens arms, & Saw that all was
prepared for action, passed
an Island in the M. R. opposit
a hard place of water Called the
Devill race ground. S 63° W
to a point on the S d Starboard Side
N 68 W to a point on Lb d Side 3 M:
Pass d a Small willow Island on
the Lb d Side to the point of a S d L d Side —
S 75° W to a point on Std Side 3 Mile,
Passed the upper point of the Island.
Crossed and in a very bad place we
got our Boat ¾ ground & She
Broke the Tow Rope & turned
the Land being a willowing the
in a Shealing three times got
off returned to the head of the
aforesaid Island, and Came up
under a falling Bank hard water
this place being the worst I ever
Saw, I Called the Retrograde bend.
Camped at an old house.

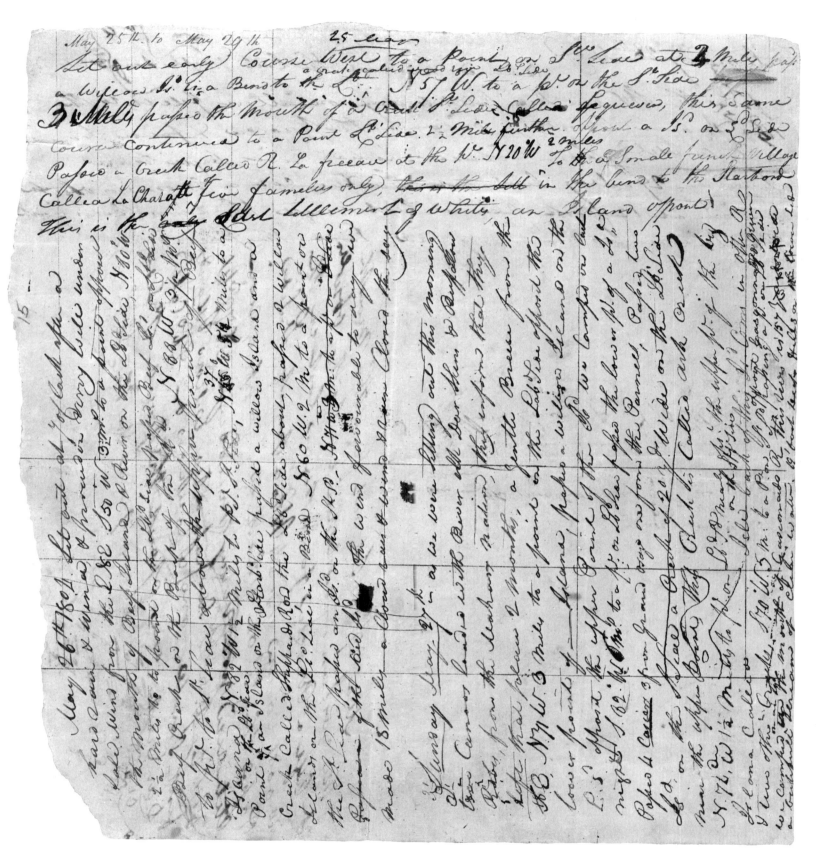

(*continued overleaf*)

Monday 28th May) rained hard all the last night stong wind
from the NW, one Deer killed to day, one Man fell in to the
18d Iniain hunting, onloaded the perogue, & found Several
articles wet, som Tobacco Spoiled. rive begin to rise
Tuesday 29th May sent out hunters, gir a Morning obsvtn
and on at 12 oClock, rained last night, the river rises fast
The Musquetors are verry bad, Load the pierogue

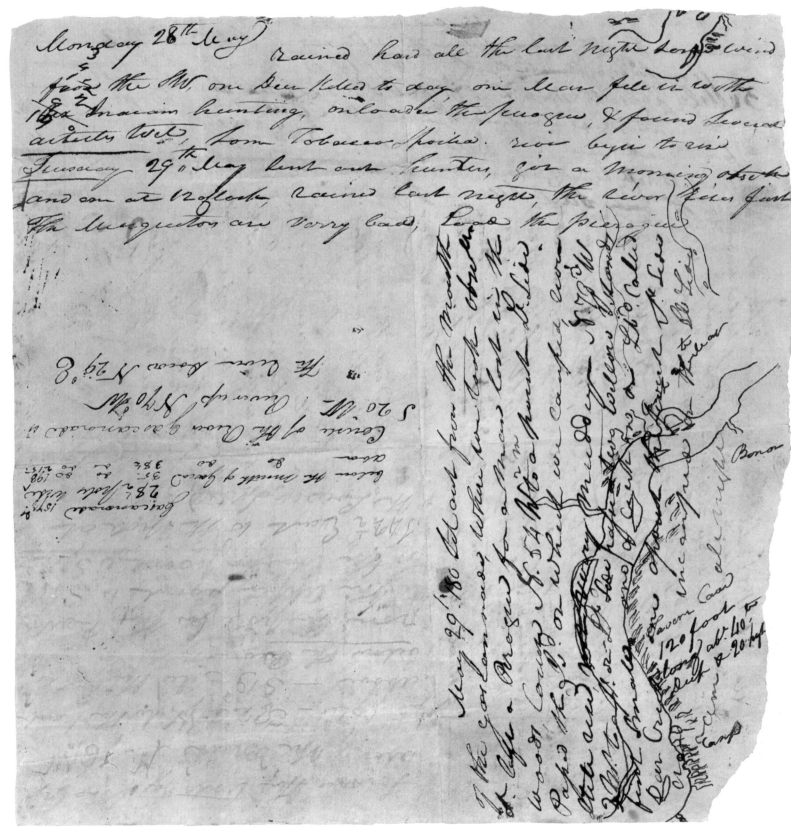

May 30 to June 1st   Doc No 16

May 30th Wednesday, Set out at 7 oClock
after a heavy rain rained all last
night, a little after dark last night
Several guns were herd below, Inspect the
French men fireing for Whitehouse who   2
was lost in the woods. Course West 2   ¾
M. to a pt. Ld Side opsd. an Isld. a Cave on
the S Side Called Monbrains Tavern, a Creek
above, S. 30° W 2 Ms. to pt. Lt Side passed an Id. on the
S. Side a Sand bar & Creek Called rush Creek on the
Ld Side Sand bar head, S 78° W 3 Ms to pt. on Ld Side psd
a willow Is. in Mid. R. a willow Island
S. 66° W 4 Ms. to a pt. Ld. Side, opposit the mouth of a small   30
River called Mary River of about   7 ds. wide a
willow Id. in the River, a large Id. above
S 46° W 5 Ms. to a pt. on L Side passed an Id. in the
Mid. Came to pt. in the mouth of a Creek Ld Side, called
one on Id. head of 60 yds wide Called little Mary   at Ithd
Passed a Creek of 15 yds. wide on the Ld Side
at 14 Miles Called Grindstone Creek & incamped
in the mouth, Low land on both Sides of the River
2d Creek ...

June 1st Friday 1804 Set out early, the Same Course
of Wednesday contd. 4 mes. passed the mouth of Little river
on the Ld. & Bear Creek on the Lard at 5 mes the
Creek is about 25 yds to the I high rent Land on the
Ld Side, S. 45° W to an Island opposite a hill on the S. S.
6 mes this Ps is on the Ld. passed the mo. of Bear creek
25 yds. wide at 2 mes. & three Small Ld. Some
Swift water and banks falling in, Wind a head
from the West, S 39° W 3 mes. to the Pt. above the
mouth of Osage River Lard Side, Camped fell
a number of trees in the Point to take observations
a fair after noon, Set up until ½ oclock to take Some
observations &
June 2nd .. took the Dist. of Son & moon &c &c
I measured the Osage & Missouris at this place
made their width as follows, the Missouri 875 yds wide
the Osage R 397 yds. wide, the distance between the
2 rivers 30 poles up is 40 ps. Took equal altitudes
& Meridian altitude also — and made them
I assended the hill in the point 80 ps.
from the Pt found it about 100 foot high, on the
top is 2 graves or mounds, a Delightfull prospect
from this hill which Comd. both rivers
Drewyer & Sheilds came to the opposite side to day at Sunset
we Sent across & brought them over, they had been about 8 days,
swam many Creeks, much worsted. they informed us

June 3ʳᵈ to 5th

Doc No 17

June Sunday 3ʳᵈ of 1804

The fore part of the day fair, attempted
to take Lunar altitudes, & the Altitudes, but
was disappointed, the clouds obscured
the Sun, took the d. of 67° Cap Lewis
& George Drewyer went out & Killed
a Deer, we Set out at 5 oclock P.M.
the murmer of heavieer theatened S.
clouds, & rain, West 3 Ms. to a pt. St. Side
Keeping along the Lb. Side 1 Ms., paſsed the
mouth of a Creek on Lrd Side 3 Ms. I cale
Cupboard, Creek, mouth behind a Rock
which projects into the river, Camped in the
mouth of the Creek aforesaid, at the
mouth of this Creek I saw much fresh
Sign of Indians, having Crosed 2
Deer Killed to day. I have a very Sore
Throat, and I am Tormented with
Musquetors & Small ticks

June 4th 1804 Monday, a fair day
Sent out 3 hunters, our Mast broke
by the boat running under a tree
paſsed an Islands a Creek on Std Side on which grow Seven
the Stard Sd at Miles on
Course N. 30° W 4 Ms. to pt. on
St Side below 2d Is. paſsed a Creek on Lb Side 15 yd.
wide, I cale Nightingale Creek, this Bad Sung
all last night and is the finest of the birds I
ever heard, below this Creek on the Lard.

(continued overleaf)

Passed a Small Is.d on the Lb.d N 25 W 3 M.
to a St. on St. B. passes a lom. Is. on Lb Sd and
Leeder Creek on the Same side 20 yd
wide passes a Creek on Lb'd Sd 20 yd wide, Scale
Mout Creek this is a Short Creek, fine land
above & below the Mouth. fentle rise
of about 50 foot, Delightfule Timber
of Ashe ash walnut hickory &c &
wind from N W by W. N 58° W. 3 M.d passed
a Creek Called foncar on the Lb Side, N 75 W
3 M.d to a pt S.d Called Batuw a de charm,
a plain on the hill opposit. I got out &
walked on the L.d thro a Charming Bottom
of rich Land about one Mile then I
assend a hill of about 170 foot on the
top of which is a plain. and about 100 ams
of Land which has gud timber on this hill
one of the party says he has found Lead on
a very extensive Cave under this hill
the Land on the
there is a very bad part
Several Deer Killed to day
by our hunters one of the horses is
the other lost his Shoes to day
Bottom on the S side to day
Batuw A derham
the best land comes to the bank on
the Lb Side and good 2 rate land.

18

June 5th Tuesday, Justed the
vennison killed yesterday, after taking
over the Scouting Party or hunters
of 3 men set out at 6 oClock
Course N 57° W to a pt on S.S. 3 ms
passed a Creek on L.S. Scale Lead 6 f
passed one on the S. Called Lit: Good-
womans Creek about 20 yd wide
Passed a Willow Id. a Beautifull Prarie
approaching near the river above Lead 6 &
extends by the Mine river in a
westerley Direction, passed the Mouth
of the Creek of the Big Rock 15 yd wide
at 4 M. on the Lb.S. at 11 oClock
brought a Caussee in Which was
2 men, (from B° Lague up the
Kansas River Where they wintered
& caught a great ofty of Beaver
but unfortunately lost it by
the burning of the plains, the
Kansa Nation hunted on the
Missourie last Winter and are
now persueing the Buffalow
in the Plains, passed a Rock called
the Prairie a Painting from
this Deawl to the mt. on Lb. Seau N 20° W
7 ½ the Sou. County run old Middleton at Nt
7 ½ M. passed a Id. on the Rt.
Side about 40 yd wide a Sand bar
in the Middle of River pass'd up between
the Sand & L. Shore one Mile to a Small
Creek 10 yd wide (Scale Sand C) We run
on the Sand and was obliged to return

(continued overleaf)

return to the Star[boar]d Side I am very
unwell with a slight fever from
a bad Cold Cought three days
ago at the Grand So R— passed
a Small Willow Is. on S Side a
large one in the Middle of the
river, York Swam to the Is.
to pick greens, and Swam back
with his greens, the Boat drew
too much water to Cross Sands
which intervened, She draws 4 foot
water, a fair wind our Mast
being broke by accident prevented
our takeing the advantage of it
passed the lower point of a
large Island, opposite this
Current divides between this
45 m. all Is. on the S. Side we
found the water excessively hard
for 1½ Miles as we were obliged
to pass up the center of this
Current below two of the Is.
round the heads of the other 2
the Current Setting immediately
against the point which was
choked up with Drift for a
mile. The Is. on
the S Side we passed along the
our Hunter or Spies discovered the
Sign of a War party of ab[ou]t 10 men

(continued overleaf)

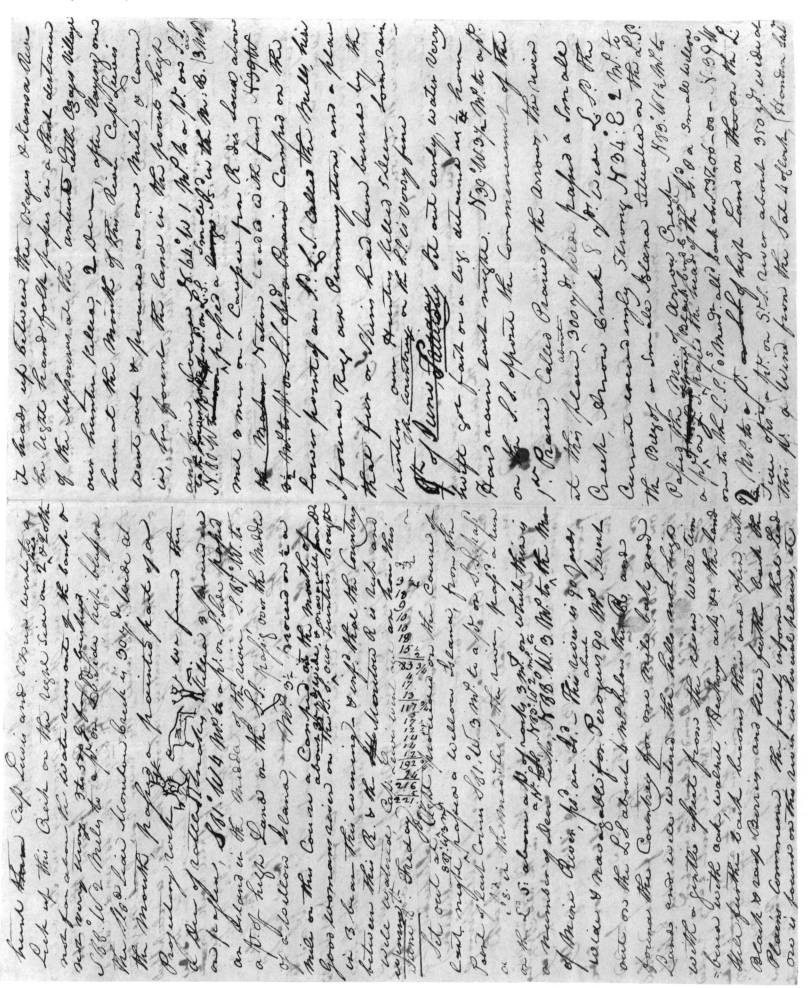

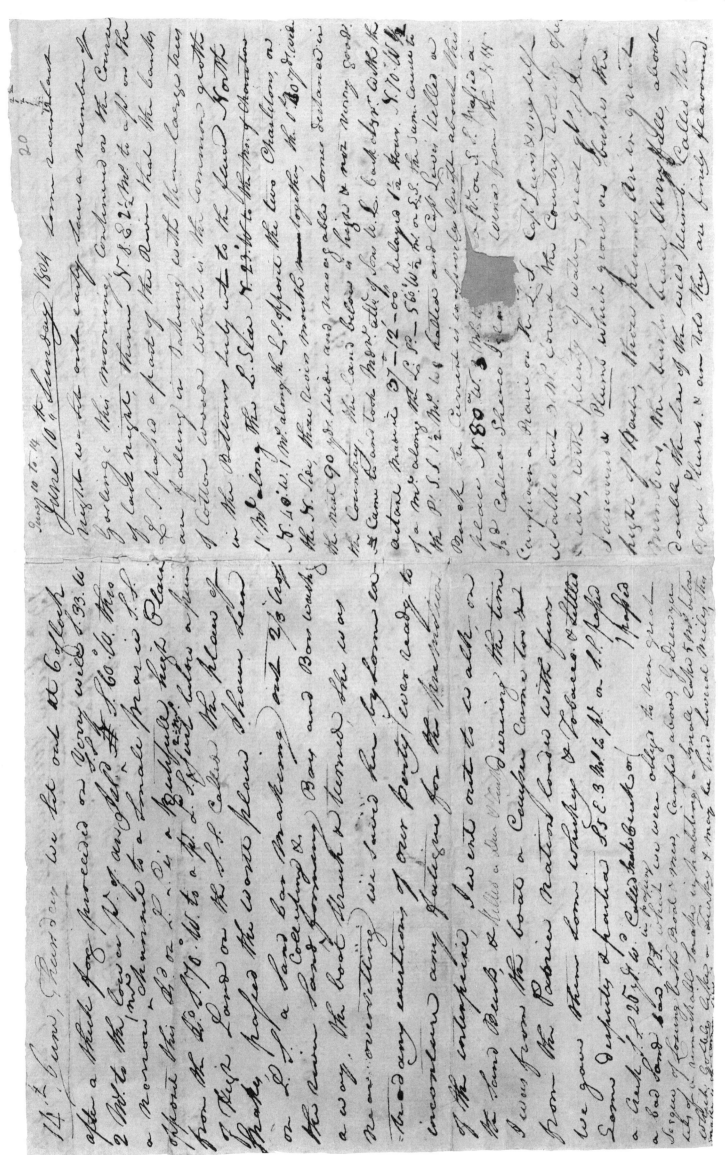

(continued overleaf)

11 June Monday – as the wind blew all this day from the N.W. which was imediately a head we Could not Stur, but took the advantage of the Delay and Dried our wet articles examined provisions and Cleaned arms, my Cold is yet verry bad – the river begining to fall our hunters killed two Deer, G Drewyer killed 2 Bear in the Prarie to day, men verry lively Dancing & Singing &c.

12th of June Tuesday we Set out early, passed thro: a verry bad bend N.75 W. 3½ to a pt. L.S. N.70°W. 2½ ms to a pt. on S.S. passed a Sand bar N 60°W 3½ ms. to a pt. on S.S. passed Plumb C at ½ a ml. on L.S. and halted to Dine, and 2 Caussease Came Down from the Soux nation, we found in the party an old man who had been with the Soux 20 years & had great influence with them, we provd. on this old man Mr. Duriaur to return with us, with a view to get Some of the Soux Chiefs to go to the U.S. purchased 300 lb. of Voyager Grease @ 5$ ⅌ Hd. made Some exchanges & purchuses of Mockasons & found it Late & concluded to encamp. Those people inform that no Indians are on the river, The Country on each Side of the River is good

13th June Wednesday, we Set out early passed ~~Passed for the Secretary~~ a verry round bend to L.S. ~~at Ham~~ passed two Creeks Called Creeks of the round Bend, between those Creeks L.S. is a butifull Prarie, in which the antient Missouri Indians had a Village, at this place 300 of them were killed by the Saukees, a fair Day. Passed the antient missouri villages on right Course N 40 W 2½ pt. L.S., S 29 W 3 Ms. pt. S.S., This nation once the most noumerous is now almost extinct, about 30 of them, liveing with Otteaus on the R. Platt, the remainder all distroyed, took altd. of S. & L with Qd. which gave N 28 W ½ Ms. to a pt. L.S. Passed Some Charming land, I have not Seen any high hils above Charlleton and the hils below for Several days Cannot be termed hills but high land, not exceeding 100 above the high water mark N 30° W, to a pt. L.S. 2 Ms. passed a verry bad Sand bar where the boat was nearly turning & fastening in the quick Sand, and camped in the mouth of Grand R. S.S. this river is about 120 yards wide and navagable for Perogues a great distance, it heads with the River Dumoin ~~Pelters~~ passing the river Carlton a butifull open Prarie Coms to the river below its mouth, we landed and walked to the hills which is abt. ½ a mile. the lower prarie over flows. the hunters killd. a Bear & Deer. this is a butifull place the Prarie rich & extensive, Took Some Looner observati:on which Kept Cap L. & my self up untill half past 11 oClock.

15. 10 16   21

15th June Friday 1804 We set out early
proceeded on about 1 M. and the Boat turned
as a Sawyer which was near doing us great
Damage, the river is rising fast & the Water
exceedingly Swift, S. 35° W 2 M. alg. S.S. S 50° W. 1 M.
to a pt. on L.S. passed a Prarie & Creek on the L.S.
S 51° W 2 m. M. to a pt. on L.S. psd. a Small willow
Island, 1 B. to pt. L.S. ¾ of a M. psd. the
Lower pt. of a Is. S. 30° W 2 M. to the
upr. pt. of an Is. on L.S. passed thro
a verry bad part of the river, the
worst moving Sands I ever Saw, the
Current So strong that the Oars
and Sales under a Stiff breeze cd.
not Stem it, we were obleged to use
a tow rope, under a bank constant
ly falling, S. 5° W 2 M. to a pt. on S.S.
psd. along a Is. on the left to the lowr.
pt. of our State on the left S 12° W 1½
M. to a pt. S.S. opd. the Village of the
little Osage passd. a bad Sand bar
on which we Stuck for a Short time
this is Said to be the worst part of the river
and Camped opd. the bend in
which the antient Villages of the little
Osage & Missouries, the lower or first
of those Villages (L. Osage) is Situated in
butifull Plain at the foot of Some
riseing land, in front of their Village
next the river is a butifull bottom
Plain in which

(continued overleaf)

they raised their Corn &c. back of
of the Village the high Prarie extends
back to the Osarge River, about 3 M.
above & in view the Missouris nation
resided under the protection of the
Osarge, after their nation was reduced
by the Saukees below, they built their
Village in the same low Prarie and
livd there many years, the war
was so hot & both nations becom
so reduced that the Little Osarge &
a few of the Missouris moovd & built
a Village near the Grand Osage, the
rest of the Missouris went and took
protection under the Ottaws or Platt
River

16th Iune Satturday set out at 7 oclock
Proceed on N. 66° W. 2½ M. passed a Cd.
Cove on the L.S. at the lower point
Drewer & Willard had Camped &
had with them 2 bear & 2 Deer we
took in the meat & proceeded on. some
rain this morning West 2 M. pass a Cd. on
L.S. & prarie to a Belge of Snag Cd. L.S. a belyfull
extensive Prarie on L.S. hills at about 9 M.
Distane. Mr. Mackey has laid down the remts.
of an old fort in this Prarie which I cannot find
S.85° W. 1 M. along the Cd. L.P. S.61 W alg L.S. 1 M. S.30 W
3. M. to pt. L.S. opsd. an Cd. & head of the Isd. S.40 W 1 M. L.S.
passed a very bad place where the sand was moovng
constantly, I walked on shore obsd. fine high Bottom
on L.S. Camped late land,
this evening.

(continued overleaf)

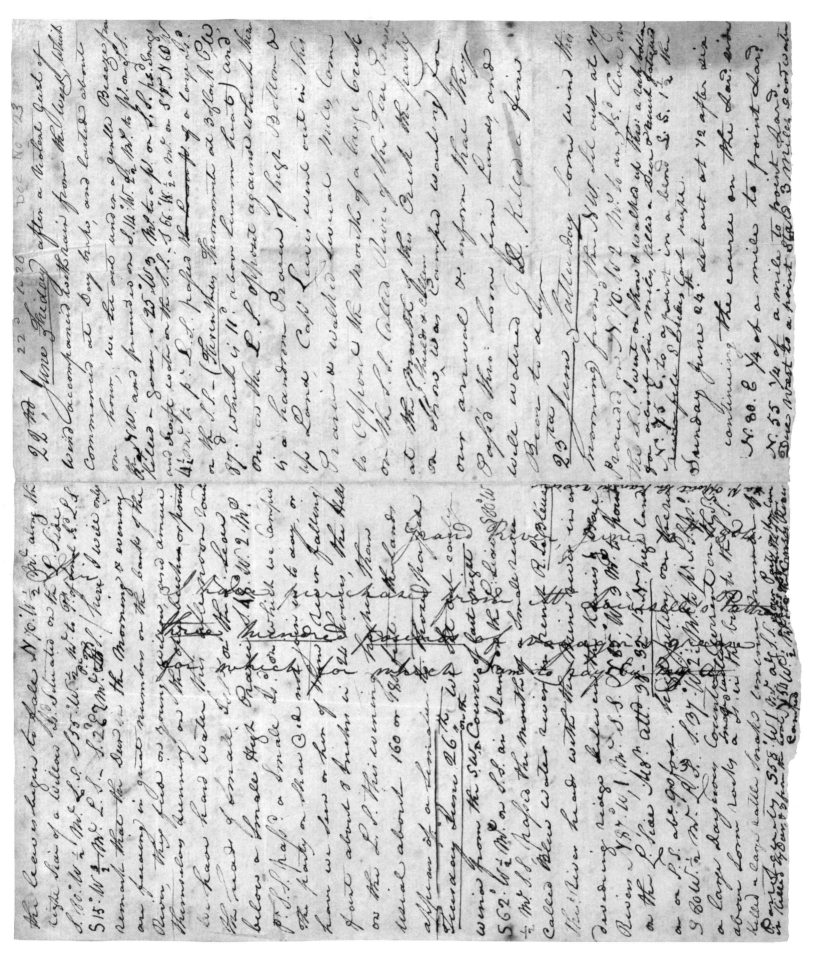

(continued overleaf)

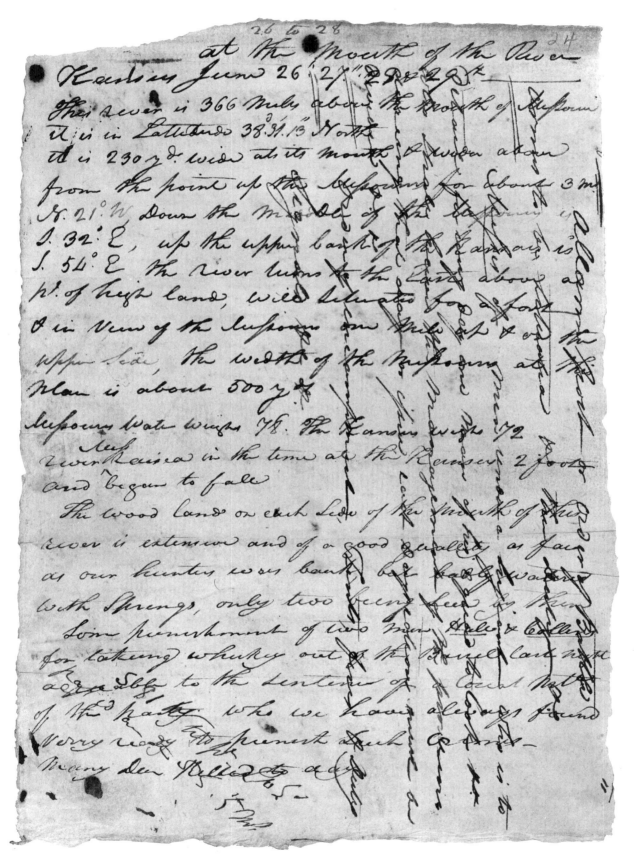

at the Mouth of the River

Kansas June 26th 27th 28th & 29th

This river is 366 Miles above the Mouth of Missouri
it is in Latitude 38° 31' 13" North
it is 230 yds wide at its mouth & wider above
from the point up the Missouri for about 3 m.
N. 21° W. Down the Middle of the Missouri is
S. 32° E, up the upper bank of the Kansas is
S. 54° E the river turns to the East above a
pt of high land, will situated for a fort
& in view of the Missouri on Mile at & on the
upper side, the width of the Missouri at a
Mile is about 500 yds

Missouris Water weighs 78. The Kansas weighs 72
river Raised in the time at the Kansas 2 foot
and begun to fall

The wood lands on each side of the Mouth of this
river is extensive and of a good quality as far
as our hunters was back bottom low watered
with Springs, only two being seen by them

Som punishment of two men Hale & Collins
for takeing whiskey out of the Barrel last night
agreeable to the sentence of a Court Mart
of the party who we have alwys found
very ready to punish such Crimes —

Many Dear Killed &c —

(continued overleaf)

✳ ⚹ passed a Sand bar in the river above the I⁰ Covered for a m⁰ with Drift Wood, Came to Cap Lewis took Med⁰ altitude & we delayed three hours, the Day being exceceding-ly hot Turkeys are plenty on the Shore, Some of the Men inform that they Saw Purkauns trees on S.S. yielded any Great quantities of Raspburies an Graps, ② pass a Creek on the L.S. Called *Tumeau* (The Frog) Creek, an Is⁰ above and in the River fellow Is⁰ on the S.S. all of the Same name, The two Willow Is⁰ has been made within 9 years & the Main Chanel runs now on the L.S. of the large Island where there was no runing water at low water from this Island the range of Hill up the River to the NW, pass a river on the L.S. a a Butifull extensive Prarie, Two Islands just above Callea (Isles des Parques) or Feela Island, those Islands are, one of our French hands tells me that the French intended to Settle here once & brought their Cows and Put them on those Island, M⁰. Mackey Says the first Village of the Kansies was a little above this Island & made use of as feelar, no trace of any thing of that Kind remains to be seen on the L⁰. fine Land on the L Side, Hills near the river all day, Camped on the lower p⁰. of I Is⁰.

✳ *Course Distance* and references by Little July

6 m⁰ on the Course's of this morning

N. 32° W. 1½ m⁰. to a p⁰ on the L. Side N W. W. to the right Side an I⁰
N 58 W. 2¼ m⁰. to p⁰. L.S. passed the head Passed a Creek on L.S. ② of the Is⁰
N. 42 W. 1½ m⁰. to a p⁰. on S.S.
N. 33 W. 1 m⁰. to North Side of a Island ③ Creek L.S.
and a Butifield extensive Pairie
N. 22° E. 1½ ——— 13
North ⑯ Hept and dry 13040

29. Jun to July 1st   DOC NO. 25

29th of June 1804, Set out from the Kansas
River ½ past 4 ofclock, proceeded on passed a
small river on the L.S. at ½ Mile a(n) Island
on the S.S. at 1½ m.s. Hills above the upr.
pt. of Iso. S.S. a large Sand bar in the
middle. Passed a very bad place of
water, the Stern of the Boat Struck
a moveing Sand & turned; within 6
Inches of a large Sawyer, if the Boat
had Struck the Sawyer, her Bow
must have been Knocked off &
in course She must has Sunk in
the Deep water below Came to & Camped
on the S.S. late in the evening

   Course & Distances Jun 29. Expansion
N. 21° W. 3½ m.s. to a pt. on L.S. passed a
Pt. on L.S. and the Lower pt. of an Isd. S.S.
(1) N. 18° W. you L.S. — opd. head of Isd. S.S. 79 ur.
3 m.s. to a pt. on S.S.
   7½

30th June, Set out very early this Morn.
Saw a Very large Woolf   on the Sand bar
this morning walking) near a gang of Turkeys
at 10 Miles above the Kansis passed the mouth
of a Small river Call the Petet Platte, or
little Shole river, this river is about 30 yd. Wide
and has Several rapids & falls, well Calculated
for mills, the land on this river is Said to be
rooling, Killed 2 Deer Swinging the river
the Wind from the S.W. here we opend the Bag—

(continued overleaf)

of Bread given us by _____ whith
we found very good, our Bacon which was
given us by _____ . . we examined and
found Sound and good some that purchased in the
Illinois Spoiled, A from a relish of this
old bacon this morning was very agreeable,
Deer to be Seen in every direction and their tracks
is as plenty as Hogs about a farm, our hunt.
Killed 9 Deer to day the Land below the
last River is good, that above, between the
two rivers which is near together is black&
and bad on the N. Side, the other Side is
good lands, Landed on the L.S. below an Isd.
Called Demond Island

July 1st 1804, Each except one of the Sintinals
Changed either a man or Beast, which run
off, all prepared for action, Set out early
passed the Demon Isd. pass a Small Creek on
the L.S. as this Creek is without name
we Call it Biscuit Creek Camped on
the upper point of of a Sand beach, the river still
falling a little a very warm Day. I took some
Medicine last Night which has worked me
very much party all in helth exsept Boils

※ ＊Course Distance & refferences Jun 30.

N. 20° W. 2 M. to pt. L.S. Boat wheeled
N. 30° W. ½ M. on L.S. — High land on the S.S.
S. 64° W. 2½ M. to pt. on S.S. psd. Little River Platt. ①
West... 1 M. on S.S. a Small Creek on L.S.
N. 60 W. ¼ M. pt. on pt. on the L.S.
July ⑩
N. 62° W. 1½ M. to S.S. Side of an Island Demond
N. 40° W. ¼ M. on L.S. of the Isd. & Sand bar on Left
N. 28° W. ¾ M. to Pt. on L.S. passed the upper point of Isd
N. 45° W. ½ mile to a pt. on S.S. Cour Cont. to tree in thr Pra

July 2 to 5

Doc No 26

July the 2nd 1804 Set out verry early this morning passd on the left of the Isles parques high butifull Situations on the L. S. the land indifferent land a Creek coms in on the S. S. Called parques, all at once the river became Crouded with drift that it was dangerous to cross this I suppose was from the caveing in of the banks at the head of Some Island above, Passed a Creek on the L. S. Called Turquie or Turkey Creek passe a verry bad Sand bar on the L. S. the 20 oars & Poals Could with much dificultey Stem the Current, passed a large Island on the S. S. Called by the Inds Wau-car-ba war-con-da or the Bear Medicin Island, at 12 oClock came to on the Island and put in a Mast, detaind four hours, exceedingly hot, wind in foupart of the day from the S. E. George Drewyer inform that the Land he pass through yesterday & to day on the S. S. was generally Verry fine he saw two Springs of fresh water near the Island, Deer has become So Common it is hardly necessary to mention them, we Camped after dark on the S. S. opposit the 1st old Village of the Kanzas which was Situated in a Valley between two points of high lands on the river Back of their Village Commenced an extensive Prarie the [struck] a large Island in front which appears to have made on that Side and thrown the Current of the river against the place the Village formerly Stood; and washed away the bank in that part. The french formerly had a Fort at this place, to protect the trade of this nation, the Situation appears to be a verry eligable one for a Town, the Valley rich & extensive, with a Small Brook Meandering through it and one part of the bank affording yet a good Landing for Boats The High Lands above the Fire river on each Side of the Missouri appear to approach each other Much nearer than below that place, being from 3 to 6 miles between them, to the Kanzas above that place from 3 to 5 Ms apart and higher Some places being 160 or 180 feet the river not So wide we made a Mast of Cotton wood yesterday to day in the Course of the evening o night it turned of a butifull red Colour

N. 22° E . . . . to a pt on the L. S. in a bend ①
N. 10° W . . W. to a pt on the S. S. passes the head of the La Da Creek S.S
N. 34° E 1 m to a pt o L. S. ps. passed Turkey Creek L. S. ③
N. 10. W. ½ m on the L. S. high land on the L S
N. 40 W. 1½ m on the S. S. an Isd ④ on S.S
S. 50 W. — To the old Village of the Kanzas on L. S.
S. 78 W ½ of a m. to a Pt on S. S. ps 2 runs on S. S. L. S. pass a Bluff of Sd
S. 81 W 2½ m to a pt on the S. S. passed the head of the Island bear ofd Sd
N. 82° W 2 m to a pt on the S. S. passed verry Swift water, & Camped.
   10½

N. 53 W. 1 md alg. S. S.
N. 50 W ½ m. alg. S. S.
N. 18° E 1 md to p. on the L S ops. an Isd N. 40 E ½ m opp of Island 1½ md.

July 3rd 1804 Set out very early this morning
and proceeded on under a gentle Breeze from the South passed
two Islands one a Small willow Island on the L.S. O the other a large
Island Called Cow I. (Isle Vache) this Island is large opposite to the head
on the S.S. is a large Pona, a Bad Sand bar on the S.S. we attempted
without Success, & was oblige to Cross back, I saw a white horse on the
L.S. in view of the Upper point of the Island, O passed a large Sand
bar at the S. point, & halted to day about a mile above the Island
and found a horse, which had been lost by the Indians, very fat
and gentle, Sent him on to Join the others which was a head on the S.S.
at this place, the french had a tradeing house, for to trade with the
Kanzes on a high bottom on the L.S. near the hills which is Prarie
proceeded on round a a large Sand bar on the L.S. & Camped (opposit a large
Sand bar in the middle of the river) on the L.S. a Butifull Small
Stream passes back of the tradeing house, beforementioned *

July 4th WEDNESDAY 1804, Set out early, passed the mouth of a Bayou
leeding from a Lake on the S.S. this Lake is large, and was once the bed of the
River, it reaches Parrelel for Several miles, Came to on the L.S. to Dine &
rest a Short time, a Snake bit Jo: Fields on the Side of his foot which Swelled much Apply Barks to the wound, pass a Creek on the L.S. about 15 yard wide
Cuming out of an extensive Prarie as this Creek has no name, and this day
is the 4th of July we name this Independance us. Creek above the Creek the
woodland is about 200 yards, back of those wood is an extensive Prarie
open and high, which may be seen six or seven below — Saw great Nos.
of Goslins to day nearly Grown, the last mentioned prarie I Call
So Field Snake Prarie, Cap. Lewis walked on Shore & Saw a large mou[nd]
we Camped in the plain one of the most butifull Plains
I ever Saw, open & butifully diversified with hills
& Valleys all presenting themselves to the river, covered
with Grass, and a few scattering trees at this place the
Kanzaws lived formerly passed a head & very large town
Tobooca Springs & other out of the bank, a good Situation

* July 3rd 1804
N 53° W. 1 Miles along the S. Side
N 50 W. ¼ m. do   do
N. 18° E 1 m. to a pt. on the L.S. Ops. two Islands one Small
N. 32° W ½ m. to a pt. or left side of the Island
N. 10° W ½ m. to pt. or L.S.
N. 60. W ¼ m. to pt. on Is. S.S
N. 78 W ½ m. to pt. on L.S. oppod. the head of the Is. Ec a pond on S.S. (2)
S. 56° W 2½ m. to Pt. on S.S. of the Missourie
N. 50 W. 1 m. or the S.S.
N 45 E 3 m. to a pt. on L.S. passed Several Sand bars (3)
N 12 E - ½ m. on L. Side round a Sand bar & Camped

July 4th 1804
N. 76. W. 1 m. on L.S. S. pa. Pona
S. 45 W. 3 m. Pt. S.S.
N 75 W. ½ m. on S.S.
N 40 W 5 m. to pt. S.S. ops. Ph
S. 12° E 2¾ m. L.S. pa. Sm 55 I.S. (2)
S 10 E 2 to a pt. S.S. opd. (3)
Passed a Creek L.S. Called
Creek of Ots. 30 y. wide
where the old Village was
on the point O

The Plains of this Country
are covered with a Leek Green
Grass, well calculated for the
Sweetest and most nourishing
hay — interspersed with Cops of
trees, Spreading their lofty branches
over Pools Springs or Brooks of fine
water. Groops of Shrubs covered
with the most delicious fruit
is to be seen in every direction,
and nature appears to have
exerted himself, by the Variety
of flours Delicately
and highly flavored raised
above the Grass, which Strikes
& profumes the Sensation, and
amuses the mind, into Conjecturing
Magnificent a Scenery
in a Country
far from the Sivilised world
to be enjoyed by nothing but
the Buffalo Elk Deer & Bear &c
which it abounds, &
Savage Indians

(continued overleaf)

243

The Names of the french
Ingagees, or Hirelens ———

1 Battest de Shone. Palm Perogue
*2 Joseph Le bartee
3   Lasoness
4 Paul Preemau
5 Chalo
6 E, Cann
7   Roie
8 Chatlo Cougee

⎫ in
⎬ Perogue
⎭

+ I. Le bartee ⎫ in the large Boat
  Rives ⎬

Peter Crousat half Indian ⎫ bow men
William La bue Mallat ⎬

1 60 M &   M to a Budg of
1 2   &   to   perro on the
3 Serg.t & 23 men for the Boat
George Drewyer. Hunter & 4 horses
1 Corp.l & 4 Privats in a Perogue to be Sent
back from Plate river
Mr Durrow intept for the Sues
Corp. Lud is my self & york ———
                in all 46 men July 4th
                4 horses & a dog

July the 5ᵗʰ 1804 ~ July 5 to ~ Set out very early this morning, Swam
the horse across the river proceeded on for two miles
under the bank where the old Kansas town formerly stood
(Say in 1724) The Cause of those people Moving from this place
I cannot learn, but Naturally conclude that War has reduced
their nation & Compelled them to retire further into the
Plains with a View of defending themselves & opposing their
enemy on Horse back / I neglecta to mention yesterday that
the Lake on the S.S. was large Say ¾ M. wide & 7 or 8 long, one
Creek & Several brooks running into it from the hills, it
contains great quantities few of fish & Goslings from which
w gave it the name / passed Some verry bad Sand bars
Situated parrelel to each other, ○ the Boat turned three times
one on the Plant of a Drift wood. the river no damage
procurocable Camage, we came to for Dinner
at a Bever house, Cap. Lewis Dog went in
drove them out. the high Lands on the L.S. is open, a
few trees Scattering ② passed a Small Creek on the L.S
in the 1 bend to the left I call Creek from the
a bank of that Mineral just above we
Camped on the L.S. under a high bank   Lat⁰ 39.—25.—41 North

Course & Distance July 8ᵗʰ 1804
N 35° E 1 M on the S.S. opposit the old village of Kanzes
S 56° E 2 M. to the L. point a large Eddy on the L.S. and a bad Sand bar
East ~ 1 M. on L.S. a Sand bar in middle &c. ○ Boat turned 3.
N. 18° W. 2 M. to a pt. on S.S op⁰. a Prairie ½. a Creek L.S ②
North 1 M. on S.S
S. 70 E 3 M. to a pt. of willow on the L.S.   wind from S.E
___
19   on the bank of this river I observe great quants
of Grapes, berries & roses Deer is not so plenty this three days
past as they were below that, Elke are plenty about those
Prarie. Some Buffalow last.

(continued overleaf)

245

July 5 to July 6 to   Doc No 27

6th July Friday) We set out early this morning &
Proceeded on/ the river falls Slowly) wind SW) passed a Sand bar in
1st bend to the right) passed a Smale Island at the S.Pt.
as Verry Worm day) (worthy of remark that the water
of this river or Some other Cause, I think that the most
Probable throws out a greater propor. of Swet than
I could Suppose Could pass thro: the human body
those men that do not work at all will wet a
Shut in a few menits & the Swet will run off
& those who work, in Streams)
oppont the 3rd point passed a Prarie on the S.S. Called
Reevys Prarie from a man of that Name being Killed
is it oppoit this Prarie the river is Confined in a
Verry Narrow Space Crouded on L.S. by coming Sand
the Hunters went in 3 Deer Jurked
(which were moving) and dificuelt to pass, or
the 6th point of to day is a Smale Island & a
Sand bar 2 Miles out in the River, this is Called the
Grand Bend, or Grando de Town, I walked on this Sand bar
found it a light Sand interspured with Smale Pebbls of
Varrous Kind, also pit Coal of an excellent quallity
was lodged on the Sand We Camped on the L.S. a Whipper will
perched on the boat for a Short time gave this name to the Creek
Coure Destance. & refferrence   July 6. 1804

N. 58° E. 1 Mi. on the L.Shore oppoit a Sand bar in the river
North 3 Mi. to a Pt on S.S. an Isd.①   (N 45 E. thro the Channel)
N. 10° W ½ on S.S. an Id.
S. 76 E ½ Mi. on S.S. to the head of the Island, a Old Batteau
S. 60° E 1¾ Mi. to a pt on the L.S. (willows)
N. 70° E 1½ Mi. along a Sand bar on the L.S. oppoit a Prarie ②
N. 50 W 1 Mi. on the L.S. passed a bad Sand
West 3 Mi. to a pt. on the S.S. a Smale Island ③ & Sand bar
──
12
(8648)   N. W. 2 Mi. I. on the SS
             N. 70 E 2 Mi. to Pt on L.S.

7th of July Satterday 1804 Set out early passed Some Verry
Swift Water on the L.S. which Compelled us to draw up by the
Cord, a Verry worm Morning, passed a butifule Prarie
on the right Side which extends back, those
Praries has much the appearance from the
river of farms, Devided by narrow Strips of wood,
those Strips of timber grows along the runs
which which rise on the hill & pass to the river
a Clift above, our Man Sick (Frasure) Struck with the
Sun, Saw a Large rat on the Side of the bank, Killed a Wolf
on the Bank passed ③ a Verry narrow part of the river, all
Confined within 200 yards, a yellow bank above, passed
a Small willow Island on the S. point, (in Low water
those Small willow Islands are joined to the
Sand bars Makeing out from the Points) a pond or
the S.S. near the prarie (up & sested) in which G.D. Saw Several Young
Swans) we Came to and Camped on the S.S. the two men
Sent out last evening) with the horses did not Join us this evening agreeable to orders — a hard wind with Some rain
from the N.E. (at 7 oClock) which lasts half an hour, with thunder &
lightning) river fall a little

Cours Distance & refferrens July the 7th
N. 40° E 2 M° on the S. point round the Sand bar
N. 76° E 3 M° to the pt. on the L.S. passed Sand bay
S. 55 E 1½ M° to a Prarie in the bend to the S.S. O P. Mackley Pro:
N. 36 W½ M° on the L.S. a Bluff on S.S. Drank Set in 2 Deer
N. 76 W ¼ M° on on L.S.
S. 66° E 2 M° to pt on S.S. from which a Sand bar make
N. 74° W 1½ on the S. Side opsd a yellow Clift river abt 200 yds wide
N. 45 E ½ M° on on S.P. a pt of a willow Island
N. 70 E ⅛ W° on L.S. — a Sand bar puts out

(continued overleaf)

8th of July Sunday Set out early this morning, the
Sick Men much better, Serjt. Ordeway was waiting at a
Creek on the S.S. below an Island, passed two Island
on the S.S. and Came to at the upper point, G Drewyer went
out R. Fields & Gutrich, five men Sick to day with
a Violent Head ake &c. and Several with Boils, we appoint
a Cook to each mess to take Charge of the Provisions. in
Serjt. Pryors = Collens in Sgt Ordeways Werner in Serjt. Floyds
Thompson, _____ The french men Killed a young Dier on
the Bank ② passed at a narrow Channel of about 80 or 100 yds
wide about 5 miles to the mouth of Nadawa River
Which Comes in to this Channel from the N.W. and
is abt. 70 yards wide at its mouth _____ feet Deep
and has a jentle Current Perogues Can Navagate
this river near its head which is between the
Missourie & the Grand river, passed up
the _____ 3/4 of a mile to the river at the
head of the _____ Island & Camped opposed the
head of this Island is another nearest the
Larbourd Shore, this Island Nadawa is
the largest I have Seen formed by a Channel washing into the Nadawa river. _____
18. or 10000 acres" _____ Course Distance & Refferce 8th July.

N. 28° E 1 Mi. on the Lfd a Sand bar
N. 60° W. 1½ to the Lower point of a Island on the S.S.
N. 25° W. 3 Mi. to a pt. on the L S passed the Sd & one on the side ①
N. 56 W ½ Mi. to the Lower point of an Island ② S 30 W. up the Chnl
West _____ ¼ mile on Lft of the Island
S 10. W. _____ ¼ Mi. to a p. on SLShore. N. 25 W. ¼ Mi. to Pt. on Isld
N. 40. W. _____ ¼ Mi. to the bend on SoS. N. 70 W ½ Mi. to a bend on the S.S.
S 70. W _____ ½ Mi. to a Bend in the Island N 32 W ½ Mi. to a bend on the S.S.
N 42 W ¼ _____ ¼ mi. to a do do S. Side _____ S 50 W ¼ Mi. to a do in do

59.39
25.41
73.41

29

July the 9th. <u>Monday</u> 1804 Sent one man back to the mouth of this Creek to ~~land~~ mark a tree, to let the party on Shore See that the Boat had passed the river, Set out ~~at the~~ early passed ① the head of the Island Situated in the middle of the river a sand bar at the head, ② passed the mouth of a ~~Cut~~ *Creek or Bayou* on the S. S. leading from a large Pond of about three miles in length, at 8 oClock it commenced raining, the wind Changed from N.E. to S.W. ③ at 6 miles passed the mouth of a Small creek on the L. S. Called Monters Creek, the river at this place is wide with a Sand bar in the middle, passed a place on the L. S. about 2 miles above the Creek, where Several french men Camped two years to hunt — ④ passed a Island on the S. S. of the river in a bend, opposite a high Land on the L. S. Wind shifted to the N.W. in the evening, opposite this Island and on the L. S. Loup or Wolf River Comes in, this river is about 60 yards wide, but little water *running* at the mouth, this river heads with the waters of the Kansas, and has a perogue navigation Some distance, it abounds with Beaver, Camped opposit the head of the Island on the L. S. Saw a fire on the S. S. Supposedly the four flankers, to be there, Sent a perogue for them, the Patroon & Bow man of the Perogue french, they returned & informed, that when they ~~approached the fire~~, it was put out, which caused them to return, this report caused us to look out supposing a pty of Indians going to ~~war~~, fired the bow piece to allarm & put our men on their guard

Course Distance & References for July the 9th ~~their guard this men on Shore every thing is readiness for Defence~~   ②
S. 66°. W. 1½ M. to the upper point of an Island in the River ① — passed the mouth of a Gut from a pond
S. 20°. W. 3½ M. to a point on the S. S. passed a Sand bar and point on L. S. — (Rains).
N. 82. W. 3½ M. to a point on the ~~S.~~ L. S. Side pd. a Sand bar, a Small creek on the L. S. ③
N. 68°. W. 3½ M. to a point on the L. S. ④ passed a Island on the S. S. — Just below the W. paso ① 12 M. ⑤

14

July 10th. <u>Tuesday</u> Set out this morning with a view to Land near the fire Seen last night, & Reconnoiter, but Soon discovered that ~~the~~ our men were at the fire, they were a sleep early last evening, and from the Course of the Wind which blew hard, their Yells were not heard by party in the perogue a mistake altogether — proceeded on, passed Peau on the upper Side of Woolf River, at 4 miles passed ① a Small Creek Called Pape, this Creek is about 15 yds. wide — and called after a Spaneird who killed himself at the mouth. ② Dined on an Island Called de Solomon and delayed 3 hours, and proceeded on, opposite this Island on the L. S. is a ③ beautifull Bottom Prairie which will Contain about 2000 acres of Land covered with wild Rye & wild Potatoes great numbers of Goslings on the Banks & in the Ponds near the river, Capt Lewis killed two this evening we Came to & Camped for the night. at a point on the S. S. opposit a Yellow clay Cliff. —

Course Distance & Reffr. July 10th.
N. 80°. W. 3 pt. to the Starboard Point passed a Sand bar.
N. 19. W. 2 M. to a point on the L. S. passed a Creek ①
North 2½ M. to Lower point of an Island ②
S. 50. W. 2½ M. to a pt. on the Left Side of the Island opd. a prarie ③
S. 50. W. 1¾ M. to a pt. on the S. ⑥ L. S. passed a bad Sand bar
N. 83° W. ~~some~~ Come to a pt. S. S.
                    10 Miles   S. 66. W.

our men all getting well but much fatigued, the river is on a Stand neither rise nor fall, the bottoms on the S. S. is very extensive & thick. the Hells or high land is near the river on the L. S. and but thinly timbered, back of those hills is open plains.

(continued overleaf)

July 11th **Wednesday**, Set out early [July 9 to 13th] proceeded on passed a willow Island in a bend to the S.S. Sent out Drewyer & Jo. Fields to hunt, Back of this Island a creek comes in on this S.S. Called by the Indians Little Tarkio Creek I went on Shore above this Island on the S.S. found the bottom subject for overflow wet and very thickly interwoven with grape Vines — proceeded on at about ½ a mile from the river about 3 m.s and observed fresh Sign of a horse, I proceed the track, with an expectation of finding a Camp of Indians on the river, when I got to the river, I saw a horse on the Bank, this horse as appears was left last Winter by some hunting party, probable the Ottoes, I joined the Boat on the Sand Island situated opposit the Mouth of Ne Mahar River, this river comes in on the L.S. is about 80 yds Wide and navagable for Perogues some Distance up the prarie Common above the mouth and continue on both Sides of this R Drewyer Killed 6 Deer to day I Killed one Several hunters sent out up the Ne Mahar R

Course Distance &c Journey July 11th 1804
N 30° W 3 M.s to a point on the S.S. above a Small prarie, & opposit a Willow Island in a bend on the S.S.
West & N.W. 3 M.s to a point on the S.S. to the south side of a Sand Island opps. a Ne Mahar R
                6

July 12th **Thursday** some hunters out on the S.S. those on the L.S. did not return last night, our Object in delaying here is to take some Observations and rest the men who are much fatigued Made Sundery observations after an early Breakfast I took five men and went up the River Ne Ma har about three Miles, to an open leavel part of an emence prarie at the mouth of a small Creek on the Lower Side, I went on Shore & passed this the plain, having several notes to the top of a high Artificial Mound from the top of this Mound I had an emence, extensive & pleasing prospect, of the Country around, I could see the Meandering of the Little River for at least 10 miles winding thro a meadow of 15 or 20000 aurs of high bottom Land Covered with Grass about 4½ feet high, the high lands which rose irregularly were toped with Mounds or antent Graves which is to me a strong evidence of this Country having been thickly settled, This River is about 80 yards Wide with a gentle Current and heads up near the Pania Vilage on River Blue a branch of Kansas, a little timbered land near the mouth for 1 mile above only a feew Trees, and thickets of Plumbs Chers &c are seen on its banks, the Creeks & little revers makeing into the river have also some timber — I got Grapes on the banks nearly ripe, observed great quantity of Grapes, plums Crab ap and a wild Cherry, Growing like a Com. Wild Cherry only larger, & grows on a small bush on the side of a Cliff ½ M. up & on Lower Side I marked my name & day of the month Sand Stone near an Indian Mark or Image of a man & a boat Tried willows & leaping on a river near our hunters killed som deer, Saw Elk & Buffalow.

14 July
16

My notes of the 13th of July by a most unfortunate accident blew over Board in a storm in the Morning of the 14th obliged me to refer to the notes Journals of Sergeants, and my own recollection the occurrences Courses Distance &c of the Day — Last night a violent storm from the N.W.⁰ Passed Tar-ki-o River, at 2 miles a Chan'd running into this river 3 ms. above forms St Josephs Isl'd Passed an illegt Prarie in the 1st bend to the left. Containing a grass exactly timothy, with Seed like flax ② passed a Island in a bind to the Sd at 12 ms. I walked on Shore S.S. lands, low & overflown, Killed three Goslings nearly Grown, Sailed under a Wind from the South all day. Camped on a Sand Island on the L. Pt opposit a high & extensive Prarie, on the S.S. the Hills about 4 or 5 Ms. off, This Plain appears extensive, great appearance of a Storm from the North W. this evening very agreeable, the Wind Stilld —
the South —

Course Distance & references July 13th 1804

N. 8° E ¼ m. to Pt. on S.S. passed the Sand Island
N. 28° E 3½ m. to pt on L.S. psd Tar-ki-o R. & S. forks &c S.S. ①
S. 70° W 3 m. to pt. on S.S. opsd a Prarie ②
N. 46° W 1½ m. on the S. point ope. the Prarie & a Hill L.S
N. 30° W 1½ m. to a pt. on L.S.
N. 45° W 4½ m. to a pt on L.S passd a Island & Sand bar ③
N. 56 W 3½ m. to a pt on S.S.
N. 8 W 2 m. to a pt. on L.S. leaving a Sand Island on Which we
20 ¼ camped to the left, on this Island I lost my notes, in a Storm

Course Distance and References July 14th 1804

N. 70° W 2 m. to a pt. on S.S. pass an Isld Small on S.S. ① a Violent Storm from W.
N. 20° W 2 m. to a pt on L.S. wind from N.W. by W.
N. 30° W 1 m. on the L.S.
N. 50° W 2½ m. to the Lower point of an Island
N. 87 W ½ to a second point of the same Island on Lad side of the Same
9   a little above
at the lower point of this island a creek falls in on the Stard
called by the Maha Neesh-nah-ba-to-na, this is a considerable
creek is as large as the nine river, and runs parallel with
the Missouri through with the greater portion of its course

July the 14th Satturday Some hard Showrs of rains accompanied with
Some wind detained us untill about 7 oʻclock, we then Set out and
proceeded on about a mile & the atmesphere became Suddenly
& dismal looking, we were in a tituation, near the upper points of a Sd Isd & the old Shore falling
in, this tituation a violent Storm of Wind from the N.E (passing over our Cuss
plain, Struck the boat nearly Harbord quatering, & blowing
down the Current) the exertions of all our men who were out
in an instant aded to the a Strong Cable and anchor was scarsely
sufficient to keep the boat from being throwe up on the Sand
Island, the Wave dashed over on the Side next to

the wind the lodgins which was covered with Tarpoling prevented the
until the boat was Creoned on the side from the wind
in this Situation we continued about 40 Minuts, the two piroques
about a quarter of a mile above, one of them in a similar situa
tion with the Boat, the other under the Charge of George Gibson
in a much better position, with her Stern faceing the wind, this
Storm Suddenly Seased, & 1 Minit the river was as Smooth as
glass, the wind Shifted to the S.E and we Set Sail, and proced
ed or passed ① an a Small Island on the S.S. and Dined — the
R: Fields who has Charge of the horses &c. on Shore did not join
us last night—. passed a old fort Where Mr. Bennet of St. Louis wal
lered 2 years & traded with the Ottoaws & Pawnies on the S.S. 1 Md. above the
little Island, I went out on the L.S. and observed two Elk on a
Sand in the river, in attempting to get near them elk observed on
near us I shot one. continued on Shore & this the bottom which
was extensive, Some Small Prarees, and a portion of high rich &
well timbered bottom, in the Glades I Saw wild Temothy lams quarter
Cuckle bur & rich Weed, on the edge Pleumbs of different kinds
Grapes, and Goose beries, Camped on the L.S. Ruben Fields & Gutrick
Joined the Party two men unwell, one a Felon on his finger, Severel falls

Course Distance and Refferinus July 15th 1804
N. 30. W. 3½ M.t to a a p.t of a willow Isl.d on the L.S. p.d. the Isl.d on S.S. ①
S. 75. W. ¼ Miles to a Sand point of the Same Island the Boat passed to Lard of Isl.
N. 84. W. ¼ The hills here projects to the river
N. 84. W. ¼ to a Lard pt. on the same island — the hills here leave the river
N. 88 W. ¼ to a point on Lard main shore opposite a Sand bar, took meed. Alt. O
Due. W. 1½ Mile to a pt. Stard. oposite which the hills again touch the river
N. 45 W ½ Mile to the mouth of Little Ne ma har on the Lard in a bend
oposit the lower point at a large Sand bar —
N. 30 E 1½ to a point on Lard. a deep bend to the right below this point
N. 30. W. ¾ to pt. Lard. Due E. from this about three miles is a large Pond
N. 15. ¾ to pt. of an Island.

July 15th Sunday 1804. a heavy fog this morning which Delaned
us untill 7 oClock, put Drewyer & Sgt. Floyd on Shore at I took two
men and went on Shore, with a view to kill Some elk, passed
this open plains, and baroney lands, Crosed three butifull Small
Streams of Water, Saw great quantity of Cherries Plums, Grapes
& Berries of Deff.t Kinds, the lands Jenerally of a good quality, on
the Streams the wood Grows Escapes the fire, at about 7 Miles I
Struck the river at the Mouth Ne ma har Creek about 40 ys
Wide, near this Creek on a high part of the Prarie I had a
Extensive View of the river & Country on both Sides on S. a low
continuation of the plain as far as I could See on the S.S. a bottom Prarie
& about 5 Ms wide & lower hilly back of this Prarie

July 16 to 19

Doc No 31

July 16th 1804 Monday Set out verry early and proceed on the Side of a Prairie pass'd the head of the Island opp'. which we Camped last night, (1) passed a Small Willow Island off the L. point, hills make near the river (2) passed a large Island on the nearest the L. S. below the p't a Small willow I'd. also one on the S. S. this large Island is Called Fair Sun the wind favourable from the South. Boat run on a Sawyer; (3) pass a place on the L. S. where at 70 acrr the hill has Sliped into the river lately Just above passed under a cliff of Sand Stone L. S. a Number of Bird Nests in the holes & crevins of this rock which Continues 2 miles. (5) passed a willow Island in a Deep bend to the S. S. river 2 mile wide at this place, not Deed Snags across passed the Lower point of a Island Called Isle Chauvin Situated on the L. Point oppost an extensive Prarie on the S. S. this prarie I call Bald pated Prarie from the range bald hills, at from 3 to 6 miles from the river, as far as my Sight will extend, we Camped in a point of wood S. Sd the L'd. or S. S. in a bend.

Course Distance & Differences July 16th 1804.

1 N. 70° W. ½ M'. to a point on the Left of the Island, opp'. to which we Camped last
2 S. 35. W. 1½ M'. to a Bend to the L. S. in a prarie opp'. the head of the Island
3 N. 30 E. 1 M'. to the lower point of a willow Isle off L. P'. (1)
4 N. 40 W. ¾ M'. up the S. Willow Island. the high lands near the river L. S.
5 N. 30 W. 2 M's. to a p'. S'd. of Sml. I'd. on S. S. p'd. a p't on the L. S. at 70 p'd. the Smale L. I.
6 N. 35 W. ¾ M'. to a L. S. of a Small willow Island, in the p'. of the large I'd. p'd. a Small willow I'd. (3)
7 N. 15 E. 1½ M'. to the lower p't. of a I'd. Called Good Sun p'd. a Smale p't. at the Low point (2)
8 N. 15 W. ¾ M'. to the S. Side of the Island, high land, 3¼ of a M'. or L'd. S. land.
9 S. 38 W. ¾ To a p'. on the left Side of the I'd. p'd. on a Sand. I'd. p'd. on L. S.
10 N. 54 W. ¾ To Lower p'. of a San'd. Will'r. I'd. on the Side of the large I'd.
11 N. 38 W. ¾ To a p't. on L. S. p'd. is the Saird Island
12 N. 52 W. ¼ To a p't. of the Island high land below or near the L'd. 40-30-12 N
13 N. 50 W. ¼ To a p't. on L. S. above the head of the Island high land at this place (4)
14 N. 58 W. 2 miles To a p't on the S. S. South on the S. Point ¼ M'. wind from S. perp'. D'. B. Cape of Sand Stone on L. S.
15 N. 40 E. 6 mile to a p't. of wood on the L. Side Some high Bald hills at about 4 or 5 miles from the river Prarie on L. Side &
20 on the S. S. pass'd a Sand bar from the S. S. a willow Island in S. bend, Camped in the upper point of a wood, in a prarie

July 17th Tuesday, we concluded to lay by to day to fix the Longitude, and get the Cromometer right (she run down day before yesterday) Several men out hunting to day Cap't. Lewis rode out to Neesh-nah-ba-to na Creek which passes thro' the Prarie (on which there is but fiew trees) within Mile of the Missouries, being from the S E. Several of the party have tumors of different kinds Some of which is verry troublesom I took a meridian altitude (43. 27') which made the Lattitude of this place 40-27-6 ⁴⁄₁₀ North. — (The Bald Hills bear N 25° W for 30 M'. The bend on S. S. passing the L'd. on the Right Side is N. 28° W. 4 M'. Took equal altitude 7-50-3 Took Suns azimuth with Compss. Cro'. Ledd'. & time 1 st. 5 h-53-10 Ⓐ "-15-28 } A M Cap't Lewis returned Saw Some obs'd on Spica* Star West "-52-55 hand'om Country, the Creek near Q. Tim Distance altitude 4-4-38 the high land is rapid and nearly 8-53-11——41-50-00 28-51-45 "-6-3 } P M as muddy as the river, & reising "-59-0——41-53-15 azimuth "-7-24 Couldte two verry fat Cat fish 9-2-58——41-54-0 N 85° W alt. 69-36-00 G Drewyer Kill'd 3 Der. & R Fields "-5-49——41-55-0 one a keep of wind broughte Swarm "-8-2——41-56-0 2d a Tim True a pass of the of Musquitors, which disapeard in two hours, blown off by a Continuation "-15-24——41-57-0 5-59-20 Cour. p'. of the Chron "-21-10——41-58-0 altitude in 40 Seconds the of the Same bree. "-25-18——42-0-0 26-35-90 water run 50 fathom Compd. as 30" x 20" in plains N. 84° W.

(continued overleaf)

alt.d North Star
Time 10-23-18 — 61°-9'-15" July 17

Chronometer too Slow 6-51 E to Sun

July 18th Wednesday a fair morning the river falling fast, set out at Sunrise under a gentle Breeze from S.E by S. at 3 miles passed the head of the Island on L.S. Called by the French Chauttes Opp.e the middle of the Island the Creek on S.S. is within 300 yd. of the back of this Island the lower point of another Island in the bend to the L.S. passed large Sand bar making out from each point with many channels passing through them, "Current runs 50 fathom in 41 Second" but little timber on either side of the river, except the Isd & points which are low wet & Covered with lofty trees, Cotton wood Mulberry Elm &c &. passed the head of a long Island in high water at this time no water passes this the Channel 3 opposite the Lower point of a Island on the S.S. pass the Island and opp.e the point 4 above & on the L.S. the hills Come to the river, This Hill has Sloped into the river for about ¾ of a mile, and leaves a Bluff of considerable height back of it this Hill is about 200 foot high composed of Sand Stone inter mingled with Iron ore of an inferior quality on lits of Soft Slate Stone

Course Distance & Referen. July 18th 1804.

N. 28° W. 3½ Ml. to Curve in the bend to the S.S. passing the Bend of a Island on L.S. the Creek near 1

S 28° W. 3½ Ml. to a pt. on the S.S. ps the head of the Island on the L.S. ow behind this 2

S 32° W. — ½ Ml. on S.S. passed a Sand bar, a long Island on the L.S. in high water

S 88 W. — ¼ Ml. on do a Sand bar to the left Wind from the S.W. h a a

S 55 W. — ¼ Ml. on do Sand bar do

N. 48 W. 2½ Ml. to a pt. on L.S. ps. a Sand bar L S water runs out to form the bd

N 64 W 2½ Ml. to a pt. on S.S. passed the head of the Island 2 and lower pt. of a Is. S.S. 3

N 50 W 5 ... Ms. to a pt. on S.S. opp. a red bank on L.S. Iron ore 4

N 3 E 1½ W. to a pt. on L.S. ops. a Small Island in the Middle of the river Camped 5 on the L.S.

we passed a very bad Sand bank a little above the hill and near appost a Small Island in the river, Saw a Dog this evening appeared to be nearly Starved to death, he Must have been left by Some party of hunters we gave him Some meat he would not Come near us Drewer brought in 2 Deer this evening

of no Consequence July 19th what was on a rooted ribs of a Deer a little and a little Coffee Walked on Shore intending only to keep up with the Boat, Soon after got on Shore, Saw Som fresh elk Sign which induced I was to know how numerals by their tract to the hills after ascending and passing thro a narrow Strip of wood Came Suddenly into an open and boundless Prairie boundless because I could not See the extent of the plain in any Direction, the timber appeared to be confined to the River & Small Creek branches, this Prairie was Covered with grass about 18 Inches or 2 feet high and Contained little of any thing else, except as before mentioned on the River Creek &c. this prospect was So Sudden & intertaining that I forgot the Object of my prosute and turned my attention to the variety which presented themselves to my view after Continueing on this rise for Som minits, I determined to make my Course to a line of woods to S.E. I found in this wood a beatiful Stream of running water, in proseing it down Several other joined it and at 3 miles fell into the river between 2 Cliffts, I went up & under one cliff of bark red Clay for ½ Ml. above this a Clay bank which had Sliped in her I found Sand Stone Containing Iron ore, this ore appear to be imbeded under the Clay but above the water

July 19th Thursday 1804   July 19 to 21

Set out early pass between 2 Islands one in Mid: & the other L.S.
Course Distance & reffur {opsd. when Prarie aproaches the river L.S.
this place is called the Bakers oven or
in french Four se tour des hass. Some

North ¼ Mo to the Lowest. of a Isd on L.S. Called Bakers oven ①
N. 10° W. 1¼ Mo to a pt. on the L.S. bad Sand bars pd. the 23d. ⊙
N. 45° W. 1¼ Me on the L. side Sand bar on L.S.
N. 35° W. 2 Mo S.S. opd. high land ② a Sand bar on the S. Side in a bend
N. 82 W. ¾ Mo to the mouth of a creek in a bend on L side above a Clift
N. 13 W 2½ Mo to Pt. L.S. Psd a Sloped in bank ③ a Do. on the S.S. a un'd S
N. 51 W 3 Mo to pt. a S.S. opd. som Clift, passed a willow Isld in Mid a Dup
      10¾ L. end to the L.S. a large Sand bar on the S.S. ④

high lands 4½ pd. above the Isds on the L.S. forming a Clift to the
river of yellow earth, on the top a Prarie, passd. many a bad
Sand bar in this distance, & the river wide & Shallow, above
this Clift 2 Smale bulf of ull runs Come from the Plains
& fall into the river, a Dee lick on the first, above
those two creeks, I found in my walk on Shore Som
Iron ore in a bank which had Slihea in to the river
about ¾ Me above the Creeks, I took a circquit
around & found that those two runs mentioned
Contained a good proportion of wood, bar and cd
by a Plain, with grass about 18 Inch. high, Capt Lewis
walked on Shore after Dinner in the first bend to the
right above those Runs passed a Smale Island Isd. of a
Sand bar I call this Island Butter Island, as at this place
we mad use of the last of our butter, as we approach
this great river Platt the Sand bars are much more
noumerous then they were, and the quick & roling
Sands much more Dangerous when the Prarie aproach
the river it is verry wide, the banks of those Plains being
much come to undermine it and fall then the wood
land passed ④ a willow Island Siturated near the middle of
the river a Sand bar on the S.S. and a Dep bend to the L.S.
camped on the right Side of the willow Island – W Braller hunting on the L.S.
Swam to the Island. Drewer Hunter Killed 2 Deer, Saw great
number of young Gees. the river Stele falling
a little Sand bars think always in view.

(continued overleaf)

Course Distance & reffr July 20th 1804

N. 18° E 3 M. to a Pt. L.S. psd. a willow Island on S.S. a Creek on L.S. ①
* took R. Fields with me and went up this Creek several
miles & Crossed thro the plains to the river above
with the view of finding Elk, we walked all day thro
those prairs without seeing any, I killed an emence
large yellow wolf — The Countrey throo which we
walked after leaveing the creek was good land covered
with Grass enterspersed with Groves & Scattering timber
near and about the head of Branches

July 20th Friday 1804, a fog this morning and very Cool George
Drewyer who proceed on over a Sand bar Bratten Ds on the river
to get his gun & Clothes left last night psd a large willow Is
on the S.S. ① feaped the mouth of l'Eau que pleure the Inglish
of what is the water which Crys this Creek is about 20 yards
wide falls into the river above a Cliff of brown Clay L.S.
oppost a willow Island, at this Creek I went on Chow *

N. 48 W __ M. to pt. Sand oposit to a deep bend and prarie
on the Star. oposite this Pt. to the right of it is the
upper point of a small Is. with a large sand bar
below it the Is. is seperated by a narrow chal from S.S.
N. 48 E. 2½ M. to a pt. on St. side of an Island. oposite the upper pt.
of a 2d Island which isdevided from it by a narrow
Channel — deep bend to S. side of this small
Island

N. 5 W 3m. to a Sand. point of an Is.
Due N. 6 M. to the point of an Isld. on Sand. side of the same.
N. 18 W 3½ M. to a Point on L.S. high land psd the Is. of Isld
a large Sand bar on the L.S. on which there
was two Swans, Capt Lewis tried to kill
one of them without Success, Camped above the
bar on the L.S. a verry agueable Breeze all
night Sergt. Pryor & Jo. Fields brought in two Deer
river Still falling. a large Spring ¾ M. below Camp

July 21 to 22   Doc No 33

July 21st Saturday, set out verry early and a gentle
Breeze from the S.E proceeded on verry well, passed a Willow
Island L.S. opsd. a bad sand bar passed some high land covered
with timber, in this Hill is semented rock & Lime stone
the water runs out and forms several little Islands in
high water on the S.S. a large Sand bar on the S.S. above
and opposit the wood & high Land, at about 7 oClock the wind
Leased and it Commenced raining passed Many Sand bars
opposit or in the mouth of the Great River Plate this river
which is much more rapid than the Missouri has throws
out imence quantities of Sand forming large Sand Banks
at its mouth and forces the Missouri close under the
S.S. the Sands of this River Comes roleing down with the
Current which is Crouded with Sand bars and not of
water at any place across its mouth, the Rapid of
the Current of this river which is greater than that
of the Missouri, its Width at the mouth across the bars
is about ¾ of a mile, higher up I am told by one of the
bowmen that he was 2 winters on this river above and that
it does not rise four feet, but Spred over 3 miles at Some
places, Cap Lewis & my self went up Some distance & Crossed
found it shallow. this water is not so muddy as the Missouri

Course Distance & References July 21st 1804

N. 22° W. 3½ M.s to pt S.S. opposit a point of high land on the L.S.
N. 28° W. 6½ M.s to a pt on S.S. ptd. pt. of willows a Willow Isd. on Lt a high pt.
N. 39° W. 3 miles to a pt on S.S. Small Channel
    13) a sand sand bar near the S.S. a large sand bar
N. 8° W. 2 M.s to a pont L.S. the Junction of Mesr & Plate Rivers
    15) a verry extensive vew of the river pass many sand
         bars in every direction thrown out by the Plate R. wind East
N. 10° W. 4 M.s the Same Course Continued up the Missouri to a Pt. L.S
    19) miles passed a Sand bar on the S.S. wind N.

Proceeded on passed the mouth of Papellion or Butterfly Creek 3 miles on the L.S.
a large sand bar opposit on that Side Camped above this bar on L.S great
number of waters about us all nite R. Fields killed a Deer hard wind N.W. Cold

(continued overleaf)

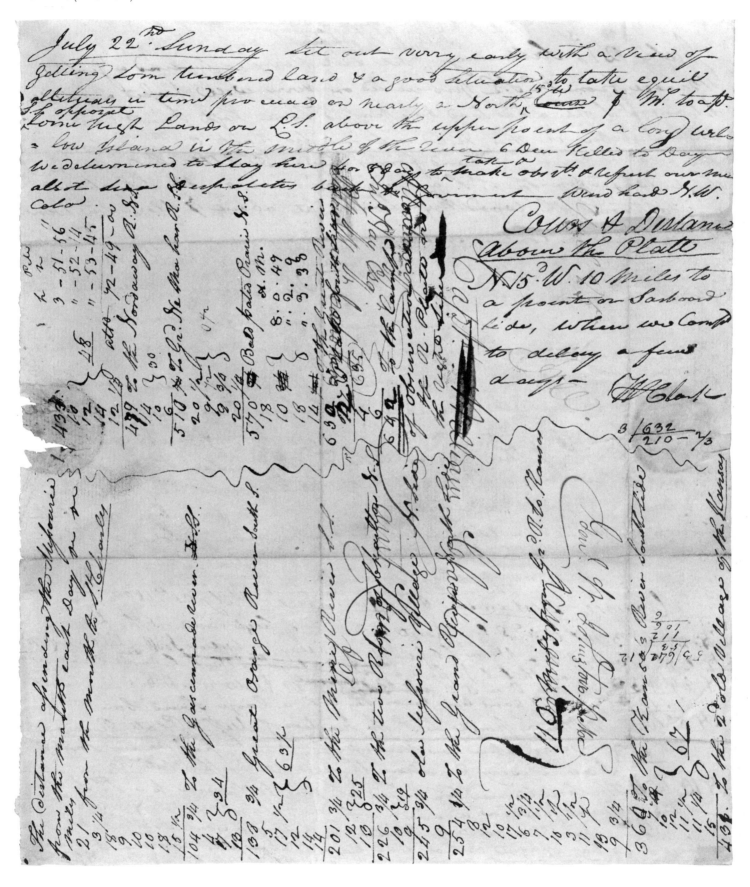

Preperation for Lunar Calculation.

Feb^{ry} 23^d. 1805 Fort mandan.

Latitude of the place of observation ———— 47°. 21'. 47".

Time by Chronometer of Obs^t. A.M. 6. 23. 45.

Chronometer too slow Apt. T at noon 2. 14. 25. 7

True time of observ^t. as shewn by the Chro^{tr}. A.M. 8 . 38 . 10 . 7

True apparent time of observation ~~reduced~~ A.M.
as deduced from Mean Time by the application of
the Equation of time with its sighn changed — 8 . 38 . 18 .

Distance of ☉^s and ☽^s nearest limbs at the time
of this observation . ☉ East ———— 66°. 20'. 31". 7

Estimated Greenwich time of the Observation —15. 15. 57. 7

☉^s Declination corrisponding with the Greenwich
time of this observation ———— 9°. 52'. 6". 8 South

True mean time of Observation at the place A.M. —8. 51. 59. 5

Hour ∠ of the A. M. observation ———— 50°. 25'. 3".

Attitude of the ☉^s Center at time of observ^t.
by M^r. Elicot's formula ———— 17°. 24'. 00"

By M^r. Patterson's Alt^d. ☉^s Center at time of
observation 18°. 30'. 56".

by a boiling motion or ebolition of it's waters occasioned no doubt
by the roling and irregular motion of the sand it
be of which it's bed is entirely composed. this sand ~~is driven in~~
the particles of
~~large bodies~~ being remarkably small and light it is easily boed
up ~~and and by the water~~ and is hurried by this impetuous ~~cou~~
in large
torrent. ~~sometimes~~ from place to place in
~~that in~~ large maßes with irristable force, collecting and
which
forming sand bars in the course of a few ~~hours~~ ~~and~~
as suddingly ~~disapated~~ ~~them~~ to form others ~~an~~ and give
perhaps to the
place ~~to the deepest~~ channel of the river. ~~where~~ it enters
changed and
the Mißouri it's ~~its~~ superior force ~~drives the~~ directs the
courant of that river against it's northern bank where it
a channel
is compreßed within ~~leß than~~ one third of the width it
had just
~~just~~ before occupyed. ~~and~~ it does not ~~then~~ furnish the
mißouri with it's colouring matter as has been aserted
by some, but it throws into it immense quantities of
courant of
sand and gives a celerity to it's ~~of~~ which it abates but
little untill it's junction with the Mißißippy. the
water of this river is turbid at all seasons of the year
is
but ~~its~~ by no means as much so as that of the Mißou
=ri. the sediment it deposits, consists of very fine particles
of white sand while that of the Mißoury is composed prin=
=cipally of a ~~dark~~ rich loam ——— in much greater quantity.

21st July.
* ~~we~~ made ~~many~~ ~~experiments to determin the~~ ~~velocity of the courent~~
~~of the Mißou in different parts~~ from the experi~~m~~ents and observations
with respect to
we were enabled to make ~~of~~ the comparitive velocities of the cou=
=rents of the rivers Missouri Mißißippi Mißouri and Plat ~~to~~
~~the following result is~~ it results that a veßel will float in
the Mißißippi ~~about~~ below the ~~mouthe~~ entrance of the Mißouri
at the rate of four miles an hour. in the Mißouri from ~~the~~
it's junction ~~with~~ with the Mißißippi to the ~~entrance~~ of the
6
Osage river from 5½ to ~~5½~~ from thence to the mouth of the Kanzas
from 6½ to 7. from thence to the Platte 5½ while the Plat ~~may~~
~~safely~~ is at least 8. —— The Mißouri above the junction
of the river plat is equal to about 3½ miles an hour as far as the
mouth of the Chyenne when it's courant ~~still~~ abates ~~to about~~
~~3 miles an hour~~ and becomes equal to about three miles an hour
from information it does not increase it's velocity for

The Lattitude of River Dubois 38°.55'.19".⁶⁄₁₀ N. and Longd. 89°.57.45" W of Greenwh.

The do — of the gasconade River 38°.44.35" N. & Longd about 91°.16.00 W.

The do of the Great Osage River 38°.31.6" N. & Longd. about 91°.38. W.

The do of the Mouth of Kanzes 39°.5'.25" North

The do of Nordaway River — 39.55.56. do

The do of the Bald pated Prarie 40.27.6. do

The do of Camp above River Platte — 41.3.19. N.

22ᵗᵈ of July 1804 Compleatly arranged our Camp, posted two Sentinals so as to compleatily guard the Camp, form bowers for the men &c. & Course from R. Platte N15°. W. 10 M.

Camp 10 M. above the river Platte Monday July the 23ᵈ —

a fair morning — Sent out a party of 5 men to took to timber for Oars, two other parties to hunt at Noflock Sent, G. Drewyer & Pete. Cruzett. & Ind.: to the Ottoaws Village about 18 M. West of our Camp, to invite the Chiefs & principal men of that nation to Come & talk with us &c., also the pawnes if they should meet with any of that nation(also on the S. Side of the Platte 30 M. higher up (at this Season of the year all the Indians in this quarter are in the Plains hunting the Buffalow from Some Sign Seen by our hunters and the Prarie being on fire in the directions of the Village induce a belief of that the nation have returned to get green Corn) raised a flag staff put out Some provisions which got wet in the french Perogue to Sun & Dry — I commenced Coppying my Maps of the River to Send to the Presd. of U.S. by the return of a party of Soldiers, from Illinois five Deer killed — one man a bad verey on his left breast. Wind from the N.W.

Equal altitudes taken at this place the two following Days Viz:

		h m s		h m s			h m s
July 22. Sunday	A.M.	8. 50. 53	P.M.	2. 58. 37	July 26.	A.M.	7. 33. 32
		". 55. 20		3. 0. 0			". 34. 55
		". 56. 48		3. 1. 28			". 36. 22
						P.M.	4. 15. 22
							". 16. 51
							". 18. 14

Given altitude 92.37'.0"

(continued overleaf)

July 22. to 27

34

White Cat fish Camp 24th of July Tuesday. a fair morning
the wind rose with the Sun & blew hard from the S. those
Southerly Brieses are Dry Cool & refreshing. the Northerly Breizes which
is more frequent is much Cooler, and moist. I continue my
Drawing. Cap Lewis also ingaged prepareing Som paper to Send
back, one of the men Cought a White Cat fish, the eyes
Small, & Pale resembling that of a Dolfin.

White Cat fish Camp 25th of July Wednesday. Several
Hunters Sent out. at 2 oclock the two men Sent to
the Ottoes of Village returned and informed that no
Indians were at the Town & they saw Som fresh
Sign near that place which they persued, but Could not
find them, they haveing taken precautions to Conceal the
rout which they went out from the Village – the Ind.
of the Missouris being at war with one & the other or other
Indians, move in large bodies and Some times the whole
nation Continue to Camp together on their hunting plS.

Those men inform that they passed thro a open Plain
all the way to the Town a few Trees excepted on the
water Courses – they Cross the Papillion or the Butterfly Creek
within a few miles of Camp and near the Village a hands-
river of 100 yards wide Called the Corne de Cherf or the Elkhorn, which mouths below the Town in the Platte N-side.
Wind from the S.E. 2 Der & a Turkey killed to Day Several
Grous Seen in the Prarie

White Cat fish Camp 26th of July. Thursday. the wind blew
Verry hard all Day from the South with Clouds of Sand
which incomoded me verry much in my tent, and as I could
not Draw in the Boat was obliged Combat with the Musgtos
under a Shade in the woods – I found the Breast of a man
the Discharge gave him ease &. 5 beaver Cought near Camp –
only 1 Deer killed to day – The Country back from Camp
on the S.S. is a bottom of about 5 Ms wide one half the Dist.
timber, the other high bottom Prarie, the ops. Side a high Hill
about 170 foot rock found also. Timbered back & below a Prarie

27. July to 30   <u>Course Distance and reference</u> July 27ᵗʰ   35

North 1 or miles to a willow point on the L.S.   with river
West. 2   do   to Sand pt. on L.S. opd. a pond L.S.
N. 10. E 3   do   to a point of high Land on the L.S. pass. a lary Sand bar
N. B. W 4   do   to a Pt. on S.S. opposit a hut part of the Prarie
N. 54 E 4½ miles to a Coops of wood in a bend to the L.S. pass. a Pt. on S.S.
___
15   opposit the Commencement of this Course I went
about 200 acres of Land imediately on the river Covered with Mouns
of Diff. hights & shapes. a pond bank & low land all round   a Bayou about
White Catfish   a Bayou about
Camp July 27ᵗʰ Friday, Charged the Boat & Perogues after a sm=
=all Shower of rain, Completed our ores & poles, Crossed over the
tow barm with a view of their going on the S.W. Side of the
Missouri and set out at Half past 1 oClock proceeded on Very
well under a gentle Breeze, pass'd a high Island on the L. Side
just above Camp, this Island is formed by a pond Supplied
by great number of Springs from this hill, this Pond has 2
out lets, & when the river is high the water pass thro the
Pond, pass'd a Sand Island in the 2ᵈ bend to the right. Camped
in a bend to the right L.S. in some wood, I walked on Shore &
killed a Deer. and did not get to the Boat untill after night
a beutifull Breeze from the N.W. the evening which would
have been very agreeable had the musquetors been tolerably
Peaceful but they were raging all night, about the size of
house flees   Cajaux

July 28ᵗʰ Satturday set out this morning early, the wind blew
from the N.W. by N. a Dark Smokey Morning, Some rain at 11
pass'd a Bluff on the S.S. it being the first high land approaches
the river above the Nodaway, a Island and Creek S.S. just above
G. Drewyer Came with a Deer & informs he heard firing to the
S.W. I walked on Shore on the S.S. found Some good Prarie out
from the S.P. The High Lands approach the river 1st bend to left
the party on Shore brought in a Missouri Indian who resides
with the Ottaws, this Indian & 2 others were Hunting in the Prarie
their Camp is about 4 miles off. This Indian informs that his nation

(continued overleaf)

Course Distances & references The 28th of July 1804 Satturday

S. 82° E 1 mile on the L. Side to pt. of a Sand bar L. S.

N. 10° W. ½ m. on the L. S. — high land approaches the river on S. S.

N. 30° W. ½ m. on L. S. — this is the first place the high land has touched
the river above the Nordaway. Nearl 3 m.

N. 77° W 3 m to a point on the L. S. passed a Island & creek on S. S. above Bluff.

N. 68 W 3 m. to a pt. on S. S. pd. the Is. S. passed the old Missouri village L. S.

N. " " ¾ m. the same course continued —

N. 63 ½ W 2 m. to a pt. S. ard. opposite to a small willow island from
10. ¾ which it is divided by a cannel of ____ yards in with

is in the Plains hunting the Buffaloe the party in which he
is encamped is about 20 family Hunting the Elk, We landed on S. S.
below an Island.

                        + Course the 29th July
                    * { North ¾ of a mile on L. S. Isld. ①
                      { N. 88° W. ½ m. to a pt. on L. S. pt. Bowyer R. ②

July 29th Sunday we Sent one Frenchman, Leliberty &
the Indians to the Camp to envite the party to med us at
the next bend of high Land on the L. S. a Dark morning wind
from the W. N. W. rained all last night — Set out at 5 oClock &
proceeded on passed the Islands, oppost this Island on the S. S.
the Creek called Indian Knob Creek which mouths several miles on a Dict
line below, is within 20 feet of the Missouri & about 5 feet higher
— * The 3 Courses of the 29th to come in here
N. 11° E. 3½ miles to an object in the bend Star. Shore. ③

N. 70° W. 2½ miles to a pt. of wood on the L. S. Saw two back eagles

S. 82. W. 2 miles to a point of timber on the L. S. below a Clean High Plain

S. 8 ___ proceeded on ½ a mile & camped on the L. S. —
      ½
Cought three large Cat fish to day very fat one of these nearly white
these Cat are so plenty that they may be Cought in any part of this
River but few fish of any other kind.

④ at the commencement of this course passed much fallen timber
apporently the ravages of a dreadfull haricane which had passed
obliquely across the river from N. W. to S. E. about twelve
months since. many trees were broken off near the ground
the trunks of which were sound and four feet in diameter.

      Willard lost his Gun in Bowyers R. R. Fields Dove & brought it up

Ale the wood Land on this part of the Missouries
appear to be Confined to the Points & Islands
Bowyers River is about presently 25 yd. Wide. Willard
Neal loosing his Gun in this river. two new husk & sword
Roots a Cold Day wind from the N. W. Some rain
the fore part of the Day.

July 30 to Aug. 1st

36

July the 30th Monday set out early & Proceeded on West 3¼ Mls. Pass.d one P.t to the L.S
and on to the S.S. to a Clear open Prarie on the L.S. which is on a rise of about 70 feet
higher than the bottom which is also a prarie covered with high grass Plumb grape vine
& Hazil — both forming a Bluff to the River, the Lower Prarie is above high water mark
at the foot of the riseing ground & below the High Bluff we came to in a grove of
timber and formed a Camp raised a flag Pole, and determined to wait for the Otto
Indians — The White horse which we found below Died last night, after posting
out the Guards &c. & sent out 4 men to hunt I am engaged in   and
drawing off my Course to accompany the map Drawn at White Catfish Camp, Cap.t
Lewis and my self walked in the Prarie on the top of the Bluff and observed the
most butifule prospects imaginable this Prarie is covered with grass about 10. Inch
high, (Land rich) rises about ½ a mile back Something higher. and is a Plain as far
as can be seen, under those high Lands next the river is butifule Bottom in=
-terspursed with Groves of timber, the River may be Seen for a great Distance
both above & below Meandering thro: the Plains between two ranges
of High land which appear to be from 4 to 10 Mls. apart, each bend of the
river forming a point, which Contains tale timber, principally Cotton wood
with Mulberry elm Sycamore & ash & lynn. Fields Killed Brarow or as the
Ponie Call it Cho car tooch, this animale burrows in the ground & feeds on Bugs
and flesh principally the little Dogs of the Prarie also Something of Vegetable kind
his Shape & Size is like that of a Beaver, his head mouth &c. is like a Dog with
its ears Cut off, his tale and hair like that of a Ground hog Something longer
and lighter, his interals like a Hog, his Skin thick & loose white & hair
Short under its belly, of the Species of the Bear, and it has a white Streake
from its nose to its Sholders, the Toe nails of its fore feet which is large is
1. Inch and ¾ qts. long and those of his hind feet which is much Smaller is
¾ long. We have this animale Skined and Stuffed.   J. & R. fields hunted
Som Deer at a Distance and Came in for a horse to bring them in, they have
not returned this evening,   a great number of Swans in a Pond &
to our Camp.   Serj.t Floyd very unwell a bad Cold &c.   Several men with
Bails, Great qts. of Catfish, Caught one Small Beaver alive, Som Turkey &
Geese killed to day.   arms & all things in order.   a fair evening. and took

(continued overleaf)

July 31st Tuesday) a fair Day) 3 hunters out this morning) J. Drewyer killed a verry, fat Buck one Inch fat on the ribs Merdn. altd. Latds. is 41° 18' 0" 5/10 North. R & Jo: Fields returned at 10 oClock. the Killed 3 Deer, and lost the horses, Cought a Small Beaver which is already tain, Several men out hunting the horse without Success. the Ottoes not yet arrived, I complete the Copy of the Course &c. Musquetors verry troublesom

August the 1st 1804 a fair morning, Sent out two men after the horses & one back to examine of the Indians have been there, Beaver Cought last night. the air is Cool and pleasent   Compt. N. 86° E. azmth 68. 47. 15 attd   Equal altitudes. & Magnetic Azmoth
A. M. 7 - 52 - 55   P. m. 3 - 50 - 42
" - 54 - 20   " - 52 - 3
" - 55 47   " - 53 - 31.

Prepared the Pipe of Peace verry flashey. Wind rose at 10 oClock and blowed from the S E

verry pleasent all Day Several men geathering grapes & two men after the horses which strayed the night before back those Grapes produce the Currnt Common in the U.S. the Goose Berry Common in the U.S. two Kind of Honeysukle, the Bush which I have seen in Kentucky, with a pale Pink flower, also one which grow in Clusters about 4 or 5 feet high, bearing a short flour in clusters of the like Colour. the leaves single. 3 Deer to day. I made a saddle of jac Johnnin, &c. all flewer &c a Reven tail to be Cooked and a Desert of Cheries, this being my birth day I order a Saddle of fat Johnnin Venison, and Currents, and Cheries, the Indians not yet arrived. a Cool fine evening Musquetors verry troublesom, the Praire Contain Cheries, apple, Grape, Currents, Rasp berry Goose berries & an Elk killed to day.   and a great variety of Plants & flours not Common to the U.S. this Country

August 2nd 1804 Wind from the S E J. Drewyer returned with the horses & one Doe Elk, three men out Hunting, one Beaver Cought this morning the Country thro which he hoped is like what we see from the Bluff above Camp

at Sunset 6 Chiefs and their waries of the Ottoes, and Missouries, with a french man by the name of Far fonge, we spoke Shook hands and gave them Some Tobacco & Provision, they Sent us water Million Three verry large & fat Bucks killed to day the wind continue hard from the S. E. — the 4 qtr. of one Buck weighed 147 lb 1½ Inch fat on the ribs

August 3rd Friday prepare a Small present for those Indians and hold a Council Delivered a Speech & made 6 Chiefs gave a few presents and, a Smok a Dram, Some Powder & Ball, the man we lost Sent not yet come up, those people express great Satisfaction at the Speech Delivered they are no Orators, beg, our Countenances, Otto, Laye Misson Small at 4 oClock Set out under a gentle Breeze from the S. E proceeded on N. 5° E 5 M Passed a Pt. on the S. S. and round a large Sand bar on the L. S. and Camped above, below a great number of Snags quet across the river, the Musquetors more numerous than I ever Saw them, all in Spirits,   we had Some rough Conversation J. Dr. about boys.

63

The Osage & Kanzies are the same language

The Ottos & Mahars speak many words of the Osarge language

The Ottos, Ayaways, & Missouris speak the same language

The Panis & Ricaries speak the same language also the Loups & repub[lican]

The Mahar, & Poncarar the same Language

The Chcaux, Mandin & Grovanter the same

The Probability is that those different tribes have one
formed 3 Great nations. Viz: the Missouris, Osarge, Kanzis, Ottos,
Mahars, & Poncaros, & ayaways, one nation.

The Panies, Loups, Republicans, Ricaries the 2nd.

The Mandans Chcaux & Grovanters the 3rd.

To tribes of the Sioux all claim the name 4th.

It is possible that the Mandan, Mahar & Poncarar may
have been a distinct nation, as they only speak some
words of the Osage. which have the same signification.

25 Days to St Tafee S of W. cross the head of Arkansas
around the head of Kanzis River 69 – 8621

after Delivering a speech informing those Children of ours of the
change which had taken place, they duty of our Government
to cultivate friendship & good understanding, the method of had
good advise & some directions, we made $1 Great chief to the
who was not present, to whom we addressed the Speech & Sent some
presents or Medels & flag, we made 2 Second chiefs one for
the Missouris & another for the Ottos (those two tribes are nearly equal)
& principal men, to those principal men to
those we gave a small comt. to each man to whom we gave
authority, a person of Br. 2d. Gar. of Paint & a med. or Cont.
a small comt. was delivered for the whole

each chief & principal man delivered a speech acknowledging
their approbation to what they had heard and promised
to pursue the good advice and caution, they were happy to
have new fathers who gave good advice & to be depended on
all Concluded by asking a little Powder & a Drop of Milk.

(continued overleaf)

267

I answered their Speech, gave them 50 balls one Canister of Powder & a Dram — after Capt Lewis Shot his air gun a few times which astonished the nativs, we Set out. rec'd from those people water millions &c.

The Chiefs & Principal men of the Ottoes & Missouris made by L. & W. the 3rd august 1804

Yrs.	Indian Name	Tribe	English Signification
1	Bde-ar-uge-nor —	Ottoe	Little Thief
2	{ Shingo-tongo —	Otto —	Big horse
	{ We tha a —	Missourie	Hospatality
3	{ Shon-Guss-can.	Ottoe —	
	{ Wan-pe-ur —	Miss: —	from this place I am told
	{ Au-ho-ning ga	do —	by Mr Fairfong the interpeter
	{ Baza con joe —	Ottoe —	that it will take a man
	{ au-ho-ne-ga —	Miss —	25 Days to go to St a fee, pass

the heads of Arkansas, round the Kansas heads, across Some mountains from the top of which the City may be Seen the Spaniards have envited those Indeans & the Panis to trade with them & some french & a few indeans are gone from the Panis to that City this Summer —

The Situation of this place which we Call Council Bluff which is handsom elevated a Spot well Calculated for a Trading establishment, the Bank high & leavel on top well Calculated for a fort to command the Country and river the low bottom above high water & will be leavel under the Command of the [...] for deuos to trade in the

[illegible rotated table text in middle of page]

other bend on either Side does the high land touch the river for Some butram &c, as I am told.

Those Bluffs afford good Clay for Brick, a great quantity on the 3 points one Ops. one abov & one below. — the Situation I am informed is, within 1 Days march of the Ottos, & 2 of the Panias, 2 of the Mahars, & 2½ of the Loups Villages, also conv-ment to the roveing Bands of Souis, those people are now at war with each other, an establishment here would bring about peace and be the means of keeping it.

Aug. 3ᵈ Camped on the upper point of a large Sand bar L. S. Musquetors verry bad.
Som place near Conncele Bluff would be the most proper place, for a trading
establishment, for many of the nations, the Ottoes one Day, Ponies 1½ days, to
the Mahar, 2 days, to Loups 2 Days & a half — and Convenient for Some the Republicans
banks of the river

(Aug. 3. to 5)

Course Distance & Refference August 4ᵗʰ Satturday 1804

S. 80° W.	1½ Mᵈ	to an old Trading house on the L. S. passed a Sand pt. Makeing from S. pt. ①
N. 25 W.	2½ Mᵈ	to a Willow pt. on the L. S. passed a a large Sand bar ② psᵈ a Creek on S. S ③
S. 70. W.	1¾ Mᵈ	to a Willow point on S. S. passed many Snags. opsᵈ a Creek of the Ponies L. S.
N. 24 W.	2½ Mᵈ	to a Willow point on L. S. passes a Sand from S. Point
N. 24 W.	3½ Mᵈ	to a Willow pt. on S. S. opsᵈ a Sand Point river verry wide & Shallow
S. 84 E.	3½ Mᵈ	to a point Lᵈ side passing a pot. on Starᵈ Side wind E.
	15	

The high land is Some distance from the river on both side
and at this place is pt. 10 or 12 Mile
apart, the tops of the high land on the S. S. appears
to Contain timber
the willow is low & not so plenty as below.

August 4ᵗʰ at 7 oClock the heavens darkened and a violent wind from the N. W.
Succeeded which lasted about an hour, with a little rain. Set out this morning
early thro a narrow part of the, the whole Channel Confined in Some parts
between the Sand on one Side & the bank on the other (which is washing in)
within 200 yards, this Chand. Crouded with Snags. at 1½ Mi. passed an old
trading house L. S. where one of our Crew passed 2 years P. C. tradeing with the
Mahar, & Ponies. — above 1 Mᵈ. a Creek Coms in opsᵈ a large bad Sand bar this
Creek is the outlett of 3 ponds, which riase their water from the Smaller
Streams running from the hills on the L. S. Great qtl. of Gees, passed
in the next bend L. S. an out let to the Ponca, Buetifule bottom Prarie
on both Side of the river, Pumey Stone is found on the Sides
of the river of various Sizes. Wind a head. Reed the man who went back
to the Camp of last night for his Knife has not Come up this evening we
Camped at the upr on the L. S. at a Beaver house. 1 Buck killed to day.

August 5ᵗʰ Set out early wind from N. E. Great appearance of wind &
rain (I have remarked that I have not heard much thunder in this Country
Lightning is common as in other Countreys) a verry large Snake was killed
to day called the Bull Snake, his Colour Some thing like a rattle Snake
Something lighter — the bends of the river to day is washing
away the banks, haveing nothing to oppose the turbulance of the
water Confined by large Sand points, forceing the Current against
the bends — the Soil of the entire bottom between the high land, being
the mud or ooze of the river at Some former period mixed with Sand & clay
easiely melts and Slips, or washing into the river — Camped on the S. S. — I went a

Course & Distance of aug. 5ᵗʰ Sunday

S. 60 E.	1½	across a large Sand bar to a point on Starbᵈ Shore below a large Willow Island on S. Bend
N. 20 W.	¾ Mᵈ	to a pt. above a Sand bar on the opsᵈ the upper pt. of the Island, (much Beaver Sign)
N. 34 W.	3¾ Mᵈ	to a pt. on the L. S. passed one on the L. S.
North	1 Mᵈ	to a pt. on the middle of a Sand Island, makeing from the L. pt.
S. 45. W.	2¾ Mᵈ	to 3 Small trees in a Bend L. S. passing over a Sand point S. S.
N. 45 W.	4½ Mᵈ	to a point on S. S. the high land Great distance from the river
North	1½	on the L. S. to a pt. of Sand bar. opsᵈ a falling in bank River narrow
N. 70 E.	½	on the S. Sand bar the same continued 4 Miles
S. 30 E.	2 Mᵈ	to the pt. of a Sand bar makeing out from the L. point, psᵈ a Sand in the Mᵈ
N. 45 E.	2½	to the lower point of an Island close to Starbᵈ Shore it behind
	20½	this Island on the Starbᵈ Side that the Olivers river disimbogues itself

(continued overleaf)

on Shore L.S. the morning Saw Some turkeys and in pursuing them Struck the river 12 miles below the place, I went out, I think the Vermon is about 370 yards across Subject to overflow, & runs into numerous Channels, Great quantities of Grapes ripe & of three different kind Some large & fine. I Killed a Turkey, and made Camp in the night, Mesquetors verry troublesom — Reed the man who went back for his Knife has not yet joined us —

August 6th Monday 1804 at 12 oclock last night a violent Storm of wind & rain from the N.W. our Perogue (Bapteist le jones Patroon) lost her colours Set out early & proceded on passed a large Island on the S.S. back of this Island River de Soldier Comes in on the S.S. — The Soldiers River is about the Size of Nodaway, Says Cane at the mouth in passing two remarkable places, where the river is a done —

we have every reason to believe that one man Desekled Moses B. Reed he has been absent three Days and one french man we Sent to the Indian Camps has not joined us, we have reasons to believe he lost himself in attempting to join us at the Council Bluff — we are determined to Send back 4 men to take Reed Dead or alive, also hunt La Liberty and to meet us at the Maha nation as soon as the can is excuted.

Corse Distance reference. 6th Augt. Monday 1804

N. 31° E. 1 mile to a pt. on the L.S. the Island opposet and also opposet Soldier's River
N. 15 E. 3½ M. to pt. in a bend below
West 1 mile to a pt. of wood above a large Sand bar making out from the L. Point
West 1½ M. to a pt. on L.S. Willows
S. 55 W. 3½ M. to a pt. of Willows on the S.S. the land naked & within 3 ms. of the R. L.
N. 10 W. to on the L. pt. a Sand bar in the middle
N. 14 E. 3 miles passing over a Sand bar on L.S. to the north Side.
North 1½ M. to a pt. on the S.S.
N. 14 W. ½ on the Sand bar from the pt.
East 3½ to a pt. Willows making from the L. point pt. a place of Snags
N. E. 1½ M. to a pt. on the S.S. an old bed of the River S.S.
20½ but fiew Snakes on this part of the river

August 7th Tuesday last night about 8 oclock a Storm of wind from the N.W. which lasted ¾ of an hour mosquetors more troublesom last night than I ever Saw them, Set out late this morning wind N.

North 2 ms. to a pt. of Willows on the L.S. opposit, Saw 10 Pelicans flying
N. 25 W. ½ M. on the L. point N. 45 W. ½ M. on the L. point of a Sand bar
N. 45 W. 1 M. to the point of a Sand bar making out from the L. pt.
S. 12 W. 2½ M. to the do. do. from the St. Point Wind fair —
S. 70 E. ½ M. to the Willows on the S.S. G Drewyer R. Fields, W. Bratten & Wm. Labiesie
Sent after Reed Deserted, La Liberty absent & a Speech to the ollow with a view
to get a fiew of their Chief to the Maha to make a peace between
them, Sent Some Tobacco Wampon, and Sheek als & pointed
order to the party in writing

N. 36 W. 2½ M. to a pt. of Willows on the L.S. a large Sand making out from it
N. 72 W. 3 M. to a pt. of willows S.S. I went out and discovered that two Bayaus
run thro the point & Cut it into Island, which Scate Detachment Island
from this bend we detached Drewyer, R. Fields, Bratten & Labuen
N. 83° E. 2½ M. to a pt. of Cotton wood passing over a Sand bar from the Said point
N. 32 W. ½ M. to a Sand point making out from the S. point
N. 12 E. ½ M. to the willows on the S.S. and Camped

38

Course Distance & refferens August the 8th Wednesday 1804

N. 20° E 2 miles to the pt. of a Sand Isld. from the S.S. the river narrow & Choked up with Snags

S. 50 E 2 mls. to a pt. of willows on the L.S. killed a Pelican

East ½ mile on the side of Sand Island from the L. pt.

North 1½ ml. to the mouth of little River de Cucour. S.S.

N. 70° W. 2 ml. to the Lower point of an Island on the no water

N. 20 W. 1 ml. to a pt. on the right Side of the Island

N. 52 W. 7 ml. to a pt. of high wood in a bend to the L.S. pased the Isd at ⅛ of a ml.
on the point of which was great number of Pelicans &c

10 Wide & Shoal, Capt Lewis took Med. altd.

	Half altitude or 0° below
	Little S. view or S.S.
	8 – 26 – 50
	8 – 23 – 29
	8 – 30 – 8
	altitude
③	80 – 14 – 15 1½ ml. below Little R. de Cour

I walked on Shore with one man Collens, — the bottoms Covrd with very
Collen killed an elk, I fired 4 times at one & have reasons to think I killed
high wees could not find him, the Musquetors were So troublesom
and thick in the Plains that I could not Keep them out of
my eyes, with a bush. in my absens Capt Lewis killed a Pelican
on Pelican Island, at which plan many hundred had collected, they
hold 3 pints which was fresh and very good, we camped on the S.S.

August the 8th 1804 Set out this morning at the usual time at
about 2 miles ① pased a part of the river So Choked up with Snags
that we found a little difficult to get this with Safty, the wind
as usual from the N.W. one of the Soldiers killed a Pelican on the Sand S.
pased the mouth of Little ② River de Cucoux on the S.S. this river is about
80 yards wide & navagable for Pirogues Some distance & runs parrelel
to the Missourie it Coms in from the River from the N E, it Contains great
Quantitys of fish Common to the Country. two miles above is ③ an Island
the Channel formerly run on the right but that Side is now filled
Hundreds of Pelicans on this Island — we calle it Pelican Isd. Capt Lewis killed one
with Sand. — This river Sous Called by the Sueoux Ea-neah Wau-de-pon is Stone R
heads in thre Leagues of the river Demoin, and passes thro a Lake about 20 Leagues
in Surf. which is also within 5 Leagues of the Demoin, this lake at one place
is confined by two rocks within a narrow Span — this Lake of different
widths, with many small Islands, from the Lake to the Mahas about
Le Soux
4 days march
dureels distant, to the Dog Plains 90 Leagus, one Principal branch of the Demoin is called
Cat river, the Lake which this river heads in is Called Despree
Capt Lewis took Merd. altitude and made the Lattetude 41 – 42 – 34 3⁄10 North.
altd of Sun 0 – 56 – 9 – 00 —

Course Distance & refferens the 9th of August Thursday

N. 30° E 2½ ml. to the pt. of a Sand bar on the L. Side Wind fair

N. 32° W. 1 ml. to the pt. of High woods on the L. Side

N. 22° W. 2½ ml. to a Pt. of high woods on S.S. — a large Sand bar makeing out from it

N. 15° W. 2 ml. to a pt. of High land, opps. to which the River latterly runs, & a circuit
of 5 Leagues has been Cut off, the old Channel is Ponds & Isds.

N. 15 W. 2 ml. across a large Sand bar to a point of woods on Lard. Shore, there is
opposite to the cut off point 6 Leagues around.

N. 46. W. 1½ ml. to willow point on Stard. Side.

N. 35° W. 55 the river now came gradualy arround to the E. of north no point offering

N. 6° E. 2½ miles, to a willow point on Lard. Side. —

N. 44. W. 3¼ Miles to point Stard. Shore.

N. about ¼ to Hd of Sand bar.

2½
3¼
5
11¼
12¼

(continued overleaf)

Aug 9 10 & 11

9th Augt. Thursday 1804 The fog of this morning detained us entill a
bout 7 oclock at which time we left our mooring and proceeded on
under a gentle Breeze from the S.E. I went on Shore found the Land the Same
as yesterday Killed a Turkey. and camped on the L.S. Great deal of Beaver
Sign to day on Beaver Creek Musquetors worst this evening than ever I have Seen them

August 10th
Course Distance and remarks 10th of August 1804 Friday .   10 3/2

N. 60° W. 2 mr. to a pt. of Sand making from the L. point
S. 50° W. 1/2 mr. on the to a Drift wood This place is called Coupe a Jarche a Maw
South 18 E. 2 1/2 mr. to a place where the river Cut through and Shortend the River 12 mr.
       Some Small willows on the S.S. passd. then the High land on L.S. in this bend 1
S. 20° W. 2 1/2 mr. to a Burt Stump on the the Bank in the bend to L.S. at which place
I was yesterday at this place within 3/4 of a mile & round the bend, 13 mr.
West 3 1/2 mr. to two Cotton wood trees at the Mouth of a Small Creek in a bend
       to the L. S. near the high land a Cliff 1 mr. above.
N. 40° W. 1 1/2 mr. to a Cliff of yellow Sant Stone on the L.S this is the first high land which
N. 52° W. 1 1/2 mr. to the pt. of a Sand bar from the S. point passed the Cliff on L.S.
N. 79° E 3 mr. to a pt. of Small willow on the L.S. passing the high timber on S.S. at 1 mr.
N. 29° E 1/2 of a mile on the L. point, the boat run on a log & detained us to Mendey
North 1 mr. to the pt. of a Sand bar makeing out from the L. point
N. 68° W. 3/4 mr. on the L. point a Sand bar makeing out from this Course .
N. 85° W. 2 1/2 mr. to the Lower point of a willow Island off the S. point - Black bird the
       late King of the Mahaus Toom or intoud Grave on the top of a high round Hill
22 1/2   of about 300 feet in the Prarie L.S. bow West about 7 miles. (Musquitors bad)

August 11th Satturday 1804 about day this morning a hard
wind from the NW. followed by rain, we landed at the foot of the hile on which
Black Bird the late King of the mahar who died 4 years ago & 400 of the nation with the Small pox
was buried and went up and fixed a white flag bound with
Blue White & Read *   [Course & Dist Aug 11th]   wind N.W
S. 52° W. 1/2 mr. on the Sand point S.S. of the Sand Island
N. 25 W. 2 mr. to a pt. of low willows from a L.W. passing over a Sand bar from the S. pt. po. the S.
       opposite the high land which the Maha King was buried Cap
N. 72 W. 2 1/4 mr. to a pt. Louis and myself being up a wind & rain Struck is fried
N. 24 W. 1/2 mr. on the Side of the willows S.S. a Sand bar passed a Creek called on the
S. 81 E 2 3/4 mr. to the begining of a pt. of willows on the L.S. at the
       Commencement of this Course is a Small Channel passing about   Wau con di Buckt
       half way thro a Praire from a bend to the L.S. within 3/4 of a   Great Sperit is bad
       mile land a mile round the point   The Flag bow S. 12° E.
N. 84 E 8 mr. to the high wood above, a Praire in the bend on S.S.   Time & Dist the Moon & Sun
       the river wide & Shallow. the wood is opsd. a pt.   D – H – M   "
N. 22° E 1/4 mr. to a pt. of Willows on the L.S. S.S. having pass   1 –13. 45 — 73 – 6. 45
       a Couple trees in a bind S.S.   " – 16. 48 — 73 – 6 – 0
North 1 3/4 mr. to a Sand pt. from the L. Side & camped   " – 18. 39 — 73 – 6 – 0
       on the S.S. Cap Lewis Killed a Duck.   " – 20. 55 — 73 – 7. 45
N. 45 W 1 1/2 mr. to a Sand pt. on the L. Side. a number   " – 22. 45 — 73 – 8. 30
18 3/4   of Blue crains flying over   " – 24. 24 — 73 – 9. 30
I have observed a number of places where the river has Changed   " – 25. 45 — 73 – 9. 30
its Bead at different times   " – 27. 49 — 73 – 10. 45
                                                                                        " – 29. 33 — 73 – 11. 30
* on the Grave which was about 12 foot Base & circulittle, on the top of   " – 31. 30 — 73 –
a Peneal about 300 foot above the water of the river, from the top of this
                                                or meanders   or 70
hile may be Seen the bends, of the river for 60 miles round & all the County
around the bend of this high land is a Soft Sand Stone Bluff of about
40 or 150 foot, the Crooked, passes a Creek Called Waucondipeach on the L.S. above
the Bluff on this Creek the Mahars had the Small pox & 400 of them Died
4 years ago, Lattitude 42° 1. 3. 8/10 taken on the Point above the Creek. the river
is verry Crooked, we are now within 3/4 of a mile of the river at a place we Shall not
gett around to untill tomorrow noon here or 3 Legues from the Mahar by land and the
Great distance here in our a belief that those people ao not hunt much.

Aug. 12 to 14

39

12th August Sunday 1804 ⟐ South wind we Set out early —
the river wider than usial, and Shaleow, at 12 we halted in a bend
to the left to take the Meridean attitude, & Dine, & Sent one man
across where we took Dinner yesterday to Step off the Destance across
Isthmes he made it 974 yards, and the bend around is 18¾ miles
above this bend about 4 miles, a yellow & Brown Bluff Commences
and Continues 3 or 4 miles on the L.S. this Bluff has Some Sand
Stone, Som reich Black mole mixed with yellow Clay, a
few Red Ceeder on the tops, which is from 20 to 150 foot high
the hille still riseing back, I think may be estemated at 200 foot
on the top is timber, the wind for a few hours this evening was hard
and from the S.E. In the evening about 5 oClock Capt L. my self wer on Shore
to Shoot a Prarie wolf which was barking at us as we passed *

45   Course Distance August 12th & Differences

N. 44° W. ½ m. to a pt. of willows on the L.S. the
S. 42. W. ½ m. on the point of a Sand bar from the L.S. the river is wider here
S. 22. E. 2¼ m. to the pt. makeing out from the L.S. passed the timber on the L.S at ½ m.
S. 78. W. 2 m. to the pt. of willows on the L.S. wind favourable from the South
S. 68. W. 2¼ m. to the upper pt. of Some Cotton trees in the bend to L.S. at this
          place the Isthobus only 973 yds wide, & 18¾ miles around the Mahar King
          grave is S. 18 E. 2½ miles   took medr. altd. 59° 8′ 6″ —
N. 49° W. 4½ m. to a pt on the S.S. oppost a Bluff, haveing passed a Sand
N. 12 W. 3 m. to a pt on the S.S. at 1 m. & one from the L.S. at 2½ m.
N. 46. E. 2¾ m. to a pt. of willows on the L.S. a Sand bar makeing out
          20¼   and Camped on the Sand Island, the Musquetos very
troublesom, both Capt Lewis & myself are much ingaged in prepar:
ing despatches to Send back, by the perogue which will return as
Soon as those despatches are ready. (Broke a favourite Diantr)
* this Prarie Wolf Barked like a large fiest and is not much
larger the Beaver is very plenty, not with Standing we are almost
in Sight of the Mahar Town — Court a very large Catfish this morn
ing, Prepared the Indian presents which we intend given to the Mahar
          S. wesa apt. Cook to Seg. Floyd Squad from to day —

(continued overleaf)

13th of August Munday 1804. Sits out this morning the day left the usial time & proceeded on under a gentle Breeze from the S.E. passed the Island. N. 66° W. 2¾ Ms. to a pt. of low willows on the S.S. a Sand bar makeing out from it & N. W. W. 5/8 Ms. to a pt. of Cotton wood on the L.S. a bend to the S.S. passing over the pt. of a Sand bar from the L. Side. wind fair

& S. 44. W. 2½ Ms. to a point on the S.S. ops. to which Mr. Mackey had a Small fort West 3/8 in which he traded with the Mahars the Winter 95 & 96 & Call the place Fort Charles

N. 50. W. 1½ Ms. to a point of high wood, in a Bend to the L.

S. 20 E 2¼ Ms. to a pt. of Willow on the L.S. passed a Creek on which the Mahars Village is Situated at 1½ Ms. a Sand bar on the S.S. & on on the L.S.

North ½ of a M. on the Sand bar L.S. Passed the Willow Island on the S.S. Wea heard

N. 69. W. 2½ Ms. to the upper pt. of Cotton wood in a Bend to the L.S. ops.d a large Island

17 he We Came to formed a Camp on the Sand L.S. & dispatched Sgt. Ordeway & Peter Crousett & 3 men to the Village of the Mahars for the nation to Corn and talk with us on tomorrow, the S.E. wind Continues high, we take Some Lunar Observations and the River is S 55° West as far as Can be Seen, the Sand bar only Changeing the Direction of the Current the Hills leave the river on the L. Side

14th of August at 12 oClock the party Sent yesterday to the Town returned and informed that they Could not find any Indians, they had not returned from hunting the Buffalow in the Praries, wind Shifted to the N.W. our party Sent after the Deserter & to the Ottoe town have not Come up as yet

August 15th Wednesday I took ten men & went out to Beavr Dam a bay of a Creek about a mile below our Camp. and with a Bresh Drag Caught 362 fish of the following kind viz. like Samon, Bass, Pirch, Red horse, Small cat, & a kind of Perch Called on the Ohio Silverfish I also Caught the Srimp which is Common to the Lower part of the Mississippi, in the Creek & on the Beavor Pond is Crumie beaver. Cat fish Very large & fat - in my absence Capt Lewis Sent the Souex interptr & a party to a Smoke which appeared to rise at no great distance to the north with a view to find Some Band of that nation, they returned and informed that the had been made Some time by Some Small party, and the head wind it to day & had Set the Prarie on fire from Some high trees, which was left burning all well, party from ottos not Come up.

(continued overleaf)

Aug.t 28th ⑩

the Bluff which show to, on the Side of the hill great quantity of a kind of Cement to Stone resembling the Cemet is Afforance thruth neither and finer than grows on a hill resembling a Lime Kin and is too far and makes a delightfull Sight above the Bluff I took my Servant and a french boy which waller on hm and Walked on Shore I Killed a Deer which I Gave to a man on his boat for the evening I Killed two Bucel Elk and two-... Amount two other which I could not finding by the Blood as they had was to lorrade & to bled them with my boys each Stir on Elk it was late and I Crofred a hand through the river above and hallo the boat and he men went out brought in the Meat ale the after part of to day it rained we on ole wd Cap Lewi and my self Continued Places this Leagues N 20° W. from the mouth of White Stone River the hills appears be a Conis fire and by to visit a high hill Situated in an emence Plain the Different nations in this quater is Suppthored to be a place of devel the

Aug.t 25th Set out on 1804 this morning Cap.t Lewis & my self & G.D. & Ordeway
Sergt.t J Fields & Colin Bratton Caws Labeech & Wearington Drewer & Joseph
set out to visit this mountain of evil spirits, we set out from the mouth
of the Whitestone creek, at 8 oclock, at 4 miles crop the creek is as open
[plain] at noon the Dog gave out & we let him back to the Creek at 12
Oclock we saw the hill a low down before we got to the hill we [took]?
great [number] of Bea[r] [hovering] about the top of this Mound Where
I got on the top from Bea[r] flew off, I assumed that they were [circling]
a kind of flying ant which were in great numbers about the top
of this hill, there [nearly] [a]t as our [foot] & hill, [h]e[ard] I [think] [h]it [me]
very short on the creek, near the top of this Mole [J]obin[ed] the hill
which [Shelfford] to & raw water or [Branch] Which are [running] in
from [plain] this hill is about [J]a [foot] [high] in the on [mond] [plain] or
from [plain] this top [conceals] [no] [views] any woods except in
level plains from the top [concealed] no [views] any woods except in
the [defferent] [points] and a few [scattering] trees on the or the this River
as [view] is the long River below the River [overflows] about [1] the one and
[road]

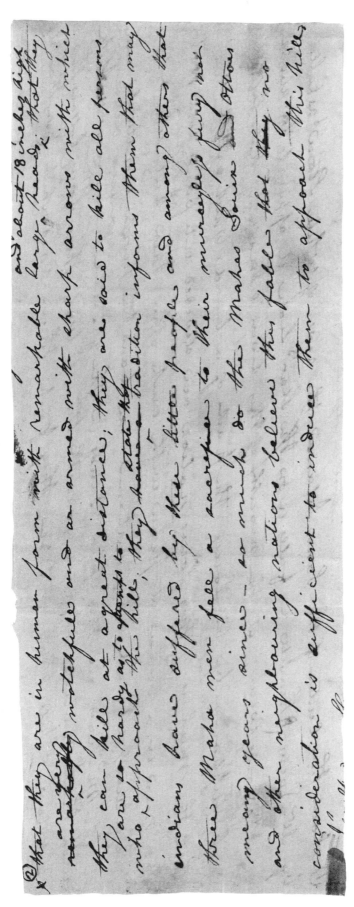

(x) that they are in human form with remarkable large heads; that they are usually noteſuls and an armed with sharp arrows with which they can kill at a great distance; they are said to kill all persons who are hardy an[d] to attempt to approach the hill. they have... inform them that may... Indians have suffered by these little people and among others that three Maha men fell a sacrifice to their savage fury met... so much do the Maha Souin Ottoes many years since — and other neighbouring nations believe this fable that they no consideration is sufficient to induce them to approach this hill

(continued overleaf)

65

about the center of this Sand Island the river of White Sand/ as called by Dr Lewis [?] Granville R. falls in on the [?] ... it appears to be about 25 or 30 yds wide; at the mouth of this river ... Cap. Clippewa be in ... the heart of a ... which are at war with the Mahas ...

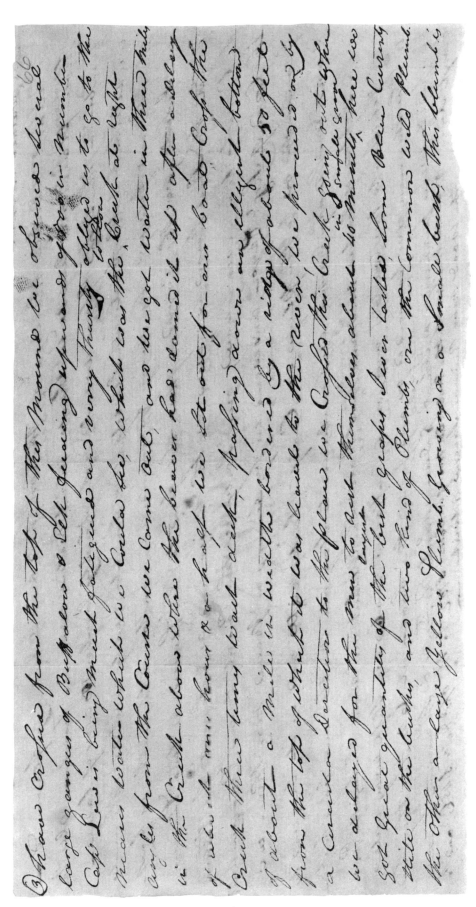

(continued overleaf)

Aug.ᵗ 25ᵗʰ Satturday ⑩ The Boat under Seg.ᵗ Pryor after Drying some goods Which got wet in the french Perogue & Jurking the Meat killed yesterday set out at 12 oClock and proceeded on six miles and Camped on the L.S. pass a Bluff of blue earth at 3 miles and a large Sand Island in a bend to the S.S. at 5 miles R. Fields brought in 5 Deer, G. Shannon an Elk this even. Rain

Course, Distance & Reference august 25ᵗʰ 1804   at 3 oClock Mercy 86 ab o,

S 72° W. 1 M.ᵈ ¼ the S.S. opposit a Bluff of Blue earth on the L.S.
West ½ m.ᵈ on the S.S. opposit the Bluff, the River verry narrow
N 22 E 3 M.ᵈ to a p.ᵗ of high willows on the L.S. opposit a Sand Is. in a bend
N. 40 W. 1 M. on the the L.S. op.ᵈ an Island afore said
S. 86 W ½ on the L.S. to a point of willows, where the Boat lay lay
Miles 6   then last night Sunset.

arrived at the boat at 9 oClock A.m.
26ᵗʰ August Sunday 1804 ^ set out at 10 oClock after Jurking the Meat & Cutting the Elk skins for a Tow Roap. and proceeded, leaving G. Drew & Shannon to hunt the horse, at the river verry full of Sand bars
and W. S. W.   Course S 66° W. 2 M.ᵈ to a Sand bar Makeing out from the S.S.
N. 82° W. 7 M.ᵈ to a p.ᵗ of willows S.S. pass.ᵈ a Island & large Sand bar on both sides, river wide and a Cleft of White earth on the L.S. of 2 M.ᵈ in length to a point of willow on the S.S. opposit Ant Creek above the Mouth of this Creek a Chief of the Maha Nation displeased with the Conduck of Black bird the main Chief came to this place and built a Town which was called by his name Petite Arch (or Little Bow) this Town was at the foot of a Isle in a handsom Place fronting the river and Contained about 100 huts & 200 men, the remains of this tribe Since the Death of Petite arch has joined the remaining part of the Nation this Creek is small — we ap. Pat. Gass Sergeant Vice Floyd Diceased, gathered great quantity of Grapes & three kind of Plumbs, one yellow loung & one red, & the Common wild Plumb. Musquitors had to night —   I have ap. 70

27ᵗʰ August Monday, this morning the Morning Star was observed to be verry large, G Drewyer came up and informed that he could neither find Shannon or the horse, he had walked all night — we Sunk Shields & J. Fields back to look for Shannon & the horses and to Come up with us on the river above at the grand Callumet or River Kalume & we Set out under a Gentle Breeze from the S.E. proceed on passd a
at 9 ms
a Bluff several miles in extent of White Clay or Marl or Chalk, under this bank we discovered large Stone resembling lime incrusted with a Substance like glass which I take to be Caboalt, also ore three m.ᵈ
to let the Soui know we wished to see the
above this Bluff we set the Prarie on fire, at two oClock we
an Indian Swam to the Perogue, we landed & two others came they were boys, they informed us that the Soui were Camped near, on the R.
Jacke one Maha boy informed us his Nation was gone to make a peace with the Panias, we proud Send S.ᵗ Pryor & a Frenchman with the Interp.ᵗ
M. Deurion to the Camp to see & invite their great Chiefs to Come and Council with us at the Callumet Bluff. Mile above on L.S. — we proud on 1½ miles further & Camped S.S.
N. 75. W. 7 M.ᵈ to the upper p.ᵗ of Cale or Chalk Bluffs on L.S. pass.ᵈ a large Sand bar on S.S. & on S.S.
North 3 m.ᵈ to a tree in the bend to S.S.   W. 2½ M. to the Mouth of river Jacque Ld. the S. side of Sd.
S 66 W ½ on the S. Side of a large Sand bar on the S.S. and camped

(continued overleaf)

28th August Tuesday, 1804 the wind blew hard last night one Indian
stayed with us all night, Set out under a Stiff Breeze from S. and proceeded
on passed a Willow Island at two miles several Sand bars the river here
is wide & Shallow full of Sand bars. The High land appear to be getting nearer to each other
passed a Bluff containing some white earth on the L.S. below this Bluff for
one mile the Shore rise gradually to the hight of the Bluff which
is 70 or 80 foot, here the Indian boy left us for his Camp — Capt Lewis
& my self much indisposed — I think from the Hommony we substitute
in place of bread, (or Plumbs) we proceeded on about 3 miles higher
and Camped below a the Calumet Bluff in a Plain on the L.S. to wait
the return of Serjt Pryor & Mr. Durion who we Sent to the Soues Camp
from the mouth of R: Jacque, before we landed the French run on
a Snag thro: their Perogue and like to have Sunk, we had her
on loaded, from an examination found that this Perogue was
unfit for Service, & Determined to Send her back by the party
intended to Send back and take their Perogue, and exchange
the loads, some of the loading was wet. Wind blew hard from
the South. J Shields & J Fields joined they did not overtake Shannon
with the horses who is a head of us.   1st Pt. Dolsey
                                          2 White Crain   } now mourning ganges
   Cours Dist   3 Little Bowl
S. 76° W. 4½ Mls to the lower part of a Bluff of white earth on the S.S. having passed
S.60° W. 4 Mls to the low part of the Calumet Bluff on the L.S. having passed
   ___   Several large Sand bars on each side of the water
   8½   a point on each Side & Several Sand bars

29th August Wednesday 1804 — rained last night and Some this
morning very Cloudy Set Some men to work to make a Toe rope of
Elk Skin, and my self to write, Sent one man to pursue Shannon
a head with Some provisions, I am much engaged writing a Speech
at 4 oClock Serjt Pryor & Mr. Durion the Soues interpeter with about
70 Soues arrived on the Opposit Side of this river we Sent over
for them Mr. D. & his Son who was trading with the Indians came over
Mr. Durion informed that the are —
Chiefs were of the party, we Sent over Serjt Pryor with young
Mr. Durion, Six Kittles for the Indians to Cook the meat
they Killed on the way from their Camp (2 Elk & 6 Deer) a
bout a bucket of Corn & 2 twists of Tobacco to Smoke intend
ing to Speak to them tomorow — G. Drewyer Killed a Deer

Serjt Pryor informs that when he approached the Indian
Camp they came to meet the supposing Capt Lewis or my
self to be of the party intending) to take us in a robe to
their Camp — he approached the Camp which was handsomly
made of Buffalow Skins Painted different Colours, their Camps
formed of a Conic form Containing about 12 or 15 persons each
and 40 in number, on the River Jacque of 80 yds wide & Deep
Containing but little wood, they had a fat dog Cooked
as a feast for them, and a fining apart for them to lodge
on their march they pised the pains four with hands &c. &c.

Aug. 30 to Sept. 1st   43

30th August Thursday 1804 a foggy morning I am much engag'd
after Blakfast we sent Mr. Durous in a perogue to the other side
ii SS. for the Chiefs and armey of the Sous he returned
at 10 oclok with the Chiefs, at 12 oclok I finished and we
delivered a Speech to the Indians expressive of the wishes
of our government, and explaining of what would be good
for themselves, after delivering the Speech we made one
Grand Chief 1st Chief and three third Chiefs and deliver'd
to each a few articles and a Small present to the whole
the grand Chief a Parole, Some Wampom & a flag in addition to his present, they with Drew and we retired to
Dinner, Mr. Durions were much displeased that he could
not dine with Cap Lewis and my self — the number of
Sous present is about 70 men — Dressed in Buffalow robes
a few fezers, Bows and arrows, and verry much Deckerated
with porcupine quills,   a Society of which only four remains
is present, this Society has made a vow never to give back
let what will happen, out of 22 only 4 remains, those
are stout likely men who stay by themselves, fond of
mirth and afsume a degree of Superiority — the air gun
astonished them verry much after night a circle was form'd around 3 fires
and these Indians danced untill late, the Chiefs looked on with
great Dignity much pleased with what they had, we retired late
and went to bed. wind hard from the South.

31st of August Friday rose early a fair Day — a curious Society
among this nation worthey of remark, i's formed of their active
Determined young men with a bow Never to give back, let the
danger or dificuelty be what it may, in War parties they
always go foward, without screening themselves behind trees
or any thing else, to this Vow they strictly adheer dureing

(continued overleaf)

their Lives, an Instance of it is last winter on a march
in crossing the Missouri a hole was in the ice which might
easily be avoided by going around, the fore most man went
on and was drowned, the others were caught by their party
and draged around — in a battle with the Crow Indians
out of 22 of this Society 18 was killed, the remaining four
was draged off by their friends, and are now here — they
associate together Camp together and are merry fellows, the
became one of the society This Custom the Sioux learned of
the de Corbeaus inhabiting the Coute Noir or Black Mountain
all the Chiefs Delivered a Speech agreeing to we sais &c &c agreed
which answers from my notes. we made or gave a Certificate to two brave men
the attendants of the great Chief gave them some
tobacco and prepared a Commission for Mr. Dorion
to make a peace with all the Chief Nations
in the neighbourhood, Mahas, Poncars, Panis
Loups, Ottoes and Missouries — & to take to the
President some of each nations who would accompany
the 3d Chiefs of
him also to certain other things, and wrote Instruc-
-tions — gave him a flag and some Cloaths — the
Chiefs Sent all their young men home, and they
leaped for Mr. Dorion — in the evening late we
gave the Comn & Instruction to Mr. Dorion & he
received them with pleasure, promised to do all
which is necessary. I took a Vocabulary of the Sioux
language, and a few answers to some queries I
put to Mr. Peter Dorion respecting the war no situati-
-on &c &c of that people which is divided into 20
tribes possessing Seperate interest they are numerous between
2 & 3000 men, divided into 20 tribes who have their interests

*

31st august Continued   45

The Distance of the Sun and moon
Sun and Moon   the moon West
Time Distance

H.	M.	S.		˚	′	″
9	— 12	— 18	=	41	51	- 00
11	— 14	— 23	=	"	48	- 00
"	— 15	— 49	=	"	46	- 00
"	— 16	— 42	=	"	45	- 30
"	— 17	— 52	=	"	46	- 30
"	— 19	— 32	=	"	46	- 30

* Interests as Different Som bands at war
with Nations Which other bands are at
peace — This Nation Call Themselves —
Dar co tar. The french Call them Souex
Their language is not peculiar to themselves
as has been Stated; a great many words
is the Same with the Mahas, Ponckais,
Osarge, Kanzies &c. Clearly proves to me
those people had the Same Orezean — this
nations inhabit the Red river of Hudson bay
St Peters. Mississippi, Demoin R. Iaqqui on the Missouria
they are at war with 20 nations, and
at piece with 8 only — they recive their
trade from the British except a few on the
missouria, they furnish Beaver Martain
Loues otter, Liknon Bear and Deer.   and

(continued overleaf)

and have forty Traders at least among
them. The names of the Different
bands of this nation are —————

1st Che cher ree or Bois rulay (the present band)
Inhabit the Soues. Jacque & Demoin Rivers —

2nd Ho in de bor to or Poles. they live on
the head of the Sueoux River ————

3rd Me ma car jo (or Make fence on the river)
the the Countrey near the Big bend of the Missouri.

4th Sou on le ton (People of the Praire) they live
North of the Missouri in the Praries above.

5th Wau pa coo do (Buds) they live near the
Praire de chaine on the Missippi —

6th Te tar ton (or Village of Praire) on the waters
of the Missippi above Praire du chain (or Dog Prairie)

7th Ne was tar ton (Big Water Town) on the Mississippi
above the mouth of the St Peters River.

8th Wau pa to (Leaf Nation). 10 Leagues up St Peters

9th Cas car ba (White man) 35 Lgs up St Peters

10 Mi ac cu op si ba (Cut Bank) reside on
on the head of St Peters river

11 Sou on ——— on St Peters in the Praries

12th Se si toons ——— 40 Leagues up St Peters.
The names of the other trebes I could not get
In

(continued overleaf)

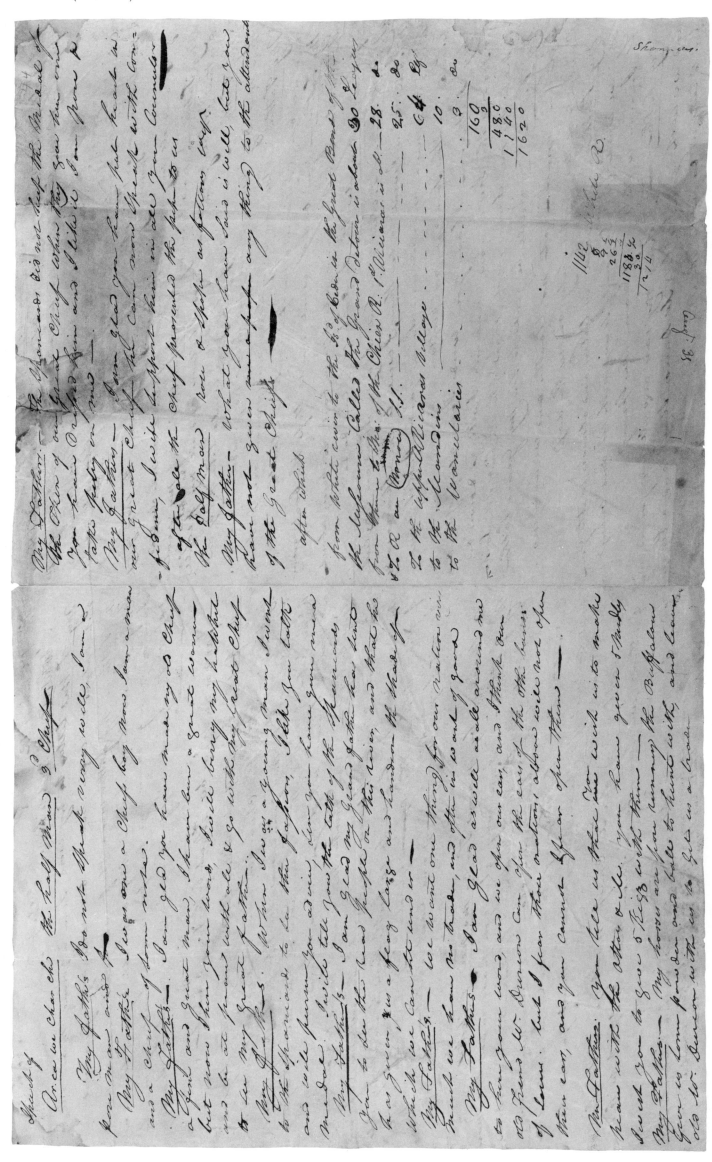

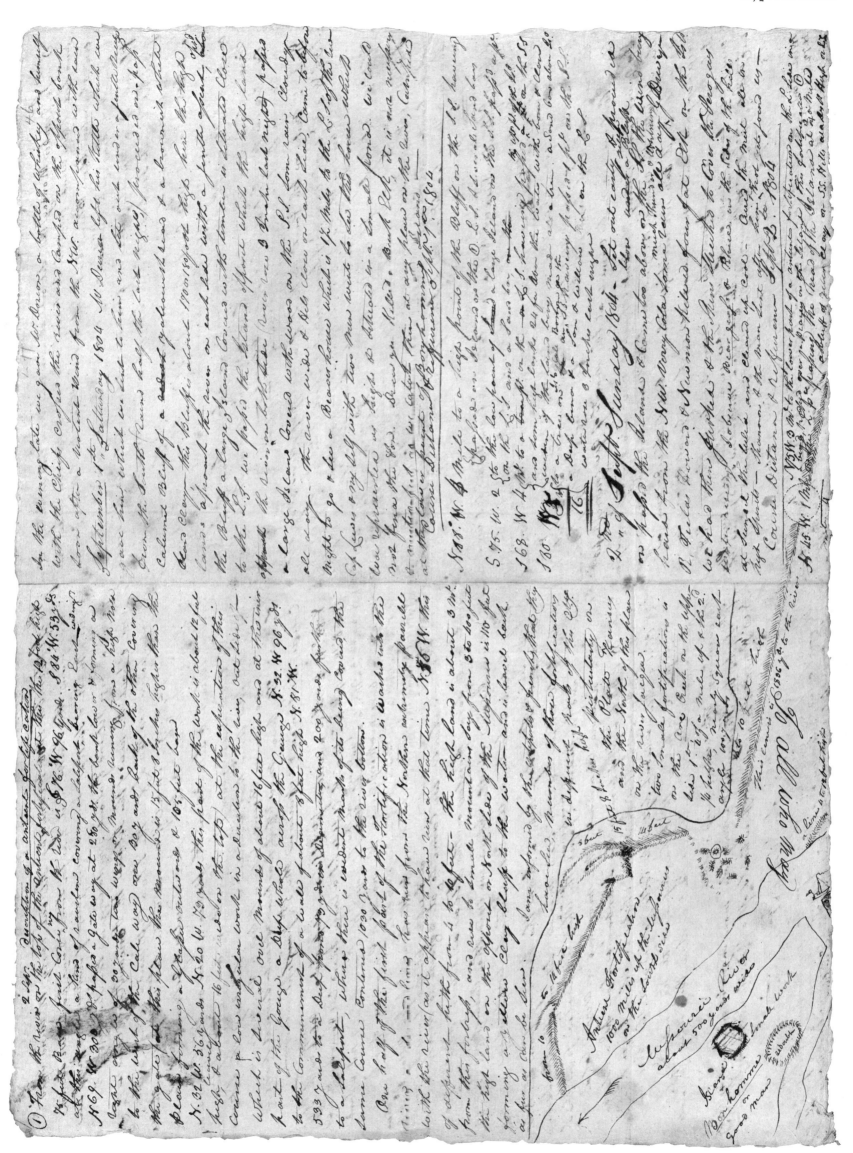

(continued overleaf)

wind SE   Sept 8. and 6 1804

The Village of those little Dogs is under the ground a considerable distance
we Dug under 6 feet thro rich hard Clay without getting to their Lodges
Some of them whole we put in 5 barrels of water without driving them out, we cought one by the water foreceing him out. their mouth
resemble the rabit, head longer, legs short, & toe nails long their tail like a
g Squirrel, which they Shake and make chattering noise their eyes like a
Dog, their colour is Gray and then Contains Soft fur

8th of September 1804 Satturday. Set out early and proceded on under a
gentle breeze from the S.E. pass'd the plain where Trodow wintered one went
below the mouth of a Creek on the S.S. at   Situated in a woods on S.S. No of rabits.
N. 35 W. 7 M. to a pt L.S. opl Trodow house
N. 88 W. 10 Miles to a pront of woods S. shore 1 mile above the commence=
=ment of this course, the lower prount of a avillow Island
17   commences, this Island 1½ in length   a small sand Island
           at its upper extremity.   high bluff an Lard begining
           at the upper point of this Island   higher hills appear
           to the West, distant about 3 miles, recently birnt —
           three small islands commence five miles from the
           commencement of this course and continue about two
           miles lying on the Stard side of the main chan?
           here met with six buffaloe bulls of which we killed two
           6½ miles farther an Island on Lard about   length
           came too at the lower point of this island and encamped.
           Jerked the meet we had taken today consisting of
           two Buffaloe, one large buck Elk & Elk fawn, three
           fawn deer, three turkies & a Squirrel

           I went out to day on the S.S with a view to find Some of
           the little Dogs, and Coats, traveled over a rigid and
           mountainous Country, without water rising to 5 or
           600 hundred feet, Islands & Sands intervening pus d
           my getting to the boat untill after night, in my
           absent Cap Lewis killed a Buffalow, I saw Gred many
           Buffalow. & White wolves. (Sailed all day)

(continued overleaf)

47

9th of Septemb Sunday, Set out at Sunrise and proceeded on passed the Island Several gangues of Buffalow on the Sides of the hils on the L.S. halted on L Side took breakfast Capt Clark walked on Shore, we proceeded on N. 32. W. 3 miles to point of an Is L.S. a creek come in opposit on N.S. passed the Island Several Sand bars above, & a willow Is on L.S. halted on S.S. at 12 oC for M. observation. above the mouth of a Small breck which came in below a grove of cottonwood Timber. — Several Sand bars N. 40. W. 2½ miles to upper point of the grove of cottonwood. the current verry rapid. above the willow Is at the bend of the river. N. 83. W. 3¾, to a point of woods on Starbrd Side passed Several Sand bars above the willow Is. passed a high Bluff on L.S. about 170 feet high & of a dark coullour. we took dinner at the ms of a Small creek which came in between the Bluffs. passed 2 more Small runs in the Same Bluff. G. Drewyer killed & put on board the perogue one Buck & 2 fauns. N. 36. W. 4 miles to lower point of wood on L Side in bend. N. 36 w. to pt S.S. Hd passed a willow Is on S.S. Several Sand bars above I.C. R. Fields came to the Boat had killed one Buffalow. passed red ceder on the edge of the hills on both Sides of the river but most on the bluff on L.S. passed a handsome round Knob on the hill on L. S. Little abv. passed a Small creek in bend at lower end of a Sand bar. L.S. and Camped on a Sand bar. Capt Clark came in, Y. — K killed a buffalow near the Boat, by the directions of the master, Capt Lewis went out with R Fields & eaut killed a buffalow. a fair Day wind from the SE Lattitd 45°.11. N. Capt Clark did not get a Goat or a black taile deer the objects of his pursuite. River falling.

10th September Monday, a Cloudy morning Set out early under a gentle breeze from the SE. passed two Small Islands one on the L.S. & the other on the S.S. both in the first Course at 10½ miles passed the lower Pt. of Ceder Island Situated in a bend to the L.S. this Island is about 2 miles long Covered with red Cedar, the river is verry Shallow opsd this Island — below the Island on the top of a redge we found a back bone with the most of the inter laying in Connected for 45 feet those bones are petrified, Som tieth & ribs also Connected. at 3 Ms abov ceda I passed a large Island on the S.S. to this Island Several Islds Elk Swam above this Island on the L.S. Middle is Situated 2 Islands Smale one above the other those Islands are Called Mud Islands and Camped on the upper Island of the, 3 Buffalow 1 Elk &c. killed to day. river falling.

Course Distance & References Sept. 10th 1804.   £13.   48

North. 5 Ms. to a Small Island in a bend to S.S. and a Bluff
     of bare black earth, pass'd a Is. on the L.S.

N. 64° W. 2 Ms. to a pt. on L.S. passed the Island on each side
found on the top of a bluff
N. 80 W. ½ Mile on the L. Side, (a few Bones Petrefied 45 longer in form

S. 80 W. 3 Ms. to Cedar Island in the middle of the pass'd Sand bar

N. 70 W. 3½ Ms. to the lower pt. of an Island in a bend to the L.S.
     having passed Cedar Island ② and a large Island on N.S.
     this Island is covered with Cedar covered with timber ③ &
     many Sand bars water Shallow.

N. 35° W. 1 Ms. to the Lower pt. of a 2d. Is. Sepd. from the first by a
     narrow Channel (one remarkable circumstance is 19/20 of the
20   buffalows here is Bulls, but the Ind. kill the Cows. —
          S.S. — a large Salt Spring of remarkable Salt water
much frequented by Buffalow, some Smaller Springs on the Side
of the hill above less Salt, the water excess Salt, and is 1½ miles
from the river on the S.W. or L.S. opposit Cedar Island —

Course Distance & References the 11th. of September

N. 35° W. 4½ Ms. to the lower pt. of a Island, having passed pt.
     the Isld. on which we & a large Sand bar from the uppr.

N. 70° W. 2 Ms. to the head of the Island on the L.S. of it

N. 45° W. 3 Ms. to a pt. on the L.S. below an Island ①

N. 50° W. 2 Ms. to the upper pt. of an do. on the S.S. passed one on
     the L.S. opd. to which L.S. opd. at ½ a Ms. is a Village of little dogs

West. 4½ Ms. to a pt. on the S.S. passed an Island on the S.S.
16   Just above the last Several Sand bars.
          we came too at the mouth of a Creek on the L.S.
at dark in a heavy Shower of rain, it Continued to rain
the greater part of the night, with a hard wind from the N.W.
Cold

Sept. 11th Tuesday 1804 Set out early a Cloudy morning the river
very wide from one hill to the other, with many Sand bars,
passed the Is. on which we lay at a mile passed three Is.
one on the L.S. (½ of a mile from it on the L.S. a little Dog
killed four, this village is 800 yards wide & 970 yd. long)
on a gentle Slope of a hill in a plain, those animals
are nomerous the other two Islands are on N.S.
the river is verry Shallow & wide, then got a ground
Several times — The man G. Shannon, who who left
us with the horses above the Mahar Village and believing us to be a head pushed on as long as he Could, 'in

(continued overleaf)

joined us, he shot away what few Bullets he had
with him and in a plentyfull country like to have starv.
he was 13 Days without provisions Subsisting on Grapes
at the same the Buffalows would come within 30 yards
of his camp, one of his horses gave out & he left him before
his last bullets wer consumed —— I saw 6 large Spotted
foxy to day a black tailed Deer, & killed a Buck elk &
2 Deer, one other Elk 2 Deer & a Porkipine killed to day
at 12 oclock it became cloudy and rained all the
after noon, & night.

Course Distance &c 12th of Septr. 1804.

N. 45° W. 4 Mills to a point of woods on the L. S. passed an Isd
Troublesom Island in the middle of the river
at the upper pt of this Island the river was so crouded
with sand bars that we found great difficulty
in getting the boat over, the turned on the sand
4 times and was verry near turning over, we
Camped on the Isd near a village of Barren dogs
some rain all day to day & cold —
I walked on Shore Saw Several foxes Several
Village of Prarie dogs, and a number of Grouse

Septr 12th Wednesday 1804 Set out early a Dark Cloudy
morning wind from the N. W. Cold passed a village of Littl
Squrels or Prarie dogs & Camped on the Isd side)

Course Distance & remarks 13th Sept. Thursday 1804
N. 45° E 1/2 M on the L. S. a sand bar making out & a Dark
wind N. W. raining morning J. D. Cought 4 Catfish verry large Bever
N. 30 E 1 M on the S. S. verry Cold day or morning
N. 60 W 1 M on the S Side to the commencement of the black Bluffs
N. 64 W 2 3/4 M on the L. S. passing under a Bluff L. S.
North 1 3/4 M to a pt of high Land on the S. S. pass sand bar on both sides rain
N. 10 W 1 M to the lower pt of a timber on S. S. passing under a Bluff S. S.
passing a large Sand Island on the L. S. & sand bars
and Camped under a Bluff on the S. S.
musquetors verry bad wors than I have
this, a pt of mud wash into the river
from a small rain

Sept. 14th Friday 1804 Course Dist. & Rfft

Set out early proceeded on passed several Sand bars water wide & Shallow N. 68° W. 2¾ Ms. to a pt. of high Land on the L. S. passed a round Island on the S. S. — Caught 3 beaver last night, some Drezzley rain Cloudy & disagreable and som hard Showers, I walked on Shore with a veew to fina an old Volcano said to be in this neighbourhood by Mr. McKey I was some distance out Could not see any Sighn of a Volcano, I killed a Goet, which is peculiar to this Country, about the bite of a Deer Shorter, its horns coms out imedeatly above its eyes broad (Short prong) the other Arched & Sofe the Color is a light gray with black behind its ears, white round its neck, no beard, his Sides & belly white, and around its taile which is Smale & white and down its hams, actively made his brains on the back of its head, his nostreals large, his eyes like a Sheep only 2 hoofs on each foot, no others/more like the antelope or Gazella than any other Species of Goat). Shield killed a Deer weighing 6½ w. Verry poor the head narrow and its ears 3 Inchs wide and 6 long, from the fore to the end of the hind foot 2 feet 11 Inch. hite 1 foot 1 ¾ its taile long & thick white, clearly the Hare of Europe, a rainy evening all wett. the Soil of those Plains washe down into the flats, with the Smaleest rain & disolves & mixs with the water, we see back from the river high hills in a level plain, evidently the remains of mountains, what bud washed into the river within those few days has made it verry mudy, passed two Small Creeks on the L. S. & Camped below a 3rd on the L. S. rained all the evening)

N. 70° W. 2½ Ms. to an object in the pt. on the L. S. passed the Mo. of a river L. S.

N. 4. W. 2½ Ms. to the Mo. of a Smale Creek in the bend to the L. S.

N. 10 E. 1¾ Ms. to the Mo. of a Creek on the L. S. passed a bad Sand bar

9¾

Pass. Course Distance & reference 15th Septr. Saturday

N. 50° E 2 Ms. to point of White River above on the L. S. above is a handsom Situation for a Town passed Several Sand

N. 26 E 1½ Ms. to a pt. on the L. S. a Bluff on the S. S.

N. 10 W. ½ M. on the L. S. to a Bluff. & Black Slate cedar & cal. Rock

N. 30 W. 2 Ms. to the upper pt. of an Island, this Island is Covred with the S. S.

North 2 Ms. to the Mouth of a Creek on the L. S. a point of hir hand opposit. under which we camped. I killed 2 Elk & see to day. White River is about 400 yds. wide & like this R.

(continued overleaf)

49

September the 15th Satturday 1804 Set out early passed the mouth of a
on the L.S. where Shannon lived or Graps waiting for McClellens boat Supposing
we had went on, Cap Lewis and my self halted at the mouth of White
River & went up a Short Crossed &c this river is about 400 yards, the water
confined within 150 yards, the Current regularly Swift, much resembling
the Missoura, Sand bars makeing out from the point, Some Islands
we Sent up two men to go up this river one Day and meet
us the Monow we proceeded on passed a Small Island Covered with
Ceden timber, & great number of rabits, no game except rabits, and Camped
on the S.S. opposet a large Creek on which there is more wood than
usial or Creeks in this quarters this Creek raised 14 feet last rain I killed a Buck elk & a Deer.

September 16th Sunday, we proceeded on 1½ Mils and Camped
on the L Side in a butifull Plain Surounded with timber
in which we saw Severale Der, we Delayed here for the purpos
of Drying the articles which were wet & the Clothes to Load the Pirogue which we had intended to Send back being the white too Small Deturmined to take also to make
Some observations for Longitude &c the two men G. & R. F. joined
us and informed that the river as far as they were up had much
the Appearance of the river about the mouth, but little timber
and that Cheifly elm, the upland between this river & the
White river is fine, great numbers of Goats, Deer of three Kinds, Buffalow, & wolves, & Barking Squrels, the fallow Deer, Cloudy, ale Day
Cleaning out the boat examining & Drying the goods, & loading
the Perogue, I Killed 2 Deer Cap Lewis one & a Buffalow, one Buffalow
& five other Der Killed. I observed Pine Burs & Burch Sticks in
the Drift wood up White river which Coms in on the L.S. immedotly
to the point is a butifull Situation for a town 3 Gentle rises, &
more timber about the mouth of this river than usial
N. 72° E. 1¼ to a Pt on the L.S. and Camped in Som Timber Sound a plain
Grea number of plumbs near Camp, a Village of
1 ¼ Barking Squrels, near Refer to the Book No 9.
from this date

and 20   Above white river   5°

17th of Sept. Monday 1804, Dried all those articles which had got wet by the last rain, a fine day Cap Lewis went hunting with a view to See the Country & its productions, he was out all day killed a Buffalow & a remarkable bird of the Species of a Corvus, long tail a greening Purple. Variegated a Beek like a Crow white round its nick comeing to a point on its back, its belly white fees like a Hawk abt the size of a tame Pigeon, Cap Lewis returned at Dark. took the Meridian & equal altitudes to day made the Lablature

Colter Killed a Goat, & a curious Kind of Deer, a darker grey than Common the hair longer & finer, the ears very large & long a Small receptical under its eye its tail round and white to near the end which is black & like a cow in every other respect like a Deer, except its runs like a goat. large.

The hunters brought in 8 fallow Deer & 5 common Deer to day, Great numbers of Buffalow in the Prarees, also a light Coloured woolf covered with hair & corse fur, also a Small wolf with a large bushy tail — Some goats of a Different Kind Seen to day, — Great many Plumbs, rabits, Porcupins & barking Squirels, Cap Lewis Killed a rattle Snake in a village of the Squirel's and Saw a hair to day— wind from the S.W.

we finished Drying our Provision, Some of which is as wet and Spoiled,

Sept. 18

J Killed a Prarie wolf to day about the Size of a Gray fox with a bushey tail the head and ears like a Fox wolf, and barks like a Small Dog — The annimale which we have taken for this Fox is this wolf, we have Seen no Foxes.

18th Sept. Tuesday Set out early wind from the N.W. modr. our boat being much litend goes much better than used

Course   N. 45° E   1 Md. to the lower point of a Island ①
N. 25° E.   3 Md. to a pt. on the L.S. passed the Isd. at 1 Md. & Som
    Isand bars makeing from it a Crak opsd. on L.S.
N. 14° E   1½ Md. to a point of willows on the L.S.
N. 10 W.   1½ Md. to a point of wood on the L.S. head wind
N. 22 W   1   Md. to a pt. of wood on the L.S. and came to
N   8   at 5 oClock to jurke the meat Killed to day
    and what was collected from what was
    Killed yesterday, i.e. 10 Deer to day 4 & an
    Elk yesterday — a Cole nyte for the Season

(continued overleaf)

Sept 19th Wednesday 1804, Set out early. a cool morning
clear & still course N. 50° W. 3 mls to a pt of wood on the S.S. a
Bluff on the L.S. opsd. here Commences a butefull Country
on both sides of the river North 4 miles to the mouth of a River S.S. ①
N. 30. W. 2½ mils to the upper pt. of the Island in the middle of the river ②
N. 43° W. 2 on the L.S. N. 54° W. 3 ml on the to a pt. of wood on the S.S.
N. 70 W. 5 ml to a Bluff on the L.S. passed a Creek ④ West 3½ mls to some
timber on the L.S. passa a Creek ⑤ Camped.   23 mils

① passed a large Island situated nearest the S.S. ½ a mile from the Lower
pt. of this Island, the 1st of the 3 rivers mouths which is about 35 yards
wide, running from the N.E. one mile above the 2nd Comes in this
is small not more that 15 yard wide a short distance above a 3d
Comes in scattering its waters thro a bottom. I walked on Shore to
see this this great Pass of the Sioux and Calumet ground, found
it a handsom situation, and Saw the remains of their Camps on the 2d rise
er, for many years passed — ③ passed a Creek on the L.S 15 yds wide we
it ④ passed a Creek 20 yds wide ⑤ passed a Creek 20 yd wide on the L.S. I call
night C. as I did not get to it untill late at night, above the mouth
of this Creek we Camped, the wind being favourable for the boat
I Killed a fat Buffalow Cow, and a fat Buck Elk, york my
servent Killed a Buck,   the Hunters Killed 4 Deer, & the boat
Crew killed 2 Buffaloes Swiming the river, handsom
Country of Plains, I saw many trous of Buffalow &
a Gangue of 30 or 40 Elk and other scattering elk &
a fine evening. I hurt my hands & feet last night —

September the 20th Thursday 1804 Dispatd 3 men across the Big
bend. Called the Grand detour, with the horse, to stay and hunt
& furch provisions untill we get around ① passed a Island
on the S.S. the river Crouded with Sand bars,   The Course
N. 50° W. 3¼ mils to the upper point of an Island on the S.S. about 2 ml long
North 4 ml to a pt on the L.S passed one on the S.S above the Island —
N. 10° W. 7½ ml to a pt. of wood on the L.S. — N. 22° W. 3 ml to the L.S.
N. 60 W. 2 ml to a Small timber on the L.S. — West 3 ml to a wood on L.S
S. 73 W. 3½ ml to a pt. of wood on L.S — South 4 mils a tree on L.S passed a
Island, situated on the L.S. this Island is Smale with a large Sand
S. 74 E 3½ mils to a point of wood on the L.S. pass Sands & Gd
S. 56 E 3½ to a pt on the S.S. opsd a high hill on the L.S.   ② &
S. 28 E 2 ml to a Cedar hill on the L.S. in a bend opposit the Gange of this bend
where the river is only 1¼ mls across & 30 mils around, the hills high
with Some low land —   this Day I refused to ① & for farther exspanion
      35½

(continued overleaf)

miles   62

From River Dubois. to St Charles ———	21	in Latitude	38.	54.	39″
from Do —. to the Mouth of Gasconade	104.	do ..	38.	45.	35.
do Do - to the Mouth of Osarge R:	138.	do ..	38.	31.	16
do Do Mene river on the South	201.	do ..			———
do do to Grand R. on the N. Side	254.	do .	38.	47.	54
do do to Kanzus R on the South.	366.	do .	39.	5.	25
do do to Creek independant at the Kanzus old village South	433.	do .	39.	25.	42
do do Nodaway River. N Side	481.	do .	39.	39.	22.
do do Nemahar R. S. Side.	561	do .	39.	55.	56
do do Bald pated Prarie N. Side	570	do .	40.	27.	7.
do do the mo. of the Great River Platte. on the South Side	632.	do at	41.	oo .	o

over

(continued overleaf)

from the mouth of Nishnabotna River
to the Council Bluffs ops. the Ottas } 682 in Lat. 41. 17. "   miles
to Little Sieoux River on N Side . . 766.   do . 41. 42. 34.
to Mahar Village . . . . S side 3 ms ofR. 864.   do . 42. 13. 41.
to Mouth of the Great River Souex } 880.   do . 42. 23. 49.
3 miles west of Floyds river on N.S.
to Mo. of River Jacque on the N. S. 970.   do . 42. 53. 13
to Mo. of River que Curre or the } 1020.   do ——
rapid river on the South side
to No preserves Island 5 miles North of } 1037. do ——
the Poncaris Village on the little
river Panca on the S. side ——
To White River on the L. S. in Disbing 1142 do.
grand . . . . 1183 do . 44. 11. 33. 3/10

(continued overleaf)

Sept 27 1804 They form their Camp in a circle &c &c No 53

Done. requesting us to take pitty on them &c. answered —

The great Chief then rose in great state and Spoke to the Same
purport and with Solemnity took up the pipe of peace and pointed it
to the heavens, the 4 quarters and the earth, he made Som dividitation
& presented the Stem to us to Smoke, after Smokeing & a Short
Harang to his people we were requested to take the meat, and
the flesh of the Dog gave us to eat — we Smoked untill Dark
at which time all was Cleared away & a large fire made
in the Center, Several men with Tambereens highly deckerated
with Der & Cabri Hoofs to make them rattle, assembled and
began to Sing & Beat — The women Came forward highly deca-
rated with the Scalps & Trofies of war of, their fathers Husbands
& relations, and Danced the war Dance which they done
with great Chearfulness untill 12 oClock, when we informed
the Chief we intended return on board, (they offered us women, which
we did not except) 4 Chiefs accompanied us to the boat and Stayd
all night — Those people have a Discription of Men which they
Call Soldiars, those men attend to the police of the Band, Correct
all errors & I saw one to Day whip 2 Squars who appeared to have
fallen out, when the Soldier approached all appeared give way and
flee with at night they keep 4 or 5 men at different distances
walking around their Camp Singing the occurrences of the night
all in Spirits this evening wind hard from the S E

I Saw 25 Squars & Boys taken 13 days ago in a battle with the Mahas, in
which they destroyed 40 Lodges, killed 75 men & boys, & took 48 prisners
which they promised us Should be delivered to Mr. Durion now with
the Yunkton Band, we gave our Mahar interpeter a few alls &c.
to gave those wretched Prisoners, I saw Hominy of Potato a Spoon of
the Big Horn animal which will hold 2 quarts

27th of Sept 1804 — The Bank as useal lined with Sioux, gave
the principal Chiefs a blanket & a peck of Corn each, Capt Lewis
accompanied the Chiefs to their Lodges, they informed us that a great
part of their nation had not arrived, & would arrive to night
and requested us to Delay one Day longer, that they might See us

I wrote a letter to Mr. Durion, & prepared Some Commissions &
a Meadel & Sent to Captain Lewis — at 2 oClock Capt Lewis return
with 4 Chiefs & a Brave man named War cha pa — (When a
those people die they penned their flesh with arrows above &
below their elbows as a testimony of their grief) after a
delay of half an hour I went with them on Shore, they left the
boat with reluctance (we suspect they are treacherous and are
at all times guarded & on our guard) They again offered me a
young woman and wished me to take her & not despise them, I waved
the Subject, at Dark the Dance began as useal and performed
as last night women with their Husbands & relations Cloths Arms
Scalps or poles &c &c Capt Lewis joined me & we Continued untill

(continued overleaf)

307

unto us about 11 oClock and 2 Chief accompand us to the boat
I with 2 Chief were in a Perogue going on board by bad Sheer-
ing the Perogue Strick the cable with such force as to brake the
Hear the Anchor Cap Lewis, and 3 or 4 men on Shore, I had all hands
up and was compelled to land & the Chief got allarmd &
allarmed the Indians, the Ship about 200 men who came down in great haste arm'd
an for action, and found it was false, about 70 of them
all night — this allarm Cap Lewis & well as my self vewed
as the Signal of their intentions, one half on guard, our
misfortune of loosing our anchor obliged us to lay under a
a falling in bank much exposed to the Accomplishment of
the hostile intentions of those Tetons who we had every reason to
believe from their Conduct intended to make an attempt to
Stop our progress & if possible rob us — Peter Crusat who Spoke Maha
Came in the night and informed me that the Maha Prisoners told
him that the Tetons intended to Stop us — we Shew'a but little
Signs of a knowledge of their intentions

28th of Septr 1804 Friday I made many attempts in deferent
ways to find our anchor without Sukkess, the Sand had covered
her up, we determined to proceed on to Day — and after Breck
fast we with great dificulty got the Chiefs out of the boat,
and when we were about Setting out the Class Called the
Soldiers took possession of the Cable — the 1st Chief who was
Still on board and intended to go a Short distance up with
us, was informed that the men Set on the Cable he went out
and told Cap Lewis who was at the Bow, they wanted tobacco
the 2d Chief demanded a flag & Tobacco which we refused
to give, Stating further reasons to them for it, after much
wrangling, we gave a Carrot of Tobacco to the 1st
Chief and he to the men & jerked the Cable from them & proceeded on under a Breeze from the S.E. we took in the 3d Chief
who was Setting on a Sand bar 2 miles above — he told us
the Rope was held by order of the 2d Chief who was a double
Spoken man — Soon after we Saw a man coming full Speed up
the bank we brought him on board, & he proved to be the Son
of the 3d Chief, by him we Sent a talk to the nation, explaining
of our hoisting the red flag under the white, if they were for Peace
Stay at home and do as we had desired them, and if they were
for war or determined to attempt to Stop us, we were ready to
defend our Selves (as I had before Said) — We Substituted large Stones
in place of an Anchor, we came to at a Small Sand bar in the
middle of the river and Stayed all night — I am verry unwell
I think for the want of Sleep —

N. 73° W. 3 m. to the Course & distance 28th of Septr
S. 80° W. 2 m. to a bend on the L.S. passed a willow &c &c
S. 6 to a bend on the S.S. at a wood &c come high land to L.S.

53

29ᵗʰ of September Satturday 1804 Set out early some bad Sand bars, at 9 oClock we observed the 2ᵈ Chief with 2 men and Squaws on Shore, they wished to go up with us as far as the other part of their band, which would meet us on the river above not far distant we refused to let him, more came on board Stateing Sevrel reasons observed they would walk on Shore to the place we intended to Camp, offered us women we objected and told them we should not Speake to another teter except the one on board with us, who might go on Shore when ever he pleased, those Indians proceeded on untill late in the evening when the Chief requested that the Peroge might put him across the river which we agreed to— Saw number of Elk on the Sand bar to day, passed an old Ricara village at the mouth of a Creek without timber we stayed all night on the Side of a Sand bar to a mile from the Shore

South 65° W. 2 miles to a point on the S.S. N. 50 W. ½ m. to a tree on the L.S. N. 16° E. 2½ m. to a point on the S.S. N. 60° W. 1¾ m. to the Mouth of a Creek L.S. N. 45° E. 2 m. to a point on the L.S. N. 25° E. 1¼ m. to a Willow Island.

30ᵗʰ of September Sunday 1804 had not proceeded far before we discovered an Indian running after us, he requested to go with us to the Ricaras, we refused to take him. I discovered at a great distance a great number of men women & children descending a hill towards the river above which the Chief with us told us was the other band, some rain & hard wind, at about 10 oClock we anchored opposit the lower of this band and told them we took them by the hand and Sent to each Chief a Carrot of Tobacco & Some to the Grinchals men and further said that after Staying with the band below 2 days to See them we had been badly treated and should not land again, as we had not time to delay— requested him to Mr. Durion for a full account of us, and an explanation of what had been Said, they appeared anxious for us to eat with them and observed they were friendly we apologised & proceeded on under a double reafed Sale. The Chief on board threw out to those that ran up Smale pieces of Tobacco & told them to go back and Show their ears, we Saw great number of white gulls. Several Indians attended us on Shore near the party with whiskey, in the evening we Saw Indians at a distance. the band came near and looked very mean, afterwards the Indian Chief on board Some tobacco and advised him to keep his men away we camped on a Sand bar. very cold & windy we gave him a Blanket knife &

N. 30° W. 3 m. to the upper point of Some woods L.S. N. 16° W. 1½ m. on the L.S. N. 10 W. 3 m. to a point S.S. N. 30 W. 1½ m. on the S.S. N. 61° W. 3 m. to a Bush on the L.S. S. 24° W. 4 m. to a point on the L.S. N. 50° W. 2½ m. passed the 2nd Band of Teton, North 2 m. to a tree on the S.S.

1ˢᵗ of October Monday 1804. The wind blew hard from the S.E. all last night. Set out early passed a large Island in the middle of the river opposit this Island the Ricaras lived in 2 villages on the S.W. Side, about 2 miles above the upper point of the Island the Chyenne River Coms in on the L.S. and is about 400 yards wide discharging but little water for a River of its Size, the current jentle and navagable, the Black mountains we haul the Boat over a Sand bar, River wide & Shoal, passed a Creek at 5 miles we call Sentinel Creek, a Smale on above, but little timber about the River, the hills not so high as usual, the upper Creek Call Lookout Creek, Camped on a Sand bar opposit a traceing house, where a Mr. Valler & 2 men had some few goods to trade with the Sioux, a boy came to us, this Mr. Valler informs us the winters last to enter 300 Leagues up the Chyenne River under the Black mountains, he Says the River is rapid and bad to navagate, it forks 100 Leagues up the N. fork enters the Black mountains 40 Leagues, same the Country like that on the Suporior lip timber more cedar, the Coal mine or Black m. is high and Some parts retain Snow all Summer, Covered with timber, green verry fine, great number of goats and a kind of animal with verry large horn, about the Size of a Smale Elk, White Bear no beaver on the Chien, great number in the Mountains, the Chyenne Nation has about 300 Lodges hunt the Buffalow, Steel horses from the Spanish settlements, which they do in 1 month, the Chanal of this River is Coarse gravel, those mountains is inhabited also by white booted Turkeys worthy of remark that the Grouse or Prarie hen is Booted the Toes of their feet to Constructed as to walk on the Snow, and the Tail Short with 2 long stiff feathers in the middle.

N. 80° W. 3 m. to the upper point of Pania Island, N. 70° W. 4 m. to the mouth of Chyenne River L.S. N. 16° W. 2 miles to a point on the S.S. N. 50° E. 4 m. to Willows on the L.S. passed 2 creek S. 53° E. 4 m. to a pt on the S.S. pt a Bluff L.S.

2nd of October Tuesday 1804. Mr. Valler came on board, Lat. 44° 19' 36. N. we observed Some Indians on a hill on the S.S. one came to the river & fired off his gun, and asked us to come, he with us to go to his camp, we refused near at hand we refused, passed a large Island on the S.S. then we expected the Siour would attempt to stop us, and prepared for action on opposit this Island on the L.S. a Smale Creek Coms in, we call this Caution Island. Camped on a Sand bar to a mile from the main Shore, the wind hard from the N.W. Cold, the Current of the river less rapid & retains less sediment than below.

N. 70° E. 2½ m. to a wood on the S.S. N. 62° E. 2 m. on the L.S. N. 15° E. 4 m. to the L.S. of an Island Situated near the L.S. N. 27° E. ½ m. to the upper pt of the Sand bar above the Island.

3rd of October Wednesday 1804. The N.W. wind blew verry hard all night, with Some rain, we set out early, at 12 examined our Store & goods, Several bags cut by the mice and Corn Scattered, Some of our cloth also cut by them also paper &c. at 1 oClock an Indian Came to the Bank S.S. with a turkey on his back 4 other boon joined him. Some rain. Saw Brant & white gulls flying Southerly.

N. 50° E. 2½ m. to a wood L.S. N. 54° E. 2 m. to a tree in a bend S.S. N. 2 m. to a point of high land on the L.S. N. 22° W. 1½ m. on the L.S. under a Bluff (Sand bars so common, impossible to number them)—

4th of October Thursday— the wind blew all night from the N.W. Some rain we were obleged to creep down 3 miles to get a Channel Suffient Deep to pass, Several Indians on the bank called to us frequently to land, one gun levels & Slipped a Ball before us, we payed no attention to them, while at Breakfast one Swam across to us, beged for powder, we gave him a Smale piece of Tobacco & put him over on land, passed a large Island in the middle of the river good hop I. passed a small creek L.S. Camped on a Sand bar at the upper part of an Island on which is the remains of an old ricara village fortified Called Lahoocat, it was circular, the village appears to have been deserted about 5 or 6 years, 17 hours get remains, the Island contains but little timber, the evening verry cold and windy, make use of drift wood for firing.

N. 18° W. 3½ m. to a point on the S.S. passed Good hope Island N. 12° E. 1½ m. on the S.S. passed a creek L.S. N. 45° E. 2 m. on the S. point passed Lahoocat Island—

(continued overleaf)

5th of October Friday 1804 Frost this morning, set out early passed a small creek on the L.S. saw 3 Tetons on the L.S. they begd some Tobacco, we proceeded on passed a Creek on the S.S. I saw a white brant in a gangue on the Sand bar, saw a large herd of Goats or antelopes Swiming the River, we killed four of them passed a small Island on the L.S. a large Creek on the L.S. at the head of the Island White Brant Creek, I walked on the Island which is covered with wild rye, I killed a Buck & a Small wolf this evening, Clear pleasant evening, Camped on a mud bar S.S. refreshd the men with a whiskey.

N 63° E 1½ miles to high land on the L.S. Course outward &c
true in a bend to S.S. N 36° W. 2 m. to a pt. of high Land on the L.S. passd a Creek L.S. N 30° E. 1½ m. to a
N.W. W. 3 to a tree on the S.S. passed an Island and creek on the S.S. N 50 W. 3 m. to a pt. on the S.S.

6th of October Saturday 1804 Cold wind from the N. Saw many large round Stones near the middle of the River
passed an old Ricara village of 80 Lodges Pickited in those lodges is nearly an octagon form, I furnishd covered with
earth and as close as they can stand, a number of their Canoes in the hills, we found Squars of 3 different
kinds growing in the village Shields kills an Elk close by — The Magpy a common here we Camped off the
mouth of otter Creek on the S.S. this Creek is 22 yds wide & heads near the R. Jacque. — Course & sentam

N 4° E 3 m. to a wood pt. on the L.S. N 8° W. 1 m. on the L.S. N 32° W. 3 m. to a pt. on the S.S. N 40° W. 2 m. to Otter Creek S.S.

7th of October Sunday 1804 frost last night, passed a River 90 yds wide the Becara Call Sar-war-kar-ne
all the water of this river runs in a chanel of 20 yards, the current appears gentle, I walked up this River a
mile, Saw the tracks of white bear, verry large, also a old Ricara village partly burnt, fortified about 60
Lodges built in the same form of those passed yesterday, many Canoes & Baskits about the hills — about 10 oClock
we saw 2 Indians on the S.S. they wishd for something, Clat & told us they were of the band we
left below on their way to the Ricaras wind hard from the S. we gave them a twist & passed a open Island covered with grass
and wild rye, I walkd on the Isd. & killd a Briaro & a Black tale Doe with a black breast, the largest Deer I ever saw, the
great numbers of Grous on it, we call it Grous Island, Camped above the Island near the S. side.

N 42° W. 2 m. to the mouth of Sar-war-kar-ne River L.S. N 30° E. ¾ mile to a Bend L.S. N 30° W. 2 m. to a pt. of
high land L.S. N 35° W. 7 m. on the L.S. N 10° W. 1 m. on the L.S. to a pt. N. 80° W. 3 m. to the Upper Side of Grous Island
N 45° W. 1 m. to the head of Isd. west 2½ m. to a point on the main S.S. high land on both sides.

8th of October Monday 1804 a Cool morning wind from the N.W. proceed on the mouth of a Small Creek
on the L.S. about 2½ miles above the L. passd the mouth of a River on the L.S. called by the Recaras
We-tar-hoo. this river is 120 yards wide, the water confined within 20 yards, throws out mud with
little Sand, great quantities of red Berries, resembling Currents near the mouth of the river
Lat. 45° 39′ 5″ N. this river heads in the Black mountain, 2 miles higher up passed a Small
River on the L.S. called Maropa 25 yards wide chocked up with mud — our hunters discovered a
Recara village on an Island a few miles above we passed the 1st Recara village about the center
of the Island, in presence of great numbers of Spectators and Camped above the Island on the
L.S. at the foot of Some high land. Mr. Gravolin a French man joined us is interpreter the Ricara is on a white
Ricara village is Situated, is about 3 miles long Seperated from the Main L. bank by a narrow Channel, these
Indians Cultivate on the Island Corn Beans Tobacco &c. after Landing Capt. Lewis with Mr Gravelin
and 3 men went to the village, I formed a Camp on Shore with the Sergts. Guard & a good watch
at anchor, Capt. Lewis returned late, a French man and a Spaniard accompany us down.

N 70° W. 2 m. to a Tree in a bend to the L.S. passd a Small Creek L.S. N 10° W. m. to a point on the S.S. N 15° E. 2 m. to the
mouth of We-tar-hoo River in a bend to the S.S. N 40° E. 1 m. on the L.S. N 90° E. 1 m. to the mouth of Maropa River L.S.
N 15° E. 1 m. to the lower point of an Island North 2½ m. to a pt. on the L.S. passed the 1st Ricara V. & 3 old Islands.

9th of October Tuesday 1804 a windey night some rain and the continued so high & cold we could not speak
or Councill with the Indians, we gave them some Tobacco and informed them we would speak tomorrow when all the great
Chiefs visited us to day about Tobacco, a trader from St. Louis — Many Canoes of a Single Buffalow Skin made in the form
of a Bowl carrying generally 3 and Sometimes 5 & 6 men, their Canoes are so light that when Waves — the Indians
much astonished at my Black Servent and Call him the big medison, this nation never saw a black man
before, the wind very high, I saw at several times to day 3 Squaws in Buffalow Canoes loaded with mud Crossing the
River at the time the waves were as high as I ever saw them in the Missouri —

10th of October 1804 at 11 oClock the wind Shifted from S.E. to N.W. Mr. Tabeau visited us we had the parade
exert us the Chiefs to be made — at 1 oClock the Chiefs all assembled under an owning near Mr. Boats and
under the American Flag. We Delivered a Similar Speech to those delivered the Ottos & Sioux, Made three
Chiefs, one for each village, and gave them Clothes & flags — 1st Chief is named Ka-ha-wissassa big moccasin Kakawissassa
2d Chief Pocasse (Hay) to the 3d Piaheto or Eagles Feather — after the Councel was over we Shot the Air
guns which astonished them, & they all departed to their lodges, we observed 2 Sioux in the Councel one of them I knew
Saw below, they Came to interseed with the Ricaras to stop us as we were on to the — the Indians much astonished at
my black Servent, who made him self more terrible in their view than I wished him to do as I told them
that before I caught him he was wild & lived upon people, young children was very good eating
Showed them his Strength &c — those Indians are not fond of liquor of any kind —

11th of October Thursday 1804 wind S.E. at 11 oClock met the 1st Chief in Council, he thanked us for what we
had given him & his people promised to attend to our advice and Said the road was open for us and no one dare
Shut it &c. we took him and one Chief on board and Set out, at our way took in the 2d Chief at the mo.
of a Small Creek, and Came too off the 2d Village which is 3 miles above the Island, we walked up with
the 2d & 3d Chiefs to their villages which is Situated on each Side of a Small Creek the Squaws were something
to eat in their way after Conversation on various Subjects & Reviewing the Artillery of those people who
are both poor & derty, we informed the Chiefs we wished them what they had to Say tomorrow and
returned on board about 10 oClock P.M. These people gave us to eat Corn & Beans, a large well flavoured
Been what they rob the Mice of in the Plains and is very nurishing — all trim hatters

12th of October Friday after Breakfast we joined the Chiefs & Indians on the bank who were waiting
for us, and proceeded to the 1st village and Lodge of the Pocasse, this man Spoke at some length, to the
purpose of the 1st Chief & Declaring his intentions of Keeping his great father from doubt as to his loyalty in
Keeping the Sioux, requested us to take a Chief of their nation and make a good peace with the Mandans
for them, that they knew that they were the Cause of the war by Killing the Mandan Chiefs
this Chief & people gave us about 7 bushels of Corn, some Tobacco of their own make and two Leggins & a Robe
we proceeded to the 3d Chiefs village which is the largest, after the usual Ceremony of eating &c.
& he spoke to near the Same amount of the last Chief & made presents by the Squaws to us, consisting of
corn, Some Beans & Simnins. after we had spoken, and gave Some Skins &c. & proceeded on & passed the

our Country, we returned to our boat... the Chiefs accompanied us on board, we gave them some Sugar Salt and a Sun Glass each, and after eating a little they returned on Shore leading on to accompany us to the Mandans, and we set out, received by men women & children of each village ... these people are able to bear arms, and the remains of ten deferent tribes of Panies reduced by the Small Pox & wars ... great quantities of corn beans &c also Tobacco for the men to smoke, they collect all the wood and ... beggery common among those Savages — their language is so corrupted that many Lodges of the same village ...

19th October Sattur dey 1804. Newman Confined for mutinous expressions, proceeded on passed a Camp of Sioux on the S.S. those people did not Speak to us. passed a creek on the S.S. 18 miles above this ...

14th of October Sunday 1804 Some rain last night we set out in the rain which continued all day passed a Creek on the L.S. Piraketo 15 yds wide, halted on a Sand bar and had the punishment inflicted on newman, which caused the indian Chief to cry untill the thing was explained to him ...

15th of October Rained all last night, passed a Ricara hunting camp on the S.S. & halted at another on the L.S. several from the 1st Camp visited us and gave meat as also those of the Camp we halted at, we gave them fish hooks &c as we proceeded on we Saw a number of indians on both Sides all day, Saw ...

16th of October Tuesday 1804 Some rain these morning ... very anxious to accompany us we set out with our Chief on Board by name Ar ke tar nar Shan (or Chief of the Town) a little above our Camp on the L.S. passed an old Chyenne Village, which appears to have been Surrounded with a wall of earth ...

17th of October 1804 Wind S.W. saw ... on Shore with the Ricara Chief who we set on Shore, the told me many extra ordinary stories, I killed a Deer ... the Chief killed a Deer and our hunter killed 4 deer in my absence the wind rose high ...

(continued overleaf)

18th of October 1804. at 6 miles passed the Mouth of La Bullet or Cannon Ball River on the L. Side about 140 yards wide, and heads near the Black Mountains above the Mouth of this River, in and at the foot of the Bluffs, and in the water is a number of round stones, resembling shells and cannon balls of different sizes, and of excellent grit for grindstones— the Bluff continues for about a mile, the water of this River is confined within 40 yards— we met 2 french men in a canoe, who informed us they wer trapping near the Mandans and wer robed of their 4 traps, & part of their Skins and several other articles, by Indians he took to be Mandans those men return with us, two emence number of goats all day our hunters Killed heaven passed a large Creek Called Che wah or fish Creek on the S.S. 28 yds wide, passed a Small Creek at 1 m on the L.S. camped on the L.S. Saw a no. of Buffalow, & in one gange 248 Elk, our hunters Killed 6 deer & 4 Elk this evening, the Country is level and some some high short hills, and ridges at a Distance, Bottoms fine and partially timbered with Cotton wood principally some ash & Elm

N. 50°. W. 2 m. to Cannon ball River L.S. N. 20°. W. 2 m. to a pt of wood on the S.S. passing Can ball Bluff L.S. North 2½ m. to a pt. of Wood on the L.S. N. 15° W. ½ m. on the L.S. opd. a Creek N. 10°. E. 2¼ to a point on S.S. pass'd a Small Creek L.S. N. 20° E. 3 m. to a point of wood on the L.S.

19th of October Friday 1804. Set out early under a gentle Breeze from the N.E. Saw more timber than common in the bottoms, passed a large Pond on the S.S. I walked out on the high land L. Side and observed great number of Buffalows, I counted in view at one time 52 Ganges of Buffalow & 3 of Elk, besides Deer & goats & all the streams falling from the hills or high lands so brackish that the water cant be drank without affecting the person making use of it as Globersalts, I saw in my walk several remarkable high Conocal hills, one 90 feet, one 60 and others Smaller— the Indian Chief Say that the Callemet Bird live in the hollows of those hills, which holes are made by the water passing from the top &c. I also Saw an old village fortified situated on the top of a high point, which the Ricaras Chief say me wer Mandans, we Camped on the L.S. 5 Killed a Deer & Saw Swans &c. our hunter Killed 4 Elk and 6 Deer to Day—

N. 60°. W. 2½ m. to a pt. on the S.S. passed a Creek S.S. N. 40° W. 2 m. to Some wood in a bend to the L.S. N. 10°. E. 1½ m. to a pt. on the L.S. N. 20°. W. 2 m. to a tree in the bend S.S. N. 33° W. 3 m. to the point S.S. N. 44° W. 1 m. to a willow pt. on the L.S. opd. a Lake L.S. N. 30° W. 2 m. to a tree in bend S.S. N. 60° W. 3 m. to a pt on the S.S.

20th of October 1804. wind from the S.E. I walked out to see those remarkable places pointed out by Lewis, and Continued all day Saw an old Village of the Mandans below the Chief who to me appeared to have been fortified, above the village on the Same L.S. is a Coal bank where we Camp'd passed a Small Creek in the S.S. and an Island on the L.S. covered with willows small timber the Country this which I passed this day is delightful, Timber in the bottoms, Saw great No's of Buffalow Elk goats & Deer as we were in want of them, I Killed 3 Deer, our hunters 10 Deer and wounded a White Bear, I saw several fresh tracks of that animal double the size of the largest track I ever Saw, great numbers of Wolves, those animals follow the Buffalow and devour those that die or are Killed, and those too fat or poor to keep up with the gange N. 30°. W. 2 m. to some timber in a bend to the S.S. at a Creek, N. 10° W. 1 m on the S.S. N. 52° W. 3 m. to W. on L.S. N. 2 miles to some timber in a bend to the S.S. opposit an Island N. 70° W. 2 m. to a point on the S.S. passed the Island N. 50° W 2 m. to the upper part of a Coal Bluff L.S. passd. Old Mandan V. L.S.

21st of October Sunday 1804 a verry Cold night wind hard from the N.E. Some rain in the night which freesed as it fell at Day began to Snow and Continued all the fore part of the Day, at ½ pa mile passed the mouth of Chiss che tar (or Heart) River L.S. 38 yards wide this River heads near Little mountain with Knife River on this River is a Smoky stone which the Indians have great faith in & Consult the Stone on all great occasions which they Say breaks are life on the Snow of that is to performs— an old Mandan Village above the mouth of the Little River, I saw a Single tree in the open Plains which the Mandans formerly paid great devotion to run round thro flesh & tie themselves to the tree to make them brave, passed an old village on a small run on the S.S. one on the L.S. & and Camped, I Killed a fat Buffalow this evening— Little game all than common

S. 80° E. 2 m. to bend on L.S. passed Chiss che tar River N. 16° W. 1½ m. to a wood S.S. N. 40° W. 3½ m. to a pt. on the S.S.

22nd of October 1804 last night at about 1 oClock I was violently attacked with a Rhumetism in my neck, which was so violently I could not move, Cap. Lewis applied a hot Stone raped in flannel which gave tempory ease, we passed a war party of Tetons on their way as was Supposed to the Mandans of 12 men on the L.S. we gave them nothing and refused to put them across the river. passed 2 old villages and a Small Island at the head of which is a bad place an old village on the S.S. and the upper of the 6 villages the mandans occupied about 25 years ago this village was entirely cut off by the Sioux & one of the others nearly, the Small Pox distroyed great numbers

N. 50°. W. 3 m. to a pt on the S.S. N. 34° W. 3 m. to the lower pt of an Island on the L.S. N. 34 W 3 m. to a pt on L. passed dry S.S. &c. N. 1 m. to a pt on the L.S. N. 44°. W. 2 m. to a pt on the S.S.

23rd of October 1804 Some Snow, passed 5 Lodges & fortified the place the two french men were robed those are the hunting Camps of the Mandans, who have lately left them— we camped on the L.S. N. 45° E. 2 m. bend S.S. N. 18° W. ½ m. on the L.S. N. 65° W. 3 m. to a River in a bend to the L.S. N. 33° W. 2½ m. to a pt on the L.S. N. 18° W. 1 m. on the L.S. N. 45° W. 3 m. to a point on the S.S.

24th of October 1804 Cloudy Some little Snow, my Rhumetism continues, not so bad as the 2 last days, a butifule Country on both sides, bottoms covered with wood, we See no game to day, passed an old of a Band of the Menetarres Called Mah har ha where they lived 40 year ago on the L.S. Came too on an Island Caused by the river Cutting through a narrow point 7 years ago, on this Island we wer visited by the grand Chief of the Mandans a 2d Chief and several other who were Camped on the Island, those Chief met our Ricaras Chief with great Cordiality, Cap. Lewis visited the Camp 5 Lodge, proceeded on & Camped near a 2d Camp of Mandan on the S.S. nearly opposit the old Ricaras & Mandan Village which the Ricaras abandoned in the year 1789

N. 80°. W. 1½ m. to a pt on the S.S. N. 10°. W. 2 m. to a pt. on the L.S. opd. 2 Islands but point — N. 34° W. 2 m. to S.S. N. 64°. W. 2 m. to a point of high land on which the Mandans & after them the Ricaras formerly lived.

N. 80°. W. 3 m. to a pt on the L.S. pass'd old Ricara Village opd. the old Mandan Village S. 20° W. 2 m. to a tree on the L.S. S. 33° W 2 m. to a point on the L.S. S. 60° W 2 m. to a pt on the L.S. N. 45° W 1 m. bend L.S. N. 70° W 1 m. to a pt S.E. S26. W. 2 m. a Camp of mandans L.S. West 1 m. L.S. N. 27 W 2 miles to S.S. passed Bluff N. 55° W 1 m. to a pt on L.S. S. 60° W 2 m. to the 1st mandan Village on the L.S.

Continued

25th of October Thursday 1804 — a Gentle Breeze from the S E b E passed an

① of a Village on a high Plain where the Mandans once lived & after they left the Village & moved higher the Recarras took possession & live untill 1799 when they abandoned it & flew from the just revenge of the Mandans, a verry extensive Bottom above the Village about the Center of which

② the Mandans lived in 2 Villages on the L. S. but little timber — Several parties of Indians on each Side of the River going up — in vew in every direction — we are informed that the Soux has lattely taken horses from the Big Bellies or Menitaires and on their way homeardwards we fell in with the Assineboins who killed them and took the horses & a frenchman Menah who resided with the Mandans for 20 years past was killed a fiew days ago on his way from the Buliehmink aftallteh minter on the Assineboin River, 150 miles N. of this place to the Mandans by the Chimibies Indians — we were frequently called to by parties of Indians & requested to land & tolt, passed a verry bad place & Camped on a Point S.S. oppsd a high hill several Indians Visit us this evening the Son of the late great Chief of the Mandans who had 2 of his fingers off and appeared to be peared in many places on inquiring the reasons, was informed that that it was a testimony of their grief for Deceased friends, they frequently cut off several fingers & pierced themselves in different parts, a mark of Savage effectio wind hard from the S.W. verry cold R. Fields with a Rhumetism in his Neck one man R. in his hips my self much better, those Indians appear to have similar customs with the Recarres, their Dress the same more mild in their languages & customs &c. &c.

(continued overleaf)

313

26th of October 1804 wind from the S.E. we Set the Ricara Chief on shore with Some Mandans, many on each Side vewing of us, we took in 2 Chiefs, (Coal, and Big Man) and halted a few minits at their Camps, on the L.S. Yorkfield is their way, here we Saw a trader from the Ossinneboin River called McCracken, this man arrived 9 day ago with goods to trade for horses & Roabs one other men with him — we Camped on the L. Side a Short distance below the 1st Mandan village on the L.S. many men women & Children flocked down to See us — Cap Lewis walked to the Village with the Chief and interpreter, my Rheumetism increy -ing prevented me from going also, and we had determined that both would not leave the boat at the Same time untele we knew the desposition of the nativs, Some Chief visited me & I Smoked with them — they appeared delighted with the Steel Mill which we were obleged to use, also with my black Servent, Cap Lewis returned late —

27th of October Satturday 1804 we Set out early and came too at the Village on the L.S. where we delayed a few minits, I walked to a Chiefs Lodge & Smoked with them, but Could not eat, which did displease them a little, here I met with a Mr. Jessomme, who had lived in this nation 13 years, I got him to interpit & he proceded on with us we proceeded on to a central point opposit the Knife River, & formed a Camp on the S.S. above the 2d Mandan village & ops. the Mah-har-ha village —

Mah har ha Village, and raised a flag staff — Capt Lewis & the Interpeters walked down to the 2d Village of Mandans, & Returned in about an hour, we Sent 3 Carrots of tobacco to the other Villages & enviting them to come down and Council with us tomorrow, — we indeaver to precure Some Knowledge of the principal Chiefs of the Different nations &. — will to give my ideas as to the impression this man makes on me is a Cunin artfull gun insonuar — he tells me he was once emplod by my brother, in the Illinois & of his discription I conceve as a Spye — upon the Brittish of Mechillimakinac & St Joseph, we think he may be made use full to us & do employ him as an interpeter — No. of Indeans bringing & in wives &c to the camps of our party on Shore &c

Cours destom &

West 2 M. to a bend on the L. S. passed a Coal bank on the L. S.
N. 16° W. 2 m to a wood on the S. S. passed the 2d Mandan V. on the S. S.
to the plan we counceld & staid untill the 1st Nov.
Cours & destance up the Missourie above the Mandans
N. 12° W. 3 M. to a Bluff 30 feet high above the wooded bottom S Side
N. 20° W. 2 M. to a tree under a Bluff of about 20 feet high on the S. S.
N. 30° W. 1½ M. to a p° of the Same Bluffs 30 feet high in which is Coal
N. 45° W. 1½ M. to the lower point of an Island, the Current on the L. S.
28th of October 1804 the wind So hard from the S. W. we could not meet the Indeans in Councils, those who visited us we Sent to the mans L Village, Consulted the Black Cat M Chief about the Chiefs of the Different villages, who gave his Oppinion to us. 29th

(continued overleaf)

29th of October 1804 a fine morning after Breakfast we were Visited by the Old Chief of the Big Bellies or Mene tarres, this man has Given his power to his Son who is now on a war party against the Snake Indians who inhabit the Rocky mountains, the Wind verry high — we met in Council under an orning and our Sails stretched round to Keep out as much wind as possible & Delivered a long Speech Similar to what had been Said to the Nations below, the old Chief was restless before the Speech was half ended, observed his camp was exposed & could wait no longer &. at the Conclusion of the Speech we mentioned the Ricaras & requested them to make a peace & Smoke out of the Sacred Stem with their Chief which I endred vod, and gave him the pipe of peace to hand around, they all smoked with eagerness out of the pipe held by the Ricara Chief Ar-ke-tar-na-Shar — we mentioned our hands that were to be discharged here, also the Robery Committed on the 2 french men below, & requested them to answer us tomorrow, gave the Chief small presents and a few presents for each village Shot the air gun which both Surprised and astonished the natives, and soon Dispersed —

our Ricara Chief Came told me he wished to return to his nation tomorrow I put him off & Said we would send a talk by him after the Chiefs had Spoken to us— we gave a Steel mill to the mandans which was verry pleasing to them

The Chiefs who received Medals to day are as follows—viz in Council

1st Mandan Village Ma-too-ton ka- 1st Chief Sha-ha-ka Big White) 2nd Ka-goh-ha-me little Crow

2 do Village Roop tan kee, 1st & grand Chief Posecop sa he Black Cat) 2nd Chief Car-gar-no-mok-She Raven man Chief — Mah-har-ha village 1st Chief Ta-tuck-co pur-re-has White Buf falows hide unfolded)

Little Menetarre village 1st Chief Omp-se-ha-ra Black moccason. 2nd Chief Oh-hark little Fox

The Grand village of Manetaries, the One Eye is the principal Chief & he is out on a hunt we Send

Oct⁰ 25. and nov. 13. 1804

we send by the Grape all the articles for this grand Chief and all the village what goods was intended for that village— The Prarie got on fire and went with such violence & speed as to catch a man & woman & burn them to death, several escapd among others a small boy who was saved by getting under a green Buffalow Skin, this boy was half white, & the Indians say all white flesh is medison, they say the grass was not burnt where the boy sat &c. & this fire passed us at 8 oClock, and look truly tremendious.

30th of October Tuesday 1804 many Indian Chief visit us to day I went in the Persgue to the Island 7 miles above to look out a proper place for to winter, it being near the turn the ice begins to run at this place, and the Country after a few leagues higher is said to be barron of timber, I found no place soutable, & we concluded to drop down to the next point below & build a fort to winter in the party danced which delide the Indians.

31st of October Wednesday 1804 The main Chief of the mandans sent 2 Chiefs for to envite us to Come to his Lodge, and here what he has to say I with 2 interpiters walked down, and with great cerimony was Seated on a Robe by the Side of the Chief, he threw a Robe highly decorated over my sholders, and after Smokeing a pipe with the old men in the circle, the Chief Spoke "he beleved all we had told him, and that peace would be good which not only gave himself Satisfaction but all his people; they now could hunt without fear & their woman could work in the fields without looking every moment for the enemy, as to the Ricaras addressing himself to the Chief with me you know we do not wish war with your nation, you have brought it on your selves, that man Pointing to the 2d Chief and those 2 young warriers will go with you & smoke in the pipe of peace with the Ricaras— I will let you see my fa- ther addressing me that we wish to be at peace with all and do not make war on any. he continued to speak in this Stile (refer to notes) he delivered 2 of the Traps to me which was taken from the french men, gave me 2 bushels of Corn,

I answered the Speech which appeared to give general Satisfaction— and returned to the boat, In the evening the Chief visited us Dresed in his new sut, & delayed untill late the men Danced untill 10 oClock which was common with them wrote to the N W Company agent on the Ossiniboin River by a Mr Mc Cruskin.

(continued overleaf)

57

1 November 1804 Visited by Several Chiefs of the lower Village who requested we would call on them & Spoke to the Same purpote with the grand Chief. we Set out in the evening & I with the Party droped down to the place we intended to winter & Cap Lewis called at the Village 3 Miles above &. &.

2nd Novr 1804 Friday — Capt Lewis returned to the Village & I fixed on a place for to build a fort and set to work Cap Lewis returned in the evening with 11 barrels of Corn, the Ricara Chief Set out for his Village accompaned by Several Mandans —

3rd of November Saturday 1804 Wind hard from the West Commence building our Cabens, Dispatched 6 hunters in a peroque down the River to hunt, Discharged the french hands, Mr. Jessomme his Squar & Child moved to camp, the little Crow loaded his Squar with meat for us also a Roabe, we gave the Squar an ax & v. Cought 2 beaver near Camp

4th of Novr. a french man by Name Chabonah, who Speaks the Big Belley language visited us, he wished to hire & informed us his 2 Squars were Snake Indians, we engage him to go on with us and take one of his wives to interpret the Snake language the Indians Horse & Dogs live in the Same Lodge with themselves

6th of Nov. Mr. Gravelin our Ricara Interpreter & 2 of our french hands & 2 boys Set out in a Canoe for the Ricaras Mr. Gravellin is to accompany the Ricaras Chiefs to the City of Washington in the Spring, great number of geese pass to the South which is a certain approach of ice —

13th. The Ice begin to run we move into our huts, visited by the grand Chief of the Mandans, and the chark Laque a Chief of the Assinneboins & 7 men of that Nation, I smoked with them and gave the Chief a Cord & a Carrot of Tobacco — this Nation rove in the Plains above this and trade with the British Companey on the Assinnebou River, they are Divided into several bands, the deundents of the Sioux & speak their lang- -guage a bad dispostd set & Can raus about 1000 men in the 3 bands near this place, they trade with the Nations of this nieghbourhood for horses Corn & Snow all Day Cap L. at the village 19

(continued overleaf)

90th in the morning early a hawk
came to the tent who offered to carry us
to bring to my flint he had some thing to say
from the nation we sat for this, and after the
two brothers He said He thought He was now
friend enough here perhaps to carry on the war —
To 8 Mandan out hunting in a tent, Decatur
from the flaw about a league after they had
made their hunt and on their return was attacked
by a large party of Sioux on of the party or
young chief was killed 2 wounded
then who made their escape say the one party of
the party who attacked them were Sioux —
the two Sioux who came here a few days ago are
was immediately sat home for fear of their
being caught by the party defeated —
Some of the attacking party was found to be Sioux
He how who was killed mentioned that after he was
wounded from that he had less at last as been
wounded Sir the boy I shall die like a man before my
Enemys told my father that New travels and so
not grieve for me —
I of the Big below who was camped near that
a missing and looking for him to their camp,
above — No one dar to go to the ground where
the battle was for fear of the Sioux being
recommenced —

1st Oct a young chief named
7 chein came to the village with a pipe & the 8 Reares who
came here a few days ago RKX off yesterday have returned
and say that the Reares & hoses are coming together

Notes at Wood River
in 1803-4

Lieut. Jonathan Clark
near Louisville
Kentucky

Nothing

The Distances of the following places as estimated from ⁶⁰
the Mouth of the Missouri, with Latitudes annexed —— ₁₈₀₆

			Miles		Latitude
To	S.ᵗ Charles Situated on the North Side		21.	in Latitude	38. 54. 39
"	The mouth of Gasconade River S. S. ——		103.	ditto	38. 44. 35.
"	The mouth of Osarge River .. S. S. ——		137.	do	38. 31. 16
"	The mouth of Grand River . N. S. ..		252.	do	38. 47. 54
"	The Mouth of Kenza River .. S.S. ..		364	do	39. 5. 25.
"	The mouth of Independance Creek S.S. ..		432	do	39. 25. 42
"	The mouth of Nodawa River. N. S. ..		480	do	39. 39. 22
"	The Mouth of the G.ᵗ Nemaha R. S.S. ..		510	do	39. 55. 56
"	The Mouth of Bald pated prarie .. N. S. ..		569	do	40. 27. 7.
"	The Mouth of River Platt .. S. Side		630	do	40. 54. 35.
"	The Councel Bluff on the S. S. ..		680	do	41. 17. 0.
"	The Mouth of the Little Sieoux R. N.S. ——		763	do	41. 42. 34.
"	The Camp opd. the Maha Village S.S. ——		866	do	42. 13. 41.
"	The mouth of Soeuex River on the N.S. ——		882	do	42. 23. 49
"	The Mouth of River Jacque on th N. S.		974	do	42. 53. 13.

(continued overleaf)

Document (continued)

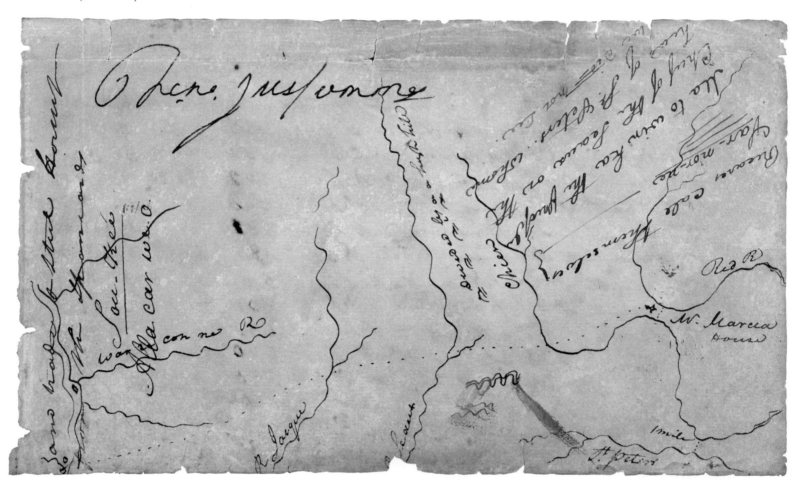

324

The Number of Officers & Men for to Protect the Indian trade
and keep the Savages in peace with the US. and each other

1805 if Soldiers act as Boatmen & Soldiers

Names of eligable Situations of Establishments	Agents	Colonel	Major	Captains	Lieuten.	Ensign	Surgeon & Surgeon Mate	Interpreter	Sergeants	Corporals	Musick	Privates	Total	Distance from one to the other
At St Louis	1	1	1	1	1	1	1	3	4	4		52	68	
at the Osarge, or Arkansaw			1	1	1	1	1	1	1	1		45	48	
" the mouth of Kanzes			1		1		1	1	2	1		23	28	366
" the Council Bluff			1		1		2	2	2		30	36	316
" Cheun or Skar Ks R		1	1	1	1	3	4	4	4		75	88	640
" Rocky Jon River	1	1	1	1	1	4	3	3	3		45	54	500
" Falls of Missourie			1	1	1	2	1	1	1		30	38	700
" Head of Kanzes or Arkansa			1	1	1	2	4	4	4		75	87	
on the Mississippi Prara du Chien	1		1	1	1	2	4	4	4		70	82	
St Peter or Falls of St Anthoney			1	1	1	1	2	2	2		30	36	
do do Sand Lake			1	1	1	1	2	4	2		40	48	
on the St Peters River			1	1	1	1	4	4	4		75	82	
	3	1	1	8	9	8	12	12	30	30	30	600	700	

(continued overleaf)

To the mouth of the River Que courre (rapid) is 1020 in Lat^d.

" The mouth of White River on the South Side 1143. do

" The Island in the Grand de tour or Big bind of the Missouree is 1200 do

" The fort on the Island of Cedars is — — — — — 1243 do. 44. 11. 33"

" The mouth of the Teton River on the So. Side 1280 do

" The mouth of the Chien / or dog River So. side 1327 do 44. 19. 36"

" The mouth of the Sur-war-kar-na River So. Side 1407 do

" The mouth of the Water-loo River So. Side 1435 do. 45. 39. 5°

" The Ricara Villages. 3 on the S.S. . . . 1440 do

" The River Boulet or Cannon Ball R. 1511 do 46. 29. a—

" The River Chiss-che-lar & old Village L.S. 1551 do — — —

" The 1st Village of the Mandans L.I. 1612 do — — —

" Fort Mandan on the N. Side is . . . . . 1609 do 47. 21. 47

" Knif River & Shoe mans village S.S 1616 —

" The Mouth of Muddy Creek — S.S — 1635.

Index

(Creeks, Forts, Islands, Journals, Maps, and Rivers are listed under those classifications.)

Abel, Annie Heloise, cited, xxxiv, 17 n., 60 n.

Air gun, use of, 7 n., 96, 97 n., 110, 123, 158, 169

Alton Quadrangle, 3 n., 4 n.

Alum, deposits of, 111–12

Amdol, ——, 29

American Bottom, 3 n., 30; settlement of, 4 n., 25 n.

American Philosophical Society, xiv, xxii, xxv, xxvii, xxxiii, 157 n., 171 n.

Amherstburg, 29 n.

Anderson, Col. Richard Clough, 9, 34

Antelope (wild goats, *cabri*), 43 n., 131–32, 134, 139–40, 146, 153–54; described, 138; numbers of, 142, 162–63

Apple trees, wild, 62, 95. *See also* Crab apple

Arapaho Indians, alliance with Cheyenne, 161 n.

Ar-ca-we-char-chi. *See* Half Man

Ar-he-tar-nar-shan. *See* Chief of the town

Arikara (Rickerie) Indians, 32, 96, 108, 165–66, 169, 172, 174, 175 n., 180–81, 188; abandoned villages of, 126, 152–56 passim, 164; decimated by smallpox, 153 n.; at war with Tetons, 153 n., with Crow, 159, with Mandans, 159; party's first meeting with, 156; previous contact with trading expeditions, 157 n.; described, 159; chief weeps at Newman's punishment, 161; rumored planning attack on Mandans, 178; council with Mandans, 184; chief returns on keelboat, 185 n.

Arkansas, 11

Arsenic, 104 n.; found by party, Lewis ill from dust of, 111–12

Ash trees, 50, 52, 60, 94, 162

Assiniboin Indians, 165 n., 172 n., 178 n.; trade with English, 166 n.; party's first contact with, 174; previous settlements of, 175 n.

Assiniboin Road, trading route to Mandans, 166 n.

Atchison, Kansas, xxxiv

Atkinson, Col. Henry, 98 n.

Atsina Indians, associated with Blackfeet, 170 n.

Au-ho-ne-ga, Missouri chief, 97

Au-ho-ning-ga, Missouri chief, 97

Aurora borealis, seen by party, 29

Ayer Collection, Newberry Library, Chicago, Ill., 134 n.

Badgers, 27, 94, 156, 186

Badgley, David, 25

Bakeless, John, cited, 6 n., 11 n., 150 n.

Baker, H., 7

Baker's Oven, 82

Bald Pated Prairie, 79, 87–88, 108, 143, 187

Baldwin, Leland D., 6 n.

Barren lands, 78 n., 184

Barton, Benjamin Smith, xxii–xxiii, xxviii, xxxii

Bass, caught by party, 107–08

Batue a De charm (plain), 50

Ba-za-con-ja, Oto chief, 97

Bear, 9, 52–61 passim; pelts in fur trade, 124; grizzly, 153, 163

Bear grass, 130

Beauvais, Vidal, 42 n.

Beaver, 51, 75, 91, 94–95, 106, 137–38, 142, 145, 172, 185, 186 n.; pelts in fur trade, 46, 124; houses 99, 130; numbers of, 103–04, 176; dams, 107, 119

Belleville, 25 n.

Benoit, François, fur trader, 37 n., 78; trading post of, 62 n.

Besernet, Lackduer. *See* Bissonette, Louis

Biddle, Nicholas, xxi, 9 n., 41 n., 46 n., 57 n., 59 n., 90 n., 131 n., 159 n., 173 n.; agrees to write history of expedition, xxv, xxxii; Clark's letter to, concerning "rough notes," xxv, xxvi

Big Ax (Nee-swor-un-ja), Oto chief, 110

Big Bend. *See* Grand Detour

Big Blue Eyes (Star-gra-hun-ja), Oto chief, 110

Big Horse (Shingo-ton-go), Oto chief, 96, 110

Big Man, Mandan chief, 166

Big White (She-he-ke), Mandan chief, 171, 173 n.

Billon, Frederic L., 10 n.

Birch trees, 139

Bissell, Capt. David, 8 n.

Bissell, Capt. Russell, 8 n.

Bissonette, Angelica, 10 n.

Bissonette, Louis (Lackduer Besernet), 8, 10 n.

Black Bird, Omaha chief: grave of, 104; causes split among Omaha, 120

Black Buffalo (Un-ton-gar-sar-bar), Teton grand chief, 148

Black Cat (Ne-ca-sa-wa), Missouri chief, 110

Black Cat (Poss-cop-sa-hee), Mandan chief, 169–172

Black Hills: habitat of Crow Indians, 123; described, 153, 156; Cheyenne Indians settle at, 161 n.; wintering place for antelope, 162

Black Moccasin (Omp-se-ha-ra), Minitari chief, 171

Blackberries, 52

Blackfeet Indians, 170 n.

Bois Brulé. *See* Sioux Indians: Teton

Boley (Boleye), John, member of expedition, 4 n.; returns to St. Louis, 33, 185 n.

Bone Lick, Ky., 135 n.

Boone, Daniel, 44 n.

Boone's Settlement, 44 n.

Boston Centinel: quoted, xxvi; cited, xxvii

Bourgmont, Etienne de, 11, 57 n., 71 n.

Brackenridge, H. M., cited, 104 n.

Brandon House. *See* Hudson's Bay Company

Brant, 142, 154. *See also* Geese

Bratton, William, member of expedition,

Bratton, William (*cont.*)
4 n., 8 n., 69 n., 75 n., 109, 112; swims Missouri, 82; in party to apprehend Reed, 101; visits Spirit Mound, 118

Brave Man (War-sar-sha-co), Oto chief, 110

Buffalo, 43 n., 51, 71, 84 n., 90, 92, 107, 109–10, 112, 116, 126, 132–35, 139 n., 140–42, 148 n., 153, 164, 178, 181, 185; hides, 46, 122, 136, 139 n., 149; numbers of, 76, 119, 131, 134, 139–42, 144–46, 162–63; hunters' preference for cows, 136 n.; party hunt to supply Fort Mandan, 181, 184

Buffalo berry (*Graisse du boeuf*), 113 n., 145

Buffalo Medicine (Tar-ton-gar-wa-ker), Teton chief, 146, 148

Bull boat, described, 158

Bushnell, D. I., 17 n.

Cahokia, 3, 4 n., 5 n., 6, 9, 10 n., 11, 16 n., 17, 24–25, 27–30, 35 n., 65 n., 139 n.

Cajeu, fur trader's boat, 46, 47 n., 48 n., 51, 53, 55–56

Calhoun, John Caldwell, 187 n.

California, xiii

Cal-ta-co-ta. *See* Grape

Calumet Bluff, 130; council with Yankton at, 121

Cameron, Murdoch, trader, 159, 172 n., 184 n.

Camp Dubois, 4 n., 33, 84 n., 90 n.; winter quarters established at, xv, xviii, 3 n., 8; map of, 2; road built from, 3; shooting matches at, 11, 35, 37; party departs from, 38, 69 n.

Campbell, John, fur trader, 29

Canada, 41 n.

Cann (Cane, Carr, Carrn), E., *engagé* with expedition, 69–70, 118

Cantonment Belle Fontaine, 41

Cape Girardeau, 42 n.; visited by Lewis and Clark, 30

Car-gar-no-mok-she. *See* Raven Man

Carolina parakeets, 62

Casa Calvo, Gov. Gen. of Louisiana, xiv

Catfish, 28, 80, 90, 93–94, 106–08, 142

Catlett (Callay, Catlet, Catlate, Chittele), Hanson, doctor at Camp Dubois, 27, 29, 37–38

Cavallos, Pedro, xiv

Cedar trees, 106, 134–35, 138, 142, 153

Cenas, Blaze, 7

Chaboillez, Charles, fur trader, 172, 173 n., 176, 181 n.

Chalo, ——, 69

Charbonneau, Baptiste (Pomp), 174–75 n.; birth of, 182 n.

Charbonneau (Chabonah), Toussaint, interpreter, 174, 176, 182 n., 185, 186 n.

Charlo, ——, 70 n.

Chauvin, Jacques, 79 n.

Cherries, 76, 78, 95

327

Wolves, 43 n., 64, 73, 82, 84, 111–12, 118, 124, 134, 139–40, 142, 154; described, 106; prey on buffalo herds, 163, 181

Woodford (Wolpard), Adam, trader, 34, 37

Worrell, Lt. Stephen, 43 n.

Wyoming, 140 n.

X.Y. Company, 181 n.; Fort Souris, 166 n.

Yankton, S.D., 121 n.

Yankton Indians. *See* Sioux

Yanktonais Indians. *See* Sioux

York, Clark's body servant, 4 n., 8, 30, 32,

York, Clark's body servant (*cont.*) 41 n., 51, 60, 69, 71 n., 110, 112, 118, 135, 141, 158, 159 n., 161 n., 166, 185; described, 119

Zinc, deposits of, 12 n.